Child Development

Child Development

GRETA G. FEIN

The Merrill-Palmer Institute

and the Editorial Staff of Prentice-Hall

Prentice-Hall, Inc.

Englewood Cliffs, New Jersey

To the spirits of collaboration, caring, and trust
that brought this book into being

Library of Congress Cataloging in Publication Data

Fein, Greta G.
    Child development

    Bibliography: p. 545
    Includes indexes.
    1. Child psychology.   I. Title.   [DNLM: 1. Child
development. WS105 F299c]
BF721.F385   155.4   77-19189
ISBN 0-13-132571-X

Printed in the United States of America

10 9 8 7 6 5 4 3 2 1

Prentice-Hall International, Inc., London
Prentice-Hall of Australia Pty. Ltd., Sydney
Prentice-Hall of Canada, Ltd., Toronto
Prentice-Hall of India Private Limited, New Delhi
Prentice-Hall of Japan, Inc., Tokyo
Prentice-Hall of Southeast Asia Pte. Ltd., Singapore
Whitehall Books Limited, Wellington, New Zealand

Cover photo by Jim Adair/The Image Bank

ACKNOWLEDGMENTS

Grateful acknowledgment is made to the following for
permission to reprint material:
Figure 1–1: From T. G. R. Bower, The visual world of in-
    fants. *Scientific American*, 1966, *215*, 80–92. By per-
    mission of Mrs. Sol Mednick and Scientific American.
Tables 2–1 and 2–2: In *From conception to birth: The drama
    of life's beginnings* by Roberts Rugh and Landrum B.
    Shettles. Copyright © 1971 by Roberts Rugh and
    Landrum B. Shettles. By permission of Harper & Row,
    Publishers, Inc.

Acknowledgments continued on page 567

Contents

Contents

x

Preface

We think of childhood as a distinctive and special period of life, but this was not always so. In ancient Greece, classical China, and medieval Europe, there was no such concept as "childhood." In the art of those times and places, children were shown as small adults, with the clothing, facial expressions, and even the musculature of adults. Before 1600, children and adults shared the same games, toys, and stories. The word *boy* was used to refer to a dependent male of any age; the word *child* was a kinship term, used without reference to age. In seventeenth-century Europe, a new attitude toward children developed. Gradually, at least in middle-class and aristocratic families, separate forms of dress for children evolved. Children began to be separated by sex and age group. They were given "special" books carefully edited for the young mind. Children were even separated from adults in the home, where they lived in nurseries with nurses and governesses. A private world for children had been created.

The study of children emerged in this context. If babies, school-aged children, and adolescents are not the same, how exactly do they differ? What are the consequences of those differences? John Amos Comenius, a seventeenth-century Czech educator, was perhaps the first to make explicit the link between children's development and the educational methods from which they would benefit. He assumed that children first understood things as real objects, then as pictures, and finally as spoken and written words. In accord with this view, Comenius designed the first picture book to teach children how to read. The results of recent research seem to support Comenius's assumption about the pattern of development. But, as the reader will discover, development is more intricate than Comenius imagined.

Child psychology is the study of the origins and development of human consciousness and behavior. The study of child development begins with the individual, but it does not end there. It inevitably touches upon sociology, the study of the origins and development of the forms and functions of human groups. The two sciences become joined in major ways when child psychologists consider that children are reared in social groups and that part of the process of development involves the child's integration in a social world. This social world—made up of cultural values, institutions, and technologies—provides the context within which children develop, the variables that influence development as well as the socially valued outcomes of that development. For the most part in Western societies, responsibility for the rearing of children rests with the family, especially with the parents. It is the parents who negotiate relations between the child and cultural institutions such as schools and hospitals, between the child and persons such as teachers and doctors. It is also parents who interpret to their children the requirements of culture—from what children should do in school to how they should feel about the teacher.

The process of social integration begins at an early age. American newborns and newborns of the Bushman tribe of Africa begin life with similar capabilities, but they become adults with vastly different skills and outlooks. The Bushman parent and child and the American parent and child live in cultures that differ in expectations, demands, and stresses. Such differences in cultural arrangements and technologies are transmitted to the young and mold them into competent members of the culture in which they are reared.

In America today, many major cultural arrangements take the form of massive and impersonal institutions—public and private—and the technologies are of the kind that require years of intensive training to master. The American parent is faced with an unusually difficult task, that of protecting and advancing the child's interest in the face of sometimes overwhelming odds. The child's interest rests upon the employment of one parent and often two, upon the parents' ability to locate and arrange health care, to supply nutritious meals, to provide intellectually stimulating experiences in the home, and to work with teachers in the monitoring of the child's schooling.

As those who study children document the important role of adults in children's development, there is a growing concern over the social conditions that increase the difficulty of rearing children at home and educating them in school. The important point is this: Although child psychologists study the development of the person, that development is influenced by factors present in the society at large. As those factors become better understood and identified, information needed to help parents and adults deal with the realities of child rearing in a complex world becomes more available. Courses in child development provide the opportunity to share such information in order that it be used to enhance the lives of families and children in America. This book was prepared in recognition of the need to communicate information about child development with those who will need it, now or in the future.

PLAN OF THE BOOK

This text is designed for introductory-level courses in child development, child psychology, and human development. Its main goal is to present basic concepts and principles of child development in a readable and engaging fashion. Important contemporary and classic research is covered in a way that reveals both the complexity and the simplicity of the basic issues as well as the common themes underlying the professional activity in the field of child development. The text shares with people new to the field a sense of respect and appreciation for the real and lively children behind the theories and experiments. The dual concern with scientific precision and a sensitivity to children as fellow human beings is reflected throughout the book.

Several key features distinguish this book:

COMPREHENSIVE COVERAGE. The book conveys the diversity of theories, methods, and research findings that mark the study of child psychology today. The influences of the cognitive, social, and behavioral points of view are presented in areas in which they have made the greatest impact. Both the clashes and the agreements between differing perspectives are examined.

READABILITY. Great effort has been expended to make the text "readable." By this we mean that general concepts have been clearly illustrated with concrete examples from the world of the student; that the richness of detail in the scientific data in the book has been carefully selected to identify general converging trends and to evoke student interest; and finally, that the use of jargon has been kept to a minimum.

FLEXIBLE ORGANIZATION. The book is organized around major periods of childhood. Within each period, the text presents discussions of physical, cognitive, language, and social development. The presentation has been planned so that the interrelatedness of different aspects of development is shown. In stressing the interrelation of thought, physical growth, language, and social behavior, we call upon what we believe to be the most challenging ideas in current theory and research. An instructor who wishes to trace a single strand—for example, the development of language from the early acquisition of basic language forms, through the use of language to communicate with others, and the eventual application and transformation of language in the process of learning to read and write—may do so by using selected subtopics in each of several chapters.

CONTEMPORARY COVERAGE. The text is contemporary in its attempt to reflect major interests in the field of child development. Contributions stemming from the *Piagetian perspective* appear in each section, reflecting the vitality of current research in the development of children's thinking. *Psycholinguistic research* is included, especially in the area of early language development, where research activity has reached the point at which alternative development theories can be fruitfully discussed. Serious research on *children's play* and on *fantasy and creativity* has mushroomed in the past decade; the high quality of this recent work merits special attention. We also have devoted attention to the development of *sex differences* and *sex-role stereotypes* and the way in which *family structures* and the *behavior of mothers and fathers* contributes to these and other aspects of development. Again the emphasis given to these topics in the text reflects current interests in the field.

IN-TEXT PEDAGOGICAL AIDS. There are several devices used in the book to aid the student in studying: (1) *Chapter introductions* present the essential ideas that will be developed in the chapter. Provocative examples often are used to give a feeling of children at various ages and periods of development. (2) *Photographs* enrich the textual discussion. The photos are positioned near appropriate passages in the text; they reinforce the discussion as they add the flavor of childhood to the book. (3) *Charts and graphs* present important data and concepts in attractive and uncluttered visual form. (4) *Chapter summaries* appear at the end of the chapters. They are convenient tools for reviewing the chapter and preparing for class discussion and exams. (5) *Baby biographies* introduce each period of childhood. These pieces of real-life baby biographies, taken from letters and journals, provide provocative and entertaining glimpses of the age period about to be discussed. (6) The *glossary* at the end of the book is a ready reference to help the student develop his or her understanding of the field of child development.

SUPPLEMENTS TO THE TEXT. In addition to the text itself, there are available to the instructor an *Instructor's Manual* containing comments on each chapter, lists of possible discussion and research topics, film lists, and suggested readings. Also available is a *Test Item File* of approximately 1,000 questions, annotated with the page reference in the text from which the question was taken. For the student, there is a *Study Guide and Workbook* which provides a battery of programmed review questions, practice tests, and lists of key terms and concepts. Each question in the guide is cross-referenced to the text page where the appropriate material is covered. The student can use the study guide to verify his or her mastery of the material covered in each chapter of the text.

ACKNOWLEDGMENTS

To study child development in the 1970s is to touch a broad, dynamic, and rapidly changing field in which old concepts are vigorously challenged and new ones replace the old at a breathtaking pace. These conditions create a special challenge to the writers and publishers of textbooks. A highly technical language must be translated, new insights must be lucidly conveyed, and the activity of science must be presented in a coherent and sensible manner. Contemporary issues must be presented in the light of traditional, perhaps eternal, problems.

Child Development represents an attempt to meet this challenge in a new way. The book is the result of a group effort orchestrated by Neale Sweet and Cecil Yarbrough and generously supported by Prentice-Hall. The essential idea—an appealing one—is to bring together a mix of scholarly, literary, and technical skills needed to ensure a book that represents the best thinking in a scientific discipline presented in a lively, readable text.

My task was to identify and organize the themes, perspectives, and research that mark the field of child development today. In this effort, I was helped by the talents and enthusiasm of Donna Cahill Solovey, Sue Eshleman, and Henry Shein, who, as graduate research assistants, spent hours in the library studying articles and abstracts and tracking down references. I culled, organized, and synthesized these research materials into a working outline providing detailed annotations for style, tone, and emphasis. A staff of able writers—Lauren Bahr, Jane Barrett, Judy Cohen, Sarah English, Martin Haydon, and Carolyn Smith—produced drafts which were then rewritten, and refined.

Ann Torbert, as manuscript editor, coordinated the transition from raw materials to readable, well-paced text. Her sensitivity to ideas, language, and people kept the project moving during its most difficult times. Were it not for Ann, this book would not exist.

Much of the revising and rewriting was guided by the thoughtful and provocative comments of reviewers. Robert T. Brown and Richard R. Rosinski helped to improve the text and to sharpen the analyses of developmental phenomena that appear in these pages. Other colleagues who provided helpful reviews at various stages of the manuscript include Gordon Finley, Mary Gander, Michael Walraven, Edward Fahrmeier, Sylvia Farnham-Diggory, and David McGrevy. Many others contributed their considerable talents to the enterprise. Irene Zakrzewski managed secretarial and typing tasks. Florence Silverman created the design and the cover. Abigail Solomon researched the photos that appear with the text. Marcia Schonzeit handled production of the book with skill and patience. Thanks to everyone for his or her contribution to the project.

GRETA G. FEIN

Child Development

CHAPTER 1

Concepts, Methods, and Theories of Development

Everybody knows what a child is, and many people know a great deal about children. They can remember what they were like and how they felt when they were young. Mothers, fathers, teachers, doctors, nurses, psychologists, and other kinds of professionals are concerned in one way or other with the well-being and development of children. And yet this most familiar of creatures, the child, poses seemingly endless dilemmas to those who seem to know the most about them. Why does one child misbehave and another conform? Why does another child learn to read easily but seem unable to grasp even simple mathematical concepts? How did two sisters, growing up in the same family, become adults with vastly different attitudes, skills, and personalities? Some dilemmas are more universal. Why are most children all over the world able to crawl during the first year of life, to speak during the second year, and to form stable peer relationships during the third year? Why can young children think only about today, whereas adolescents can comprehend the distant past and anticipate the unseen future?

Human beings are rarely passive in the face of things they do not understand. They try to find out about the things they want to know. They consult with relatives, friends and neighbors, and sometimes professionals. They seek expert advice from newspapers, magazines, and books. Often, though, the layman's most plausible answers rest upon assumptions that are wrong and yet seem so obviously right that they are never challenged.

The Ptolemaic theory of the heavenly bodies illustrates how difficult it often is to detect an incorrect but appealing assumption. The theory, current during the second century A.D., took as its starting point the idea that the earth was the center of the universe around which the sun, the stars, and the planets revolved. That idea was firmly embedded in the religion, myths, folk tales, and belief systems of the time. These belief systems, or *world views,* were shared by astronomers and philosophers as well as by ordinary folk. For many centuries, it was almost unthinkable to believe that the universe could operate in any but the Ptolemaic way. It took a slow accumulation of evidence that did not fit the theory before this basic premise could be challenged. The history of science offers many other examples of how widely accepted and unquestioned beliefs became the foundation of scientific theory. Michael Polanyi, a philosopher of science, claims that "the premises of science on which all scientific teaching and research rest are the beliefs held by scientists on the general nature of things" (1964, p. 11).

Long before scientific methods were used to study human behavior and development, philosophers posed the problems that psychologists are still trying to solve. In Chapter 2, for example, we will discuss individual differences and how environmental and biological factors contribute to these differences. Although the contemporary controversy is informed by recent scientific evidence, the ideas used to organize the discussion can be traced to the distant past. Hippocrates, a Greek physician (known as the "father of medicine") who lived in the fourth century B.C., thought it obvious that the minds and personalities of human beings were largely determined by environmental factors. Speaking of the "human inhabitants of Asia," Hippocrates noted:

Such a climate does not produce those mental shocks and violent bodily dislocations which would naturally render the temperament ferocious and introduce a stronger current of irrationality and passion than would be the case under stable conditions. It is invariably changes that stimulate the human mind and that prevent it from remaining passive. (cited in Toynbee, 1952, pp. 145–146)

Although we may be amused by Hippocrates's mistaken geography, climatology, and cultural characterizations, his observation of the role of stimulus change in the development of mind is echoed in contemporary developmental research. If the role of environment was obvious to Hippocrates, the role of genetic factors was equally obvious to the philosopher Aristotle, a contemporary of Hippocrates:

For man is generated from man; and thus it is the possession of certain characters by the parent that determines the development of like characters in the child. (cited in McKeon, 1973, p. 259)

These arguments of environment versus biology continued, and thinkers made new distinctions and refined some of the old ones. Descartes (1596–1650), for example, distinguished the universal characteristics of mind from those that vary from person to person:

Good sense or reason, is by nature equal in all men;...the diversity of our opinions consequently does not arise from some being endowed with a larger share of reason than others, but solely from this, that we conduct our thoughts along different ways and do not fix our attention on the same objects. (cited in Veitch, 1974, p. 39)

How then do beliefs influence scientific activities? Beliefs might determine which hypotheses scientists choose to investigate. If Hippocrates were to use the methods of contemporary psychology, he might study hypotheses about the relation between climate and human abilities. Aristotle might hypothesize about how genetic differences affect individuality. Descartes would study the relation between endowment and experience. But hypotheses are only tentative answers to significant questions. Beliefs also influence the questions that scientists ask and how they go about finding answers. We call such beliefs *models* (Reese and Overton, 1970).

Hippocrates saw man as adaptable, formed by the external forces of the physical environment, whereas St. Augustine saw man formed by the social environment. With strikingly different models of man, Aristotle and later Descartes stressed the fixedness of at least some human characteristics. General models such as these are useful — indeed, unavoidable — as a framework for study. Two models — the *mechanistic* and the *organismic* — have dominated the study of child development (Reese and Overton, 1970; Anderson, 1957; von Bertalanffy, 1967). The mechanistic model derives largely from the thinking of a group of philosophers referred to as *empiricists*; the organismic model comes from a group referred to as *rationalists*. The mechanistic model describes the behavior of a developing child as if it were performed by a machine (not that the developing child *is* a machine). The organismic model likens the child to a biological system.

A *model* of reality does not describe reality. Rather, it provides the premises upon which a theory rests; it helps determine what needs to be described. Therefore, a model of development — whether mechanistic or organismic — cannot be judged as either true or false, but only as more or less useful. Theories, on the other hand, *are* used to explain and predict phenomena. They can be judged by their truthfulness, that is, whether their explanations and predictions are supported by evidence.

THE CONCEPT OF DEVELOPMENT

In general, *development* refers to what happens to living things as they move forward in time. But development does not refer to change alone. The term also includes the notion that change is systematic and that it characterizes the life cycle of a species. How and why such change takes place are the subject of developmental psychology. Both the mechanistic

and the organismic/structural models attempt to explain how and why developmental changes come about.

Among the issues arising from the differences between the two models is that of *continuity* versus *discontinuity*. Does development take the form of a continuous, gradual transition from one stage to the next, or does it proceed in a series of discontinuous steps involving successive reorganizations of the total system? Consider talking as an example: How does the infant progress from babbling, to single words, to two-word "sentences," to proper grammatical constructions?

Mechanistic models argue that the transition is quantitative. If, for example, the transition from babbling to single words were monitored continuously, mechanists believe that the change could be shown to be gradual and *continuous*. There would be a gradual increase in some measure such as frequency of intelligible utterances.

Organismic models, on the other hand, say that simple measurement of development misses the point. Organismic theorists are not antimeasurement per se. They argue that mechanists measure the wrong things, that most measures fail to describe the increasing complexity of the organism's competencies. Organismic theorists believe that development is characterized by the appearance of new *structures*. Structurally, the transition from babbling to proper sentences involves a sequence of major

Developmental psychology studies changes that occur to children as they move forward in time—how and why they change from newcomers with limited means of understanding the world to adults capable of composing symphonies, curing diseases, managing corporations, raising children of their own. (Michael Hardy)

reorganizations of the cognitive, auditory, and vocal systems. Because such structures are different, development in this model is thought to be *discontinuous*.

Mechanistic and organismic theorists also disagree about what constitutes and characterizes *stages* of development. Stage is merely a descriptive concept in mechanistic theory. For a statement such as "The child is in stage *x*," the mechanist could easily substitute something like "The child is 4 years old." To the mechanist, the difference between being 4 years old and 14 years old might be in the speed of conditioning or in the kind of strategy used to recover information stored in memory. Belief in stages is fundamental to organismic theorists. Their theories are based on the existence of a sequence of stages; each stage is characterized by certain patterns of behavior. In terms of ability to perform mental acts on objects at hand, the world of the 2-year-old child is qualitatively different from that of the 11-year-old child.

THE MECHANISTIC MODEL

As we indicated earlier, the mechanistic model likens the behavior of a developing organism to the working of a machine. The machine may be simple (a light switch) or immensely complex (a computer), but it is characterized by what are called *input-output relations*. A stimulus (or input) applied to the organism results in a change in the behavior or condition of the organism (the output of the machine). Investigators who work in the mechanistic tradition are concerned with the process of change, the principles that can account for the relation between input and output. The organism is at rest unless provoked by a stimulus, and change over time is determined by sequences of input-output events. Change is seen as essentially *quantitative* (measurable) in nature: The child speaks more words, makes finer discriminations, coordinates more complex actions.

The writings of seventeenth-century philosopher John Locke (1632–1704) did much to promote the mechanistic world view. He compared the mind to a blank page, a "white paper, void of all characters, without any ideas." This is the famous *tabula rasa* (blank slate) image. Locke's organism was not entirely "empty." It lacked preformed ideas, but it had the "faculties" (abilities, such as reflection and abstraction) with which to construct notions about the world. Locke argued that the mind first becomes furnished with simple ideas conveyed through the senses (such as ideas of yellow and white, hot and cold). Then these simple ideas combine to produce more complex ones.

How does such a world view shape theories of child development? First, it says that in order to find out how children acquire knowledge, one must study how simple experiences become associated. Second, it stresses the malleability of children. Locke wrote, "I imagine the minds of children as easily turned, this or that way as water itself'' (cited in Ulich, 1954). Further, Locke believed that the way to get children to learn something is to have them practice it over and over again, until it becomes a habit. The mechanistic model as formulated by Locke became the pattern for what psychologists call *learning theory*.

According to learning theorists, behavior is shaped by external events. Changes in behavior involve *associative* processes. Learning theorists see the organism as reactive, as responding to particular external stimuli with particular responses. This is symbolized as *S* (stimulus) → *R* (response). The *stimulus* can be any action or agent that causes or changes an activity of the subject. The *response* is the reaction of the organism to the stimulus. Raindrops falling on your head (stimulus) may make you raise your umbrella (response). The smell of baking bread (stimulus) may make you raid the refrigerator (response). The S⟶R model can be modified in various ways, but it excludes behavior attributable to genetic or maturational factors. Traditionally, learning theorists have used two processes to account for the formation of regular associative connections—classical conditioning and operant conditioning.

Learning Theory

CLASSICAL CONDITIONING. The basic work in classical conditioning was done by Ivan Pavlov, whose studies demonstrated that dogs could be conditioned to salivate at the sound of a bell. In *classical conditioning*, an association is achieved through the paired presentation of stimuli. One stimulus, the *unconditioned stimulus* (UCS), normally elicits an *unconditioned response* (UCR). The unconditioned response is basically a reflex action of the organism that occurs regularly in response to a natural external stimulus. Pavlov's dogs, for example, normally salivated (UCR) when given food (UCS). Pairings then are made of the unconditioned stimulus and a new, neutral stimulus, called the *conditioned stimulus* (CS). With repeated pairings of the unconditioned and the conditioned stimuli, the organism comes to associate the two. Eventually the conditioned stimulus is enough, without the unconditioned stimulus, to produce the response, which is called the *conditioned response* (CR). In the case of Pavlov's dogs, initially they did not salivate at the sound of the bell (CS); with repeated presentation of the food (UCS) and the bell (CS), they began to salivate (CR) when they heard the bell, even in the absence of the food.

John B. Watson, a psychologist in the United States, was enthusiastic about the implications of Pavlov's work for the modification of human behavior. Believing "children are made, not born" (1928, p. 7), he said:

Give me a dozen healthy infants, well-formed, and my own specified world to bring them up in and I'll guarantee to take any one at random and train him to become any type of specialist I might select—doctor, lawyer, mer-

chant, chief, and yes, even beggar-man and thief, regardless of his talents, penchants, tendencies, abilities, vocations, and race of his ancestors. (Watson, 1958, p. 104)

Watson also stressed the importance of studying observable behavior. He set out to demonstrate that fears and other emotional responses could be acquired and subsequently eliminated through conditioning. In a famous experiment (Watson and Raynor, 1920), Watson conditioned fear in an 11-month-old infant named Albert. First, Watson showed Albert a white rat. The infant showed no fear and approached the animal to play with it. Then Watson made a loud clanging noise whenever Albert reached out to stroke the animal. The noise caused the baby to cry and pull away from the rat. After a few pairings of rat and noise, the baby responded fearfully at the sight of the rat alone. Soon Albert's fear spread to other white and furry things—his mother's muff and even Santa Claus's beard. Watson did not stop there. In other experiments, he went on to show how the same principles of classical conditioning could be used to break the association between a conditioned stimulus and a conditioned response. Watson demonstrated that fear could be extinguished as it had initially been conditioned.

OPERANT CONDITIONING. *Operant conditioning* is another way of producing associative learning. In operant procedures, a behavior (or *operant*) first occurs spontaneously. The operant is a voluntary action produced by the subject. It is followed by application of a particular stimulus that gradually causes a change in the frequency of the behavior. Thus operant conditioning changes the frequency of a behavior by introducing a stimulus *after* the behavior occurs. Stimuli that increase the frequency of behavior are called *reinforcers*. Stimuli that suppress behavior are called *punishments*. In operant conditioning, the associative connection is between the operant behavior and the stimulus consequence (the reinforcement) of that behavior. As B. F. Skinner, the best-known exponent of operant conditioning, puts it, "We must take into account what the environment does to an organism not only before but after it responds. Behavior is shaped and maintained by its consequences" (1971, p. 16).

An important aspect of operant conditioning is *extinction*—the return of the operant behavior to its previous state when the reinforcement or punishment is discontinued. The length of time that it takes for the operant behavior to disappear is related to the strength of the conditioned response. In some cases, extinction may be slow or may seem to fail to occur. This happens when a behavior is reinforced after some occurrences and not others. Take the case of a young child who tries several times during the day to get attention from his or her mother. The mother's responses are irregular and often occur after the child's most frequent and intense—some would say obnoxious—efforts. From the standpoint of operant conditioning, it can be predicted that the child's attention-seeking behavior will continue to occur at the frequency and intensity that have previously been reinforced. Parents may not even recognize that they may be reinforcing undesirable behavior. An example is the attempt of parents to reduce the amount of time that a child spends crying in bed before falling asleep. Going in to see the child after it has cried for 20 minutes reinforces, rather than reduces, long periods of crying. The undesirable behavior continues and becomes more difficult to extinguish the next time it occurs.

Learned responses may be *generalized* to situations similar to that in which the response was learned. Such generalization is sometimes desirable, as when a child has been reinforced at home for helping others and generalizes that behavior to school and other places. Sometimes *overgeneralization* occurs, as Albert's behavior illustrates. Albert developed an "irrational" fear—a phobia—of all fluffy objects, which was clearly maladaptive. Similarly, a 3-year-old child who had been frightened by a large, noisy St. Bernard developed an intense fear of all dogs, even small, relatively quiet ones—a situation that made it difficult for his parents to take him to the homes of friends who had dogs of any kind. Many other phobias—fear of crowds, of elevators, of high places, and even of schools—begin in this way.

Generalization alone, therefore, does not result in effective learning. *Discrimination* is required as well. A child must discriminate, for instance, between the kind of aggressive behavior that will be punished (picking on a younger child) and the kind that will be rewarded (performing well in a boxing match). A child must learn to discriminate between attention-seeking behaviors that irritate adults and those that do not; between the wrong time and the right time to make demands upon adults. The 3-year-old just mentioned eventually learned to discriminate between dogs that might be dangerous to him and those that would not hurt him.

According to Skinner and others, operant conditioning can be used to teach a complex behavior by means of *shaping*, in which rewards are given for performance that comes closer and closer to the desired behavior. Skinner's debt to Locke is revealed in the following passage:

Operant conditioning shapes behavior as a sculptor shapes a lump of clay. Although at some point the sculptor seems to have produced an entirely novel object, we can always follow the process back to the original undifferentiated lump, and we can make the successive stages by which we return to this condition as small as we wish. At no point does anything emerge which is very different from what preceded it. The final product seems to have a special unity or integrity of design, but we cannot find a point at which this suddenly appears. In the same sense, an operant is not something which appears full grown in the behavior of the organism. It is the result of a continuous shaping process. (Skinner, 1953, p. 91)

Traditional learning theories face a crucial problem, however, in attempting to explain how behavior is shaped. That problem is, How are novel responses acquired in the first place? As Bandura and Walters (1963) point out,

It is doubtful . . . if many of the responses that almost all members of our society exhibit would ever be acquired if social training proceeded solely by the method of successive approximations [i.e., shaping]. This is particularly true of behavior for which there is no reliable eliciting stimulus apart from the cues provided by others as they exhibit the behavior. (p. 3)

It appears that certain behaviors are learned by observation, a process variously termed *modeling, identification, copying,* or *role playing.* If children are to learn the language of their community, a "verbalizing model" is indispensable. Moreover, there is evidence that learning may occur through observation, even when the child does not immediately reproduce the model's behavior and therefore receives no reinforcement. As Mischel (1971) notes, "What you know and how you behave depends on what you see and hear and not just on what you get." (p. 71)

SOCIAL LEARNING THEORY. *Social learning theory* explains learning processes as based on the observation of a model. Considerable study has recently been directed toward the role of imitation in learning. It appears that imitative role playing (for example, scolding baby brother with mother's words and inflections) permits the child to learn an entire class of interrelated behaviors as a group without going through a long period of discrimination training. In other words, children do not do what adults *tell* them to do but what they see adults *doing* (something parents have known for a long time).

In an experiment by Bandura (1962; cited in Bandura and Walters, 1963), children were shown a film in which an adult performed four aggressive responses. Some children saw a version in which the adult model was severely punished; others saw a version in which the model was generously rewarded; and still others saw a version in which the model's behavior was neither rewarded nor punished. The behavior that each child later exhibited varied according to whether the model he or she had seen had been punished or not.

In modern society, many models are symbolic. They are presented through instructions (oral or written), through pictures, or through a combination of the two. Children spend much of their time watching films and television. Therefore, these symbolic models have a strong influence on their behavior (hence the debate over violence on television). Parents also use exemplary models, such as George Washington and Martin Luther King, Jr., to indicate to their children the kinds of behavior they consider desirable. Such models often reflect the norms of a particular society.

FIGURE 1–1
*Information-
processing
experiment
(From Bower, 1966,
courtesy of Mrs. Sol
Mednick and Scientific
American)*

It seems, then, that the *acquisition* of a particular behavior may result primarily from observation; the *performance* of that behavior depends on the anticipated consequences. Thus, to the S → R equation of operant (and classical) conditioning, social learning theory adds the concept of *modeling,* which requires the introduction of an information-processing stage. In that stage, the observer watches, processes, and stores information, and waits for an appropriate time to produce the observed behavior. The behavior thus learned is "grasped" all at once, from exposure to models. It is not acquired piecemeal, by external reinforcement and slow learning curves. Social learning theory thus represents a departure from the orthodox behaviorism of Watson and Skinner.

Information-processing models follow the mechanistic tradition. Information-processing theorists are attracted by experiments such as the one illustrated in Figure 1–1. First the infant is conditioned to respond (with a head-turning motion) to a visual stimulus. The response is reinforced by a "peek-a-boo," which the infant enjoys. After a while, though, the infant gets bored. An expressive infant might indicate the lack of interest

*Information
Processing*

by a yawn; others might fret; still others go to sleep. Operant theorists dismiss these findings by saying that "peek-a-boo" no longer functions as a reinforcer (by definition). Information-processing theorists want to find out *why* the effect of the same stimulus changes over time. Kagan (1969), for example, claims that infants pay more attention to events that deviate moderately from familiar events than to either completely familiar or completely novel events. Although his findings are not conclusive, they suggest that discrepancy plays a role in what infants do. Thus, varying the peek-a-boo game somewhat would help hold the infant's interest. (Kagan's research will be discussed more fully in later chapters.)

The information-processing approach seeks to discover what is actually happening between the S and the R of the S → R equation. That is, it examines the processes that convert specific inputs into specific outputs. Thus, information-processing theorists are particularly interested in such processes as perception, memory, attention, recognition, problem solving, and thought. Recent information-processing models depend heavily on mathematical and computer metaphors. They view the flow of information through the system as a series of operations similar to the subroutines of a computer program. Such models begin with the question "How is the human organism programmed?" Information-processing models have been useful in the study of memory (Hagen, Jongeward, and Kail, 1975). Bruner (1973a) has applied the computer metaphor to the acquisition of skilled performance.

Another example of information processing is the work of Craik and Lockhart (1972). They proposed a model of memory in which incoming stimuli are analyzed at several levels. The product of these analyses is a particular memory trace, which is stored as information is stored in a computer. The persistence of a trace varies according to the level at which the stimuli have been processed. At the simplest levels, the physical and sensory features of the stimulus are analyzed, and the result is a temporary memory trace. Deeper levels are concerned with pattern recognition and meaning, and they result in memory traces that are more resistant to forgetting.

From the standpoint of child development, the information-processing approach is a useful framework for studying the changes in children's capacity to use memory as a tool, particularly during the years between ages 5 and 11. These changes appear to occur gradually and to be related to the child's own efforts to remember. In terms of Craik and Lockhart's model, the child plays an increasingly active role as information is analyzed at "deeper" levels. As the child grows older, he or she uses these deeper levels more often in order to increase the likelihood that certain information will be remembered (i.e., memorized). Bruner (1966) asks what processes are operating when motor skills become organized in infancy. How does an infant come to pick up one small cube and then a second and then a third? The key, he believes, is feedback. From birth, the infant is busily trying to correlate what it sees with what it can do, that is, to correlate perception and action. The sensory feedback that accompanies movement helps the infant make this correlation. The computer metaphor is also seen in Bruner's use of the term *subroutine* to describe the component acts of each complete action. According to Bruner (1973a), the three themes that are central in the development of skilled action are intention, feedback, and the action patterns that mediate between them. Bruner, and most other information-processing theorists, believe that learning in the traditional sense of classical and operant conditioning can account for only a small part of the organization of skilled behavior, memory, and other cognitive phenomena.

THE ORGANISMIC/STRUCTURAL MODEL

The organismic/structural model of development takes as its pattern a biological system. In this model, the organism is thought of as the source of its own activity and as a self-regulating system. The concept of the child as a system emphasizes the *relations* among its parts or properties (Reese and Overton, 1970). The significance of any part is derived from the larger context in which it occurs. Vision, for example, is more than just a property of the cornea, retina, and so on. It is a property of the visual *system* interacting with other *systems* (such as nerves and brain) in the body. To use a familiar phrase, the whole is more than the sum of its parts.

Students of development who start from the organismic model concentrate on *structure* or *competence* (abilities). Development consists of changes in the structure (organization) of the system over time and is *qualitative* in nature. Today the baby forms more understandable sentences and uses 50 words, but last month it said only 2 words. The language system has become sufficiently organized during that time to allow for a new competence (ability to use phrases and to talk in sentences). Moreover, the organismic model sees the child as a system characterized by activity and change—activity and change that come from within rather than as a result of external forces.

The organismic metaphor owes much to the philosophy of Gottfried Wilhelm von Leibniz (1646–1716). He asserted that the essence of substance is activity, consisting "in a continuous transition from one state to another as it produces these states out of itself in unceasing succession." The "whole" is organic, not mechanical in nature.

The educational philosopher Jean-Jacques Rousseau (1712–1778) voiced the practical implications of a view of the organism as self-motivating and self-regulating. His book *Émile* (1762) was a milestone in the evolution of the view that children are not merely little adults, to be rewarded for good behavior or punished if they do not live up to adult expectations.

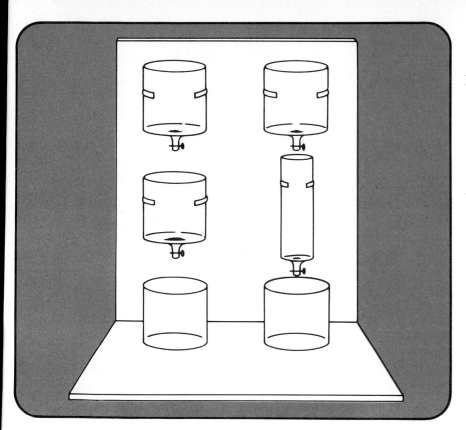

FIGURE 1-3
*Experimental
apparatus for
learning the concept
of conservation of
quantity*
(*Adapted from
Inhelder, Bovet,
and Sinclair, 1967*)

THE CONCEPT OF STAGES. Thus far, we have used the term *stage* or *level* of development in a very general way, simply to indicate how far the child has progressed along the road from conception to maturity. But to Piaget, these terms have a more precise meaning. As the child progresses toward maturity, he or she goes through a series of stages. These stages occur in a fixed order because each one is a *prerequisite* for the one that follows. At each stage, certain organized patterns of behavior, or *schemes,* appear; these may be either behavioral (e.g., thumb-sucking) or intellectual (e.g., classification of objects). The term *scheme* includes both the child's activities and the structures underlying those activities.*

Piaget's stages are classified into four major periods: (1) the sensorimotor ("sensory-motor") period; (2) the preoperational period; (3) the period of concrete operations; and (4) the period of formal operations. These periods and their subdivisions will be described at length in later chapters; here we will present a brief summary by way of introduction.

The *sensorimotor* period extends from birth to about age 2. During this period, the first organized patterns of behavior appear. At first, the infant is completely egocentric—it does not distinguish between its own body

*Many authors refer to the same concept by the term *schema* (plural: *schemata*). *Schema* is a mistranslation of the French word for "scheme."

To organismic theorists, abilities of thought are structural properties that define what the child can and cannot do in his or her interactions with the outside world at various stages of development. (*Stock, Boston*)

Rousseau was interested in persuading his contemporaries to abandon authoritarianism in favor of freedom and independence. Accordingly, he urged educators to "give children full liberty to use their natural abilities." (cited in Ulich, 1954, p. 392)

Those who take the organismic approach to the study of development generally stress *structure-function* relations rather than stimulus-response relations. They take it as their task to describe the structures present in the behavior of the organism at any given time, the order in which they appear, and the rules determining the transition from one stage to another.

The study of structure—both biological and psychological—is justified by the argument that one cannot understand how the child functions or develops until one understands exactly *what* is functioning or developing. Structural analyses are illustrated by Jean Piaget's study of the structure of children's thought, and by the psychoanalytic analysis of feeling and emotion.

Jean Piaget may be the most eminent developmental psychologist of our time. He has linked research about early development to a comprehensive theory of how children move from one stage to another, with successively more stable and sophisticated modes of thought appearing at each stage. Piaget began his professional career as a biologist; thus it is not surprising that he would base his theory on an organismic model. Later, while working in Alfred Binet's laboratory in Paris, constructing an intelligence test for children, Piaget became interested in the *wrong* answers that children gave while being tested. He considered the possibility that those wrong answers came not as a result of children being less smart than adults, but from a totally different way of thinking and viewing the world. The problem that attracted Piaget was the origin of knowledge: What do children know and how do they acquire this knowledge? It was from the writings of the rationalist philosopher Immanuel Kant (1724–1804) that Piaget drew inspiration. Kant asserted that the mind at birth could not be "blank," for if it were, human beings could never acquire the ability to reason.

Piaget

According to Kant, the capacity to make causal judgments, to comprehend time, space, and number are inherent properties of mind that make it possible to make sense out of experience. Piaget set out to study how the categories of reason develop in young children. Does the infant at birth comprehend causality, time, space, and number? Or are there simpler, earlier structures that become transformed with experience into adult categories of reason? Beginning with the concept of structure as consisting of three key ideas—wholeness, transformation, and self-regulation— Piaget roughly defines a structure as "a system of transformations" and states that the structure as a whole (the system) is defined by laws governing the relations among its parts or elements.

What Piaget means is easier to illustrate than to explain. An example is his classic study of the "conservation problem," which Piaget used in order to study the origins of the child's concept of quantity. A child is shown two identical beakers (A and B) filled with equal amounts of liquid, as illustrated in Figure 1–2. He is asked whether the two contain the same amount, and most children agree that they do. The liquid from one beaker (say B) then is poured into a third beaker (C), which is shorter and wider. The child is again asked whether the two beakers (A and C) contain the same amount. In the same manner, the liquid is poured back into the original beaker (B), and then into another beaker (D), which is taller and thinner. If the child always says that the amount of liquid is the same, he is said to have conserved continuous quantity. The child who conserves quantity recognizes that pouring the liquid into beakers of different

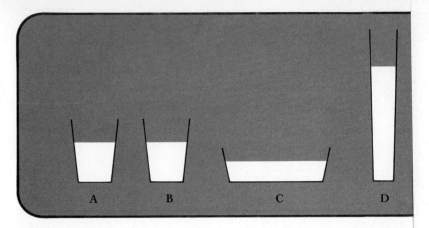

FIGURE 1–2
Conservation of continuous quantity

shapes does not change the amount. If the child does not assert th quantity of liquid remains the same, then he has failed to conserve.

When the child performs the conservation problem ("same? less?") by reference to the surface appearance of things (that is, hei width), and again when he or she shifts from height to width w sensing a contradiction, the child is demonstrating *structural* cha istics of thinking. In the first case, the child's cognitive structure is ized on the basis of surface appearances such as height or width. second case, the child has replaced these properties with the "l conservation of quantity" as an organizing principle. To Piaget, modes of thought are structural properties. Their existence in the defines what the child can and cannot do in his or her interactions the outside world (Flavell, 1963).

In an elaboration of this study (Inhelder, Bovet, and Sinclair, the child was shown transparent jars filled with equal amounts of li Instead of being poured out, the liquid emptied through taps into c ent-shaped jars and finally into jars identical to the original ones Figure 1–3). By experimenting with this arrangement, the child car form both dimensional and quantitative comparisons and event arrive at an understanding of conservation of quantity. The results experiment showed, according to Piaget (1970), that the ease with wh child acquires a logical structure such as conservation depends o child's level of development. For example, most very young children unable to learn the logic underlying the principle of conservatior higher levels of development, the ability to learn the principle of conse tion—that is, to demonstrate a structural characteristic of thinking creased progressively. If the child understood quantitative relat before taking part in the experiment, he or she could learn the princ of conservation from the comparisons made during the experiment. the farther the child was from that ability, the less likely he or she wa use the experimental sequence to arrive at an understanding of conse tion. It is at this point that Piaget's notion of the stages of developn comes into play.

and outer reality. At about 8 months, the infant begins to become aware of its environment as separate from itself. The beginnings of symbolic play also occur during this period, starting at about 18 months.

During the *preoperational* period, from ages 2 to 7, the child gradually prepares for the period of concrete operations. At the beginning of the preoperational period, the child responds primarily to external appearances, as the conservation problem illustrates. The preoperational child believes that a row of four objects tightly grouped contains fewer items than a longer row of four objects loosely grouped. Only after considerable experience can the child go beyond surface appearances. After counting both rows of items many times, the child will come to understand the equivalence of both rows. During this period, the child also learns to use language and to form mental images.

The period of *concrete operations* extends from age 7 to age 11 or 12. The term *concrete operations* refers to mental acts that the child can perform on objects at hand. The child can mentally add and subtract items from groupings and can consider subgroupings within a larger category. For example, he or she can mentally consider whether a box of balls contains more blue or more red balls without having to physically divide the balls to establish a one-to-one equivalence. Such operations, however, are still limited to the child's concrete experiences; he or she cannot yet think logically about abstract ideas.

The period of *formal operations* begins in early adolescence. During this period, the child gains access to principles of propositional thought and begins to "operate on operations," that is, to think about thought itself as well as about concrete things. The adolescent can perform operations on hypothetical statements and can work through to a logical conclusion despite the validity of the content. Such thought leads eventually to the ability to program computers, to work out the structures of atoms, to navigate aircraft, and so forth. From the standpoint of intellectual development, the child has reached maturity.

PIAGETIAN PRINCIPLES OF CHANGE. We have seen that development in Piagetian theory proceeds through a series of stages characterized by different behavioral and intellectual schemes. But how does this happen? What forces are at work in the child to propel him or her along a particular developmental path?

Piaget's theory of change begins with organization and adaptation. *Organization* refers to the tendency to combine physical and psychological structures into coherent systems. These tendencies are inherited, but the ways in which a particular individual adapts and organizes are determined by the environment in which the individual grows and learns. In Piagetian theory, the term *adaptation* means more than Darwinian fitness to survive; it means the ability to modify the environment as well.

Adaptation takes two forms: accommodation and assimilation. *Ac-*

commodation refers to the tendency to change in response to the environment. Suppose an infant is shown a shiny plastic cube he has never seen before. In order to grasp the cube, he must adapt (or accommodate) to its features — its size, location, squareness, slipperiness, weight. As he reaches for the cube, his eyes and arms accommodate to its location, his hands accommodate to its size, shape, and texture. In lifting the cube and bringing it closer, his body muscles must accommodate to its weight as his eyes and hands accommodate to the changing visual perspective and motor activity. Simple actions thus involve a series of linked accommodations that must occur if the cube is to be brought to its final destination — usually the mouth.

But Piaget is quick to point out that accommodation cannot occur without the complementary process of assimilation. *Assimilation* is the incorporation of elements of the external world into the child's own activities. By the age of 4 months, the actions of reaching for an object, grasping it, and bringing it to the mouth are a well-coordinated pattern of behavior. When the child sees a new object, he or she acts upon it by using such well-established and familiar patterns of behavior. In a sense, the child incorporates — assimilates — new objects into familiar ways of dealing with objects. Piaget likens assimilation to a digestive process in which new objects act as foods for sensorimotor schemes.

Accommodation and assimilation are complementary processes. One (accommodation) involves transforming structures in response to the environment. The other (assimilation) involves dealing with the environment in terms of previously formed structures. Children are continually trying to reach a balance between the two: in drinking, between too much and too little water; in eating, between too much and too little food; in experiencing the world around them, between what they already know and what is novel and puzzling. Piaget terms this process *equilibration*.

To Piaget, equilibration is the mechanism underlying growth (again, we are speaking here of both physical and psychological growth): "In a sense, development is a progressive equilibration from a lesser to a higher state of equilibrium" (Piaget, 1967, p. 3). Once a particular equilibrium has been achieved, however, what stimulates the child to go on to higher stages of development? In other words, *why* does cognitive development occur?

Piaget believes that cognitive development results from the child's efforts to understand the physical world. Each step toward understanding gives rise to new questions. As any parent can tell you, and as you probably remember from your own childhood, a child's favorite question is "Why?" Questioning continues until a final equilibrium is reached between the individual's cognitive structures and the information coming in from the environment, at which point formal reasoning takes over. From a need to understand what is happening in his or her experience, the child *constructs* his or her own intellectual development. Carrying the analysis one step further, we may ask, What is the source of the child's endless curiosity? To this question, Piaget answers that the need to know is an inherent characteristic of the organism itself. This need guides the organism toward its end state, intellectual maturity.

Psychoanalytic Theory: Freud and Erikson

Psychoanalytic theory is "structural" in that it deals with the organization of emotion and experience; with structures that can be substituted for each other (generosity for greed, hate for love, and so forth); and with stages of development that represent *transformations* from preceding stages. Despite these general similarities to Piagetian theory, however, there are significant differences. Most notably, the emphasis of psychoanalytic theory is on *individual* personality structure rather than on the universal structure of mind. Psychoanalytic theory focuses on the partially resolved and partially unresolved conflicts of the individual and on the individual's adaptations to those conflicts.

Sigmund Freud (1856–1939) was the founder of psychoanalytic theory. The essence of the theory is that basic *drives* (or instincts) must be gratified at each stage of development. Biological maturation moves the child from stage to stage, but experiences in each stage affect the psychological outcome of that stage on the child. Too much frustration or too much gratification in any stage promotes fixation on the needs at that stage. Freud labeled these stages according to the body zones that gratify the drives. Thus the young child moves through the *oral, anal,* and *phallic* stages as the child's source of instinctual satisfaction shifts from the mouth to the genitals. When children are in the phallic stage (between the ages of 3 and about 6), they experience the Oedipal (or Electra) conflict. According to Freud, boys have an unconscious sexual attraction for their mothers, and girls have a similar attraction for their fathers. Because the object of the attraction cannot be obtained, the child suppresses these feelings and identifies with the parent of the same sex. This identification ushers in the *latency* period, which lasts until adolescence, when physiological changes prepare the way for the *genital* stage and sexual interest in people of the opposite sex.

Freud believed that children acquire basic personality structures in the course of psychosexual development. The first structure to appear is the *id,* which represents the infant's unregulated pleasure-seeking instincts. When hungry or lonely, the infant storms and rages until its needs are met. Later, during the preschool years, the child becomes able to control his primary drives according to the demands and expectations of the environment. The structure that monitors the relation between drives and reality is called the *ego.* The ego of the preschool child enables the child to wait for gratification and to recognize more than one way of finding satisfaction. Finally, having resolved the Oedipal conflict by identifying with the same-sex parent, the child acquires a conscience. The moral standards of the parents become internalized, and the child acquires a *superego* (conscience) that will always be there to make him feel uncomfortable when he violates a moral prohibition. According to Freud, adult character traits are formed when the natural developmental events of childhood are frustrated.

Erik Erikson described how *social events* in the child's life influence later personality. Erikson's work, therefore, is described as psycho*social,* pertaining to the psychological development of the individual in relation to his or her social environment. Freud's approach, on the other hand, is described as psycho*sexual,* having to do with the psychological aspects of sexuality.

Erikson views human growth

from the point of view of the conflicts, *inner and outer, which the vital [i.e., healthy] personality weathers, re-emerging from each crisis with an increased sense of inner unity, with an increase in the capacity "to do well" according to his own standards and to the standards of those who are significant to him. (Erikson, 1968, p. 92; emphasis added)*

Erikson outlined eight stages that occur during the human life cycle. Each stage involves a particular kind of encounter with the environment and a resultant *crisis* (meaning not a catastrophe but a turning point). The crisis is a period of high vulnerability together with immense potential. It is therefore the source both of strength and of maladjustment in the individual.

Erikson called Freud's oral stage of infancy the *incorporative* stage. It is a period of receptivity and acceptance and, later, a period of taking and holding on to. The baby's "encounters" are more varied than one might at first realize:

APPROXIMATE CHRONOLOGICAL AGE	FREUD'S STAGES	ERIKSON'S STAGES
Infancy	Oral	Trust vs. mistrust
1½–3 years	Anal	Autonomy vs. shame and doubt
3–6 years	Phallic	Initiative vs. guilt
6–12 years	Latency	Mastery vs. inferiority
Adolescence	Genital	Ego identity vs. identity confusion
Young adulthood	—	Intimacy vs. isolation
Mid-adulthood	—	Productivity vs. self-absorption
Maturity	—	Ego integrity vs. despair

TABLE 1–1
Comparison of Freud's and Erikson's Stages of Development

Some people think that a baby, lest he scratch his own eyes out, must necessarily be swaddled completely for most of the day and throughout the greater part of the first year, and that he should be rocked or fed whenever he whimpers. Others think that he should feel the freedom of his kicking limbs as early as possible, but also that as a matter of course, he should be forced to cry "please" for his meals until he literally gets blue in the face. (Erikson, 1968, pp. 98–99)

Ideally, the outcome of this stage should be a feeling of trust—in oneself as well as in others—but all too often the outcome is a deep mistrust of both self and others.

The stage that Freud identified as the anal stage involves the contradictory impulses to hold on and to let go. The key encounter of this period is with the process of toilet training, and the ideal outcome, according to Erikson, is a feeling of autonomy. Quite often, however, the child ends up with strong feelings of shame and doubt.

Early childhood (Freud's phallic stage) is, in Erikson's terms, an *intrusive* stage characterized by "intrusion into space...; into the unknown...; into other people's ears and minds...; upon or into other bodies..." (Erikson, 1968, p. 116). The "encounter" is with the realization that the child will not be able to replace the father in the mother's affections (or vice versa). The rival parent becomes the ideal for the child, and the result of the child's efforts to approach that ideal may range from a strong sense of initiative to a deep sense of guilt.

Erikson's later stages show the same pattern of biologically and socially based encounter, crisis, and outcomes stated as polarities (such as identity versus identity confusion). The school-age child, for example, learns to produce things and develops a sense of mastery and industry—but may also develop a sense of inferiority. And the adolescent's encounter with society results in either a sense of identity or the familiar "identity crisis." In addition to these stages in childhood, Erikson has outlined a series of stages that extend beyond adolescence and into adulthood, based on the same structural principles (see Table 1–1).

Psychoanalytic theory has had a substantial influence on studies of children's development. The first studies of infant attachment to a mothering figure were inspired by psychoanalytic notions. Studies of femininity and masculinity examined the child's early identification with the same-sex parent. Implications for rearing children have also been derived from psychoanalytic theory: "The relationship of the individual's later feelings and character traits to earlier experiences suggests that manipulation of these experiences in a 'healthy' direction may favorably influence later development" (Caldwell and Richmond, 1962, p. 76).

Ethology

The term *ethology* refers to the observation and study of the ways organisms adapt to environmental conditions. This kind of research has for the most part developed out of Darwin's theory of evolution, especially through the work of Konrad Lorenz. Ethologists ask *why* an animal (whether human or nonhuman) behaves in a particular way—that is, what the survival value of a behavior is. In keeping with the organismic model, ethologists investigate the behavior of the total organism and its relation to the physical and social environment. Ethologists stress (as does Piaget) the behavior patterns of an animal; a catalogue of these patterns is called an *ethogram*. Each behavior pattern is described in detail, often using slow-motion film to capture behavior sequences that ordinarily happen too quickly to permit fine description (Eibl-Eibesfeldt, 1970).

Recently, the field of ethology has broadened to include the study of humans—particularly children. Moreover, its scope has been widened to include "social ethology," in which group behavior is studied in ways similar to those used to study individual behavior. It is expected that research of this sort will yield insight into matters such as mother-infant attachment and development of sex differences.

In attempting to answer questions concerning why children behave in particular ways, ethologists begin with close observation and description of behavior. In studying different kinds of smiles, for example, the physical appearance of the smile is described and then the conditions under which the smile occurs are analyzed. The reason for doing this is that, as mentioned earlier, it is difficult to study "how" without knowing "what."

Ethologists emphasize that there is more than one way to answer the question of why an animal behaves in a certain way. The answer may be either immediate or historical, and it may be either individual or related to the species. For example, the answer to why a young child shows a particular pattern of sleep may have to do with the current state of the child's central nervous system, with the way the child's central nervous system has developed since birth, with the possible function of sleep in all children, or with the evolution of sleep as an adaptation serving a particular function. Answers of the first two types have been traditional in psychology, but answers of the last two types have recently become more important. The ethologist points out that observational and descriptive research are indispensable in answering basic questions in terms of human status as "a biological organism with an evolutionary history" (Hess, 1970, p. 9).

RESEARCH DESIGNS AND METHODS

We have seen how different world views lead to differences in the theories and hypotheses proposed by various researchers in the field of child development. The research designs and methods used by investigators also tend to follow from their overall world views. Those who are concerned with developmental stages and the structure of behavior at each stage tend to emphasize detailed descriptions of what children do. Piaget, for example, described in great detail how the pattern of sucking, looking, and grasping behaviors of his babies changed with age. The emphasis on careful description is in keeping with the notion that stages emerge in a regular sequence. It follows, then, that one of the major questions of interest to stage, or organismic, theorists is whether it can be shown that any given set of patterns constitutes an *ordinal scale*. That is, do all children pass through stage 1 before entering stage 2, and then pass through stage 3?

Those who see development as a continuous process, who study children's learning as how children process information, adopt a strikingly different research strategy. These theorists are interested in finding reliable measures of the processes under investigation—number of trials in learning, number of items remembered, time spent looking at a stimulus. Whereas Piaget is interested in how children arrive at eight right or wrong solutions, researchers in the mechanistic tradition focus on inferences based on how output changes as a function of input variations. For example, when children observe an aggressive model, does their subsequent aggression vary as a function of whether the model was punished? Will children look longer at a familiar object than at an unfamiliar object?

These differences are profound ones that subtly influence other aspects of research. Although theorists who work in different traditions use observational procedures in different ways, all child study begins with the description and classification of children's behavior.

Observational Methods

Historically, the baby biography was the first step in the development of systematic observation of children. A baby biography is a diary that is usually kept by the child's parents. The first published baby biography recorded the infancy of Louis XIII. It was a detailed description of all his activities kept by the court physician Hérouard (and, incidentally, has proved exceptionally useful to modern researchers studying attitudes toward children and child-rearing practices of the seventeenth century). During the nineteenth century, baby biographies became quite popular. Charles Darwin's record of the behavior of his 3-year-old son is perhaps the best-known example.

Baby biographies were a rich source of information about early development, but they had certain disadvantages. For one thing, there was no way of knowing whether the reported behavior was typical of children of a particular age. Moreover, one could not be sure that the observers were accurately reporting what had happened. It is difficult to believe, for example, Hérouard's observation that the 2-month-old Louis responded "Erouad" (Hérouard) when the wet nurse asked, "Who is that man?"

Early in the twentieth century, a new method—the questionnaire—was introduced. In a study of curiosity in children, for example, Theodate L. Smith and G. Stanley Hall (1907) asked parents to "describe the first sign of curiosity or wonder in the infant" or "give instances of destructive curiosity." Note, however, that the questionnaire method still required the investigator to trust the observational reliability of parents. Researchers still use questionnaires or, more often, interviews to find out about parents' child-rearing beliefs or about children's perceptions of family, teachers, and friends. Sometimes these procedures are necessary. Whenever it is practical, though, contemporary researchers prefer to observe what children do rather than to rely on what other people or the children themselves say they do.

The next step toward accurate observation was field observation in natural settings or in "naturalistic" laboratory settings. This method uses trained observers in either natural or arranged situations. Children are studied in natural situations because their development is undoubtedly influenced by their ordinary, everyday experiences, and it is often misleading to *guess* what these experiences might be. In naturalistic studies, the purpose is to study the relationship between events that occur naturally and the response of the child to such events. The researcher might observe how children play, how they interact with teachers, or how they use materials in home and school situations.

Experimental Methods

For some research purposes, uncontrolled natural situations are inadequate. For example, in ordinary life, children may have few opportunities to exhibit altruistic behavior although they are capable of this behavior when the occasion arises. Since opportunities in the real world differ, some children may *seem* to be more generous, helpful, and thoughtful than others. In such cases, children can be observed in experimental studies deliberately arranged by the investigator. These situations have the advantage of being standardized; that is, they are the same from one child to the next. Also, experimental studies are designed so that comparisons may be made among the specific features of events that might influence children's behavior. The researcher can create situations that bear specifically upon the problem being investigated and eliminate factors that detract from the study of that problem. The experimenter can control which elements in the situation change, in order to compare the reactions of different groups of children. For example, in a study of children's play, one group of children was observed playing on a climbing apparatus with many attractive parts, while another group was observed playing on an apparatus with few parts (Scholtz and Ellis, 1975). The experimenter recorded how often the children touched the apparatus and how often they touched one another, in order to determine how variations in the complexity of play equipment influence play. The experimenter might also vary the size of the play group, or whether or not an adult is present, depending, of course, on what he or she wishes to study. It must be recognized, though, that the information obtained in experimental studies refers only to behavior in such standardized situations.

Planned experiments can take place in natural settings or in laboratory settings. In a field experiment (such as the play study described above), deliberate variations are introduced into natural settings. In a laboratory study, on the other hand, the experimenter attempts to approximate settings found in the real world. Whether in the field or the laboratory, experimental researchers are concerned with children's perceptions and feelings as they participate in the study. Do the children view the experimenter with apprehension? Is the setting an unfamiliar one? Do participants understand the problem they are being asked to solve? These and similar factors influence results.

Correlational Analyses

Recall Hippocrates's hypothesis that climate influences human ability. It would be exceedingly difficult to examine this hypothesis in a controlled experiment. People would have to be randomly assigned to different climates, and temperamental and intellectual differences would have to be studied over successive generations. Such difficulties do not mean, though, that it is impossible to study how climate influences human ability. The hypothesis could be changed into a statement about *relationships* instead of causes. That is, the words "is related to" could be substituted for the word "influences." A study to test the hypothesis "climate is related to human ability" could much more easily be done.

Much research in child development is about relationships between one factor and another. These relationships are expressed as *correlations*. Correlational analyses have made important contributions to the understanding of how different behaviors are related. For example, some investigators report a *positive* correlation between parental punishment of children and children's aggression with peers. This simply means that a great deal of punishment is associated with a great deal of aggression. A *negative* correlation means something quite different. In the above example, a negative correlation would mean that a great deal of punishment would be associated with relatively little aggression. It is often tempting to interpret correlations as causal statements, especially when relations between adults and children are being studied. But to do so would be to draw an unwarranted conclusion from the data. For example, children sometimes influence their parents as much as parents influence their children, as we will discuss in later chapters. In this instance, an active, impulsive, explosive child might precipitate parental punishment.

Development refers to change—usually change that occurs over a substantial period of time. In order to study developmental change, researchers often compare children at different ages. They use one of two types of studies—longitudinal or cross-sectional.

Longitudinal Versus Cross-Sectional Studies

In a *longitudinal study,* the same children are observed on several occasions over an extended period of time. For example, in studying children's vocabulary, the investigator might observe a group of 15-month-olds, then observe the *same* group at 19 months, and again at 24 months. The data thus obtained can provide information about sequence of development, since each child becomes his or her own standard for comparison. Stage theorists prefer longitudinal studies, especially during periods of rapid growth, because they are interested in changes in the patterning of behavior rather than in what children are able to do at any given age. Longitudinal methods are also used to study the stability of behavior. For example, in studying the stability of scores on intelligence tests, the same people might be tested at regular intervals from infancy to adulthood in order to determine whether a person's performance at one age correlates with his or her performance at a later age. Finally, longitudinal methods are used to study the way early experiences influence later behavior. Interactions between mothers and infants when the children are 12 months old might be correlated with school grades in the same children.

There are drawbacks to the use of longitudinal studies. Longitudinal studies can be troublesome because children who begin a study do not always continue to its end. Also, with repeated testing over time, children might become familiar with the test materials. And it takes a long time to find the answers to the questions posed by the study. However, for some problems, longitudinal procedures are preferred; for others they are essential.

In a *cross-sectional study,* different children in various age groups are observed. Suppose the investigator wants to compare children's vocabularies at several different ages. He or she might select groups of children at different age levels—say, 15, 19, 24, and 27 months. Of course, there would be different children in each group. Such a study would provide information about how children differ from one age to another. But it would not tell the investigator anything about the sequence of development, such as which kinds of words appear first, which appear next, and whether early features of vocabulary influence later language skills. Clearly, cross-sectional studies are unable to address many consequential questions. Yet, they do not have the problem of losing participants over time, and the results can be known in considerably less time. For these reasons, cross-sectional studies are more popular than longitudinal studies. Consequently, they are the source of much of what we know about children.

SUMMARY

Two models—the mechanistic and the organismic—have dominated the study of child development. The *mechanistic model* likens the workings of an organism to those of a machine. Investigators who work in the mechanistic tradition are concerned with the process of change, the principles that account for the relation between input (stimulus) and output (behavior).

Mechanistic and organismic theorists hold different views of the nature of development. One difference is the issue of whether development is continuous or discontinuous. Mechanistic and organismic theorists also disagree about what constitutes and characterizes *stages* of development.

Learning theory, for example, comes out of the mechanistic tradition. Learning theorists study the shaping of behavior by the formation of regular associations between *stimulus* and *response.* Traditionally, learning theorists have used two processes by which associative connections are made—classical conditioning and operant conditioning.

Classical conditioning, based on the work done by Pavlov, pairs an unconditioned stimulus, which normally elicits an unconditioned response, with a neutral stimulus (the conditioned stimulus). After repeated presentations, the conditioned stimulus will be enough to reproduce the original response.

Operant conditioning changes the frequency of a spontaneous behavior (or *operant*) by introducing a stimulus after the behavior occurs. Stimuli that increase the frequency of behavior are called *reinforcers;* stimuli that suppress behavior are called *punishments.* In operant conditioning, the associative connection is between the operant behavior and its consequence. *Extinction* is the return of the operant to its previous state when the reinforcement or punishment is discontinued. Learned responses may be *generalized* to situations similar to that in which the response was learned. Sometimes, *overgeneralization* takes place. Operant conditioning can be used to teach a complex behavior by means of *shaping,* in which rewards are given for performance that comes closer and closer to the desired behavior.

Social learning theory investigates learning processes based on observation of a model. The acquisition of a particular behavior results primarily from observation (modeling); performance of that behavior depends on the anticipated consequences.

The *information-processing* approach examines the processes that convert specific inputs into specific outputs. Information-processing theorists view the flow of information through a system as a series of operations similar to the subroutines of a computer program.

The *organismic/structural model* of development takes as its pattern a biological system. The concept of the child as a system emphasizes the relations among its parts or properties. The organismic model concentrates on *structure* or *competence,* and development consists of changes in the structure of the system over time. Structural analyses are illustrated by Piaget's study of the structure of children's thought, and by the psychoanalytic analysis of feeling and emotion.

Piaget has formulated a theory of how children move from one stage of thought to another. Each stage is a prerequisite for the one that follows. Piaget's four major stages are (1) the sensorimotor period; (2) the preoperational period; (3) the period of concrete operations; (4) the period of formal operations. Changes occur through *organization* and *adaptation.* Adaptation takes two forms: *accommodation* and *assimilation.*

Psychoanalytic theory focuses on the conflicts of the individual and on his or her adaptations to those conflicts. Freud founded psychoanalytic theory, which states that basic *drives* must be gratified at each stage of development. Freud proposed that the child moves through the following sequence of stages: *oral, anal, phallic, latency,* and *genital.* In the course of psychosexual development, basic personality structures—the *id,* the *ego,* and the *superego*—emerge. Erikson described how social events influence personality. He outlined eight stages during the human life cycle; each involves an encounter with the environment, and each can be a turning point of strength or maladjustment for the individual.

Ethology, a research method that seeks to discover the behavior patterns of animals (including humans), takes an organismic/structural approach.

Baby biographies were the first step in the systematic observation of children. Other observational methods that followed were the questionnaire and field observation in natural settings.

For some research purposes, however, uncontrolled natural settings are inadequate. In those cases, experimental methods are used. In experimental studies, the researcher can control which elements in the situation change.

Much research in child development deals with relationships between one factor and another. These relationships are expressed as *correlations,* and are measured as positive or negative. Correlations are not, however, causal statements.

In order to study developmental change, researchers compare children at different ages. They use two types of studies to do so—longitudinal or cross-sectional. In a *longitudinal* study, the same children are observed on several occasions over an extended period of time. In a *cross-sectional* study, different children in various age groups are observed. Each method has particular advantages and disadvantages for the researcher.

PART I

A Child Is Born

Quite some time ago, I decided to jot down a thing or two about my daughter, Susan. But somehow, the time passed too quickly, and she is now almost 3 years old.

What do I remember?

She was born on March 3, 1956, at 10:05 A.M. The doctor said that the birth was easy—only 6 hours of labor. I can remember hardly any of it. They knocked me out soon after the contractions began to come at 5-minute intervals. I begged them not to, but they just pushed the mask over my face. Next time, it's going to be natural childbirth. I think I missed something important.

We waited a long time for this baby—more than the 9 months it took for her to grow inside me. The first baby miscarried in the fourth month. And then we tried and tried and nothing happened. We were thrilled to discover Susan was on the way.

In the meantime we began to build a house for her (and the others who will come later). Mike and I both grew up in a city, but we've decided to build our house in the country—only an hour's ride from Mike's job. Susan will have her own room and a place to play outdoors. We want to do for her the best that we can.

CHAPTER 2

Heredity and Environment: The Origins of Individuality

THE DEVELOPMENT OF INDIVIDUALITY

Although all human beings share many characteristics, no two individuals are ever exactly alike. Each of us is the product of a unique set of genes and a unique pattern of experiences. Even identical twins, whose genes are exactly the same, develop as unique individuals. They may be different in size at birth because of their different positions in the uterus, and afterwards their individualities continue to be shaped by their unique interactions with the world.

The environment with which individuals interact is constantly changing, in ways that may be subtle or dramatic. The most drastic—and potentially most dangerous—passage from one environment to another occurs at birth. Another "natural" change is the transition from childhood to adulthood, when most people go from being cared for by their parents to having their own children and caring for them. Being born and giving birth are inevitable transitions in the human life cycle. Anthropologists, however, have recognized for a long time that different cultures can heighten the natural transitions or provide new ones. As Benedict (1938) noted in her pioneering work on cultural conditioning, our own society, where children are expected to be nonresponsible, submissive, and (despite Freud's discoveries) sexless, makes the transition from childhood to adulthood more stressful than in cultures where small children work and take some responsibility for the family's well-being. In the same way,

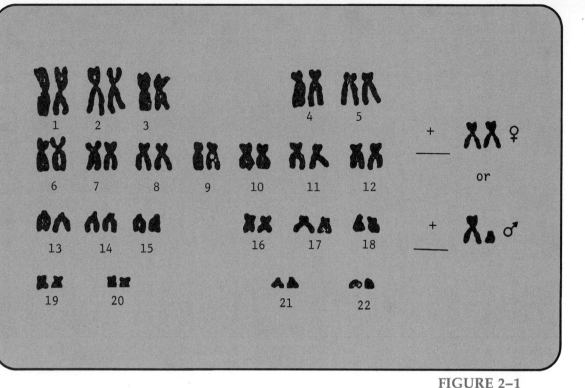

FIGURE 2–1
The 23 pairs of chromosomes in females and males, arranged in pairs. Note that the twenty-third pair of chromosomes (the sex chromosomes) is different in the female (top) and in the male (bottom). The female has two X chromosomes. The male has one X and one Y chromosome. (Landrum B. Shettles, M.D.)

our culture adds to the difficulties that come with the physical changes of aging by forcing older people to retire from their jobs and encouraging them to live in retirement "villages" or nursing homes where they are isolated from younger people.

This chapter will discuss the genetic and cultural basis of individuality. First, we will examine the genetic component of individuality, and then the aspects of individual personality that are shaped by culture and environment. These two components represent the smallest and the largest—the microstructural and the macrostructural—origins of individuality.

GENETIC TRANSMISSION

Debates about whether a person's fate is determined by character or by outside circumstances have gone on for a long time. In Shakespeare's plays, for example, characters ponder whether their destinies were determined by "the stars"—their astrological charts at the moment of birth. This debate began to take new forms in the seventeenth century after the invention of the microscope enabled scientists to see human cells and to form more precise ideas about how the body works. Sperm were first identified in 1677, but not until 200 years later did scientists explain the role of the sperm and the egg in fertilization.

FIGURE 2–2

Watson and Crick's double helix model of the DNA molecule. Each "rung" on the molecule consists of a pair of chemical bases—either thymine (T) and adenine (A), or guanine (G) and cytosine (C).

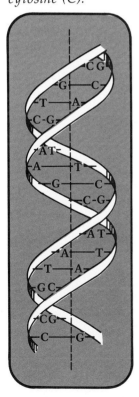

Research in biology discovered that there are two kinds of cells in the body—*somatic cells* and *germ cells*. Somatic cells are all of the cells in the body except the reproductive or germ cells (the sperm and the ova). Somatic cells govern the body's formation of bones, muscles, and organs. Each of these contains *chromosomes,* the threadlike structures that convey heredity. All members of a species have the same number and types of chromosomes, and every somatic cell in an individual's body has the same grouping of 23 pairs of chromosomes (see Figure 2–1). The members of each pair are arranged together, although each may contain different genetic information.

Each chromosome, in turn, is made up of *genes,* the smallest units of heredity. Scientists estimate that about 44,000 genes are strung like beads on each chromosome pair, which means that there are as many as one million genes distributed across the 23 pairs of chromosomes. Each gene differs from any other, and each has a "message" to contribute to the individual's total genetic code. This message is contained in the chemical structure of the gene. Some genes are common to our species and ensure that humans develop smooth skin rather than fur, lungs rather than gills, hands rather than paws, and a spinal column that enables us to stand and walk upright. Other genes determine individual characteristics such as skin, eye, and hair color, susceptibility to certain diseases, or other variations that are thought of as temperamental characteristics. Genes thus carry two kinds of messages: One kind makes an individual distinctively human, and the other makes a human who is a unique individual.

Genes and chromosomes are composed largely of a complex chemical called deoxyribonucleic acid, or DNA. DNA is the chemical code carrier for all the cells in the body. Although scientists knew that DNA existed in the cells of the body, it was not until 1953 that two researchers, J. D. Watson and F. H. C. Crick, proposed a model for its structure (see Figure 2–2). It is a giant molecule made of five chemical elements: carbon, hydrogen, oxygen, nitrogen, and phosphorus. Each DNA molecule has thousands of possible arrangements. Different arrangements of the DNA molecule cause the differences among genes. DNA directs certain cells to become bones, others to form organs, and so on. Biologists now believe that it does so by producing another nucleic acid, RNA (ribonucleic acid). RNA, unlike DNA, can circulate freely among the cells and direct the building of various proteins. Thus it functions as a "messenger" from the DNA in the cell nucleus to the rest of the cell.

In the course of development, somatic cells divide and reproduce in a process called *mitosis.* As we have mentioned, every cell in an individual's body has the same genetic content as every other cell. The reason for this is that during cell division, each gene makes a copy of itself. The 46 chromosomes in each cell grow and then split lengthwise to double in number to 92 chromosomes. Half of each identical set moves toward opposite poles of the cell. The cell then reorganizes itself into two equal parts with the normal number of chromosomes (46) in each. The two identical daughter cells that result are exact replicas of the original cell (see Figure 2–3).

Germer cells (or *gametes*) are similar to somatic cells in their basic chemical composition. They are distinct, however, in that they form only the reproductive cells of the body—sperm in males, ova in females. Each germ cell contains only 23 chromosomes—*half* the number of chromosomes of the other cells in the body. When a sperm and ovum combine, the resulting organism thus has the correct number of 46 chromosomes.

    Germ cells reproduce in a halving process called *meiosis*. During meiosis, the chromosome pairs separate *twice* (rather than once, as in mitosis) to form *four* daughter cells, each containing 23 chromosomes (see Figure

Germ Cells

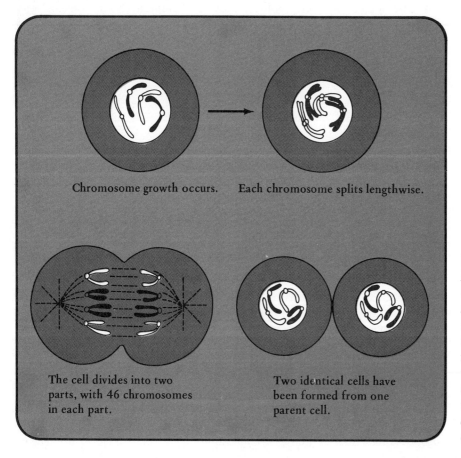

Chromosome growth occurs.   Each chromosome splits lengthwise.

The cell divides into two parts, with 46 chromosomes in each part.

Two identical cells have been formed from one parent cell.

FIGURE 2–3
Mitosis, the process by which the somatic cells in the body divide and reproduce. The two identical cells that result from mitosis are exact replicas of the original cell; each contains 46 chromosomes.

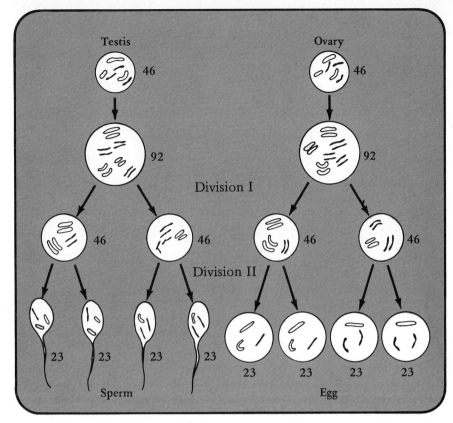

FIGURE 2-4
Meiosis, the process by which the germ cells in the body divide and reproduce. The four cells that result from meiosis contain only 23 chromosomes each.

Testis 46

Ovary 46

92

92

Division I

46 46 46 46

Division II

23 23 23 23

Sperm

23 23 23 23

Egg

2-4). Each sperm or ovum produced in meiosis contains only half of each parent's pool of about a million genes. A process called *crossover* ensures that genes from each parent are not always transmitted in blocks. Shortly before the germ cells divide, each member of the 23 chromosome pairs wraps itself closely around the other member. At this point, parts of each paired chromosome may break off, and the parts may attach themselves to the other chromosome in the pair rather than to the chromosome from which they broke away. When the final division of meiosis occurs, crossover helps to ensure that the 23 chromosomes in each of the four daughter cells contain a random assortment of genes from the original pool.

The process of sexual reproduction, in which the genes of two individuals combine to produce a new person, ensures genetic variation within any given species. It is remarkable that, even when conception occurs, the genes in the sperm and ovum already contain the instructions for producing germ cells that will someday contribute to the heredity of a new human being. The system of genetic transmission accounts for the immense variability within the human population. It ensures a range of variations that make it possible for humans to survive in vastly different environments.

DOMINANT	RECESSIVE
Dark brown hair	Light brown and red hair
Black hair	All other hair colors
Curly hair	Straight hair
Baldness (dominant in males)	Baldness (recessive in females)
Normal skin pigmentation	Albinism
Brown eyes	Blue eyes
Normal color vision	Red-green color blindness (sex-linked)
Astigmatism	Normal vision
Far-sightedness (hyperopia)	Normal vision
Double-jointedness	Normal
Diabetes insipidus	Normal
Normal	Diabetes mellitus
Sickle cell anemia	Normal
Normal	Hemophilia (sex-linked)

TABLE 2-1
Some Dominant and Recessive Characteristics

Source: Adapted from Rugh and Shettles, 1971, Appendix D, pp. 227–230.

The Mathematics of Variability

Genetic variability comes from two sources: the separation of chromosome pairs during meiosis, and their recombination into a new set of 23 pairs at fertilization. How chromosome pairs separate in meiosis is random. Since each new human being at fertilization inherits 23 chromosomes from each parent, 2^{46} combinations are possible. Each chromosome, moreover, contains thousands of genes which can be reshuffled to different chromosomes by crossover. The possible combinations of genes number in the trillions. During intercourse, from 50 to 500 million genetically different sperm enter the vagina. Only one of these will fertilize the ovum. The possible combinations of genes that a child could inherit from one set of parents are beyond the human imagination. The miracle is that, among the 23 chromosomes waiting in the ovum, at fertilization every chromosome from the father finds the "right" chromosome from the mother with which to pair up.

Of the 23 pairs of chromosomes in human cells, 22 shape the individual's general mental and physical characteristics. The chromosomes of the twenty-third pair determine what sex the organism will be. In the first 22 pairs of chromosomes, genes that affect the same trait, such as eye or hair color, are paired off. Often one member of a gene pair may be *dominant* and the other *recessive*. As the names suggest, dominant genes win out over recessive ones and determine individual characteristics. The gene for brown eyes, for example, dominates the gene for blue eyes. Thus, an individual who receives a gene for brown eyes from one parent and a gene for blue eyes from the other parent will have brown eyes. Although there are exceptions, desirable genes tend to be dominant. Table 2–1 lists some dominant and recessive characteristics.

The Genetic Basis of Sex

Biological research has identified two types of chromosomes—X and Y—that appear in the twenty-third pair of chromosomes in humans. They are the sex chromosomes, and they determine whether an individual will be male or female. An organism with two X chromosomes is female. An organism with one X chromosome and one Y chromosome is male. When ova are formed by meiosis, every ovum contains an X chromosome, since all the female's cells contain two X chromosomes. When males form sperm, half the sperm carry an X chromosome, half a Y chromosome. The woman always contributes an X chromosome. Thus, the sex of a baby depends on whether an X or a Y chromosome is contained in the sperm that fertilizes the ovum (see Figure 2–5).

The X and Y chromosomes not only establish the sex of an individual but also determine sex-linked inheritance. A number of hereditary defects in males are caused by recessive genes carried on the X chromosome. Such recessive genes, for example, cause color blindness, hemophilia (a disease in which the blood fails to clot), and baldness. In female offspring, the recessive characteristic on the X chromosome contributed by the mother will be masked by genes for the dominant characteristic on the X chromosome contributed by the father. In males, the fact that the Y chromosome is shorter than the X chromosome means that there may be ordinarily recessive genes on the X chromosome for which there is no counterpart on the Y. Therefore, the effects of the recessive gene will be expressed. Because females contribute the recessive gene, they are carriers of these conditions, but only rarely are they sufferers.

The Sex Ratio

Despite the popular idea that more girls are born than boys or that first-born children more often are girls, in fact more boys are born than girls. Approximately 106 boys are born for every 100 girls, and in first children the percentage of boys is even higher. Why are there more boys? Scientists speculate that the imbalance may result from the fact that sperm carrying Y chromosomes are smaller and lighter than those carrying X chromosomes. Therefore, they move more quickly to fertilize the ovum.

Another reason that more boys are conceived may be that boys are more vulnerable than girls. Two or three times more boys than girls are miscarried early in pregnancy; 130 boys die at birth for every 100 girls; many more boys are born defective; and at almost every stage of life, the death rate is higher for males than for females (Scheinfeld, 1972). The percentage of boys may be higher in first children because the more fragile male needs good prenatal conditions to survive, and such conditions exist more often in a woman's first pregnancy.

Throughout the ages, some people have tried to ensure that their baby will be either a boy or a girl—by choosing different positions for intercourse or having intercourse at particular times during the woman's cycle. But there is no reliable way to guarantee the sex of the child being

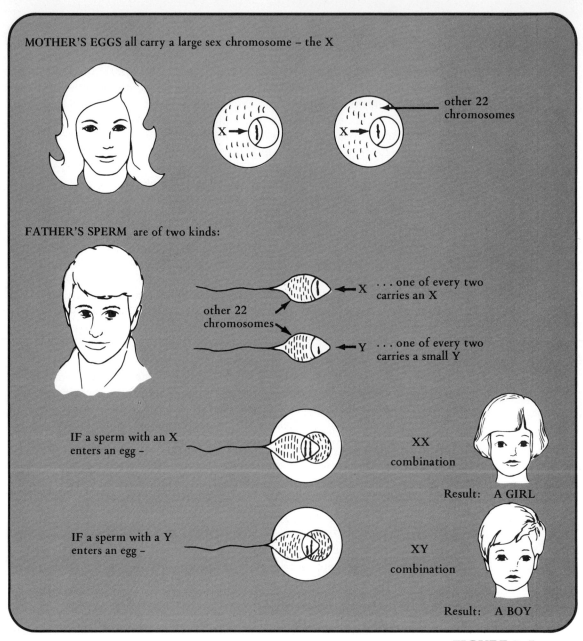

MOTHER'S EGGS all carry a large sex chromosome – the X

other 22 chromosomes

FATHER'S SPERM are of two kinds:

other 22 chromosomes

X . . . one of every two carries an X

Y . . . one of every two carries a small Y

IF a sperm with an X enters an egg –

XX combination

Result: A GIRL

IF a sperm with a Y enters an egg –

XY combination

Result: A BOY

FIGURE 2–5
How a baby's sex is determined (Adapted from Scheinfeld, 1972, p. 28)

conceived. However, parents can find out the sex of their baby before it is born. This is done in a procedure called *amniocentesis,* in which an obstetrician inserts a needle into the uterus and extracts some of the amniotic fluid. Analysis of the loose cells floating in the fluid reveals the baby's sex. Either a Y chromosome or a structure called a Barr Body, which is found only in female cells, indicates the sex of the fetus. The procedure is still too risky to be used routinely simply to determine sex. It is not usually recommended unless one of the parents has a known genetic abnormality or the mother is old enough (over 35) that Down's syndrome (mongolism) is a serious risk.

Genetic Anomalies   There are a number of genetic anomalies (abnormalities) that have impli-cations for survival and later development. They may be inherited in several ways. Some genetic defects, as we have seen, are caused by reces-sive genes on the X chromosome. The usual pattern of inheritance for such X-linked disorders is for carrier women, themselves unaffected, to pass on the defective gene to half their daughters, and for half their sons to be affected by the disease itself. Other genetic defects can be caused by paired recessive genes on the *autosomes,* the 22 pairs of chromosomes that do not affect sex. One type of paired recessive gene, for example, causes people to develop as albinos. The gene for albinism might run in a family for generations without being expressed, until a family member mated with someone who also carried the recessive gene. Then, statistically, 1 in 4 of their children might be albinos. Marriage between close relatives increases the likelihood that recessive genes will be paired.

Some genetic defects are caused not by single or paired genes but by what are called *gross chromosomal abnormalities*—the absence of a chromo-some or a part of one, or the presence of an extra one. These defects in-volve a great deal of DNA content and are apt to affect the individual's development in many ways, physically and intellectually. Chromosomal abnormalities are usually caused by a failure in the last division of meiosis or by defective division of the fertilized egg. The tendency to produce such abnormalities can be hereditary or can be caused by environmental factors, such as the age of the mother.

Different kinds of genetic anomalies, of course, have different psycho-logical and medical consequences for affected individuals and their families. Genetic "defects" run a full gamut from color blindness to dis-orders so severe that they cause spontaneous abortion or death during infancy. There are at least four kinds of genetic anomalies, classified not by their causes but by their effects:

1. Severe genetic anomalies with early death (such as Tay-Sachs disease).
2. Chronic genetic anomalies with good life expectancy (Down's syn-drome).
3. Treatable genetic anomalies with recurrent severe episodes (hemo-philia, sickle cell anemia, diabetes, cystic fibrosis).
4. Remediable genetic anomalies with amelioration of symptoms (Turn-er's syndrome, Klinefelter's syndrome, PKU). (Reed, 1975)

Chapter 16 will present these anomalies in more detail, but we will look briefly at specific examples of each of the four categories.

Diseases that result in early death can be devastating to parents, who may feel guilt about "causing" their child to have a genetic defect. Tay-Sachs disease, a metabolic disorder, causes substances to accumulate in the brain that cause degeneration of the nervous system and brain tissue. This results in mental and motor deterioration, blindness, convulsions, emaciation, and death by the time the child is 3 or 4 years old (Reed, 1975). There is no known cure. Tay-Sachs disease is produced by two recessive genes, so that parents who are both carriers have a 25% chance of having a child with the disease.

Diseases like Down's syndrome (mongolism) which cause chronic defects but are compatible with living to old age pose different, long-term problems for affected individuals and their families. Down's syndrome is associated with defects of the heart, eye, and skeleton. The average IQ of children with Down's syndrome is between 25 and 45, well below the population average of 100. Affected children used to die young, often of pneumonia or heart disease. Antibiotics and heart surgery now allow these children to live much longer, so that the birth of an affected child raises a number of questions for the parents: whether to choose complicated and expensive heart surgery; whether or when to institutionalize the child; what will be the effects on themselves and their other children of caring for a severely retarded person. (Reed, 1975).

Treatable genetic anomalies that can cause severe, even life-threatening, crises cause other types of problems: prolonged and expensive medical care; pain and fear associated with the crises; the difficulties of living within the restrictions posed by the disease. Sickle cell anemia is one such severe chronic blood disease. During crises, the red blood cells change their shape and block the flow of blood through small blood vessels, causing pain and possible tissue death if the condition is not treated promptly. Crises can be caused by infection, lack of oxygen due to high altitudes, or strenuous exercise—or they may have no discernible cause at all. Sickle cell anemia occurs most frequently in people whose ancestors came from malarial regions in Africa. (The sickle cell trait may be a protective reaction of the body against a form of malaria.) Ten percent of American blacks are carriers of the trait, and they can be easily identified by blood tests, even though they are relatively symptom-free. Two carrier parents have a 25% chance of having an afflicted child. Sickle cell anemia, like hemophilia, diabetes, and other diseases that require restrictions on activity or diet, has special psychological consequences. Affected children or their parents may become overanxious or overprotective, and some adolescents may rebel against their disease by exercising too strenuously, picking fights, or ignoring dietary restrictions.

A few genetic anomalies can now be treated and their worst symptoms prevented. PKU (phenylketonuria) is a metabolic disorder. If the condition is untreated, it causes mental retardation, irritability, and hyperactivity. If the condition is diagnosed early (in most states all newborns are tested for it), a restricted diet during childhood can prevent retardation and many of the behavioral problems. PKU is caused by two recessive genes, so that all the children of affected individuals will be carriers. PKU women, especially, may be advised not to have children (Reed, 1975).

Today, many genetic anomalies can be detected in the fetus by the process of amniocentesis. If the fetus is found to have a serious disease caused by a genetic "defect," a therapeutic abortion may be the recommended course of action. The percentages listed in the above discussion illustrate the mathematical probabilities—and the realities—of genetic transmission. Additionally, they support the logic of genetic counseling, particularly for couples who suspect they may be in a high-risk category.

As we discussed earlier, some genetic anomalies are sex-linked. Others come from the workings of dominant and recessive traits, and still others come from chromosomal anomalies. Special environmental stresses can sometimes influence the occurrence of genetic or chromosomal aberrations, as well, as we will see in Chapter 3. We have already noted that the likelihood of harmful recessive traits inherited from both parents is always greater in closely related people. Scientists speak of "hybrid vigor" in plants and animals to explain the phenomenon in which hybrid offspring display greater size and health than their parents. Observations of people who have been closely inbred show that the notion of hybrid vigor holds true for human beings as well. In isolated rural communities, for example, certain inherited traits are prominent. In the European royal families, where inbreeding was common, entire dynasties became proverbial for madness, and Queen Victoria's children carried hemophilia to half the royal houses in Europe. Several studies of children produced by incest—the most extreme form of inbreeding—show that approximately half of them either die in infancy or are extremely retarded. Inbreeding may be becoming rarer in contemporary advanced societies, where people are more mobile and fewer communities are isolated than in the past. Studies in France and England (Dubos, 1969) have shown that availability of the bicycle alone increases tenfold the area in which one looks for a mate!

Family Resemblance By the simple workings of heredity, the child receives a random selection of about half the parents' genes. Thus parents and children resemble each other, and children usually show some resemblance to their other relatives. Parent and child have about 50% of their genes in common, as do siblings. Genetic inheritance, however, changes in the case of identical twins.

TWINS. What is the genetic difference between fraternal and identical twins? Fraternal twins are *dizygotic* (DZ): They are formed when the mother releases two ova during one menstrual cycle and each is fertilized by a *different* sperm. Identical twins are *monozygotic* (MZ): They are formed when one ovum that has been fertilized by one sperm divides completely soon after conception, giving rise to two separate individuals (see Figure

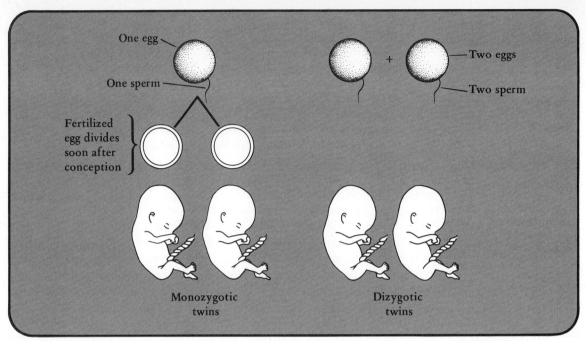

FIGURE 2–6
*How monozygotic
and dizygotic twins
are formed*

2–6). Monozygotic twins are genetically identical because they came from one fertilized egg. Dizygotic twins, genetically, are no more alike than any other siblings.

Studying identical and fraternal twins enables researchers to examine the influences of genes and environment on the development of psychological characteristics. Since monozygotic twins have the same genetic inheritance, any differences between the members of an MZ pair are thought to be caused by the environment. Differences between the members of a DZ pair, on the other hand, may be attributed to both heredity and environment. The influence of heredity on intelligence, for example, can be calculated by studying twins. A summary of such studies shows that the closer two individuals' genetic inheritances are, the closer their IQ scores will be (Scarr-Salapatek, 1975). MZ twins are much more alike in IQ than are DZ twins, whether or not the twins were reared together. Twin studies have also been used to measure the inheritance of psychosis. When both members of a twin pair have a particular trait or disorder, they are called *concordant;* if only one does, they are *discordant.* A study by Kallmann (1953) showed that schizophrenia in MZ twins is concordant 86.2% of the time; in DZ pairs, only 14.5% of cases are concordant. Such findings suggest that a predisposition to schizophrenia may be inherited.

SHARED HEREDITY. The workings of probability allow geneticists to estimate how likely it is for individuals to inherit certain characteristics. Table 2–2 shows the genetic inheritance that different family members have in common. Children share approximately 50% of their parents' genetic characteristics; 25% of their grandparents'; 25% of their uncles' and aunts'. Shared heredity accounts for many physical resemblances between family members.

Family resemblances, moreover, are increased by *assortative mating*— the tendency for "likes" to marry "likes." People tend to choose partners who resemble themselves in background and intelligence. Assortative mating may well be increasing in modern societies. Geographical mobility, as we already have seen, allows people to choose from a wider range of marriage partners than when they were limited to their own town or neighborhood. Likewise, in the United States, young people are increasingly grouped on the basis of social status or academic achievement. Performance on IQ tests administered as early in life as grade school may determine who is in which high school class and who goes where to college and professional school. To the extent that children from artistic, business, or intellectual families tend to marry others from similar families, offspring within a family will tend to have similar talents. At the present time, within the white population of the United States, the IQ correlation between parents—who are not genetically related at all—is approximately .40. A correlation of 0 would occur if mating were totally random. The IQ

Monozygotic twins share 100% of their parents' genetic characteristics. Dizygotic twins share 50% of their parents' genes and are no more alike than any other two siblings. (Shelly Rusten)

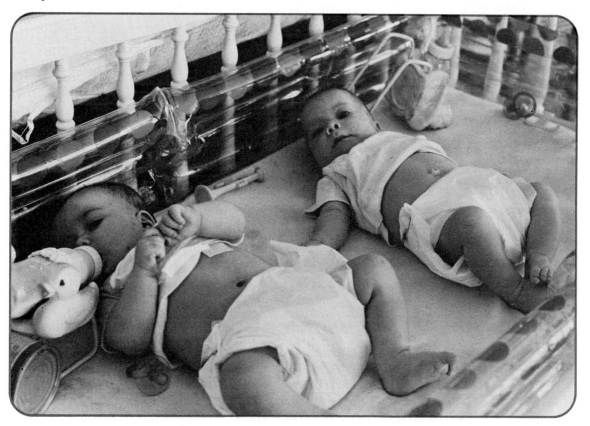

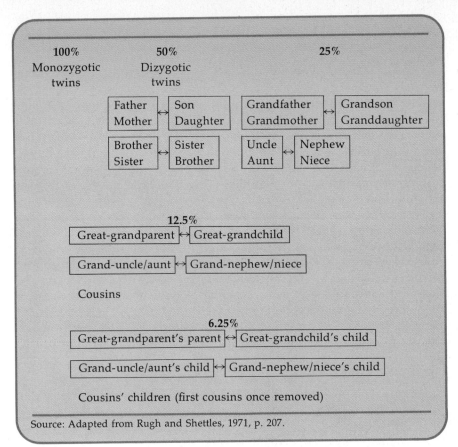

Source: Adapted from Rugh and Shettles, 1971, p. 207.

TABLE 2-2
Degrees of Shared Heredity Among Family Members

correlation between siblings is .55, rather than .50 which would be expected if parents mated on a random basis. Since assortative mating makes family members more alike than simple probability would suggest, it also makes for greater differences *between* families.

Polygenic Models of Inheritance

Earlier we discussed how some characteristics like eye color, color blindness, and certain genetic abnormalities are inherited through combinations of single genes that are dominant or recessive for those characteristics. Many other characteristics, however, are the products not of one gene but of many genes.

Behavioral geneticists believe that characteristics like height, intelligence, and some mental illnesses result from the cumulative effect of multiple genes whose "messages" are small and similar. Inheritance for such characteristics is termed *polygenic*. Intelligence, for example, seems to be influenced by a combination of at least 20 genes, and perhaps by as many as several hundred (Scarr-Salapatek, 1975).

The polygenic model of inheritance proposes that, given random mating, family members will become less similar with each successive generation and over each degree of difference in kinship. The model also suggests that the abilities of offspring will tend to move toward the population mean. A parent of above-average intelligence will have children who are not as bright, and the grandchildren will be even closer to the average. Genius seems rarely to be passed on to succeeding generations. In fact, over the span of six to eight generations, family members are, genetically, practically unrelated (Scarr-Salapatek, 1975). There is considerable evidence to support the theory of polygenic inheritance. A study comparing performance on intelligence tests in three generations (grandparents, parents, and children), for example, found the correlations for grandparents and grandchildren much smaller than for parents and children. Interestingly, among immediate family members, fathers and sons were most alike in intelligence (92% positive correlation); mothers and sons least alike (67% positive correlation); and mother-daughter and father-daughter pairs were in the middle (Honzik, 1971).

All told, there is considerable evidence that many human characteristics have a genetic component, whether it is singular or polygenic. There is also, however, a large body of evidence indicating that the environment contributes to how a person develops and to what a person will be like as an adult. In the next section we will look at some of the ways in which the environment influences individual development.

GENOTYPE AND ENVIRONMENT

The Concept of Expression

The human infant inherits the core characteristics of the species *Homo sapiens* in addition to the potential for individuality. *Endogenous* (internal) biological factors determine the physical form and potential competencies of the child and the patterns of changes that will mark his or her development. *Exogenous* (external) societal factors—the material, economic, and social conditions of life—constitute the immediate environment in which the child lives, the environment that determines whether a child will become a farmer, a teacher, or a machinist. These two environments are in constant interaction. Endogenous factors, for example, enable the human child to learn the use of tools and of symbols (language). Exogenous factors determine which language the child will speak and provide the raw materials of experience from which tools and symbols are constructed. The biological inheritance that sets the course of development is called the *genotype*. The group of characteristics that emerges from the interaction of genetic potentials and the workings of the environment on the individual organism is called the *phenotype*.

Reaction Range

Any genotype is capable of producing a variety of phenotypes, and environment is a key ingredient in the mixture. The truth of this is obvious: A child brought up as a member of a large family in an urban area will be

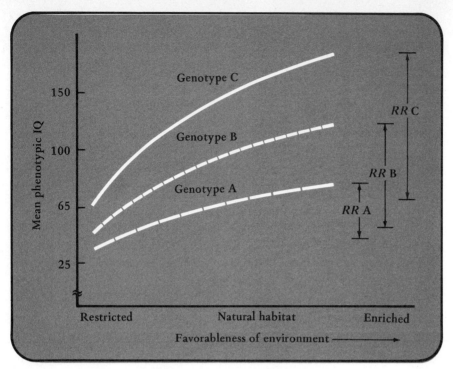

FIGURE 2–7
Hypothetical intellectual reaction ranges of three genotypes in more and in less favorable environments (Adapted from Gottesman, 1963)

quite different from the same child had he or she been raised in a medium-sized family in a rural section of the country or even in a small family in a suburban area. Psychologists term the range of different possible phenotypes a *reaction range.*

Simply stated, the reaction range is the variation in skills and abilities that can develop from the same genotype under varying environmental conditions. The genotype sets the boundaries within which individual characteristics can develop. Figure 2–7 shows hypothetical reaction ranges of IQ for genotypes in more or in less favorable environments. The phenotypic reaction range for each genotype is indicated by the letters *RR.* The greater the genotypic potential, the greater will be the influence of environmental variation upon its expression and the larger the reaction range. An example of this is what happens to children's performances on intelligence tests if they are placed in severely deprived environments. Performance of all children declines, but those children with the highest initial IQs show far greater losses over a given period of time than children whose IQs were low to start with (Skeels, 1966).

Or, consider a trait such as musical ability. A child with little inherited musical ability will develop some musical skills in a musically enriched environment. However, this child will not show as much musical talent as will a child who has inherited a greater genetic potential and lives in the same enriched environment. High genetic potential widens the reaction range. Figure 2–7 shows that even on the more restricted end of the scale of environments, the more highly endowed Genotype C still does better than the less well-endowed Genotype A. Different genetic traits

48

may interact with each other. Musically talented children, for example, may be better able to develop their potential, even in limited environments, if they also have a high capacity for asserting themselves.

Environment as Threshold

The environment can be seen as a threshold, or a launching pad, for individual development. The environment must provide a minimal level of physical support and intellectual stimulation if individuals are to fulfill their genetic potential. Placement in an environment less adequate suppresses development of ability. As simple an environmental factor as nutrition can have a marked effect on intellectual development. As the next chapter will show, malnutrition during the first 2 years of life can lower children's IQ scores permanently. Beyond nutrition, however, no one has determined exactly what characteristics of an environment constitute an adequate threshold. As yet we know little, for instance, about how individuals are affected by the total emotional and intellectual climate of their time.

The *duration* of deprivation may also be a factor in its effects on individuals. Some of the damage caused by a deprived environment in early childhood can be undone—if the environment is improved early enough. In a study by Skeels (1966), babies removed from an orphanage and placed in a home for retarded adolescents early in life showed dramatic improvements in mental abilities. In the orphanage, the babies were isolated in cribs; their only contact with adults took place when they were fed and changed. As they grew older, they were removed to rooms with 35 children for every attendant, where they spent large amounts of time sitting in chairs staring at the walls. There was very little human interchange and contact among the children themselves or between children and attendants. Although the orphanage was designed for mentally normal children, a number of them developed symptoms of mental retardation. Then, due to a reorganization of the orphanage, 13 of the babies were removed to a home for retarded adolescent girls. The orphans were placed in wards with older, brighter girls, where they received much attention. Competition developed among the wards to see which group would have "its" baby walking or talking first. Almost every child was informally "adopted" by one adult and developed an intense one-to-one relationship; they benefited from playgrounds, nursery schools, and excursions. During a year and a half of living in this "enriched" environment, the children showed a mean increase in IQ of almost 28 points, with some children showing an increase of over 50 points. During the same period, the IQs of a control group of children who remained in the orphanage declined almost as markedly.

Research by agencies of the U. S. government has led to the establishment of a list of nutritional "minimum daily requirements" required to maintain the body's physical well-being. Just as the human body needs an array of nutrients, so the human mind needs many subtle elements in order to receive a complete and balanced "mental diet." Characteristics of an environment that permits genetic potential to maximize have not yet been identified. The environment that the babies experienced in the home for retarded adolescent girls, for example, was—by middle-class standards—not enriched in terms of learning materials and toys. But it *was* sufficiently rich in attention and human interaction to be beneficial to the children from the orphanage. Environmental sustenance results from many elements acting together. Continuing research in child development may eventually give us a model of the elements necessary for maximizing development.

Individual variation in a given population can be explained only by a concept that takes into account the contributions of genes and environment as they operate independently or in combination. Accordingly, investigators have invented a statistic called *heritability*. It measures the proportion of individual variation attributable to genetic inheritance relative to that attributable to environment. The statistic is derived from the correlations of test scores for MZ and DZ twins, siblings, parents and children, and other kin. Estimates of heritability will differ depending on several factors—the reliability of the tests, the ages of the individuals, and the range of test scores—because these factors influence the correlations from which heritability is estimated.

Heritability

As we have seen, a disadvantaged environment suppresses the expression of phenotypic variation, including mean IQ scores. If a child's environment favors athletic over intellectual skills, for example, more time and energy will be put into athletic activities. Mom may take Judy to a daily tennis lesson or serve dinner late every night when David gets home from playing basketball. In these cases, then, the environment may work against the expression of intellectual skills. Investigators have suggested that environmental variation is an important factor in estimating heritability in a total population. In populations where most families share the same standard of living and there is little variation in environmental "favorableness," most of the differences between people will come from genetic factors. For example, if MZ twins are reared apart in similar middle-class families, differences in the twins' environments are not likely to be very large and the estimate of heritability will be relatively high. Observations of different societies support this hypothesis. The population of Great Britain, for example, is relatively similar, and the government ensures a minimal standard of living. There, genetic factors account for a higher proportion of differences in ability than in the United States where population and socioeconomic factors are more diverse (Bane and Jencks, 1973). Estimates of heritability thus depend on the range of environmental differences in a particular population.

All studies of the relative influence of heredity and environment must contend with the factor of *covariance*—the ongoing process in which genotype and environment mutually influence each other. Children who are at the outset slow in learning or behind their age-peers in test performance may be assigned to "slow" classes and taught to think of themselves as hopelessly dull. Thus, they continue to fail to learn for psychological reasons.

Debate about the relative influence of heredity and environment goes back a long time and is likely to continue for some time to come. Even today, geneticists, who are trained as biological scientists, may ignore the influence of the environment on individual development. Sociologists and behavioral scientists, on the other hand, may know little about genetics and will approach the question with preferences toward environmental explanations of behavior (Eckland, 1967). Debates about heredity may, moreover, stir up more than abstract passions. Studies of heritability do not usually measure "neutral" characteristics like height, running speed, or physical strength. Instead, the vast majority measures intelligence, which to most people means the ability to do well enough in school to go on to college and, perhaps, to think like Einstein (who, by the way, did poorly in school). As the next section will show, Americans tend to overestimate the importance of intelligence, some seeing it as the sole factor that determines success in life. The conclusion that there is a substantial hereditary component in intelligence can easily be misused by anxious parents who think their slow child is doomed for life or by politicians who argue that there is no point in trying to improve the schools or fund programs for preschool education. Comparisons of intelligence among different socioeconomic groups or races are especially controversial. There is a growing consensus that there is no way of attributing some portion of intelligence to nature and another portion to nurture. Every genetic characteristic requires an environment in which to function. The act of functioning, in turn, changes the environment. The outcome—in this case, intelligence—is the result of a process in which one force transforms another. The process is *transactional.* As Medawar argues, "the contribution of nature is a function of nurture, and of nurture a function of nature, the one varying in dependence on the other, so that a statement that might be true in one context of environment and upbringing would not necessarily be true in another" (1977, p. 14). One consequence of the current controversy over heritability is that the concept itself is being challenged. As so often happens in science, the controversy may be resolved by the invention of a new and better concept to account for the relevant facts.

GROUP DIFFERENCES IN INTELLIGENCE

Data show that blacks and low-income whites as a group have slightly lower average IQ scores than do middle-class white children. Individual differences in performance among middle-class children, most researchers agree, arise far more from genetic than from environmental differences. Until recently, however, scientists assumed that differences *between* groups were caused by environmental disadvantages. But in 1969 Jensen advanced the controversial suggestion that social-class and racial differences in IQ were the result of the genetic makeup of these population groups.*

Social-class differences in children's performance on IQ tests have been well established. By the time children have reached age 3, their IQs are correlated with their parents' education, their father's occupation, family income, and social class (Bayley and Schaefer, 1964). As Jensen (1969) points out, "this is a world-wide phenomenon and has an extensive research literature going back 70 years." Interestingly, though, during the first 9 months of life boys from lower-class families (and girls to a lesser extent) develop much more rapidly than middle-class children, scoring higher on tests of ability for those ages. By 18 months, however, children from upper-class groups do the best.

Social Class

Jensen argues that these differences have a hereditary component. In America, he asserts, intelligent people tend to achieve high occupational status and work at jobs that pay well. He believes that children of these high-income parents receive a slightly better genetic inheritance for intelligence than do other children. However, the simple appearance of differences *between groups* does not indicate whether the differences were caused by genes or by environment. We know, of course, that disadvantaged environments tend to suppress the development of genetic potential. Undoubtedly, many more disadvantaged children would do well on IQ tests if they had been raised with the scholastic/achievement orientation that is characteristic of the American middle class.

Social mobility may mean that some of the IQ differences between different social classes *are* genetic. Several generations ago, social status tended to be conferred by reason of a person's family origin. Within each family and each class there was likely to be a wide range of IQ scores. Today, social status tends to be based to a greater degree upon an individual's occupation and education. Thus, members of each social class are more alike than in the past, which means that there are greater differences between classes. Therefore, the classes tend to be breeding groups with sharper differences in IQ levels (Scarr-Salapatek, 1975).

The average IQ of black children, like that of white children from low-income families, is slightly lower than that of middle-class whites. Jensen (1969) reports that IQ test scores of blacks are about 15 points below the

Race

---

*Traditionally, psychologists, educators, and health workers have prepared tables that indicate terminology used to describe the intellectually exceptional. We will not do that in this text because such a system transforms a score into a label for a child which, in view of the issues raised in this chapter, is indefensible. By way of providing some sort of perspective, however, we *can* say that most people receive a score of around 100 in IQ tests. Relatively few people score below 70; those who do so function poorly, especially in school. Likewise, relatively few people score above 130, and those who do generally do well in school.

average scores of the white population and argues that the difference can be explained by genetics. There *are*, indeed, some established differences between blacks and whites: Black children are a little smaller than white children at birth, and their bone development is more rapid, as is their motor development during early childhood. But our earlier cautions about drawing conclusions from comparisons between groups apply here too. Since racial differences in America are associated with economic disadvantage, the simple appearance of IQ differences cannot bear directly upon genetic or environmental determinants. We should also note that when gross socioeconomic differences are taken into account in research studies, the difference between races is only about 11 IQ points—about the average difference between siblings in the same family (Jensen, 1969). This is a trivial difference, half of which can be accounted for by test motivation alone. (Motivation, as we will see in the next section, has a lot to do with performance on IQ tests).

How Should *Differences Be Interpreted?*

We have already noted some of the difficulties in interpreting IQ differences between different population groups. Some theoretical justification for genetic differences between social classes can be made, as we noted above. But, such justification does *not* apply to differences between races. Moreover, between-race comparisons are complicated by cultural differences. Black and white children grow up in much different social and cultural environments, even when black and white parents have identical occupations and incomes (Bane and Jencks, 1973). Black children may learn a different set of language rules (linguists are beginning to study Black English as a language in its own right) and a different style of thought (Scarr-Salapatek, 1971a). There is still no way to measure the effects of these cultural differences. Therefore, a number of responsible investigators have concluded that between-race comparisons of IQ are not possible (Bane and Jencks, 1973; Scarr-Salapatek, 1971a and 1971b; Loehlin, Lindzey, and Spuhler, 1975).

Studies of adopted children offer another perspective on the influences of heredity and environment on intellectual development. Are the IQ scores of adopted children likely to be closer to those of their adopted parents or those of their natural parents? A classic study by Skodak and Skeels (1949) found that the IQs of the adopted children studied were, in fact, higher than those of their natural parents. The IQs of the natural mothers averaged 85. The natural fathers were not studied, but if we estimate their IQs at the population average of 100, the children could have been expected to have an average IQ of about 94. In fact, the average IQ of the children was around 106. Researchers assume that the rise in IQ scores was the result of the social environment that the children experienced in the adoptive families) Scarr-Salapatek, 1971b).* Although chil-

*Readers interested in further discussion of hereditary and environmental influences on IQ should consult Kamin, 1974; Fulker, 1975; Loehler, Lindzey, and Spuhler, 1975; Block and Dworkin, 1976.

dren's genetic abilities might be related to those of their parents, the complex relationships between genetic endowment and environmental opportunities are such that the level of a child's performance on an IQ test will vary considerably according to the child-rearing environment. What are the implications of these findings for the possibility of attempting to improve IQ scores?

The question of how home and school conditions can enhance what children do, in fact, do is a very different—and perhaps socially more important and scientifically more interesting—question than the genetic or environmental limits of that performance.

    A growing body of studies suggests that IQ scores can be substantially changed when children are placed in enriched environments. We have already noted that the genotype of an individual does not confer a fixed set of characteristics but merely a *range* of potential reactions. An enriched environment can raise the IQ level closer to the top of an individual's own reaction range. Skeels' classic study of children raised in an orphanage and then transferred to a home for retarded girls showed that an enriched environment could cause genuinely dramatic changes in children's IQs (see Figure 2–8). And the lowered scores of the children who remained in the orphanage showed how drastic the effects of extreme deprivation can be (see Figure 2–9). A study of low birth-weight siblings confirms the importance of the environment in intellectual development (Scarr-Salapatek, 1975). Fifty low birth-weight children were found to score, on the average, 13 IQ points lower than their normal-weight siblings—even though they were reared in the same homes and, given random distribution of the parents' genes, had the same average genetic endowment.

    Improving children's intellectual environments raises their IQ scores. One researcher has tutored from birth to 3 years of age a group of children whose mothers' average IQs were under 70 (their fathers' IQs were unknown). These children might have been expected to have an average IQ of 80 to 90 if they were raised by their retarded mothers. Instead, the infants registered average IQs of about 120 (Heber, 1969).

    Observations of children reared in kibbutzim in Israel also indicate the importance of environment in intellectual development. Children in kibbutzim are reared under the same conditions, in nurseries, and separated from their parents during most of the day. The children studied came from a mixed population of Oriental and European Jewish families. The two groups had different cultural heritages and, since they have been separated for so many centuries, constituted different genetic pools. Oriental Jewish children reared at home had an average IQ of about 92, compared to about 108 for European Jewish children. But children reared in the kibbutzim had, at all ages, "equivalent, and high, average IQs" of 115 (Scarr-Salapatek, 1975). There, the environment seemed to wipe out between-group differences.

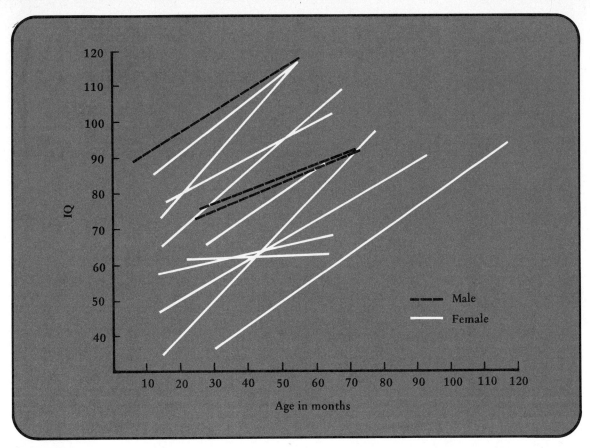

Male
Female

FIGURE 2–8
*Changes in IQ
scores of 13 children
moved from
orphanage to school
for retarded girls
(Adapted from
Skeels, 1966, Table 1,
p. 10)*

Studies indicate that appropriate intervention can increase IQ scores. How such scores relate to those of one's parents may not be so important as the issue of whether increased scores reflect substantially improved functioning in socially valued skills. Short of gross genetic abnormalities, there is probably no genetically based reason why every human child cannot acquire the basic skills (reading, writing) for which human beings have been so generously endowed. The trick may be to ensure that the circumstances in which children grow provide *equally* generous opportunities for all individuals to acquire such skills.

*Does IQ Have
Anything to Do with
"Intelligence"?*

Throughout this chapter we have been referring to "intelligence" and "IQ," and in the rest of this book we will continue to do so. Therefore, it is relevant at this point to ask what, exactly, behavioral scientists mean by the term "intelligence." In casual speech, most of us use the word rather loosely, to refer to a number of different human qualities. The statement, "Chris is very intelligent," might mean: "He gets really good grades"; "She is really funny—has a terrific sense of humor"; "He is very tactful—sensitive to other peoples' feelings"; "She and I usually agree about people—we think the same things are important." In fact, all these

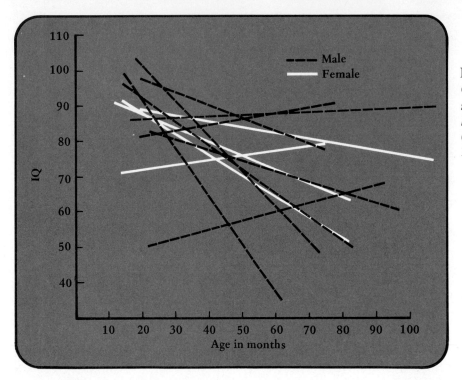

FIGURE 2–9
*Changes in IQ
scores of 12 children
left in an orphanage
(Adapted from Skeels,
1966, Table 2, p. 13)*

statements may describe intelligence—in combination with other personality traits.

Of all the statements about intelligence given above, the first—"Chris gets really good grades"—actually comes closest to the psychologist's definition of intelligence. The first intelligence tests, devised by the French psychologists Binet and Simon in 1905, were used *to predict school performance.* Binet and Simon observed children in school and worked with teachers to devise a series of graded tests that could accurately predict school performance better than a teacher after hours of observation of a particular child. It is no surprise, then, that results of IQ tests correlate with school achievement. Yet, they also reflect the peculiarities of our educational system. Neither schools nor tests have changed much since 1905, and both tend to reward the same narrow range of skills:

an attention span long enough to encompass the teacher's utterances and demonstrations, the ability voluntarily to focus one's attention where it is called for, the ability to comprehend verbal utterances and to grasp relationships between things and their symbolic representations, the ability to inhibit large-muscle activity and engage in covert "mental" activity, to repeat instruction to oneself, to persist in a task until a self-determined standard is attained—in short, the ability to engage in what might be called self-instructional activities, without which group instruction alone remains ineffectual. (Jensen, 1969, p. 7)

Some people might question the high value we give to these skills—or that we demand them from small children at all.

Although IQ tests may measure basic intellectual skills, these skills *in isolation* have little to do with success as an adult. IQ tests do not predict whether people will make lots of money in their jobs. Over a hundred studies have shown that differences in IQ explain only 12% of the variations in income. A difference of 5 IQ points "translates into an income advantage of a few hundred dollars a year" (Jencks, Smith, Acland, Bane, Cohen, Gintis, Heyns, and Michelson, 1972).

Traditional IQ tests measure only a narrow range of basic intellectual skills that do not necessarily predict cognitive capacity nor competence in general.
(Van Bucher, Photo Researchers)

Not only are IQ tests based on a narrow view of human intelligence, but a child's performance on an IQ test can be affected by situational factors. Motivation influences test performance. Children whose experiences have led them to be fearful and wary in strange situations may respond "I don't know" to questions that they could answer, simply to minimize the time they must spend with the strange adult tester (Zigler and Butterfield, 1968). Learned differences in motivation account for a good deal of the apparent IQ differences among ethnic groups. A number of studies have demonstrated the importance of motivation to test performance.

Other studies showed that children score higher on IQ tests if they know and like the examiner or if the examiner plays with them for a few minutes before administering the test. Such play periods helped children overcome the anxiety produced by the testing situation (Zigler, Abelson, and Seitz, 1973). The play periods, moreover, had stronger effects on the IQ scores of children from disadvantaged backgrounds than on those of middle-class children. The children from disadvantaged backgrounds seemed more sensitive to changes in the emotional atmosphere.

IQ tests may, as well, be culturally "loaded." Typically they do not take into account the child's own culture. Psychologists have called for a broader view of competence and greater sensitivity to cultural and situational factors in the assessment of competence. After an extensive review of the literature concerning cross-cultural differences in cognitive development, Glick (1975) concluded that we should be cautious about

inferring cognitive abilities or lack of them from performance on any specific behavioral test. We do not know the relationship between cognitive capacities and the conditions of their application. *(p. 647)*

Cultural factors have a demonstrable influence on test performance. In one experiment, for example, Kpelle rice farmers from Liberia and Yale sophomores were asked to make estimates of volume by guessing the number of cups of rice in each of several bowls. The rice farmers were more accurate at the task than were the Yale students. Yet, it would be incorrect to conclude that Kpelle superiority at a task for which they were culturally prepared indicates that they are generally more competent than the college students (Cole and Bruner, 1971).

CULTURE AND THE ASSESSMENT OF COMPETENCE

Measurements of competence in different cultures—South Pacific tribes or American ethnic groups—may be distorted by the researchers' own cultural biases. The failure to take culture into account has often led to what is called the *deficit hypothesis*. The deficit hypothesis is the assumption that children from poor families, for example, are culturally "de-

Studying Differences

prived"—by inadequate mothering (by middle-class standards), by the father's absence, by an "unstimulating" environment, by inadequate language skills, or by the children's own inability to defer gratification. The combination of factors may vary, but the assumption remains the same: that minority group children suffer intellectual deficits when compared with their "more advantaged" peers (Cole and Bruner, 1971). Labov (1970) has attacked the deficit hypothesis, focusing on the concept of "linguistic deprivation" and the assumption of cognitive incapacity. He has found that children who remain monosyllabic in conventional testing situations become lively and articulate when the examiner goes to the children's own homes and talks to them about subjects that interest them.

It is difficult to compare competence, then, even in different subcultures in the United States. The problems we have already mentioned—language barriers, differences in motivation, and the researcher's bias—may be intensified when comparisons are made between widely separated cultures. Yet cross-cultural research is well worth pursuing.

Whiting and Whiting (1975) conducted an interesting study comparing children's behavior in different cultures. They observed children in their natural setting in six cultures (Kenya, Mexico, the Philippines, Okinawa, India, and the United States). The Six Cultures study, as it is called, reveals subtle and diverse differences in child-rearing practices and their effects on development. The Whitings found, for example, that cultural complexity is a key variable. Children in simpler societies tend to be nurturant and responsible. They begin to perform "adult" roles sooner—even though the competence underlying such chores would probably not be reflected in school-oriented intelligence tests. Cross-cultural research such as that of the Whitings is one way of exploring the factors that underlie and determine child development. Its aim is to separate biological, environmental and cultural determinants of development, and it may broaden our understanding of how the human mind works.

What Are Differences?

What children *can* do and whether they will do it are two very different questions. A growing body of evidence shows that cognitive performance depends on two factors: capacity (what a person can do) and application (whether the capacity will be applied). Behavioral scientists do not yet know much about the conditions that influence the performance of skills in different contexts. Skills such as categorizing objects, for example, may be part of people's daily routines—but they may resist categorizing them in new ways. Psychologists assume that sorting objects according to categories (food, tools, and so forth) is intellectually more advanced than sorting objects according to how they go together (cup and saucer). But when people of the Kpelle tribe were asked to sort out types of food, clothing, and cooking utensils, they persisted in grouping items in categories of two items each, with each pair related by function: a knife with an orange, a potato with a hoe, and so on. As Glick (1975) recorded:

When asked, the subject would rationalize the choice with such comments as, "The knife goes with orange because it cuts it." When questioned further, the subject would often volunteer that a wise man would do things in this way. When an exasperated experimenter asked finally, "How would a fool do it?" he was given back sorts of the type that were initially expected— four neat piles with foods in one, tools in another, and so on. (pp. 635–636)

Here the subject was perfectly capable of "advanced" cognition but saw no sense to it.

In sum, cross-cultural tests suggest, as do experiments with American children, that IQ tests are based on a narrow view of competence and that situational factors contribute to performance. Because of these difficulties, a growing number of researchers are beginning to take an anthropological approach to the study of competence. Using this approach, researchers observe capacities applied in normal, everyday life, or what is called mundane cognition. *Mundane cognition* can involve the daily application of very complex skills. The people of the Pulawat Atoll, for example, with little technology or formal education, have worked out a complicated and accurate system that enables them to navigate over long distances using relationships among winds, currents, and direction to guide them (Gladwin, 1970).

The observation of cognitive skills that are a part of daily life raises new problems of its own. It is difficult to determine how those skills were first developed, whether their application involves cognition or rote learning, whether cognitive skill applied in one area could be transferred to other areas. Would the Pulawat navigator do well in an American school— or would the average American be able to learn the Pulawat system of navigation?

Observations of mundane cognition in other cultures, as well as Labov's observations of linguistic skills in "culturally deprived" black children, may lead to new and better ways of measuring competence. These observations can then become the basis for sophisticated, flexible experiments to measure competence in contexts familiar to the subjects. A growing number of psychologists are urging that the same approach be taken in American education. Teachers of "disadvantaged" children, they argue, should use relevant materials in order "to get the child to *transfer* skills he already possesses to the task at hand" (Cole and Bruner, 1971, p. 874).

It should be noted, in conclusion, that even behavior that seems "undesirable" may be functional in different cultures. Few of us might consider dependence-dominance to be likeable traits in adults. Complex societies such as our own require that individuals be competitive and achievement-oriented in school and on the job. Child-rearing practices are societies' ways of shaping children into the kinds of adults they need. Just as cultures vary in the kinds of adults they need, so they also vary in the characteristics they are likely to consider "intelligent." We must be cautious about implying that the skills we value in contemporary American society are valued by others, were always valued by us, and will continue to be valued in the future.

SUMMARY

No two individuals are ever exactly alike. Each of us is a product of a unique set of genes and a unique pattern of experiences. These are micro- and macrostructural components of individuality.

The human body is composed of two kinds of cells: somatic cells and germ cells. *Somatic cells* govern the formation of bones, muscles, and organs. Every somatic cell contains 46 *chromosomes,* the threadlike structures that convey heredity. The chromosomes, in turn, are made up of *genes.* Each gene differs from any other, and each has a message, contained in its chemical structure, that contributes to the individual's total genetic code. Genes and chromosomes are composed largely of a complex chemical called *DNA* that directs the differentiation of cells into blood, bone, muscle, and so on. In the course of development, somatic cells divide and reproduce in a process called *mitosis.* The 46 chromosomes double in number, and the cell then divides and reorganizes itself into two equal parts with 46 chromosomes in each new cell. The two identical daughter cells that result are exact copies of the original cell.

Germ cells are similar in structure to somatic cells, except that each contains only 23 chromosomes. They form only the reproductive cells of the body—*sperm* in males, *ova* in females. Germ cells divide by a process called *meiosis,* in which the chromosome pairs separate twice to form four identical daughter cells, each containing 23 chromosomes. When the sperm and ovum unite, the individual thus formed has a total of 46 chromosomes—half from the father and half from the mother. The process of *crossover* that occurs during meiosis ensures that genes from each parent are not transmitted in blocks. *Dominant* and *recessive* genes on the chromosomes determine general physical characteristics.

Of the 23 pairs of chromosomes, 22 shape the individual's general physical and mental characteristics. The twenty-third pair determines the individual's sex. In this pair, females have two X chromosomes; males have one X chromosome and one Y chromosome. The sex of the baby depends on whether the ovum (containing an X chromosome) is fertilized by an X or a Y chromosome from the father. Fertilization by an X results in a female; fertilization by a Y results in a male. The X and Y chromosomes also determine sex-linked inheritance. Some hereditary defects in males—color blindness, hemophilia, and baldness, for example—are caused by recessive genes carried on the X chromosome.

The sex ratio at birth is 106 males for every 100 females. One possible explanation for this ratio is that sperm carrying Y chromosomes are smaller and lighter than those carrying X chromosomes and may reach the ovum more quickly. Another possible explanation may be due to the fact that baby boys are more vulnerable than girls. More boys may be conceived in order to offset the higher vulnerability.

There is no reliable way to guarantee the sex of a child at conception. However, a relatively new procedure called amniocentesis can tell parents the sex of their unborn baby and whether it has any of several genetic abnormalities. The procedure is still too risky, however, to be used casually to find out the sex of the fetus.

A number of genetic anomalies may be inherited. Some genetic defects are caused by a recessive gene on the X chromosome. Other genetic defects are the result of *gross chromosomal abnormalities*—the absence of a chromosome or part of one, or the presence of an extra one. The tendency to produce such abnormalities can be hereditary or can be caused by environmental factors. Many genetic anomalies can be detected by amniocentesis in time for therapeutic action to be taken. Genetic counseling for couples who may be in a high-risk category is also recommended.

By the workings of heredity and probability, parent and child have about half of their genes in common. Siblings, too, have about half their genes in common. The exception to this rule of family resemblance is the case of *monozygotic* (MZ) twins. They are formed when one ovum, fertilized by one sperm, divides completely into two separate individuals. Such twins have the same genetic inheritance and thus are called identical twins. Twins formed when the mother releases two ova that happen to be fertilized by two different sperm are *dizygotic* (DZ) or fraternal twins. Studying twins enables researchers to examine the relative influences of genes and environment on various individual characteristics. Family resemblance is determined by degrees of shared heredity and by *assortative mating*—the tendency for likes to marry likes.

Some characteristics (such as eye color) are inherited through the workings of single genes that are dominant or recessive. Other characteristics (such as height and intelligence) result from the effects of many genes working together. Inheritance for such characteristics is termed *polygenic.*

Individuals are born with a particular genetic makeup, but environment will influence the *expression* of certain genetic traits. The interaction between genes and environment seems especially crucial in the expression of intelligence. The range of possible expressions of any characteristic is called *reaction range.* The greater the potential of the genotype, the wider the reaction range will be. No one has yet identified the minimum environmental threshold that will provide normal development. But we do know that there is no single element that will ensure such development.

Heritability is a statistic invented to measure the proportion of individual variation caused both by genetic inheritance and by differences in environment. In populations where there is little variation in environmental "favorableness," differences between people will tend to come from genetic factors. Debate about the relative influence of heredity and environment raises questions about the hereditary component in intelligence—a question that is so controversial that it challenges the entire concept of heritability.

The question of whether IQ test scores are the result of heredity or environment may not be a useful one. Children's IQs *are* correlated with social class. Children from upper-class families tend to score higher on IQ tests than do those from disadvantaged families. Yet, research indicates that the interactive effects of biological and social factors are too subtle and intertwined to be easily separated. And, investigators have concluded that between-race comparisons of IQ are not possible. The *level* of performance may be more important than the range of differences between children.

Intelligence tests were first designed to predict school performance, and they continue to do so today. IQ tests do not, however, predict how a person will do in the real world of jobs and income. In addition, performance on IQ tests depends on such situational factors as motivation, anxiety in unfamiliar settings, and cultural familiarity with the experimental task. Thus, we cannot generalize overall competence from IQ scores.

Measurements of competence differ by culture and by problems that arise in the process of "translating" testing situations to other cultures or subcultures. Thus, growing numbers of researchers are beginning to study capacities in everyday life, rather than in test situations. Such observations of *mundane cognition* may lead to better ways of measuring competence.

CHAPTER 3

Prenatal Development and Birth

THE IMPORTANCE OF THE PRENATAL PERIOD

A character in John Updike's novel *Couples,* when asked to name the most wonderful thing in the world, replies, "A baby's fingernails." She explains her response: "I mean the whole process, all the chemistry...the way it produces out of nothing, no matter almost what we do, smoke or drink or fall downstairs, even when we don't want it, this living *baby,* with perfect little fingernails. I mean... what a lot of *work,* somehow, ingenuity, *love* even, goes into making each one of us" (Updike, 1968, p. 238).

When we think of human growth as a long, slow, continuous process, we are apt to forget the extent to which individuals develop even before they are born. During the first 10 weeks after conception, the fertilized egg becomes a recognizably human fetus, with a head, arms and legs, and a central nervous system that responds to changes in the environment— the mother's womb.

Because so many important changes take place before birth, health during the prenatal period is of great practical importance. As this chapter will show, the unborn are especially vulnerable to environmental stresses such as maternal malnutrition, drugs taken by the mother, and her exposure to diseases.

THE EMBRYOLOGICAL MODEL OF DEVELOPMENT

The prenatal period has theoretical as well as practical importance. A number of developmental theorists, among them Sigmund Freud, Jean Piaget, and Erik Erikson, have argued that there are similarities between the development of the embryo and development *after* birth. In both kinds of development, individuals with specific sets of genetic instructions react to, and to some extent are shaped by, their environments. Prenatal development is usually described as primarily *structural,* relating to physical and anatomical changes, whereas postnatal development is seen as primarily *functional,* relating to changes in behavior. There are four ways in which prenatal and postnatal development are similar (Fishbein, 1976).

First, as we saw in Chapter 2, human growth depends on both the inner timetable, set by the genetic code, and the outside world to which a person responds (Fishbein, 1976). Individuals must reach certain stages or levels of maturity before they are affected by certain environmental influences. Recent evidence suggests, for example, that children cannot be taught to read before certain structures in their brains have matured. Likewise, prematurely born infants learn to hold their heads up and walk no sooner than babies conceived at the same time and carried to full term — even though the premature infants have been exposed to stimuli from the environment longer (Tanner, 1970).

Second, both prenatal and postnatal development proceed by stages (Fishbein, 1976). The stages in the development of the unborn baby can be charted almost week by week, and they follow one another in a specific order. The stages of development *after* birth are, of course, less distinct, with more individual variations. Still, postnatal growth follows certain regular patterns; for example, babies hold their heads up before they sit, and crawl before they walk. Each stage, moreover, must be preceded by changes both in the brain and in the muscle structure. As people mature, the stages of growth become increasingly complex. What we call adolescence, for example, involves not only hormonal changes, but emotional and behavioral development as well (Tanner, 1970). Erikson, among others, has suggested that even adults pass through predictable stages of development. It should be emphasized, though, that behavioral development *after* birth is far less predictable than physiological development before birth. Different systems seem to be involved in the different kinds of development, and these systems may mature and change relatively independently of one another.

Third, some developmental changes are irreversible. The physiological development of the embryo, with the differentiation of cells into the nervous system, the digestive system, the cardiovascular system, and so on, cannot be turned around once it has begun. Physical abnormalities that develop before birth also are irreversible, at least by the body's own action. (Some abnormalities can be corrected by surgery after birth.) Behavioral and psychological development in general, however, seem far more responsive to change. For example, Guatemalan infants who live in barren huts during the first year of life show behavioral retardation as measured by American standards. Then, during the third year of life, they leave the confines of the hut and join the active play and games of village children. By 10 years of age, they perform as well as middle-class American children (Kagan and Klein, 1973). Likewise, children may forget a first language after long exposure to a second one. But children do not ordinarily forget how to construct or use symbols.

The fourth similarity is that prenatal and postnatal development proceed by "differentiation and hierarchical integration" (Fishbein, 1976, p. 47). In other words, development, whether physiological or psychological, is not simply a matter of getting bigger. Psychological development involves making increasingly complex responses to the outside world. One of the first things babies learn is to distinguish their parents from the rest of the world. During the first few years of life, children's responses to significant others—mothers, fathers, sisters and brothers, playmates, teachers—become increasingly sophisticated. The physical development of the embryo shows the same kind of increasing complexity.

Individual development may be explained by the concept of *canalization,* *Canalization* as proposed by Waddington (1957). As we have seen, some genetic patterns are constant across a species: most human beings are born with two eyes and a nose. Other genetic traits like height and coloring vary with individuals. Waddington suggested that the development of a specific genetic trait may be compared to a ball rolling down a canal. Where the canal is deepest, it is hardest for an environmental force to deflect the ball. At certain sensitive periods in development, however, several shallow canals may intersect, as illustrated in Figure 3–1. During these periods, the pressures of the environment may cause the ball (the genetic trait) to be deflected from one canal to another (Fishbein, 1976.)

We are used to the idea that some elements of postnatal development take different directions because of environmental pressures. A person with a tall body build may end up being a basketball player; a person with a short body may become a jockey. During periods of rapid growth, even physiological development may be deflected by environmental influence. In human beings and many other mammals, for example, the visual system develops rapidly right before birth and during the months immediately following birth (Tanner, 1970). Research has shown that if kittens are deprived of light until 3 months after birth, they are never able to see afterwards. Light deprivation *after* this sensitive period has no such effect (Hubel and Wiesel, 1963). Different periods appear to be crucial for the development of different specific traits. And during these periods, the organism is more vulnerable to environmental stress than at other times.

What is remarkable about human development is the spontaneous tendency of individuals to fulfill their genetic program in spite of environmental stress. Tanner has compared human growth to the flight of a rocket:

Children, no less than rockets, have their trajectories, governed by the control systems of their genetical constitution and powered by energy absorbed from the natural environment. Deflect the child from its growth trajectory by acute malnutrition or illness, and a restoring force develops so that as soon as the missing food is supplied or the illness terminated the child catches up toward its original curve. (Tanner, 1970, p. 125)

The concept of canalization is important because it illustrates how genetic endowment interacts with environmental conditions to influence

FIGURE 3–1

The canalized landscape. The ball represents a specific genetic trait. At certain points in development (labeled "decision point") developmental pathways intersect, and environmental pressures will cause the ball to move into one canal or another (Adapted from Waddington, 1957)

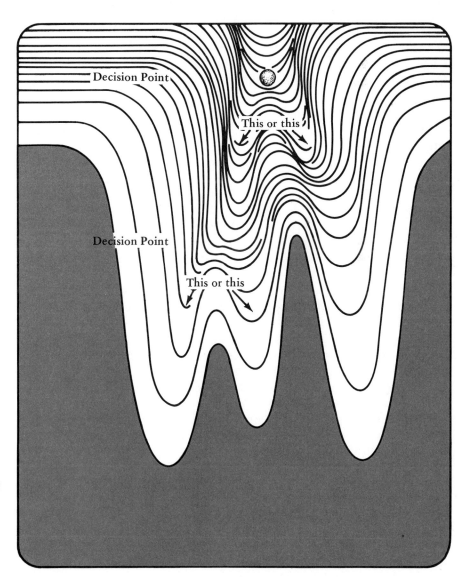

an individual's phenotypic characteristics. Even during the prenatal period, the nature of this interaction is quite complex.

PRENATAL DEVELOPMENT

Prenatal development begins at the moment of *fertilization* when against great odds a sperm penetrates and fertilizes an egg cell. This event marks the beginning of the period of the ovum, which lasts from 1 to 2 weeks after conception. Fertilization is a more active and competitive process than we may realize. In fact, most sperm have very little chance of ever reaching an egg cell. Guttmacher (1973) views this process from the perspective of mathematical probability: "The baby the sperm engenders has a far greater mathematical chance of becoming president than the sperm had of fathering a baby" (p. 19). The sperm's chances of success are very low from the moment during intercourse when they are deposited in the vagina. Most of the hundreds of millions of sperm die in the vagina, never reaching the protective confines of the cervical canal. Only one sperm enters and fertilizes the egg. Almost immediately after fertilization, a membrane forms around the penetrated egg and prevents other sperm from entering. Indeed, if more than one sperm enters the egg at the same time, the fertilized egg will no longer be able to live (Avers, 1974).

The Period of the Ovum

As we saw in the previous chapter, a sperm and an egg each have 23 chromosomes, half the number of chromosomes in all the other cells of the body. During the first 12 hours after fertilization, the *pronucleus* of the sperm and that of the ovum, in which the chromosomes are contained, move slowly to the center of the ovum to meet and join. The chromosomes —23 from each pronucleus—then pair off, so that the fertilized ovum, called a *zygote,* has 23 *pairs* of chromosomes.

The zygote is now ready to begin the next step in development— *cleavage* (or mitosis), in which the zygote divides into two complete, equal parts, or cells. During the next 2 days, the cells in the zygote continue to divide by the same process. As noted in Chapter 2, during the first cleavage the two new cells sometimes separate completely, forming two zygotes that then divide independently, producing identical twins. By the fourth day, when the zygote may contain as many as 60 or 70 cells, one cell separated from the rest can no longer produce a separate individual. At about the fourth day, the zygote is a sphere-shaped solid mass of cells, called a *morula.* Even though the number of cells in the morula is doubling about every 12 hours, the diameter of the morula itself increases very little. Rather, its cell content divides into increasingly smaller units (Guttmacher, 1973).

As the cells continue to divide, the morula moves through the Fallopian tubes (where the ovum was fertilized) into the uterus. Some time between the third and fifth days, the solid mass of cells takes on a new form. The cells rearrange themselves along the outer surface of a hollow sphere, whose center is filled with fluid. This hollow sphere of cells is known as a *blastula* (Guttmacher, 1973). At 5 or 6 days after conception, cells within the blastula begin to specialize. Cells clustered on one side of the cavity will subsequently become the embryo. The remaining cells form the placenta and the intrauterine fluids in which the embryo floats.

Between 7 and 9 days after conception, the blastula makes contact with the uterus, and implantation of the embryonic mass in the lining of the uterus begins. Secretions of the hormones progesterone and estrogen have prepared the uterus for implantation. The embryonic mass becomes firmly embedded in the lining of the uterus and begins to receive nourishment from the mother's blood. The embryo then grows at an accelerated rate, doubling in size every day for the next few days. By a week after conception, the embryonic mass is 1/1,000 of an inch long.

Soon after implantation, the *placenta* begins to form on the section of the blastula's outer wall deepest within the uterine tissue (Guttmacher, 1973.) The placenta is a total life-support system for the developing embryo. Through it, the embryo receives food and oxygen and excretes waste. In addition, the placenta acts as a barrier between the mother and the embryo. Without it, the baby would be rejected by the mother's immunological system as a foreign growth (Bleier, 1971). To some degree, the placenta is also a barrier between the embryo and infections the mother might contract during pregnancy.

The Embryonic Period

The *embryonic period,* the second through the seventh week after conception, is particularly crucial in human development. Not only does the appearance of the embryo change radically during this period—from a mass of cells to a recognizable human infant—but by its end, all of the major organ systems and body parts have been formed. Figure 3–2 shows the major events that occur in the first 7 weeks of development. As we have noted, periods of rapid development are also periods when the organism is most susceptible to environmentally produced defects. For human beings, the embryonic period is the most sensitive of all.

Between days 18 and 28 after conception, the central nervous system begins to develop. The central nervous system will give directions about the development of most other systems (Wyden, 1971). Development of the nervous system begins with the appearance of the *neural groove,* which undergoes further differentiation until it takes the form of a rudimentary brain and spinal cord (Avers, 1974).

Other critical body systems develop at about the same time as the central nervous system. During the third week, the blood vessels and stomach begin to form. A tube that will develop into a heart begins to pulsate in the fourth week. At 28 days, the embryo has the beginnings of 40 pairs of tissue segments that will later become muscles, connective tissue, and bones. By the end of the fourth week, dramatic changes have occurred

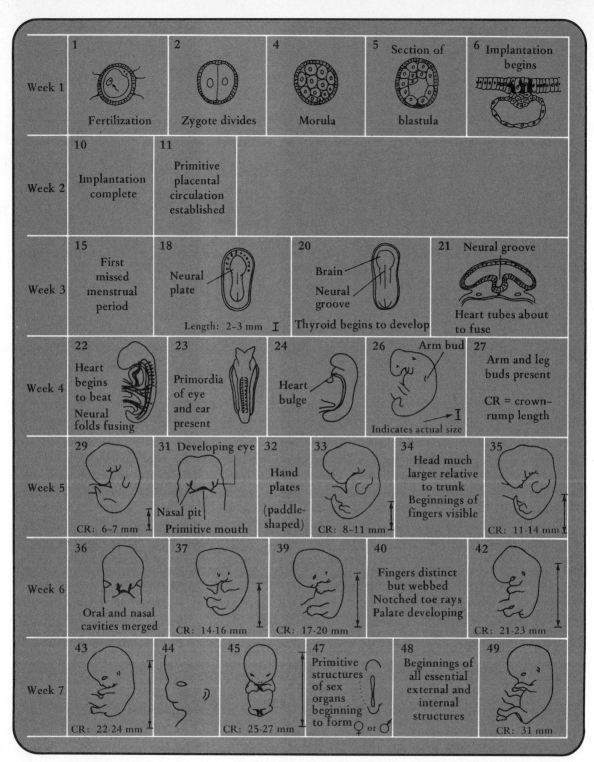

FIGURE 3–2 *Highlights of development in the first 8 weeks of life (Adapted from Moore, 1977)*

in the embryo, and it has increased in mass about 7,000 times (Avers, 1974). Nevertheless, by its appearance alone, the human embryo cannot yet be distinguished from the embryo of a pig, rabbit, chick, or elephant (Guttmacher, 1973). The end of the embryonic stage—28 to 30 days after conception—marks the beginning of a woman's awareness of her pregnancy. She has missed a menstrual period, and pregnancy tests register positive.

During the last 3 weeks of the embryonic period—weeks 5 through 7 after conception—the embryo continues to develop along a predetermined timetable. Because functions of the brain and heart are needed by the developing embryo sooner than functions of the digestive organs, the upper part of the body develops before the lower. During the fifth week, the embryo's brain bulges out of proportion from the rest of its mass (Guttmacher, 1973). The extraordinary size of the brain is accompanied by increased structural differentiation. The cerebral cortex, the part of the brain that governs both motor activity and intellect, may be seen for the first time (Rugh and Shettles, 1971). The fifth week is also marked by the complete formation of the chest and abdomen. In addition, the eyes become recognizable through closed lids; lung buds as well as hand and foot plates appear; and the olfactory lobe, which governs the sense of smell, begins to form. During the fifth and sixth weeks, the heart undergoes significant structural and functional changes. Its tubular shape is transformed into a four-chambered heart (Avers, 1974). By the end of the fifth week, the embryo is still only ½-inch long (11–14 millimeters) and weighs only 1/1,000 ounce. By day 36, all the muscle blocks are present, and the arm and leg buds are formed. By day 47, the primitive structures of the sex organs, the urethra, and the anus begin to take form, although it is still impossible to tell from the appearance whether the embryo is male or female. By the end of the embryonic period, at about the forty-ninth day after conception, the beginnings of all the baby's organs are present. The developing organism is now called a *fetus*.

The Fetal Period

The structural development of the fetus is less dramatic than that of the embryo, but structural changes continue to occur. During the third month after conception, the first signs of external genitalia appear, making it possible to determine the sex of the fetus through visual observation. In addition, bony structures begin to replace the soft cartilaginous tissue of the skeleton. Because the muscles and nervous system are now connected, movement of the legs and arms is possible. These movements are imperceptible to the mother; she will not feel fetal activity until the fourth month or after. The first reflexes of the fetus are "total," with the entire body reacting to any stimulus, but gradually this reaction becomes more sophisticated so that only the stimulated area responds (Rugh and Shettles, 1971). During the fetal period, "details" are beginning to develop. By the end of the third month, the fetus has eyelids, fingernails, and even the

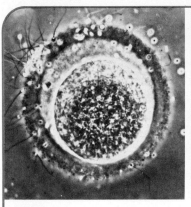
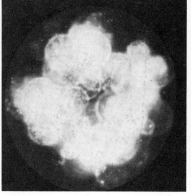
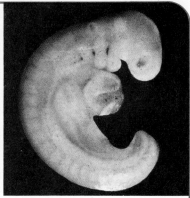

*Fertilization, showing penetration
of sperm into ovum*

Morula, 3½ days after fertilization

Embryo at 28 days

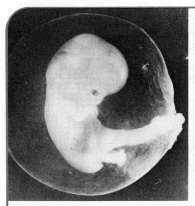
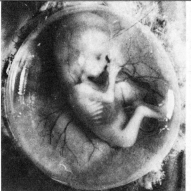
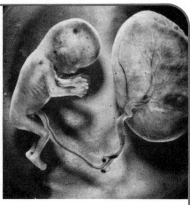

An 8-week-old embryo

Fetus at 14 weeks

A 16-week-old fetus

*Prenatal
development at
various stages.
(Landrum B. Shettles, M.D.)*

buds of the "baby teeth" (Bleier, 1971). During the fourth month, eyebrows and eyelashes begin to appear. In the fifth month, hair appears on the head, and the skin takes on a wrinkled and folded look. By the beginning of the fifth month, the fetal heartbeat can be heard through a stethoscope. Hearing the heartbeat can be thrilling evidence of the baby's development.

The final trimester of pregnancy—months 7, 8, and 9—marks the first time the fetus could survive outside the uterus if born prematurely. (Medical advances are making it possible for some babies born during the sixth, and on rare occasions during the fifth, month to be kept alive in intensive-care nurseries.) During the sixth month, the fetus can already breathe on its own, but survival becomes more likely during the seventh month because of the amount of brain and central nervous system development that takes place during this period.

Other significant changes also take place at this time. The fetus develops hair on the head that may be as long as 1 inch and nails that extend beyond the edges of the fingers and toes (Guttmacher, 1973). In addition, during the ninth month, antibodies pass from the mother's bloodstream into the fetus. Since newborns do not manufacture their own antibodies for 1 to 2 months after birth, immunities acquired in this manner are important for survival (Avers, 1974).

The size of the fetus also increases during the final trimester. However, during the ninth month, the rate of growth begins to slow down (Avers, 1974). The fetus also develops an extra layer of fat and a thickened, smooth, and polished skin, which is now almost free of the downy layer of hair that covered its entire body earlier (Guttmacher, 1973).

At birth, the average full-term baby weighs about 7 pounds, 5 ounces (3,276 grams) (Final Natality Statistics, 1976). This weight is good preparation for life outside the uterus, for most babies lose a little weight during the first week or so after they are born. During the last 6 weeks of pregnancy, with the fetus's increase in size, some mothers feel Braxton Hicks contractions. These are the muscle spasms that extend the uterus to accommodate the fetus; they are sometimes mistaken for the onset of labor. The longer the fetus remains in the uterus during the final trimester (up to a maximum of about 40 weeks after the last menstruation), the better its chances for survival. Guttmacher (1973) describes the likelihood of survival during the final trimester in terms of increasing percentages. A child born alive during the seventh month has about a 50% chance of living; during the eighth month, its chances increase to better than 90%; and at the end of the ninth month, its likelihood of survival rises to 99%. The last stage of prenatal development is less sensitive or crucial than the earlier ones—with the embryonic period, as we noted earlier, the most sensitive of all.

The Vulnerability of the Embryo

There are, as we have seen, three basic stages in prenatal development: the period of the *ovum,* between 1 and 2 weeks after conception; the *embryonic* stage, between 3 and 7 weeks after conception; and the fetal stage, from 8 weeks until birth. The effects of environmental stresses—*teratogens*—on the developing organism depend on the stage in which the teratogens occur. Teratogens encountered during the embryonic period—and, to a lesser extent, during the period of the ovum—may result in prenatal death; 30% of embryos are spontaneously aborted. Teratogens also may cause malformations—called *congenital defects*—in the baby. These are environmentally caused structural deformities that do not affect the embryo's chromosomal structure and are therefore not passed on to the next generation. After about the tenth week, teratogens usually do not produce congenital defects except—and the exception is crucial—in the brain and nervous system (Fishbein, 1976). The eyes and external genitalia can also be affected after the tenth week of development. It is important to keep in mind that environmentally and genetically caused abnormal-

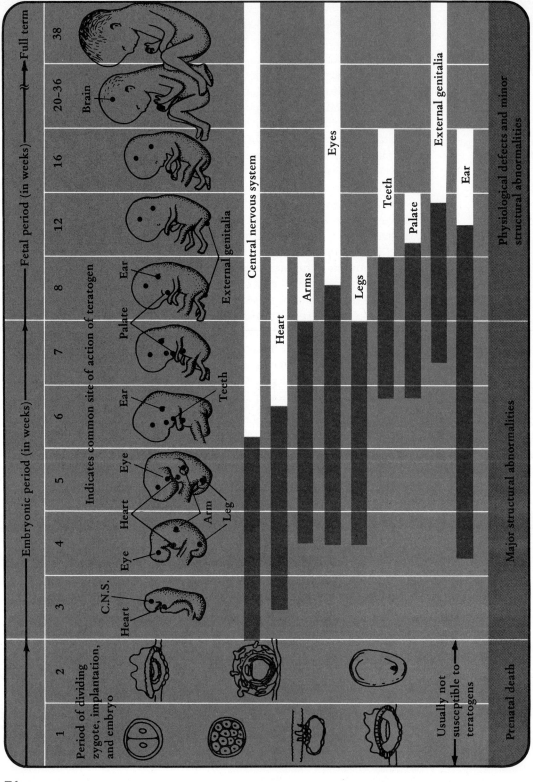

FIGURE 3-3 *Sensitive periods in prenatal development. Dark shading indicates highly sensitive periods; white indicates less sensitive periods.* (*Adapted from Moore, 1977*)

ities affect only 2.5% of infants, and most of these represent minor defects. Only 1 in 200 deliveries is stillborn because of congenital defects. In addition, 1 in 200 babies dies before its first birthday because of birth defects. Serious abnormalities affect only 1% of the 199 infants who survive (Guttmacher, 1973).

The embryonic period is sensitive, of course, because so many basic structures are developing very rapidly. As we noted earlier, during periods of rapid development, a particular genetic trait is vulnerable to being deflected from its normal course of development. During crucial periods of development, the organism is especially susceptible to stresses that would have little effect earlier or later. Waddington (1957) has called such sensitive periods *epigenetic crises.* During the days when a particular organ, such as the heart, is developing, it is vulnerable to being deformed by teratogens. Moreover, as Figure 3–3 shows, the *same* teratogen affects development differently, depending on when it occurs. The effects of thalidomide, a tranquilizer widely prescribed during the early 1960s, provided a natural laboratory demonstration of this process. The effects of thalidomide on babies depended on the specific days when their mothers had taken it. Taken between the thirty-fourth and thirty-eighth days after conception, thalidomide caused babies to be born without their outer ears. Between the thirty-eighth and the forty-sixth days, it caused the absence or underdevelopment of arms. Between the fortieth and forty-sixth days, it had the same effect on the legs. Between the forty-eighth and the fiftieth days, it resulted only in an extra bone in the thumb (Saxen and Rapola, 1969).

Embroyos, then, are especially vulnerable to environmental stresses because they are passing through a number of epigenetic crises. Once basic anatomical structures are formed, the fetus becomes more resistant to stress. The embryo is also vulnerable simply because it is little. A dose of radiation that could irreversibly damage a developing embryo might have little effect on an 8-month fetus. The entire prenatal period, however, seems important for the development of the brain, although the exact degree to which stresses irreversibly affect the brain is not yet known (Tanner, 1970).

PRENATAL VULNERABILITY AND MATERNAL HEALTH

Eighty percent of all birth defects are caused not by heredity but by an unfavorable fetal environment. As facts accumulate regarding the process of prenatal development, scientists have become increasingly able to identify and remedy prenatal conditions that will have harmful effects on later development. The technique of amniocentesis allows obstetricians to detect chromosomal abnormalities and blood diseases. Since chromosomal abnormalities occur most often in babies whose mothers are over

40—and to a lesser extent in mothers who are having their *first* pregnancy after about age 32—amniocentesis is often recommended for women in those age groups. Prenatal medical care, along with a sound diet and common-sense precautions about infections, drugs, and radiation, can prevent many kinds of birth defects. One of the most common causes of developmental abnormalities in infants and children is an ancient and obvious one: malnutrition.

As many as two-thirds to three-fourths of the children born in developing countries may not be getting enough to eat. Malnutrition, both prenatal and postnatal, is not just a problem of the developing nations. It occurs in the United States as well, and not just among low-income mothers:

Malnutrition

Statistics show that prosperous mothers as well as low-income mothers suffer from protein deprivation. Women who snack on empty calories (soft drinks, salty tidbits, sweets), who get a significant proportion of their daily calories from alcohol, fats and carbohydrates rather than proteins, vegetables and fruits, or—at the other extreme—women who diet to neurotic excess do not provide the healthiest environment for a naturally greedy fetus. (Wyden, 1971, p. 93)

Recent research has focused on the effects that malnutrition in the prenatal period and during the first 6 months after birth has on mental development. Children malnourished at this stage may not achieve their optimal physical growth, and they may be unable to realize their full potential for mental development (Dayton, 1969). Evidence indicates that malnutrition has a direct effect on brain growth:

It a fetus does not receive enough nourishment, the rate of brain cell division slows down. A seriously deprived fetus may have 20% fewer brain cells than normal. If a newborn is seriously undernourished during the six months after birth, cell division is also slowed down—again by as much as 20%. If an infant should have been malnourished both in utero **and** *after birth, the arithmetic is tragic. The brain may be 60% smaller. (Wyden, 1971, p. 93)*

Studies in Chile, Guatemala, and South Africa show that children malnourished early in life never catch up to the intellectual performance of their peers, even if they are given dietary supplements afterwards (Wyden, 1971; Dayton, 1969). Those findings are confirmed by a recent study of American children whose mothers suffered from excessive protein loss during the second half of pregnancy, when the protein needs of the developing fetus are greatest. Compared to a control group of children whose mothers were healthy, the children of protein-deprived mothers weighed less at birth. In tests of mental and motor development and IQ, which were continued until the children were age 4, the protein-deprived chil-

PHASES	DEVELOPMENT	EFFECT OF MALNUTRITION
Phase I: Conception to birth Hyperplasia	Number of cells increases	Interferes with cell division; causes permanent damage
Phase II: Birth to 1 year Mixed hyperplasia and hypertrophy	Number and weight of cells increase	Causes permanent damage
Phase III: 1 year and on Hypertrophy	Weight of cells increases	Causes smaller than normal cell size; can be corrected by adequate nutrition

Source: Adapted from Winick and Noble, 1965, 1966.

TABLE 3–1
Three Phases in Growth of the Brain and the Influence of Malnutrition

dren did significantly worse. The average IQ of the control children was a little over 100; the children deprived of protein during the fetal period scored an average IQ of only 84 (Rosenbaum, Churchill, Shakhashiri, and Moody, 1969).

How does malnutrition exert its effect on brain development? Scientists can answer this question more precisely now than years ago, when the only measure of malnutrition was physical height and weight and perhaps the circumference of the head. Such measures are relatively crude; some individuals, after all, are simply genetically small. New techniques allow scientists to measure growth not just by physical size, but by determining the number and size of individual cells (Dayton, 1969; National Research Council, 1970).* Such achievements make it possible to examine the number and size of cells in the brain.

In order to answer the question of how malnutrition affects brain development, we will look at the different kinds of cell growth. Cells increase in number by division. Individual cells also increase in size. Scientists have identified three phases in the growth of the human brain, as shown in Table 3–1. During the first phase, the prenatal period, brain cells increase in number by cell division, or *hyperplasia*. The second phase, the first year after birth, is characterized by mixed brain growth. Cells continue to increase in number by hyperplasia, and individual cells also increase in size by enlargement of the components of the cell, or *hyper-*

*Researchers can now use radioactive techniques to measure the *total* DNA content and the total protein content of any given organ. Scientists assume that the DNA content in the nucleus of any given cell is constant across a species. Thus, by dividing total DNA content of an organ by the amount of DNA known to be present in one cell, researchers can determine the *number* of cells in the organ. Protein content, unlike DNA content, varies with the size of the individual cell. By dividing the organ's total protein content by its total DNA content, researchers can measure the *size* of its cells (Sweet, 1973).

trophy. The third phase begins by the end of the first year of life, at which point all increase in brain weight comes about by hypertrophy (Dayton, 1969). By the end of the second year of life, the brain has almost reached its adult size. Some developmental theorists think a fourth stage of brain development—formation of connections between nerve cells—should be added to the first three (Wyden, 1971). The fourth stage may continue long after the brain has reached its full physical size.

To return to our earlier question: How does malnutrition affect the development of the brain? The answer depends on when the malnutrition occurs. During the first two phases of brain development, malnutrition interferes with cell division, and its effects are permanent. Dr. Myron Winick, a leader in research on brain growth, explains, "The brain never gets another chance. We found that cell division stops at approximately the same age in both undernourished and well-nourished children" (Wyden, 1971, p. 93). Malnutrition after the first 12 months of life results only in cells of smaller than normal size. These can be corrected by adequate nutrition (Dayton, 1969). Recent research has shown that children can show remarkable resiliency following periods of malnutrition. Their growth, once they are given adequate food, accelerates rapidly, even to the point where they reach their full genetically indicated height.

CATCH-UP. One of the clearest examples of the human system's tendency to be self-regulating is the phenomenon of catch-up growth. Children deprived of food experience stunted growth. But when food is restored to them, they grow much faster than average for their age. Their accelerated rate of growth continues until they approach their own growth curve—the genetically programmed curve that determines their height and rate of growth. Catch-up growth is illustrated by the case of a child who underwent two periods of starvation because of anorexia nervosa, a psychological disorder that causes people to refuse to eat (see Figure 3–4). At the end of each episode of the disease, the child's growth accelerated until it approached the normal growth curve. Researchers have observed catch-up growth in children with hormone disorders, in malnourished children, and even in genetically tall children born to small mothers, who grow more rapidly than average during the first 6 months after birth (Tanner, 1973).

Catch-up is not always complete, however. Experiments show that rats, if starved for a period immediately after birth, will never reach normal size, even if they are fed without restriction afterwards (Tanner, 1970). The experiments suggest that the completeness of catch-up growth depends on two factors: when and how long the period of malnutrition lasts, and how fast the normal rate of growth is when the malnutrition occurs. Interestingly, females in all species of mammals seem better able to catch up after undergoing environmental stress.

The phenomenon of catch-up growth raises a number of questions.

FIGURE 3–4

Catch-up growth of a young child following 2 periods of anorexia nervosa (Adapted from Prader, Tanner, and von Harnack, 1963)

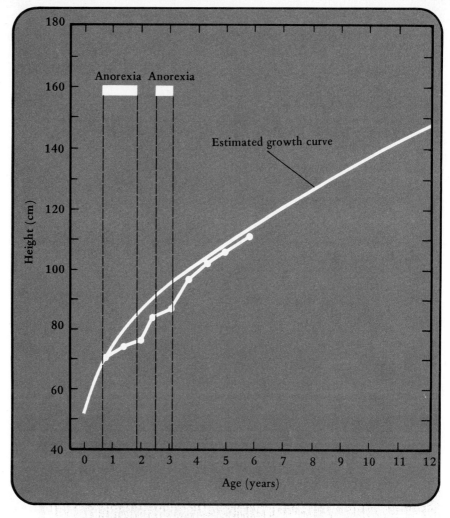

Why does it occur at all? What causes the rate of growth to slow down when individuals approach their growth curves? Why is catch-up incomplete if malnutrition occurs during sensitive periods? Scientists do not know all the answers to those questions. The stimulation to catch up affects the entire system and probably has no single course, but is a response involving several hormones (Tanner, 1973).

TIME TALLY. Tanner's theory of the "time tally" helps to explain catch-up growth. He suggests that once the central nervous system has developed to a certain point—perhaps at about 3 months after conception—"a substance accumulates, or some cells mature, in a manner which traces out the brain's growth curve" (Tanner, 1970, p. 128). This hypothetical substance then signals to the system the *time tally*—the growth tempo for each individual. The body's current actual size, he suggests, may be represented by a second substance, produced by the cells during growth (Tanner, 1973). Thus the more an individual grows, the more of this second substance there will be. Tanner calls the second substance "the inhibitor." The rate of growth for an individual during any given period of time, Tanner suggests, is determined by the distance of *mismatch* between the time tally and the individual's actual size at the time, as shown in Figure 3–5.

Admittedly, this system is hypothetical, and may well be oversimplified. It is likely that there are more than two "substances" or sets of signals that determine growth (Tanner, 1973). As a theoretical model, however, Tanner's concept does explain the phenomenon of catch-up growth. The time tally signals to the entire system its own growth curve, and the individual grows until approaching this curve, when the inhibitor — the measure of the individual's actual size — increases and signals that growth may slow down. If individuals undergo starvation or other kinds of environmental deprivation, the mismatch between actual size and the time tally widens. Once the deprivation is removed, growth takes place at an accelerated rate until the original growth curve is approached. Tanner's model also explains the failure to catch up when starvation occurs during critical periods. If starvation occurs when the brain and central nervous system are themselves undergoing rapid growth through cell

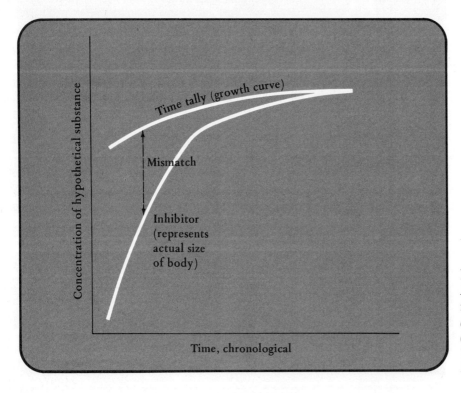

FIGURE 3–5
Hypothetical relations of growth-controlling agents (Adapted from Tanner, 1970, p. 130, Figure 31)

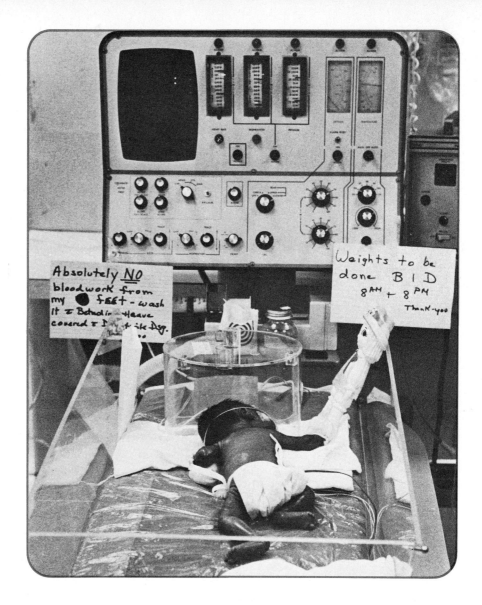

Low birth weight caused by malnutrition and low birth weight caused by short gestation are different phenomena that require different, but essential, postnatal treatment.
(Harry Wilks, Stock, Boston)

division, then the time tally—which is produced by the brain—will be affected (Tanner, 1970). Catch-up growth suggests that malnutrition deflects the normal progress along the genetically given pathway. If the deflection is not too severe or prolonged, when the reason for it is removed, the normal developmental timetable is reinstated through the catch-up mechanism. If the deflection is severe, the time tally is damaged and another pathway—presumably defective—is taken.

Low Birth Weight

A common consequence of maternal malnutrition is low birth weight. Until recently, doctors assumed that all newborn babies weighing less than 5½ pounds (2,500 grams) were *premature*—born before 37 weeks of gestation. But research in the early 1960s showed that many low-birth-weight babies—perhaps as many as one-third of them—had actually been carried to full term and had suffered malnutrition within the uterus (Sweet, 1973). Low birth weight caused by malnutrition and low birth weight caused by short gestation are very different phenomena. Thus babies that weigh less than 5½ pounds (2,500 grams) at birth are now called *low-birth-weight infants;* babies born before 37 weeks of pregnancy are called *short-gestation-period infants* (Tanner, 1970). Researchers have established standards of fetal growth, so that we now know the range within which the infant's weight should fall at any given gestational age. And doctors have developed sophisticated techniques for assessing gestational age of newborn babies by physical signs such as skin color and texture, the form of the ear, even the lines on the soles of the feet, and by neurological tests of the baby's posture and how far the wrists, ankles, and legs can bend (Sweet, 1973). Thus a baby born at any given gestational age can now be identified as *average for date of birth* (AFD) or *small for date of birth* (SFD).

The distinction between the low-birth-weight infant and the short-gestation-period infant has practical importance because the two require different postnatal treatment. Short-gestation infants may need intravenous feeding or help in breathing. Low-birth-weight infants are often born with hypoglycemia (pathologically low levels of sugar in the blood). Unless they are injected promptly with glucose, their condition may result in severe brain damage. Scientists believe that attention to the problems of low-birth-weight infants may cut in half the infant death rate and, perhaps, eliminate the major cause of brain damage ("How Children Grow," 1972).

However, despite advances in the medical care of the newborn, small-for-date babies still seem to suffer disadvantages in their later intellectual development. There is no correlation between premature birth and later intellectual development. But a study comparing average-for-date and small-for-date babies born during the 1960s showed that the SFD babies scored significantly lower in various measurements of IQ. The mean IQ of the AFD babies was 99.2; that of the SFD babies was only 92 (Francis-Williams and Davies, 1974). Another study found that SFD babies show significant deficits in total brain weight (Hill, 1975).

SOME STATISTICS. The incidence of low birth weight varies sharply from country to country. In the United States in 1975, 7.4% of all live births weighed less than 5½ pounds (2,500 grams). In the poorest Indian and Guatemalan villages, the rates of incidence of low birth weight are as high as 40% or more. In all countries, however, the incidence of low birth weight varies with socioeconomic levels. In the United States, the percentage of low-birth-weight babies among nonwhites, who are often at an economic disadvantage, is 13.1, more than twice that of whites. In very poor populations, birth weight also is correlated with the mother's height; the highest incidence of low birth weight occurs in the poorest families with the shortest mothers (Ricciuti, 1976).

Low birth weight is associated with prenatal and infant mortality. Up to a certain point—about 8 pounds (3,629 grams)—the more a baby weighs at birth, the better are its chances of survival. The infant death rate for babies who weigh about 5½ pounds (2,500 grams) at birth is 58 in 1,000; for babies who weigh under 5 pounds (2,000 grams), the mortality rate is 207 in 1,000 (United States Bureau of the Census, 1975). Studies of several European countries showed that the rates of prenatal and postnatal mortality were correlated with the incidence of low birth weight. In Sweden and Bulgaria, where about 5% of children weighed less than 5½ pounds at birth, there were fewer than 20 stillbirths for every 1,000 live births. In Hungary, where over 10% of newborns weighed less than 5½ pounds, the number of stillbirths was 35 (World Health Organization, 1972).

Birth weight, then, is important for a number of reasons. It is correlated with chances of survival after birth. It is also a convenient index of growth and is highly correlated with other indices such as height, head circumference and brain size, and intellectual development.

LOW BIRTH WEIGHT AND INTELLECTUAL DEVELOPMENT. Studies in countries where malnutrition is severe indicate that low birth weight is associated with retarded intellectual development. In one Mexican town, researchers found that the smaller children were for their age, the lower their scores on tests of learning and behavior tended to be. Research in a Mayan Indian village where most of the preschool children showed retarded growth confirmed these findings (Scrimshaw, 1969). The children were asked to perform three kinds of tests to measure their ability to integrate information from the various senses. In those tests, the smallest children did consistently worse than the others. It should be noted, though, that such test results are valid only when small physical size is the result of malnutrition. In Guatemala City, among middle- and upper-class children, whose size was a function of genes rather than malnutrition, researchers found no correlation between small stature and poor intellectual development (Scrimshaw, 1969).

The consequences of malnutrition may be heightened by poor environmental conditions. In fact, it becomes difficult to separate the biological consequences of malnutrition in children from other sociological factors that can retard intellectual development. Homes where mothers and children are malnourished also tend to be homes where sanitation and health care are poor, families are large, and parents are poorly educated. Although it is difficult to distinguish among the consequences of malnutrition and other adverse environmental influences, one fact does emerge from all the studies: The adverse consequences of early malnutrition are greatly heightened by a poor environment afterwards. Children who suffer *both* undergo a dual risk (Ricciuti, 1976).

Since the causes of retarded development in children are so complex, there are any number of ways of trying to prevent it: better schools, the education of parents, food supplements both for pregnant women and for their newborn infants. One of the simplest ways of reducing the number of stillborn and low-birth-weight babies is to improve the diets of pregnant women. The results of this can be dramatic. Food rationing in Great Britain during World War II provided a "natural experiment" that illustrated the effects of food supplements:

Under the food-rationing policy, pregnant women were given special priority, and the quality of the diets of pregnant women, especially those in the low-income groups, was significantly enhanced. Between 1929 and 1945, the stillbirth rate fell from a previously rather stable rate of 38 per 1,000 live births to 28, a fall of about 25 percent during a period when many aspects of the physical environment were deteriorating. (National Research Council, 1970, pp. 122–24)

Experiments in Colombia and Mexico showed that nutrition supplements to pregnant women and to children improved the children's intellectual development and even the behavior of parents and children toward each other (Chavez et al., 1974).

Maternal Nutrition

The results of intervention studies strongly suggest that the improvement of maternal diet has positive effects on newborn children. However, maternal and fetal health are shaped not only by the mother's diet during pregnancy but by her health before she became pregnant. Dr. Merrill S. Read, director of the Growth and Development Program of the National Institute of Child Health and Human Development, argues that "a mother's nutritional reserve...cannot be suddenly accumulated during pregnancy. These assets are the cumulative result of a lifetime." He adds that even the healthiest woman should not "just trust that her body will somehow have the reserves that are needed for her infant" (cited in Wyden, 1971, p. 94).

Some common-sense advice about diet applies to most pregnant women. It is better to obtain calories from the four basic food groups—meat and fish, milk and dairy products, fruits and vegetables, bread and cereals—than from candy, soft drinks, and potato chips. A pregnant woman's daily diet should include:

- 4 servings of items in the milk and dairy group (1 quart of milk will take care of all 4 servings);
- 2 or more servings of meat, poultry, fish, or eggs;

	NONPREGNANT WOMEN 18–22 YEARS OLD*	RECOMMENDED DAILY ALLOWANCES ADDED FOR PREGNANCY
Calories	2,000	200
Protein (grams)	55	10
Vitamin A (international units)	5,000	1,000
Vitamin D (international units)	400	0
Vitamin E (international units)	25	5
Ascorbic acid (milligrams)	55	10
Folacin (milligrams)	0.4	0.4
Niacin (milligrams)	13	2
Riboflavin (milligrams)	1.5	0.3
Thiamin (milligrams)	1	0.1
Vitamin B_6 (milligrams)	2	0.5
Vitamin B_{12} (micrograms)	5	3
Calcium (grams)	0.8	0.4
Phosphorus (grams)	0.8	0.4
Iodine (micrograms)	100	25
Iron (milligrams)	18	30–60
Magnesium (milligrams)	300	150

*Height: 65 inches (162.5 cm); weight: 128 pounds (57.60 kg).

Source: National Research Council, Food and Nutrition Board, 1970.

TABLE 3–2

Comparison of Nutritional Requirements for Pregnant and Nonpregnant Women

- 4 or more servings of vegetables and fruit, including green leafy and yellow vegetables, as well as a serving of a fruit high in vitamin C;
- 4 or more servings of whole-grain, enriched and restored bread, and cereal products (U.S. Department of Health, Education and Welfare, 1973).

Milk, especially, is an important source of calcium for the developing fetus's bones and teeth.

Pregnancy is not a reason to eat without restriction *or* to go on a starvation diet. Doctors used to recommend that pregnant women gain no more than 10 or 15 pounds. Since research showed that low weight gain tended to result in low-birth-weight babies, most doctors now suggest a weight gain of around 25 pounds (Wyden, 1971; National Research Council, 1970). Table 3–2 compares the nutrients the average woman needs during pregnancy to those needed by a nonpregnant woman. As the table indicates, a pregnant woman usually needs about 2,200 calories per day, or 200 more than her nonpregnant intake (National Research Council, 1970). Table 3–3 provides a sample daily menu for pregnancy.

Drugs

People who live in Western industrialized nations may be less likely to suffer from malnutrition than any other population group in history.

TABLE 3–3
*Sample Daily Menu
During Pregnancy*

BREAKFAST

Fresh fruit—½ grapefruit, 1 medium orange, ½ cup citrus juice, or 1 cup tomato juice
Cereal—½ to ¾ cup whole-grain cereal
Eggs—1 to 2
1 slice whole-grain or enriched bread or toast, with margarine or butter if weight gain is normal
Coffee—with sugar and 1 ounce cream if desired

LUNCH

Main dish such as macaroni with cheese, or cream soup—¾ cup; a serving of meat may be substituted
Fresh salad, with dressing if desired
Whole-grain or enriched bread—2 slices with margarine or butter if weight gain is normal
Milk—8-ounce glass
Fruit—½ cup

AFTERNOON SNACK (4 P.M.)

Milk—8-ounce glass
Fruit, if desired

DINNER

Meat, fish, or poultry—¼ pound
Potato
Green vegetable
Whole-grain or enriched bread—1 slice, or 4 whole-wheat crackers
Salad, with dressing if desired
Simple milk dessert such as custard, pudding, or ice cream—½ cup

BEFORE BEDTIME

Milk—8-ounce glass, or equivalent amount of cheese

Source: Adapted from Guttmacher, 1973, pp. 109 and 110.

Modern societies, though, contain new hazards for pregnant women and their fetuses. Environmental pollutants—chemical and nuclear—can cause birth defects, and the drugs that women take voluntarily are another potential threat to fetal development.

Drug use is an especially serious problem in pregnant women since almost all drugs cross from the mother's circulatory system to that of the fetus by way of the placenta. A study of 911 mothers shortly after delivery showed that 82% of the women had taken an average of four prescribed drugs during their pregnancy (not counting iron), and that 65% had medicated themselves with an average of 1.5 drugs (Forfar and Nelson, 1973). Of course, not all drugs have harmful effects on the developing fetus. Many, however—including some that are available without a prescription—are potentially hazardous to fetal development. Pregnant women should not take *any* drug at all—even aspirin—without consulting their doctors.

Rugh and Shettles (1971) list the drugs that should be avoided by all women during pregnancy:

1. *Androgens* and other sex hormone treatments, sometimes prescribed to prevent miscarriage. They can affect the sexual development of the fetus during early pregnancy.
2. *Tolbutamine,* sometimes prescribed for diabetes.
3. *Anticoagulants* and drugs that affect blood pressure. These can cause the fetus to hemorrhage and die.
4. *Adrenocorticosteroids* (cortisone), which cause congenital malformations, notably cleft palate.
5. *Thyroid or antithyroid* treatment. It can cause congenital goiter or damage to the fetus's thyroid and pituitary glands.
6. *Cytoxic* (cell-destroying) and *antimetabolic* drugs used in chemotherapy for cancer. These either cause the fetus to be aborted or result in severe damage.

Various nonprescription "drugs" can be dangerous to the fetus, as well. Although it passes from mother to fetus very quickly, *alcohol* is not harmful to the fetus when taken in moderation. Heavy consumption of alcohol, however, is potentially harmful to the fetus as well as to the mother. In extreme cases, babies born to severely alcoholic mothers suffer from delirium tremens. *Heroin* and *narcotics* are associated with low birth weight. In addition, the babies of addicted mothers are themselves born addicted and undergo withdrawal symptoms within 24 hours after delivery. They become irritable and overactive and have convulsions; if not treated, they may die (Guttmacher, 1973). *Cigarette smoking* may also be hazardous to the fetus. A number of recent studies show that smoking by pregnant women is associated with lower birth weight, shorter body length, and higher neonatal mortality (Meredith, 1975). A British study found that the mother's smoking was more often correlated with low birth weight than any other factor (Sweet, 1973). Scientists are not sure *how* smoking causes reduced birth weight, although they speculate that it causes the fetus to be deprived of oxygen (Wingerd, Christianson, Lovitt, and Schoen, 1976).

Radiation

Before the 1954 publication of findings linking radiation to potentially harmful effects on the fetus, X-rays were used on pregnant women without restraint. They were even given as a test for pregnancy and as a way of verifying the physician's impression of the fetus (Guttmacher, 1973). Today, scientists acknowledge that radiation can cause both hereditary and congential defects. Cells that are dividing and becoming differentiated are especially vulnerable to radiation; thus exposure that might be acceptable for an adult would be harmful to a fetus. Heavy radiation in the pelvic area during the early stages of pregnancy can cause congenital abnormalities. When this occurs before either doctor or patient is aware of the pregnancy, a therapeutic abortion is often recommended. Radiation of areas other than the mother's pelvis—dental X-rays, for example—are safe if the pelvis is shielded.

Rh Factors

Rh factors are inherited substances in the red blood cells. Rh factors are classified as either positive or negative, and Rh-positive is dominant over Rh-negative. Rh factors are compatible in babies whose mother's blood is Rh-positive and whose father's blood is Rh-negative. That is, because Rh-positive is dominant, the baby will have Rh-positive blood, which will "match" that of the mother. Incompatibility of Rh factors affects about 10% of babies whose mother's blood is Rh-negative and whose father's blood is Rh-positive. During her first pregnancy, an Rh-negative mother manufactures antibodies against the Rh-positive factor in her baby's blood. These antibodies are usually manufactured when Rh-positive fetal blood cells enter the mother's bloodstream at the time the placenta separates and is delivered from the uterus. The child born from a first pregnancy is not affected by these antibodies. In subsequent pregnancies, however, the antibodies pass through the placenta to the fetus's bloodstream, where they attack the baby's Rh-positive blood cells (Guttmacher, 1973). This condition is called *erythroblastosis*. When it occurs, the fetus may suffer from severe anemia, jaundice, or mental retardation or be stillborn. A vaccine was developed in 1968 which, if given to a mother within 72 hours after her first delivery, abortion, or miscarriage, can prevent antibodies against the Rh positive factor from developing (Seligmann, Gosnell, and Shapiro, 1976).

Diseases

The diseases a woman contracts during pregnancy also are a potential hazard to the developing fetus. The placenta acts as a barrier between the fetus and many maternal diseases. It is almost always effective in preventing the passage of bacteria, which (with the exception of the one that causes pneumonia) are too large to cross the placental barrier. But some viruses do cross the placenta and affect the developing fetus. Among the diseases a pregnant woman can transmit to her fetus are smallpox, chicken pox, measles, mumps, scarlet fever, syphilis, influenza, and German measles. The following diseases are known to have damaging effects on fetal development.

1. *German measles* (rubella) can cause a variety of fetal defects including congenital cataracts and other eye damage, heart malformations, deafness, microcephaly ("pinhead"), mental retardation, slowing of intrauterine growth, and chromosomal changes. In addition, an increased incidence of miscarriages and stillbirths is associated with the rubella virus (Guttmacher, 1973). The type of abnormality that develops is directly related to the week during pregnancy in which the virus occurred. A woman intending to have children can take the hemagglutination inhibition (HI) test to determine whether she has acquired immunity to rubella through past exposure to the disease. If she has not, she can take a live-virus vaccine that enables her system to develop immunity to rubella. Since the vaccine contains the rubella virus, which even at its weakened form can cause damage to the fetus, it must be taken at least 90 days before the woman becomes pregnant (Guttmacher, 1973).

2. *Syphilis* can be transmitted to the fetus through the placenta. When the disease remains untreated, there is an 80% chance that the fetus will be infected. The infection causes stillbirths and prematurity in 25% of the cases, the death of the infant soon after birth in 25 to 30% of the cases, and serious residual injuries in infants who survive (Dwyer, 1976). The time the mother contracted syphilis affects the likelihood of fetal involvement. The more recent the infection of the mother, the more likely it is that the fetus will be affected. Treatment dramatically reverses the outlook for the fetus. In almost all cases, treatment with massive doses of penicillin, which crosses the placental wall, eliminates the possibility of congenital syphilis in the infant (Dwyer, 1976). To diagnose syphilis in pregnant women, most states require a simple blood test called the "Wassermann."

3. *Diabetes* is a noninfectious hereditary condition in which the body fails to produce enough insulin, a hormone needed by cells to absorb sugar. When insulin injections are given, diabetes almost never threatens the life of the mother during pregnancy. However, even when maternal diabetes is properly controlled, fetal complications are common. These complications include fetal death during the last weeks of pregnancy. To avoid this risk, babies of diabetic mothers are often delivered 2 to 6 weeks before the expected delivery date through induced labor or Casarean section (an operation in which the obstetrician cuts open the uterine wall and removes the baby directly). With expert care, including medication and careful regulation of diet, diabetes can be brought under total control. Diabetic women who are receiving care, therefore, can safely have children (Guttmacher, 1973).

Many babies born with serious birth defects could have been normal had their mothers followed a few simple rules. These rules include getting adequate prenatal care as soon as pregnancy is suspected; never self-medicating—to be more exact, never taking *any* drug without the advice of a doctor; avoiding diagnostic X-rays; and preparing herself in advance for pregnancy by determining exposure to rubella and syphilis and by checking for diabetes and Rh incompatibility (Guttmacher, 1973).

HAPPY BIRTHDAY!

According to the National Center for Health Statistics, 3,144,198 babies were born alive in the United States during 1975. Of this number, there were 60,258 multiple deliveries in which two or more infants were born. For every 1,000 girls born, there were 1,054 boys. The median birth weight was 7 pounds, 5 ounces (3,276 grams). The gestation period for these infants was usually between 259 and 293 days, although 8.9% of the recorded births were premature (occurring before 259 days) and another 8.7% were born at 301 days or more of gestation (Final Natality Statistics, 1975). Unless delivered by Caesarean section, babies are born following two stages of labor. During the first stage, the cervix dilates sufficiently to accommodate the baby's head. During the second stage, strong contractions of the uterus push the baby through the birth canal and out into the world. The duration of labor varies widely, although it usually takes longer for the first child. The mean duration of labor is 13 hours. It can last less than 4 hours or more than 30—the point at which it is clinically classified as "prolonged" (McLennan and Sandberg, 1974).

Some Facts

Different cultures vary widely in their attitudes toward childbirth. The Araucanian Indians in South America view childbirth as a sickness. The people of Alor (an island in eastern Indonesia) and the Jarara tribe of South America, on the other hand, consider childbirth a natural and normal phenomenon (Mead and Newton, 1967). Anthropologists have noted that modern Western cultures tend to equate childbirth with illness. Most women have their babies in hospitals—places where one usually goes only when sick. Our culture also tends to see pain as an inevitable part of childbirth.

*Childbirth
Without Pain*

MEDICATION. Since the nineteenth century, when James Simpson first administered chloroform to a woman in labor, medical science has searched for drugs that would alleviate the pain of childbirth. The search has not been entirely successful; a recent obstetrical text concludes that *"No completely safe and satisfactory form of obstetric anesthesia is currently available"* (McLennan and Sandberg, 1974). A number of drugs, though, may be routinely administered to women in labor: anesthetics that numb tissues, analgesics that ease pain, sedatives that quiet anxiety and relax muscles, and even amnesic drugs that cause women to forget the pain afterwards. The problem with most drugs is their possible adverse effects

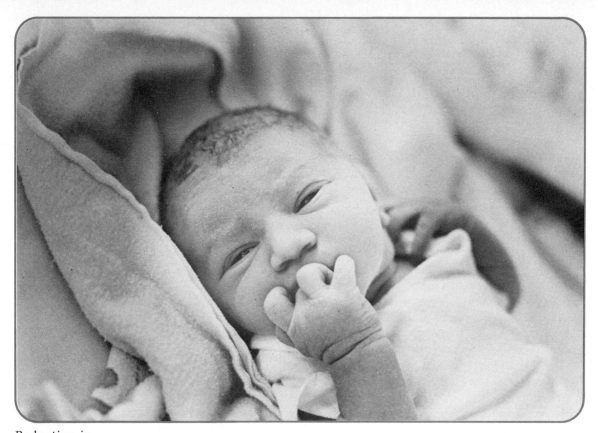

Reduction in medication given to mothers during delivery may benefit their infants. This baby girl, born "naturally" in a hospital, is 1 hour old. (Suzanne Arms, Jeroboam)

on the fetus: "A dosage high enough to relieve pain in a 120-pound woman will in most cases affect a 6-pound baby" (Seligmann et al., 1976).

Drugs that affect the fetus's breathing or the placenta's transfer of oxygen are especially dangerous, since depriving the fetus of oxygen during birth can result in permanent brain damage. The drugs ordinarily administered during delivery, of course, do not have such drastic effects—but they do carry some risks. Even the widely popular spinal anesthetics sometimes cause a sharp reduction in the mother's blood pressure, leading to a slower fetal heart rate and a lowered oxygen supply from the mother to the fetus. A recent study found significant correlations between the potency of delivery medication and infants' performance on tests of muscle tension, vision, and general maturation. The more powerful the medication, the more poorly the infants performed; the influence was apparent not only at 2 and 5 days after birth, but persisted over the next 3 weeks (Conway and Brackbill, 1970). The American Academy of Pediatrics has recently decided "to recommend officially that the least possible medication during childbirth is probably the best" (Seligmann et al., 1976, p. 60).

"NATURAL" METHODS. A number of recent efforts to reduce the pain of childbirth have focused not on drugs but on "natural" techniques such as mental concentration, exercises, and the psychological preparation of women for childbirth. Grantly Dick-Read, who pioneered "natural child-birth" in the early 1950s, proposed the now-familiar theory that fear during childbirth causes muscle tension, which causes pain, and that if fear could be lessened, both the physical and psychological problems of childbirth would be eased. The Lamaze method of painless childbirth, more widely used now, is based on the principle of *psychoprophylaxis*, a Pavlovian concept of the conditioned reflex developed in the Soviet Union in the 1940s as a way of reducing the pain of labor. Dr. Lamaze's technique involves education about the physical process of labor and exercises that improve muscle tone and flexibility. The exercises teach women to control their breathing, relax their muscles, and coordinate breathing with control of the diaphragm and muscles. Fathers participate in "training" for labor, learning how to contribute to their wives' comfort, and are present throughout labor and delivery (Birkbeck and Moore, 1975). The Lamaze method allows women to understand and control labor and delivery and prepares them both mentally and physically to help the process along. Few people would climb a mountain or run a marathon without preparation; labor, like those activities, is hard and prolonged work.

Advocates of the Lamaze method argue that it results in shorter labor; a reduction of pain and, therefore, in the amount of medication the mother will need; healthier babies; and a more satisfying psychological experience for the parents. Several studies of "prepared childbirth" tend to confirm these assertions. Women who attended prepared childbirth classes were found to need less sedation, to have shorter and less traumatic labors, and to have healthier babies than women who did not. Those studies, how-ever, have been contradicted by others and are questionable because of the absence of adequate control groups. Parents who seek prenatal in-struction are a self-selected group that may be highly motivated to achieve a successful labor and delivery, and their attitudes may affect labor as much as actually attending classes and practicing Lamaze techniques. The results of studies of prepared childbirth are, as a whole, skimpy but en-couraging. They suggest "in general that length of labor and occurrence of complications are probably not much affected by programs of preparation or education but that less medication and spontaneous delivery are more likely" (Grimm, 1967, p. 29). The reduction in medication may, in turn, be beneficial to infants.

Ceremonies of birth reveal much about different cultures' attitudes toward children. For the Siriono tribe in Bolivia, who value children very highly, every birth is the occasion for a 3-day celebration. Siriono parents change their own names with the birth of each child. The new baby is breast-fed within half an hour of birth, kept in constant contact with the mother afterwards, and usually not weaned before 3 years of age. In many other cultures, birth is a public celebration. The Navaho Indians welcome any- *The Ceremony of Birth: Warm or Cool* one who comes to lend moral support to the mother during childbirth (Lockett, 1939). In our own culture, by contrast, birth is private. Most American women delivering their first babies have never witnessed childbirth, except perhaps on film. In many hospitals, fathers are not allowed in the delivery room, and mothers and babies are routinely separated after birth, with no visitors allowed except for the immediate family.

Leaving mother and baby together after birth is part of a new and radical ceremony of "birth without violence" developed in France by Dr. Frederick Leboyer. Leboyer, influenced by the Freudian concept of the birth trauma, believes that a difficult birth can cause permanent psychological damage to the individual—and that birth in most hospitals is unnecessarily traumatic. Leboyer proposes a different method:

First, the delivery chamber is kept shadowy and dim, as an unlit room at twilight, and silence is maintained by everyone present. In this way the baby's eyes are not blinded by the sudden onslaught of harsh surgical lights, and its ears are not suddenly violated by strident sounds. Second, when the baby is born, it is not picked up by the heels and slapped on the behind, but, instead, laid softly on the mother's stomach—umbilical still unsevered—where for the next four or five minutes it is tenderly massaged. Finally, at the end of this peaceful time, the cord is cut and for another few minutes, the baby is gently bathed in the basin of warm water. (Englund, 1974, p. 113)

Leboyer argues that his methods ease the transition from the uterus to the outside world. Many mothers whose babies he has delivered maintain that they can see the results in the personalities of their children. Those children, they observe, are "gay, open, and easily satisfied"; their parents feel that their children show fewer difficulties with sleeping, eating, and maternal relationships and are more socially adaptive than other babies (Englund, 1974). As yet, there are no data to prove these results. Leboyer's methods have been very controversial. Many physicians argue, for example, that they need bright lights in the delivery room so that they can see such things as skin color in order to assess the newborn's health. Traditionally, an infant's first act is crying, and many doctors argue that that first squall is an indispensable sign that the baby's lungs are working properly.

Traditional medical techniques of delivering babies are being challenged by innovations even more radical than Leboyer's. A number of parents are dissatisfied by medical techniques such as the use of forceps and drugs, which may leave mothers feeling little control over labor and rob them of the feeling of achievement during childbirth. One of the most articulate critics of hospital delivery is an obstetrician, Dr. A. Atlee. Dr. Atlee (1963) asserts that most labor rooms in hospitals are sterile and frightening, especially for the woman having her first baby. Atlee argues that hospital maternity wards should be more pleasant and more suppor-

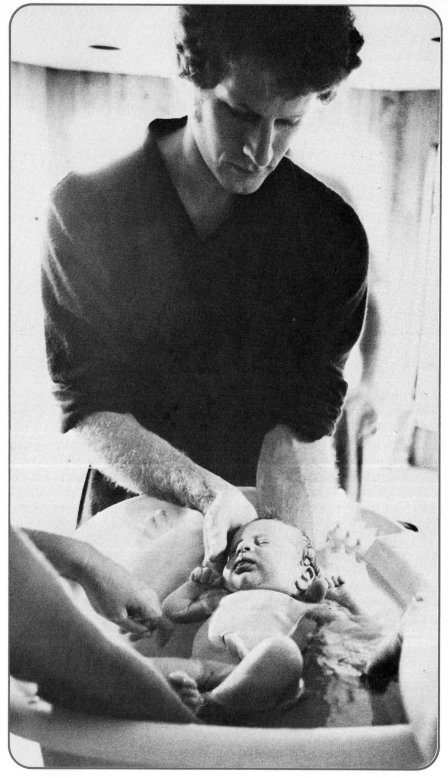

A father bathes his newborn daughter in warm water, "Leboyer style," after her birth at home. (Suzanne Arms, Jeroboam)

94

tive. But since hospitals are slow to change, a growing number of parents are bypassing them altogether and going to places like the Childbearing Center in New York, where fathers and children are welcome during labor, mothers can walk in a room or garden before delivery—and midwives deliver the babies. The number of midwives in the United States is growing, and their services are often sought by women who feel they can talk more easily to midwives than to doctors. More women are choosing to have their babies at home, and one obstetrician in Pennsylvania has specialized in teaching fathers to deliver their own babies (Morrone, 1976). Midwives and home delivery are much less expensive than delivery in a hospital, where a woman who has a healthy baby without complications pays for elaborate equipment she and her baby do not need, and for a doctor who has been trained for 7 or more years to handle every conceivable complication of labor and delivery. Home birth, its advocates argue—and most of them are college-educated professionals—is a more satisfying psychological experience for the parents.

Most births do not involve complications, but between 10 and 15% do require special attention. As we have seen, oxygen deprivation, whether caused by drugs or by the constriction of the umbilical cord, can cause permanent brain damage—so that the few minutes it could take to get from home to hospital could affect the baby for life. It is ironic that parents are becoming more mistrustful of doctors and hospitals at the same time when doctors are using increasingly sophisticated techniques to ensure the welfare of the fetus and to aid the baby's survival afterwards. New instruments allow obstetricians to see the fetus's position before birth and predict whether complications will arise. A recently developed oxygen monitor can measure the baby's oxygen level continuously, both before and after birth (Altman, 1976). Other monitors measure the fetal heartbeat and the mother's contractions, so that a Caesarean section can be performed at the first sign of trouble. Perhaps because of these devices, the percentage of babies delivered by Caesarean is rising, from 5% of births nationwide in 1968 to almost 10% in 1974, with the rate at some hospitals as high as 20% (Seligmann et al., 1976). For the majority of births, of course, such techniques are not necessary. However, women considering home delivery should exercise common sense and some caution. Statistically, second and third pregnancies are safest, with the risks of stillbirth highest in fourth and subsequent pregnancies. The risks for the first pregnancy are intermediate (World Health Organization, 1972). The best candidates for home delivery are probably women who have delivered one healthy baby without complications—in a hospital.

The new ideas about childbirth are beginning to shake established medical procedures. Most hospitals now offer classes to prepare couples for childbirth, and a growing number are accepting the presence of fathers in the delivery room. Whether the more radical ideas of Leboyer and others will take hold remains to be seen.

SUMMARY

The prenatal period has theoretical as well as practical importance. Developmental theorists argue that prenatal and postnatal development are in some ways similar: (1) development depends on the interaction of an individual's genetic code and environmental influences; (2) development proceeds by stages; (3) developmental changes are irreversible; (4) development proceeds by differentiation and integration.

Individual development may be explained by the concept of *canalization*. Each of us carries a unique set of genetic instructions. At sensitive points in development, genetic traits may be deflected from their normal course of development by environmental pressures.

Fertilization starts a process of changes through which a one-celled organism becomes a human baby. The fertilized ovum is called a zygote. Within the first day after conception, the process of *cleavage* (or mitosis) begins. By the fourth day, the zygote has grown to a sphere-shaped solid mass of cells, called a *morula*. The morula moves through the Fallopian tubes into the uterus, and there the solid cells of the morula rearrange themselves around the outside of a sphere filled with liquid. The hollow sphere of cells is known as a *blastula*. Cells of the blastula specialize into those that will form the placenta and the intrauterine fluids, and those that will become the embryo. At 7 to 9 days after conception, the blastula implants itself in the lining of the uterus and begins to receive nourishment from the mother's blood.

The *embryonic period,* between the second and seventh week after conception, is crucial. During this stage, all of the major organ systems and body parts form. At the end of the seventh week, the developing organism is called a *fetus.* Structural changes continue to occur during the *fetal period,* the eighth and subsequent weeks after conception. The fetus grows larger, and its responses become more integrated throughout the remainder of pregnancy. By the seventh month after conception, the fetus has a good chance of survival if born prematurely.

The developing organism is vulnerable to the effects of environmental stresses—*teratogens*—throughout the prenatal period. The organism passes through crucial periods when it is susceptible to stresses that would have little effect earlier or later. Such sensitive periods are called *epigenetic crises.* The embryonic period is especially sensitive.

Maternal health determines the quality of the environment for the developing organism. Good nutrition is important throughout pregnancy. Although the phenomenon of *catch-up growth* shows the tendency of the human system to be self-regulating, malnutrition during pregnancy permanently affects brain development, preventing individuals from reaching their genetically indicated physical size and intellectual potential.

A common consequence of maternal malnutrition is low birth weight. A distinction is made between low birth weight caused by malnutrition and that caused by prematurity. Babies born before 37 weeks of pregnancy are called *short-gestation-period infants;* babies carried to full term but weighing less than 5½ pounds (2,500 grams) at birth are called *low-birth-weight infants.* New techniques of assessing gestational age of newborns enable doctors to classify babies as *average for date of birth* (AFD) or *small for date of birth* (SFD), and to treat them accordingly. Small-for-date babies seem to suffer disadvantages in later intellectual development. Experiments have shown that simple nutritional supplements for pregnant women and their babies can reduce stillbirths, increase birth weight, and improve intellectual and social development of children.

Prescription and nonprescription drugs, alcohol, cigarettes, X-rays, and diseases such as German measles or syphilis, and conditions such as diabetes and *erythroblastosis* (resulting from incompatibility of RH factors) pose hazards for the developing fetus. Medical care early in pregnancy and common-sense precautions can prevent the occurrence of birth defects from these causes.

Birth occurs after a gestation period of approximately 259 to 293 days. Unless delivered by Caesarean section, babies are born following two stages of labor. Medication to reduce the pain of labor and childbirth can be given. But drugs are being found to have an adverse effect on the newborn, and women and their doctors are coming to believe that the least possible medication is probably the best. A growing number of parents are turning to simpler, more natural ways of giving birth.

PART II

Infancy

May 10, 1959

After 3 years, it's hard to remember much about the first weeks of Susan's life. It's the nights that stand out most in my memory.

Why didn't someone tell me that babies cry all night? Every night! Maddeningly! I nursed Susan at 10 or 10:30. Oh, she went to sleep so peacefully. But then the clock struck one. For the next 3 hours, she nursed, dozed, and howled. Mike covered his head with a pillow and slept through it all. What long, lonely hours she and I spent together, walking from window to window through the dark house, looking out at empty streets, stars, and snow; frantic rocking, rubbing, and crooning; now a bottle, then a search for an open pin. Call the doctor? Wake up Mike?

The worst was over by 3 months. Suddenly, one night she slept all the way through from 11 P.M. to 7 A.M. Through another night and then another. What a luxury—whole nights of blessed, uninterrupted sleep!

If the nights were unbearable, the days were bliss. Susan loved her bath, and her grandma loved to give it to her. From the kitchen, I could hear them cooing to one another.

When Susan was 5 months old, she pulled herself to a sitting position in her crib. At 9 months, she managed to walk around the house holding on to things, and at 13 months, she walked by herself.

The experts say that babies don't really talk until they are about a year old. But Susan began to talk at 6 months. She said "dada," "mama," "cookie," and "bye-bye." Were we imagining it? Did she know what she was saying?

The new baby is due next week. Can I face those sleepless nights all over again? Maybe this baby will be different.

May 21, 1959

It's a boy! Name: Jonathan Daniel. Weight: 7 lbs, 2 oz. A feisty, black-haired, squinty-eyed, beautiful baby.

We go home tomorrow. . . .

CHAPTER 4

The Competence of the Newborn

A baby is born with many skills and responses. In this chapter, we will explore these skills and the manner in which they develop. What are the sensory stimuli that dominate the world of the baby? How does the relationship between newborn and environment change and expand? These are basic questions for all students of infant development. In describing the newborn, researchers have used widely divergent methods and arrived at markedly different conclusions. To encompass as much of this research as possible, we will look at the baby in several ways. The baby may be viewed as a bundle of reflexes, a cluster of emerging behaviors, and a sensory surface. The baby is also a learner, a thinker, and a social partner (Kessen, Haith, and Salapatek, 1970).

The extent of a newborn's abilities is quite impressive. The baby is a well-functioning, though by no means independent, system. What do we mean by the newborn's competence? Competence, according to the dictionary, can include both potential capacity and actual performance. The baby enters a world full of people who want to test its competence. Doctors and nurses poke, slap, and inject; mothers worry if their babies are all right. New techniques in neonatal assessment enable medical workers to give a fast report on how this baby compares to most newborns.

NEONATAL ASSESSMENT

Within minutes after a baby's birth, medical workers check for any major abnormalities in development that might need emergency attention. Then they determine where the baby falls within the normal range of variation found in newborns. Since the mid-1950s, the Apgar score has been used to assess the condition of the newborn. Administered 1 to 5 minutes after birth, the Apgar score measures five items: pulse, respiration, muscle tone, reflex irritability, and skin color. Scores of 0 to 2 are given for each

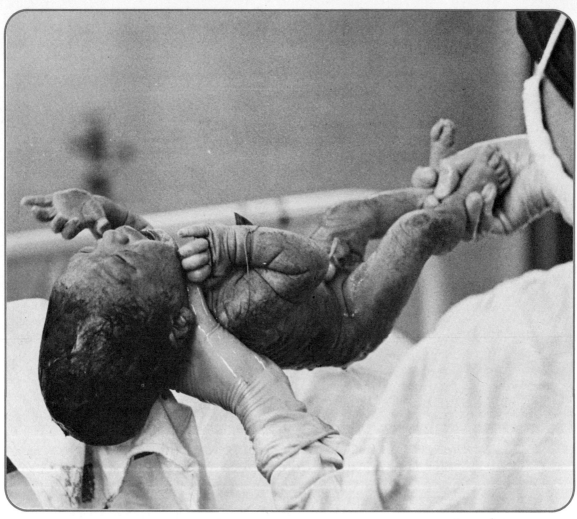

*A newborn
infant.
(Josephus Daniels,
Rapho/Photo
Researchers)*

item. A "perfect" Apgar composite score is a total of 10; a score of 7 to 9
predicts a good chance of the infant's survival; 4 to 6 is fair; 3 or below
calls for immediate medical attention.

*What a Newborn
Is Like*

Newborns are often quite frightful sights. They emerge from the birth
canal covered with a white, waxy material that helps protect their skin
during the prenatal period. Their skin is red and wrinkled. Some babies
are bald at birth; others have a full head of hair, which soon falls out. Many
are covered with a fine matte of body hair, which adds to a generally comic
appearance. Mothers who anticipated infants looking as if they crawled
out of a diaper ad may be horrified.

A baby's head appears very large, since it comprises one-quarter of
total body length (compared to one-tenth in adults). The bones of the
skull have not yet fused, and the top of the head is soft. Following the

tremendous struggle of delivery, most babies fall into a deep sleep and some have trouble for a few days staying awake long enough to nurse. During this period, the baby will stabilize breathing, circulatory, and digestive functions. The baby generally will lose some weight during this time, although fat deposits tide the baby over until he is ready to nurse. The sucking reflex, however, is already present. The baby will cry, but no tears are secreted.

Weight at birth varies, depending on prenatal care, genetic factors, season of birth, and other variables. Average weight is within a fairly constant range from one cultural group to another. Indian newborns average about 2.74 kilograms (6 pounds); American Indian newborns weigh an average of approximately 3.6 kilograms (8 pounds); Japanese and American blacks fall in between at 3.1 kilograms (6¾ pounds) (Meredith, 1971).

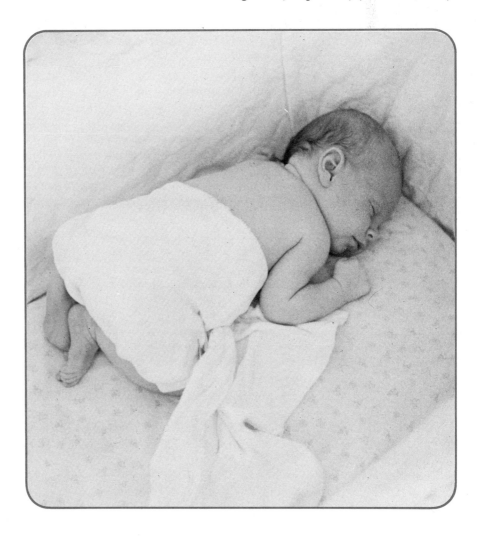

In the first 4 to 6 weeks of life, babies spend a great deal of their time sleeping. (James R. Holland, Stock, Boston)

Because nutritional standards and medical resources vary greatly among these cultures, it is hard to say how much of this variation stems from environmental and how much of it can be attributed to inherited characteristics.

The newborn is a person of many talents. Within a short time of his rude expulsion from the dark and cozy home that brought everything to him, he is coping with a new world. He can draw in air and extract its oxygen, actively search for food, and swallow it down the right tube. He can turn his head from side to side and yell for help with those tasks he cannot manage alone.

The newborn is also a busy person. In order to learn and master so many new skills, the newborn's body operates at a much faster rate than does an adult's. He breathes twice as fast as a grown-up and his heart contracts 120 times a minute (compared to the adult pulse of 70). The baby urinates up to 18 times a day and may move his bowels up to 7 times. To rest from all this activity and recharge for the next day, he sleeps more than 14 hours out of every 24 (Caplan, 1973).

Brain and Nervous System at Birth

The coordinating center for all this work (the brain and the central nervous system) is buzzing with newly established neural circuitry. The rate of brain growth is at its highest point just before birth. No other system in the body develops at such a rapid pace (Kessen et al., 1970). At birth, myelinization is almost complete. *Myelinization* is the development of a myelin sheath around cranial nerves which marks the capacity for full neural functioning. Two major exceptions are the *optic* nerves (controlling vision) and the *olfactory* nerves (responsible for the sense of smell). In both these areas, the myelin sheath is not yet fully developed. In addition, the newborn's hearing apparatus is almost completely formed. Both the middle and the inner ear structures reach adult size by the fifth fetal month. In the sixth month, the auditory nerve fibers start to myelinize. At that point, the fetus shows a response to pure tone. The newborn baby, then, is equipped with many of the structures necessary to respond to the sounds of his new world (Eisenberg, 1975).

State

In assessing newborns, researchers have asked what infants do in the absence of stimulation: What are the self-generated behaviors of the baby, and in what patterns do they occur? The concept of *state* has played an important role in such studies. State refers to a pattern of self-generated behavior that recurs over time. State has been defined as a behavioral condition that (1) remains constant for a certain length of time; (2) recurs often in an individual infant; and (3) can be observed in other infants (Hutt, Lenard, and Prechtl, 1969).

There is controversy over how to define the different states observed in newborns. Some researchers believe that each of the states is distinct, marked by unique neurophysiological conditions (Hutt et al., 1969). Others view the various states as points on a continuum, sharing important similarities and distinguished mainly by differences in degree.

Most investigators who subscribe to the latter view use a scale ranging from deep sleep to awake excitement. How many categories they use depends on how they treat transitions from one state to another. Some researchers characterize transitions as separate states in their own right; others disregard them.

DEVELOPMENTAL CHANGES IN STATE. Regardless of which classification system is used, we know that newborns demonstrate all the different states in the first days of life. The time they spend in each state changes, however. The newborn's transitions follow a developmental pattern from rapid transitions during the first few days to establishment of one predominant state after little more than a week (Beintema, 1968). Although state changes during the first few days of life, infants differ at birth in the way state is organized.

During neurological examinations of infants, Beintema (1968) identified five categories as follows:

- State 1: regular respiration; closed eyes; no movements.
- State 2: irregular respiration; closed eyes; no gross movements.
- State 3: open eyes; no gross movements.
- State 4: open eyes; gross movements; no crying.
- State 5: open or closed eyes; crying.

She found six developmental patterns in the organization of these states. In three of the patterns, the infant showed a predominant state from the first day of life. On day 1, about one-quarter of the infants had a predominant State 3; a similar number exhibited predominant State 4. A very few babies had predominant State 5. As Figure 4–1 illustrates, gradually over the course of 9 days, more and more infants exhibited State 4. The occurrence of State 3's relative inactivity decreased markedly, and State 3 supports the principle that increased waking activity and movement rapidly becomes the dominant mode of activity in the newborn.

INDIVIDUAL DIFFERENCES. Not all infants readily settle into a predominant state. Remember that of Beintema's six patterns, only three were marked by early establishment of a predominant state. The other three patterns involved infants who consistently moved from greater to lesser activity, lesser to greater, or who showed no pattern at all. Only one out of two infants showed a predominant state on day 1, but over the course of a week they not only settled into one state, but the overwhelming majority settled into State 4. By day 9, only a handful of consistently uncharacter-

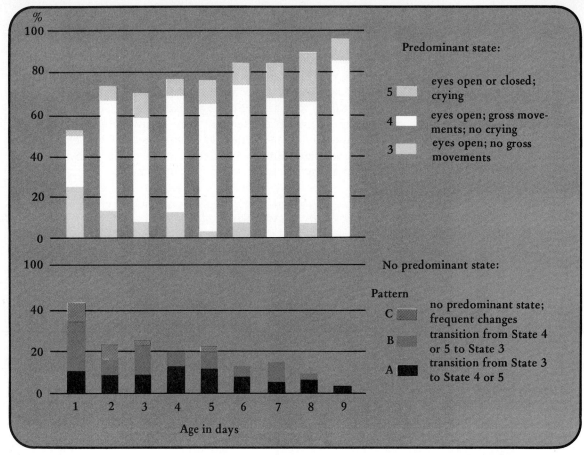

FIGURE 4–1
Predominant states and state patterns in the first 9 days of life
(*Adapted from Beintema, 1968, p. 35*)

izable infants had not adopted an organizational pattern of activity (Beintema, 1968). State patterns affect caregiving; infants with irregular patterns may be more difficult for parents to manage and to feel comfortable with because their states are less predictable.

Interestingly, Beintema found that during the first 2 days, the infant's state pattern did not change much in response to handling by adults. After that period, the state pattern was more easily influenced by handling involved in the examination.

We should note that the range in individual state patterns is wide. There is variation in the amount of time spent in each state. Infants also differ in the distinctiveness of their behavioral style (Thomas, Chess, and Birch, 1968, 1970). Some well-organized infants give clear cues to their mothers; others give weaker or more ambiguous cues. Another point of variation is the proportion of time spent in states of greater equilibrium or intense activity. Mothers know this individual difference well. One baby sleeps sweetly, but an older sister may have been a red-faced screamer at the same age.

WHAT DO INFANTS DO WHEN STIMULATED?

Remember that the infant's state is a pattern of self-generated behaviors rather than a series of responses to stimuli. It is important to establish the infant's state before judging the response to a given stimulus, since the same stimulus can elicit two different responses from the same infant. Presentation of a nipple, for instance, may evoke little response from a sleepy infant, whereas it may increase the activity of an alert—and hungry—infant.

Reflex Systems

The baby has not yet learned to make smooth, voluntary movements; nevertheless his muscles are capable of remarkable feats. Moving in automatic, involuntary patterns called *reflexes,* the newborn demonstrates a number of skills that help him cope with the outside world. Figure 4–2 illustrates some major infant reflexes.

The *rooting reflex* helps the newborn locate food. When the baby is stroked on the cheek or near the mouth, his head turns toward the stroking object in search of the nipple. This reflex is activated most readily by stroking inside the baby's mouth. Once food is found, the *sucking reflex* follows. Rooting has been observed in awake infants only 30 minutes old; it does not occur in sleeping states (Gentry and Aldrich, 1948).

Some reflexes have a protective function. The *optical blink reflex* causes the eye to close in order to protect it from excessive light. The *gag reflex* enables the newborn to spit up liquids blocking breathing passages. An infant also has a *withdrawal reflex* that causes him to pull away from a source of pain and cry in outrage.

One of the most dramatic reflexes of the newborn is the *Moro reflex.* This muscular response is a reaction to a sudden and intense change in stimulation and is thought to be part of our evolutionary heritage from the apes. If the baby is exposed to a loud noise, bright light, sudden change in head position, or other alarming situation, he arches his back and tosses back his head. Arms and legs flail out and then are hugged closely to the middle of the body. Moro, the scientist who first described this reflex, theorized that it is a vestigial form of primate clinging (Kessen et al., 1970). The Moro reflex generally disappears when the infant is 3 to 6 months old. Persistence of the reflex past this age may indicate damage to the central nervous system.

The *Babinski reflex* is another reflex that appears in newborns but disappears after a while. Stroking the sole of the baby's foot triggers the Babinski reflex, in which the toes of the foot spread apart. The reflex disappears 4 to 6 months after birth and, like the Moro, may indicate neurological damage if it persists past the age of 6 months.

Many reflexes, like the Moro, involve a complex set of responses by several different parts of the body. For example, the *tonic neck reflex* requires movement of the arms and legs as well as the neck. If the baby's

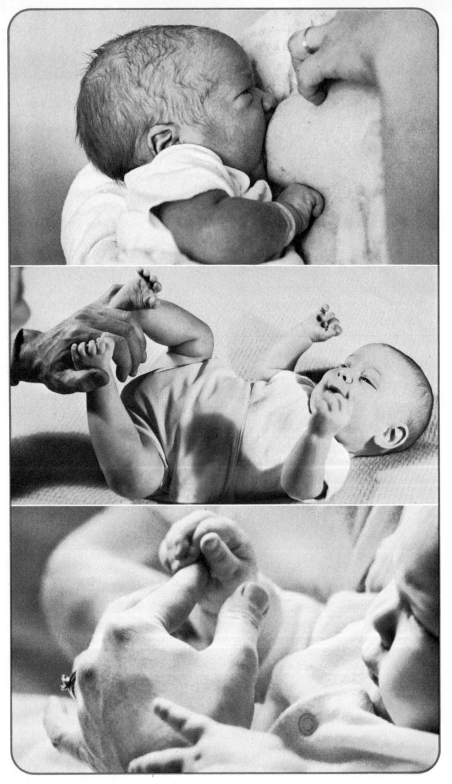

FIGURE 4–2
Major infant responses: (top) sucking reflex, (middle) Babinski reflex, (bottom) palmar response (Eve Arnold, Magnum; Edna Bennett, Photo Researchers; Elizabeth Wilcox, Photo Researchers)

head is turned sharply to one side and held, the arm and leg on that side extend, while the other arm bends at the elbow. The *palmar response* requires delicate finger coordination. If you place an object in the baby's palm, all his fingers will flex around it.

The newborn's pediatrician looks for these reflexes and many others. Faulty reflexes may be evidence of neurological or other damage. Assessment of newborns is particularly important since many signs of abnormality may vanish in the first few days or weeks after birth, to be followed later by irrevocable damage (Prechtl and Beintema, 1964). Early detection is an important tool in treating such birth defects.

For example, the absence of the optical blink reflex may indicate impaired light perception. Recall that the baby's visual apparatus is not yet fully developed and that vision plays a major role in early learning. Without early detection, the infant suffering from this defect may encounter severe learning problems and be diagnosed incorrectly as having low intelligence.

Some reflexes are normally absent more than they are present. For example, a constant, clearly defined tonic neck reflex in a newborn may be indicative of some neurological dysfunction. It is usually observed in infants 2 to 3 months old.

THE NEUROLOGICAL EXAMINATION. Prechtl and Beintema were pioneers in the effort to standardize procedure and refine diagnoses in the area of neurological examinations. They emphasized the importance of controlling the environment in which the examination takes place, including light, temperature, and the examination surface. They described in detail the technique for handling the infant in each diagnostic test. Finally, they stressed the influence of the infant's internal state on the examination. Factors like the time from last feeding, drugs from labor remaining in the infant's bloodstream, and incipient infection can alter response patterns. The work of Prechtl and Beintema paved the way for development of other neonatal scales, most notably the Brazelton Neonatal Behavior Scale. The Brazelton Scale sets out a number of criteria and lists nine possible ratings for the infant's performance on each item (Brazelton, 1973).

During the neurological exam, as we mentioned before, the physician looks for asymmetries—reflexes that are noticeably stronger or weaker than average—as indicators of neural abnormality. Such asymmetries can also result from the drug addiction of the mother. In tests using the Brazelton Scale, infants who were born addicted showed a number of important differences from nonaddicted babies. They became irritable more easily during the testing and cried more often than normal infants. This behavior in turn elicited more help from the infant's caretaker, but the addicted infant did not take readily to nestling and cuddling. These motor responses were impaired by the withdrawal syndrome. Addicted infants spend less time in an alert state than do nonaddicted newborns, and they perk up less in response to consolation. This is likely to make the addicted infant more difficult to take care of (Strauss, Lessen-Firestone, Starr, and Ostrea, 1975).

DEVELOPMENT WITH AGE. As we mentioned above, the Moro reflex disappears between the age of 4 to 6 months and changes into the adult "startle" reflex. There are three possible explanations for this development. The Moro and startle reflexes may be two distinct patterns, the former simply being replaced by the latter. Or, the startle reflex may be present at birth but may be obscured by the similar but grosser movements of the Moro reflex. The third theory is that the Moro reflex degenerates into the adult response; both responses have many characteristics in common. At present, it is not possible to say with certainty which of these three developmental theories is correct (Hunt, Clarke, and Hunt, 1967).

Another interesting developmental progression is that of infant swimming. Infants only a few weeks old show competence in swimming. Their movements in water are smoothly coordinated and forceful enough to propel them through the water. When the head is submerged, the infant's breathing stops briefly so that he does not inhale water. However, at approximately 4 months, swimming behavior becomes very disorganized and ineffective. Infants may make struggling movements or sink without moving at all. Toward the end of the second year, children regain the ability to swim, this time through voluntary muscle control. McGraw (1939) suggests that the intervening disorganized phase is due to inhibitory messages from developing areas of the brain.

Development of walking skills follows a similar pattern. Stepping reflexes appear in the first week of life; with support, a newborn is able to step when his weight is supported by the examiner and to navigate his way over low obstacles (André-Thomas and Autgarten, 1966). Like swimming skills, these stepping motions also disappear temporarily at about 8 weeks. This precocious display may still serve a developmental purpose, however, in facilitating the infant's learning to walk. One group of researchers found that active exercise of infants before their stepping motions disappeared at 8 weeks significantly lowered the age at which they took first voluntary steps (Zelazo, Zelazo, and Kolb, 1972). Perhaps, then, infantile reflexes are not aimed solely at ensuring immediate survival but also at preparing the baby for later accomplishments.

In animals, genetic messages in each species produce reflexes that are constant in form. These are called *fixed action patterns*. Genetic messages also create the disposition to learn the right thing at the right time. The same concept applies to humans. It is difficult to state conclusively that nature rather than nurture causes development of certain reflexes, because the relation between activity and stimulation is so close. For instance, deaf children begin to babble and vocalize at the same age as infants who

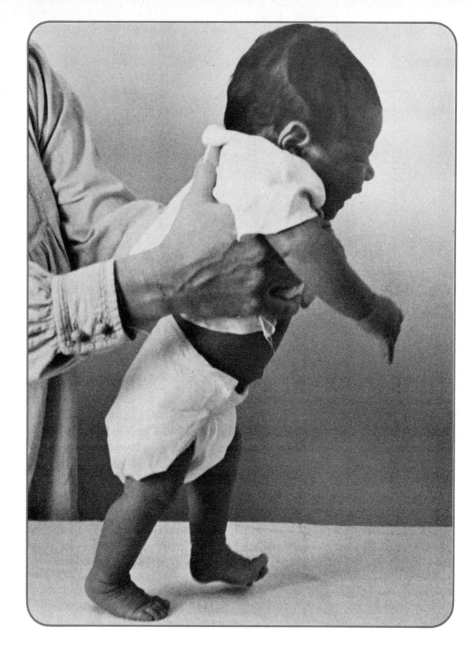

Stepping reflexes appear in the first week of life and disappear at about 8 weeks. (Suva, DPI)

can hear. And yet by 1 year of age the spontaneous sounds of deaf children do not resemble the sounds of their hearing playmates. Children who are born blind show the smiling reflex (Eibl-Eibesfeldt, 1967). Yet the circumstances that evoke smiling differ, and so the role of smiling in later social interaction will differ. Thus it is probably safe to conclude that although many of the infant's reflexes stem from genetic commands designed to ensure complete development and adequate learning, stimulation from the environment determines whether and how the reflexes will be used.

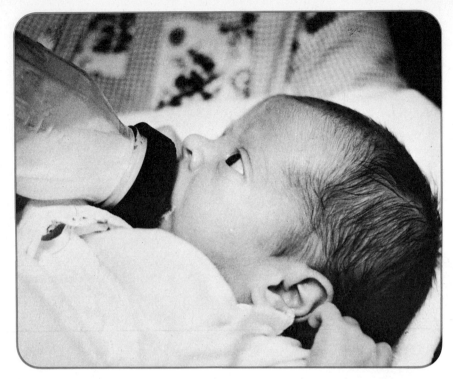

Sucking is an organized congenital pattern of behavior that an infant uses for both nutritive and nonnutritive purposes. (George Ross, DPI)

Organized congenital patterns of behavior are somewhat similar to reflexes in humans and fixed action patterns in animals. The main difference is one of degree. Organized congenital patterns of behavior denote behavior that is sustained longer, copes with a wider range of tasks, and incorporates more of the external environment than reflexes and fixed action patterns.

This is a rather broad concept, but it does have several limiting characteristics. The pattern must be present at birth (congenital) and may or may not be genetically determined. The behavior pattern is at least to some extent the result of the child's act, rather than of those around him. It appears to be important in the life of the child and can be described in terms of when and where it appears (Rheingold, 1967).

SUCKING. Sucking is a good example of an organized congenital pattern of behavior. There are several important components in this behavior pattern. We mentioned earlier the rooting reflex, which enables the infant to locate a nipple. Once this is accomplished, the infant begins a two-part sucking action. He creates suction inside his mouth, drawing a flow of milk from the bottle. At the same time, the newborn presses the nipple between his gums, squeezing milk out. This second process is called *expression*.

Swallowing is a complex process that requires coordination of swallowing, sucking, and breathing. Swallowing occurs in the pause between inhaled and exhaled breaths. To keep up an uninterrupted stream of milk and air, nature has equipped newborns with a swallowing reflex that is three times faster than the adult reflex (Halverson, 1944).

Feeding cycles partially govern the desire to suck. (Newborns also engage in nonnutritive sucking, as we shall see.) Feeding practices are a source of ongoing controversy. Some experts advocate demand feeding (in response to hunger urges); others believe that scheduled feeding is the best practice. If fed on demand, newborns may feed up to 14 times a day. Within a few weeks, however, infants usually settle down to three to six nursings a day. Infants who are allowed to regulate their own nursing sessions seem to approximate the 4-hour intervals commonly prescribed in fixed-interval feeding (Aldrich and Hewitt, 1947).

Nonnutritive sucking is commonly observed in newborns. Researchers have even observed and photographed a fetus sucking its thumb in the uterus. Newborns suck their thumbs and hands, often as a result of some kind of distress. Nonnutritive sucking seems to serve a pacifying function.

In nursery observations by Kessen, Leutzendorff, and Stoutsenberger (1967), it was found that sucking reduces movement both before the first postnatal feeding and afterward. Moreover, infants who sucked actively enjoyed a significantly greater quieting effect than those who sucked poorly or refused the nipple. Interestingly, the investigators observed similar effects between feeding and movement in a severely brain-damaged child who had developed only a brain stem. They concluded that the relationship between sucking and movement is present at birth and may be organized at subcortical levels.

The above discussion suggests that sucking is a highly stable pattern of behavior. This is not to say, however, that it is inflexible. We mentioned earlier that sucking is composed of both suction and expression. Normally, there is one suction motion for each expression of the nipple. In a set of experimental feedings, however, this relationship was altered. When infants were rewarded with milk for expression but not suction, the frequency of suction decreased. On the other hand, when suction was reinforced and expression was not, the frequency of expression remained the same (Sameroff, 1968). Thus, expression seems to be the more stable of the two sucking actions.

In addition to the relationship between sucking and movement reduction, some researchers believe that there is a link between sucking and seeing. Bruner (1969b) argues that ongoing sucking stimulates the baby to scan his environment for more visual information. Other researchers (Mendelson and Haith, 1975) argue that the two processes are independent of each other. They point out that sucking is organized subcortically and is well developed at birth, whereas visual functioning is centered in the cortex and is still incomplete at birth. They conclude that the two neurological systems are too different to possibly influence each other at this stage.

CRYING. Crying is a subject that produces anxiety in parents and conflicting advice from experts. Some people advise immediate attention to the fussing or crying infant; this is a cultural pattern often found in simple societies. Others, including Dr. Benjamin Spock, advise parents to let the newborn cry for 15 to 20 minutes when establishing a feeding schedule, unless the cry is clearly a hunger cry. There is even controversy over the meaning of the infant's cry. Some researchers believe that all cries are purposive (that is, contain a message), whereas others think that at least some cries are random and undifferentiated.

Cries may or may not be purposive, but they have been shown to be distinctive. In some cases, certain kinds of cries can be related to a particular initiating event such as pain or hunger. Analysis of infant cries has been greatly facilitated by sophisticated devices, including magnetic tape and spectrographs, which produce a graph tracing the rise, fall, and volume of a cry.

There are four basic situations in which cries occur. In each case, the sound and behavioral patterns are distinct. The *birth cry* is, naturally, the baby's first. It often occurs before the entire body has emerged from the mother. Typically, the baby takes two gasping breaths and then gives the familiar wail. The birth cry lasts about 1 second and has a flat or falling tone (Wasz-Hockert, Lind, Vuorenkoski, Partanen, and Valanne, 1968). The *basic cry* is also known as the *hunger cry*, since it is most often heard 4 hours after feeding. It is not, however, necessarily caused by hunger. The basic cry follows a rhythmical pattern of cry, silence, inhaling whistle, and rest. The *pain cry* has been clinically identified by recording newborns as their skin was pricked for blood tests or vaccinations. The pain cry follows a pattern of one long cry followed by an even longer silence as the infant holds his breath, and then a series of basic cries of various lengths (Wolff, 1969). Additionally, the pain cry is accompanied by tensed facial muscles, frowns, and clenched fists. The *mad cry* is similar to the basic cry, except that the infant forces a greater amount of air through his vocal cords, creating greater turbulence and a more exasperated sound (Wolff, 1969).

Can adults distinguish these different cry signals? Experiments show that, with experience, people can learn to identify properly much infantile communication. Midwives, nurses, and mothers scored the highest in a test requiring identification of taped pain, birth, hunger, and mad cries. Even this group, however, had problems correctly identifying the birth cry, probably because they did not hear it as regularly as they heard the other cries. Individual differences among infants also affect how clearly others understand the message of a cry. The more atypical a cry is (the more it varies from the standard pattern), the more difficult it is for the caretaker to know what an infant wants (Wasz-Hockert et al., 1968). In addition, markedly atypical cries can be an important diagnostic tool in

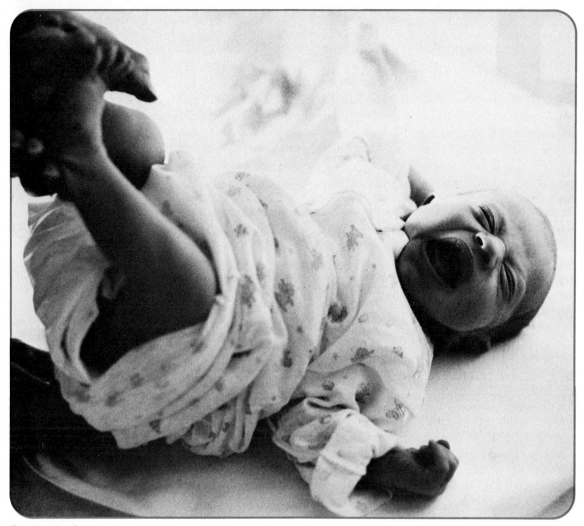

Crying is the infant's first means of communication; with experience, parents learn that different cries convey different messages. (Shelly Rusten)

detecting neurological abnormalities. Children suffering from Down's syndrome also have distinctive, shrill cries that may signal trouble to the alert pediatrician (Wolff, 1969).

Crying may be an important signal, but what parents want to know about it is how to stop it. The first step is feeding. If this is ineffective, pacifier sucking may help by reducing the diffuse activity that stimulates and arouses the baby. Other techniques that often prove effective are rhythmic tapping and swaddling. Picking up the crying baby is a technique well known to mothers, as is rocking. Studies have shown that faster rocking is more effective than slower rocking, possibly because of its effect on the autonomic nervous system (Ter Vrugt and Pederson, 1973). Infants who are carried on their mothers' backs receive this kind of steady rocking and often stop crying readily.

THE NEWBORN AS PERCEIVER

All the time the infant is being pricked, watched, and slapped by others, he is making observations of his own. Some of his perceptual processes are more sophisticated than others, but his environment nevertheless makes a profound impression on him. What exactly is the extent of the newborn's ability to sense stimuli? The answer depends on which sensory capacity is under consideration.

VISUAL COMPETENCE. The newborn does not see objects in sharp focus; *Sensory* he has a tendency to nearsightedness. Nor can he alter his focus very *Capabilities* readily. Usually, he focuses on objects about 19 centimeters (7½ inches) in front of him (Haynes, White, and Held, 1965). He is sensitive to the intensity of light and will shut his eyes if light is too bright. If an object is moved slowly in front of him, he can follow it with both eyes, although convergence (simultaneous focus of both eyes on the same spot) does not always occur. More often, his eyes will converge on a nonmoving object.

AUDITORY COMPETENCE. The infant's hearing apparatus is highly developed at birth. The auditory portion of the cortex, however, is still immature, and the right and left hemispheres of the brain are not fully coordinated. The newborn may have difficulty integrating sound from both ears in the first few months (Conel, 1952; Dreyfus-Brisac, 1966).

During the first 2 weeks after birth, the newborn has a high auditory threshold due to fluid that is trapped in his middle ear. A strong stimulus is required to get a response. After the fluid is absorbed, however, the threshold drops rapidly. Newborns react demonstrably to sound. A loud tone causes a marked increase in pulse rate; a softer tone produces a smaller acceleration in heartbeat. Intense stimuli produce a reaction after a shorter interval than that produced by softer sounds.

Sounds affect newborns in three different ways—they soothe, they alert, and they distress. Rhythmic, low-frequency sounds are particularly soothing. Those sounds that fall within the frequencies most characteristic of the human voice are most effective in getting the infant's attention. On the other hand, several different types of sounds are distressing to newborns. Very high and very low tones make infants fuss and cry, and loud or sudden sounds elicit a Moro reaction and accelerated heartbeat.

Newborns show an ability both to habituate to and to discriminate between different sounds. *Habituation* refers to the phenomenon that occurs when the same stimulus is repeatedly presented. After a certain number of repetitions, the infant shows no response; he has habituated to the sound. *Discrimination* is evidenced when an infant who is habituated to one auditory stimulus reacts to a very similar, but slightly different sound. These are important elements of the learning process. Newborns less than a week old can discriminate between sounds of different intensity, pitch, and duration (Hirschman and Katkin, 1974). Newborns 1 to 4 days old also can discriminate between sound sources located in different places (Leventhal and Lipsitt, 1964).

OTHER SENSES. Although vision and hearing have received more attention in neonatal assessment than have other faculties, they are not the only sensory capacities important to the developing child. Tactile sensitivity is demonstrated by the rooting reflex and the Babinski reflex. The newborn also shows an ability to track a tactile stimulus across his face. As a finger moves in front of him, the baby turns his head in such a way as to try to bring the finger and his mouth as close together as possible (Blauvelt and McKenna, 1960).

Sensitivity to temperature is not as marked. Infants tend to respond to both hot and cold stimuli and have difficulty discriminating between similar temperatures. They do, however, adjust their total caloric intake in response to changed environmental temperature (Cooke, 1952).

The newborn's sensitivity to pain undergoes a change in the first 2 postnatal days. On the first day, the threshold of pain is relatively high; a strong stimulus is required to produce a sensation of pain. In the following 3 days, sensitivity increases noticeably. There is some evidence of a sex difference here. One study showed that girls react to less intense stimuli than boys. A second study, however, has cast some doubt on this conclusion (Lipsitt and Levy, 1959).

Taste is an important sensory capacity for the newborn. Newborns actively regulate the amount of fluid they consume, depending on how pleasing or distasteful it is to them. Newborns find plain water aversive and drink as little of it as possible. If the feeding solution is sweet, infants will drink more of it. (This fact has been exploited by manufacturers of commercial formulas, which contain large amounts of sugar and create a "sweet tooth" even before the baby has any real teeth.) If the solution is sour, infants will drink less, but if the taste is either bitter or salty, they do not seem to mind at all (Desor, Maller, and Andrews, 1975).

The Organization of Sensory Information

The foregoing discussion attempts to map some of the more important sensory abilities of the newborn. The question remains, however—what happens to the sensory information between the time it is received and the time a response is formulated? The organization of sensory information into meaningful patterns and hierarchies is the process known as *perception*. The classic debate about the origins of perception swirls around three main theories. Some theoreticians feel that perception is innately organized. Others believe that it is the result of accumulated sensitivity to the environment. Still others, among them Piaget, claim that perception stems from developing motor acts (Kessen et al., 1970). Research on neonatal perception is a valuable tool in providing information to this ongoing controversy.

PATTERN AND FORM PERCEPTION. The first question to be asked is how a newborn perceives pattern and form. Is there some congenital mechanism that is receptive to information about the whole, or does the newborn originally respond to one part only? And how does the infant's perception mature and change into the adult mode?

It is generally agreed that up to 7 weeks of age, newborns may process elements of a form, but they do not respond to an entire configuration (Appleton, Clifton, and Goldberg, 1975). For example, when newborns look at real faces, they scan high-contrast areas such as the hairline. By 7 weeks infants show increased preference for looking at faces, and it is the eyes that attract their attention (Bergman, Haith, and Mann, 1971). In Chapter 5, we will deal with attention patterns in older infants.

Salapatek and Kessen (1966) have proposed an "attractive elements" hypothesis that offers a major new approach. They theorize that newborns refer to attractive parts of the figure rather than to the figure as a whole. In an experiment with two groups of infants, they displayed a black triangle on a white ground to one and a plain black ground to the controls. Cameras recording the infants' eye movements revealed some interesting data. The control group scanned the plain black field widely. Their scanning was dispersed more in horizontal directions than in vertical directions, indicating that horizontal scanning is probably somewhat easier for the infant. The group that saw the triangle exhibited a very different response. Not only was their scanning less dispersed, but they concentrated on particular parts of the triangle—the corners. There was little scanning across the center of the figure, which would have indicated a response to the figure as a whole. Salapatek and Kessen concluded that the angles were highly attractive to the infants, who lacked the capacity to integrate them into a whole figure. A later study by Kessen, Salapatek, and Haith (1972) indicated that vertical edges are much more attractive to newborns than horizontal edges. Newborns do not scan horizontal edges unless they are close to the natural resting place of the eye (Haith, 1976).

COMPLEXITY AND CONTOURS. A great deal of experimentation has been done to demonstrate the hypothesis that as infants mature, they prefer stimuli of increasing complexity. Unfortunately, the definition of "complex" has been applied both to stimuli with a great deal of sensory input and to stimuli that are unfamiliar to the child. The results of this research have been ambiguous. For example, increasingly older groups of infants did choose increasingly complex checkerboards in one experiment, but individual children studied over a period of time did not follow this pattern (Appleton et al., 1975).

A theory that fits the experimental results somewhat better is the contour theory. This approach stresses the number of transitions from one area to another, rather than the complexity of the stimulus per se. It seems there may be a physiological basis to this theory. At the age when children show increased preference for complexity (at about the age of 4 months), the child's eye develops the ability to anticipate regular patterns of movement and to stare at patterns for relatively long periods of time (Appleton et al., 1975).

SCANNING AND ATTENTION. At first, the newborn devotes little time—only 5 to 10%—to visual sweeping of the environment. By the tenth week, however, scanning occupies 35% of waking time (White, 1971). Scanning covers wide ranges and frequently changes directions. As we mentioned, vertical surfaces are more attractive, and thus are scanned more than horizontal ones. Scanning is altered when a pattern appears in the line of vision. The infant adjusts his eye sweep to fit the pattern, concentrating on its most attractive parts. Kessen and his colleagues (1972) maintain that infants get stuck on elements of the stimulus. Is the infant "captured" by the stimulus, or is he intensely absorbed in processing as much information as possible? The answer to such questions will help us to understand how infants are able to increase what they know about objects and events.

It is important to keep in mind the relationship between variable patterns and infant scanning ability. For example, a 1-month-old looks primarily at the outer boundaries of a face, such as the line between chin and clothing or forehead and scalp. Only a few weeks later, however, he pays more visual attention to internal factors such as eyes. This in turn is related to the maturation of the eye itself. Haith (1976) suggests that what is attractive to an infant depends on what the infant can do. He theorizes that infant scanning is an attempt to maintain a high level of neural activity and that scanning stimulates parts of the visual cortex.

Haith observed infant scanning patterns in both lit and darkened rooms. He found that infants showed better eye control, smoother movements, and wider eye openings in the dark. He concluded that infants are initially equipped to cope with darkness and the simplest of visual stimuli, and that they follow three rules in their scanning. These are: (1) If awake, and alert, open the eyes; (2) in the absence of light, scan the potential field in an intensive search; and (3) in the presence of light without pattern, scan widely (perhaps to find the edges).

THE NEWBORN AS LEARNER

Learning theorists use the term *learning* to refer to changes in behavior caused by reinforcement—whether positive or negative. The Pavlovian dog conditioned to salivate at the sound of a bell exhibits learned behavior. A baby who is played with when he coos is likely to vocalize more frequently than the baby who is ignored. A child spanked for drawing on the wall with crayons or burned by touching a hot stove learns not to repeat those behaviors.

What is the earliest age at which infants are capable of learning? The question is a controversial one, as learning is defined in formal laboratory studies. Yet Marquis (1941) demonstrated in a naturalistic setting what every mother knows: Infants quickly learn to anticipate service of the next meal at a particular time. Marquis put one group of infants on a 3-hour feeding schedule; another group was placed on a 4-hour regimen. After 7 days, they were switched. Each group continued to show increased motor activity when food was due according to the previous schedule. Although Marquis made no recordings of it, the autonomic nervous system was probably also aroused at the accustomed time of feeding (Hirschman and Katkin, 1974).

Learning Paradigms

Classical conditioning has been used in attempts to condition sucking responses and eyelid closure in newborns. Although some experiments claimed success, the designs were methodologically flawed, and their results have not been duplicated. Some recent studies claim that in 1-month-old infants, some stimuli and some responses are more readily conditioned than others (Abrahamson, Brackbill, Carpenter, and Fitzgerald, 1970). It is "generally recognized that classical conditioning is not obtained with any facility in neonates and older infants" (Millar, 1974, p. 56). One possible explanation for this is that the infant is neurologically immature (i.e., he cannot make an association between the conditioned stimulus and the response). Another explanation is that the stimuli are novel to the baby and elicit a defensive response rather than the orienting behavior required for conditioning.

Operant conditioning has been demonstrated much more successfully with infants than has classical conditioning. We have already mentioned Sameroff's (1968) modification of the suction-expression pattern through the use of reinforcement. Other experimenters have successfully conditioned smiling, head turning, and vocalization by rewarding the desired behavior when it occurs. Seligman (1970) has emphasized the general role of preparedness in operant conditioning. He suggests that there is a continuum of preparedness to associate stimuli with responses. Some stimulus-response associations are physiologically well prepared for. Others are not prepared for or are counterprepared and, thus, are unlikely to occur. For example, head turning is already a well-integrated pattern of behavior; the only association that is needed is that between head turning and the reinforcement. It would obviously be a lot harder to associate the same reinforcement with sitting up alone, for which the infant is not prepared.

In an adaptation of the formal paradigms of learning, Papoušek, a Czech psychologist, used both classical and operant methods in an experiment

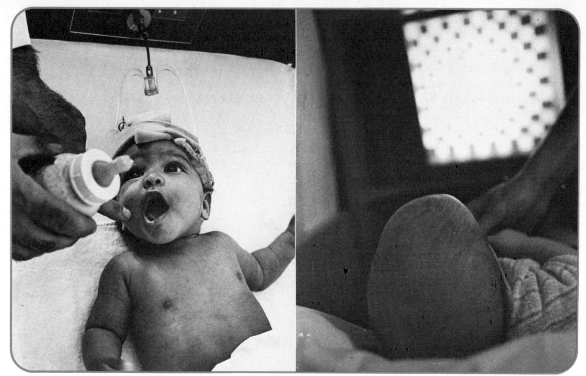

Experiments done with infants demonstrate that conditioning is most efficient when it builds upon infants' natural dispositions or reflexes and when the amount of reinforcement depends on the amount of effort expended by the infant.
(Jason Lauré)

to condition head turning. He used milk as an unconditioned stimulus and as a reinforcement. Milk was presented from the left side while a bell was rung. If the infant turned his head, he received milk. If he did not turn his head, the left corner of the mouth was touched with the nipple. If he still failed to respond, his head was turned, the milk was presented, and the head was returned to the middle position. With 10 trials per session, it took 3 weeks and 177 trials for most newborns to learn (Papoušek, 1967). Papoušek's method has revealed that infants *can* be conditioned. But conditioning cannot be efficient when events and responses are arbitrary. As Sameroff (1968) points out, conditioning is efficient probably only when it builds upon or takes advantage of the infant's natural dispositions to respond to certain events with certain behaviors.

In addition, the contingencies associated with response feedback and the next response are important. In a study of conditioning of 9- to 14-week-old infants, Watson (1967) presented an interesting visual stimulus to infants who turned their heads to a particular side. Watson found that infants who turned their heads again 5 seconds later were most likely to turn them to the preferred side. However, infants who turned their heads either *before* or *after* a 5-second interval were as likely to turn to the "wrong" side. Watson theorized that conditioned behavior depends on a functional awareness that response and feedback are contingent. According to Watson, infants who turned their heads before 5 seconds had passed had not had enough time to analyze the relationship between the stimulus

121

and the reward; after 5 seconds, their memory span for contingency experiences had begun to decline. It is clear that the time gap between the response and the reinforcement is important for conditioned learning. If infants are to perceive that there is any connection between a particular behavior and its reward, then the interval between the two must be short. Some practical implications can be derived from the above results. Parents who wish to influence their child's behavior must respond almost immediately to the baby's activities if they are to be successful.

In general, then, conditioning in newborns is weak and unstable and takes many more trials than it does with older infants. In older infants, though, situations in which the *infant* controls the reinforcement produce especially rapid and effective learning. The learning paradigm in which the amount of reinforcement depends upon the amount of effort expended by the subject is called *conjugate reinforcement*. Infants from 2 to 5 months old who were allowed to operate a mobile by kicking learned quickly to increase their kicking rates in order to increase the mobile's movement (Rovee and Rovee, 1969). Infants also can learn to increase their sucking rate in order to bring a visual display into focus (Siqueland and DeLucia, 1969).

Habituation

Recall from our earlier discussion that habituation results when a stimulus is repeatedly presented until it no longer elicits a response. Why is habituation of interest? It provides clues to how behavior change may occur in newborns and is also helpful in studies of memory and discrimination. On a theoretical level, repetition of the stimulus enables the infant to build at least a primitive internal representation of the stimulus. Each repetition adds information to the model until it is complete. The infant's decreased responses indicate that the stimulus is familiar and remains at least partially in the memory between presentations (Appleton et al., 1975).

The habituation process is initiated by the "orienting response," the first reaction to a new stimulus. According to Sokolov (1963), the orienting response plays a particular role in learning by heightening perceptual processes, receptivity, and consolidation of information. As the internal model of the stimulus becomes more complete, the orienting response occurs less frequently. We will discuss in more detail in the next chapter the role of the orienting response in the control of the infant's attention.

THE CAREGIVING ENVIRONMENT

The infant and his or her caregiver share many common goals, primarily the nurturance and growth of the infant. At the same time, the caregiver is an experienced adult with a view of the world very different from that of the infant. The relationship between infant and caregiver is best conceptualized in the terms of *transactions*.

The newborn and the caregiver are involved in an exchange process in which one response begets another, which in turn elicits a reciprocal response, and so forth. The exchange process begins shortly after birth. Caregiver and infant need to achieve a basic coordination of their respective schedules. This is generally easier if the infant is placed in the same room with the mother immediately. In this situation, with a demand feeding schedule, mother and infant establish a whole network of reciprocal responses. For example, within 1 week a relationship between the infant's state and the mother's response time has developed. The infant's state also begins to show a stable series of responses to the mother's way of holding and talking to him. The mother's 24-hour schedule has begun to adjust to the baby's pattern of naps and waking periods. The mother, in turn, tries to "shape" the baby's schedule to best coincide with that of the household (Sander, 1976).

The synchronization between infant and caregiver is very subtle. Condon and Sander (1974) have shown that even in the first postnatal day the infant responds to adult speech. By correlating speech in the infant's presence with his movements, they found that points of articulation in adult speech generated increased motor activity in the infant. Condon and Sander suggest that this early experience is one important foundation upon which later learning of language rests.

Individual Differences and Caregiver Characteristics

Infants come into the world with many different predispositions. Some are quiet and peaceful; others are restless and fretful. Other individual differences have been noted in intensity of responses and sensitivity to pain. Drug-addicted and brain-damaged infants are generally more unstable than normal newborns. All of these individual differences will affect the interaction between infant and caregiver.

According to the Brazelton Scale, one of the most important indicators of social interactive capacities is cuddling. The scale of responses on this item runs from active thrashing and refusal to cuddle at one extreme, to aggressive cuddling, molding, nestling, and grasping at the holder at the other extreme. Some babies are difficult to satisfy and others are easy (Thomas, Chess, and Birch, 1968).

Cultural characteristics also affect infant and caregiver interaction. For example, swaddling both restricts movement and has a calming effect. Swaddled infants sleep more and show fewer responses to light tactile stimulus while asleep than do nonswaddled infants. When unswaddled, babies show more startle responses than when movement is slightly restricted (Lipton, Steinschneider, and Richmond, 1965). Circumcision is another custom that affects newborn behavior. Circumcision is commonplace in the United States but rare in Europe. Some studies have revealed disruption in sleep patterns following circumcision; other have found prolonged fussiness and wakefulness. It is not clear how long these effects persist (Richards, Bernal, and Brackbill, 1976).

Some cultures have a tendency to handle their babies roughly, and such roughness will affect the baby's social interaction with his caregivers. Individual differences among parents also play an important role. When a difficult baby meets a tense mother, for example, their problems compound each other. The result may be extreme infant irritability, refusal to cuddle and be consoled, and inability to quiet self. This is a situation that calls for intervention and counseling before communication between infant and caregiver is permanently impaired. In general, however, newborns will find caregiving environments more or less disposed to accommodate them.

The long-term effects of individual differences are not clear, but there is some evidence of persistence. Yang and Halverson (1976), for example, found a relationship between fussy, protesting infant behavior and disruptive behavior in nursery school. Infants who did not show this negative behavior were rated positively in nursery school by their teachers.

SUMMARY

The newborn baby is a well-functioning, though by no means independent, system. Within minutes after birth, medical workers assess the newborn's conditions by means of the Apgar score. They determine where this infant fits within the normal range of variations of newborns. After about a week, during which the functions of breathing, circulation, and digestion stabilize, most infants settle into a predominant *state*.

Various reflex actions help the newborn cope with the outside world. The major infant reflexes are the following: the *rooting* reflex; the *sucking* reflex; the *Moro* reflex; the *Babinski* response; the *tonic neck* reflex; the *palmar* response; and the *optical blink* reflex. Faulty or absent reflexes may signal neurological or other damage. Some reflexes, such as the Moro reflex, and swimming and stepping reflexes, disappear with age.

Organized congenital patterns of behavior are similar to reflexes except that they are sustained longer and involve a wider range of tasks. Sucking and crying are examples of organized congenital patterns of behavior. In studying crying, researchers have found four basic cries: the birth, hunger, pain, and mad cries.

At birth, some sensory capacities are more fully developed than others. Visual competence, for example, is incomplete. Newborns tend to be nearsighted; they are sensitive to bright light; they can follow a slowly moving object but cannot always focus both eyes on it. Auditory competence is highly developed by 2 weeks after birth. Newborns react to sound with changes in pulse rate. Additionally, newborns show an ability both to habituate to and to discriminate between different sounds.

Other sensory capacities are present in newborns in more or less developed states. Tactile sensitivity is demonstrated by the the rooting reflex and the Babinski response. Newborns are not especially sensitive to temperature and have difficulty in discriminating between hot and cold stimuli. In the first 2 days after birth, infants have a high pain threshold, which decreases thereafter. Taste is a developed sensory capacity, and infants have preferences for various tastes early in life.

The organization of sensory information into patterns and hierarchies is known as *perception*. Studies of infant perception indicate that newborns seem to process parts of a form rather than the whole. As they grow older, infants devote more time to scanning the environment, pausing to investigate interesting stimuli. Elements of the stimuli that infants find attractive seem to change with age.

Learning refers to changes in behavior. In general, conditioned learning in newborns is weak and unstable and takes longer to achieve than it does with older infants. For infants 2 months of age and older, situations in which the infant controls the reinforcement (called *conjugate reinforcement*) can produce rapid and effective learning.

The relationship between infant and caregiver is best thought of in terms of transactions. An exchange process between infant and caregiver begins shortly after birth and continues to become more subtle and better synchronized with time.

CHAPTER 5

Motor and Cognitive Development: The Baby as an Active System

In the first 3 years of life, infants undergo rapid physical and cognitive development—which, as noted earlier, involves more than simply getting bigger. As babies grow, they make enormous progress in motor development and coordination. Born with a few simple reflexes like sucking, looking, and grasping, babies gradually learn to reach, to manipulate objects, to crawl and walk and run. Along with this development of motor skills comes growth in *cognition*—the child's ability to know and understand the world. It is, in fact, through motor responses that the infant begins to organize and to deal with the environment. By the age of 3, children have achieved an understanding of the major dimensions of two worlds—the world of people and the world of things.

Understanding the correlation between the development of motor and cognitive skills in infants poses special problems for researchers, because babies cannot explain why or how they are doing something. Determining what infants perceive and understand is difficult, since babies cannot simply *say* that they feel surprised or happy, that they see the color blue or red, that they think one picture is more interesting than another. Therefore, it is difficult for an external observer to determine what an infant actually "knows." As adult observers, we see *performance*, and from performance, we infer *competence*. As Chapter 2 showed, such observations can be misleading. A child's failure to wind up a toy, for example, may be caused by lack of interest, fatigue, inability, or any combination of these. When an examiner says, "Bring me the toy," and points, to what does the infant respond? Does he or she react to the verbal request, to the adult's gesture, or to a combination of the two? How can we tell whether babies enjoy looking at a picture? If they look at it quickly? for a long time? or often?

As adults studying child development and behavior, we need to remember that the infant's *world* is the environment as the child sees it. This world may bear little correspondence to adult reality. There is no justification for believing that infants think like adults. But if we assume that the infant has an "infant theory" of reality, the study of infant cognition becomes that of constructing theories about the infant's theory. How we can tell what infants "know" will be the focus of our attention in this chapter.

MOTOR DEVELOPMENT

Before exploring some of the theories that explain how infants perceive and respond to their environment, it is important to take a brief look at the development of babies' motor skills. As stated earlier, cognitive development goes hand in hand with the development of motor skills. Building a tower of blocks, for example, involves being able to make judgments about spatial relationships, but infants cannot even begin to play with building blocks until they have mastered the motor skills of grasping, reaching, and placing. The infant capable of building a tower of blocks concentrates upon the placement of blocks. This activity depends on some cognitive understanding of spatial relationships, with reaching being smooth and almost automatic. The infant who is just beginning to reach must focus, instead, upon the act of reaching itself. How, then, does motor development proceed?

As we have seen, infants are born with several systems of reflexes that disappear during the first few months after birth. Newborn babies held upright make "walking" movements; if their hands are placed on a bar, they can actually grasp strongly enough to suspend themselves. If they are placed prone (face down) in the water, they make swimming movements forceful enough to move their bodies for a short distance (McGraw, 1939). These reflexes disappear by the time babies are about 4 months old. Once reflexive swimming movements disappear, children do not make swimming movements again until they are about 2 years old, after they have learned to walk, and then those movements are voluntary and purposeful rather than reflexive (McGraw, 1939).

During the first 3 years of life, babies' primitive sensorimotor systems become elaborated and coordinated. Both the *gross* (large) *motor system,* which governs movement of the head, torso, legs, and arms, and the *fine* (manual) *motor system,* which governs the smaller movements of eyes, hands, and fingers, come to be under the infant's own control. At 1 month of age, babies cannot yet hold up their heads. They turn their heads if their cheeks are touched, can follow a horizontal movement of a ball, and can grasp a finger placed in their hands. At about 3 months of age, babies' large motor systems have developed so that they can hold up their heads when they are lifted to a sitting position and can lift their heads and upper chests when placed in a prone position. Their eyes can follow the vertical movement of a ball, and they can look at their own hands and clasp and unclasp them. At this point, babies may bring an object grasped in their hands to their mouths, but they cannot yet coordinate the movement of eyes and hands (Sheridan, 1975).

By the time they are 6 months old, babies have achieved a greater degree of gross muscle control. They can sit straight when they are supported and can kick strongly and grasp their own legs. Their fine motor systems have matured to the point where they can grasp objects with both hands, move them to their mouths, and suck on them (Appleton, Clifton, and Goldberg, 1975). At 9 months, babies can sit by themselves, pull themselves to a standing position, and begin to crawl. They can hold small objects and strings between thumb and forefinger (although they cannot yet deliberately release them). At 1 year, babies can crawl, and some can walk by themselves. They can put pegs in a pegboard and manipulate toys in a variety of ways without immediately putting them in their mouths; they can use everyday objects, such as combs, for their appropriate purposes; they also are learning to retrieve hidden objects (Sheridan, 1975). By around 18 months, babies learn to walk up and down stairs with help, to push and pull wheeled toys, to walk while carrying a toy, to build towers with blocks, and to enjoy looking at picture books when the pages are turned for them. At 2 years, babies hold pencils and scribble, turn the pages of a book one by one, build tall towers with blocks, and drink while standing up. By the age of 3, they can walk up and down stairs while carrying a large toy (Sheridan, 1975).

Some of these developments may seem quite simple — we laugh at the idea of an adult who cannot walk and chew gum at the same time. But for a child, learning to drink while standing up or to go up and down stairs while carrying a toy involves coordinating the large and fine motor systems. A child just learning to reach and grasp or to walk has to concentrate completely on that one activity until it begins to be automatic. For instance, a simple activity such as picking up a bottle and bringing it to the mouth — an activity that babies have ample time to practice — requires the coordination of three separate acts: looking, grasping, and sucking. Eye, hand, arm, and mouth have to work together before a baby can actually pick up the bottle and bring it to the mouth. Most other activities,

Learning to spoon-feed oneself requires coordination of separate motor acts—and plenty of concentration and practice. (Shelly Rusten)

such as building with blocks, involve the same sort of combination and integration of simple acts into complex behaviors.

In addition to enabling babies to perform more complex activities, the increasing development of motor coordination opens the world of the infant to new areas of exploration. Being able to stand enables the child to see the coffee table from the top instead of only from the bottom, for example. And the top, with its whole new world of interesting objects, presents the opportunity to touch and move—and sometimes break—the items that the infant finds there. Thus, as motor skills develop, infants are able to explore and interact with more and more of the world. With this increased interaction comes the development of the cognitive processes that contribute to an understanding of that world.

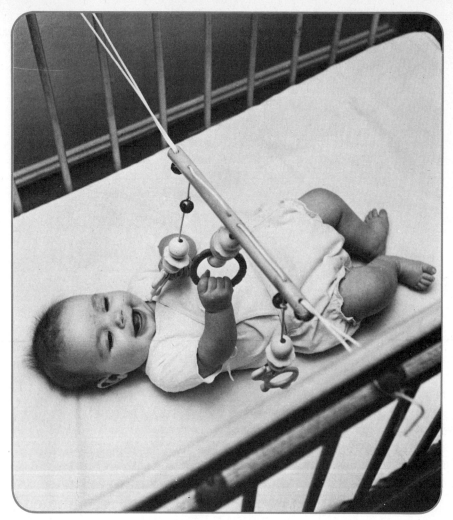

COGNITIVE DEVELOPMENT AND EXPLORATION

During the first 3 years of life, children coordinate and develop the reflexes and seemingly unorganized movements of the newborn into skills that give them the ability to deal more and more successfully with the environment. Until 1959, when Robert W. White published his classic study of infant motivation, *drive reduction theories* explained human activities, including those of the infant, as efforts to satsify basic physiological needs. These theories required that an external force or a tissue deficit such as hunger or thirst exist in order to set an organism into motion. The problem with these theories, however, was that they did not explain such activities as the play of small children—or, for that matter, an adult's reading a detective story or even a kitten's playing with string or knocking a pencil off a table.

White's article, entitled "Motivation Reconsidered," marked a major shift in theories of children's motivation. He argued that the motivation of the seemingly purposeless activity in infants and small children is *competence*—a term he uses to refer to an organism's capacity to interact effectively with its environment. Babies who laugh when they shake a rattle and the rattle makes noise, he suggested, are pleased by a feeling of efficacy, or *effectance*—the perception that their actions can cause the environment to respond in ways that they can control. According to White, effectance motivation is aroused by stimulus conditions that offer "difference-in-sameness." Children can produce novelty by their own actions upon things. They can make balls behave differently by dropping them and by rolling them, and they can use blocks to make new structures. In addition, children seek out novelty in their environments. Children at play need some novelty to keep up their interests; their attention is most absorbed by situations that are mainly familiar but that contain small elements that are new to them (White, 1959). They respond with attention and exploratory behavior to special kinds of attractive events.

The Development of Attention

One form of attention is the *orienting response.* When babies are confronted with a new event, their heart rates slow a little, they turn their heads toward the stimulus, and they cease their other activities. With repeated presentations of the stimulus, infants become habituated to the stimulus and the orienting response diminishes. When the same sound is repeated over and over again, for example, most people—babies and adults—stop listening. With repeated exposure, a strange smell or a novel sight becomes familiar.

What causes habituation? Some theorists believe that habituation is a kind of learning that occurs when infants are able to recognize a stimulus and at least partially remember it in the time between exposures to it (Sokolov, 1960). Shortly after birth, infants are able to "tune out" stimulation that does not change from moment to moment or day to day. They may, for example, become used to the sound of the stereo in the background at nap time. When babies are presented with a stimulus that differs from the old stimulus in any way, however, the orienting response occurs again. A change in a repetitive sequence of stimulation represents a form of novelty; babies who have become habituated to one sequence of notes or tones react to a change in the sequence of notes (McCall and Melson, 1970).

Attention patterns change with age. Kagan (1972) has found that newborn infants attend to stimuli that move, that have sharp contours, or that have a light-dark contrast. Newborns may prefer objects with strong contrasts because their visual systems are not yet fully mature. By the time babies are about 2 months old, though, they enter a second phase in the development of attention; they begin to pay more attention to stimuli that differ moderately rather than markedly from those usually encountered. According to Kagan, infants begin to acquire *schema*—mental representations of events—as a result of encounters with the environment. The attention of children at this second stage may be less a function of the *novelty* principle—attention to events simply because they are new—than of the *discrepancy* principle—greater attention to events that differ moderately from an infant's schema than to events that are either totally familiar or totally novel. Infants in this phase spend more time looking at objects that are only slightly different from those that they are used to looking at than at objects that are completely new or completely familiar. They pay more attention to phrases that are moderately different from phrases they have already heard than to phrases that are identical or very different; they look longer at moderately different mobiles than at mobiles that are greatly or slightly different (Kagan, 1972). During the second stage of attention, infants show decreasing interest in masks of the human face. Presumably, the reason for this loss of interest is that the child has formed a mental representation of the general schema of a face. Most faces the infant sees offer little discrepancy in terms of position of eyes, nose, and mouth; thus they offer less interest.

According to Kagan, at about 9 months of age, infants enter a third phase in the development of attention. Attention to masks of human faces increases at this point and continues to do so until about 3 years of age. This U-shaped curve of attention (high interest—low interest—high interest) holds true for American children and for children from isolated villages in Latin America and Africa, regardless of whether the stimuli are familiar masks or abstract designs. Discrepancy can no longer be the primary factor in explaining attention time. If it were, time spent watching familiar objects would decrease as a child got older.

A growing body of evidence suggests that during the third phase of attention, a new cognitive structure or process emerges. The infant begins to form hypotheses in order to interpret discrepant events. These hypotheses represent the child's attempts to transform a discrepant event into a familiar form—the schema. Support for the notion that infants are capable of generating hypotheses about experiences comes from studies of heart-rate changes. When adults and older children attend to interesting stimuli, their heart rates decrease, just as do those of infants. But when adults and children are actively thinking, whether memorizing or making calculations, their heart rates *increase*. Recent studies show that when infants over 9 months old are exposed to *masks* of human faces, their heart rates increase as well. One-year-old infants who watch a toy car rolling down an incline and knocking over a plastic object begin to anticipate the car's motion and look toward the object. As they do so, their heart rates increase. Kagan (1972) suggests that if an increase in heart rate in infants indicates an increased rate of mental activity (as is the case with older children and with adults), then the data suggest that children begin active thought at about 1 year of age. This achievement marks the third stage of

*The game of peek-a-boo becomes fun when a child learns to anticipate the reappearance of the "missing" person.
(Alice Kandell, Rapho/Photo Researchers)*

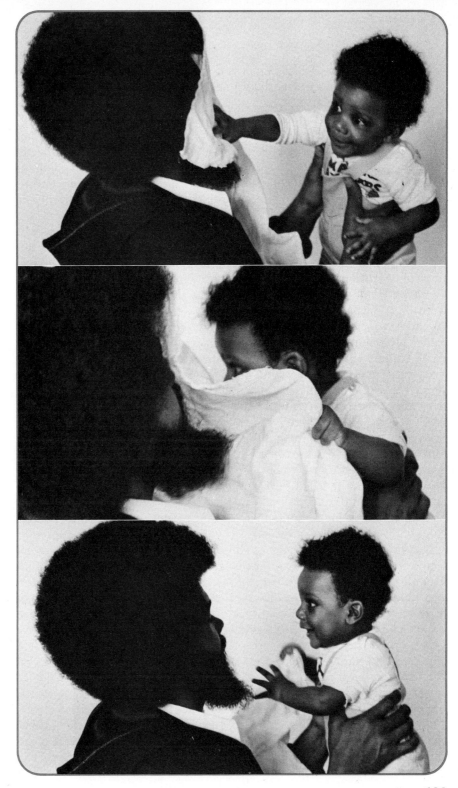

attention, the *activation of hypotheses,* in which infants begin to think about how new events fit into their previous experiences.

Another measure of cognitive development appears in studies of children's reactions of "surprise." Surprise occurs when incoming information does not agree with stored information, when expectations are not fulfilled. According to traditional theories, newborn babies are not capable of being surprised, although they can be *startled* by sudden and intense stimuli, such as loud noises. A newborn would not necessarily be surprised, for example, to see a stuffed animal disappear behind a blanket and a toy truck reappear in its place. Neither, however, would a newborn be startled by such an event, as is evidenced by the fact that infants do not demonstrate the same reactions to the disappearance of an object as they do when a sudden, loud noise occurs behind them.

Contrived Events and Surprise

Infants cannot be surprised until they have begun to formulate expectations. If infants are surprised when objects disappear or are replaced as if by magic, their reactions indicate that they have developed the notion — called *object permanence*—that absent objects continue to exist. Through daily contact with the world, children gradually learn what is possible and what is not possible, and they develop heightened sensitivity to departures from the possible (Charlesworth, 1969). By 4 or 5 months of age, babies who are "tracking" an object that disappears behind a screen seem surprised if a different object appears on the other side; they look back as if searching for the original object. Nine-month-olds do not seem surprised if one toy is hidden in a box and a different toy is found when the box is opened; but 18-month-olds refuse the new toy and continue to search for the first toy (LeCompte and Gratch, 1972). Thus events that elicit surprise cause the child to respond with attention and to seek out information about the event that might explain the discrepancy between expectations and what actually happened.

Although there is no single, universally accepted theory on the distinction between startle and surprise, there is agreement that they do differ. The human's capacity to be startled is present in the first few days of life and persists throughout life. Young infants, however, are only capable of a reflexive startle response. Only after reaching a certain age are they capable of secondary responses associated with surprise, such as exploratory behavior. The capacity to be surprised requires the ability to recognize a signal and to anticipate or expect the event the signal signifies. At one age, a child can be completely insensitive to the experience of a particular series of events not being fulfilled, and a few months later show a pronounced surprise reaction if the same sequence is violated.

As babies interact physically with the environment, it is apparent that they also begin to develop the cognitive abilities that enable them to make sense out of the events and situations that take place around them. The development of these cognitive skills seems to progress in stages.

I place the string, which is attached to the rattle, in [Laurent's] right hand, merely unrolling it a little so that he may grasp it better. For a moment nothing happens but, at the first shake due to chance movement of his hand, the reaction is immediate: Laurent starts looking at the rattle and then violently strikes his right hand alone, as if he felt the resistance and the effect. The operation lasts fully a quarter of an hour during which Laurent emits peals of laughter. (Piaget, 1952, p. 162)

Jacqueline holds a rectangular box, deep and narrow, whose opening measures 34 x 16 mm. . . . she tries to put my watch chain into it (45 cm. long). During the first fifteen attempts, she goes about it in the following way: First she puts one end of the chain into the box (2 to 4 cm.), then she grasps the chain about 5 cm. from this end and thus puts a second segment into the box. She then gets ready to do the same with a third segment when the chain, no longer supported by the child's hand, slides out of the box and falls noisily. Jacqueline recommences at once, and fourteen times in succession sees the chain come out as soon as it is put in. (Piaget, 1952, p. 318)

Lucienne looks at the box. The chain spreads out on the floor and she immediately tries to put it back into the box. She begins by simply putting one end of the chain into the box and trying to make the rest follow progressively. This procedure which was first tried by Jacqueline, Lucienne finds successful the first time (the end put into the box stays there fortuitously), but fails completely at the second and third attemps.

At the fourth attempt, Lucienne starts as before but pauses, and after a short interval, herself places the chain on a flat surface nearby (the experiment takes place on a shawl), rolls it up in a ball intentionally, takes the ball between three fingers and puts the whole thing in the box. (Piaget, 1952, pp. 336–337)

PIAGET'S STUDY OF INTELLECTUAL DEVELOPMENT IN INFANCY

In 1923, Jean Piaget began the study of intellectual development in infancy. He spent an enormous amount of time observing the behavior of his own children—Jacqueline, Laurent, and Lucienne—during their first 3 years of life. From these observations, he constructed his theory of intellectual development, which describes development as taking place in a series of stages, with successively more stable and sophisticated modes of thought appearing at each stage.

Piaget's Clinical Method

Piaget's "clinical method" for studying babies involves careful observations over a long period of time as well as testing the limits of children's abilities by setting simple tasks for them to perform. The rules of Piaget's method are the basis of the scientific method in every science: observe in natural settings; generate hypotheses about underlying competence; probe or experiment to check out the hypotheses; observe results; revise hypotheses; then probe again. These procedures may be illustrated by a sequence of observations that Piaget made of his son Laurent. Piaget observed Laurent trying to manipulate the circular rotating tier of a table that worked like a lazy Susan, by pulling the tier toward himself. Piaget probed: "I immediately placed an interesting toy beyond his reach" on the tier. Laurent tried to pull the tier toward himself again and again, and as he did so, the tier sometimes turned by chance. Finally, Laurent noticed that the object had accidentally gotten closer, and he gained success. Piaget observed: "The child's behavior does not yet give the impression that he has understood the role of rotation; he simply repeats a movement which was once efficacious, without turning the tier intentionally." Piaget probed again by repeating the experiment over the next few days. Not until more than 2 weeks later did Laurent rotate the table from the outset, demonstrating that he had definitely acquired the new scheme (Piaget, 1952).

A number of similar experiments by Piaget, carried out in his own home with his own children and without controls, were the foundation for his theory of intellectual development as a progression through a series of stages. Piaget's experiments have been fruitful bases for further research, and his results and conclusions have been replicated many times by other researchers.

The Sensorimotor Period

Piaget identified the first period of intellectual development as the sensorimotor (sensory-motor) period, extending from birth to 2 years. Piaget observed that intelligence during this stage is "essentially practical—that is, aimed at getting results" (Piaget and Inhelder, 1969). Children at this age do not yet use language or symbols; their learning occurs through *action*. Sensorimotor intelligence is, literally, thinking with bodily sensations and movements. According to Piaget, concepts of the permanence of an object and of space, time, and number gradually emerge as a result of fundamental changes in the way children organize the relationships between actions and consequences. At birth, the world of infants is centered on their own bodies. During the sensorimotor period, children come to see themselves as existing in "a universe that is made up of permanent objects" (Piaget and Inhelder, 1969).

Piaget identified six distinct stages within the sensorimotor period. Each stage is characterized by the type of reactions that the infant is capable of in that period. Timetables for the beginning and end of each stage are only approximations. Piaget is neither concerned about measuring individual differences in intellectual development nor about setting up norms (averages) for development. His focus is on the structure of the most advanced behaviors that a child is able to produce. He is interested in identifying the *sequence* in which these behaviors appear and, therefore, the process of development by which individuals come to understand the world. The order of the stages in the sensorimotor period does not vary; a child cannot "skip" a stage or go back entirely to an earlier stage. But, at a given time, a child might be at a certain stage in terms of one measurement of ability and at a less advanced stage in terms of another measurement. And a child who one day demonstrates behavior that is characteristic of the next stage of development might wait 2 weeks before demonstrating such behavior again.

STAGE 1. Stage 1 (birth to 1 month) is characterized by congenitally organized patterns of behavior. Such patterns form the basis of the infant's understanding of the world. Looking and sucking are the primary patterns of behavior for the Stage 1 child. Yet even during the first month, these patterns begin to be modified by experience. Infants learn to search for the nipple instead of simply waiting for it to be presented to them. Thus they are already beginning to coordinate two organized patterns of behavior—sucking and rooting. In Stage 1, babies begin to demonstrate curiosity by choosing to look at moderately novel objects within their view. They also begin to imitate noises made by adults. If a baby is uttering the sound "rra" and the adult responds with "a ha, ha, ha, rra," the baby will try to repeat the same sound—although at this stage babies cannot actually reproduce sounds they have not first made themselves.

STAGE 2. Stage 2 (1 to 4 months) is characterized by the presence of what Piaget calls *primary circular reactions.* At this stage, if an infant's behavior produces interesting results accidentally, the infant will try to repeat the action in order to obtain the same result again. For example, babies suck on their fists or fingers if they accidentally come to their mouth, and through a process of trial and error, infants gradually learn how to bring their hands to their mouths. These repeated (that is, circular) reactions, Piaget calls primary because they still involve only the baby's own body. The baby has not yet begun to manipulate objects in the outside world.

STAGE 3. In Stage 3 (4 to 10 months), *secondary circular reactions* begin to appear. Children's actions begin to center on objects and events outside their own bodies. Infants will try to manipulate objects in order to repeat an accidental occurrence that they find interesting. Laurent's shaking his rattle is an example of a secondary circular reaction: To continue to make the rattle shake, Laurent had to establish a connection between his action and its result. Then he had to learn to repeat the necessary hand movements.

In Piaget's first three sensorimotor stages, children's response systems give them their first definitions of physical objects. Babies come to know objects as things to look at, to grasp, and to suck. They begin to discover that objects are different according to the way they look and feel. Children learn how to prolong an interesting event—how to intentionally repeat activities that had interesting consequences. Even during Stage 3, though, children's behavior is not fully intentional. Infants do not have a goal in mind from the start but discover the goal by accident.

STAGE 4. In Stage 4 (10 to 12 months), the child's behavior becomes intentional. Piaget calls this *coordination of secondary schemes.* Stage 4 children have goals in mind, and they discover that behaviors can be means for achieving particular ends. Suppose that something is in the way of an object that the child wants. Children already know that an object can be moved, and at this stage they make the simple connection: Move this in order to get that. The child can intentionally apply old behavior patterns to new situations. Established behaviors become part of a voluntary action system, so that the child can select from among a number of possibilities behaviors that can serve the desired purposes. An object becomes more than just something to be mouthed; it can be dropped, pulled, squeezed, thrown. More important, it can be moved in order to get at something else.

Another ability that characterizes Stage 4 is that of imitation. During earlier stages, children are able to imitate the movements of others only when they can watch their own movements and match them to those of a model. In Stage 4, children can imitate movements, like blinking, that they cannot see themselves make. They begin to try to imitate actions that they have not performed before, though such efforts may not be successful. In attempting to blink, babies may open and close their mouths instead of their eyes and may even close their eyes and keep them shut instead of blinking them.

STAGE 5. Behavior in Stage 5 (12 to 18 months) is characterized by an interest in novelty for its own sake. Piaget terms experimentation of this type *tertiary circular reactions.* In Stage 5, children experiment to see what will happen to various objects. Piaget's son Laurent dropped objects on the floor from different heights and positions—an "experiment" most parents come to know well. Piaget calls such behavior "directed groping."

Stage 5 is also marked by the discovery of new means to achieve goals. How does the child invent new solutions to abstract problems? Initially, the invention may be accidental. The child reaching for a toy that is sitting on top of a pillow finds out *by accident* that the toy comes closer when the pillow is moved. Then the child pulls the pillow until the toy is within reach. The child can take advantage of accidental, unexpected happenings and so create new means (pulling the pillow) to reach a familiar goal (grasping the object). The important accomplishment at Stage 5 is that children can solve problems by disconnecting a familiar goal from the behaviors typically associated with attaining that goal; they can quickly insert new behaviors to try to reach the same end. If these behaviors prove unsuccessful, they can then identify other actions that might be linked to solving the problem. Finally, children can integrate new behavior patterns and familiar goals.

Eventually, children become able to vary their actions deliberately and systematically. This competence permits them to imitate actions that they have never before performed. At Stage 5, Piaget's daughter Jacqueline was able to imitate her father when he touched the tip of his tongue with his forefinger. Imitation has often been treated as a mechanical behavior, but in order to imitate, children must relate one event in space to another. That is, children must recognize a correspondence between the thing being imitated and the parts of themselves capable of performing the imitation. Jacqueline, for example, saw the correspondence between her mouth and her father's mouth, her finger and her father's finger, her tongue and her father's tongue. One important side effect of the child's new control over means and ends is that spatial arrangements can be mapped and modified. The relations of "one thing above another," "one thing below another," or "one thing beside another" can be put together and taken apart.

According to Piaget, Stage 5 is the turning point in children's mental development. It is the *peak* of sensorimotor development. It is the last stage in which behaviors are limited to present and immediate actions and things. From this stage on, the child acquires an increasingly complex array of mental images and mental codes that can represent actions not actually occurring and things not actually present.

STAGE 6. At Stage 6 (18 to 24 months), children can represent actions by thinking about them. Pretend play begins to appear; for example, children can treat a doll as if it were a baby. They can ponder different solutions to problems without overt trial and error. They can imitate a model when the model is no longer present. The difference between the child's way of solving problems in Stage 5 and in Stage 6 is illustrated by a comparison between the ways two children, one at Stage 5 (Jacqueline) and one at Stage 6 (Lucienne), solved the problem of how to put a chain in a box. The difference between the two solutions to the problem is striking. Jacqueline at Stage 5 makes the same mistake 15 times. Finally, she gropes her way to a solution. In contrast, Lucienne at Stage 6 works out a solution without overt groping and repeated failure. Whatever might have gone on in Lucienne's head, it permitted her to derive a solution to the problem rapidly and efficiently. The ability to represent mentally various objects and actions implies an organization of space in which more than one path to a goal is possible.

Principles of Change

As discussed in Chapter 1, Piaget views intellectual development as guided by two basic tendencies in the organism: organization and adaptation. *Organization* is the tendency to combine different processes into coherent structures or systems. Prehension is an example of the organization of looking, grasping, and sucking into a more complex system of action. *Adaptation* is simply the organism's tendency to adapt to the environment. Adaptation, in turn, takes place through two processes: assimilation and accommodation.

Assimilation is the incorporation of a new event into an existing scheme. Babies who suck every object they can bring to their mouth demonstrate the process of assimilation. When infants categorize a rattle as a "suckable," they have assimilated the rattle into an existing sensorimotor scheme (sucking). Thus assimilation enables infants to incorporate elements of the outside world into their past experience.

Accommodation is the modification of an existing scheme or the creation of a new one in response to a novel event. Through accommodation, infants modify their internal structures in reaction to events outside themselves. Newborn babies, for example, can change their sucking patterns in order to obtain milk delivery; this is an early example of accommodation (Kessen, 1967). As infants grow, their accommodations become increasingly sophisticated. Stage 5 tertiary circular reactions are examples of more advanced accommodations. What happens when children are confronted with an event they cannot understand, an event that cannot fit established structures? If the event is very remote from what they can understand, they will ignore it or become frightened. But if the event is only moderately different from previous experience, children's conceptual categories can change. Within the Piagetian framework, cognitive change—the formation of new structures or categories of knowledge—occurs when children confront problems and experiences that are familiar and yet somewhat different from those that they know.

CONSTRUCTION OF THE PERMANENT OBJECT

According to Piaget, during the sensorimotor period, children come to see themselves as objects in a world made up of other permanent objects. Very young infants, however, do not know that they live in a world of permanent objects. Although they soon learn to recognize certain things—mother, father, breast, bottle—they seem not to know that these things exist when they are out of sight. A major milestone of cognitive development occurs when a child comes to know that physical objects continue to exist even though they are not actually, physically present. Piaget has called such knowledge *object permanence*. According to some philosophers, a cornerstone of thinking is that an absent object can exist in the mind. As important, perhaps, is the person's belief that mental objects are "real"—that mother, father, bottle can "happen" under the proper circumstances. Thus it can be argued that the child's attainment of the concept of object permanence marks the beginning of thinking.

STAGE 3. Children in Stage 3 (4 to 8 months) begin to show that they can maintain contact with absent objects. When an object falls to the floor, they will lean over to look for it rather than simply stare at the point from which it disappeared. In addition, they can anticipate that a whole object exists when they have seen just a part of it. If a large enough part of an object shows from behind a screen, they will reach for it. But if the visible part is made smaller, the infant's reaching hand will stop abruptly. At this stage, children make no attempt to recover objects that have disappeared from view behind an obstruction such as a cloth or cup, even though they are physically capable of doing so.

STAGE 4. Stage 4 children (8 to 12 months) show substantial progress in the development of the concept of object permanence. If an object is covered by a cloth or a cup or if it is moved behind a screen, the child will search for it. However, the child's object concept is still limited to looking for an object where it was first hidden. Suppose an object is hidden behind one screen (A) and the child repeatedly finds it there. Now, if in full view of the child, the object is hidden behind a different screen (B), the child will continue to search where it was first hidden (A), although he or she *watched* it being hidden somewhere else. Infants' behavior at this stage shows that they realize that objects continue to exist when hidden. However, such knowledge appears to be accompanied by the belief that objects are located at some *particular* point in space (behind screen A, for example). There is as yet no realization that objects continue to exist if moved from place to place.

STAGE 5. During Stage 5 (12 to 18 months), children become able to disassociate the object from the place where they are accustomed to finding it. They will search for the object where it was last seen, no matter where it was previously hidden. But suppose a small object, hidden from sight by the adult's hand, is moved from one hiding place to another. Children will search for the object in the place where they saw it last. At this stage, children do not yet reason that the object must have been moved to another place while it was covered by the adult's hand.

STAGE 6. During Stage 6 (beginning at 18 months), children acquire a full-fledged concept of object permanence. If a small object is hidden in an adult's hand and then placed in one hiding place after another, children will search in all of the hiding places and even in the adult's hand until they find the object.

Piaget has carefully observed the development of object permanence during the first 3 years of life. Before the age of 4 months (Stages 1 and 2 of object permanence), the infant behaves as if an object that is "out of sight" is also "out of mind." Infants in Stage 3 of object permanence (4 to 8 months) grasp objects and retrieve a partially hidden object, but they do not search for an object that disappears.

In Stage 4 of object permanence (8 to 12 months), infants will search for a hidden object but only in the *first* place in which they saw the object. By Stage 5 (12 to 18 months), infants realize that an object does exist even when it is moved from place to place. Stage 5 infants will always look for the object in the place in which it was *last* seen. In Stage 6 (beginning at 18 months), infants acquire an image of absent objects and the understanding that objects can be moved from place to place. They will continue to search until they find the hidden object (Piaget, 1954).

Using Piaget's findings as a basis, investigators have tried to interpret the status of object permanence at different stages. Their studies have explored a number of questions. One important question, for example, is how the senses of vision and touch contribute to the development of object permanence. Six-month-old infants (Stage 3), who can recover a partially hidden object, are unable to retrieve an object they have already grasped if an opaque cloth is placed over their hands. The same children can remove the cloth if it is transparent (Gratch, 1972; Gratch and Landers, 1971). These studies suggest that for 6-month-old infants, *seeing* an object contributes more to belief in its permanence than does touching it (Appleton et al., 1975).

If the child's concept of object permanence is not completely established until Stage 6, what are children doing when they search at Stage 4? Do infants really expect to *find* something when they search for a hidden object? Evidently they do. In one group of studies (Charlesworth, 1966), investigators made an object "disappear" through a trap door while an adult's hand covered the object. Twelve-month-old children showed puzzlement at the disappearance, and they actively searched for the missing object. In another study (LeCompte and Gratch, 1969), a hidden object was "mysteriously" transformed. This was done by using two toys—a big, shiny plastic one and a small, drab one. One of the toys was placed in a trick box. When the children looked inside the box, they sometimes found the toy they saw being hidden, and they sometimes found the other one. Nine-month-old children (Stage 4) were mildly puzzled by this trick, but they accepted the new toy and did not search for the other one. The investigators found the mild puzzlement and confusion consistent with Piaget's description of the Stage 4 infant, who is able to recognize the object that disappeared but not yet able to *imagine* the absent object. However, in the same experiment, children at 18 months were deeply surprised and puzzled and searched for the missing toy. The investigators concluded, therefore, that children in Stage 6 do have a definite object in mind and search for it even when they have not seen it disappear, because they can imagine where the object might be likely to be found (LeCompte and Gratch, 1969).

These findings pose a curious problem. Apparently, Stage 4 infants expect to find something when they look for it, yet they do not search for the original object if they find something else. Why not? One suggestion is that for infants an object is a "thing-of-place"—under a hand or behind a screen. Apparently, once children learn that one screen (A) is the place where objects are *found,* they discount the place where objects are *hidden.* When they see the object placed behind another screen (B), they will continue to look for it behind screen A. Even when the children were *shown* the experimenter finding the object behind screen B, they continued to look for the object behind screen A (Landers, 1971). For young children, objects, places, and their own behavior seem to be intertwined. Neither "object" nor "place" is assumed to have independent, stable coordinates. However, between 12 and 18 months, children's concepts of object and place become independent of their own activities. Gradually, the child's world comes to contain representations of particular things and particular places. Children begin to reason that if the object is not in one place, it might be in another.

Most of the studies of object permanence have dealt with infants 6 months of age and older. But, in a provocative study, Bower (1971) has attempted to demonstrate that even younger infants have a primitive concept of object permanence. In this study, an object was placed in front of the infants; then a screen came between them and the object; and when the screen was moved, the object had "disappeared." A change in heart rate indicated that infants as young as 20 days showed surprise at this trick. Bower reasoned that even very young infants will expect to see an object reappear after it has been hidden; but if the time during which the object is hidden is prolonged, they will simply forget about the object.

Bower (1971) also found that 8-week-old infants will track a moving object that disappears behind a screen, as if they expect it to come out on the other side. Very young infants, though, continue to track a moving object even if it stops right before their eyes:

It was as if the infants had been tracking a moving object, had noticed the stationary object that the moving object had become, had looked at it for a while and then had looked farther on to find the moving object again. It seems that they had not been aware that the stationary object was in fact the same as the moving object. (p. 35)

Bower found, moreover, that infants under 16 weeks who were tracking a moving object were not surprised if a different object emerged from the other side of the screen—as long as the new object appeared at the time when the original object should have appeared. But if either an identical or a different object appeared from behind the screen *before* it could have been expected, given the speed at which the first object had been moving, the infants were upset and stopped watching. Bower concluded that younger infants are not affected so much by *features* of objects as by movement. Infants over 4 months old, by contrast, were surprised both by the appearance of the new object and by the appearance of an object before it was expected; they looked back at the screen as if anticipating the appearance of the original object at the expected time. Bower remarks that infants under 4 months live in "a grossly overpopulated world. An object becomes a different object as soon as it moves to a new location....The infant must cope with a large number of objects when only one is really there." (pp. 37–38). The discovery of the permanent object simplifies and depopulates the world of the infant. Separating an object from its particular location in time and place becomes a foundation for the child's eventual acquisition of concepts of space, time, and causality.

For the young child, space seems to possess elastic dimensions. The actual distance from one point to another point is not as important as the fact that a chair is in the way. At 3 years of age, children believe that the distance between one point and another is *increased* if an obstacle is put in the way. The basis of this belief may be that in order to cover the distance, the child must bypass or remove the obstacle. If so, the notion of *distance* is practical and not abstract, based on sensorimotor activity, not on measurement.

Space, Time, and Causality

According to Piaget, children's concept of time is confounded by their concept of space. In a classic study, Piaget showed children a racetrack on which two little men run. One man runs 4 feet while the other, taking the same amount of time, runs 1 foot. Young children believe that the first man ran for a longer period of time than the second man; they insist that the man who ran only 1 foot stopped first, even though both men stopped at the same time (Flavell, 1970). Distance and time are not yet clearly differentiated.

Yet time is an important dimension of children's comprehension of simple causal relationships. By 18 months children know that a switch turns on the vacuum cleaner, a knob turns on the TV, a button rings the doorbell, and a lever releases water in the toilet bowl. Children acquire such knowledge easily because these events are closely linked in time. At least the physical distance between the light switch and the light, between the object that "causes" and the event that "happens," does not seem to bother them.

During the second year of life the child begins to explore cause-effect connections in simple situations. While playing with a ball, the child experiments with how to make it roll—by hitting it with a stick, by kicking it, by releasing it on an inclined plane. While turning the cap of a screw-top jar, the child discovers how the cap becomes fastened when it is turned. Opportunities to explore rather ordinary household objects help children discover how their actions influence things and how one thing is related to another. From such exploration comes the ability to classify objects.

Classification of Objects

Objects can be classified according to two systems. One system *defines* the object. The other *identifies* the object when it is present. An object—a blanket, a doll, a dog—can be *defined* according to how it is used, according to its appearance, and in terms of its likeness to other objects. *Identifying* objects involves applying a definition to a particular instance, which enables a child to recognize his or her *particular* blanket, doll, or dog. How do young children define objects? And how do they use their definitions to identify objects in the world around them?

Investigators have suggested that the earliest object categories have a functional basis (Nelson, 1974). An object *is* whatever can be done with it. According to a functional scheme for grouping objects, an object can be an "edible," a "pushable," a "rollable," a "throwable," and so on. Piaget argues that functional categories constitute the child's early knowledge about objects. Children's first definitions are practical; they learn what an object "is" by acting on it.

For the most part, researchers interested in children's classification schemes have asked *how* children put different objects together. Children usually are shown an array of objects and asked to group the objects.

Young children may not classify objects in the same way that adults do. Suppose a child is shown these six shapes:

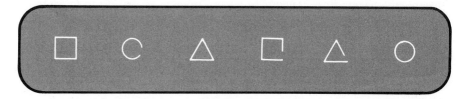

If the task is to sort the shapes that go together, two kinds of groupings can be made: a grouping based on the properties of the forms, or a grouping based on the geometric figures. A grouping based on the properties of the forms is a *topological* grouping; a grouping based on the geometric figures is a *euclidean* grouping. Such groupings would look like those shown in Figure 5–1. Young children tend to group according to topological properties. They prefer the properties of openness and closedness to the geometric features of squares and circles.

Children demonstrate their interest in topological relations in a variety of ways. An 18-month-old is enchanted by the relationships between keys and keyholes, jars and jar tops, pots and pans of various sizes—by objects that fit into or onto other objects. Topological properties seem to lend themselves to active manipulation—to doing things. Piaget described

A topological grouping
(closed forms vs. open forms)

A euclidean grouping
(square vs. triangle vs. circle)

FIGURE 5–1
Two types of groupings in object classification

how Jacqueline tried to solve a topological problem at 15 months of age: Given a toy made of hollow blocks that fit into one another, she tried at first "to put the little ones in the big ones and the big ones into the little ones, varying the combination" (Piaget, 1952). Within a few days, she had mastered the toy.

Children's capacities to group objects is often evaluated in terms of what adults would do with the same materials. If children do not put squares in one pile and circles in another in a euclidean grouping, the inference is drawn that children are unable to classify at all. This judgment ignores the possibility that children might classify according to other principles.

Such classification experiments illustrate the problem of studying children's behavior. By age 2, children have learned to attend to multiple dimensions. They are able to *identify* particular objects that can be seen as different only if attention is paid to two or more characteristics. But 2-year-olds do not simultaneously *classify* objects according to more than one dimension. When 2- and 3-year-olds are given colored shapes, they "mess around" with them without making simple groupings according to shape or color. Yet when they are given the opportunity to observe an adult grouping objects according to shape or color, they will begin to do so too. Clearly, young children *can* use dimensions such as shape and color to classify objects. However, they apparently do not always use these dimensions spontaneously.

THE ORGANIZATION OF PROBLEM-SOLVING SKILL

The ability to represent mentally various objects and actions and the ability to comprehend simple cause-and-effect relationships enable children to tackle more complex problem-solving situations. Piaget is interested in the child's understanding of the world—how the child selects problems and then goes about solving them. Bruner's interests begin where Piaget's leave off. Bruner's studies ask how the child becomes a skillful and efficient problem solver, or, put another way, how the separate components of problem-solving skills become organized into smooth and coordinated actions. Take, for example, the simple (to an adult)

146

problem of rotating a lever to obtain a toy. In an experiment based on one of Piaget's, Koslowski and Bruner (1972) presented the problem of obtaining an out-of-reach toy placed on a rotating lever. Children between 1 and 2 years of age were shown a lever attached to a rotating platform similar to a lazy Susan. An attractive toy was placed on one end of the lever so that the child could obtain the toy only by using the lever. The child had to move the lever in order to bring the toy within reach. Koslowski and Bruner found that children of different ages used different strategies to gain access to the toy and that the strategies became more sophisticated with age.

According to Bruner, a major component of the organization of skill is the acquisition of voluntary control or intention. By introducing the concept of intention or voluntary control, Bruner is saying that it is necessary to attribute to babies a capacity for "planfulness" and forethought in order to account for changes in ability that occur during the first 2 years of life. The concept of voluntary control, as Bruner has analyzed it, includes several important features of behavior: the ability to anticipate an outcome, the ability to choose means for achieving a goal and to employ those means appropriately, the ability to correct and coordinate behavior in order to reach the goal, and the recognition that the goal can be achieved by alternate means (Kalnins and Bruner, 1973). The notion of an active, selecting infant implies that the infant manages his own transactions with the environment.

When are babies capable of voluntary control? Until recently, psychologists assumed that very young infants could not exert voluntary control, perhaps because the behavioral repertoire of newborns is limited. As we have seen, very young infants cannot coordinate their large and fine muscle movements as well as older children can. Several studies, though, suggest that infants can exert voluntary control remarkably early— when the tests they are given are appropriate to their capacities. Psychologists know, for example, that by the time babies are 5 weeks old, two response systems—sucking and looking—are perfected. In one study (Kalnins and Bruner, 1973), babies between 5 and 12 weeks of age were shown a silent film whose clarity was contingent on their sucking on a dummy nipple. When they sucked vigorously, the film came into clear focus; when they ceased sucking, the film became blurred. The infants quickly learned to maintain a high rate of sucking when sucking led to clarity. So far, the study demonstrates that infants respond to reinforcement contingencies in their environments. When externally arranged contingencies do not suit them, they arrange their own. When the infants became tired of sucking, and the film began to go out of focus, they simply looked away from it—demonstrating an alternate means of reaching the "goal" of not having to look at a blurred film.

Very young infants, then, resort to their own devices—sucking and gaze avoidance—to control stimulation, which goes along with White's theory of competence (1959). Even the youngest babies seem to take pleasure in mastering their environment, which goes along with White's theory of effectance.

LOOKING

Much of the cognitive development discussed thus far in the chapter depends on the baby's ability to see and to look at objects. Looking is a more complex process than we may realize. The learning of visual forms seems to be the result of informal visual training that begins at birth. Babies initiate this training; they explore the world with their eyes long before they explore it with their hands and feet. During their first month, babies spend between 5 and 10% of their waking time scanning the environment; by 2½ months, 35% of their time is occupied by looking (Appleton et al., 1975).

As noted in Chapter 4, the visual system of newborn infants is not fully mature. A newborn baby is unable to adjust his or her focus to varying distances; the eye movements necessary to keep visual images on the retina are not completely controlled; the newborn may be unable to track moving objects. By about 3 months, depth perception and muscular control are much finer, and the infant's vision has sharpened. Even at birth, though, infants are sensitive to brightness and color.

What Can Babies See?

An interesting aspect of visual competence is the perception of color. What do infants see when they see "color"? Is the perception of color inborn, or do children learn to see red as red, and blue as blue when they learn the names of colors? The color world is infinitely complex: It has been estimated that the human visual system can discriminate 7½ million different colors (Nickerson and Newhall, 1943). Psychophysicists measure color by wavelengths of light; less scientifically trained people deal with color as a perceptual *category* (such as red). Do babies see broad color categories, and are those categories the same as or different from the categories of adults? A recent series of experiments demonstrates that babies do indeed perceive broad color categories—and their categories are much the same as those of adults. Long before infants know language and the *names* of hues, they organize wavelength into hue categories of blue, green, yellow, and red (Bornstein, Kessen, and Weiskopf, 1976a, 1976b). Even babies' color preferences parallel those of adults. Bornstein has found that, like adults, babies seem to prefer red, blue, yellow, and green, in that order (Flaste, 1976).

Until recently, scientists did not know what babies were actually able to see, apart from light, color, and movement. Researchers now can determine what babies are looking at by observing reflections in a baby's

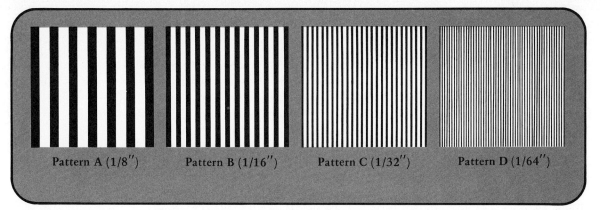

Pattern A (1/8")   Pattern B (1/16")   Pattern C (1/32")   Pattern D (1/64")

FIGURE 5–2
Patterns of black and white stripes shown to infants to determine visual acuity. Newborns were able to see the stripes in pattern A; 6-month-old infants could see the stripes in pattern D. (Fantz, 1961, p. 171)

cornea. If a baby is looking directly at an object, the object will be mirrored in the center of the eye. Observations of corneal reflections have enabled scientists to measure visual acuity in the perception of forms. In an ingenious study, Fantz (1961) showed patterns of black and white stripes of decreasing width to a group of infants (see Figure 5–2). Each pattern was paired with a gray square of the same size. The researchers knew that infants tend to look more often and longer at patterned stimuli than at plain stimuli. They reasoned that the finest (smallest) pattern that consistently was preferred to the gray square would indicate how narrow a stripe infants can perceive at various ages. Newborn babies were able to see stripes ⅛-inch wide (Pattern A in Figure 5–3) at a distance of 10 inches; 6-month-olds could distinguish the ¹/₆₄-inch stripes (Pattern D) at the same distance (Fantz, 1961).

What Do Babies Look At?

Babies' attention patterns change gradually during the first year of life. The attention of newborns is easily distracted from one stimulus to another. By about 2 months, babies move to what Bruner (1969a) calls "a stage of 'stuckness.'" Their attention is now "caught" by various targets in the outside world. Sometimes babies even look as if they are trying unsuccessfully to pull away from a target; they turn their heads, only to have their eyes remain fastened on the object. Between 4 and 5 months of age, babies' eyes begin to move smoothly and easily to anticipated objects. Bruner calls this stage *biphasic attention*. By this, he means that babies continue to watch outward objects, but they seem to have developed an inner control over their attention. They no longer give the impression that they are stuck on their target. They still can place attention, but they now can shift or withdraw it as well (Bruner, 1969a).

Attention studies conducted in laboratories pose certain theoretical problems. Such studies are based on the premise that if babies look longer at one object than another, they "prefer" that object. As Haith and Campos point out, this theory does not explain "what a baby is actually doing while he is 'attending' to a preferred stimulus, what he is doing while

149

attending to a nonpreferred stimulus . . . , what he is doing when attending to neither (about 50% of the time) and, in fact, what happens when no 'preferred' stimulus is available. Clearly, the system does not shut down in the latter case" (1977, p. 266). Perhaps, they conclude, we should not think of babies as showing "preferences" but as processing stimuli or collecting information.

Nor do infants always seek out stimulation. As we indicated earlier, they may in fact, actively avoid it. Babies seem to have a system of buffering, which helps them to break off contact with the outside world. Buffering mechanisms include the sleep states described in Chapter 4, crying, gaze aversion, and nonnutritive sucking (Bruner, 1973b). Sucking on a pacifier or fingers seems to reduce babies' irritation or discomfort. Lipsitt (1967) found that infants are especially likely to suck on pacifiers when they are tired or in pain or when they are faced with new stimuli. We should not, then, view babies as systems constantly seeking stimulation from the environment. There is evidence that they sometimes actually shut out such stimulation. Finally, theories about infant attention should take into account the fact that for babies—just as for adults—there is a difference between objects that *attract* attention and objects that *hold* attention. Babies are quickest in turning to look at objects that are large or moving, but they look longest at objects that are novel or complex (Cohen, 1972).

Infants' interest in faces extends to interest in their own faces when they see them in mirrors. Indeed, mirrors seem to hold deep fascination for most infants. Babies first notice their reflections at about 18 weeks of age. But at this point, they do not realize that the face is not that of someone else. Self-recognition occurs sometimes between 12 and 20 months of age; accounts vary on this point.

Self-Recognition

An innovative approach to the study of self-recognition as revealed in the infant's responses to his reflection is that taken by Papoušek and Papoušek (1974). These investigators used two TV screens to present an infant with varying images of itself. They wanted to discover just what it is about the infant's reflection that elicits responses from the infant. Various films (including a videotape of the infant himself) and a live mirror image were used to determine to what extent a baby responds to the fact that the mirror image does exactly what it does; to eye contact; to the babyish features of the mirror image; to smiles and friendly expressions.

The results of the experiment showed that eye contact with the image in a film is more likely to elicit a response from 5-month-old infants than is the simultaneous mirror image. But as babies grow older, they become more interested in the relationship between their own movements and those of the mirror image. There is some evidence that this is a "learned" response. Papoušek and Papoušek noted that several of the infants

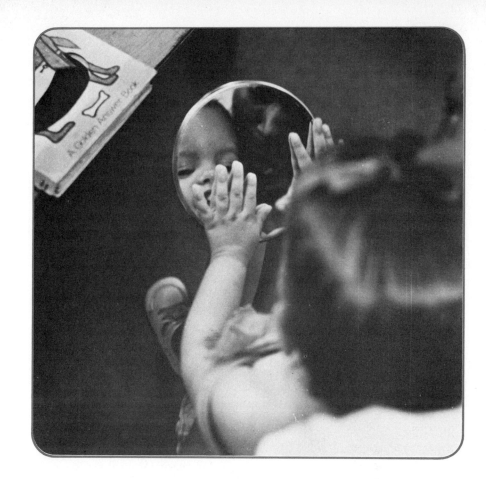

Mirrors seem to hold deep fascination for most infants, but they must see their reflections many times before they realize that they are watching themselves. (Jason Lauré, Woodfin Camp)

watched the mirror image without interruption while waving their arms in the air. Babies must see their reflections many times and watch the reflections mimic their own actions before they are finally able to recognize themselves in a mirror.

An experiment conducted by Amsterdam (1972) attempted to pinpoint the age at which self-recognition appears by the simple expedient of putting a spot of rouge on the child's nose and observing the child's reactions to seeing the spot in the mirror. If the child touched the spot or used the mirror to examine his or her nose, the researchers assumed that self-recognition had occurred. Amsterdam found a developmental pattern of three distinct phases in children's responses to their reflections. At first the child believes the reflection is another child. In fact, at about 1 year, he or she may look behind the mirror in an effort to find that child. This stage is followed by a period of apprehension and withdrawal from the mirror. During the second stage, however, the child also shows signs of self-consciousness—either embarrassment or self-admiration. Some observers feel that these behaviors indicate self-recognition, but, according to Amsterdam, there may be other explanations for these responses. In the case of self-admiration, for example, the child may be imitating behavior he or she has observed in adults looking at mirrors.

The third phase is the period in which true self-recognition appears. In Amsterdam's experiment, self-recognition was established as occurring at 20 to 24 months of age. At this stage the child can locate the spot of rouge on his or her nose by looking in the mirror. Despite such evidence, there is continued controversy over the age at which self-recognition first appears. Some investigators put it as early as 6 months—and further research on this subject clearly is in order.

Visual Comparison

One process that scientists are only beginning to study is visual comparison. When babies are presented with two stimuli, they stare alternately at each, a behavior that is called *shifting* (Ruff, 1975). Piaget considers shifting the beginning of visual comparison. When adults shift attention between two stimuli, we assume—and can verify the assumption by asking—that they are comparing the two. But when babies shift attention from one stimulus to another, are they actually comparing them? Ruff's findings suggest that they are. Infants 3 months of age and older shift more when two stimuli are similar than when they are different. Just as adults do, the infants gradually decrease shifting as the two stimuli become familiar. Ruff's data suggest that infants control and distribute their attention in relatively complex situations and do so in ways that are remarkably efficient and appropriate.

Infants first explore the world with their eyes. By about 5 months, they can shift their attention smoothly from one place to another. Research indicates that babies' attention is held by objects that are novel or complex, but as was pointed out earlier in the chapter, in infant's reaction to a novel stimulus depends on previous experience. If a baby is habituated to one particular stimulus and responds with attention to presentation of a novel stimulus, we can conclude that the baby has *remembered* something about the previously experienced stimulus.

MEMORY

What and how much do infants remember? Piaget observed what he called *recognitory assimilation* in his three children. At 6 months, when Lucienne observed dolls she had shaken, she would outline the movements of swinging them with her hand; at 7 months, she would open and close her hands briefly (Ginsburg and Opper, 1969). Piaget believed that during the sensorimotor stage, infants represent the world in terms of actions: "Everything takes place as though the child were satisfied to recognize these objects or sights and to make a note of this recognition, but could not recognize them except by working, rather than thinking, the schema helpful to recognition" (Piaget, 1952, p. 185).

That infants remember *something* is apparent from casual observations; babies recognize their parents, for example. Reactions to familiar stimuli provide further evidence for infant memory. Obviously, if an infant responds in different ways to a familiar stimulus and to an unfamiliar one, the infant is showing some memory of the familiar one (Cohen and Gelber, 1975). Infants' responses to unfamiliar stimuli can be measured in two ways: by habituation and by paired-comparison tests. In habituation studies, babies may be shown a single pattern for a fixed number of times or until they have become habituated to it (decreased their attention to it); then they are shown a different pattern. The amount of time they spend looking at the new pattern is compared to the time they spent looking at the familiar one. In paired-comparison procedures, infants are shown two patterns simultaneously over a number of trials; then they are shown one familiar pattern and one new one. The percentage of time they spend looking at the new pattern is measured. Infants demonstrate recognition in a shorter time in paired-comparison tests than in habituation tests, but both measures show that infants are capable of visual memory.

How long can an infant remember? Some of the evidence is contradictory. Different studies have shown that 4-month-olds can recognize geometric patterns for as long as 24 hours after seeing them initially; a more recent study using paired-comparison techniques, however, demonstrated that 5-month-olds could recognize geometric patterns after 48 hours and photographs of faces after a delay of 2 weeks (Cohen and Gelber, 1975; Fagan, 1973). Interestingly, though, when infants in the same study were shown three-dimensional face masks, they did *not* recognize them 3 hours later. What caused the difference in retention? Or, to ask the question another way, what interfered with the infant's ability to remember? The researchers hypothesized that the infants failed to recognize the face masks because during the 3-hour interval, they were exposed to very similar stimuli in the natural environment—human faces. The hypothesis was tested in a fourth experiment: 5-month-olds were exposed to photographs of a face and then divided into three groups. Subjects in the high-similarity group were shown photographs of new faces very much like those they had originally seen. Subjects in the medium-similarity group were shown the new photographs rotated 180 degrees. Subjects in the low-similarity group were shown line drawings of the new faces, also rotated 180 degrees. All the infants were then tested for recognition of the original photographs. Infants in the low- and high-similarity groups recognized the photographs. But for infants in the medium-similarity group, exposure to the rotated photographs interfered with recognition. A final experiment showed that exposure to similar material interferes most with recognition if it occurs immediately after infants have seen the first photograph. If exposure to intervening stimuli is delayed for 3 hours, it does not interfere with recognition (Fagan, 1973). Infants, then, are capable of long-term visual memory. But infants, like adults, can forget, and one cause of their forgetting is diversion of attention by material *similar* to the material to be remembered (Fagan, 1973).

Other investigators have been interested in what elements of colored patterns an infant remembers. When babies remember a colored form, do they remember the form or the color? Saayman, Ames, and Moffett (1964) habituated a group of 3-month-old infants to a colored geometric pattern. They then showed the babies the familiar pattern and a pattern that differed in color and/or form. The investigators found that 3-month-old infants store both color *and* form in memory; they do not respond to a change in either the form or color by itself. By the age of 8 to 12 months, however, infants store color and form separately. By that age, they are able to respond to a change in either form *or* color (Collard and Rydberg, 1972).

Besides varying with age, the capacity of memory varies with individual children. Some infants habituate more rapidly than others. Recent studies suggest that so-called "fast" and "slow" habituators do not differ in the *time* it takes them to actually process and store visual information. The difference between them is in the number of *trials* necessary before each judges the stored representation to be the same as the one he is looking at. Some infants get involved in a habituation task right away; thus they peak and habituate very quickly. Other infants take longer to get involved in the task and may spend a number of trials looking but not remembering; once they do begin to store information, they peak and habituate as quickly as do so-called "fast" habituators (Cohen and Gelber, 1975).

Research indicates that much of infant behavior is dependent upon memory and that the ability to remember is present in very young infants. The ability to remember enables infants to begin storing information about their environment, which inevitably helps them when they actively begin to interact with the world around them.

EXPLORING, PLAYING, AND PRETENDING

During the second half of the first year, babies are no longer content with looking at and listening to the world around them. They touch and manipulate every object they can reach. Novelty is especially important for infants who are just beginning to explore the world. Between 8 and 13 months, children prefer novel toys to old ones and relatively complex toys to simple ones (Ross, 1974; McCall, 1974). (These preferences follow the patterns of attention discussed earlier.) Infants explore a toy to discover all aspects of it. They are as interested in its sensory characteristics—its shape and weight, its texture to feel with their hands *and* with their mouths—as they are in what it "does" (McCall, 1974). They are beginning

Through play and exploration, children learn about physical relationships and sensory characteristics such as shape, weight, and texture.
(Eileen Christelow, Jeroboam)

to know objects as things to look at, to grasp, and to suck. Parents and caregivers often fail to appreciate the variety of information a toy offers an infant. Exploration of the toy can be as interesting to a child as learning what the toy does. When children's interest is attracted to an object, they use what they know—mouthing, pounding, throwing—to explore and experience the object. In that process, they may learn something new, although what they learn may not be what an adult might expect or predict. As children mature, though, they gain interest in how a toy works and what it can do. The process of mental growth seems to thrive on interplay between a changing and varied environment and an active, curious child.

Children's modes of play activities change dramatically between the ages of 12 and 26 months. Play directed at discovering an object's physical properties becomes less central. Instead, make-believe play and activities in which an infant combines objects (such as putting a spoon into a cup or making a pile of blocks) become more frequent, as well as more complex and sophisticated. On the one hand, the child's use of objects becomes increasingly organized and ordered. The child's behavior shifts from attention to loose spatial relations (putting things on top of or next to other things) to attention to relations that produce multiple rows or piles or that separate one kind of object from another. These behaviors demonstrate the child's knowledge of things "as they are." On the other hand, make-believe play increases. Pretend play gradually becomes more detached from the specific properties of objects. At 19 months, children may pretend to feed a doll; by 36 months, they may pretend to feed a stick. Thus two major cognitive transitions occur during the second year of life. One transition is marked by the appearance of activities in which the child fits and orders objects according to increasingly constraining temporal and spatial relationships. And, in apparent contradiction, the other transition is marked by the appearance of pretend activities in which the child ignores these physical relationships and symbolizes things "as if they were." As children become able to organize the physical world, they are able symbolically to represent objects according to a concept of what the object is and does.

Pretend Play

Pretend play has considerable significance in theories of cognitive development. When children pretend, an activity is taken out of its typical context. Means are disconnected from ends. For example, the child "eats" without consuming food. Objects that are present are treated "as if" they were something else—a large box as if it were a car, for example. The act of pretending thus implies a symbolic transformation of the immediate physical environment. What makes the appearance of symbolic activities so important is that symbols—mental representations of actions and objects—are essential elements of mature thought. Arithmetic, logical reasoning, and language all require the ability to "think" actions and things. To Piaget, pretend play marks the transition from functional, practical activity to operational, representational activity.

Piaget's analysis of pretend play emphasizes its cognitive-structural features. He traces the development of this play through a number of stages. The earliest form of pretend play that Piaget describes is the *sym-*

bolic scheme, which is first detectable around 12 months of age. It consists of the child's performing a well-established sensorimotor routine *out of its usual context*—children "sleep" by closing their eyes or "drink" from an empty cup. The most complex form of pretend play is sociodramatic play, which does not usually appear before age 3. It involves several children playing roles, imagining settings, and evoking interpersonal relations.

There is some evidence that the pretend play of young children is dominated by the immediate characteristics of available toys, whereas older children adapt materials to "pretend" themes. The pretend play of 2-year-olds is dependent on the actual presence of objects that are similar to real things—toy telephones, toy trucks, cuplike cups, babylike dolls. Three-year-olds are more likely to use a stick for a telephone, a box for a truck, a rag for a doll, a leaf for a cup (Fein, 1975). Thus the imaginative quality of the pretend play of young children is partially a function of the available materials.

Pretend play is also sensitive to other kinds of situational factors. Children's play tends to be disrupted and inhibited when strangers are present or when mothers or primary caregivers are absent. One study (Fein, Robertson, and Diamond, 1973) showed that 2-year-old girls, more than boys, pretended more in the presence of a familiar adult than in the presence of a stranger. Children's play also becomes inhibited when adults tell them how to play. Play flourishes in a familiar environment in which the material resources are interesting and diverse, in which the child commands the initiative and adult expectations are scaled to the child's capacities. Allowing play to flourish provides children with an important opportunity to develop the cognitive abilities and intelligence that enable them to interact in the world.

INTELLIGENCE TESTING

Cognitive development in babies as well as in older children can be measured through the use of certain types of tests designed to measure various factors—including environment and personality—that contribute to mental development or intelligence. Infant mental development was first measured by Arnold Gesell in 1919. Gesell and his colleagues undertook to survey the normal behavior of children in infancy and early childhood. They observed children in various settings in order to establish behavioral norms for the ages of 3 to 4 months, 6 months, 9 months, and 1 year. The Gesell Developmental Schedules are lists of behaviors arranged by age to show development in four major areas: motor behavior, adaptive behavior, language behavior, and personal-social behavior. The Gesell Schedules are used to measure "developmental age" and have been the foundation of other tests of young children.

Bayley's motor and mental scales, first developed in 1933, used the Gesell *Bayley's Scales*
Schedules as a source of material. Bayley's original mental scale included
185 items extending through 3 years of age. It measured sensory perception, fine motor skills, adaptability to social situations, and some language
items. Bayley's original motor scale included 76 items that measured large
motor skills such as crawling, walking, and balance, from birth to 3½
years of age. In 1966, Bayley revised both scales, adding new items. She
is also developing an Infant Behavior Profile, which measures such items
as attention span, reactivity, and happiness (Thomas, 1970).

The Bayley Infant Scale (BIS) has been shown to be both reliable and
internally consistent. The reliability of the scales has been demonstrated
by studies of infants who were tested and then retested after a short interval. One study found that after one week, test-retest agreement was
achieved on 76% of the items for both the mental and motor scales (McCall,
Hogarty, and Hurlburt, 1972).

Although the Bayley Scales are internally consistent, they do not predict *Predictive Validity*
performance on IQ tests given later in childhood or adulthood. Bayley *of Infant*
herself concludes: "It is now well established that we cannot predict later *Intelligence Tests*
intelligence from the scores on tests made in infancy" (1955, p. 806).

Why is there so little correlation between scores on infant tests and later
IQ? One reason may be sampling problems. The subjects of infant tests
are often simply any that are available—what Kessen (1960) has called
"'unsampled' samples." Bayley, for example, did attempt to obtain a
representative sample of English-speaking infants from Berkeley, California, but the infants on whom she based her original scales turned out
to have a mean IQ score of 120 when they grew older. Such a sample was
very select; later tests therefore show low correlations.

Another explanation for the low correlations between scores on infant
developmental tests and IQ tests may be simply that the two kinds of
tests measure different kinds of skills. Psychologists have tended to assume that intelligence is a fixed characteristic that remains constant
throughout development. But the nature of intelligence may change with
development, or intelligence at various levels of development may consist
of skills that change and/or disappear (McCall et al., 1972).

The home environment, as we might expect, influences the intellectual *Influences on*
development of children. Until rather recently, there was no standardized *Intellectual*
way for investigators to measure different home environments. In 1966, *Development*
however, a group of researchers developed and standardized an "Inven- *of Infants*
tory of Home Stimulation" that measures items on six subscales: (1) responsiveness of the mother, (2) avoidance of restriction, (3) organization
of the environment, (4) provision of appropriate play materials, (5) maternal involvement with the child, and (6) opportunities for variety in daily

stimulation (Elardo, Bradley, and Caldwell, 1975). Scores are based on observations in the home and interviews with the primary caregiver. Investigators used the scale to assess the baby's environment at 6, 12, and 24 months. They also tested the babies at 6, 12, and 36 months. They found little relationship between home environment and babies' performance on infant development tests. But they did find that the home scores of infants at 6 months were highly correlated with Binet IQ scores at 3 years of age. The provision of appropriate play materials and the organization of the physical and temporal environment seemed to have an especially strong influence on IQ scores (Elardo et al. 1975). The home environment also predicts *changes* in IQ test scores. Bradley and Caldwell (1976) found that "infants who come from homes rich in appropriate kinds of experiences have mental test scores that show a progressive *increase* during the first 3 years of life. By comparison, infants who come from homes poor in certain kinds of experiences have mental scores that progressively *decrease*" (p. 96, emphasis added).

The finding that home environment seems to have little impact on performance on early infant tests suggests that early development may simply be a function of physical maturation. However, the quality of a child's interactions with the environment is important for *cognitive growth*. One study suggests that the home environment may be more important for the mental development of girls than of boys (Yarrow, Rubenstein, and Pederson, 1975). Another study (Bradley and Caldwell, 1976), assessing the effect of home environment on IQ scores of 3-year-olds, found that among the boys tested, those who had egalitarian, positively evaluating mothers recorded the highest scores. Girls with the highest scores were those whose mothers were loving and accepting and who expected high achievement from their daughters.

The personality of the baby seems also to be related to IQ. Birns and Golden (1972) studied the relationship between personality measures of babies at 18 and 24 months of age and their performance on IQ tests at 3 years. They found a baby's apparent pleasure in performing a task at 18 and 24 months to be highly correlated with performance both on infant development tests and on IQ scores at 3 years. Birns and Golden suggest that pleasure in problem solving contributes to and facilitates cognitive development. They also found that two other personality measures—cooperation and attention-persistence—seem to contribute to high IQ scores. How children perform on tests reflects not just what they know but how they feel. As we said in earlier chapters, performance is not the same as competence. Social and intellectual factors are always intertwined in performance. It may be that some home environments make for happy, sociable babies who like doing things with people, including testers. To the extent that tests are social situations, it is reasonable to believe that scores reflect social as well as mental characteristics.

PIAGETIAN SCALES OF INTELLIGENCE

Of all the *theories* of infant development, Piaget's is the most coherent and comprehensive. But Piaget is not particularly interested in formulating abstract definitions of "intelligence." His definitions of intelligence vary, although his concern with intellectual development as an ongoing, active process does not. His writing, though, often implies a connection between intelligence and *intention*. Piaget suggests that we can infer intention from a child's behavior when there is a goal in mind at the start and some distinction between means and ends: "In an act of intelligence, ...the end is established from the outset and pursued after a search for the appropriate means" (Piaget and Inhelder, 1969, p. 9). Determining a child's intentions, of course, is more difficult than observing what the child actually does. Piaget recognized this difficulty and attempted to deal with it through flexible and individualized kinds of experimentation.

Several investigators have devised developmental scales based on Piaget's theory of development. The most comprehensive of these scales have been developed by Uzgiris and Hunt (1975). The Uzgiris-Hunt tests must be administered by trained examiners. The items in the Uzgiris-Hunt scales, unlike those in traditional tests, are *ordinal:* They are presented in an invariant sequence. Traditional tests assume that infants' progress is the result of maturation; little attention is given to how abilities at one level relate to abilities at subsequent levels. Piagetian scales (including the Uzgiris-Hunt scales), on the other hand, assume that success in one item is a prerequisite for success in the next. For example, the ability to follow a slowly moving object is necessary if the infant is then to notice the disappearance of a slowly moving object (Uzgiris and Hunt, 1975).

Traditional and Piagetian scales are based on profoundly different notions of intelligence. Unlike the designers of traditional scales, Piagetians are not interested in individual differences in "intelligence." Uzgiris (1976a) for example, argues that "if sensorimotor intelligence is the foundation for subsequent intellectual development, it will be coordinated and then reorganized by most children at an early age. Are the differences of a few months in achieving some level of functioning of real interest?" (p. 160). Therefore, Piagetians are not concerned with the predictive validity of their scales or even with whether a child's high level of performance on early Piagetian scales will be matched by a similarly high level of performance at a later age. Infant's performance on Piagetian tests is not very highly correlated with their performance on traditional tests of infant development, and their early performance on Piagetian tests does not predict their later scores (Uzgiris, 1976a). Uzgiris (1976b) argues strenuously against the use of Piagetian scales to provide measures of individual differences.

As we have seen, infant tests, whether Piagetian or traditional, are not valid predictors of later intelligence. At the very least, infant tests should be used with some caution. There is no justification for classifying infants at 2 or 3 years of age as irrevocably "slow" or "bright" or "average." Lewis (1973) argues that intelligence tests should not be used, as they are now, to evaluate infant intervention or enrichment programs. The skills enhanced by intervention programs and the skills measured by intelligence tests may be quite different. After all, providing children with an interesting and pleasant environment, whether at home or in child-care centers, might be more sensibly seen as an end in itself than as part of an anxious effort to boost future IQ scores.

SUMMARY

In the first 3 years of life, infants undergo rapid motor and cognitive development. Understanding the correlation between developing motor and cognitive skills in infants poses special problems because babies cannot explain why or how they are doing something. The study of infant cognition involves *constructing* theories about the infant's theory of reality.

Cognitive development goes hand in hand with motor development. Certain displays of cognitive development cannot take place until the motor abilities that support the cognitive tasks are coordinated and perfected. Babies' sensorimotor systems become elaborated and coordinated in the first 3 years of life. The *gross motor system* governs movement of the head, torso, legs, and arms. The *fine motor system* governs the movements of eyes, hands, and fingers. Activities that involve coordination of the gross and fine systems are the most complex and take longer to develop. As motor skills develop, infants become able to explore and to understand more of the world.

White has suggested that the motivation for the seemingly purposeless activity in infants and small children is competence. Even very young children are pleased by a feeling of effectance. They respond to attractive events with attention, one form of which is the orienting response. Repeated presentation of a stimulus results in diminution of the orienting response and habituation to the stimulus. Attention patterns change with age; infants go through three phases in the development of attention. The final phase appears to mark the beginning of active thought. Another measure of cognitive development appears in children's reactions of surprise. Infants cannot be surprised until they have begun to formulate expectations about the permanence of the objects around them.

Development of cognitive skills seems to progress in stages. From observations of his children, Piaget constructed his theory of intellectual development, which describes development as progressing in a series of stages. The first stage is the sensorimotor period, from birth to 2 years, during which time children come to see themselves as objects in a world made up of other permanent objects. Piaget identified six distinct stages within the sensorimotor period, each characterized by the type of reactions which the infant is capable of in that period and through which infants progress in the development of object permanence. By about 18 months, infants acquire a full-fledged concept of object permanence. According to Piaget, cognitive development is guided by organization and adaptation. Adaptation consists of two processes: *assimilation* and *accommodation*. Assimilation is the incorporation of a new event into an existing scheme. Accommodation is the modification of an existing scheme or the creation of a new one in response to a novel event.

Infants' notions of time, space, and causality are not yet clearly differentiated. Opportunities to explore ordinary household objects help children discover how things are related to one another and how objects may be classified. Young children tend to group things according to properties that lend themselves to active manipulation. The ability to comprehend cause-and-effect relationships enables children to tackle more complex problem solving. A major component of the organization of problem-solving skills is the acquisition of voluntary control. Even very young infants demonstrate voluntary control, when tests given them are appropriate to their abilities.

Cognitive development depends to a large extent on the baby's ability to look at surrounding objects. At birth, infants are sensitive to brightness, color, and movement. Visual acuity improves over the first few months of life, as does the ability to focus and to track moving objects. Babies prefer to look at objects that are novel or complex. They first notice their own reflections in a mirror at 18 weeks, and self-recognition occurs between 12 and 20 months of age. Habituation and paired comparison tests show that even very young infants are capable of visual memory.

At about 6 months of age, babies begin to touch and manipulate every object they can reach. Such exploration is the beginning of play and leads to pretend play, in which children become able to represent objects symbolically. To Piaget, pretend play marks the transition from functional, practical activity to operational, representational activity.

Cognitive development can be measured by tests such as the Bayley Infant Scale which are internally consistent but do not predict later performance on IQ tests. Traditional developmental tests measure individual differences in performance. Several investigators have devised developmental scales based on Piaget's theory of development. Piagetian tests measure where the child is in the sequence of development although performance on these tests does not predict later scores, nor is it highly correlated with performance on traditional developmental tests.

CHAPTER 6

Language Development: The Communicating Infant

FOUNDATIONS OF LANGUAGE

The Gift of Speech   Newborn infants confront a challenge that seems almost overwhelming. First, they must communicate basic needs: For a while, crying is the major means of doing so. Then they must learn a complex language, composed of strange sounds that bear no physical resemblance to the things to which they refer. Yet, the infant starts with an advantage that solves the problem easily in the normal process of growing up. The advantage is a capacity for thinking in ways conducive to the acquisition of language.

Human language and the thought processes which accompany it differentiate us more distinctively from nonhuman primates than any of our other abilities and attributes. Even the experimenters who claim they have taught something approximating human language to chimpanzees and gorillas acknowledge that the trained animals do not acquire language in the way children do. There is little evidence that trained animals acquire syntactic rules that permit language to convey subtle and diverse meanings to others; the concept of naming; or the idea that language can be used to describe events never before experienced.

Humans have, then, a unique capability that no other species can approach. There must be something in our mental and physical mechanisms that accounts for our remarkable capability to acquire and use human languages in the course of maturation. The mystery of the origin and development of human language has challenged philosophers from Aristotle to Descartes, but their speculations have yielded more controversy than enlightenment. In recent times, psychologists have taken up the inquiry. They, too, have generated volumes of controversy, but their methods have given us useful and, occasionally, testable hypotheses supported (or contradicted) by observational data. The principal investigators are psycholinguists, so called because they view the subject of language acquisition and use as a psychological phenomenon. Their work is aided by the contributions of neuropsychologists, who are concerned with the anatomical structures and neurological processes involved in the language function.

Investigators who study language are interested in such questions as the relationship between language and communication; the innate factors that predispose the infant to perceive and learn human language; the relative effects of the child's environment and maturational development on language acquisition; the difference between what the child understands and what he speaks. Finally, they ask, how does human language, in its various native tongues, influence our thought?

Language and Communication

Although we are accustomed to identify language with communication, we must distinguish between them. Language is only one form of communication, and communication is only one function of language. Certainly, a lighthouse beacon and a railroad crossing signal are forms of communication. An animal's footprints convey meaningful information to the hunter. So does a baby's cry to its mother. These are nonverbal *signals*—visual and auditory—but how do they differ from language? What, indeed, is language?

Critchley's (1975) definition of language—"the expression and reception of ideas and feelings"—seems too general and comprehensive for purposes of discrimination. He sharpens this definition by distinguishing human language, or *speech,* as "the expression and reception of ideas and feelings by verbal symbols." (Later we will consider another definition that specifies the characteristics of language.) In any case, Critchley's second definition uniquely identifies *human* language, which we will refer to by the shorter term, *speech.*

Speech does more than just communicate. We use it also to regulate (inhibit or activate) our behavior (Luria, 1961). Think of the occasions when you silently tell yourself to "go slow" or to "watch the ball." We use speech to verify a result of an action or a test: "They match—good!" We will also consider how speech affects our view of the world.

Smiles, frowns, and gestures are signals that are part of our nonverbal communication system. (Camilla Smith)

To get a better grasp of the broad concept of language, let us distinguish some of its principal elements. *Signals* are stimulus patterns associated with a particular object—for example, smiles, frowns, cries, gestures, tones, smells, tracks. When signals occur with some regularity or consistency, they constitute a *signaling system*. At the visual level, human and nonhuman primate signals have much in common—for example, facial expressions that indicate anger and pleasure.

Signals are directly linked with their respective objects and, hence, are restricted in flexibility and variability of message. The child eventually learns to represent an object (or the concept of an object) by a distinct *symbol,* which stands for the object, yet is separable from it. The *signified* object need not be present to be realized (Sinclair-de-Zwart, 1969). Thus, the child may say "meow" while pushing a lump of clay that symbolizes a cat. Note that the child invents the symbol or adopts a suggested symbol, which may be changed from time to time. *Signs* are introduced at more sophisticated levels of representation. A sign is an arbitrary *signifier* whose meaning is agreed on by social convention. Words are the signs that make up human language. Their relationship to the signified object or concept is not only purely symbolic, but fixed by convention. In addition, words can be both spoken and written. Words lend themselves to elaborate meaningful combinations (sentences) capable of expressing any conceivable human thought.

165

The concept of innate mechanisms that may predispose the infant to "recognize" the sounds of his native language and gradually learn to use them effectively raises questions about biological structures and processes in the human organism.

It has long been argued that the human vocal tract (larynx, pharynx, and mouth, including the tongue) is well designed to produce phonetically articulated speech, and that the lower primates cannot develop our form of speech because they do not have our vocal anatomy. From this fact of comparative anatomy, a motor theory of speech has been proposed and widely accepted. It states that the ability to articulate *phonemes* (the "atoms" — that form words — /m/, /b/, /a/, etc.) is a necessary skill for comprehending, as well as producing, speech. As evidence, neuropsychologists point out that people who have lost control over their mouth, lips, and tongue as a result of brain damage also develop disturbances in speech comprehension and writing (Luria, 1971).

Other researchers consider the motor theory evidence uncertain, however. Wind (1976) says that the vocal tracts of chimpanzees and baboons could produce understandable phonemes. The primates' deficiency lies in the lack of a central nervous system faculty for encoding and decoding each other's sound signals in linguistic form.

Blaming the monkey's brain for its linguistic incompetence seems to make sense in the light of anatomical differences between ape and human cortical structures. The human brain is richly endowed with so-called *association areas* that link the primary sensory centers of vision, audition, and touch. The associations that are responsible for speech functions are focused in one hemisphere of the brain (generally the left). This *lateralization* of function provides the specialized association structures that perform the necessary processing of visual and auditory signals into verbal constructs. Levy (1976) found that where hemispheric function was not strongly lateralized, interference with speech was noted.

If, as noted, speech has biological foundations, there should be some relation between the development of language competence and physiological maturation. Lenneberg (1966) demonstrates that speech presents the "hallmarks" of maturationally controlled behavior: a regular sequence of development, a constant state of environmental stimulation, emergence of behavior without direct reference to need or purpose. Table 6–1 shows how the sequence of speech development parallels motor development, indicating a corresponding maturational process. Of course, the correlation between speech and motor development does not establish a *causal* link between the two processes. In fact, Lenneberg disclaims such a direct, causal relationship. In support of the independence of language acquisition from articulation (which is subject to motor control), he points out that babies babble with speechlike sounds and intonation — and hence are physiologically qualified to utter sentences — long before they actually do

Biological and Maturational Factors

AGE	MOTOR DEVELOPMENT	LANGUAGE DEVELOPMENT
12 weeks	Supports head when in prone position	Smiles when talked to and makes cooing sounds
16 weeks	Plays with rattle when placed in hands	Turns head in response to human sounds
20 weeks	Sits with props	Makes vowellike and consonantlike cooing sounds
6 months	Reaches, grasps	Cooing changes to babbling which resembles one-syllable sounds
8 months	Stands holding on; picks up pellet with thumb and finger	Increasing repetitions of some syllables
10 months	Creeps; pulls self to standing position; takes side steps while holding on	Appears to distinguish between different adult words by differential responding
12 months	Walks when held by one hand; seats self on floor	Understands some words; says mama, dada
18 months	Can grasp, hold, and return objects quite well; creeps downstairs backward	Has repertoire of between 3 and 50 spoken words, said singly
24 months	Runs, walks up and down stairs	Has repertoire of more than 50 words; uses two-word phrases
30 months	Stands on one foot for about 2 seconds; takes a few steps on tiptoe	Tremendous increase in spoken vocabulary; many phrases containing three to five words
3 years	Tiptoes 3 yards; can operate a tricycle	Vocabulary of about 1,000 words; pronunciation clear
4 years	Jumps over rope, hops on one foot	Language apparently well established

Source: Lenneberg, 1967, pp. 128–130.

TABLE 6–1

Milestones in Infant Language and Motor Development

speak. Further, mutes who cannot articulate speech sounds do acquire written and sign language.

Maturational control of speech development is evident in the regularity and fixed sequence of the onset of various stages, even in the case of children handicapped by such abnormalities as blindness, deafness (of

child and/or parents), and general retardation. Children with these handicaps proceed through the language development process in the sequence
outlined in Table 6–1, although lack of vocal interaction between deaf
parents and children may limit the vocabulary size. The language development sequence also seems to hold for different languages and cultures
and, hence, is independent of environment.

Each stage of this maturational process must be accomplished properly
in preparation for the next stage. A consequence of this principle is that
there is a right time for each stage. Lenneberg (1969) has proposed a
critical age hypothesis that sets approximate age boundaries for language
acquisition. These boundaries correlate with levels of brain maturation.
The association areas of the brain, essential to the speech functions,
develop throughout childhood. The human brain at birth weighs only 40%
as much as the adult brain. The late-developing association areas account
for most of the difference. It is in these areas that lateralization is most pronounced. During the lateralization process, speech functions are not
completely localized in one hemisphere. Children who suffer brain damage in the dominant hemisphere before the age of 2 continue the language
acquisition process with no noticeable effect. If the damage occurs between ages 2 and 4, a transient aphasia (loss of speech function) soon
gives way to resumption of language learning as the other hemisphere
takes over the speech function. As the brain matures further, the aphasia
lasts longer and causes more persistent disturbance of speech function
with increasing age, through the midteen years. After age 16, when the
brain has reached its mature stage, most functions are locked in and
traumas cause lasting dysfunction.

The epigenetic process sets progressive limits to the brain's capability
for language learning. Preteen children learn two or three languages at
the same time as easily as they can learn one. Yet when older children or
adults try to learn a new language, the process seems to be less "natural"
and more difficult.

If our genetic endowment gives us a unique speech capability, can other
biological constructions accomplish the same result? Can our nearest
relatives, the nonhuman primates, match our capability for language
acquisition? The possibility has inspired some fascinating research. So
far, however, experiments designed to teach language to primates seem
to have raised more questions than they have answered. Success in teaching chimpanzees American Sign Language (ASL) and other symbolic
systems of communication has provoked considerable controversy over
the issue of whether the apes have really learned anything like human
language. The core of the argument is a matter of definitions: What is a
language? How does *language* differ from *speech?* Hockett (1960) identified
13 *design features* that qualify human language. Four of the most significant
are the following:

Animal Language

1. *Displacement.* The fact that human language can refer to events and objects that are distant in both time and space, not just the here and now.
2. *Productivity.* The ability to combine old words into new statements that are understood by the listener.
3. *Traditional transmission.* The fact that, although the details of a language (that is, the words) are learned, the ability to learn a language is probably genetically determined.
4. *Duality of patterning.* The fact that a large number of words are made up of a small number of sounds that have no meaning in themselves (phonemes).

We can apply those criteria to the primates' language to determine whether or not the apes are catching up with us.

The two most famous "talking" chimpanzees are Washoe, who has been taught to communicate with a limited ASL vocabulary, and Sarah, who has learned to combine plastic symbols in sentence order (Premack, 1971). The claims of primate language acquisition have been challenged on the grounds that (1) the animals have merely learned associations by an operant conditioning process (food reinforcement); (2) their expressions show no syntactical production—for example, no flexible use of phrase structure—but just mimic the word order presented in their training models; (3) their communications are concerned exclusively with their immediate environmental situation, food, and drink; and (4) although they can discriminate between same-different and all-none, they fail on relations between relations (such as, the object called "apple" is different from the object called "banana"). We can add to these challenges the fact that monkey language meets none of the four requisites for human language specified among Hockett's design features.

THE PRELINGUISTIC PERIOD

Sound Perception

The newborn infant enters the world with a perceptual and vocal apparatus that is incapable of articulate speech but genetically programmed to acquire that capability as the central nervous system matures (Menyuk, 1972). There is evidence of this from recent experiments in newborn speech perception. These studies have used the infant's sucking reflex and heart-rate orienting response to indicate categorical perception of speech sounds.

Eimas et al. (1971) found that 2- to 3-month-old infants could distinguish between speech sounds of different categories (that is, different places of articulation). The infants responded to between-category changes (for example, switching from [ba] to [ga]) but not within-category changes ([ba] to [pa]). The infant's ability to process phonetic features gives children a means of segmenting a stream of sounds into discrete units even before they learn that language is made up of such units. A child's natural responses to sounds in the parents' speech reinforce the social bond between them as members of the human species.

The first sounds the infant produces are, of course, cries. After about a month, crying is interspersed with cooing, as the infant develops a vocabulary of signals. At 3 to 6 months of age, babbling enters the repertoire. Now the infant seems to be practicing first speech sounds in a kind of vocal play. Consonant and vowel combinations can be heard in the babbling. At first, the infant's babbling produces almost all of the sounds in human language, including difficult pronunciations from European and Asian languages. As the baby's babbling progresses, the exotic sounds drop out (Jesperson, 1922). Learning theorists attribute this selection process to the reinforcement by the parents' speech, although other theorists, notably McNeill (1970b), say there is no basis for that interpretation.

Sound Production

The babbling speech sounds are *phonemes,* the phonetic elements that compose words. According to McNeill, the infant's babbling goes through a regular sequence of vowel and consonant types, combinations of which eventually merge into meaningful utterances, such as "mama" and "papa" (although not necessarily referring to the proud parents!).

During the babbling period, the infant shows signs of mimicking pitch variations, speech rhythms, and vocal intonations that are imitated from the parents' speech. Brazelton and Young (1964) have identified imitative vocal behavior in infants as young as 9 weeks.

The special problems of blind babies throw some light on the function of early vocal interaction between parent and child. Blind infants engage in no eye contact with caregivers, seldom smile, and present a limited repertoire of signals (hunger, contentment, rage, sleepiness). They show no obvious signs of interest (focusing of eyes on target objects), although Fraiberg (1974) learned that blind children explored objects with their hands while their faces were averted and expressionless. She also found that vocalizing was not initiated by the child, was sparse, and usually occurred in response to the mother's or father's voice. Apparently, the absence of signs of attention, warmth, and interest on the part of the blind child reduced the amount of parental vocalizing which, in turn, reduced infant vocalizing. Lack of visual stimuli, which normally evoke vocalization in sighted infants, further depressed cooing and babbling. Yet, in spite of the sparse vocalizing during the first year, by the end of the year blind children were emitting differential vocalizing and smiling toward their mothers. By the second year, they were at the same level of language competence as sighted babies. Even with restricted resources, the blind child will acquire language (Fraiberg, 1974).

What has been said about the infant's predisposition to discrim-

The babbling of young infants is a form of vocal play in which the infant produces almost all of the speech sounds that occur in human language. (Anna Kaufman Moon, Stock, Boston)

inate and produce speech sounds implies some innate speech mechanisms. But we must restrain our inclination to take that capability as evidence for the innateness of language acquisition processes. The significance of this distinction will emerge in the review of conflicting theories—innateness versus learned behavior—of language acquisition.

THEORIES OF LANGUAGE ACQUISITION

There are three fundamental theories that attempt to explain the process of language acquisition. They are (1) learning theory, formulated in terms of the operant conditioning concepts of Skinner; (2) linguistic theory, as developed principally by Chomsky; and (3) cognitive theory, which is associated with the work of Piaget. These three theories stand as the points of reference for various interpretations that modify and combine their basic concepts.

B. F. Skinner is widely recognized as the "father" of operant conditioning, *Learning Theory* which he has applied, with few modifications, to the process of language acquisition (Skinner, 1957). In essence, operant theory holds that all learning—including that of language—results from the reinforcement of the learner's behaviors. The reinforcement is provided by people in the learner's environment on a continuous or intermittent schedule. Parents reinforce some of the infant's babbling by smiling, patting, or uttering happy sounds. Differential reinforcement by parents of infants' desirable utterances increases the frequency of those utterances and reduces the frequency of unreinforced utterances.

How does the infant "decide" what to utter in the first place? According to learning theory, infant vocalizations are initially part of the child's behavioral repertoire. These vocalizations are then reinforced when parents recognize them as elements of their language. As the child grows up, he or she perceives words and then sentences uttered by adults, imitates them, and continues to be reinforced (usually by understanding responses on the part of adults and peers) for correct usage. In this way, infants acquire a conception of grammatically correct structures.

Skinnerian theory of verbal learning runs into some serious problems. As Chomsky (1959) points out in his critique of it, a language acquisition theory that depends on imitation and observation of adult speech cannot account for the great number of entirely novel sentences produced by children. Skinner's principle of stimulus control states that operant responses in some cases are evoked by certain stimuli (as a ball evokes the response "round"). Chomsky questions the effectiveness of that principle as a learning device on the grounds that there are too many alternative responses possible, and that many responses are expressed in the absence of the relevant stimuli. Clark and Clark (1977) pose a particularly damaging challenge to the reinforcement effect with evidence that parents pay little attention to their children's syntactic errors, offering a minimum of feedback essential for learning through reinforcement.

Reinforcement of children's utterances undoubtedly plays a significant role in language learning, but it fails to account for a number of critical events in the process.

Linguistic Theory

Chomsky (1957) extends the hypothesis of innate speech-processing mechanisms to include the claim that children are born with built-in models of language structure that enable them to determine the rules of syntax of any language to which they are exposed. At the heart of the theory is the concept of linguistic *universals,* the basic syntactic forms that Chomskians claim are common to all languages—for example, sentences composed of noun and verb phrases.

The child's innate sense of syntactic structures equips him to analyze the sentences he hears and to reconstruct the grammar of his native language. This competence enables the child to compose essentially correct (or, at least, acceptable and understandable) sentences that have never been heard before. A system of rules that can produce such an unlimited variety of acceptable sentences is called a *generative grammar.**

The linguistic model comprises a two-level structure: an internal representation of the speaker's intended meaning *(deep structure)* which is transformed into an external utterance *(surface structure)* by means of the innate, syntactic, sentence-forming system (the *grammar*). The internal process constitutes the native speaker's language *competence,* which Chomsky distinguishes from external *performance.* Competence is assumed to be ideal, whereas performance is vulnerable to errors caused by carelessness, distraction, and memory deficiency.

Implicit in the concept of innateness is the notion of *linguistic universals.* Obviously, children are not born with a built-in grammar of their native language, so their fixed, innate, rule-finding mechanism must be capable of deciphering any of the world's profusion of languages.† This mechanism requires a common syntactic basis for all languages; that is, all languages function within certain syntactic constraints. For example, the noun-phrase/verb-phrase combination is universal in all languages. Universal constraints make a statement such as "John will order which sandwich and?" grammatically unacceptable in an inquiry about John's preferences for sandwiches along with, say, coffee. The universal rule tells us that components ("sandwich and") cannot be separated from *coordinate structures* ("sandwich and coffee").

Sharp attacks have been leveled against the innateness hypothesis with its implicated concepts (the competence-performance distinction and linguistic universals). In spite of extensive efforts, linguistic theorists have not yet succeeded in specifying a universal grammar that would apply to even one of the large number of known languages. Nor have they managed to discover more than a few universal linguistic structures,

---

*In psycholinguistics, *grammar* does not refer to terms such as noun, verb, or adjective, but to a rule system that guides speakers in learning the relations and structures of their language.

†The psycholinguists' classic anecdote concerns the British couple who adopted a French infant and then proceeded to study the French language so that they could understand the child when it began to talk.

although the principle of semantic and syntactic universals would presume an abundance of such forms.

Opponents argue that the only meaningful innateness in the human organism is in its biological predisposition to interact with its environment in certain ways (such as subjects acting on objects). Syntactic structures (noun-verb, for example) merely reflect such relations. Hence, the emergence of common syntactic and semantic structures — universals — in all languages. Therefore, opponents conclude, there is no need to postulate an innate grammar.

The development of language competence as a consequence of children's *Cognitive Theory* interaction with the world is the fundamental thesis of cognitive theory, whose principal exponent is Piaget. Although Piagetians disclaim cognitive theory as an explicit theory of language acquisition (Sinclair-de-Zwart, 1969), it does provide the basic ingredients and causal relations for such a theory. Essentially, Piaget sees the child's action experiences as the basis for the development of language skills. The process begins during the sensorimotor period, when objects are represented by the child's actions in playing with them, or by their natural functions. These are the preparatory experiences that provide the form and content for higher concept formation as the child enters later developmental stages.

Imitation plays a key part in the child's learning of new behaviors. Gradually the child delays imitation of observed behaviors for hours or days, a procedure necessary for the development of a facility for abstract representation, the basis for words (Appleton, Clifton, and Goldberg, 1975). The child's acquisition of object permanence during this period is also essential for representational thought.

As the child proceeds into the second — preoperational — stage (at about age 2), he gains skill in symbolic play, representing objects by symbols and breaking away from here-and-now to take in past and future events. The child begins to internalize the symbolic representations of his action schemas, thus engaging in the early stages of reflective thinking. This major step leads to the "progressive freeing of speech" from the action context of the objects and conditions to which it refers. Now language becomes a means of developing "decontextualized knowledge," the process of learning new things by thinking about old ones in new ways (Bruner, 1972).

What we see, then, is the development of the child's cognitive skills through a process of *adaptation* to the environment and *assimilation* of knowledge through symbolic play. Practice with symbols is prerequisite for the stable acquisition of meaning. Since symbolic play (not language) is the source of cognitive development, cognition must precede and provide the substance for, the child's language.

Piaget's cognitive model, like Chomsky's linguistic theory, is incompatible with the fundamental thesis of learning theory — that language is acquired by a process of imitation and reinforcement of word and sentence utterances in situational contexts. Between Piaget and Chomsky there are basic disagreements, yet they share some common ground (Sinclair-de-Zwart, 1969). Both cognitive and linguistic theories agree on language acquisition as a creative, rather than a conditioned, function. Although both theories distinguish between competence and performance, Piaget would stress the possibility that performance may sometimes surpass competence where imitation produces what he calls "pseudo-structures" not yet mastered by the child. Both postulate an internalized grammar as part of an acquisition device.

The main differences between Piaget and Chomsky are these: Linguistic theory assumes the child's innate understanding of language as a system of signs (that is, words) instead of symbols; cognitive theory focuses on the vital function of the child's preverbal, sensorimotor activity, which is given virtually no attention by the Chomskians; and linguistic theory considers language an object of knowledge rather than a result of the child's experience with the symbolic process.

DEVELOPING LANGUAGE COMPETENCE

Whatever theory of language acquisition one adopts, it is clear that a major developmental transition occurs when babies are about a year old. At this age, *sounds* heard and reproduced (babbled) by babies first become words. With this breakthrough, we can begin the study of language acquisition by examining children's verbal productions—their form, content, and progression—as a means of determining how they master their native tongues.

Comprehension-Production Gap

We have already noted that infants as young as 2 months of age perceive speech sounds. Thus, shortly after birth, infants have a rudimentary ability to divide a stream of speech sounds into words. Additionally, children quickly learn to distinguish variations in intonation and to relate them to situational events. By the end of the first year, children respond appropriately to commands like "no," "don't touch that," and "come to Daddy," long before they can produce any words of their own.

Such behavior suggests comprehension. Yet many months can pass before the child produces his or her first word. The gap between comprehension and production presents another problem for learning theory, which says that the child's abilities to comprehend and articulate words should lead directly to their use under the control of the relevant stimuli. The gap may be attributable to inadequate neural maturation.

Children's First Words

In considering the child's first speech productions—words and sentences—we begin by looking at their semantic content (or meaning) and speculating on how the child acquires and refines word meanings. However, the semantics of first words cannot be isolated, for the way children learn word meaning is related to their use of words to express intentions. This involves syntactic relations. So we will have to discuss semantics and grammar together in order to understand how children learn language.

Children's first linguistic utterances are single words. As Fishbein (1976) notes, the average child starts using single words at about 1 year of age and increases his vocabulary to about 50 words over the next 6 to 12 months. There appears to be a logical sequence to the occurrence of certain types of words. Although we might expect children to start with the most familiar words—those addressed to them by their parents—these words are generally not among the first to appear. Instead, first words relate to children's immediate interests and to objects present in their environments: play ("peek-a-boo"), food ("cookie"), toys ("ball"). The objects named first are likely to be those whose function involves action: playthings that children manipulate (rattle, toy animal, ball), and those normally in motion (dog, bird, horse, car). Moving and movable objects are, of course, most likely to engage the child's attention. Sound-producing objects (stereo, TV, radio) also demand notice, with consequent naming. Nelson (1973a) found considerable variation in the rate at which children learn to speak their first 50 words. But she also found that the rate of word acquisition is not related to subsequent rate of language development.

Two types of words comprise the child's early vocabulary: substantive and function words. *Substantive* words include object names, action verbs, and event labels. Bloom (1973) says these words appear, disappear, and reappear in the child's vocabulary with "a high mortality"—presumably since the action schemas have not all been internalized and hence are unstable. This would make their occurrence dependent on immediate situational contexts.

Function words include a variety of designations for direction, request, and inquiry (such as "up," "more," "where?"). Since they relate to common physical functions, they are more stable and remain fixed in the child's vocabulary.

Descriptive words are represented with minimal frequency in the early vocabulary. Adjectives—color names, in particular—refer to the static attributes of objects and, as noted, the child is more attentive to the dynamic properties of action and sound.

While the early naming of objects and actions may be the simple result of imitation and association, by the time children approach the end of the sensorimotor period, they are internalizing their action schemas. This, as Piaget indicates, involves the use of symbols. Words now are not merely labels *on* objects in present context, they are symbols *of* objects in mental representation. The child can use word-symbols (which are then, of course, signs) as representatives of the objects or events in symbolic play—substituting one object for another (a stick becomes a "fish") and acting out imaginary events (the child makes believe she is asleep).

Symbolic play develops what Morehead and Morehead (1974) call "double knowledge"—the association of the word with the function of the object or the conditions under which it is used, separating the word from the object. Thus, the stick can be a "fish" when it floats on the water and a "bird" when it is thrown into the air. One child applied the word "afta" to a drinking glass, the contents of the glass, a pane of glass, and an entire window (Werner, 1948). This suggests a mode of categorical perception that differs from an adult's selection of common features. How does the child acquire the semantic content of words? We will examine three explanations.

How Are Meanings Learned?

Nelson (1974) addressed the question of how semantic content is learned as a problem in determining the child's method of concept formation during the sensorimotor period. In an earlier series of experiments, Ricciuti (1965) determined that 12- to 24-month-old children are capable of rudimentary category recognition—that is, the children can separate A-objects from not-A-objects. Nelson (1973a) then found that *function*, rather than color or form, is a preferred cue for such categorical recognition. On the basis of that hypothesis, she developed a *functional core* model to explain how the child acquires meanings.

The process proceeds in a sequence of steps: (1) The child identifies— but does not necessarily name—a new, whole object, say, a ball. (2) The child identifies significant relationships, primarily functional—mother, brother, or other person throwing, rolling, bouncing the ball, in the house, in the schoolyard. (3) On observing more instances of ball-in-use, the child selects invariant characteristics that define *ball* (rolls, bounces), and places them in the semantic *core* of the object, eventually discarding the irrelevant, specific agent and location attributes. Finally, (4) the child names the object. Nelson's functional core model conforms with Piaget's action-based concept formation. However, Nelson describes the actual process by which the child develops and refines the action schema into a named concept.

Another explanation for concept naming has been proposed by Clark (1973) in the *semantic feature hypothesis*. She defines features in terms of the child's perception of object-attributes, which constitute the meaning of the word that is associated with the object. Thus, the word "bow-wow" will be associated with the feature *four-legged* when the first instance of a dog is observed. The child will generalize the word "bow-wow" by over-extension to other four-legged animals such as cows. He or she will eventually add other perceived features, for example, *barking* and *mooing*, to the list of features that characterize an object. Cows will then be identified separately from dogs and other four-legged animals. Eventually, accretions of specific features will narrow the groups represented by each name until the child's words correspond in meaning to adult usage.

Clark's hypothesis centers on the child's perception of features (or attributes) in contrast to Piaget's principle of hands-on action as the source of meaning-concepts. She is somewhat closer to Nelson, whose model assumes acquisition by perception, but stresses the child's focus on dynamic function (as does Piaget) rather than on static features of form and color. Since some objects (tables, houses) are immobile, their static features (size, form, color) would undoubtedly be perceived by the child. Clark acknowledges that her hypothesis does not provide a model of the semantic core of the word's meaning, as Nelson's does.

A third conception of the way children acquire meaning depends on innate structures and semantic universals. Bierwisch (1967) proposed a *universal primitives hypothesis* that traces the child's learning of meanings to a biological mechanism of perception and cognition. The primitives are not the external physical features but the psychological perceptions of features that are "wired in" to the organism. Bierwisch suggests that our environment is processed by this internal mechanism that selects and translates perceived features into semantic components. For example, our perception of same-different relations is predetermined according to an innate primitive. In other words, we see what we are biologically constructed to see. Such a process implies that the semantic components are universal to all languages. We have no way of testing this hypothesis, which is an extension of Chomsky's theory.

So far we have been considering the child's single words as discrete units with individual meanings. However, when the child uses them in communication, there is evidence that there is more in a word than just a name of an object or action.

When children utter single words, they are usually not just showing off their growing vocabularies. They are making requests, expressing feelings, or calling attention to their observations. As a means of communication, a word is no longer an isolated linguistic element; it becomes a sentence expressing the speaker's intention. Such single-word sentences are called *holophrases.*

Holophrastic Speech

It comes as no surprise to parents to learn that their children take their first verbal steps with complete sentences wrapped up in single words. Mother easily knows that when Junior looks at a slipper on the floor and says "Daddy," he is telling her "That's Daddy's slipper." Not only the child's intent look and the situational context, but his intonation reveal his meaning. If he says "Daddy?" with a rising intonation, in Daddy's absence, she interprets his question as "Where's Daddy?" Holophrastic patterns of intonation, called *frequency contours,* differ characteristically for statements, questions, and exclamations, indicating that the child knows what he wants to say, but is not ready to supply the apparently redundant words.

Clearly, children's one-word sentences involve syntax as well as word meaning. The two are inseparable in speech. Does this mean that the children are working with a grammar in forming their first words? Probably not. Piaget would say that they are merely applying their action schemas to the "expression of a possible action" (1951), and that their internalization of a grammar will develop from these verbal propositions.

The judgment of holophrastic words as equivalent to adult sentences comes down to a question of the child's comprehension of the way linguistic structures represent actual events—a dubious hypothesis. De Laguna (1927) offered this interpretation of holophrastic utterances: Since, as we have seen, the child knows the ways in which objects are used, and by whom, as part of his lexicon of word meanings, he utters the word, which carries its loose bundle of properties, and more often than not, the adult hearer fills in the blanks properly, with the help of contextual and intonational clues. As de Laguna said, "In order to understand what the baby is saying, you must see what the baby is doing."

Thus, we can consider holophrases as rudimentary sentences in which the word, supplemented by the context, conveys the child's meaning. Sometimes the word is the predicate with an obvious subject ("Dolly" = "I hold the dolly"). Sometimes the word is the subject for which the context provides a likely predicate ("Dada!" = Daddy, throw the ball!"). De Laguna refers to this function of holophrastic speech as *predication*.

Telegraphic Speech

Children launch their first two-word utterances when their vocabularies contain about 50 words (at about age 2). These two-word combinations, which soon increase in length, show certain syntactic regularities. At first glance, they resemble telegrams: "Read book," "See cow," Where go?" It seems as though redundant words—prepositions, articles, auxiliary verbs, conjunctions—have been omitted. Appropriately, Brown and Fraser (1963) called it *telegraphic speech*.

However, unlike telegrams, the abbreviated sentences do not leave out just the redundant items with the least information content. English plurals and possessives and past tense endings are dropped, along with main verbs whose meaning must be inferred from situational context. Russian children omit important inflections high in information content (Slobin, 1966). Clearly, something other than mere redundancy determines the omissions. Psycholinguists have tried to find clues to the child's competence at this stage by looking at the syntactic patterns of telegraphic speech.

Syntax in Early Utterances

Pivot-open grammar was proposed by Braine (1963) as a result of his observation of the regularities of position of certain words in two-word utterances. On the basis of a distributional analysis of the speech of three children, Braine divided the words into two main classes: *pivot* and *open*. Pivot words always appear in the same (first or second) position. First-position pivots (P_1) never appear in second position (P_2) and vice versa, nor do pivots appear alone in holophrases. Open-class words appear in either position, with a pivot, with another open-class word, or alone. These are the possible combinations:

$P_1 + O$: see dog
$O + P_2$: dog allgone
$O + O$: nice dog
O : dog

The pivot words are few in number and stable in membership. Pivots generally serve as modifiers ("this," "that," "big," "my"). The open class includes a growing list of names of objects and people, nonpivot verbs, and adjectives. Miller and Ervin (1964) found a similar dichotomy in their studies. They used the terms *operator* (= pivot) and *nonoperator* (= open) to designate their classes.

The prohibited combinations (P; $P_1 + P_2$; $P_2 + P_1$) suggest that the child has a rudimentary grammatical competence which is reflected in what he says. However, the evidence in the actual speech of a number of children denies that the child's grammar has the pivot-open rule structure. In Braine's own study, some of the pivots (for example, "more") violated the never-alone prohibition. Other pivots did not appear exclusively in fixed positions. Bowerman (1973) found in her studies that a number of the pivot-open combinations were restricted. That is, some pivots combined exclusively with certain types of open-class words—for example, pivot locatives ("here") only before open nouns, pivot names only before open verbs.

Perhaps the most telling criticism of pivot grammer was Bloom's (1970) argument that it did not fully represent the child's intentions. Pivot grammar allows no discrimination between different meanings for identical pivot-open combinations. Thus, "*Mommy sock*" can mean either "*Mommy's sock*," "*Mommy puts on sock*," or "*Mommy, give me sock*." Only the context can indicate the child's intention, but, in any event, the pivot-open grammar, lacking case structure, does not represent fully the child's competence. Bloom proposes a Chomskian-type *deep structure*, which is an internal representation of the child's intended meaning. This requires phrase structure rules which break the sentence into noun and verb phrases, permitting representation of subject-object, genitive (that is, possessive), attributive (or adjective), and locative (or place) relations. A reduction transformation boils the full deep-structure meaning down into the telegraphic form. Transformations are performed on deep-structure sentences according to the syntactic rules of the innate grammar postulated by Chomsky. We will see this operation in more detail when we discuss his transformational grammar.

A more elaborate system for representing the child's semantic relations is Fillmore's (1968) *case grammar*. Fillmore adopts Chomsky's concept of innate linguistic structures. His deep structures are *propositions* modified by *modalities* (for example, tense or negation). The propositions are composed of verbs and nouns which fill different *case roles*. The cases are:

- *agentive* (*John* opened the door);
- *instrumental* (The *key* opened the lock);
- *dative* (John told *Mary*);
- *factitive* or *resultant* (John made a *bookcase*);
- *locative* (John is in the *kitchen*);
- *objective* (John opened the *door*).

The cases all relate to verbs, that is, to actions. The cases are universal to all languages. Fillmore's case grammar thus provides a meeting ground for Piaget and Chomsky.

Fillmore's case roles are a collection of semantic relations that give the child the means of representing any intention in a deep-structure proposition that is transformed, according to a set of internal rules, into a surface utterance. For example, "*Sit chair*" is the surface transformation of the verb +locative in the base sentence, "*Sit in the chair.*"

These and other case grammars constitute an approach to the analysis of early speech that is called *rich interpretation,* in contrast to the lean interpretation of pivot-open grammar and learning theory. Rich interpretation credits the child with knowing more than he can express and instinctively using extralinguistic cues (such as gestures and imitative sounds) to complete his meaning. The child's utterances seem to convey relations associated with his activities. His use of agent-action, action-object, recurrence ("*more ball*"), and disappearance ("*allgone ball*") reflect his sensorimotor experiences. Notice how the concept of language universals presents a superficial compatibility with the Piagetian view of action schemas. Both are based on the natural ways that things work in the world, as in Fillmore's case roles. Let us take a closer look at Chomsky's linguistic theory to see the essential difference between the two views of language acquisition.

Transformational Grammar

Chomsky's theory of language acquisition comprises a two-level model that relates the speaker's intended meaning with the overt utterance. At the base, there is the *deep structure,* which consists of *kernel* sentences, usually simple assertions. The kernel sentences are transformed by an internal device, called a *grammar,* which consists of a set of rules that the speaker discovered during his developmental period. His discovery of the rules was made highly efficient by an innate predisposition to distinguish between correct and incorrect sentences that he heard, and to extract the appropriate syntactic rules.

The transformation process is accomplished by means of a set of *rewrite rules* that break the kernel sentences into their constituent noun and verb phrases and the phrases into their component *morphemes*. (Morphemes are the semantic elements that compose words: *play + ing* are two morphemes.) Certain specified operations are then performed on the revised kernel sentences (for example, deletion, inversion, negation), resulting in the *surface structure*—the sentence uttered by the speaker. Here is an example of the process.

1. Kernel sentences: (a) A man is wise. (b) A man is honest.
2. Revised kernels: [A man [man is wise] is honest.]

$$\frac{\overline{NP_1 \quad \underline{NP_2 \quad VP_2} \quad VP_1}}{\dfrac{S_2}{S_1}}$$

   S = sentence; NP = noun phrase; VP = verb phrase;
3. Transformation: Replace NP_2 with *who = A man who is wise is honest.* Delete *who is = A man wise is honest.* Invert *man* and *wise = A wise man is honest.*

The last sentence—*A wise man is honest*—is the surface structure sentence.

How does the child learn to break down the kernel sentences into their revised form, and how does he know which transformation operations to use, and when? What tells him that implicit questions are formed by reversing subject and verb? Chomsky (1957, 1965) answers these questions by postulating a *Language Acquisition Device* (LAD) with an inherent capability for learning any language to which it is exposed. LAD receives a steady flow of utterances that include grammatically correct and incorrect sentences. With a built-in sense of universal semantic and syntactic relations (for example, all sentences include noun and verb phrases), LAD performs a continuous distributional analysis of the sentence input to sort out various acceptable patterns. In this way, LAD acquires a workable set of rewrite and transformation rules. Since these rules constitute a productive, as well as an acquisitive, device, they constitute a *generative grammar*, capable of producing an infinite series of correct, and no incorrect, sentences. That is what is meant by the child's ideal *competence*. The child's *performance*, of course, is often faulty.

The child's ability to understand adult admonitions and instructions before he can utter more than a few simple words, and his use, in novel contexts, of sentences that he has never heard, are cited as evidence of innate linguistic mechanisms. Strong support is also offered by children's errors in word formation. A child will say "hisself," which is consistent in the possessive form with other reflexive pronouns: "myself," "yourself." Why does he attempt to correct the inconsistent form, "himself?" Because the child is not merely learning words and phrases by rote but is engaged in a process of learning and using construction rules. McNeill (1969) argues that all languages must be learnable by all children and must, therefore, be constructed with universal linguistic components that are within the children's capacities. Looked at in this way, children's genetically determined capacities impose universality on the world's languages.

LANGUAGE AND THOUGHT

You might think that language universals would imply similar ways of viewing the world, and indeed, in the early 1900s it was commonly believed that all human beings, regardless of what language each speaks, think in similar ways. In the 1920s, however, Edward Sapir and Benjamin Whorf restated and elaborated an earlier hypothesis that challenged the notion that people think alike with the assertion that people do not even perceive the world in the same way. Instead, the *Sapir-Whorf hypothesis* proposed that both perception and thought are determined by language. The idiosyncrasies of particular languages affect the way people observe and evaluate their environments and experiences.

For example, people who speak European languages (including English) see time as a dimensional entity, somewhat like a ribbon marked off into segments labeled "past," "present," and "future." The Hopi Indians, by contrast, have no words or tenses to indicate periods of time as we do. Our language enables us to think of such concepts as "morning" or "summer" in terms of quantities of time. But the Hopi say "when it is morning" instead of "in the morning" or "summer is only when the weather is hot" instead of "summer is hot" (Carroll, 1956.)

Siklóssy (1976) uses the Sapir-Whorf hypothesis to explain the greater difficulty in learning a second language later in life, when the world representation implicit in our first language has become habituated in our thinking. Children are not handicapped by fixated world views; hence, they readily learn more than one language.

Piaget's *cognitive hypothesis* contradicts the Sapir-Whorf hypothesis by placing thought before language. To Piaget, thinking is just one form of intelligence. Intelligence comes first, in the early stages of the sensorimotor period, when the child can deal only with actions on objects in the here-and-now. As the child internalizes his action schemas, and learns to operate on abstract objects and distant events, he acquires the ability to use symbols separate from their referents (Piaget and Inhelder, 1969.) The child develops concepts of space, time, causality, and object permanence from his sensorimotor experiences. Out of the cognitive concepts come the first words. The Piagetian sequence is thus opposite to the Sapir-Whorf relation.

LANGUAGE DIFFERENCES AND DEFICITS

This chapter has stressed similarities among children in the acquisition of language. There is evidence that the sequence of steps through which children progress in learning language is universal (Piaget and Inhelder, 1969; Slobin, 1973), and the age at which children begin to babble and to speak shows little variation (Lenneberg, 1969). But there are some differences, caused by inconsistencies in the treatment of children of different sexes and by variations in environmental factors.

Sex differences have been found in infants' earliest vocalizations. Zelazo *Sex Differences*
(1967, 1969) found that 3-month-old-girls vocalize more to male experimenters than to female experimenters; male infants showed no significant differences in this behavior. Earlier development of girls may explain this discrepancy.

Parent-infant verbal interactions play an important part in the speed of language acquisition. Cherry and Lewis (1976) found that mothers talked with their 2-year-old daughters more than with their sons; the mothers encouraged verbalization from their daughters more than from their sons. Mothers maintained conversation by asking and answering questions and by repeating the child's utterances. Cherry and Lewis conclude that "mothers of girls are providing a richer language environment compared with mothers of boys." Since the evidence is correlational, it is difficult to rule out the possibility that girls provide their mothers more responsive language partners.

Drawing conclusions about the effects of parent-child vocalizing interactions on the rate of language acquisition is a risky exercise in view of the observation by Lenneberg (1967) and other neuropsychologists that girls' brains mature earlier, particularly in the lateralization of speech function in the dominant hemisphere. This earlier cortical development could certainly expedite vocalization and the rate of language acquisition.

Since the child learns a language by attending to its use by people around *Environmental* him, we are interested in the effects of variations in the environment on *Differences* language acquisition. In the situation of extreme deprivation—where the child neither hears nor sees any language—he will acquire none. Hewes (1976) reported the case of a 13 ½-year-old girl who had been confined without communication up to that age. She was completely "languageless." The potential for language is not enough to assure its development in the absence of language in the environment. Given some speech in the

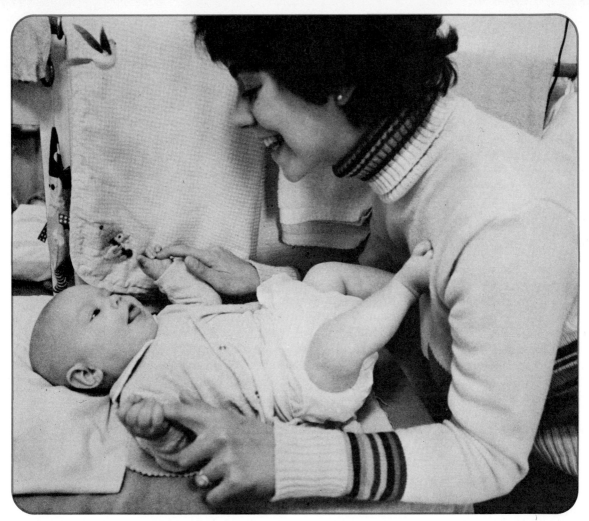

Verbal interactions between parents and children may affect the speed of language acquisition. (Suzanne Arms, Jeroboam)

environment, is there a correlation between its quantity or quality and the child's language development?

The parent is the child's principal source of language modeling and interaction. Bell and Ainsworth (1972) found that when mothers responded more promptly to their infants' crying and other vocal signals, the children soon directed the signal to other uses. Prompt response to cries of hunger led to early generalization of the signal to other needs, a first step toward extended use of signals for a variety of specific purposes.

Children of deaf parents learn to speak in a somewhat impoverished environment with respect to vocal interactions. In infancy, such children make the same amount of noise and go through the same cooing sequence as do children of hearing parents. But babies of deaf parents do not vocalize in response to their parents' speech as babies of hearing parents do. However, Lenneberg (1969) found that both groups of children proceeded through the early vocalization and later verbal stages in the same sequence and at about the same pace. In fact, children of deaf parents readily learn two languages simultaneously, vocal and sign (ASL).

As the child matures through successive stages of language development, environmental effects are so complex that psychologists and educators are sometimes misled in deriving conclusions from the evidence. For example, in 1961 Bernstein presented an analysis of language style differences among lower- and middle-class British families. As a result of more subtle and rational verbalization by middle-class, in contrast with lower-class, parents (for example, "Please be quite so I can hear the radio," instead of "Shut up!"), middle-class children learned a more sophisticated code suitable for intricate verbal communication and complex intellectual activity. The lower-class child's code was restricted and less suited to abstraction of thought. However, other studies did not support Bernstein's thesis. Templin (1957) detected no significant differences in the complexity of sentences (the use of subordinate clauses, for example) between lower-class and middle-class children.

Robinson (1965) attempted to relate the lower-class child's restricted code to social situations among the child's peers although the elaborate code is available for formal situations such as school. The lower-class children's letters written to a friend (social) showed the restricted code, whereas letters to a school official (formal) showed no interclass differences.

One of the most impressive demonstrations of the nature of language differences arising from differing environments was presented by Labov, Cohen, Robins, and Lewis (1968). They showed that black speech, generally viewed as the result of social-class deprivation, corresponds with standard English in the systematic pattern of its grammatical structures. For example, they noted regularity in black and white children's treatment of copulas (forms of *to be*) with noun phrases and pronouns. The extensive, side-by-side comparison of black speech and standard English revealed the former as a formal language governed by rules—a distinctive language rather than an impoverished or illogical jargon.

Black speech is an example of a cultural difference, although the black culture shares most of its customs with its surrounding white culture. Do differences between widely separated cultures pose special problems for children's language acquisition? Slobin (1973) has compiled data on acquisition patterns for more than 40 different languages. He found that "the rate and order of development of the semantic notions expressed by language are fairly constant across languages, regardless of the formal means of expression employed" (p. 187). In other words, Chinese and Latvian children progress through the same preverbal and linguistic stages at approximately the same ages as children who speak English or Japanese. This, of course, is not surprising, whether we subscribe to the Chomsky-McNeill theory of linguistic universals or to Piaget's hypothesis of cognitive primacy in language development.

It would appear, then, that differences in environment may retard language acquisition where gross deprivation exists — for example, absence of language, cognitive deficits due to genetic or nutritional factors, traumatic influences on maturation. However, when the child is exposed to even a restricted language environment, he or she will make the most of the available materials to serve the natural impulse to acquire speech.

SUMMARY

The ability to think and to communicate in language is the major distinguishing feature between human beings and other animals. What accounts for this unique human capability has been the subject of a great deal of speculation. As a result of investigations by psycholinguists, who consider language acquisition and use as a psychological phenomenon, and by neuropsychologists, who study the anatomical structures and neurological processes involved in language, some of the controversy is being cleared up.

An understanding of language must begin with an understanding of the distinction between language and communication. Human language is only one form of communication, and communication is only one function of language. Nonverbal signals are also forms of communication. And language is used to regulate behavior as well as to communicate. Language is made up of *signals, symbols,* and *signs.*

Researchers studying the biological structures and processes relating to the production of speech have developed a motor theory of speech, which states that the ability to articulate phonemes is unique to the human vocal tract and is a necessary skill for comprehending as well as producing speech. Other researchers, however, believe that the vocal tracts of some primates could produce understandable phonemes, and they claim that these primates are unable to do so because of a lack in the central nervous system.

If speech has biological foundations, then there should be some relation between the development of language competence and physiological maturation. Lenneberg has demonstrated that speech development parallels motor development and that speech presents all the characteristics of maturationally controlled behavior. He has proposed a *critical age hypothesis* that sets approximate age boundaries for language acquisition.

Studies relating to the biological components of speech have raised questions about whether nonhuman primates can match human capability for language acquisition. Success in teaching chimpanzees American Sign Language and other symbolic systems of communication have provoked controversy about what exactly language is. Hockett identified design features that qualify human language; primate language meets none of Hockett's criteria.

The newborn comes into the world genetically programmed to acquire speech capability as the central nervous system matures. The first sounds the infant produces are cries. After about a month, crying is interspersed with cooing, and then babbling enters the repertoire. The babbling sounds are actually phonemes, combinations of which eventually merge into meaningful utterances.

There are three fundamental theories that explain the language acquisition process: (1) The learning theory formulated by Skinner states that infant vocalizations are part of the child's natural repertoire and are reinforced when parents recognize them as elements of language—operant conditioning applied to language acquisition. (2) The linguistic theory developed by Chomsky claims that children are born with built-in models of language structure—*linguistic universals*—that enable them to determine the rules of syntax of any language to which they are exposed. The linguistic model is made up of two levels: an internal representation of the speaker's intended meaning (the native speaker's language *competence*) that is transformed into an external utterance (external *performance*) by means of the innate, syntactic, sentence-forming system (the *grammar*). (3) The cognitive theory associated with Piaget explains the development of language competence as a consequence of children's interaction with the world. Piaget believes that cognitive development must precede and provide the substance for language development and that cognitive skills develop through a process of adaptation to the environment and assimilation of knowledge through symbolic play.

Whatever theory of language acquisition one ascribes to, it is clear that at about the age of 1 year, the sounds babies hear and reproduce first become words. But even before children produce their first words, they are able to distinguish variations in intonation and to relate them to events. In other words, they can respond to commands long before they can produce words of their own.

Children's first linguistic utterances are single words. Two types of words comprise the early vocabulary: *substantive,* including names, action verbs, and event labels; and *function,* including a variety of designations for direction, request, and inquiry. Although the early naming of objects and actions may be the result of imitation and association, by the end of the sensorimotor period words become more than mere labels on objects in present context; they become symbols of objects in mental representation.

There are three basic explanations of how children learn the semantic content or meaning of words. Nelson's *functional core model* says that children acquire meaning in a sequence of steps: (1) identifying but not naming a new, whole object; (2) identifying significant relationships, primarily functional, that have to do with the object; (3) after observing more instances of the object in use, placing them in the semantic core of the object and eventually discarding the irrelevant, specific attributes; (4) naming the object. Clark's *semantic feature hypothesis* states that children's perceptions of object-attributes constitute the meaning of the word that is associated with the object. Eventually, additions of specific features will narrow the groups represented by each name until children's words correspond in meaning to adult usage. Bierwisch's *universal primitives hypothesis* traces children's learning of meanings to a biological mechanism of perception and cognition that determines how the environment is processed and selects and translates perceived features into semantic components. This hypothesis implies that semantic components are universal to all languages.

To children, a single word is not an isolated linguistic element but usually represents a sentence expressing the speaker's intention. Such single-word sentences are called *holophrases*—rudimentary sentences in which the word, supplemented by the context, conveys meaning.

Children make their first two-word utterances when their vocabulary contains about 50 words. Their two-word combinations resemble telegrams and thus have been called *telegraphic speech.* To understand the omissions in telegraphic speech, psycholinguists look at syntactic patterns. Braine's *pivot-open grammar* divides words into two main classes: pivot words that always appear in the same position; and open words that appear in either position. Evidence from the actual speech of a number of children, however, denies that children's grammar follows the pivot-open structure rule. Fillmore's *case grammar* adopts Chomsky's concept of innate linguistic structures. According to Fillmore, children's *deep structures* (internal representations of intended meaning) are *propositions* composed of verbs and nouns that fill different *case roles.* The case roles are a collection of semantic relations that give children the means of transforming any intention in a deep-structure proposition into a set of internal rules. This and other case grammars constitute the *rich interpretation* approach to an analysis of early speech that credits children with knowing more than they can express and instinctively using extralinguistic cues to complete their meaning.

Chomsky's *tranformational grammar* theory of language acquisition begins with deep structures that consist of *kernel* sentences, which are transformed into overt utterances by an internal device, called a *grammar* and consisting of a set of rules discovered by the speaker during the developmental period. The transformation process is accomplished by means of a set of *rewrite rules* that break down the kernel sentences into their noun and verb phrases and these phrases into their component *morphemes.* These are then revised by certain specified operations and result in the *surface structure*—the sentence uttered by the speaker. Children learn to break down kernel sentences as a result of a *Language Acquisition Device*

(LAD)—an inherent capability for learning any language—that performs a continuous analysis of all sentence inputs and sorts out various acceptable patterns. The child thus acquires a workable set of rewrite and transformation rules. These rules are productive as well as acquisitive and, therefore, constitute a *generative grammar* capable of producing an infinite series of correct sentences. Children's performance, however, is never as perfect as their ideal competence.

McNeill claims that since all languages are learnable by all children, they must be constructed with universal linguistic components. This does not necessarily mean that all human beings have similar ways of viewing the world. The *Sapir-Whorf hypothesis* proposes that both perception and thought are determined by language and that the peculiarities of particular languages affect the way people observe and evaluate their environments and experiences. Piaget's *cognitive hypothesis* contradicts the Sapir-Whorf hypothesis by placing thought before language.

Although there are many similarities among children in the acquisition of language, there are some differences caused by inconsistencies in the treatment of children of different sexes and by variations in environmental factors.

CHAPTER 7

Social Development: The Baby as Social Partner

AFFECTIONAL SYSTEMS

Social development, the subject of this chapter, refers to how children deal with social experiences—how they accommodate to such experiences, how they control them, how they feel about them. We will consider the people who make up the baby's social world—adults (friends and strangers) and peers. We will also examine the behaviors that infants use to mediate social interaction.

Social development begins with the relationship between caregiver* and infant, a relationship that has been characterized by those who study it as a *system*. The concept of system has become a central theme of contemporary research in child development. The concept has been especially useful in describing the infant's development of social ties with significant others—parents, relatives, baby-sitters, or peers. In large measure, the baby's social development revolves around interpersonal exchanges with parents and other adult caregivers, although as we will discuss later in the chapter, recent research suggests that peers may become important

*We prefer to use the term *caregiver* in place of *mother* because it includes other adults who may provide most or all of an infant's care and who are relatively stable figures in the baby's world. We do defer to customary language usage in considering caregiver a feminine noun, although we applaud and heartily support—even urge—the participation of men in child-care activities.

INFANT → MOTHER	MOTHER → INFANT
The infant-mother affectional system proceeds through a definite sequence of stages:	The maternal affection system goes through three basic stages:

INFANT → MOTHER	MOTHER → INFANT
1. *Reflex.* The first stage is a brief one. The infant's reflexes serve to guarantee survival by bringing it into contact with the mother's body and the source of nourishment. Reflex behaviors include hand and foot grasping, rooting, sucking, and visual tracking of the mother.	1. *Maternal attachment and protection.* The first stage is characterized by total acceptance of the infant; it serves the interrelated functions of providing for the baby's nutritional and other needs, giving it intimate physical contact, and protecting it from external threats.
2. *Comfort and attachment.* The affectional bond between the baby and the mother is not formed until the second stage, when the infant's responses have become voluntary or semivoluntary. During this stage, the infant develops a feeling of safety in the presence of the mother.	2. *Ambivalence.* During this transitional stage, the mother gradually allows the infant to explore more of its environment; she also begins to discipline the baby, though not brutally. This helps reduce the infant's dependence on the mother, in preparation for the next stage.
3. *Security.* The sense of security developed during the attachment stage allows the baby to leave the mother for brief periods to explore its surroundings, returning every once in a while to "touch base." A significant outgrowth of this stage is the self-assurance it provides, which is a prerequisite for the stage that follows.	3. *Maternal separation or rejection.* The third stage may arrive quite suddenly in some monkey species, in which the mother will give all her attention to a new baby and reject the older child. In other species, however—and in humans—the young maintain a close relationship to the mother for many years.
4. *Separation.* In this stage, relationships with age-mates or peers gain in importance; the mother ceases to be the dominant influence in the child's life.	

Source: Harlow and Harlow, 1966.

TABLE 7–1
Stages of Development in Affectional Systems of Mother and Infant Monkeys

to babies at an early age. An *affectional system* is a reciprocal relationship between two persons, marked by strong feelings and mutual caring. In two-person systems, *bidirectionality* is an important issue. Each person contributes to a social exchange: The baby cries, the adult approaches, the baby quiets, the adult vocalizes, the baby looks into the adult's eyes, and the adult smiles. The baby expresses emotion by smiling, laughing, and crying. Sometimes it is the baby who initiates an encounter, and sometimes it is the adult. Either one might terminate it. The behavior of one person influences the behavior of the other, although sometimes the influence of one person may be more pronounced than the influence of the other.

Much of the research on affectional systems has been based on observations of the behavior of various lower primate species. Though the young of these species mature much more rapidly than human young, there are similarities between the developmental stages through which each species passes (Harlow and Harlow, 1966). Harlow and his colleagues have studied the development of affectional systems in infant monkeys. The researchers observed mothers and infants in normal laboratory situations. They also created artificial situations in which infant monkeys were separated from their mothers and reared in isolation. Infants reared in isolation were maladaptive in their social behavior as adults. The Harlows's observations suggested that the infant monkey's attachment to others goes through a sequence of stages, as does the mother monkey's attachment to the infant. These stages are described in Table 7—1. Because monkeys have simpler social systems and because researchers can experimentally create good and bad social environments for the monkeys, the development of stages in affectional systems is more clearly identifiable in monkeys than in humans. Yet, the Harlows's research with

Infant-caregiver affectional systems are bidirectional: The behavior of one person influences the behavior of the other.
(Marlis Müller)

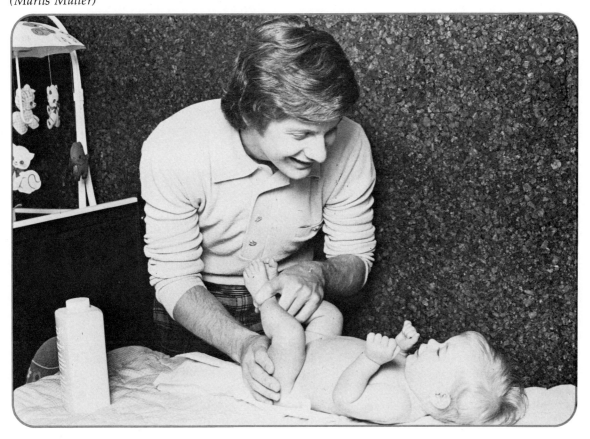

monkeys provides us with a useful model against which to view the development of affectional systems in humans. The important point that comes out of that research is that *each* member of a reciprocal system develops, but the development of one is always in relation to the development of the other.

The preceding discussion illustrates the bidirectional nature of affectional systems. Caregiving makes the infant feel comfortable; the infant smiles; the adult responds with enthusiasm. The recent emphasis in developmental research on the bidirectional nature of adult-child interactions leads to a concern with the question of "fit." Research has shown that as infants develop, they elicit different and unique responses from caregivers. Over the course of a study of mother-infant interactions, Sander (1969) observed:

[*we had*] *the impression that we were watching a sequence of adaptations, common to all the different mother-infant pairs, although acted out somewhat differently by each. Each advancing level of activity which the child became capable of manifesting demanded a new adjustment in the mother-child relationship. . . . (p. 191)*

Through a process of mutual modification, the infant and the caregiver "negotiate" the developmental issue confronting them — say, learning the difference between night and day or learning how to use a spoon. The result is a fit between a particular child and a particular home and family. In this chapter, we use the term *interaction* to refer to what infants and caregivers do when they are together. The term *transaction* refers to the process of social modification in the behavior, feelings, and understanding of those who participate in the exchange.

The influence of babies on adults may be as important as that of adults on babies. This is a subject that has been neglected until recently. Yet one can easily appreciate the survival value of the infant's effect on its parents. Prolonged eye contact and exchange of smiles lead parents to feel that their babies "know" them. At that point, the infant emerges as a member of the human community and as an active participant in social transactions. During this early interchange, the caregiver may develop an enduring attachment to the baby. In fact, Lorenz (1943) has suggested that "babyishness" itself — the physical appearance of the infant — has an effect on the adult. Cann (1953) conducted a study in which adults were shown Lorenz's pairs of pictures like those in Figure 7–1. Each pair consisted of a baby and an adult of the same species. Responses to the pictures showed that adults tended to prefer the "babyish" ones. It appears, therefore, that babyish-

FIGURE 7–1
Comparison of features of infant and adult forms of four different species. The infant features tend to release protective responses in adults, whereas the adult forms do not. (Lorenz, 1943)

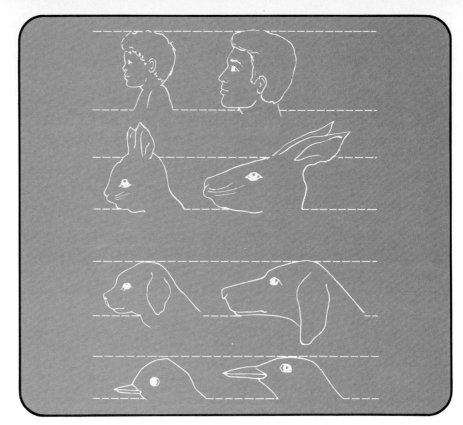

ness serves as a "releaser" of protectiveness in the adult—a response that is independent of social custom.

In addition to a babyish appearance, the infant's helplessness may induce adult protectiveness, and of course the crying or fussing of the baby has a significant effect in getting adult attention. The distinctive feature of crying is that it is one of the few infant behaviors not welcomed by adults. The sound of an infant's cry arouses strong feelings in the caregiver. The reaction usually takes the form of a variety of efforts to stop the crying (and to reduce the likelihood that it will occur again): holding the baby, talking to it, giving it a pacifier, rocking it. Korner (1974) has studied the effects of these various efforts. Her tests show that holding a young baby to the shoulder has the greatest soothing effect, whereas talking to it has the least effect. (It should be noted, however, that the infant's crying *can* exceed the adult's tolerance limits, sometimes causing the caregiving system to break down.) In addition, the infant stimulates the adult to respond to it on a social level. The baby accomplishes this in several ways, of which smiling is the most effective. Bowlby (1957) hypothesized that smiling, like babyishness, makes the infant more appealing and thus increases its chances of survival.

195

SMILING

The baby's smile is one of its first social acts, an evoker of positive social responses from others. Like the affectional system itself, the infant's smile goes through several phases (Bowlby, 1969; Sroufe and Waters, 1976). The first phase, which lasts from birth to about 5 weeks of age, is one of *spontaneous smiling*. The smiles of this period are brief grimaces of the mouth, correlated with fluctuations in the activity of the central nervous system. These smiles are not accompanied by crinkling of the muscles around the eyes, which characterizes later, social smiling. Early smiles may be spontaneous, occurring in the absence of any external stimulation, most commonly during sleep. Or they may be elicited by stroking the infant's cheek or stomach or by various sounds, especially that of a human voice (Wolff, 1963). Because these early smiles occur in response to a wide variety of stimuli, they are not considered truly "social."

The second phase of smiling, beginning during the fifth week of life and extending through the fourteenth week, starts with *unselective social smiling* and changes to *selective social smiling*. During this period, the number of stimuli that elicit a smile narrows considerably. The most effective smile-producing stimuli at this point are human voices and faces —although the baby does not yet distinguish those of particular individuals. Wolff (1963) observed that smiling babies in the second phase are alert and bright-eyed. The smiles themselves are broader than before and are accompanied by a crinkling of the skin around the eyes, but they do not last long. By about the fifth week, the baby begins to smile at a moving face, and by 8 weeks the baby begins to smile consistently at a stationary face. This development marks the beginning of a period of *selective social smiling*, in which babies will smile just as readily at strangers as they will at caregivers (although they may smile a bit more generously at familiar faces). Yet, from 6 weeks to about 6 months, infants smile at familiar and at strange faces, as well as at painted masks.

The baby becomes increasingly able to process stimulus content, to recognize familiar faces and other events. Finally, at the age of 6 to 7 months, *differential social responsiveness* begins. In this final phase in the development of smiling behavior, the infant smiles differently in response to different individuals. The baby will smile freely at familiar people, but will greet strangers with some wariness (Bowlby, 1969).

In order for the first truly social smile to occur, infants must have reached a certain level of development. They must have acquired fixation of glance, be able to follow a moving object with their eyes, and be able to examine the internal features of an object. When they can do these things, they can observe human faces and look into the eyes of another person. It is true that the infant has already "smiled" many times. But these smiles were fleeting ones, based on stimulation and lacking social meaning. The first true smile is dramatically different, and the caregiver's

Smiling in response to the human face may be a biologically determined act that increases the infant's attractiveness to adults. (Jon Rawle, Stock, Boston)

response is equally dramatic. Wolff (1963) reports that within several days after social smiling begins, caregivers recognize the change and make such comments as "Now the baby is fun to play with," or "Now the baby can see me." Suddenly at that point caregivers spend more time playing with the baby. In short, the infant has made its first social conquest.

For many years it was believed that the infant's smile was a learned behavior—a conditioned response to the caregiver's face—and that it was associated with feeding and attention to the infant's other needs. However, several studies suggest that the tendency to smile in response to a human face may be biologically determined (Bowlby, 1957, 1958; Wolff, 1963). Extensive research carried out in the last 10 years has provided some explanation of the process by which infants learn to recognize and respond to the human face.

The Infant's Response to the Face

Earlier in the chapter we discussed babyishness as a releaser of protective impulses in adults. Similarly, it appears that the human face attracts the baby's attention and serves as a releaser of the smiling response. Social smiling is a specific response to the human face or voice. Initially the eyes alone will elicit a smile, but as the infant grows older the stimulus must resemble a complete face (and not a profile) more and more closely if it is to elicit a true smile (Vine, 1973; Zelazo and Komer, 1971).

197

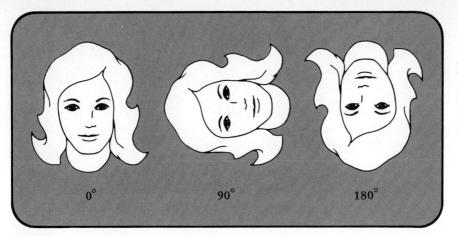

FIGURE 7–2
*Illustration of 0°,
90°, and 180° facial
orientations.*
(Watson, 1972, p. 325)

There is some evidence that infants gradually begin to discriminate emotions revealed by facial expression. By 4 months of age, infants look longer at a joyful expression than at an angry or a neutral one (LaBarbera, Izard, Vietze, and Parisi, 1976).

Watson (1972) studied infants' smiling in response to the human face as a process of operant conditioning. He hypothesized that the infant gradually becomes aware that certain responses of caregivers are contingent on his own actions. For example, caregivers may make sounds after the baby has made a sound, or they may tickle him when he moves his legs. Watson calls such interactions "The Game." In order to discover what effect facial orientation would have on "The Game," Watson conducted an experiment in which infants were shown faces in the three orientations pictured in Figure 7–2. He found that during the third and fourth months, the baby smiles vigorously only in response to faces in the 0° orientation (1966). Watson interpreted these results as indicating that the baby, through experience, associates the 0° orientation with social interaction and responds accordingly. This interaction is a variant of "The Game," in which the infant becomes aware that he or she can win a response from the caregiver by smiling at her while she is in the 0° orientation. In other words, Watson believes that the 0° facial alignment is the "marker" of a special situation.

In another experiment (Kagan, Henker, Hen-Tov, Levine, and Lewis, 1966), 4-month-old infants were shown four different three-dimensional faces: a regular face; one in which the features were rearranged; one with no eyes; and one without any features. All were in 0° alignment. The investigators found that the regular face elicited much more smiling behavior than the other three faces. For example, smiling responses to the regular face were three times as numerous as comparable responses to the scrambled face. These results indicate that recognition of or familiarity with facial patterns are a factor in eliciting the infant's smile.

The experiments just described seem to indicate that a variety of factors contribute to the development of the infant's response to faces. Some investigators believe that the eyes and the face are special kinds of configurations that innately elicit smiling (Spitz and Wolf, 1946). The sequence in which the infant scans the face, fixates the eyes, and within a few seconds smiles seems to support the idea of an innate releasing mechanism. Other investigators offer a more cognitive explanation (Kagan, 1971; Sroufe and Waters, 1976). Their position holds that with repeated experience, the infant forms mental images (or schemas) of events such as faces. When a face enters the infant's visual field, he examines it and tries to associate it with already formed schemas. That is, he tries to recognize the new event. The activity of recognition involves uncertainty that produces a certain amount of tension. Recognition is followed by release of tension, and smiling is an expression of that tension release. Smiling, then, reflects the infant's sense of accomplishment or mastery in social as well as nonsocial situations.

Smiling can also be seen as a distinctively social response. Investigators, like Watson, who hold this view emphasize the social implications of smiling rather than the general mechanisms responsible for it. Babies are more likely to smile when they are with others than when they are alone. And smiling encourages friendly approaches and sustained attention from others (Bowlby, 1969; Vine, 1973). During the infancy period, smiling increasingly becomes a behavior with which the infant can exert control over the social environment.

Each viewpoint has something to contribute to the story of smiling. The infant's response to the configuration of the human face may be adaptive and contribute to the infant's survival. Cognitive-affective mechanisms may account for the relation between perceived events and the smiling response. With age, the infant can anticipate the response of others and thus gains control over his role as a social reinforcer. Soon the baby comes to master the situations in which smiling is a desirable and useful form of social behavior.

LAUGHTER

When people play games with babies, much of the fun is in making them laugh. Laughter appears at about the fourth month of life. Little research has been done on this subject, though as Sroufe and Wunsch (1972) point out, "Laughter may provide a rich source of information concerning cognitive and emotional development in infancy" (p. 339). Sroufe and Wunsch conducted a series of studies of the development of laughter in infants in the first year of life. The studies utilized both longitudinal and cross-sectional designs. Sroufe and Wunsch hypothesized that "laughter would result from contact with the unexpected, the incongruous, the familiar yet unfamiliar" (1972, pp. 339–340). This assumption is related to White's concept of effectance motivation—the notion that children are aroused by novelty, by stimuli that are neither strange enough to be frightening nor familiar enough to be boring. White proposes that "children most enjoy that which lies at the growing edge of their capacities" (1959, p. 335), and Sroufe and Wunsch suggest that the development of laughter might provide an index of the infant's cognitive development. Accordingly, amount of laughter should be expected to increase with age.

Sroufe and Wunsch devised a number of stimulus situations that might elicit laughter in infants. The stimuli represented four categories: auditory, tactile, social, and visual (though all of the items might be considered somewhat social, since in each case the mother did something in the baby's presence). The auditory category included items such as "lip popping" and "boom, boom, boom"; the tactile category included "kissing stomach" and "coochy-coo"; the social category consisted of gamelike items such as "gonna get you" and "peek-a-boo"; and the visual category included items such as "disappearing object" and "shaking hair." The investigators hypothesized that visual and social items would make more sophisticated cognitive demands upon infants than would tactile and auditory items. Accordingly, visual and social stimuli should become more potent at eliciting laughter as infants grow older.

In fact, Sroufe and Wunsch found, in both the cross-sectional and the longitudinal portions of the study, that the amount of laughter did increase with age and that there were developmental trends with respect

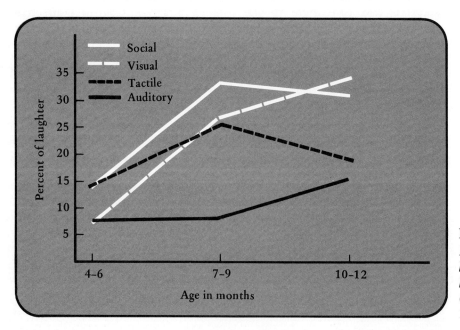

FIGURE 7–3
Percentage of laughter in the longitudinal study (Sroufe and Wunsch, 1972)

TABLE 7–2

Percentage of Laughter by Item in Cross-Sectional Study

	AGE IN MONTHS		
ITEM	4–6	7–9	10–12
Auditory			
Lip popping	12	25	14
Aaah	17	46	32
Boom, boom, boom	12	21	23
Whispering	12	25	18
Squeaky voice	4	38	32
Tactile			
Blowing hair	8	17	9
Kissing stomach	29	83	54
Coochy-coo	8	46	41
Bouncing on knee	12	46	9
Jiggling over head	25	75	86
Social			
Playing tug	4	42	45
Cloth in mouth	4	25	59
Gonna get you	21	54	82
Covering baby's face	12	42	36
Peek-a-boo	12	62	82
Chasing, crawling after	4	38	68
Visual			
Covered face	4	25	54
Disappearing object	4	25	32
Sucking baby bottle	4	17	36
Crawling on floor	4	21	36
Walking funny	4	33	54
Shaking hair	21	54	86
Holding in air	8	42	68
Total	10	37	43

Source: Sroufe and Wunsch, 1972, Table 7–1, p. 341.

to the type of stimulus that evoked laughter. Table 7–2 records the percentage of laughter elicited by each item in the cross-sectional portion of the study. The amount of laughter, averaged across the four item categories, increased from 10% for infants 4 to 6 months of age, to 37% for 7- to 9-month-olds, to 43% for the 10- to 12-month-old group. Figure 7–3 shows the percentage of laughter in the longitudinal study. At 4-6 months, social and tactile stimuli evoked more laughter than visual or auditory stimuli. From 7 to 9 months, although social stimuli were still the most effective items, visual items were slightly ahead of tactile ones. The effectiveness of visual stimuli continued to rise until at 10–12 months they led all other types of stimuli.

Sroufe and Wunsch settled on a functional interpretation of the significance of infant laughter. They suggested that tension results when an incongruous event occurs that is appropriate to the infant's cognitive level but that does not match developing cognitive schema. Laughter discharges the tension. The investigators observed that "laughter builds from smiling responses on initial trials and fades again to smiling on later trials" (p. 350). They suggested that infants laugh when the tension between existing schema and incongruity has reached its peak. The discharge of tension by laughing allows the infant to continue to consider and to process the incongruity. Smiling on later trials may indicate that the infant has processed the incongruity of the stimulus (Sroufe and Wunsch, 1972).

The infant's crying, cooing, smiling, and laughing play crucial but varying roles in initiating and maintaining interaction between the infant and the caregiver. Some interactions involve basic care, whereas others may be considered purely social. At first, of course, most infant-caregiver interaction centers around caring for the baby's needs. But social interaction appears early in the baby's life and strong affectional relationships — called *attachments* — develop toward the end of the first year of life.

ATTACHMENT

The term *attachment* refers to the affectional bond between the child and a particular individual. The development of an attachment assumes the existence of at least one stable, long-term relationship between the child and another person. Children show attachment behavior by clinging, by asking to be picked up, by following, and by crying when left — generally, by seeking and maintaining proximity to another person.

As we have said, most children form their first attachments before they are a year old. The child's first attachment circle almost invariably includes the primary caregiver — usually the mother — but it can include others as well.

Schaffer and Emerson (1964a) have proposed a sequence of three stages in the development of attachment. The first is an asocial stage in which infants seek contact with various parts of their environment. Eventually they realize the significance of humans as a special part of the environment, and they make efforts to be with or near other humans. This development marks the beginning of the second stage of attachment. During the second stage, babies protest separation from *any* individual. They appear concerned over loss of proximity to a human being, although they have not yet narrowed their attachment to specific individuals.

The third stage, attachment to particular individuals, appears between

*Most children
form attachments
by the time they
are a year old;
a child's first
attachment is
usually to his
or her mother.
(Camilla Smith)*

6 and 9 months of age and becomes more pronounced in the next few months. Attachment behavior is accompanied by strong feelings. When the caregiver appears, the infant greets her with joy; her disappearance will create sorrow and probably anger. At this age, children often become intensely upset when separated from attachment figures as, for instance, when left with a baby-sitter or at a child-care center. Many infants begin to show wariness or uneasiness toward strangers by 8 months of age (Bronson, 1972). Apprehensiveness increases between 8 and 12 months of age, especially if the baby is confronted with a stranger who initiates contact without giving the baby a chance to "warm up" (Greenberg, Hillman, and Grice, 1973; Morgan and Ricciutti, 1969). In some cases, this distress diminishes during the second year. In others, however, it may persist until the child is 3 or even 4 years old. By this time, the child will have developed a complex set of attachments to other people, as well.

Until recently, the father was not considered an important figure in the infant's early attachment circle. At best, he was viewed as an occasional mother-substitute. Since infants spend most of their time with their mothers, investigators had assumed that a baby's strongest attachment is to its mother. But as Lamb (1975) points out, "the opportunity for brief yet highly emotionally charged interaction with the father each evening may offset the longer hours spent with a harassed and dissatisfied mother during the day" (p. 249).

One study recently tested the strength of the infant's attachment to its father. Kotelchuck, Zelazo, Kagan, and Spelke (1975) devised an experiment in which a child was placed in the center of a playroom with toys; the infant's parents and various strangers entered and left the room as instructed by the experimenter. The child was left alone with one or two adults in all possible combinations of parent and stranger: two parents; one parent and one stranger; two strangers. The infants' responses to these combinations showed that they were disturbed by being left alone with a stranger in an unfamiliar room, but were comforted by the presence of either parent. Moreover, the departure of either parent would elicit protest, whereas the departure of the stranger would not. The investigators found that over 70% of the children were responsive to their father's presence (Kotelchuck et al., 1975). Similarly, a longitudinal study of 60 Scottish infants revealed that at first 65% of the infants were attached only to their mothers, but by the time they were 18 months old, 79% were attached to their fathers as well (Schaffer and Emerson, 1964a). Thus, attachment is not necessarily an exclusive relationship with the mother. In cases in which the infant becomes attached to someone other than the mother, the attachment figure is likely to be someone who tends to respond to the infant frequently and promptly, who plays with the baby, and who gives comfort when the baby is distressed (Schaffer and Emerson, 1964a; Schaffer, 1971; Stayton and Ainsworth, 1973).

In the initial steps of the development of attachment behavior, the infant must learn to distinguish between itself and its environment, between people and inanimate objects, and between familiar and unfamiliar people. These capacities appear in an orderly sequence, but they do not emerge fully formed. Each appears in partially developed form and is refined over time.

There are various theories that attempt to explain the origin of attachment. These differ according to the area of psychological interest from which they come. In the case of psychoanalytic theory, the attachment relationship is described as an *object relationship,* and the mechanism at work is considered to be gratification of the infant's basic needs (Freud, 1938). The source of gratification becomes a "love object." In the case of social learning theory, the term used to describe attachment is *dependency.* One view of this approach explains that the caregiver's responses serve as reinforcers of the infant's smiling and similar behaviors (Gewirtz, 1976). Another view sees dependency as an acquired drive resulting from the association of the mother's presence with primary drive reduction (for example, the reduction of hunger when the mother feeds the baby). The term *bonding* comes from ethological studies and is used to describe the development of social ties in various species (Bowlby, 1969). The

Theoretical Origins of Attachment

study of attachment behavior in primates other than humans (as in Harlow's work) and in primitive hunter-gatherer cultures helps to clarify how such behavior might favor the survival of a species under different environmental conditions. In this view, certain behaviors serve to bring the child—whether animal or human—into proximity with the caregiver and to elicit a loving, protective response. Despite their differences, each of these theoretical approaches considers the caregiver-infant relationship to be reciprocal. The nurturant attention of the caregiver elicits smiles, babbling, and movement in the baby; these in turn prompt further caregiving behavior. The responsiveness of the caregiver appears to be a major factor in the type of attachment that develops.

Factors Influencing Attachment

Ainsworth and her collaborators have studied the relation of maternal behavior to infant attachment. They found that by the end of the infant's first year, different babies have organized attachment behavior toward the caregiver in different ways (Stayton and Ainsworth, 1973). They identified two types of attachment behavior. An infant who is *anxious* (or insecure) in its attachment cries intensely and for long periods when it is separated from the caregiver and again when baby and caregiver are reunited; the baby also will cry when put down. The researchers suggest that such an infant is anxious about the caregiver's continued accessibility. The infant who has a *secure* attachment relationship, by contrast, shows milder protest upon separation from the caregiver, greets her happily when she returns, and tends to accept being put down. The infant seems to show confidence in the caregiver's accessibility. The anxious pattern just described was found to be related to the caregiver's unresponsiveness to the infant's crying and other signals. Bell and Ainsworth (1972) showed that the amount of the baby's crying was related to the caregiver's habit of ignoring or delaying a response to the crying. It is likely that the infant develops confidence in the caregiver—and consequently a secure attachment—in proportion to her consistency and promptness in responding to its signals (Ainsworth, Bell, and Stayton, 1971; Clarke-Stewart, 1973).

Another factor in the development of attachment is the amount of social stimulation the child receives. Researchers have found correlations between high levels of stimulation and secure attachment. "Stimulation" includes different types of social interaction, as well as the availability of a variety of play materials. Clarke-Stewart (1973) studied the relationship between attachment and various maternal behaviors. The higher a mother scored in each of these behaviors, the more securely attached her infant tended to be. Figure 7–4 illustrates the relationships found between attachment behavior and the mothers' expression of affection, responsiveness, and provision of social stimulation. Two other criteria that researchers have used to measure the strength of attachment are separation anxiety and reactions to strangers.

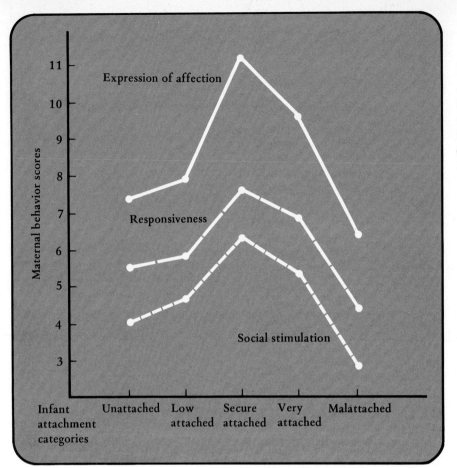

FIGURE 7–4
Relations between maternal behaviors and categories of infant attachment.
(Clarke-Stewart, 1973, Figure 6, p. 78)

As infants develop attachments, they become uncertain when the caregiver departs. They protest and try to follow when the caregiver leaves, behaviors which are thought to reflect *separation anxiety*. Many studies have been made of how children behave when they are separated from their caregivers. Bowlby and his colleagues (1969), for instance, have noted the following sequence of attachment behaviors typical of a child 15 to 30 months old who has a reasonably secure attachment with his caregiver.

Separation Anxiety

1. *Protest.* Crying, screaming, and trying to follow the departing caregiver; unconsolable sobbing at bedtime. Protest behavior is strong during the first 3 days of separation.
2. *Despair.* A lessening of protest accompanied by sadness and withdrawal. Some children become hostile and reject friendly overtures; others become indiscriminately and joylessly clinging, frequently to one particular temporary caregiver.
3. *Detachment.* Observed when child and caregiver are reunited. The child

turns away when the caregiver approaches; he or she is quiet, impersonal, or tearful. It appears that the child is very frightened at the possibility of another separation.

Reactions to separation (and, as we will see, to strangers) vary according to the situation in which the separation occurs. A very young child may react more strongly to a strange environment than to the absence of the caregiver. Some observers have found that as the environmental situation becomes increasingly different from the home situation which the infant is used to, the separation reaction will become more intense (Ainsworth et al., 1971; Yarrow and Pederson, 1972). In a familiar environment, on the other hand, infants who can walk are likely to make positive and active efforts to end the separation by following the caregiver when she leaves the room (Stayton, Ainsworth, and Main, 1973).

Separation anxiety may be explained in a number of ways. One possible explanation is that a large discrepancy from the child's expectations produces fear. When the baby is in the living room and the mother steps into the kitchen, the baby might be quite casual. But if the mother steps into the closet, something which does not happen often, the baby might become upset. It is interesting to note that after the child has developed the ability to symbolize objects, at about 24 months, the reaction to brief separations becomes less intense. The child seems to become less afraid that the caregiver will be permanently lost if allowed to disappear. That faith may be a fragile one. When ill or in a frightening new environment, the child might become intensely distressed when the caregiver leaves. Separation anxiety is governed by how the child feels about the situation as much as it is governed by how the child feels about the caregiver.

Reactions to Strangers

Fear of strangers, like separation anxiety, is usually viewed as an indicator of attachment. Both show that the child can distinguish between a stranger and persons with whom he or she has established a special relationship. Reactions to strangers are less intense in familiar environments than in unfamiliar ones. Also, the child's degree of control makes a difference. The rapid approach of a stranger may cause a child to respond with alarm, but the same child may approach the same person at his or her own initiative without showing fear. Interestingly, cross-cultural studies indicate that fear of strangers may be universal among babies (Konner, 1972; Goldberg, 1972).

Wariness toward strangers first appears at about the time that the infant begins to distinguish one adult from another, that is, at 4 or 5 months of age (Bronson, 1972). Not all children are fearful of strangers, but most show distinctive behaviors toward them that change with age. Four-month-old infants make a long, continuous inspection of the stranger's face. But by 9 months the baby will avoid looking at a stranger, and wariness may have increased to the point of fearfulness.

Infants and young children often demonstrate attachment by showing anxiety over separation. (Joel Gordon)

TABLE 7–3
Why Children Show
Fear of Strangers

A COGNITIVE EXPLANATION		
The child cannot classify the stranger	$\longrightarrow$	The incongruity produces distress
A BEHAVIORAL EXPLANATION		
The child cannot find a suitable response to the stranger	$\longrightarrow$	Behavior disruption produces distress
A CONTINGENCY EXPLANATION		
The behavior of the stranger is not predictable	$\longrightarrow$	Loss of control produces distress

There are several popular (and likely) theories that explain infants' fear of strangers. They are summarized in Table 7–3. Note that each of the theories concerns itself with a different aspect of stranger anxiety; therefore the three are not necessarily in conflict. First, some investigators attribute fear of strangers, as well as separation anxiety, to the incongruity principle. By 5 months of age, the infant begins to identify the faces of its mother, father, and other people who play important roles in its life. As it examines the face of a stranger, the baby discovers that this face differs from other, well-known faces. The incongruity is disturbing. If this cognitive explanation is correct, fear of strangers should be influenced by the baby's ability to distinguish a stranger perceptually. Also, it should increase as the baby's ability to identify and compare visual images improves. The available evidence suggests that this is the case.

Another explanation for fear of strangers emphasizes behavioral responses rather than perceptual comparisons. According to this point of view, the infant needs to *do* something when it experiences an unfamiliar stimulus (a strange face). A familiar face evokes a familiar response (such as a smile or a vocalization), and the infant's tension subsides. If, however, the infant cannot associate the new image with something familiar, he will be unable to find a suitable response and his tension will increase. Eventually the stress becomes too great, and the child terminates the encounter by turning away, seeking the mother, or crying.

A third explanation, the contingency explanation, differs considerably from the first two. We know that babies take great delight in events that occur in response to their own acts (such as social smiling). The contingency explanation proposes that when infants are exposed to strangers, the interaction is no longer predictable. That is, the stranger may not respond according to the baby's expectations. Wariness and distress appear because the baby feels that it has lost control over its social environment. As we pointed out in our discussion of smiling, different theories often provide plausible explanations for different parts of a problem. Stranger reactions change with age. It is likely that perceptual incongruity accounts for the reactions of young infants, whereas social control is more of an issue in the reactions of older infants.

Psychologists have suggested that the presence of a trusted caregiver supports exploratory behavior and the emergence of autonomy and mastery by reducing the child's anxiety. A 1-year-old child, for example, may become upset and cling to the caregiver if she tries to leave the infant alone in an unfamiliar place. Yet the same child might casually wander over and inspect the same unfamiliar place if the caregiver were nearby. There seems to be an important difference between "being left" and "leaving." In the former case the caregiver, not the child, controls the situation, and crying may be the only way to restore the caregiver's presence. In the latter case, by contrast, the child can regain contact with the caregiver at will.

The concept of the caregiver as a *secure base* will sound familiar to anyone who takes a young child to the park and sits on a bench while the child plays. The child seems to maintain a delicate balance between exploring his or her surroundings and staying close to the adult. The child will wander away to investigate an interesting object and then return to the caregiver before setting out on another expedition. This behavior clearly has survival value from an evolutionary standpoint. The child's attachment to the caregiver ensures protection, nourishment, and so forth, and exploratory behavior helps the child learn about the world in which he or she will eventually have to live without the caregiver's continual support.

In a study of attachment behavior shown by young children in outdoor settings, Anderson (1972) found that up to the age of 2½ years, children will stay within sight or sound of the caregiver. They seem to establish their own boundaries (which generally coincide with what the caregiver will tolerate). Their movements take the form of "bouts" in which they walk or run either away from or toward the caregiver, pausing after each bout. The pauses tend to be longer (but less frequent) when the child is close to the caregiver.

Children observed in outdoor settings do perform a variety of actions that indicate attachment (Anderson, 1972). They often pick up objects and take them to the caregiver; they may wave to the caregiver (this occurs not before a departure but just before a return); they may lift both arms straight up in the "pick me up" gesture, even when at a distance from the caregiver; and they may point. The caregiver usually responds to these overtures by taking the offered object, by waving, talking, smiling, and looking in return. What all these actions have in common is that they are two-way transactions that serve to maintain contact between the child and the caregiver.

Attachment research has drawn its full share of criticism. Cohen (1974), for example, argues that behaviors such as smiling, following, crying upon separation, and exploring from a "secure base" have not been shown to be directed *selectively* toward the attachment figure. Babies sometimes smile at strangers. They do not always cry when the caregiver leaves. They can be comforted by people other than the caregiver. And yet the presence of an attachment figure seems to be a condition that facilitates friendliness to strangers, and the departure of the attachment figure is likely to cause distress. There are clearly qualitative differences between the way children respond to unfamiliar people and the way they respond to people who are stable members of their social world. There are also problems in relating individual differences in children's attachment to the way that attachment develops during the first 2 years of life. Some babies make friends easily and seem to enjoy new situations; they are most likely to show separation or stranger distress when they are tired or ill. Other children are edgier about new experiences and show intense distress when things change. These patterns of individual differences change with age, and so far, it has been difficult to separate developmental from personality patterns. Despite such criticisms, however, attachment research has unquestionably made a significant contribution to our knowledge of the nature of social ties and the development of social responsiveness.

RELATIONS WITH PEERS

As infants grow older, the social boundaries of their worlds expand. Their mobility enables them to explore the environment and to meet an ever-increasing number of children other than brothers and sisters. Most children begin to react positively toward peers by 8 months of age (Greenberg et al., 1973). They begin to form relationships with peers during the second or third year of life. Gradually they become less dependent on the caregiver to supply all of their social stimulation. A new affectional system then comes into play.

An important early study of social relations between young children was conducted by Maudry and Nekula (1939). They put two children of about equal ages together in a playpen. Various toys were put in the playpen during the course of the experiment. Sometimes each child was given a toy; sometimes only one toy was provided for the two children; for a while, the children were left alone together with no toys. The interactions between the children were observed from behind a screen. The observations revealed that children's social interactions vary by age. Between 6 and 8 months of age, infants were quite insensitive to one another; nor were they particularly interested in the toys. This behavior began to change at around 9 months. The babies then became interested in the toys

and reacted negatively to the other baby in the playpen. The negative reaction did not occur, however, when there were no toys in the playpen.

The period between 14 and 18 months appears to be a transitional phase. When both children were given a toy or when neither child had a toy, they showed positive social attitudes. But if only one child had a toy, negative attitudes were likely to prevail. After the age of 19 months, however, children became more interested in their partners than in the experimental materials. Social interactions were usually positive, regardless of the availability or lack of toys.

Maudry and Nekula stressed that the negative social reactions they observed were largely due to conflicts over toys, not to personal aggression. Negative social reactions were most noticeable in children between 9 and 13 months of age. After 18 months, there was a steady increase in cooperative play. In short, the child regarded the partner first as play material (6–8 months); then as an obstacle to play material (9–13 months); and finally as a playmate (19–25 months).

Experiments such as the one just described have been influential in the study of children's responses to their peers. Unfortunately, early research on this subject suffered from methodological problems. For example, the children studied had spent little time together prior to the observation, which often was made in unfamiliar surroundings. We still lack systematic information about how peer relations change over time in naturalistic, relatively long-term situations. Yet recent studies confirm the finding that, between 12 and 24 months, children's behavior is increasingly influenced by the presence of peers. Eckerman, Whatley, and Kutz (1975), for example, studied in a laboratory setting pairs of infants who were unfamiliar to each other. They reported an increase in peer interaction and a decrease in interaction with the caregivers between the ages of 10 and 24 months. Support for these findings comes from another study reporting that in the presence of familiar peers, children between the ages of 17 and 20 months spend 59% of their time in peer interaction (Rubenstein and Sandberg, 1975). However, we know relatively little about the *quality* of the interaction, its evolution over time, and how it is influenced by various circumstances in naturalistic, relatively long-term situations.

Questions about long-term interactions in natural settings have given rise to a number of studies of peer interaction in play groups (Mueller, 1972a; Mueller and De Stefano, in press). The results of these studies suggest that at an early age social interaction is organized around objects and that contact between children is fleeting. At about 14 months of age, however, children begin to show interest in one another, and 2 or 3 months later, the beginnings of reciprocal interaction are seen (Mueller, 1972a). Other observers have found that even from the earliest beginnings of peer interaction, children differ in their abilities to negotiate access to materials, in their attractiveness to other children, and in their overall control over social situations (Lee, 1973).

Preliminary observations by the author of infants receiving group care suggest that by 18 months there are striking differences in the ways children manage encounters with peers. Some children consistently maintain considerable spatial distance between themselves and others. If another child approaches, these children move away from a desired toy, to return only when the invader has departed. Such children spend much of their time observing group life, always on the perimeter of group activity. Other children seek out proximity to others, even though their interactive skills are primitive. Still other children provoke active, often disturbing contacts with others. These children are frequently in the middle of commotions. For instance, they may grab things and provoke grabbing from others. But they may also offer and receive affection, as well; they are visible and impossible to ignore. The context of the child's day-to-day experience is created in part by the child's behavior and in part by the way others respond to the behavior. The peer system that emerges is codetermined by predispositions that a child brings to the group setting, and by human and material resources in the setting that enhance, submerge, or modify those predispositions.

What about the long-term effects of early group experience? Recent studies give cause for concern regarding the influence of early peer contacts on subsequent behavior in group settings. One study reported that children who entered a group setting for the first time at 3 years of age engaged in fewer social interactions with peers than did children who had experienced 2 or more years of group care (Schwartz, Krolick, and Strickland, 1973). Yet, a follow-up study of the same children 3 months later reported that the children who had been in day care since infancy were more aggressive and less cooperative with adults than were the children who had entered the group setting as 3-year-olds (Schwartz, Strickland, and Krolick, 1974). Such findings disagree with observations of children in the kibbutz, who at an early age exhibit highly sophisticated forms of positive social behavior (Neubauer, 1965). Thus there is obviously a need for further research on early peer relations in group settings.

SOCIAL INFLUENCES ON EARLY DEVELOPMENT

Individual differences in the development of reactions to peers are, of course, influenced by the kinds of early attachments that children develop. And those early attachments are determined in large part by caregiver behavior. There is considerable recent evidence to support the idea that the characteristics of the interaction between infant and caregiver are related to the child's cognitive development, as well.

The Influence of Parents

One source of evidence regarding influence of the caregiver on early cognitive development comes from Clarke-Stewart's (1973) longitudinal observation of mother-child interactions. Her findings suggest that an interactive style characterized by warmth, responsiveness, and social stimulation at 9 months was related to children's later performance on the Bayley Scales of Mental Development and other indexes of intellectual and social competence. Clarke-Stewart found positive correlations between various caregiver behaviors and child performance. One such correlation was between adult verbal stimulation and the child's ability to comprehend and express language. Another correlation was between the amount of time the caregiver spent with the child playing with materials and the child's level of cognitive development and complexity of play with objects. Interestingly, stimulation inherent in the physical environment did not seem to be related to cognitive development. Clarke-Stewart interprets this finding to suggest the importance of the caregiver as a mediator of play materials. That is, the time spent playing with a child may be more important for cognitive development than the richness or amount of stimulating materials available to him or her.

Various investigators suggest that the quality of interactions between caregivers and children—and, possibly, the course of cognitive development—can be improved by courses in "parenting."

Parent Education Programs

Some "parenting" programs have already been undertaken. One example is the "educational intervention" research conducted by Karnes,

Teska, Hodgins, and Badger (1970). This program involved group meetings with mothers (10 per group) and their children. The meetings were divided between group discussions with the mothers (on subjects such as child discipline and health care) and activities directed toward the children (usually centering on use of toys such as puzzles and boxes that fit inside other boxes). The mothers were encouraged to repeat these play activities with their infants at home between meetings. Staff members made home visits each month. At the end of the 2-year program, the children in the experimental group scored significantly higher on the Binet IQ test than did children in a control group. Another result, perhaps more important, was the greater involvement of the mothers with the children, the family, and even the community at large.

Up to now, programs of this kind have focused on the parents of disadvantaged children. It is likely, however, that similar programs would be welcomed by many middle-class parents. The current interest in "parent effectiveness training" may be a sign of increasing concern on the part of middle-class parents. In a recent book for parents, for example, Koch (1976), a psychologist who has worked with babies at the Institute for the Care of Mother and Child (in Prague, Czechoslovakia), describes 333 exercises and games to play with babies during the first 2 years of life. Babies who participated in Koch's activities showed marked advances in their development.

Child Care

Many parents are concerned that separation of the child from the primary caregiver for long or frequent periods may be harmful to the child. Part of this concern arises from the belief that the separation itself, which causes distress in many children, may disturb the child's social and intellectual functioning. There is also some doubt as to whether the child will receive adequate social stimulation, affection, and attention in the absence of the primary caregiver. This concern characterizes the long-standing opposition in this country to group day care for infants and toddlers (although this opposition is weakening in the face of increasing maternal employment).

The effects of separation differ depending on the age and general well-being of the child, the kind of substitute care involved, and the quality of the relationship between caregiver and child. There are many kinds of separation — long or short, single or repeated, regular or irregular. Children who are separated from their mothers on a regular basis (for example, in day-care centers) have not been studied extensively. The research that has been done so far suggests that such arrangements do not necessarily lead to the kinds of disturbances feared. In addition, children raised in Israeli kibbutzim, who undergo far more extensive separation from their parents, do not show adverse effects (Fein and Clarke-Stewart, 1973). Children who have experienced long separations in hospitals and other institutions, by contrast, have often suffered considerable distress and, sometimes, severely impaired development. These disturbances may sometimes be reduced by the presence of an adequate substitute for the caregiver.

The *quality* of child care is especially important to the development of the child. Few people would argue that a day-care setting in which children are merely cared for physically is an adequate substitute for parental care. An "enriched" day-care program that provides the child with regular attention and with stimulation in such areas as language and cognitive development, on the other hand, may have positive results not only for the child but also for the parents. This has been demonstrated in many studies. Fallender and Heber (1975), for example, periodically tested both mothers and children who participated in an enriched day-care program on tasks involving reciprocal interaction. The researchers were interested in finding out whether there would be a responsive interaction pattern between mother and child even though the child was away from home every day.

The children who had participated in the program were found to use "significantly more verbal information-processing behaviors and more verbal and physical positive feedback" than did control children (Fallender and Heber, 1975, p. 833). More important, perhaps, were the effects on the participating mothers, who were more likely than control mothers to give the child verbal instructions on how to perform a task (rather than showing the child how to do it), and to give praise or encouragement. These results, according to Fallender and Heber, indicate that both children and parents profited from the children's interactions with adults other than their mothers. Such findings should not be surprising in view of our knowledge that the infant's behavior toward the caregiver influences her responses to the infant. Once again we are reminded that the infant-mother affectional system is a bidirectional one. Other studies have been less successful in finding positive outcomes from quality infant day care. Kagan, Kearsley, and Zelazo (1976) concludes, though, that having been in such a program does not appear to harm children. Unfortunately, studies of infant day care are sparse. Little is known about the way different aspects of surrogate care, whether in a neighbor's home or in a group program, influence young children. This lack of information reflects more general cultural values regarding the out-of-home care of young children.

A society that is not "ready" for day care will not accept it. Nor will it expend much effort to find out how to develop programs that protect and even enhance infant development. The situation is parallel to the question of children's attachment to their fathers. In a recent article, Gornick (1975) points out that "observations made before their time ... are treated as curiosities, perhaps aberrations.... The culture commands that

The quality of substitute child care is important to the social and emotional development of the child.
(Elizabeth Crews, Jeroboam)

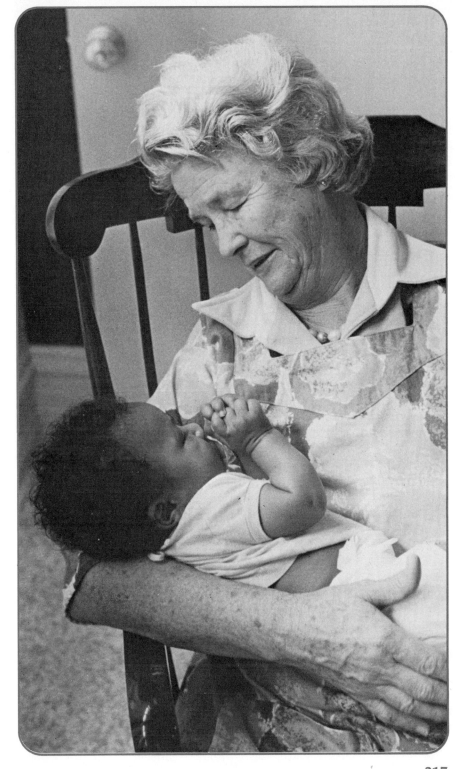

the mother is more important to the child than the father, and the social scientists will be damned if they'll discover otherwise." Similarly, a society that believes that it is "natural" for a mother to be available to her child at all times is unlikely to attempt to reconcile conflicting reports. Worse yet, if society insists that caregiving is only for women (while fathers secretly long to do it) and that women are the only persons able to rear happy children (while increasing numbers of women join the work force), children may suffer in the end far more from these contradictions and the conflicts they produce than from the thwarted need for a particular caregiver or a particular child-care environment.

SUMMARY

Social development begins with the relationship between caregiver and infant described as an *affectional system*—a reciprocal relationship between two persons, marked by strong feelings and mutual caring. In two-person systems, *bidirectionality*—how the behavior of one person influences the behavior of the other—is important. As a result of their research with monkeys, the Harlows have come up with a useful model against which to view the development of affectional systems in humans.

The bidirectional nature of adult-child interactions indicates that through the developmental process certain transactions take place that result in a fit between a particular child and a particular home and family. *Interaction* refers to what infants and caregivers do when they are together. *Transaction* refers to the process of social modification in behavior, feelings, and understanding of those who participate in the exchange.

The influence of babies on adults may be just as important as that of adults on babies. The infant's effect on its caregiver has a certain survival value. "Babyishness"—the physical appearance of the infant—serves as a "releaser" of protectiveness in the adult. The infant's helplessness may induce adult protectiveness, and crying or fussing has a significant effect in getting adult attention and help. Infants use a variety of methods, of which smiling is the most effective, to stimulate adults to respond to them on a social level.

Smiling, one of the infant's first social acts, is an expression of the affectional relationship with the caregiver. The infant's smile goes through several phases, beginning with *spontaneous smiling* which occurs in response to a wide variety of stimuli and is not considered truly "social." The second phase—*unselective social smiling*—is smiling in response to a smaller number of stimuli, particularly human voices and faces. *Selective social smiling*, the third phase, is marked by smiling consistently at a stationary face, as readily at strangers as at caregivers. The fourth and final phase—*differential social responsiveness*—consists of smiling differently in response to different individuals. The first truly social smile cannot occur until the infant has acquired fixation of glance, is able to follow a moving object with its eyes, and is able to examine the internal features of an object. The first true smile is dramatically different from earlier fleeting smiles and is quickly recognized by caregivers, who usually respond by spending more time playing with the baby. Recent studies suggest that the infant's tendency to smile in response to a human face may be biologically determined rather than a learned behavior.

It appears that the human face attracts the infant's attention and serves as a releaser of the smiling response. Experiments indicate that a variety of factors contribute to the development of the infant's response to faces. Some investigators believe that the eyes and the face are special kinds of configurations that elicit smiling. Others propose that cognitive-affective mechanisms may account for the relation between the human face and smiling. And still others feel that smiling at the human face is a distinctively social response by which the infant can exert control over the environment.

Laughter appears at about the fourth month of life. The work of Sroufe and Wunsch indicates that the amount of laughter increases with age and that there are developmental trends affecting the type of stimulus that evokes laughter. Their functional interpretation of infant laughter suggests that tension results when an incongruous event occurs that is appropriate to the infant's cognitive level but that does not match developing cognitive schema. Laughter releases the tension and allows the infant to continue to consider and to process the incongruity.

Social interaction appears early in the infant's life, and toward the end of the first year, strong affectional relationships begin to develop. These relationships, called *attachments,* refer to the affectional bonds between the child and a particular individual and assume the existence of a stable, long-term relationship between the child and another person.

Schaffer and Emerson have proposed a sequence of three stages in the development of attachment: (1) an asocial stage in which infants seek contact with various parts of the environment; (2) a second stage marked by the infant's realization of the significance of humans as a special part of the environment and characterized by the infant's protest against separation from any individual; and (3) a third stage, characterized by attachment to particular individuals and accompanied by strong feelings of distress when those individuals disappear. Studies have shown that attachment is not necessarily an exclusive relationship with the mother.

Various theories attempt to explain the origin of attachment. The psychoanalytic theory describes attachment as an *object relationship* with gratification of the infant's needs acting as the underlying mechanism. Social learning theory describes attachment as *dependency*. Ethological theory describes attachment as *bonding,* which occurs as a result of certain behaviors that serve to bring the child close to the caregiver and to elicit a loving, protective response. Each of these theoretical approaches considers the caregiver-infant relationship to be reciprocal and indicates that it is the responsiveness of the caregiver that appears to be a major factor in the type of attachment that develops.

Researchers have identified two types of attachment behavior. An *anxious* attachment is marked by the baby crying intensely when it is separated from the caregiver, crying when they are reunited, and crying when it is put down. A *secure* attachment is marked by the baby making a milder protest upon separation from the caregiver, giving a happy greeting when they are reunited, and accepting being put down. Anxious attachments usually develop if there is a lack or inconsistency of affection, responsiveness, or social stimulation from the caregiver.

Separation anxiety refers to the fear and uncertainty infants experience when the caregiver leaves. The anxiety is governed as much by how the child feels about the situation as by how the child feels about the caregiver. Three basic forms of behavior relating to separation anxiety have been isolated: (1) protest, (2) despair, (3) detachment.

Fear of strangers, like separation anxiety, is usually considered an indicator of attachment. Both show that the child can distinguish between a stranger and persons with whom a special relationship has been established. Reactions to strangers are less intense in familiar environments and when the child has some control over the situation than in unfamiliar environments or when the child has little control. There are three popular theories to explain stranger anxiety: (1) cognitive, which says that the child cannot classify the stranger and this incongruity produces distress; (2) behavioral, which says that the child cannot find a suitable response to the stranger, and the behavior disruption produces stress; and (3) contingency, which says that the behavior of the stranger is not predictable, and the child's sense of loss of control produces distress.

Psychologists suggest that the presence of a trusted caregiver, a *secure base*, supports exploratory behavior and the emergence of autonomy and mastery by reducing the child's anxiety. Attachment behavior often differs markedly from child to child and in varying situations.

As infants get older, the social boundaries of their worlds expand to include other children, and a new affectional system comes into play. Children's social interactions vary by age. Children regard partners first as play material, then as obstacles to play, and finally as playmates. Despite these findings, there is still a lack of systematic information about how peer relations change over time in naturalistic, relatively long-term situations.

Individual differences in the development of reactions to peers are influenced by the kinds of early attachments that children develop. In addition, there is considerable evidence to support the idea that interaction between infant and caregiver is related to the child's cognitive development. Studies strongly suggest that the time a caregiver spends playing with a child may be more important for cognitive development than the richness or amount of stimulating materials available to the child.

The study of attachment and affectional systems leads to the important question of which types of child care are beneficial or harmful. Studies of infant day care are sparse, and little is known about the way different aspects of surrogate care influence young children. This lack of information reflects general cultural values regarding out-of-home care of young children, although as more and more women work, the need for such information becomes vital.

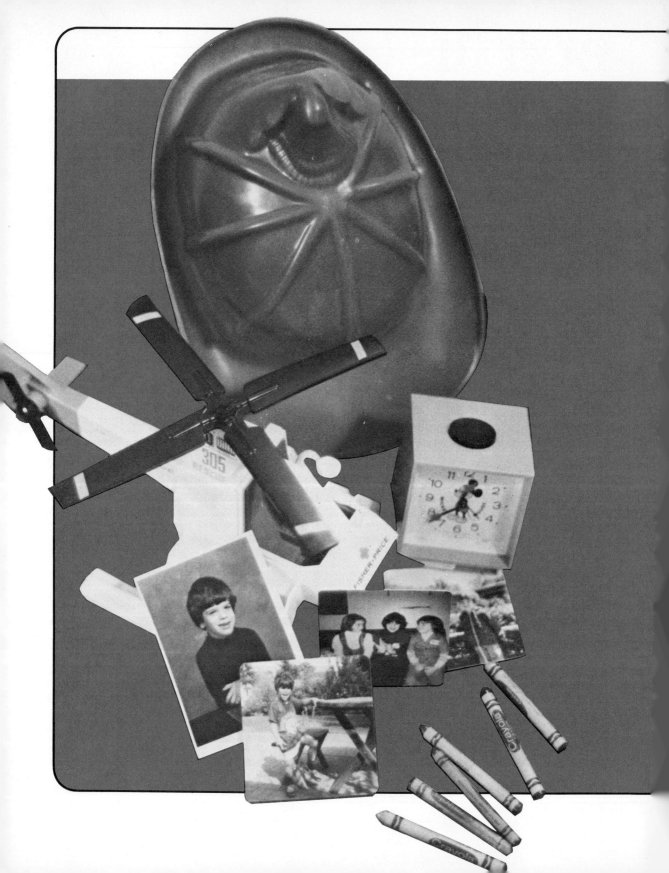

PART III

Early Childhood

September, 1960
Susan started nursery school today. Her best friend Beverly went too. When I took them in the morning, they marched in hand and hand. No looks backward. Much chatter on the way home. One of the boys cried and cried. He held the teacher's hand all day. They felt sorry for him—and very critical of his mother for leaving him.

February 12, 1961
Today the children in Susan's class celebrated Lincoln's birthday. When she came home, all she could talk about was Lincoln—what a good man he was because he didn't let white people hurt black people. She felt strongly about this because one of her closest friends is black. She could not see why anyone would want to harm Beverly.

May 24, 1964
Jon was 5 years old last Thursday. The house was jammed. A dozen kids and as many grownups. Susan (8 years old) managed the whole affair and ruled the children with an iron hand: pin-the-tail (everyone in line—no peeking), peanut hunt (outdoors), and so on.

Grandma and Grandpa gave Jon a pair of roller skates for his birthday. For 3 days now, it's been roller skates morning, noon, and night. Stand up; fall down; stand up again. His legs are painted with antiseptic, and band aids decorate knees and elbows. Today, raw determination paid off. He was up for a whole length of the driveway. There's no holding him now.

CHAPTER 8

Thought, Language, and Communication

In previous chapters, we traced the development of the infant. We described the status of the newborn and discussed the early stages in the child's formation of stable concepts of people, things, and the relations among them. We also described the remarkable process by which the child begins to create a symbolic system for the representation and, eventually, communication of those concepts. During the sensorimotor period (0–2 years), the child develops the abilities necessary to construct and reconstruct objects symbolically using an elementary form of reasoning, by means of mental images without the aid of language. During the second year of life, the child seems to acquire the basic elements of thought. In Piaget's terms, the child's sensorimotor intelligence is reconstructed at a symbolic level. At this point, the child is entering Piaget's "preoperational period."

The preoperational period usually extends from age 2 to about age 7. During those years, the child develops further the abilities that have to do with representing things. Piaget calls this the *symbolic function*. The preoperational period is characterized by the acquisition of language, by evidence that the child has dreams and sometimes nightmares; by symbolic play; and by the first attempts at representational drawing and painting. By the end of this period, the child can distinguish clearly between words and symbols and what each represents, and can recognize that names are arbitrary designations. The child also acquires understanding of conservation, which achievement marks the change to the concrete operational period.

During the period of concrete operations (around 7–11 years), the child begins to think about objects. Piaget describes concrete operations as internalized actions that permit children "to do in their head" what before they would have had to accomplish through real actions. Concrete operations also enable children to understand the relations among classes of things.

THE PREOPERATIONAL CHILD

The preoperational period is characterized by a transition from thinking with the body to thinking with the mind. We saw in Chapter 6 how the infant's sensorimotor intelligence determines the formation of concepts and the acquisition of language. The young child is unable to *reason* about reality, because he or she has not yet separated words and symbols from the objects they represent. For example, the child may become upset if someone steps on a stone that he or she is using to represent a turtle (Elkind, 1968). By the age of 7, however; the child has reached the "age of reason" and can clearly distinguish between words and symbols and the objects they represent.

A striking phenomenon of the preoperational period is the development of the child's use of language. Weir (1970) studied the monologues produced by her 2-year-old son as he was drifting off to sleep. A typical sequence is the following:

What color — What color blanket — What color mop — What color glass.... Not the yellow blanket — The white.... It's not black — It's yellow ... Not yellow — Red.... Put on a blanket — White blanket — and yellow blanket — Where's yellow blanket.... Yellow blanket — Yellow light.... There is the light — Where is the light — Here is the light. (p. 19)

This passage would not require much change to sound like a lesson in a course for non-English speakers.

The most remarkable feature of the child's linguistic "play" at this age is the spontaneous invention of new forms of words. Many examples of this phenomenon can be found by listening to young children. Chukovsky (1963) records some good examples:

Having been told by a little boy that a big horse "hoofed" him, I used this word [hoofed] at the first opportunity in a conversation with my young daughter. Not only did she understand at once the meaning of the word, but she did not even suspect that it did not exist, for it seemed to her completely normal. (p. 5)

FIGURE 8-1
Berko's "wugs"—drawings used to elicit children's addition of inflections to nonsense words
(Berko, 1958)

This is a wug.

Now there is another one.
There are two of them.
There are two _____ .

A two-year-old girl was taking a bath and making her doll "dive" into the water and "dive out" of it, commenting: "There, she drowns-in—now, she drowns-out!" . . . Notice the exquisite plasticity and the refined meaning of these words. "Drowns-in" is not the same thing as "drowns"—it is to drown only temporarily with a definite expectation implied that the doll would be "drowning-out" again. (p. 7)

The child's inventions often reveal the acquisition and application of rules. An example is the formation of plurals. Parents are continually correcting errors of this kind. The child may say *goose* for one and either *gooses* or *geese* for two. If the child has been told to say *geese*, he or she may overgeneralize and use *meese* as the plural of *moose*. Thus children invent a "regular" form—often insisting on it in the face of adults' attempts to correct them—in an effort to compensate for the irregularity of the language. The child is consistent, although the language is not.

Why do children try to correct inconsistencies in the language? Because they are in the process of learning general rules of construction, not just the collections of words and phrases they happen to hear. Berko (1958) found that children as young as preschool age use rules to add inflections (endings) to words. Berko showed the children pictures of objects new to them and called these objects by nonsense names. She asked questions to discover whether the addition of inflections is rule-regulated or the result of children's memorization of forms heard elsewhere. For example, Berko

227

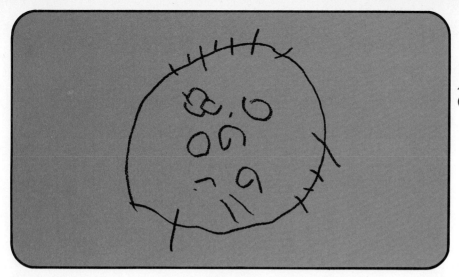

FIGURE 8–2
A "scribble picture"
(Golomb, 1974)

showed the children a drawing like the one in Figure 8–1 and told them, "This is a wug." She then showed them two wugs and said, "Now there is another one. There are two of them. There are two _____." A large number of the preschoolers supplied the appropriate inflections. Thus, even at an early age, the inflections are rule-regulated. The task of the linguist is to understand the child's rules for generating plurals from singulars and for applying the terms learned in one context to other contexts, especially new contexts or contexts for which words have not yet been acquired.

The originality of children when they are free to express themselves is rarely equaled after the age of 7. This originality seems to occur only while the child is mastering the basic principles of his or her native language. When mastery has been achieved, the child's inventive talent begins to fade. But during this period the child becomes, in Chukovsky's (1963) words, a "linguistic genius," delighting parents with words like *rainbrella, stocks* (for socks and stockings), *unihorn* ("I'm a horse with a unihorn"), *soupcase, fig nuttin's,* and so on. Who but a 5-year-old would say, "When you're standing on your head and you're sick, you 'throw down,' right?"

Equally fascinating as an indicator of the development taking place during the preoperational period are the changes that occur in children's drawings between the ages of 2 and 7. Drawings have been the subject of extensive study. Not only parents but educators and psychologists as well have long been puzzled by young children's art.

The child's earliest drawings bear very little resemblance to reality. They tend to be "scribble pictures" such as that in Figure 8–2. The child is not at all concerned with the results but is very pleased with the activity of drawing. After a few months, however, the child becomes somewhat more skillful and begins to show pride in the results of his or her efforts. These creations are still prerepresentational, but now the child makes up

228

stories to "explain" the picture: "It's a person with a lot of hair—he is having a shampoo" (Golomb, 1974, p. 5). The drawing serves as a starting point for the story, which may have little to do with any resemblance, intended or accidental, between the picture and reality.

At about 3 years of age, the child begins to see the representational possibilities of art. He or she starts drawing "things" and exploring the nature of lines and forms. However, a single form can stand for many different objects. The first drawings of people appear at this stage (see Figure 8–3). These representations are global in character—they stand for the whole person. (When asked to draw the whole person—not just the head—the child may draw a rudimentary stick figure *within* the original circle.)

The next step in the development of children's drawings is the peculiar "tadpole drawing," which appears at about 4 years of age. The primitive global figure is replaced by a circle with two vertical lines extending downward from it. This figure is still incomplete. In Figure 8–4, for example, the body is "open." During the remainder of the preoperational period, the figure gradually becomes more differentiated and more complete in a conventional sense, as in Figure 8–5. But there is still a long way to go before the figure takes on any resemblance to reality.

It is clear from the preceding paragraphs that children's spontaneous drawings show a developmental sequence in which the child's drawings of an object gradually come to resemble what we—as adults—think a drawing of that object ought to look like. But the odd, "faulty" character of children's drawings—their deviation from adult conventions—presents a dilemma. Do the earlier drawings represent a deficiency in the child's concept of "person" or in sensorimotor coordination? Apparently not. If

FIGURE 8–3
First representations of people, drawn about age 3 (Golomb, 1974)

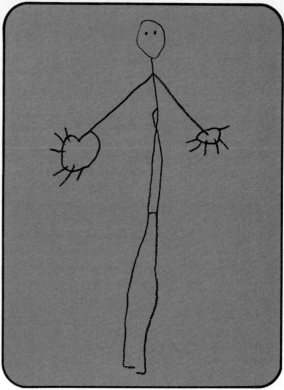

FIGURE 8–4
A "tadpole
drawing"
(Golomb, 1974)

FIGURE 8–5
Drawing from
preoperational
period
(Larry Smith, age 4)

the child is told what to draw or given forms to assemble, the end product is surprisingly sophisticated. Clearly, children know what the human body looks like, but they cannot reproduce it accurately without help.

In considering children's development from the standpoint of Piaget's stages, it is important to recognize that the achievements that occur at one level of development may be "reconstructed" at a higher level. This idea is best conveyed by an illustration (from Flavell, 1963):

Late in the sensory-motor period, the child gradually develops a precise behavioral map of his immediate surroundings. He can quickly and efficiently go from A to B to C and back to A; he can make detours when obstacles block his path, etc. . . . In other words, his motor movements definitely possess a strong structure, a tight organization as regards spatial relationships. It will be several years later, however, before he can represent the terrain and its relationships symbolically, in contradistinction to direct motor action with respect to it. He will for a long time be incapable of drawing a simple map of his immediate environment, or even of correctly filling in objects on a map constructed by others. (p. 23)

At first glance, there may appear to be little in common between the movements of the young child and the map-making project of the older child.

230

But there are structural similarities between the two activities. The map-making project constitutes a performance on a symbolic-representational level of an activity that originally was mastered on a sensorimotor level. Speaking, reading, writing, understanding, and drawing pictures, listening and telling stories—all (according to Piaget and others) reflect a leap forward in the development of intelligence. Just as the child gained mastery over sensorimotor systems, the child now extends this mastery to new media.

Throughout this chapter, we will be discussing the acquisition of concepts that represent reconstructions during the preoperational period of achievements originally attained during the sensorimotor period. During the preoperational period, two important changes occur: the emergence of the symbolic function and the advent of intuitive thought.

The Symbolic Function

The symbolic function emerges between the ages of 2 and 4. You may recall this concept from Chapter 6. It refers to the ability to make an object, symbol, or word represent something that is not immediately present. This ability allows the child to operate on a new level. He or she is not restricted to acting on the immediate environment but can conceive of the past and future and can talk about things that are not present.

Note, again, that words and symbols refer not to the actual objects they represent but to the child's knowledge of those things. To one child, the word "dog" may refer to a delightful fluffy creature that approaches her gently with its tail wagging and licks her hand. To another, the same word may refer to a frightening animal that runs at him at lightning speed, snarling and snapping. The two concepts may have some elements in common—four legs, a tail, the ability to run and bark—but one child's concept of "dog" is quite different from the other's.

MENTAL SYMBOLS. According to Piaget, the first indication of the emergence of the symbolic function is the formation of mental symbols. One example of the use of mental symbols involves *deferred imitation*. Consider the following example:

[*Jacqueline*] *had a visit from a little boy . . . whom she used to see from time to time, and who, in the course of the afternoon, got into a terrible temper. He screamed as he tried to get out of a play-pen and pushed it backward, stamping his feet. J. stood watching him in amazement, never having witnessed such a scene before. The next day, she herself screamed in her play-pen and tried to move it, stamping her foot lightly several times in succession.* (Piaget, 1951, p. 63)

Because Jacqueline's imitation of her playmate's tantrum occurred on the following day and not immediately, Piaget reasons that she must have formed a mental image of the tantrum that enabled her to produce it at a later time. In other words, it appears that the child can "store" another person's actions and reproduce them later.

How does the child accomplish this? Piaget believes that symbols (or images) are derived from imitation. At first, the child imitates through actions. For example, seeing her father riding his bicycle, Piaget's daughter Lucienne swayed to and fro in imitation of the motion of the bicycle. Lucienne's behavioral imitation of the bicycle was the forerunner of the preoperational child's internal imitation, or mental image, of the same object.

Another example of mental symbolism can be seen in the child's ability to find hidden objects, which occurs during stage 6 of the sensorimotor period. Piaget observed this ability in his daughter Jacqueline when he hid a small pencil in his hand and then put his hand first under a beret, then under a handkerchief, and finally under a jacket, where he left the pencil. Jacqueline immediately reached under the jacket and found the pencil. She did not look for it in her father's hand, which is the last place she had seen it.

Since Jacqueline's behavior could not be considered an accident, because she had acted the same way many times before, Piaget concluded that Jacqueline formed a mental image of the pencil, which enabled her to follow its movements even though she could not actually see them. When Piaget covered the pencil in his hand, Jacqueline believed in its continued existence. When his hand was placed under a succession of objects, the use of the mental symbol enabled her to follow mentally the invisible movements.

At this point, it is necessary to introduce the distinction between the *figurative* and *operative* aspects of intelligence. To Piagetians, this distinction is important. The operative aspect refers to the actions (physical and mental) with which the child deals with changes in the environment. Getting a chair in order to climb onto the kitchen counter in order to reach the cookie jar represents the operative aspect of intelligence. The child's mental image of the chair or the word "chair" represents the figurative aspect. It is the figurative aspect of intelligence that produces images. Note, however, that these images are not "copies" of reality in the sense of a photograph. Rather, they are schematic diagrams such as the child's "tadpole people."

Since the construction of a mental symbol involves imitation, it also involves a process of *accommodation*. This is because the symbol is an internal imitation, and imitation entails modifying behavior to meet the demands of the environment. For instance, in place of actually swaying back and forth, Lucienne might imitate the bicycle by making slight and almost imperceptible movements of her muscles. The child's muscles perform an abbreviated imitation of swaying, and those bodily sensations constitute the mental symbol of the bicycle. This internal imitation or accommodation provides the child with symbols. Yet the meaning of these symbols is biased by the child's previous experience and individual characteristics. The result is a *personal* symbol that in some way resembles the object referred to. It is not equivalent to a word, which is social rather than personal, and only arbitrarily related to the object. For example, a child's mental symbol of a dog is personal. The word "dog" is social and arbitrary—we could equally well agree to use "cat" or "shoe" to stand for the animal we refer to with the word "dog."

SYMBOLIC PLAY. The development of the symbolic function is also expressed in symbolic play, which occupies a large portion of the preoperational child's time. Here again, Piaget's daughter Jacqueline provides an example:

[Jacqueline] *saw a cloth whose fringed edges vaguely recalled those of her pillow; she seized it, held a fold of it in her right hand, sucked the thumb of the same hand and lay down on her side, laughing hard. She kept her eyes open, but blinked from time to time as if she were alluding to closed eyes.* (Piaget, 1951, p. 96)

According to Piaget, this incident illustrates the playful use of concrete (as opposed to mental) symbols. Jacqueline knew that the cloth was not her pillow; she used it to represent the pillow. Whereas formation of mental symbols involves accommodation, symbolic play involves *assimilation*. The behaviors associated with one object (the pillow) are extended to another (the cloth). The cloth is therefore absorbed into behavioral schemes that previously were applied only to the pillow. This process gives the symbol meaning for the child.

Piaget believes symbolic play is essential to the child's emotional growth. The 2- to 4-year-old child is in a vulnerable stage. Many aspects of the child's environment are difficult to understand, and the child's capacity for self-expression is limited. Through symbolic play, the child can incorporate the environment into his or her own needs and desires, sometimes acting out the conflicts of real life to his or her own advantage—as in the classic case of giving a doll a spanking. Thus symbolic play helps the child adjust his or her own perceptions of the world to reality.

Intuitive Thought

Between the ages of 2 and 4, the child first begins to carry out "actions in thought"; that is, the child demonstrates intuitive thought. Consider the following example, illustrated in Figure 8–6. If three balls, A, B, and C, are rolled through a cardboard tube and the child is asked to predict the order in which they will emerge at the other end (that is, the original order), the child can do so. However, when asked to predict the order in which the balls will emerge if they are rolled back through the tube (the reverse order), the child cannot do so. In fact, some children, having seen ball C

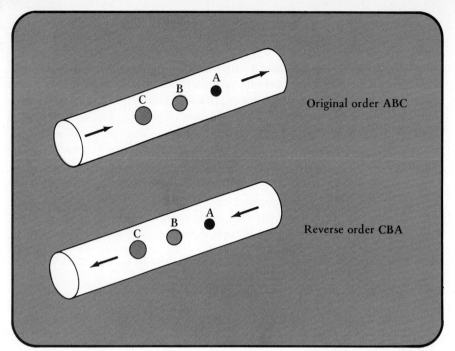

Original order ABC

Reverse order CBA

FIGURE 8–6
Between the ages of 2 and 4, children can predict the emergence of the original order (A, B, C) of balls rolled through a tube, but not the reverse order (C, B, A)

emerge when the three balls are rolled back through the tube, expect ball B to emerge as the "leader" the next time the balls go through the tube.

The child's inability to predict the reverse order of the three balls in the tube illustrates the difference between *preoperational* intuitive thought and the form of cognitive activity that Piaget terms *concrete operational.* Operations are *systems* of cognitive actions—organized networks of related acts. Examples include "logical" operations such as adding or subtracting and "infralogical" operations involving time, space, quantity, and the like. The preoperational child is limited in the mental operations he or she can perform, because those operations are isolated instances that have not yet merged into a system. Again taking the balls in the tube as an example, if the tube is turned 180 degrees, as shown in Figure 8–7, the order in which the balls will emerge is again reversed. Before the age of 7, the child cannot predict this result. Even when the child has seen that a 180-degree turn will reverse the order of the balls, he or she cannot predict that a 360-degree turn will reverse the order yet again. In short, the child does not understand the *system* of changes that determines the order in which the balls will emerge from the tube.

The classic study of preoperational intelligence is Piaget's beads-in-glasses study. This experiment is conducted as follows:

Two small glasses, A and A_2, of identical shape and size, are each filled with an equal number of beads, and this equality is acknowledged by the child, who has filled the glasses himself, e.g., by placing a bead in A with one hand every time he places a bead in A_2 with the other hand. Next, A_2 is emptied

234

into a differently shaped glass B, while A is left as a standard. Children of 4–5 years then conclude that the quantity of beads has changed, even though they are sure none has been removed or added. If the glass B is tall and thin they will say that there are "more beads than before" because "it is higher," or that there are fewer because "it is thinner," but they agree on the non-conservation of the whole [i.e., that the total quantity of beads has changed]. (Piaget, 1973, pp. 129–130)

The child bases the decision regarding the quantity of beads in the glass on his or her perception of the level reached by the beads. But this is not simply a case of perceptual illusion. What happens, according to Piaget, is that the child "centers" his or her attention (or thought) on only one aspect of the problem—the heights of A and B—and ignores other aspects such as the widths of the two glasses.

If glass B is emptied into another glass, C, that is very tall and thin, the child may say that there are fewer beads in C because "it is too narrow." The child has "centered" on width instead of height. But the decision as to which glass contains more beads is still an intuitive one. If the child were able to "decenter" and consider mentally all the relationships involved in a situation—in this case, both the heights and widths of A and B—as well as the reversibility of the action (what would happen if

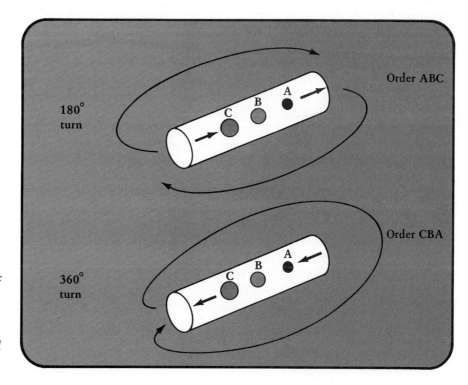

FIGURE 8–7
Children between the ages of 2 and 4 cannot yet understand the system of changes that determines the order in which balls emerge from a tube rotated 180 or 360 degrees.

B were poured back into A₂) he or she would recognize that the quantity of beads remains the same. In other words, the child would be thinking in terms of a system of relationships and would therefore be performing a cognitive operation.

It is interesting to note that when the quantity of beads placed in each glass in the preceding experiment is small—say, four or five beads—the preoperational child is able to understand that the two collections of beads are equal. However, when larger quantities are used and the shapes of the containers change noticeably, the preoperational child ceases to recognize that the quantities in the two glasses are equal. The child cannot yet deal adequately with *changes* in the physical world.

Conservation

THE CONSTRUCTION OF INVARIANCES. To Piaget, one of the most important cognitive achievements of childhood is the construction of stable and permanent concepts—"invariances"—in the face of the continuous change occurring in the environment. The child's world is full of change—both in objects themselves and in the way objects look from different perspectives. Trees lose their leaves and grow them again. People dye their hair. Even ordinary objects such as a chair or a cup look different depending on whether they are viewed from the side, the top, or the bottom. Yet somehow the child constructs from the diversity of experience some fundamental beliefs or concepts. The concept of the object as a permanently and constantly existing thing is one such belief. It is one that is acquired, as mentioned earlier, during the second year of life.

Having acquired the concept of object permanence, the child is ready to grapple with the permanence of *attributes* of objects such as amount, number, weight, and volume. In experiments designed to test the child's understanding of this concept—termed the *conservation paradigm*—the child is first asked to establish the equivalence of two sets: water in two glasses, lumps of clay weighed on a scale, or, as just described, collections of beads. Then the appearance of one set is changed in some way, and the child is asked to predict whether the appropriate attribute (the amount of water, the weight of the clay, the number of beads) remains constant or whether it changes too.

All of these experiments are similar in that they involve the following three steps: (1) The child is asked to recognize that two amounts are equal (most 4-year-olds can do this); (2) the experimental materials are transformed while the child watches (sometimes this is actually done by the child); and (3) the child is asked to judge whether the amounts, which now *look* different, are still equal.

Piaget's studies (as well as replications of Piaget's work) have repeatedly indicated that the child goes through a sequence of stages in acquiring the concept of conservation. At first, the child is unable to recognize that

Having learned that objects are permanent, the child can now focus attention on the attributes of objects, such as the noises made by tapping various sized containers with a drumstick. (Alice Kandell, Rapho/Photo Researchers)

the quantity of the item being measured is conserved throughout the experiment. At 4 or 5 years of age, the child can see that the amounts presented in the first step of the experiment are equal because they "look the same." But after the amounts have been transformed so that they no longer look the same, the child cannot grasp the fact that they are still equal. When asked if the amounts are different or the same, a 5- or 6-year-old will waver between two different answers when the amounts no longer look the same. In the case of the glasses of water, the child will sometimes say that the taller glass contains more to drink and sometimes that the wider glass contains more.

As the child approaches 7 years of age, the concept of conservation is finally acquired. The child's ability to understand conservation marks the change from preoperations to concrete operations. The child may give any of several reasons to explain why the amounts are equal. He or she may point out that if the liquid in glass C were returned to glass B, glasses A and B would contain identical amounts of liquid. Or the child may say, "It's the same water"; that is, no water has been added or subtracted from the original amount. A third argument is that, although glass C is shorter than glass B, it is also wider. The extra width compensates for the loss in height, so the amount of liquid is the same.

OPERATIONAL THOUGHT. At about the age of 7 years, children begin to enter what Piaget calls the concrete operational period. In this period, the child can perform *operations*—actions that the child does mentally that are, however, *concrete*—applied only to objects that are present. In other words, the child is able to perform certain actions in his or her head but is not yet able to deal with abstract concepts.

Take the following example of an experiment conducted by Piaget with a concrete operational child. Piaget instructed:

Take the same number of pennies as there are there [there were 6 in set A]. (He made a row of 6 under the model, but put his much closer together so that there was no spatial correspondence between the rows. Both ends of the model extended beyond those of the copy.) Have you got the same number? — Yes — *Are you and that boy [referring to the hypothetical owner of set A] just as rich as one another?* — Yes. — *The pennies of the model were then closed up and his own were spaced out.)* — And now? — The same. — *Exactly?* — Yes. — *Why are they the same?* — Because you've put them closer together. *(From Piaget, 1926, p. 79)*

The concrete operational child notices that his line of pennies has become longer than the line of pennies in the model and that the line of pennies in the model has become denser than the child's line of pennies. Mentally, he or she is able to coordinate the two dimensions and realize that while the length of his own line of pennies increases by a certain amount, the density of the model line of pennies increases by an equivalent amount. The preoperational child, on the other hand, notices only that his line of pennies has become longer than that of the model, ignoring the fact that the line of pennies in the model is now denser.

The preoperational child fails to conserve because he or she centers attention on only a limited amount of the available information—length in this case—rather than coordinating both dimensions of length and density. In contrast, the concrete operational child is able to decenter attention and coordinate two dimensions.

This ability to coordinate represents one form of reversibility. The concrete operational child mentally realizes that since the increase in length counteracts the increase in density, the result is a return or a reversal to the original situation. The preoperational child may realize that if the pennies in the model were returned to their original positions, there would be one penny for each penny in his or her own set, but the child is not helped by this knowledge. He or she is still strongly influenced by perceptual factors and feels that the number of a set changes when its appearance changes.

It is important to understand, however, that the course of development is continuous. According to Piaget, the child moves gradually from stage

1—centering on one dimension only—to stage 2—centering alternately on one dimension then the other—to stage 3—decentering and coordinating both dimensions at the same time. The child is not one day in stage 1 and the next day in stage 2. Rather, the transition takes place over a long period of time.

Although they involve similar mental operations, conservation of number, weight, and volume do not appear all at the same time. This irregularity, called *horizontal décalage,* refers to the fact that the child masters the conservation of number at about 6 or 7 years; does not achieve stage 3 of the conservation of weight until 9 or 10 years; and does not understand the conservation of volume until about 11 or 12 years. Having mastered the concept of conservation in one area, such as number, the child is still not able to generalize to another area, such as weight. This décalage, or lack of ability to generalize, points up the degree to which the thoughts of children between 7 and 11 years are concrete. Their mental ability is tied to specific situations and objects and cannot be applied to other situations and objects. The child can profit from outside information—be it reinforcement, adult explanation, or other sources—only when his or her cognitive structure is ready to understand it.

CONSERVATION TRAINING. The fact that the principle of conservation is gradually constructed by the child is well established. But what experiences of the child make it possible for him or her to accomplish that construction? This question has given rise to a large number of studies of "conservation training."

The typical training study works in the following way. A number of children are given a pretest to determine whether they understand the principle of conservation. "Nonconservers" are then given a set of experiences intended to help them understand conservation in a particular domain. Each child is tested again to discover whether he or she can now conserve in the domain tested and, more important, whether the training can be generalized to other domains.

One of the earliest training studies was conducted by Smedslund (1961). The subject of the study was the conservation of weight. First, young children were asked whether two balls of clay were equal in weight. Then one of the balls was shaped into a sausagelike form. The children judged the ball and the sausage to be unequal in weight. Smedslund attempted to teach the children the principle of conservation by having them weigh the ball and the sausage. This method, however, was not very successful. The children continued to be easily convinced that the weights were unequal. And, if they were able to understand that the weights were equal, they did not generalize this ability to new situations.

A more sophisticated study was conducted by Gelman (1969). Her approach was to train nonconservers to attend to relevant *cues*. For example, in the glasses-of-water experiment, the child is faced with several cues: size, shape, height, width, water level, and actual amount of water. From the investigator's point of view, only one cue—the amount of water—is relevant, but from the child's point of view any cue may appear relevant. Gelman's tactic was to train the child to focus on the relevant cue and to screen out the irrelevant ones. The method used was to present the child with a large number of problems containing many different cues but having one cue in common. The child was rewarded for choosing the common cue.

Gelman's method succeeded in experiments dealing with conservation of length and number (which generally are acquired earliest). It did not work with conservation problems involving mass or amount (of liquid). These results support Piaget's claim that children can profit from training if, and only if, their cognitive structure is ready to assimilate the new information. In other words, development does not occur as a result of learning. Rather, *learning is a result of development.*

CONSERVATION AND OTHER CAPACITIES. To Piaget, the child functions as a coordinated and integrated system at all levels of development. The mental structures that limit the preoperational child's understanding of the principle of conservation are responsible for other beliefs that, on the surface, have little to do with conservation. A case in point is children's explanation of dreams. Here again, we find a sequence of stages. At first, the child believes dreams come from outside and take place in the child's room. Later, he or she guesses that the source of dreams is in the head but that the dreams themselves still exist externally. Finally, the child comes to see dreams as internal both in origin and in the experience of them. These three stages may be seen in the following examples (from Piaget, 1951), in which children respond to questions about the source and location of dreams:

Stage 1
When do you dream? — At night. — *Where is the dream when you are dreaming?* — In the sky.... *Can you touch the dream?* — No, you can't see and besides you're asleep.... *When you are asleep, could another person see your dream?* — No, because you're asleep. — *Why can't one see it?* — Because it is night. — *Where do dreams come from?* — From the sky. *(pp. 93–94)*

Stage 2
What is a dream? — You dream at night. You are thinking of something*(!)* — *Where does it come from?* — I don't know. — *What do you think?* — That we make them ourselves*(!)* — *Where is the dream while you are dreaming?* — Outside. — *Where?* — There *(pointing to the street, through the window).* *(p. 107)*

Stage 3

Where do dreams come from? — In the eyes. — Where is the dream? — In the eyes. — Show me where. — Behind there (pointing to the eye). — Is a dream the same as a thought? — No, it is something. — What? — A story. (p. 117)

In the first stage, the child's judgment is governed by the appearance of things. Just as there appears to be more water in a taller glass, a dream *appears* to take place somewhere outside of the child. In the second stage, the child vacillates between an "external" and an "internal" explanation of dreams. The same child who said we "make dreams ourselves" also said later that dreams are made "in the bed... from air." Similarly, children in the middle stage of the development of conservation may say at one time that a taller glass contains more water and at another time that a wider glass contains more. The third stage, in which the child recognizes that dreams are internal, is parallel to the stage at which the child acquires the concept of conservation.

The stages in children's understanding of conservation can also be related to their appreciation of humor. A study of this relationship was conducted by McGhee (1976). He predicted that the child would show greater appreciation of humor soon after the concept of conservation involved in a joke had been acquired and less appreciation both before acquiring the concept and several years afterward. Table 8–1 presents examples of the conservation-related jokes used in the study. The results

TABLE 8–1
Conservation Jokes Used in McGhee Study

1. Mr. Jones went into a restaurant and ordered a whole pizza for dinner. When the waiter asked if he wanted it cut into six or eight pieces, Mr. Jones said: "Oh, you'd better make it six! I could never eat eight!"

2. Joey lives near an ice cream store where they give really big scoops of ice cream. One day Joey asked for two scoops, and the man asked if he wanted them in one dish or two. "Oh, just one dish," said Joey. "I could never eat two dishes of ice cream."

3. Johnny's mother walked into a restaurant and ordered a whole cake to eat. When the waitress asked if she wanted it cut into four or eight pieces, she said: "Just cut it in four pieces; I'm trying to lose weight."

4. One day George and Bobby found an old raft, and they decided to take their picnic lunch and eat it on the raft. When they got out in the middle of the lake, George took his big thermos of lemonade and drank it all at once. Just then, the raft started to sink. George said: "That'll teach me! Drinking all that lemonade made me too heavy for the raft."

Source: McGhee, 1976, Table 1, p. 422.

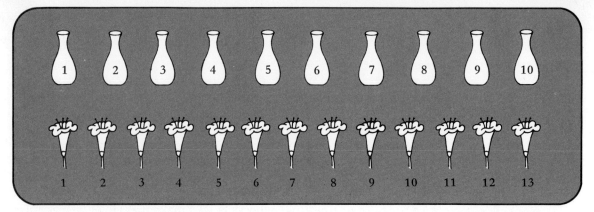

FIGURE 8–8
*Piaget's experiment
testing children's
understanding of
one-to-one
correspondence
(Piaget, 1965)*

of the experiment confirmed McGhee's hypothesis: The highest "funniness ratings" were found among children who had recently acquired the concept of conservation of mass and would soon apply the principle of conservation to weight as well. The jokes apparently presented the greatest challenge to children at this level of development. College students, on the other hand, did not find them very funny.

As we have seen, the concept of conservation relates to many areas, including dreams and even humor. One of the most important concepts in the child's mental development relates to numbers. The preoperational child is unable to conserve and believes that the number of items in an array changes if the arrangement of those items is altered.

THE CONCEPT OF NUMBER

Piaget's studies of the structure of children's thinking have stimulated much research on this subject as well as, more recently, interest in applying his theories in the classroom. One major area of investigation of the development of the concept of conservation involves the child's concept of number. Here, however, we are not dealing with computational abilities such as simple addition and subtraction. Piaget is not interested in facts that can be memorized. He is concerned with the basic ideas underlying those abilities—one-to-one correspondence and conservation of number.

One-to-one correspondence is the operation that establishes that two sets of objects are equivalent in number. The sets may contain completely different objects—apples and oranges, shoes and socks. The question is whether the child can recognize that both sets contain the same number of objects. An adult can do this by counting; a child has to put the objects in set B next to those in set A in order to understand that they are equal in number.

Piaget conducted an experiment to test children's understanding of one-to-one correspondence. He presented the children with a set of 10

*One-to-One
Correspondence*

vases and a bunch of flowers. Each child was asked (in appropriate words) to construct a set of flowers equal to the set of vases. A typical response was that of a 4-year-old who assembled a row of 13 flowers equal *in length* to the row of 10 vases (Piaget, 1965), as illustrated in Figure 8–8. He could see that the rows were the same length, and, therefore, he assumed that the number of flowers and the number of vases were the same. Again, we see how the young child is deceived by physical appearance.

Before a child can count, he or she must understand the concept of one-to-one correspondence. Each number goes with one and only one object, and each object, no matter what it looks like, gets one number, the next in the series. It is often amazing how children find ways to simplify this complex task. This was illustrated by the behavior of a 4½-year-old boy who wanted to find out the number of letters in his name. Before trying to count them, he carefully drew a line beside each letter; he then successfully counted the lines.

Conservation of Number

To find out whether the child realizes that two sets are equivalent in number even when their appearance is changed, the boy was told to put a flower in each vase (the extra flowers were set aside). The boy in Piaget's experiment then watched while each of the 10 flowers was taken out of its vase. Next, the flowers were bunched in front of the vases so that the 10 flowers formed a shorter row than the 10 vases. Piaget continued his questioning:

Is there the same number of vases and flowers? — No. — *Where are there more?* — There are more vases. — *If we put the flowers back into the vases, will there be one flower in each vase?* — Yes. — *Why?* — Because there are enough. [*Piaget then closed up the spaces between vases and opened spaces between the flowers.*] *And now?* — There are more flowers. (Piaget, 1965, p. 50)

Thus, even when the boy himself had established a one-to-one correspondence between the flowers and the vases, he failed to *conserve* their numerical equivalence. Conservation of number is the mental operation whereby equivalence is preserved even though the perceptual array has been modified (see Figure 8–9). When the rows of flowers and vases looked different, the child believed that they actually *were* different.

The child goes through three stages in acquiring the concept of conservation of number and in the transition from preoperational to operational thought (as will later be the case with conservation of mass or volume). In the first stage, the child fails to conserve, as illustrated by the experiment just described. The child centers on only one dimension — the length of the rows — and ignores other dimensions such as the space between the objects in the rows.

In the second stage, the child can construct two sets that are equivalent

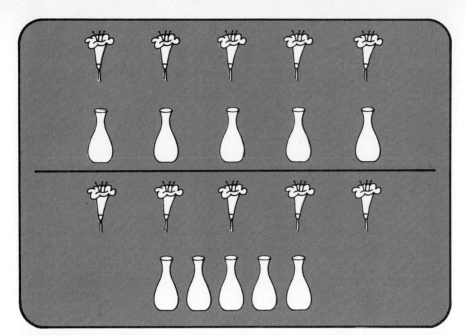

FIGURE 8–9
Conservation of number experiment (Piaget, 1965)

in number. But the child fails to conserve their equivalent when the spatial arrangement is altered. The stage 2 child may vacillate, however. In the case of two rows of pennies, for example, the child may say at one time that there are more pennies in the longer, widely spaced row "because it's a longer line." But after a minute, the same child may say that there are more pennies in the shorter row "because there's a little bundle." In Piaget's terms, the child centers first on length and then on density but does not yet coordinate the two dimensions.

In stage 3, the child does two things. First, the child constructs a set that is numerically equivalent to another set. Second, the child conserves numerical equivalence when the spatial arrangement of the two sets is changed. The child recognizes (1) that the number of objects in the rows is the same since nothing was added or subtracted, (2) that row B can be lengthened or shortened to match row A, and (3) that the greater density of one row compensates for the greater length of the other. The child recognizes the numerical relationship between the two sets and now knows that changes in appearance do not signify changes in number.

The term *numerosity* refers to "how many," that is, to the number of items *Numerosity* in a set. Pre-Piagetian studies of children's concepts of numerosity simply assessed children's knowledge of "number facts." Beckmann (1923) and Descoeudres (1921), for instance, studied the ability of 2- to 6-year-old children to "produce" numbers. They wanted to find out at what age most children understood the concept behind the "name" of a number. Among the tasks used was one in which the children were asked to take a certain number of objects (1, 2, 3, 4, or 5) out of a box. Since the children did not have another set of objects to match (that is, a model) they were required to respond to numerosity alone.

Table 8–2 presents the percentage of children in each age group represented in the Beckmann and Descoeudres studies who could produce each number consistently. By the age of 3, most children can reliably

Children's concepts of numbers progress in stages in the transition from preoperational to operational thought.
(J. Berndt, Stock, Boston)

AGE	NUMBER								
	1*	2		3		4		5	
		B	D	B	D	B	D	B	D
2	40	30	40	0	0	0	—	0	—
2½	79	70	74	0	16	0	0	0	0
3	100	70	100	20	19	4	4	0	4
3½	100	84	97	20	67	12	13	4	0
4	100	90	97	63	78	39	25	17	11
4½	100	99	100	83	87	55	61	36	32
5	100	100	100	82	96	64	81	45	33
5½	100	100	100	93	100	87	73	70	14
6	100	100	—†	96	100	92	100	74	93

*Data for the number 1 were collected only in the Descoeudres study.
†Dash indicates that data were not collected.
Source: Adapted from Gelman, 1972, Table 1, p. 124.

TABLE 8–2
Percentages of Children in the Beckmann and Descoeudres Studies Able to Produce Each Number Consistently

produce the number 2, but not the number 3. They become capable of producing the number 3 between the ages of 3 and 4. They cannot produce numbers larger than 3 until they are 4½ or 5 years old.

Descoeudres also found that a young child will pay attention to the numerosity of an array if that array is small enough for the child to estimate the number of objects in it accurately. However, the young child's ability to estimate numerosity breaks down at some number between 2 and 5. The typical 3½-year-old can estimate the numbers 1, 2, and 3 reliably in a variety of tasks and can sometimes estimate the number 4. Any number larger than 4 is regarded as "a lot," or arbitrarily labeled "twenty" or "a hundred." Descoeudres called this the "1, 2, 3, beaucoup (many)" phenomenon.

Piaget made an important contribution to research in the area of children's concepts of number. Early investigators were concerned with the child's mastery of number facts. Piaget added the question of *how* children construct a concept of number. Recent studies have elaborated on some of the implications of earlier research in the light of Piaget's work.

ESTIMATORS AND OPERATORS. *Estimators* are the cognitive processes by which one determines some quantity, such as how many items there are in an array or whether one array has more items than another. In the case of numerosity, the estimate can be a guess (how many pennies in a piggy bank); it can be based on counting; or it can be derived from the configuration of the items (such as they way values are shown on playing cards). *Operators* are the processes by which one determines the consequences of transforming a quantity in various ways (Gelman, 1972). If coins are added to the piggy bank, the amount increases; if coins are taken out, the amount decreases. But if the coins are taken from the bank and spread out on the table, the amount is unchanged. Estimators involve a "lower" level of processing than operators and are more closely tied to perception. For example, one cannot estimate the quantity of coins unless the coins are actually present, but one can state that pouring the coins from one container to another will not change their numerosity, even though the coins and the containers are not present. Preoperational children can accurately *estimate* small numbers, but they lack the *operators* that would enable them to see that the number of objects in a group of any size is not changed when the objects are rearranged. According to Piaget, operators are necessary to a mature concept of number.

NUMEROSITY VERSUS OTHER CUES. How children estimate numbers changes during the preoperational period. First, children count and later they estimate small quantities by glancing at an array. When asked how they know the answer, these children say, "It looks like two" or "I can see it's three." Recall that in our earlier discussion, we presented Piaget's claim that young children center on the length or density of an array rather than its number. And yet other research suggests that with small arrays, young children respond to numerosity. In a study investigating how children estimate number, Gelman (1972) examined which features (density, length, numerosity) of an array form the basis of an estimate. This study used the "triad" method. From among three arrays, children were asked to choose two that had the "same number" of items. Each pair of arrays was alike in only one feature. Hence, choice of that pair had to be based on that particular feature. In Figure 8–10, for example, choice of A and B would be based on numerosity; choice of A and C would be based on length.

The results of the study showed that 4-year-olds consistently responded

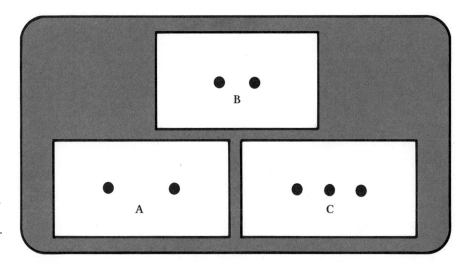

FIGURE 8–10
An array of three stimuli, with variations in density, length, and number (Gelman, 1972)

to numerosity when the arrays contained two or three items. When the arrays contained three or five items, the response to numerosity was less consistent, and the child was likely to estimate on the basis of the *length* of the array. Similar results were obtained with 5-year-olds. However, arrays containing five or nine items elicited different results: 4-year-olds no longer responded to numerosity, and 5-year-olds did so only in some cases. Older children, on the other hand, based their estimates on numerosity in all cases.

There is evidence that young children have a concept of number, at least to some extent. They can respond to numerosity in small arrays, as shown in the "triad" experiment. They can understand that a change in the number of items in an array involves addition or subtraction of items whereas a rearrangement of the items does not. However, these abilities apply only to numbers that the child can estimate. In Piagetian terms, estimators, and not operators, are at work. The young child's concept of number thus is *pre*operational.

LANGUAGE AND THOUGHT IN THE PRESCHOOL CHILD

The thought/language controversy discussed in Chapter 6 has provided fuel for extensive research on the development of both thought and language in children. In general, such research has found that patterns of thinking establish the course of early language development (a Piagetian position). A child cannot talk about a concept or an event he or she does not understand. Thus language development reflects the limitations and the creativeness of thought in the preschool child. We have already mentioned the inventiveness in children's growing ability to recognize and know permanent objects and to have some hypotheses about how objects are named. Children label objects within their own rather limited frame of reference, and it is their remarkable ability to synthesize information and observations that astounds and amuses adults. One boy, for instance, began to call horses "forses" when he observed that horses have four legs. Because the child has learned that objects are permanent fixtures of his world, he is now ready to consider those objects as long-term, and he focuses attention and curiosity on the attributes of objects. In short, he is constructing a *system* out of formerly fleeting and diverse things, and he has need for a vocabulary to match and describe his system. He now comes to need and to learn words that denote relations among items and among events in time and space. Thus, as preschool children begin to understand the principle of conservation, they begin to acquire the vocabulary of conservation—words relating to number, size, weight, height, space, and time.

Cromer (1974) has studied children's expressions of concepts such as temporal order. He argues that even though children have the words and

An understanding of conservation is accompanied by the acquisition of words relating to number, size, weight, space, and volume. (David Strickler, Monkmeyer)

the syntactic capacity to express concepts about time, they do not—indeed, *cannot*—do so before they understand the concepts themselves. They may say things like "I can't whistle any more" (meaning *yet*); "I told you later" (meaning *earlier*); and "the day before (meaning *after*) tomorrow." In other words, children cannot use language to express relations they have not mastered.

Another group of experiments bearing on the relationship between language and thought dealt with the words used by children during Piagetian conservation tasks. Sinclair-de-Zwart (1969) observed that children who have learned to conserve quantity use comparative terms, such as *more,* when describing different quantities. Children who have not yet acquired the conservation concept tend to use absolute terms, such as *a lot* and *a little.* Interestingly, children used comparatives for discrete units (such as marbles) before they did so for continuous quantities (such as clay)—and the conservation of discrete units (that is, number) is acquired earlier than the conservation of quantity.

Among the conclusions suggested by Sinclair-de-Zwart's study is that relational terms such as *more, less, as much as,* and *none* form a class whose use is linked to operational ability (such as conservation of quantity). The difficulty encountered by the child in learning to use such words appears to be parallel to the difficulty he or she encounters in developing operations such as conservation. The words, like the dimensions, are not yet coordinated into a system.

Moreover, children who conserve use different terms for different dimensions (long-short, fat-thin), whereas nonconservers tend to use one word for several dimensions (big for either long or wide). More important, children who conserve are able to coordinate two dimensions in their descriptions: This pencil is longer but thinner, and this one is shorter but thicker. The nonconservers describe only one dimension at a time.

The investigators then tried to teach nonconservers the language used by conservers to describe objects. The results were striking; it was easy to teach nonconservers different terms for different dimensions but extremely difficult to teach coordinated descriptions. In subsequent tests of the conservation of liquid, only 10% of the children showed improvement although more than half could describe the relation between the higher level of the liquid and the narrower glass. Sinclair-de-Zwart concludes that verbal training might lead children to recognize different dimensions of the problem, but it does not bring about operational thought. It should be clear from the preceding discussion that children's language capacities undergo continuing refinement related to their ability to understand more complex concepts.

Language as a Mediator

It has been proposed that language acts as a mediator in the solution of problems — that linguistic capacities assist the child in problem-solving situations. Verbal mediation enables the child to generalize — to extend the same label (word) to include many objects, all of which evoke the same response. This is a controversial proposition, and investigators of the relationship between language and thought have often focused on it. Careful attention has been given to the verbal labels used by children during problem solving in order to determine whether those who verbalize have an advantage over those who do not.

Consider first the transposition problem. Suppose children are shown two squares, one of which is larger than the other. The child has to figure out which of the two squares is the "correct" one, that is, which one, when chosen, will earn the child a reinforcement. Suppose the experimenter reinforces the child (with praise or a piece of candy) every time the larger square is chosen. Eventually, the child solves the problem and chooses the larger square on every trial. Now the experimenter substitutes a new pair of squares for the old ones in order to test whether the child "transposes" — that is, continues to choose the larger square. What happens if the squares in the new pair are *considerably* larger than the squares in the

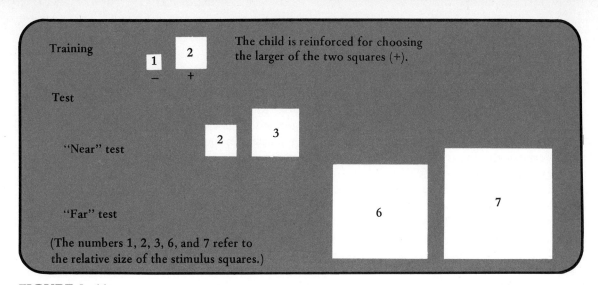

Training — The child is reinforced for choosing the larger of the two squares (+).

1 − 2 +

Test

"Near" test — 2 3

"Far" test — 6 7

(The numbers 1, 2, 3, 6, and 7 refer to the relative size of the stimulus squares.)

FIGURE 8–11
The ability to verbalize the size relation seems to determine whether children transpose on a "far" test

old pair? The problem is illustrated in Figure 8–11. When the test pair differs slightly from the training pair, the test is called a "near" test; when the test pair differs considerably from the training pair, the test is called a "far" test. What happens with this new test depends on the age of the child. Children between the ages of 3 and 6 years tend to choose the larger square (number 3) on a near test. That is, they all transpose from the old test to the new test. It is the children's choices on a far test that help us understand the mediating function of language.

In one study (Kuenne, 1946), 3-year-olds were less likely than 5-year-olds to transpose (to choose number 7) on a far test. In addition, none of the 3-year-olds but almost all of the 5- and 6-year-olds used words such as "big," "small," "bigger than," or "smaller than" to explain their choices. It appears that the ability to verbalize the size relation determined whether children transposed on a far test. Verbal ability appeared to function as a mediating link between the physical stimulus (S) and the overt choice response (R). Investigators who work within the framework of traditional S → R learning theory argued that in order to explain the difference between the performance of the older and the younger children, it is necessary to attribute to the older children a mediating process (such as language) that permits the child to abstract and retain the relationship even when the physical appearance of objects changes dramatically. Younger children, without language ability, remain fixed on a specific size square and are unable to transpose the idea of relative size from one test to another. Older children, with verbal ability, are able to remind themselves, using words, to pick the larger square in the second test.

Still another shift seems to occur between 5 and 8 years of age. Children at both these ages transpose on a far test. When instructed to choose the "same" stimulus on a near test of transposition, the younger children transpose (they choose stimulus number 3). But older children are more

251

likely to choose stimulus number 2 when instructed to choose the "same" stimulus. Although both groups use mediation (as indicated by their performance on a far test), in this context, the word "same" has different meanings at these ages (Fein, 1972). The younger children choose the square that maintains the same relationship as that learned in the training pair—that is, the *larger* square (number 3). The older children interpret "same" to mean same *size,* when that option is available. Thus, on a near test, they choose square number 2, which is the same size as the correct answer in the training pair.

Flavell, Beach, and Chinsky (1966) have proposed that there is a difference between children who have not acquired language (and therefore cannot use verbal mediators) and children who have acquired language (and could use verbal mediators if they knew how). The very young child who does not produce relevant words in the first place has a "production deficiency." The somewhat older child who produces these words but does not use them to solve problems has a "mediation deficiency." In an ingenious study, Flavell et al. used lip reading to observe the verbal behavior of children between the ages of 5 and 10 years who were engaged in a problem-solving activity. Most of the older children and few of the younger children "talked to themselves," suggesting that it is only the older children who spontaneously use language to help themselves in problem-solving activities.

On the other side of the question of language as mediator, Blank (1974) points out that children often cannot use the relevant words even when they are supplied. This, of course, is the point made by Piagetians. They would say that these children lack the necessary cognitive structures to use the words effectively. The children cannot apply words to problems they do not understand.

The eminent Soviet psychologist Vygotsky (1934, 1956) proposed that there is a directive function of language. At first, language is used to express the child's activity; that is, language accompanies action. Gradually, though, language becomes more than a means of communicating action. Eventually, it becomes able to regulate motor activity. If, for example, a 2-year-old is asked to put a doll on the bed, he or she will do it. If the child is told, "Don't put the doll on the bed," he or she will probably do it anyway. And if the child is asked to say "Don't," he or she is still likely to put the doll on the bed. It is as if the language guidance function is only partially effective. It is tied to positive action; it can direct action but cannot direct nonaction.

Directive Function of Language

The child must be able to dissociate language and action before language can *guide* behavior. For example, in one experiment (Tikhomirov, 1958), children were instructed to press a bell every time a red light flashed and not to press it when a blue light flashed. They were further instructed to say "Press" or "Don't press" as the lights flashed. A 3½-year-old could easily respond to the signals with the appropriate words. But as the child said "Don't press," he or she not only pressed the bell but pressed it even harder. Not until the age of 4 or 4½ does the verbal response "Don't press" actually inhibit the child's behavior.

COMMUNICATION DURING THE PRESCHOOL YEARS

In Chapters 6 and 7, we saw that communication does not depend on language alone. The child becomes a part of several communication systems long before speech is acquired. He or she "reads" nonverbal signals —smiles, gestures, physical contact—and produces nonverbal signals that are "read" by others. With respect to the exchange of information, however, words have special advantages over nonverbal signals.

But language is much more than a means of sharing information. It is used to express feelings, to control the behavior of others, to maintain social contacts, to entertain. A child who is acquiring language must find out not only what it consists of but also what it is used for and how it is used. He or she must learn the social rules governing what can be said, to whom, and when.

Role Taking The acquisition of speech greatly enhances the child's ability to communicate with others. However, it is important to distinguish between linguistic competence and the effective *use* of language in interpersonal communication. Such use involves the ability to take the listener's point of view— *role taking*. Children achieve a reasonable amount of linguistic competence by the age of 3½. They can express feelings, make their needs known, and discuss in general ways items and events that are part of their daily experiences. But even at age 10, they do not approach adult levels of communication competence. For example, they cannot yet always consider another person's point of view, and their powers of persuasion are still developing.

The distinction between *linguistic* and *communication* competence is illustrated in a classic experiment by Krauss and Glucksberg (1969). In the experiment, two children are seated facing each other but separated by a screen that prevents each from seeing the other. In front of one of the children is a stack of six wooden blocks, each of which is stamped with a design (see Figure 8–12). In front of the other child is a matching set of six blocks spread out in a random order. The child with the set of stacked blocks is designated as the speaker. He or she is asked to describe the forms on the blocks so that the other child (the listener) will be able to stack his or her blocks in the same order as those of the speaker. After each trial, the children compare their stacks. They then repeat the task with a different stacking order each time.

In order to determine what the listener needs to know to stack the

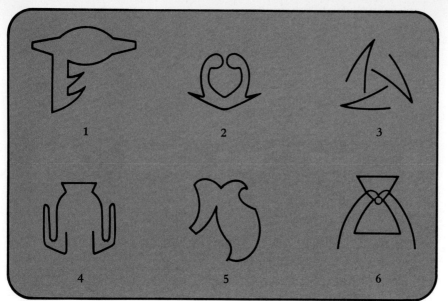

FIGURE 8–12
Forms used in experiment to distinguish linguistic competence from communication competence (Krauss and Glucksberg, 1969)

blocks successfully, the speaker must take the point of view of the listener. A child who identifies Form 6 to the listener as looking "like Mommy's hat," for example, does not realize that this information is useless from the other's point of view. Young children have trouble conveying information, because they are firmly tied to their own points of view. One child in the Krauss and Glucksberg experiment demonstrated this fact quite well by describing Form 5 as "a pipe, a yellow part of a pipe." The addition of the word "yellow" could have had absolutely no meaning to the listener, since the forms were stamped in black ink on the wooden blocks.

The results of the Krauss and Glucksberg experiment showed that young children were incapable of taking the listener's point of view. Kindergartners showed no improvement in ability to communicate even after eight trials at the task. Flavell et al. (1969) found that when asked to explain a game to a blindfolded listener, young children do not take into account the listener's special status, often saying things like "and then you move it there." Older children in the Krauss and Glucksberg experiment, however, did demonstrate improved ability to match their communications to the point of view of the listener. Improvement in ability to describe the six forms so that their partners could identify them was least in first graders and greatest in fifth graders, indicating that communication competence does develop with age (Krauss and Glucksberg, 1969).

Private Speech

When two young children talk with each other, very little communication may actually occur. They may appear to be talking to each other, but in reality they are simply verbalizing in each other's presence, as the following dialogue (or "collective monologue") shows:

254

Peter
I'm throwing it, I'm throwing it.

How far it goes, how far it goes.

I'll run after it.

See you there.

(Danziger, 1976, pp. 157–158)

Paul

This box is heavy.

It's full of stones.

It won't move, it won't move.

I'm going to empty it.

Piaget characterizes the speech of young children as *egocentric,* because it reflects their inability to distinguish between their own points of view and those of others. According to Piaget, communication does not take place in such situations, because there is no *desire* to communicate. The child's use of speech is purely expressive. In one experiment (Piaget and Inhelder, 1956), children were placed in front of a scale model of three mountains and asked to select a photograph showing how the mountains

As shown in tests devised by Piaget, young children have difficulty distinguishing their own point of view from that of others. (George Roos, DPI)

would look from another position, such as the opposite side. Young children tended to select the photograph showing the mountains the way they themselves had seen them. In Piaget's terms, they could not *decenter* from their own perspective.

On a verbal level, the same sort of decentering is necessary if the child is to consider other points of view. Parallel to the experiment just described is one in which children were asked to make up a story about a picture containing three people and then retell the story from the point of view of each person in turn (Feffer and Gourevitch, 1960). Younger children's stories dealt mostly with what they saw in the pictures. Older children took into account the supposed thoughts, emotions, and intentions of the characters and introduced appropriate changes of perspective when they retold their stories. In short, the role-taking skills of the older children increased as they became able to attribute coherent patterns of motivation and thinking to others. Such skills are fundamental to the development of skill in interpersonal communication. According to Piaget, the egocentric speech of young children must give way to role taking if true communication is to occur. Other investigators, however, take issue with Piaget's claim that young children's speech is entirely egocentric.

The speech of young children, which is not addressed or adapted to a listener, is often called *private speech* by researchers who feel that Piaget's label of egocentric speech has too many negative connotations.

According to Vygotsky (1962), the failure of private speech to communicate does not indicate the child's lack of intent or ability to communicate. Vygotsky claims that there is a social intent behind the child's speech, but that what is happening is that the child is really addressing himself. He believes that the child does not distinguish clearly between the self as listener and others as listeners. According to Vygotsky, private speech does reflect some social communicative ability or intent even though the self becomes the listener. The self, he proposes, is a more intimate and understanding listener than another person, and, therefore, the conversation can be abbreviated, as are conversations between very close friends, which may be unintelligible to others. Piaget claims that the speaking child is egocentric, because he or she does not differentiate the self as speaker from the listener; according to Piaget, the child *cannot* differentiate between private speech and social speech. In either case, the effect is the same: Young children speak to themselves or to the air around them rather than *to* each other.

PEER CONVERSATION. Numerous studies have investigated children's conversations with each other. Although such conversations are often "egocentric," they also can be high in social and informational content. Garvey and Hogan (1973), for instance, found a surprising amount of mutual responsiveness among 3½- to 5-year-olds. These investigators made videotapes (through one-way mirrors) of pairs of children in a playroom. The children produced many collective monologues like the one quoted earlier. But they also produced exchanges such as the following:

Speaker A	Speaker B
(Hums theme song from television show)	
	We watch that.
Me, too.	
	Isn't it funny?
I know, it sure is.	
	My group got shot.
	Did your group ever get shot?
No.	
	Well, mine did.
Will you put this hammer in (tool belt) for me?	
	(Puts hammer in)
Thank you, I'll take it (tool belt) now.	
(Garvey and Hogan, 1973, p. 564)	

Obviously, social speech does occur in young children.

Mueller (1972) examined the factors that determine whether an utterance will receive a response. In addition to the utterance itself, he examined factors such as the listener's visual attention and the physical distance between the children. A response might consist of nonverbal behavior, such as shaking the head, as well as verbal replies. Mueller found that 62% of all the children's utterances produced a definite response from the listener. Significantly, the most powerful predictors of success involved the *listener's* behavior. That is, when the listener was watching the speaker at the beginning of the utterance or when the utterance was itself a response to something the listener had said, a reply was most likely.

These results do not contradict Piaget—there *is* a good deal of egocentric speech among young children—but they do accentuate the positive: Much of children's speech *is* social, and skillfully social at that.

ADJUSTING TO THE LISTENER. Some psychologists question the methods used to determine the egocentrism of young children's speech. Shatz and Gelman (1973) point out that communication tasks that involve role taking focus on the ability to make ordered statements. It can be argued that children perform poorly on such tasks because they lack the ability to provide the required explanations, even to themselves. But preschool children have been known to "talk down" to younger children, and what is this if it is not adjusting their speech to the listeners?

Shatz and Gelman conducted a series of three studies exploring young children's ability to adjust their speech to the listener. In the first (Study

A), 4-year-old children were asked to tell an adult about a toy and then to tell a 2-year-old about the same toy. In Study B, tape recordings of similar, but uncontrolled, conversations were obtained. In Study C, tapes of 4-year-olds talking to their peers were obtained. The results were as follows: When talking to younger children, the 4-year-olds used shorter, simpler utterances than when talking to adults. Their speech to peers, on the other hand, resembled their speech to adults. Clearly, young children can adjust their speech to the listener. But this ability is evident only when the child is talking about objects and events he or she understands. The child can more readily talk about a familiar toy than about an unfamiliar picture or form. The 4-year-old adjusts differently to listeners of different ages. The younger the listener, the greater the tendency to use simple utterances. Children are also influenced by the listener's ability to pay attention. There is some evidence that they are aware of younger children's cognitive limitations. Thus speaker and listener *interact* to produce an environment that is favorable to communication.

LINGUISTIC ENVIRONMENTS

The preceding discussion shows that even 4-year-olds participate in producing a linguistic environment suited to the needs of the child who is just beginning to speak. The particular environment in which a child learns to speak may have a strong influence on his or her later use of language. For example, Nelson (1973b) has identified two different patterns in the way parents use language with their children. When interactions between parent and child contain numerous references to things, the child's early speech will contain a large number of object names. Highly social interactions, on the other hand, result in the use of a large number of expressive phrases such as "go by-bye." There is no question that the home environment is a fundamental factor in the child's language development. Parents seem to sense this and to modify their speech to suit their perceptions of the child's needs. Hence the prevalence of "nursery talk" as well as the use of simple words such as "dog" and the avoidance of longer words such as "poodle" or "animal."

It is well known that parents naturally adapt their speech to the language abilities of their children. But how is this accomplished? Moerk (1975) has studied this question in detail, considering not only such factors as the length of parents' and children's statements but also the *types* of interaction involved. (Such interactions include "mother describes her own acts," "mother answers a question," "child imitates," "child expresses a need.") It appears that parents use slightly longer utterances than those used by the child but shorter utterances than those they would use with another adult. The parents' utterances are within the range of the child's competence, but the child has to put some effort into under-

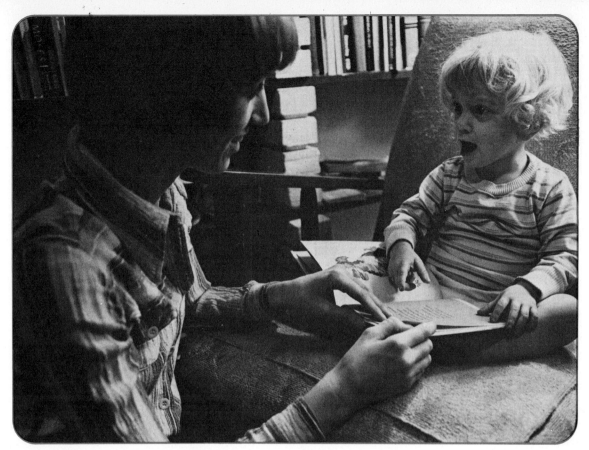

One-to-one interactions between the child and an adult provide opportunities to practice developing language skills. (Joel Gordon, DPI)

standing them. In other words, adults pace their speech slightly ahead of the child's current level of performance and so stimulate the child to reach higher levels of mastery.

The types of interactions that take place between parent and child also change as the child gains in language competence. Certain communications become more frequent, and others diminish in frequency. Among those that become more frequent are "child describes a past experience"; among those that diminish in frequency are "child imitates." According to Moerk, more "primitive" forms of interaction (such as imitation) are replaced with more complex forms. The correlations between parent and child behaviors again show a high level of mutual adaptation. For example, as the child begins asking more questions, the parent provides more answers, explanations, and descriptions of objects, events, and actions including past experiences and future plans.

Environments other than the home also influence the child's speech. Sometimes this happens in ways parents do not favor, as when the child comes home from the playground, saying words that have been carefully avoided at home. If the child goes to a nursery school, the "instructional language" used there will play a role in his or her linguistic development.

And peers and siblings have a significant effect as well. It has been suggested that baby talk, parent talk, peer talk, and teacher talk can be viewed as a series of subsystems of the total language system. As the child encounters each subsystem, he or she learns something new about the total system. In addition, the child learns *how* language is used in different situations.

Language Teaching

It is apparent that much teaching and learning of language take place during adult-child interactions. But who ordinarily speaks to the child, and what is the child likely to hear? In a study designed to answer this question, Friedlander (1970) recorded the speech occurring in the homes of two 12-month-old babies. The recordings showed that about 70% of the speech directed toward the babies come from the mother, 20% from the father, and 10% from guests. This speech consisted largely of attempts to teach the baby new words, imitation of the baby's utterances, questions, and word play. Along the same lines, Brown (1970) has observed that young children are not especially encouraged to use correct grammar, since adults generally understand and respond to badly formed sentences. Most of us recall having our grammar corrected by parents and other adults. But upon reflection, one realizes that this happened only a small percentage of the time. Had we been corrected at every error along the way, communication would have been very difficult indeed. Thus it does not appear that children's grammatical progress is a result of explicit attempts to teach them grammar.

Yet, one-to-one interactions between children and adults are known to be effective in helping the child learn certain aspects of language. In addition, children can benefit from specific instruction in language skills, so long as such instruction is geared to the child's capacities. The adaptation of a lesson to the language skills of two different children is illustrated in the following examples. One of the children was a well-functioning boy who did not need the instruction. The other was a girl who had been in a tutorial program for about 3 months. Although she had shown some improvement, she continued to withdraw from cognitively demanding situations.

The conversation centered on a children's book entitled *Are You My Mother?* The first excerpt is from the conversation between the teacher and the well-functioning boy.

Teacher: *Do you know what we call a person who writes books?*
Child: *(Shakes head.)*
Teacher: *Do you think it might be a pilot or an author?*
Child: *Author.*
Teacher: *Yes. Why wouldn't it be a pilot?*
Child: *Cause pilots fly planes.*
(Blank, 1973, pp. 158–159)

In this exchange, the teacher directed the child toward the correct information by giving him a verbal choice. The teacher then *extended* the discussion by asking him to explain why the choice of "pilot" would have been incorrect. Compare the following conversation, on the same subject, with the girl who had been participating in the tutorial program.

Teacher: *Do you remember the name of the person who writes a book?*
Child: *Uh, uh (shakes head).*
Teacher: *Do you think that person's called a doctor?*
Child: *No, doctors check people?*
Teacher: *That's right. You know who writes books — an author.*
   You say "An author writes books."
Child: *An author.*
Teacher: *Say the whole thing — an author writes books.*
Child: *An author writes books.*
(Blank, 1973, pp. 176–177)

Here, the teacher offered only a clearly incorrect choice, because the child had a tendency to guess wildly. Then the child was asked to repeat the correct choice to help focus her attention and to give her practice in using full sentences.

The effectiveness of strategies such as those just described leads to the question of what can be done to improve linguistic environments. Numerous studies have explored the differences between middle-class and economically disadvantaged children in terms of language performance. They have found significant differences in such areas as length of utterance, use of tenses, vocabulary size, and word comprehension. There is some controversy over whether such differences represent deficiencies or simply differences in language behavior (for example, the child may be performing adequately in some dialect such as black American). Yet, it is generally agreed that day-care and similar programs should put some of their efforts into encouraging the development of children's linguistic capacities.

Parental Language and Cognitive Development

It is generally agreed that children who do well in intellectual and academic endeavors come from families in which the parents show interest in their children's intellectual development. But what exactly do parents do to influence cognitive development?

To answer this and related questions, a longitudinal study of mother-child interactions was conducted by Hess and Shipman between 1965 and 1969. The subjects were a group of black mother-child pairs. At the beginning of the study, the children were 4 years old. Hess and Shipman found major differences in the teaching strategies used by the mothers. For example, suppose the mother's task was to teach the child how to group a small number of toys into categories. One mother might explain the task to the child and then let the child proceed, as follows:

"All right, Susan, this board is the place where we put the little toys; first of all you're supposed to learn how to place them according to color. Can you do that? The things that are all the same color you put in one section; in the second section you put another group of colors, and in the third section you put the last group of colors. Can you do that? Or would you like to see me do it first?"

   Child: "I want to do it." (Hess and Shipman, 1965, p. 881)

Another mother might be less precise in her instructions and rely more on nonverbal communication:

"Now, I'll take them all off the board; now you put them all back on the board. What are these?"

   Child: "A truck."

   "All right, just put them right here; put the other one right here; all right, put the other one there." (p. 881)

A third mother might give even less information:

"I've got some chairs, do you want to play the game?" Child does not respond. Mother continues: "O.K. What's this?"

   Child: "A wagon?"

   Mother: "Hm?"

   Child: "A wagon?"

   Mother: "This is not a wagon. What's this?" (p. 882)

When the teaching session was over, each child's achievement was scored on the basis of accuracy of performance and ability to verbalize the principles on which that performance was based. The most effective teaching strategies were those in which the mother accompanied her instructions with reasons, used praise, carefully oriented the child to the task, and gave the child specific feedback.

These results have been replicated in more recent studies (Bee, Nyman, Sarason, and Van Egeren, 1968; Bee, Van Egeren, Streissguth, Nyman, and Leckie, 1969). Bee and her colleagues concentrated on the following aspects of mother-child interaction, on a task of building a house of blocks like a model house:

1. The form in which suggestions were given, whether declarative or interrogative. *The mother could say, for example, "Start with the front of the house," or "Should we start at the front of the house or the back?" Both types of suggestions deal with the same information, but the interrogative form requires some decision from the child, perhaps encouraging more autonomy and more reflection.*

2. The specificity of the suggestions. *All of the mothers' task-oriented*

statements were scored according to three levels of specificity starting with very general orienting suggestions ("Look at the lady's house"), to statements giving a clue but not the solution ("Try this block next"), to statements giving the entire solution ("Put this block right here"). The least specific suggestions require the most thought and allow the greatest latitude of choice for the child; the most specific suggestions will perhaps help him build the house, but would be less likely to generalize to other learning situations.

3. The nature of the feedback. *Both positive and negative feedback (i.e., praise and criticism) may be helpful to the child coping with a complex task. But positive feedback is not only a more effective teaching strategy. Repeated negative reinforcement may well result in general avoidance of similar problem solving or learning situations.*

4. The extent to which the mother became physically involved herself with the task. *Again, the extent to which the mother gets involved building the house herself rather than encouraging or instructing the child to build seems to have strong implications for the child's feeling of participation and autonomy in working toward a solution himself. (Streissguth and Bee, 1972, pp. 164–165)*

The mothers who used more questions, more praise, less criticism, and less specific suggestions and who intruded into the task less often had children who were more persistent, better able to profit from instructions, better able to think before making a choice, and more imitative of an adult model. Bee and her associates, like Hess and Shipman, believe their results support the hypothesis that parental teaching strategies are related to children's cognitive development. However, they caution that this is not necessarily a *causal* relationship. Perhaps the relationship could better be described as a mutual adaptation that develops over a period of years.

In fact, there is a growing body of evidence suggesting that parental behaviors need to change as children grow older. For the infant, cognitive development is associated with social stimulation, parental attention, and affection. During the preschool years, parents must, on the one hand, deal with the increasingly assertive behavior of their children, so that discipline becomes an issue. On the other hand, children require more specific intellectual guidance and help during this period than social stimulation alone could provide.

SUMMARY

During the second year of life when children begin to acquire the basic elements of thought, they are entering Piaget's preoperational period. This period, extending from age 2 to about age 7, marks a transition from think-ing with the body to thinking with the mind. A striking phenomenon of the preoperational period is the development of the use of language, the most remarkable feature of linguistic play being the spontaneous invention of new forms of words. Equally fascinating as an indicator of development are the changes that occur in children's drawings, which gradually become more and more representational. As intelligence develops, the achievements that children mastered at a sensorimotor level can be reconstructed at a higher symbolic-representational level.

The symbolic function, which enables children to make an object, symbol, or word represent something that is not immediately present, emerges between the ages of 2 and 4. One example of the use of mental symbols involves *deferred imitation,* or the ability to "store" another person's actions and reproduce them later. To Piagetians, the distinction between the *figurative* and *operative* aspects of intelligence is important. The operative aspect refers to the actions (physical and mental) with which children deal with changes in the environment. The figurative aspect refers to the mental image of the object or the word that stands for the object. The construction of a mental symbol involves a process of *accommodation.*

The development of the symbolic function is also expressed in symbolic play, which occupies a large portion of preoperational children's time. Whereas formation of mental symbols involves accommodation, symbolic play involves *assimilation.* Symbolic play helps children adjust their own perceptions of the world to reality.

Between the ages of 2 and 4, children first begin to demonstrate intuitive thought. But preoperational children are limited in the mental operations they can perform. They do not yet understand operations as systems, as organized networks of related acts. Young children "center" on only one aspect of a situation. They are unable to "decenter" and to consider mentally either all the relationships involved or the reversibility of an action.

To Piaget, one of the most important cognitive achievements of childhood is the construction of stable and permanent concepts — invariances — in the face of continuous change in the environment. The concept of the object as a permanently and constantly existing thing is acquired during the second year of life. Then children are ready to grapple with the permanence of attributes of objects (such as amount, number, weight, and volume) — the concept known as *conservation.* Studies have repeatedly indicated that children go through a sequence of stages in acquiring the concept of conservation. At about age 7, children begin to enter what Piaget calls the concrete operational period. They can now perform *concrete operations* — mental actions applied only to present objects. They can perform certain actions in their heads but are not yet able to deal with abstract concepts. Concrete operational children are able to decenter attention and coordinate two dimensions, but their mental ability is tied to specific situations and objects. Children do not acquire conservation in all domains at the same time. It may take months or years before they can apply what they learned in one task to another task, even though the same concept is involved. Piaget calls this display of different levels of achievement in problems involving similar mental operations *horizontal décalage*. Experiments designed to test conservation indicate that even with training, children cannot solve certain types of problems if their cognitive structure is not ready to assimilate the new information.

To Piaget, children function as coordinated and integrated systems at all levels of development. The mental structures that limit preoperational children's understanding of the principle of conservation affect other areas as well, notably children's explanations of dreams and their appreciation of humor.

One major area of investigation in the development of conservation involves numbers — one-to-one correspondence and conservation of number. *One-to-one correspondence* is the operation that establishes that two sets of objects are equivalent in number. Preoperational children have to put the objects in one set next to those in a second set to understand that they are equal in number. *Conservation of number* is the mental operation whereby equivalence is preserved even though the perceptual array has been modified. Children go through three stages in acquiring the concept of conservation of number: (1) Children fail to conserve; they center on only one dimension and ignore other dimensions. (2) Children can construct two sets that are equivalent in number, but they fail to conserve their equivalence when the spatial arrangement is altered. (3) Children construct a set that is numerically equivalent to a second set, and they conserve numerical equivalence when the spatial arrangement of the two sets is changed. The concept of *numerosity* — the number of items in a set — also develops over time. Until about age 5, any number larger than 4 is regarded as "a lot"; this has been called the "1, 2, 3, beaucoup (many)" phenomenon. *Estimators* are the cognitive processes used to determine some quantity, such as how many items there are in an array or whether one array has more items than another. *Operators* are the processes used to determine the consequences of transforming a quantity in various ways. Preoperational children can accurately estimate small numbers, but they lack the operators that would enable them to see that the number of objects in a group of any size does not change when the objects are rearranged.

The same is true of language and the relationship between thought and language ability. Piaget has found that thought is a prerequisite for language; therefore children cannot talk about a concept or an event that they do not understand. As preschool children begin to understand conservation, they begin to acquire the vocabulary of conservation — words relating to number, size, weight, height, space, and time. Relational terms such as *more, less, as much as,* and *none* form a class whose use is linked to operational ability (such as conservation of quantity). The difficulty encountered by children in learning to use relational words appears to parallel the difficulty they encounter in developing operations such as conservation. The words, like the dimensions, are not yet coordinated into a system. Children's language capacities undergo continuing refinement related to their ability to understand more complex concepts.

It has been proposed that language acts as a mediator in the solutions of problems, that linguistic capacities assist children in problem solving. Verbal mediation enables children to generalize, to extend the same label (word) to include many objects, all of which evoke the same response. Studies of transposition problems support the idea that mediational processes influence the way people solve problems. Some investigators have proposed that there is a difference between children who have not acquired language (and therefore cannot use verbal mediators) and children who have acquired language (and could use verbal mediators if they knew how). Young children who do not produce relevant words in the first place have a "production deficiency." Somewhat older children who produce these words but do not use them to solve problems have a "mediation deficiency." In addition, children often cannot use the relevant words even when they are supplied. Piagetians would say that these children lack the necessary cognitive structures to use the words effectively; they cannot apply words to problems they do not understand.

The directive function of language also develops in stages. At first, language accompanies action. Gradually, it regulates motor activity. For children up to about 4 years of age, language can direct positive action but cannot direct nonaction. Children must be able to dissociate language and action before language can guide behavior.

Children who are acquiring language must find out not only what it consists of but also what it is used for and how it is used. The effective use of language in interpersonal communication involves *role taking*— the ability to take the listener's point of view. The ability to speak (*linguistic* competence) develops earlier than the ability to exchange information (*communication* competence). Communication competence improves with age.

Piaget characterizes the speech of young children as *egocentric*, because it reflects their inability to distinguish between their own points of view and those of others. Other investigators, taking issue with Piaget's claim, call young children's speech which is not addressed or adapted to a listener, *private speech.* Vygotsky claims that there is a social intent behind children's speech but that they do not distinguish clearly between the self as listener and others as listeners. He believes that children are really addressing themselves, and therefore conversation can be abbreviated. In either case, children speak to themselves or to the air rather than to each other. Despite these observations, children's conversations can be high in social and informational content and can produce a good deal of mutual responsiveness, either verbal or nonverbal. Other studies have found that young children can adjust their speech to the listener, but only when they are talking about objects and events they understand.

The particular environment in which children learn to speak may have a strong influence on their later use of language. When interactions between parents and children contain numerous references to things, the children's early speech will contain a large number of object names. Highly social interactions, on the other hand, result in the use of a large number of expressive phrases. In addition, parents adapt their speech to the language abilities of their children and pace their speech ahead of the children's current level of performance in order to stimulate higher levels of mastery. Environments other than the home also influence children's speech. It has been suggested that baby talk, parent talk, peer talk, and teacher talk can be viewed as a series of subsystems of the total language system.

The speech of adults who interact most often with children consists largely of new words, imitations of the babies' utterances, questions, and word play. Few attempts are made to encourage use of correct grammar, since adults generally understand and respond to badly formed sentences. Thus, children's grammatical progress does not appear to be a result of explicit attempts to teach them grammar. One-to-one interactions between children and adults are known to be effective in helping children learn certain aspects of language. In addition, children can benefit from specific instruction to language skills as long as such instruction is geared to their capacities.

CHAPTER 9

Exploration and Play

WHAT IS PLAY?

Everybody, whether adult or child, knows that play is fun. Adults tend to think of play as the opposite of work, as something they do not have to do but like to do. Children, too, play when they do not have other things to do, when they are physically and emotionally comfortable, when they can think of interesting things to do alone or with others. But children's play represents more than mere recreation. As we will see, play is important to development.

Because children spend so much time playing, a great deal of attention has been devoted to defining just exactly what play is. But a definition has been especially elusive. Some psychologists stress the motivational aspects of play. According to this view, play stems from the natural desire of the increasingly sophisticated brain and central nervous system to explore and master the environment. Other psychologists have emphasized the self-expressive nature of play. They believe that children at play are expressing their own understanding of the world.

We shall simply define play as a nonserious and self-contained activity engaged in for the sheer satisfaction it brings (Dearden, 1967). Such a definition allows considerable range in the behaviors that can be classified as play. The hallmark of play is the player's high degree of choice in what to do. He or she can engage in activities without regard to achieving a particular goal. The player can experiment and elaborate, can put obstacles of one sort or another (such as rules in games) in his own way. By our definition, the insistence that a child "go out and play" will not ensure that the activities that take place are play behaviors. One young boy made this point when he said, "I have to play; that's my job." The player must have the option to choose whether or not to play—to define an interesting problem or situation and to solve it or react to it in his or her own way. Freedom of choice produces in play such diverse activities as pouring sand from one container to another in a sandbox; running a make-believe grocery store; solving a jigsaw puzzle; hitting a fuzzy ball back and forth over a net. But why, when they have a combination of ample time and interesting materials, do people choose to play?

FUNCTIONS OF PLAY

We have said that play is an important aspect of child development. What are the purposes of childhood play and what functions does it serve? For one thing, play suspends ordinary rules and consequences of behavior in favor of rules and consequences that are less demanding, less serious, and often less efficient. The suspension of the usual consequences of behavior is most clearly seen in mock battles. Mock fights are commonly observed in young children, baboons, and chimpanzees (Miller, 1973). Often they are initiated by younger, weaker, or more submissive children and animals, who could reasonably expect to lose or to be hurt seriously if combat were "for real."

One necessary part of such feigned aggressiveness is an early communication that "this is play" (Bateson, 1956). Such a message is important because many movements, sounds, and facial expressions can be interpreted as either hostile or harmless, depending on the context in which they occur. After this initial message has been given and received, children and young animals at play adhere to the agreement (to have fun and not inflict harm) in several ways. Their blows are exaggerated and often miss the mark; they give ample warning and make their actions unnecessarily complicated. Miller (1973) calls this kind of fanciful, inefficient behavior *galumphing*. At the outset of any interaction between children, galumphing behavior is a way of communicating that what follows is to be understood as play.

Within the context of play, children are granted opportunities for discovery without risk. For example, in make-believe play, children can experiment with dominant and submissive roles with few adverse consequences. The child learns to recognize and to act in his or her own fantasies, as well as in those of others. One play session may find the child taking a variety of roles, ranging from cowhand to lion to baby. Children can learn behaviors appropriate to each play situation in a relatively risk-free setting. They can test without fear the outer limits of what is acceptable. Later on in life, failure to abide by social hierarchies may prove more costly.

A second function of play is to permit the dominance of process (means) over goals (ends). The child at play is free to practice certain behaviors without pressure to produce. Thus children will busily place pegs in holes or small boxes inside larger ones, without regard for any further result or achievement. When children first discover switches, they spend hours (if parents let them) turning on and off lights, vacuum cleaners, radios,

In play situations, children are free to choose activities that interest them, without regard to achieving a particular goal. (left, David Powers, Jeroboam; center, Marlis Müller; right, Shelly Rusten)

and TVs without caring much about illumination, cleaning, listening to the radio, or watching television. Sometimes a child elaborates on the process by voluntarily placing obstacles in his path. For example, a child may learn to place plastic rings over a post, then he may try to stack them on his finger, and finally he may attempt to stack them alone. He has purposely tried more difficult variations of the stacking activity.

Rather than establishing a rigid pattern of "problem—most efficient method of resolution—result," children learn through play to be flexible. Dissociating means from ends yields mastery of techniques that may seem unnecessary now but may be useful later (Miller, 1973). Children can try new and varied combinations of behaviors that may, or may not, be helpful in nonplay settings. For example, a child will happily pour water from one container to another for quite some time. Later, if the child wants a glass of milk, he or she may remember from water play that a short round container will hold the liquid better than a plate. Through process-oriented play, children can learn and perfect basic skills.

Some psychologists believe that play functions as a means of reliving and partially resolving early conflicts, as well as of releasing tension and relieving frustration. This view of play is termed *psychogenic,* stemming primarily from the needs and motives of the individual child. In terms of theory, the psychogenic interpretation of play is closely associated with psychoanalysis. One of the foremost interpreters of the psychogenic function of play is Erik Erikson, whose work *Childhood and Society* (1964) contains fascinating case studies using play as both a diagnostic and a therapeutic tool. Play therapy provides a safe opportunity for uncovering emotional conflicts and for acting out emotions in make-believe situations, without adult retribution. It can also set up low-risk learning situations in which the child can practice new coping skills.

In summary, play expands the child's understanding of the world by allowing him or her to explore, without serious risk, objects, relations among objects, and social roles. Just as cognition proceeds in stages, so does play. The play activities that interest a 2-year-old are considerably different from those that capture the attention of an 8-year-old. As we have seen, children are most fascinated by events that are familiar yet novel, events that lie at the boundary between what they understand and what they do not understand. Play indexes cognitive development by showing us where a child is in terms of cognitive ability. We shall look at the development of play activity and its relation to development of cognitive abilities in the following sections. There we will consider two varieties of play activity — exploratory play and symbolic, pretend play.

PLAY AS EXPLORATION AND DISCOVERY

It is an observable fact that most animals, including humans, spend a great deal of time extracting information from their environments. The desire for information can be a powerful force, overcoming drives like hunger, thirst, and fear. Hungry rats in laboratory settings may stop to examine a new object in their environment before dashing over to their food. Birds may come close to a strange, new object, even though it is threatening and could possibly kill them. This is *exploratory behavior,* behavior directed toward seeking information (Berlyne, 1966).

Scientists divide exploratory behavior into two categories. Specific exploration occurs when an animal has insufficient information about the environment. This condition arouses a feeling of uncertainty, which we term *curiosity;* as a result the animal makes an effort to find the particular information that will reduce its uncertainty (Berlyne, 1966). Specific exploratory behavior in children is commonly observed when they receive a new toy, especially one with buttons, switches, and knobs that ring buzzers, turn on lights, open doors, and start up motors. Children explore and manipulate the toy—pushing the buttons, turning switches and knobs until all the possibilities have been tried. Asking questions is another form of specific exploratory behavior—and one of the young child's favorite activities. It has been estimated that questions comprise up to one-fourth of all utterances of 3- and 4-year-olds (Ross, 1974).

Animals also explore their surroundings out of a more general need for stimulation, variety, and change. When a child finishes exploring a new toy, what does he do with it? He might try out *different* combinations of buttons and switches, put things into the doors, use the toy together with other toys. He might even incorporate the toy into a pretend game. This is *diversive exploratory behavior,* stemming not from curiosity over an incomplete set of facts but rather from the desire for change for its own sake (Berlyne, 1966). Other investigators have called this form of behavior "play" (Weisler and McCall, 1976). Every mother knows that children have plenty of motivation in this regard. Because children have a short attention span relative to that of adults, they require a great deal of stimulation and variation. Diversive exploration enables them to meet this need and to overcome boredom.

A number of factors determine the amount of exploration a child will exhibit. One such factor is novelty. Recall from our discussion in Chapter 5 that response to a given stimulus can decline through habituation. The child gets accustomed to the stimulus, which gradually loses the power to evoke curiosity. As he gathers more data about the stimulus, his inner representation of it becomes more and more complete. Soon he loses interest in seeking out more information.

Another factor that determines the degree of curiosity is complexity. Berlyne (1966) found that the more a stimulus is varied, irregular, or packed with perceptual data, the more it is likely to elicit exploratory behavior. The exploring child is filling two needs at the same time. He or she is dispelling present uncertainty about a particular object. The child also is internalizing information for later storage and retrieval. In other words, he or she is learning. The factors that encourage exploration also facilitate learning. Novelty, complexity, and incongruity lead a child to a greater number of questions of increasing sophistication.

Novelty, Complexity, and Incongruity

As children grow older, they are increasingly eager to explore new things. In general, the older the child is, the more novelty is likely to entice him or her. Mendel (1965) demonstrated this principle with several groups of children ranging in age from 3½ to 5½. First the children were habituated to a collection of eight small toys. Then they were offered four more collections from which to choose. The four additional collections were designed to differ increasingly from the original grouping of toys. They contained two, four, six, and eight different toys, respectively. As the children selected one of the new sets, they were observed and rated on an anxiety scale. Generally, the children showed stronger preferences in direct relation to the toys' novelty. However, the older children preferred the high degrees of novelty, whereas the younger ones showed no signficant preference between the toy groupings that were somewhat novel and those that were extremely novel.

There are several types of novelty. Abrupt change in a steady pattern is novel and arouses interest. So does a familiar object in an unfamiliar setting, like a fly in a bowl of soup. Finally there is literal novelty in a stimulus presented for the first time, such as a view of the moon's surface (Nunnally and Lemond, 1973).

Children also prefer relative complexity. Switzky, Haywood, and Isett (1974) noted that increased complexity aroused different behavior in different age groups. Two-year-olds preferred objects of moderate complexity; such toys increased both total play time and total exploration time. Older children showed an interesting difference in their responses. Not only did 4- to 7-year-olds prefer objects of high complexity, but their response to such objects was increased exploratory behavior and decreased play activity.

There is some evidence that too much complexity (that is, more than can be processed) is undesirable. Hunt (1965) refers to this as "the problem of the match." If the difference between the stimulus and what the child has already learned is too great, he or she will exhibit stress and avoidance behavior. On the other hand, if the difference is too small, the child will be bored. The optimum level is one of small discrepancies that challenge the child, yet can be readily assimilated to already acquired knowledge (Switzky et al., 1974).

Incongruity also attracts exploratory behavior. Nunnally and Lemond (1973) explain this effect in terms of *information conflict.* Two or more pieces of information compete for attention, making it more difficult to identify, categorize, and analyze each of them. Information conflict is greatest when two or more cues that normally identify an object point to opposite conclusions. For example, a creature with a head of a lion and the body of a sheep would be hard to categorize. When the cue is very dominant, however, there is less information conflict and the encoding task is easier. A blue horse is extremely unusual, but it is still clearly a horse.

The foregoing principles of novelty, complexity, and incongruity have great practical significance for childhood education. They can be integrated into teaching methods and materials so that children will be drawn into new learning experiences. If the materials presented to them are too familiar, simple, or predictable, children will be bored. If materials are too far removed from the children's experiences, too complex, or so strange as to be frightening, children will avoid them. It takes an artful and talented teacher or parent to find the proper balance.

PRETEND PLAY

"Let's pretend" is the archetypal play of children (and sorely missed by many adults). As we saw in Chapter 5, pretend play has significance for cognitive development. The act of pretending implies that the child has transformed the physical environment into a mental symbol. Piaget believes that the ability to construct mental codes of actions and things marks the beginning of operational, representational activity.

When it first appears, at about 18 months of age, symbolic play may include simple motions like eating from an empty spoon or drinking from an empty cup. Gradually, though, play becomes an increasingly organized childhood activity, though still informal. Two or three young children who *appear* to be playing together may actually be playing at two or three separate fantasy situations, into which each has worked the presence of the other children. In the play of older children, however, shared rules and norms are clearly visible. Their play has remarkable internal coherence, especially regarding a collective agreement to pretend. Children as young as 2 years old recognize that "let's-pretend" messages suspend the rules of the real world and cross into the realm of fantasy (Sutton-Smith, 1970, 1971). As children grow older, rules and definitions become more elaborate and even more closely adhered to. There are provisions for taking turns, adopting and reversing roles, beginning and ending, succeeding and failing. Such techniques preserve the social agreement that "this is play."

Let us not forget that make-believe play as an ordinary activity represents a rather special challenge to young children. First, they must know something about the roles and relationships of people in the real world around them. Second, children must learn the rules and the roles required in the particular game they want to play. Third, they must coordinate their roles with those of the other players.

Viewed from the perspective of developmental psychology, pretend play follows a rather unusual developmental course. It appears rather abruptly at 18 months of age. It blossoms in the form of dramatic play between 3 and 4 and reaches its height between ages 5 and 6. Play that began as a few simple gestures now includes intricate systems involving reciprocal roles, ingenious improvisations of needed materials, coherent themes, and nicely woven plots. Play then begins to decline. By middle childhood, children rarely engage·in spontaneous and complex role enactments. Instead, their interests shift to games, both formal and informal. The underlying processes at work here have not been a focus of sustained research. It may be, as Piaget suggests, that the child increasingly addresses his concern to the logic of relationships in the real world. The child has come to master enough knowledge about the world as it is to know that pretending is only pretending, and that the real challenge is to master the rules of interpersonal systems. Other theorists believe that dramatic play may disappear as overt behavior, but that it persists in the daydreams and fantasies of later life (Singer, 1973). Perhaps pretending "goes underground" because the conflict between reality and fantasy is so profound and personal that it can not be expressed in a free-for-all group game. It may also be that the child's capacity for conceiving of the fantastic simply exceeds possibilities for acting out. Reading, thinking, or watching TV may be more appropriate means of expressing the reality-violating capacities of the mind.

The Concept of Role

In pretend play, what consequences flow from describing someone as "little sister," "mother," "doctor," or "teacher"? What do children learn from assuming different roles in dramatic play? Young children play out roles in various ways, as if they were working from a collection of role features, some subset of which is at any time sufficient to constitute the character. When children play "mother," their voices become soothing or strident, their attitudes become pleading or demanding, their gestures become punishing or accepting. A "doctor" is crisp and authoritative; a "fireman" is deep-voiced, active, and commanding. Role features consist

Young children are interested in the role features of such awe-inspiring figures as doctors and fire and police officers.
(George Zimbel, Monkmeyer)

of what characters do, how they do it, and how other characters respond to the style and to the message. This issue is more easily discussed in terms of specific examples. Note how the following make-believe situations both reflect and mock reality. The children alternately adopt one role, then suddenly shift into a very different role.

Doris is playing at the carriage. Janie, "I wanna play with you." Doris, "Only if you are the little sister." When she has completed fixing the carriage to her satisfaction she tells Janie, "You're little sister. Hold here and help me push the baby. Now walk." Doris has arranged the carriage with a broom across it. Janie takes the broom away. Doris pulls her back ordering, "stay here," and then, "no, no, no." They walk along, Doris pushing the carriage and Janie holding on at the side. The teacher greets them: "Hello! Nice baby you have." Janie, looking at Doris, says, "You play with me." But Doris quickly answers, "No, she's just the little sister." Rickie yells for no apparent reason and Janie still standing beside Doris imitates him. Doris hits her on the head. She offers no resistance. They walk back across the room, Janie holding on. Doris orders her, "Now turn, we have to go to the store." Janie says, "I wanna go to the park." She is told by Doris, "Well,

you can't." Janie finally says, "I don't wanna play," but is told by Doris,
"Well, you have to," and she continues. (Hartley, Frank, and Goldenson,
1952, pp. 29–30)

Harvey was playing with Karen, his twin sister. Karen began to push
the carriage. Harvey said, "Let me be the baby, Karen," and started to talk
like a baby. He got into the carriage. Karen pushed him around the room as
he squinted his eyes and cried. She stopped the carriage, patted his shoulder,
saying "Don't cry, baby." He squirmed around, put his thumb in his mouth,
and swayed his body.

Josie came to the carriage and wanted to push Harvey. He jumped out
and hit her in the face. She walked away almost crying. He went to her,
put his arm around her and said, in a sympathetic manner, "Come, you be
the baby, I'll push you in the carriage." She climbed in. He ran and got the
dog and gave it to her saying, "Here, baby." She smiled and began to play
with the dog. He went to the housekeeping corner, got a cup and held it to her
mouth. He smacked his lips, looking at her, smiling. He pushed her around
in the carriage. Karen ran to him and said, "Harvey, let me push the
carriage, I'll be the mamma, you be the daddy." Harvey said "O.K.," and
reached his hand in his pocket and gave her money. He said, "Bye, baby,"
waving his hand. (Hartley et al., 1952, pp. 70–72)

In the first selection, Janie adopted the role of little sister. Little sister
is someone who complies with an older sister's (Doris's) commands,
walks by her side, and has to ask permission to go to the park. The core
characterization of little sister is infantile incompetence and dependency,
whereas big sister is portrayed as competent in an adult way and having
independent contact with the outside world.

Beyond these core concepts of roles, children elaborate in endlessly
creative ways. Harvey's baby was active and obstreperous. Josie's baby,
on the other hand, was sweetly compliant, taking cues from Harvey and
playing on her own with the dog, a less dominant being. Note also how
the children support these characterizations with a host of devices — body
postures, physical contact, tonal variations, and props. For example, Doris
hit Janie to subdue her; Janie, the little sister, did not resist. Harvey
climbed into the carriage to secure his role as baby; he, in turn, reinforced
his parental role to Josie's baby by offering her a drink. As the play progresses, roles can be shifted, modified, or reversed — but only within
limits. It is not unusual for a child to assert "sisters don't do that." (To make
sure that Doris stayed in her role, Janie said to her, "You play with me.")

Although the suggestion has yet to be pursued in depth, Bateson (1956)
speculated that the power of such play is not in the child's original learning of role characteristics, since the play itself presupposes mastery of the
role. What children may learn from dramatic play is that there is such a

thing as a role; that roles are reversible, distinguishable sets of demeanors; and that dramatic play requires the cooperation of others.

Role playing in dramatic play also contributes to the child's social identity. Kohlberg (1969) views role playing as a means of building shared social relationships. According to his theory, in role playing the child imitates someone else in the hope of being rewarded for showing similar competence. Thus he or she comes to make the first distinction in the social world — that between self and others.

A certain amount of independence from adults is a necessary condition for role playing. However, children do not, as Kohlberg suggests, confine themselves to displays of superior competence. In our examples, the children frequently sought out the role of baby and younger sibling. Children also love to act as animals, both real and imaginary. They reenact scenes that are inherently interesting and wonderful to themselves; this often has nothing to do with admiration from adults.

As children grow older, play themes become more serious, yet roles are still adopted and changed with remarkable fluidity. Harvey plays mother, father, and baby. At the same time, there are limits. No one but Karen can play the role of mother when Harvey is the baby. For children who have played together a great deal (like the twins, Karen and Harvey), role transitions are smooth and effectively communicated.

One of the fundamental characteristics of sociodramatic play is that it combines fantasy and reality. Viewed this way, sociodramatic play is a method of divergent thinking about social relationships. Children are free to generate hypothetical questions and answers about complementary social relationships. What would it be like to be a mother? How would I act as a baby? Although children formulate these hypotheses at least partially from their own experience, they are dependent on group consensus of role boundaries. This is clear from Doris' insistence that the little sister role for Janie includes submission to authority. Through such interactions, children learn methods of behaving that they may then carry into real life.

Despite the fact that some theorists have traditionally treated sociodramatic play as an inevitable aspect of development, it does not flourish in all countries. Cross-cultural studies suggest that some societies encourage rich fantasy play, whereas others exert strong inhibitory pressures. And, as we have already mentioned, sociodramatic play is often molded by the functions it serves — to teach children the norms and values of power relationships and conflict. Another factor that influences the form that play takes is material wealth.

In a comparative study of advantaged and disadvantaged Israeli kindergartners, Smilansky (1968) investigated the role of economic wealth in promoting sociodramatic play. Two groups were observed in free-play situations in similarly equipped classrooms. There was a startling dif-

Play helps children generate questions and answers about complementary social relationships: What would it be like to be a mother? How do babies act? (Marlis Müller)

ference in the amount of sociodramatic play between the groups: It appeared in 78% of the observed play periods of the privileged youngsters, but in only 10% of the observed play periods of the disadvantaged children. There were other differences between the two groups, as well. The advantaged children were more likely to engage in imitative role play, make-believe, and verbal communication. They had more activities going at any one time, and they organized themselves into small groups whose play persisted for relatively long periods. They emphasized diverse real-life roles and elaborate episodes in their play, rather than getting involved with special toys.

The disadvantaged children, on the other hand, did not stay in groups for even moderate lengths of time. They liked to manipulate replicas of real objects, but they rarely incorporated them into stories or fantasies of any complexity. They found it difficult to pretend without the use of props. These behavioral differences, according to Smilansky, were due to one of two factors. Either the disadvantaged children lacked information on how to organize play episodes, or they had not acquired the techniques for initiating and maintaining them.

Observations of disadvantaged children in the United States indicate that similar socioeconomic differences exist here as well (Rosen, 1974). A growing body of evidence suggests that play behaviors are very sensitive to situational factors, such as available play materials and partners, the emotional state of the child, and the emotional climate of the setting. If this is indeed the case, then changes in situational factors should result in changes in play behavior.

PROMOTING PLAY

Play Skills
Enrichment

Smilansky followed up her initial observation with a series of experiments designed to enrich the disadvantaged children's play (1968). On the strength of the hypothesis that either information or technique was deficient, she provided four different training programs to the disadvantaged children. One group received intensive instruction in specific play themes. Another group learned play techniques from teachers who intervened in ongoing sequences and suggested new directions for the play to take, such as a role, interaction with another child, or make-believe with an object. A third group received both types of instruction. A control group received no instruction. The most dramatic change in play occurred in the third group, although the second group also showed improvement in the frequency and quality of play. Smilansky interpreted these results as meaning that social symbolic play is most efficiently enhanced by *techniques* learned from adults or from other children.

SOCIODRAMATIC PLAY AND PROBLEM SOLVING. Enrichment training can be aimed specifically to stimulate sociodramatic play and increase problem-solving abilities. Rosen (1974) was particularly interested in promoting sociodramatic skills as a means of bolstering social problem-solving abilities. She provided 40 hours of instruction to a group of underprivileged children. A group of control subjects received no extra training. First, teachers worked with individual children, analyzing their particular weaknesses and offering appropriate remedial activities. Then they worked with the group as a whole. The teachers introduced props such as firefighter hats to prompt role playing. They intervened in group play, interjecting new themes and complications. For example, if the children were spontaneously playing mountain-climbing, the teacher would propose that a member of the party had slipped and now needed group assistance.

Again, the results of intensive training in play skills was gratifying. Not only did the children show remarkable individual improvement in their sociodramatic skills, but they also showed increased ability as a group to solve problems requiring maximum cooperation and minimum competition. This improvement can probably be explained as a result of each child's greater ability to quickly adapt to role demands and to communicate such role changes smoothly to others.

FANTASY TRAINING. Specific training can be remarkably effective in improving fantasy play of young children. Freyberg (1973) demonstrated this with a group of 80 disadvantaged children in New York City. She divided them into high- and low-fantasizers, plus a control group. Both high- and low-fantasizers received eight separate sessions in creative play. Using such toys as pipe-cleaner people and blocks, Freyberg acted out stories and adventures. The children quickly took the initiative in inventing their own plots. At the end of eight sessions, both groups of fantasizers scored much higher than before on scales of imaginative play. They also showed more positive emotions and better concentration. These results persisted in a follow-up study 2 months later. The control group exhibited none of these gains (Pulaski, 1974).

THE ROLE OF TELEVISION IN PROMOTING MAKE-BELIEVE. To explore the use of television as a means of enhancing fantasy and make-believe play, Singer and Singer (1974) conducted an experiment over a 2-week period with four groups of 15 children apiece from the same day-care center. All children were between the ages of 3 and 4. The first group watched "Mister Rogers' Neighborhood," a popular children's show, for a half-hour each day. A second group also watched the show, but they were simultaneously instructed by a live adult. She interpreted parts of the show, calling attention to details and encouraging the children to imitate Mister Rogers' actions. A third group watched no television but instead received an equivalent period of live instruction by a teacher in guided fantasy and imaginative play. The fourth group, the controls, followed the normal nursery school routine, including organized play around artistic activities and some formal game playing.

The results were surprising. The control group, which initially scored somewhat higher than average on scales of imaginative play, showed a striking decline. All three groups receiving intervention showed an increase in imaginative play. The experimenters had anticipated that the television-plus-live-intermediary arrangement would turn out to be the most stimulating, but in fact it was the live teacher working without television who produced the greatest increase in spontaneous make-believe. The least effective enrichment program was the television-only format. (The experimenters note that 15 children around one television set is

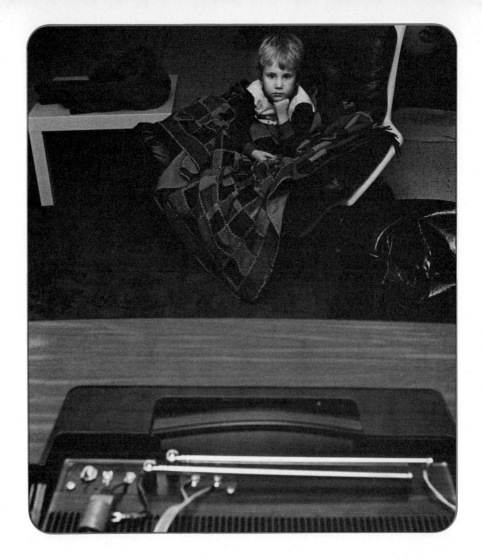

Singer believes that television widens children's horizons and provides them with information that can be used in make-believe play.
(Terry Evans, Magnum)

neither a typical nor an optimal arrangement.) They concluded that the live teacher was most successful because she alone was able to engage the children directly and give them immediate feedback on their responses. In this sense, television had little impact on these 3- and 4-year-old children. Singer and Singer suggest that to increase imaginative play, full utilization of a television program like "Mister Rogers' Neighborhood" would require carefully structured adult mediation, probably in much smaller groups. Jerome Singer believes, however, that television does have an impact on the development of make-believe play in those children whose parents do not pass on fairy tales, myths, and legends to them. According to Singer, "in this sense, television has widened their horizons ...and provided them with a great deal of material that can be used in the course of make-believe" (cited in Pulaski, 1974, p. 74).

Where does creativity come from? Can parents do anything to stimulate *Parental* creativity in their children? Bishop and Chace (1971) have studied these *Contributions* questions in terms of the generally accepted notion that creativity is *to Creativity* related to playfulness. Believing that playfulness, in turn, is related to the child's home environment, these investigators have identified several psychological characteristics that determine whether parents will tend to inhibit or encourage playfulness in their children. These characteristics may be placed on a continuum ranging from concreteness to abstractness. The abstract end of the continuum is characterized by "openmindedness, adaptability, unorthodoxy, low authoritarianism, the ability to entertain multiple viewpoints, and the ability to grant a certain amount of auton- omy to the child." The concrete conceptual system is characterized by "simplicity, high absolutism and closedness of beliefs, high authoritarian- ism, high conventionality, and high rigidity and thus relatively low adapta- bility" (Bishop and Chace, 1971, p. 324).

The results of the study demonstrated that mothers whose attitudes approach the abstract end of the continuum tend to provide a play en- vironment that stimulates flexibility, exploration, and autonomy in their children. (For reasons that are not clear, similar differences were not found for fathers.) These children are more likely to show complex and varied behaviors in a performance task. Although the study did not answer the question of how a high degree of playfulness influences creativity in the child, the performance of the children on a task used in the study was similar to the kinds of behaviors required for creative endeavors, such as tolerance for incongruous, novel, complex elements and varied choice and decision patterns.

The objects and settings that nurture play and fantasy change with age. *The Importance* Children of about 2 years of age prefer to play with realistic toys; they *of Situational* engage in more fantasy play with such toys than they do with less realistic *Factors* ones (Fein and Robertson, 1975). Five-year-old children, for whom make-believe capacities are well established, prefer relatively unstructured, less realistic objects, used in combination with complex symbolism and highly diverse role playing (Pulaski, 1970). For them, open-ended en- vironments are more stimulating than restrictive roles and rules. In an early play study, Markey (1935) noted that younger children typically engaged in imaginative play related to the materials around them, whereas older children engaged in complicated make-believe involving relations and themes. Two-year-olds, for example, used sand with digging toys such as shovels and pails; 4-year-olds used sand as a make-believe lubri- cant for a make-believe train (a tricycle). Three implications for early education arise from these observations. First, physical materials must be age-appropriate. Second, rules for older children should be flexible enough to permit them to use materials in several different ways. Finally, and most

Younger children typically use materials they find around them as the basis for imaginative play. (Marion Faller, Monkmeyer)

important, children need contact with other children for the full exercise of their symbolic powers.

The effect on play of spatial arrangements in child-care settings is hard to pinpoint because there are such a high number of variables. It does seem clear, though, that in outdoor play areas, at least, a certain amount of play equipment is indispensable. In a recent study (Scholtz and Ellis, 1975), groups of children were offered play apparatus that varied in complexity: simple climbers and slides versus climbers and slides plus rope ladders and cut-out hiding and climbing boxes. The children played more with the more complex materials than with the less complex materials. Over several episodes, contacts with the materials declined whereas contacts with other children increased. In a sense, a playmate is a more enduringly complex stimulus than an arrangement of inanimate objects. Positive social interactions, interspersed with quarrels and combats (mock and serious), create endless novelty, surprise, and challenge.

Play is also affected by the emotional state of the child. Play is most likely to occur when the child is not under the influence of strong biological or emotional drives. Although some play contains components of anxiety and aggression, too much stress will disrupt play. Frustration or separation from the caregiver (in the case of very young children) will inhibit play. Mendel (1965) found that levels of anxiety influence children's willingness to seek out or to avoid new things. Children with low anxiety were more likely than very anxious children to explore newly offered toys. Clearly, then, a fairly steady emotional state is a threshold requirement of happy and efficient play. The child's emotions will affect short-term play. General personality factors have long-term effects on the child's play.

PLAY AND PERSONALITY

The personality of the individual child interacts with the personalities of playmates, the environment, and the available play materials to define the course of play. As we have already noted, the child's emotions affect short-term play, often by inhibiting it. Personality factors are more persistent and exert greater influence over development of play skills and play habits. Singer (1961) found in one of his experiments on daydreaming that children with vivid imaginations will sit quietly for longer periods than will children with lower imaginative capacity. He tested this finding by dividing children into groups of high- and low-fantasizers on the basis of preliminary tests and interviews, using questions such as "Do you have an animal or a make-believe person you talk to?" Then he told the children he was looking for astronauts "of the future" who would have to endure long periods of solitude on their intergalactic voyages. He asked each potential astronaut to sit quietly for 15 minutes. The candidates signaled when they had had enough. Even though the mean waiting time was only six minutes, the high-fantasizers consistently outlasted the low-fantasy "astronauts." Those who lasted longest were the children who went through elaborate countdowns and blastoffs. They launched themselves into orbit with rolling eyes and engine noises. While they were waiting out in space to be recalled, they turned an imaginary steering wheel.

Patience and calm are not the only attributes associated with ability to fantasize. High-fantasizers are often among the older children in the family and are emotionally close to their parents, especially their fathers. Amount of early story reading by parents does not seem to be a significant factor, but life style is. Singer (1973) describes the optimal conditions for development of a rich fantasy life as follows: parental interest and encouragement of the imagination, adult role models to emulate, and the opportunity to practice fantasy by being alone.

Pulaski (1974) drew on this material to suggest that fantasy encouragement could be used as a means of calming hyperactive children and increasing their attention spans. This approach is buttressed by data from projective tests. Children who perceive human movements in inkblots tend to have good control over their own movements. On the other hand, children who perceive few movements on projective tests tend to be impulsive and very active. Apparently, children with the ability to envision action (especially human action) in their own minds seem to have less need to act it out (Pulaski, 1974).

Pulaski found that the predisposition to fantasize is already well formed at the age of 5. She gave both structured and open-ended materials to a number of 5-year-olds and asked each to make up a story. Surprisingly, the degree of complexity in the children's stories had little relation to the type of toy each had been given. Rather, story complexity seemed closely related to ability to fantasize. Pulaski suggests that low-fantasizers are also less creative, less flexible in their thinking, and less adept at communication. She also found that low-fantasizers tend to be more physically active (1974). These findings have been confirmed by Singer and Singer, who found that boys who are low in imaginative ability tend to be more physically aggressive than high-fantasizers.

Ability to fantasize can help a child cope with feelings of aggression. Biblow (1973) demonstrated this with a group of fifth graders that included both high- and low-fantasizers. He subjected all of them to a task designed to frustrate and anger them. The task was very difficult and was made worse by a group of older children who stood by and teased. Next Biblow rated the level of aggression each child exhibited. He then divided the children into three groups and showed each group a different movie. One group saw an aggressive film full of punching, shouting children. Another was shown an episode from the fantasy movie *The Adventures of Chitty Chitty Bang Bang*. The third group saw slides of mathematical problems. Then Biblow observed the subjects at play, watching for remaining aggression.

High-fantasizers exhibited less aggression than low-fantasizers, regardless of which film they saw. Low-fantasy children showed no decrease in aggression, and those who saw the aggressive film became even more hostile than they had been before seeing the film. Children who saw the math slides exhibited no mood change. Bilbow suggests that extensive training in fantasy may help children cope with feelings of aggression.

Although make-believe play shows some promising potential as a therapeutic tool, it is first and foremost a normal and essential part of growing up. It is closely linked to development of communicative skills, patience, concentration and attention spans, flexibility, creativity, and imagination. Subtle signals from parents can easily discourage this rich source of growth and inspiration. Some parents worry that their child spends too much time in imaginative play and not enough time with other children. Other parents worry that their child spends too much time in play and not enough in more serious activities. Parents can make a conscious effort to facilitate the development of make-believe play by placing a high value on imagination and by creating opportunities for the child to be alone to mull over his experiences or to play with others if he wishes. After all, fantasy trips are one of the best and earliest means of escaping temporarily from the domain of parental authority and creating adventures, alone or with others.

SENSE AND NONSENSE

As we have seen, early symbolic play is centered around clear functions of familiar objects. The child's symbolic adventures quickly grow bolder, and soon, more drastic violations of functional rules occur. For example, a bowl can be worn on the head like a hat. A fur collar may be used as a wonderfully comforting pillow. A paper cup in a bathtub becomes a boat. To children, these propositions can be very funny. They know a standard rule has been violated. Part of the joke is the deliberately created gap between the dictates of the serious world and the child's vision of a silly world (Piaget, 1945). Sutton-Smith (1967) contrasted the calculated upset and imbalances of play to most other life tasks, which are aimed at maintaining equilibrium and stability. Play, according to this view, is structured precisely in a manner designed to make nonsense out of ordinary expectations.

Sutton-Smith characterizes play as open-ended and divergent (varying from the norm). This interpretation is sharply at odds with the psycho-analytic tradition, which views play as a safe release of neurotic energy. The divergent view of play also runs counter to Piaget's belief that children strive for clarity, consistency, and equilibrium and that symbolic play is part of this quest for order. Sutton-Smith believes that both the psycho-analytic and the cognitive theorists have failed to take account of the special nature of play.

In what way does "disequilibrium on purpose" represent divergent

One way in which children reorganize familiar material for the purposes of novelty and humor is to play with their food— to eat bread into unusual shapes, to blow bubbles in a glass of milk with a straw, to make decorative patterns out of peas before eating them. (Cary S. Wolinsky, Stock, Boston)

thinking? Consider what happens when the child wears a cereal bowl for a hat. Although bowls and hats are usually not used in similar ways, they do have common physical characteristics. The child's actions and words are a kind of speculation about the common features that could make them interchangeable in the world of play. In grouping bowls and hats together, functional and physical characteristics are allowed to diverge to the point of absurdity. This is primarily a process of reorganizing old material, rather than adding or adjusting to new information. One of the most delightful qualities in children's play is to take an old, familiar object and make it seem totally and ridiculously different by putting it in another context.

Play as divergent thinking also has an affective component, best described as wonder. This quality captures some of the free-ranging speculation, the tentativeness, and the reflection on alternatives that mark the young child's outlook on life. Play probably increases the child's ability to form new and rich associations. At least, Sutton-Smith (1967) showed that a greater variety of functions were attributed to toys that were frequently played with than to toys that were usually neglected. Other researchers have noted that games are more effective than workbooks in helping children learn the identical material (Humphrey, 1965, 1966). Children who receive special training in acting out fantasy stories (such as the Billy Goats Gruff or Little Red Riding Hood) are better able to reconstruct new stories from picture sequences and to recognize causal relations between one event and another (Saltz and Johnson, 1974).

Clearly, play is a very important element in the development of thinking. Serious theoretical treatment of play is still rudimentary, but at least child psychologists have begun to accept it as a major influence to be reckoned with.

SUMMARY

Play is defined simply as a nonserious and self-controlled activity engaged in for the satisfaction it brings. The hallmark of play is the player's high degree of choice in what to do. For children, play represents more than recreation; it is important to development.

Within the context of play, children are granted opportunities for discovery without risk. Play suspends the ordinary rules and consequences of behavior in favor of less demanding, less serious, and less efficient rules and consequences, as seen most clearly in mock fights. At the outset of any interaction between children, *galumphing* behavior—fanciful, inefficient behavior—is a way of communicating that what follows is to be understood as play. Play also permits the dominance of process (means) over goals (ends). Children at play are free to practice certain behaviors without pressure to produce. Rather than establishing a rigid pattern of "problem—most efficient method of resolution—result," children learn through play to be flexible.

The *psychogenic* view sees play functioning as a means of relieving and partially resolving early conflicts as well as a means of releasing tension and relieving frustration. This approach to play is closely associated with psychoanalysis. Play therapy provides a safe opportunity for uncovering emotional conflicts and for acting them out in make-believe situations, without adult retribution. It can also set up low-risk learning situations in which children can practice new coping skills.

Exploratory behavior—behavior directed toward seeking information—is a part of animal activity. *Specific* exploration occurs when an animal has insufficient information about the environment. This condition arouses a feeling of uncertainty, which we term *curiosity;* as a result, the animal makes an effort to find the particular information that will reduce its uncertainty. Examining a new toy and asking questions are specific forms of exploratory behavior common among children. Animals also explore their surroundings out of a more general need for stimulation, variety, and change. This is *diversive exploratory behavior,* stemming from the desire for change for its own sake. Some investigators call this form of behavior "play." A number of factors—novelty, complexity, and incongruity—determine the amount of exploration children exhibit. These same factors also facilitate learning, because they lead children to a greater number of questions of increasing sophistication.

The older children grow, the more novelty entices them. Young children also like complexity, but at an optimum level of small discrepancies that are challenging yet can be readily assimilated to already acquired knowledge. Incongruity also attracts exploratory behavior, which is explained in terms of *information conflict*—two or more pieces of information competing for attention, making it more difficult to identify, categorize, and analyze each of them. Information conflict is greatest when two or more cues that normally identify an object point to opposite conclusions.

Pretend play is the typical play of children. The act of pretending implies that children have transformed the physical environment into a mental symbol. Piaget believes that the ability to construct mental codes of actions and things marks the beginning of operational, representational activity. Make-believe play appears rather abruptly at 18 months of age, blossoms between 3 and 4, reaches its peak between 5 and 6, and then begins to decline. At that point, children's interests shift to games, both formal and informal. Piaget suggests that children increasingly address their concerns to the logic of relationships in the real world. They have come to master enough knowledge about the world as it is to know that pretending is only pretending and that the real challenge is to master the rules of interpersonal systems. Other theorists believe that dramatic play may disappear as overt behavior but that it persists in the daydreams and fantasies of later life.

In pretend play, young children play out roles in various ways, as if they were working from a collection of role features, consisting of what characters do, how they do it, and how other characters respond to the style and to the message. Children's make-believe situations often both reflect and mock reality. Role playing in dramatic play also contributes to children's social identity, helping them distinguish between self and others. A certain amount of independence from adults is a necessary condition for role playing. Children reenact scenes that are inherently interesting and wonderful to themselves. As children grow older, play themes become more serious, yet roles are still adopted and changed with remarkable fluidity.

One of the fundamental characteristics of sociodramatic play is that it combines fantasy and reality and, therefore, is a method of divergent thinking about social relationships. Children are free to generate hypothetical questions and answers about social relationships. Although children formulate these hypotheses at least partially from their own experience, they are dependent on group consensus of role boundaries. Through such interactions, children learn methods of behaving that they may then carry into real life.

Sociodramatic play does not flourish in all countries. Some societies encourage rich fantasy play, whereas others exert strong inhibitory pressures. Material wealth also influences the form that play takes. Advantaged children are more likely to engage in imitative role play, make-believe, and verbal communication. They emphasize diverse real-life roles and elaborate episodes in their play, rather than getting involved with special toys. Disadvantaged children, on the other hand, like to manipulate replicas of real objects but rarely incorporate them into stories or fantasies, and they find it difficult to pretend without the use of props. A growing body of evidence suggests that play behaviors are very sensitive to situational factors such as available play materials and partners, the emotional state of the child, and the emotional climate of the setting. A fairly steady emotional state is a threshold requirement of happy and efficient play.

This evidence suggests that changes in situational factors should result in changes in play behavior. Enrichment training can be aimed specifically to stimulate sociodramatic play and to increase problem-solving abilities. Specific training can be remarkably effective in improving fantasy play of young children. In some situations, television seems to have little impact on young children. Some theorists suggest that full utilization of television to increase imaginative play requires carefully structured adult mediation. Others believe that television does have an impact on the development of make-believe play for children whose parents do not pass on fairy tales, myths, and legends.

The objects and settings that nurture play and fantasy change with age. Children about 2 years old prefer to play with realistic toys; they engage in more fantasy play with such toys than with less realistic ones. Children of about 5 years of age, for whom make-believe capacities are well established, prefer relatively unstructured, less realistic objects used in conjunction with complex symbolism and highly diverse role playing. For them, open-ended environments are more stimulating than restrictive roles and rules.

The personality of the individual child interacts with the personalities of playmates, the environment, and the available play materials to define the course of play. Children with vivid imaginations will sit quietly for longer periods than will children with lower imaginative capacity. Low-fantasizers are also less creative, less flexible in their thinking, less adept at communication, and tend to be more physically active.

Make-believe play is a normal and essential part of growing up. It is closely linked to development of communicative skills, patience, concentration and attention spans, flexibility, creativity, and imagination. Parents can make a conscious effort to facilitate the development of make-believe play by placing a high value on imagination and by creating opportunities for children both to be alone to mull over their experiences and to play with others.

CHAPTER 10

Social Development

In Chapter 8, we discussed features of the child's thinking between 3 and 7 years of age. According to Piagetian theory, the child is midway between the sensorimotor thinking of infancy and the concrete, operational logic of middle childhood. The child has become a symbol-*making* person, and now his or her task is to become a symbol-*using* person. Investigators who prefer to define cognitive processes in terms of mediating mechanisms— whether considered as storage or productive systems, using words, images, or some other representational unit—also see the child as acquiring a new mental capacity during this period. Although the relation between language and thought is still a controversial issue, between infancy and middle childhood, children achieve a harmony between thinking and speaking that makes new forms of social encounters possible. There still may be a strong egocentric flavor to their speech, but a substantial part of their communication is responsive to those around them. In Chapter 9, we described how pretend play changes from the brief, symbolic episodes of infancy to the extended and elaborated sociodramatic group play of preschool children. In this chapter, we will examine the social world of children and how they expand their participation in it.

The social world of the infant is composed primarily of adults. By age 3, however, children begin to come into increasingly frequent contact with other children of their own age or slightly older—siblings, cousins, neighbors, strangers—in the yards, streets, and fields of rural communities or in the playgrounds, nursery schools, and day-care centers of urban ones.

The details of this transition vary from one environment to another. In a small-town black community, for example, the "knee-baby" of 2 or 2½ becomes a member of a children's gang under the care of a "nurse child." A younger child becomes the "knee-baby" and the 3-year-old's easy-going relationship with the gang replaces the knee-baby's closeness to the caregiver. This separation usually occurs without distress, in marked contrast to the tears of the middle-class child starting nursery school. The activities of the children in the gang are oriented primarily toward the real relationship among them, with little imaginary play and almost no use of toys. The children themselves "are the playthings and the players.... [They] sit close to one another, rub bare feet with each other, tease, tell stories and jokes" (Young, 1970, p. 283). Peer group activity among white middle-class children is quite different. The white middle-class child's activities at 2 and 3 years of age typically involve sandbox, paper and crayons, dressing up in Mommy's old shoes or Daddy's hat. The routine of the typical white middle-class child is highly structured, with breakfast at 8, nursery school from 9 to 12, and so on through bath at 7 and bedtime at 8. The same basic transition—from complete dependence on the caregiver to greater interaction with peers—occurs in both instances, but under quite different circumstances.

Family groups, peer groups, work groups—all provide opportunities for face-to-face encounters with others who play crucial roles in the acquisition of new social knowledge and in the transmission of knowledge already gained. Many observers have argued that the peer group is a universal element of human culture (Hartup, 1970). All over the world, children associate voluntarily with one another in activities initiated and maintained by the children themselves. But the role of the peer group varies from one culture to another. It is generally recognized that the peer group fulfills a socializing function. In the United States, children's groups perform a socializing function that is in some ways informal and dependent on the group's own rules. On the other hand, in other countries (such as the Soviet Union), the effect of the peer group as a socializing agent is institutionalized; the social mores are those of the government and the society at large. In Soviet schools, for example, children are held responsible for one another's discipline and scholarship. Adults expect the peer group to carry out more serious socialization tasks in addition to the spontaneous play associations of the members (Bronfenbrenner, 1970).

Certain behavioral characteristics—helping, cooperative, altruistic (or *prosocial*) behaviors on the one hand and aggressive (or *agonistic*) behaviors on the other—are crucial factors governing the quality of group life. They are factors that may determine how well a group can transmit knowledge to its members and how successful it is in its problem-solving efforts. A moment's reflection will produce numerous examples in support of this statement. How much learning takes place in a classroom full of noisy children? How much will a committee accomplish if its members dislike one another? How well does a family function when its members are in continual conflict? Among the questions we will be considering are how children acquire prosocial and agonistic behaviors and how these behaviors change as children grow older. Another question we will consider is how the immediate group situation—its rules, its rewards, the characteristics of its members—influences peer group behavior.

THE DEVELOPMENT OF PEER RELATIONS

There is little doubt that children's abilities to initiate and sustain social interactions with peers change substantially between the ages of 2 and 7. But of what does this change consist?

By the age of 2, children are already responsive to peers, although investigators disagree about the quality and quantity of the responsiveness observed. Maudry and Nekula (1939) claimed that infants ignore other infants except when toys are present, and that whatever social contacts do occur resemble contacts with inanimate objects, consisting mainly of exploratory looking and grasping. However, a recent study by Mueller (1973) demonstrates that although toys may be used as vehicles for social contact, the children do not actually treat each other like objects. Moreover, Lee (1973) has shown that social contacts differ from one child to another—that some babies are more "popular" (more often sought as playmates) than others. Lee's observations revealed differences in interactional styles among 8- to 10-month-old babies in a day-care center. The most popular of the children was "a responsive, adaptive social partner." Thus, although the baby's social repertoire is limited, these social behaviors do constitute efforts at interaction, and they are responded to as such by other infants.

The presence of a familiar peer has several important effects on the social behavior of young children. In a study of 17- to 20-month-old toddlers, Rubenstein and Howes (1976) found that toddlers play with, imitate, and offer objects to peers significantly more than they engage in these behaviors with their own mothers. Over 50% of the time during which the peer was present was spent in social interaction; less than 3% of that interaction involved conflict. The toddler's mother was practically ignored. The presence of a familiar peer also enhanced a toddler's competence with his own toys. Interaction with a peer stimulated the child to make use of the unique properties of toys and to find creative and unusual ways to use them (Rubenstein and Howes, 1976). The researchers were unable to determine whether peers actually teach each other new skills or whether they simply encourage each other to display existing skills. Either way, the result is greater utilization of the potentials of the toy.

By the age of 3, children have acquired some specific techniques for initiating and maintaining social encounters. One such technique takes the form of ritualized patterns of turns and rounds (Garvey, 1974). Consider the examples in Table 10–1. Each "turn" consists of the contribution (verbal and/or nonverbal) of one child. The content of the second child's turn may be the same as or complementary to the content of the first child's turn. In either case, one turn is contingent on another, forming patterns, which Garvey terms *rounds,* of interaction. These episodes are

TABLE 10–1
Sample Round Pattern of Two Preschoolers

X'S TURN	Y'S TURN
Bye, mommy.	
	Bye, mommy.
Bye, mommy.	
	Bye, mommy.
Bye, daddy.	
	Bye, daddy.
Bye, daddy.	
	Bye, daddy.
Hello, my name is Mr. Donkey.	
	Hello, my name is Mr. Elephant.
Hello, my name is Mr. Tiger.	
	Hello, my name is Mr. Lion.
I have to go to work.	
	You're already at work.
No, I'm not. I have to go to school.	
	You're already at school.
No, I'm not.	
I'll be the dragon and you be St. George that killed him.	
	(shoots the dragon, X)
(falls dead)	Now, I'll be the dragon.
(shoots Y, the dragon)	
	Do it again, I'm not dead.
(shoots again)	
	(falls dead)

Source: Garvey, 1974, p. 167.

marked as nonliteral by devices such as chanting (as in "Bye, mommy," in which neither child shows any intention of leaving) or role assignment (as in "I'll be the dragon... you be St. George..."). They often are punctuated with exaggerated gestures and giggles. As Garvey points out, turn patterns constitute mutually adaptive behavior. Both children recognize that a play situation exists, that the rules of the interaction apply to both children, and that the theme around which the interaction is organized can be modified by either child.

Developmental Changes in Peer Play

As children grow older, turn patterns like the one just described become longer and more varied. Other aspects of peer play change too. An early study of these changes was conducted by Parten (1932). Parten identified six ways in which 2- to 5-year-olds behave in group situations:

1. *Unoccupied behavior.** The child does not appear to be playing, but watches whatever is taking place nearby. When nothing is going on, "he plays with his own body, gets on and off chairs, just stands around ... or sits in one spot glancing around the room" (p. 249).
2. *Onlooker.* The child is interested in watching other children play and often talks to them (for example, asking questions or giving suggestions) without actually entering into the play.
3. *Solitary independent play.* The child plays alone with a separate group of toys without trying to get close to other children and without paying attention to what they are doing.
4. *Parallel activity.* The child plays independently, but with the same toys other children are using and in close proximity to them. The child is playing *beside* other children rather than *with* them.
5. *Associative play.* In this type of play, the child can be said to be playing with other children. They talk about what they are doing, borrow toys from each other, follow one another around, and sometimes try to control the membership of the group. All are engaged in similar activities.
6. *Organized supplementary play.* Here the group is organized around a goal or theme. One or two children direct the activities of the others. This type of play involves "division of labor, taking of different roles by the various group members and the organization of activity so that the efforts of one child are supplemented by those of another" (p. 251).

These types of interaction are increasingly sophisticated, and as might be expected, Parten's study revealed that the more sophisticated forms are observed in older children. Between the ages of 2 and 3, play is predominantly parallel, with relatively little time spent in cooperative enter-

*The child is not really unoccupied; *unfocused* might be a better term.

296

prises. By age 5, associative and cooperative play have increased in frequency, and less mature forms are infrequent.

Another early study (Green, 1933) came to similar conclusions. In this case, the primary object of study was the amount of group play among preschool children. Green observed that group play increases regularly with age; at the same time, the amount of solitary play decreases. These results are charted in Figure 10–1. In addition, the size of the play group increases as children grow older. Whereas the 2- or 3-year-old is more likely to play alone or with one other child, the 4- or 5-year-old shows an increased tendency to join in associative and cooperative play with two

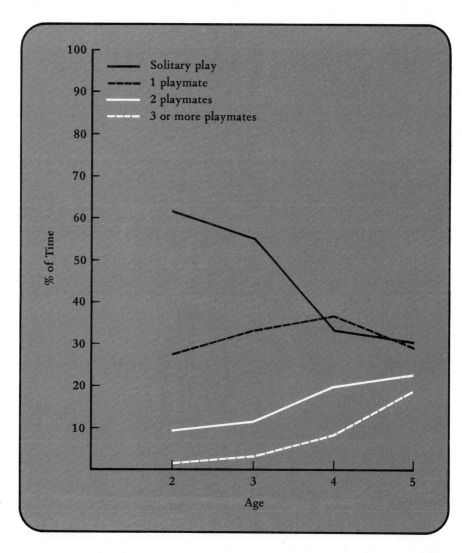

FIGURE 10–1
Percentage of time spent playing in different-sized play groups at various ages
(Adapted from Green, 1933, pp. 303–304, Table 7)

or more children. Interestingly, the number of quarrels peaks between 3 and 4 years of age, as the child shifts from solitary play to play with one child (Green, 1933).

A recent replication of Parten's study conducted by Barnes (1971) shows a similar developmental progression but some significant differences as well. Barnes compared the play behavior of preschool children with the behavior observed by Parten 40 years earlier. The data suggest that today's 3- and 4-year-olds are much less socially oriented in their play than the children in Parten's study. Barnes hypothesizes that the change may be due to the amount of time modern children spend watching television and to the decrease in average family size that has occurred since the 1930s.

With age, the overall pattern of group behavior changes. There is an increase in sociodramatic play: games in which children take various roles—"I'll kill the rattlesnakes and you cook them, but first Danny has to cut off the head and rattles." Children also become more verbal in their social exchanges—but most of these changes occur in the language used in dramatic play and not in the language used in ordinary social contacts. Marshall (1961) observed that as children become older, both prosocial and hostile behaviors increase within the context of dramatic play, but not in reality situations. This suggests that cooperative sociodramatic play serves as a safe vehicle for acquiring and experimenting with various social skills.

Marshall's data show a correlation between participation in dramatic play and home environment. Environments that promote social play are those in which parents and children discuss topics that are of interest to children and that can serve as a basis for dramatic play. In other words, children who participate most actively in dramatic play have easy access to a wide range of information in their homes. This is the type of environment that is usually described as intellectual. But since these children are also accepted by their peers and not dependent on teachers, it may be inferred that their home environments are socially as well as intellectually stimulating.

We will discuss the effects of parental attitudes more fully later in the chapter. Here, let us turn our attention to the effects of peer interaction.

The Importance of Peers

How crucial for children's social development is the opportunity for peer interaction? So far there is no clear-cut answer to this question. Studies of rhesus monkeys (Harlow and Harlow, 1965) suggest that deprivation of early peer contacts results in failure to acquire the control systems needed for later social relations. There is little evidence of similar patterns in human children, however.

Does this mean that early peer contacts do not play a role in children's social development? Not necessarily. Close relations with parents provide skills that optimize children's peer contacts; this, in turn, seems to lead to successful peer relations as the child grows older. However, as indicated in Chapter 7, there is evidence that in some cases early peer interactions result in increased aggressiveness in later years (Schwarz, Strickland, and Krolick, 1974). Thus, in human children, the *quality* of the peer behavior acquired at an early age may be more important for social development than the number of opportunities for social interaction.

It is also possible that peers can provide social nurturance and protection if they are otherwise lacking. This has been demonstrated not only in studies of infant monkeys raised without parents, but also in the dramatic case of six children whose parents were killed in concentration camps during World War II and who subsequently lived together for several years. The children were flown to England after the war. They were then between 3 and 4 years old. Since they were so young, it was decided that they should be given some time to adjust to the change in their circumstances before being placed among larger groups of children. Arrangements were made for them to live in a country house for a year. There they showed no interest in forming attachments with adult caregivers. In fact, they behaved toward them with active hostility. When angry, they would hit and bite, shout, scream, and spit at the adults. In contrast, the children were strongly attached to one another, as the following passage shows:

The children's positive feelings were centered exclusively in their own group. It was evident that they cared greatly for each other and not at all for anybody or anything else. They had no other wish than to be together and became upset when they were separated from each other, even for short moments. No child would consent to remain upstairs while the others were downstairs, or vice versa, and no child would be taken for a walk or on an errand without the others. If anything of the kind happened, the single child would constantly ask for the other children while the group would fret for the missing child. (A. Freud and Dunn, 1951, p. 131).

In short, though they had suffered greatly from the loss of their parents and the upheaval of their lives (they were "hypersensitive, restless, aggressive, difficult to handle"), these children had developed positive social attitudes toward one another. There was no sign of envy, jealousy, rivalry, or competition within the group.

Peer Group Processes

When children become members of a peer group, they often acquire new behaviors. Some of these behaviors may be undesirable. Within weeks after starting nursery school, for example, a child may display language or behavior shocking to his or her parents (like the 3½-year-old who decided to practice his new vocabulary of reproductive organs while on the crowded spiral ramp of New York's Guggenheim Museum). But children also acquire desirable social behavior from peers. They learn to take turns, to share toys, to help each other in the performance of various tasks. The processes by which children influence each other's behavior include modeling, direct reinforcement, and teaching.

PEERS AS MODELS. Children serve as models—often very effective ones—for other children. One study reveals that children will pick up aggressive peer behaviors even when those behaviors are portrayed on film (Bandura and Walters, 1963). Children have also been observed to pick up prosocial behaviors from peers. One study even showed that preschool children who are fearful of dogs become less fearful when they observe other children who like dogs (Bandura, Grusec, and Menlove, 1967).

Preschool children are more likely to choose as models those peers with whom they have had positive social exchanges in the past. Hartup and Coates (1967) observed a group of nursery school children and recorded positive social exchanges among the children. Later, in a laboratory setting, each child observed other children engaging in sharing behavior. The amount of imitative sharing that resulted from those observations depended on the child's past experience with the child who served as the model.

Although children readily imitate the behavior of their peers, adults probably provide better models in areas such as language learning. Children obviously imitate the language of their peers and acquire new words from them, but they are much more likely to imitate the language of adults (Hamilton and Stewart, 1977). Moreover, imitation of adult language increases with age, whereas imitation of peer language decreases. Adults, incidentally, are more likely to reinforce children's imitative responses than are peers.

PEERS AS DIRECT REINFORCERS. Peers reinforce each other's behavior, but the conditions under which such reinforcement occurs are complex. If a child is hit by another child, hits the aggressor back, and the aggressor withdraws, two things happen: (1) The original victim becomes more aggressive; and (2) the aggressor is likely to attack someone else (Patterson, Littman, and Bricker, 1967). The withdrawal of the aggressor has reinforced the victim's defensive behavior, but lack of reinforcement has not diminished the aggressiveness of the attacking child. However, in such cases, the peer group may help adults modify the attacking child's undesirable behavior. For example, if the teacher in a preschool class makes it clear that a particular child's behavior is undesirable, the other children are likely to change their behavior toward that child. Often, the combination of adult and peer nonreinforcement has the desired result of changing undesirable behavior.

An experiment by Wahler (1967) has demonstrated that peer reinforcement can be manipulated by adults. Children in a nursery school class

Younger siblings learn behaviors and some cognitive skills from older brothers and sisters.
(Shelly Rusten)

were instructed to ignore particular children when they behaved in a certain way, but not when they behaved in other ways. Wahler found that young children are able to follow such instructions, and the procedure resulted in the desired change in the behavior of the selected children. (Reversal of the procedure resulted in a shift back toward the original behavior.)

There are many potential applications of this method. It can be used not only to reduce aggressive behavior, but to reinforce desired behaviors as well. Suppose, for example, that one child is particularly withdrawn. The teacher can enlist the support of the other children in the class to reinforce any friendly overtures that child may make. Thus the teacher can use children as allies, either explicitly or otherwise, in bringing about behavioral changes in selected children.

PEERS AS TUTORS. Peers may also function as sources of new information. Older children are often effective teachers of younger children. For example, older siblings may acquire teaching techniques from adults and then apply those techniques when they interact with younger siblings. Thus big sister may teach little brother to add and subtract numbers under 10, using flash cards like those she has seen at school, before little brother enters kindergarten.

Cicirelli (1974) has investigated the effects of older siblings' instruction on younger siblings' performance of cognitive tasks. His study used an object-sorting task in which children were asked to form groupings of familiar objects. There were two trials. In one, the older sibling was present to help the younger sibling; in the other, the younger sibling performed the task alone.

The results of the experiment were rather complex, but the following generalizations may be made on the basis of the data obtained. (1) Children are more likely to use inferential categories (groupings of objects based on a shared characteristic other than physical appearance) when they are helped by siblings 4 years older than when they are helped by siblings 2 years older. (2) Verbal instruction by the older sibling leads to greater use of inferential categories by the younger sibling. The use of inferential categories is believed to indicate more mature concept formation. In short, young children are able to profit from teaching behaviors of older siblings, but this effect is more marked when there is a 4-year age difference between the siblings than when they are closer in age.

ON HAVING FRIENDS

In the preceding section, we mentioned that a toddler will interact more positively with a familiar child than with an unfamiliar one. It seems that the child is beginning to understand what it means to have a friend. An early sign that a child has acquired the concept of "friend" is the appearance of imaginary companions in the absence of (or in addition to) real ones.

Imaginary Companions

Parents often amuse their grown children with stories of their childhood companions—"Waldo," who could fly away if someone was chasing him, or "Yehudi," who lived in the refrigerator and turned off the light when the door was closed. Piaget's account (1951) of how his daughter Jacqueline created an imaginary playmate, "Marécage," is typical. Like most children who invent such "friends," Jacqueline used her imaginary companion to compensate for what she considered to be defects in real life. When required to take a nap, for example, Jacqueline said, "Marécage never lies down in the afternoon, she plays all the time" (p. 132). She also made up stories about her companion's activities. She entertained her father with the following account while walking along a mountain path: "[Marécage] rolled right to the bottom of the mountain into the lake. She rolled for four nights. She scraped her knee and her leg terribly. She did not even cry. They picked her up afterwards. She was in the lake, she couldn't swim and was nearly drowned" (p. 134).

Children may also create an imaginary *self* and then come up with imaginary companions to go with the imaginary self. For example, at age 3, one boy shifted back and forth from being himself to being "Billy the Kid." His stuffed rabbit became Billy the Kid's horse. Still another form of imaginary companion is the toy that takes on a name and a personality. The little boy's stuffed rabbit later became a spaceman. The rabbit, in the role of spaceman, had certain needs and requirements to which the family was expected to respond: "Pumie says he's going on a trip, so please leave his things alone while he's gone."

The phenomenon of imaginary companions has not been studied extensively. However, Manosevitz, Prentice, and Wilson (1973) have observed that imaginary companions are more frequent among first-born and only children. The data suggest that the companion makes up for the child's loneliness. The child for whom real friends are not available can and often does invent the friends he or she needs.

Friendship and Popularity

Friends are those people with whom an individual chooses to interact most frequently. They are people that we like to be with—and who, in turn, like to be with us. Observations indicate that acquiring a friend takes time for a preschool child, as it does for older children and for adults. During the early stages of acquaintanceship, the degree of friendship between any two children fluctuates markedly. After having been in the same group for a long time, however, children tend to be more stable in their friendships with each other than with newer members of the group. Stability of friendships is also directly related to the age of the children; friendships become more stable as children grow older (Witryol and Thompson, 1953).

Investigators measure the presence of friendship in young children in two ways. The first is the *sociometric test,* which identifies patterns of relationships among children. In such a test, children who belong to the same preschool or play group are asked questions such as "Who is your best friend?" or "Whom do you like to play with?" or "Who are the best kids in the class?" The results of sociometric tests are presented graphically in the form of a *sociogram,* as shown in Figure 10–2. The alternative way of measuring children's friendship is to observe them in group settings. The observer records which children a particular child chooses to play with or to sit beside during lunch or story time. Friendship patterns are determined on the basis of these choices. Observations of preschool children have shown that by age 4, children prefer some companions to others and that these preferences are moderately stable. Sociometric analysis confirms these findings (Marshall and McCandless, 1957b). In fact, sociometric scores correspond fairly well with the opinions of teachers concerning the friendships and popularity of children in their classes.

Sociometric analyses indicate that some children are more popular than others. Popularity is measured by peer acceptance—the degree to which peers want contact with a particular child (Hartup, 1970). The fact that some children are more popular than others does not mean that less popular children do not form stable friendships; they often do. Moreover, popular children may be fickle in their relationships with others. It should be noted, too, that friendliness is not a *cause* of popularity. The relationship between friendliness and popularity is probably a reciprocal one.

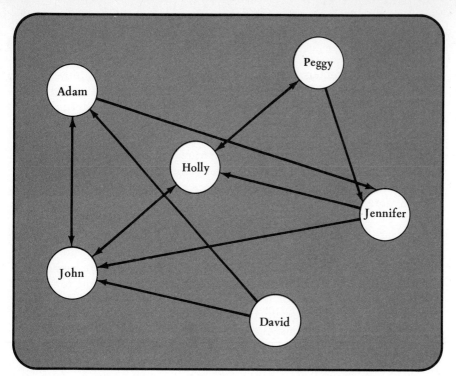

FIGURE 10–2
Sociogram showing hypothetical choices of two favorite companions of each of six children. Note that John and Holly were chosen most often, and David was not chosen at all.

That is, sociable children are more easily accepted by the group, and being accepted encourages sociability (Moore, 1967).

Many investigators have explored the question of what makes some children more popular than others. However, as Hartup (1970) points out, no single aspect of behavior in isolation from other aspects has been shown to determine popularity. There are several characteristics, though, that taken together are consistently associated or correlated with popularity. (Remember that the fact that the measures are associated does not mean that one *causes* the other.) Popular children are outgoing in their behavior. They are kind, sensitive to the social overtures of their peers, and cooperative. They accept routines, do not fuss about rules, and are eager partners in group enterprises (Hartup, 1970). Popular children are also more likely to be imitated than less popular children.

Another factor associated with young children's popularity is dependence. Dependence on adults interferes with acceptance by peers; dependence on peers may enhance a child's popularity (Hartup, 1970). The relationship between dependency and popularity is not a simple one, however. The quality of the child's relations with others is an important variable as well. For example, investigators have found that socially mature behaviors with adults, such as seeking help or approval when it is needed, are often associated with peer acceptance. Socially immature behaviors, such as clinging or whining, are associated with low popularity (Marshall and McCandless, 1957a; Marshall, 1961). More mature behavior with peers also seems to facilitate peer acceptance (Hartup, 1970).

Aggressive children are usually rejected by peers, although nonaggressive children are not necessarily popular. It appears that popularity involves nonaggressiveness combined with an orientation toward other children and a willingness to accommodate to their wishes. In sum, popular children tend to seek help and support from peers, and they are generally more outgoing than less accepted children. Their relations with other children may be described as "easy-going, relatively nonaggressive give-and-take" (Hartup, 1970).

By the age of 4, then, children's group experiences may already be characterized as positive, negative, or middling. The socially accepted child

In early childhood, children form preferences for some peers over others. These preferences lead to moderately stable friendships. (Marion Faller, Monkmeyer)

has acquired different skills from the child who is socially rejected. These early peer experiences have lasting effects. Waldrop and Halverson (1975) observed that 2½-year-olds who are highly involved with peers, who are friendly, and who actively cope with problems have more friends and a more active social life five years later, at age 7½.

Young children clearly are responsive to each other. They seek out companions, even invent them when real ones are not available. They readily acquire the behaviors and routines with which social encounters are initiated and maintained. They also form preferences for one child over another, and these preferences lead to moderately stable friendships. Some children are more sought after as playmates than others; "popularity" emerges at a remarkably early age.

As children grow older, their social behavior becomes more refined and differentiated. Some behaviors are prosocial in character; they reflect empathy and helpful concern for others. Other behaviors are clearly aggressive in character. In the next section, we will discuss the prosocial behaviors that appear during the preschool years. In the section that follows, we will turn our attention to aggressive behaviors.

PROSOCIAL BEHAVIOR

Most parents and teachers would agree that they want children to acquire prosocial behavior—to be generous and helpful toward others, to share, and to empathize with others. Although parents may not recognize altruistic behavior when it first appears, it has been observed in very young children. Some children begin to show concern for others by the age of 2. If a child falls down and cries, another child may spontaneously offer a toy. Or an unhappy child fussing in an adult's lap may receive a friendly, sympathetic pat or kiss from a peer. Such behaviors are not frequent, but they do occur.

The Generous, Helpful Child

By the age of 4, generosity has become a stable dimension of children's behavior. However, generosity involves a rather diverse set of behaviors. One form of generosity is the giving of help to those who need it. Baumrind (1971) has observed that helpful children are helpful in a number of ways. For one thing, children who offer help to others are generally more *nurturant* than less helpful children. That is, they tend to give positive attention to their peers. They tend to be emotionally expressive and to seek help as well as give it (Bryan, 1975). In one study, for example, children who were more likely to aid a puppet in distress also expressed their own emotional distress more often (Lenrow, 1965). Generous children are also more aggressive. It is likely that their aggressiveness is a result of the greater number of social contacts in which these children participate.

Moreover, as Marshall (1961) has suggested, this aggressive behavior may have a playful, make-believe quality.

Why are some children more likely to help others? It may be that the giving of aid requires a general quality of "outgoingness" (Hartup and Keller, 1960). This kind of "social courage" may make it possible for helpful children to reveal their own vulnerability (by expressing distress or seeking help when necessary); to achieve control over their own environment (by helping themselves whenever possible); and to extend these attitudes to situations in which others are expressing distress or seeking help. It is also possible that such children are more easily aroused emotionally, so that they respond more readily to threats both to themselves (hence the aggressive behavior noted earlier) and to others. Finally, in the language of "contingency reinforcement," such children may have learned that a request for help leads to the giving of help, and this may have become a rule governing their own social behavior (Bryan, 1975).

Another characteristic that has been related to generosity is lack of competitiveness. Children who are generous tend to be less competitive in situations in which competition is possible but not encouraged. Rutherford and Mussen (1968) studied competitiveness in nursery school boys. The boys were first scored on a situational test of generosity. They then participated in various activities designed to measure competitiveness. One such activity was a racing game in which a boy raced a doll along a yardstick, competing against the doll of the researcher. Since the researcher raced his "entrant" at a slow but constant speed, the child could win or lose the race by as small or large a margin as he chose. The boys made themselves win in every race. But the average margin of victory for the highly generous boys was about one-third less than the average margin of victory for the nongenerous boys. The generous child appears to have less need to outdo a competitor by a large margin. However, in situations that encourage competition, even generous and helpful children go for personal gain rather than social sharing. And although children become more helpful and generous as they grow older, their capacity for generosity does not appear in competitive situations.

The Development of Empathy

Another measure of altruism is *empathy* — the ability to perceive and understand the feelings or motives of others. Many observers believe that preschool children not only are aware that other people have feelings but also make an effort to understand those feelings.

According to Borke (1971), even 3-year-olds are aware of other people's feelings. In Borke's experiment, children 3 to 8 years old were told stories that portrayed the characters in situations likely to produce an emotion of some sort. Such situations included eating a favorite snack, losing a toy, getting lost in the woods at night, being forced to go to bed. Borke used two methods to assess the children's empathy with the characters in the story. In one, the child was shown a picture of one of the characters and asked to add the face. (The children chose the face from a set of four drawings of faces showing happiness, sadness, fear, and anger.) In the other method, the child was asked to point to the face that indicated how the story character felt. The results of the experiment showed that between the ages of 3 and 3½, children can connect situations with the emotions of happiness, sadness, and anger. Fear is not identified until the age of 4. It was also evident that children's sensitivity to the feelings of others increases with age. This trend was not consistent among the four emotions portrayed, however. Apparently, it is easier for children to differentiate between pleasant and unpleasant feelings than to distinguish among unpleasant feelings. In Borke's view, the fact that 3-year-olds can distinguish between happy and unhappy feelings in other people suggests that they are aware that other people have feelings that are different from their own.

Shantz (1975) has reviewed recent research on empathy in young children and confirms Borke's conclusion that 4-year-olds can reliably identify situations that evoke happy responses. She found that between the ages of 4 and 7, there is increasing accuracy in children's identification of situations that evoke fear, sadness, and anger. But, she asks, if children can identify the feelings of others, does it follow that they *share* those feelings? In an attempt to answer this question, Feshbach and Roe (1968) presented story and slide sequences depicting anger, happiness, sadness, and fear to a group of 6- and 7-year-olds. After each sequence, the children were asked "How do *you* feel?" The sequences were presented a second time to half of the children in the group, who were then asked "How does this child [the one in the story] feel?" A greater number of answers were obtained to the second question than to the first one. Apparently, young children are able to identify (that is, understand) the feelings of others in a story situation without necessarily sharing those feelings.

By the age of 5 years, children become sensitive to what others are intending to do as opposed to what they do "by accident." King (1971) investigated children's attitudes toward intentional versus accidental behavior by means of film sequences. For example, one sequence showed two boys running and then one boy tripping and getting up unhurt. The other sequence showed the boys running and then one boy pushing the other against a tree; the victim appeared to be hurt. Again, the results showed an age-related trend. Preschool children paid little attention to intent in judging the boys' behavior, whereas children of kindergarten age judged intentional harm more severely than accidental harm. Similarly, kindergarten children judged deliberate kindness as more kind than accidental kindness (Baldwin and Baldwin, 1970).

The results of these and similar studies lead to the conclusion that attention to multiple aspects of the perceptions and feelings of others increases in early childhood. It is evident that communicative, roletaking, and spatial (perspective) skills are highly correlated (Rubin, 1973), and all increase with mental and chronological age. Meanwhile, the child becomes less "egocentric"—perhaps because he or she is increasingly able to "center" on the feelings of others.

Acquiring Concern for Others

Two factors appear to play major roles in the acquisition of altruistic behavior: cognitive development, and adult modeling and nurturance. Not surprisingly, increased altruism is associated with certain aspects of cognitive development. If children are generous or helpful to others or share the feelings of others, they must be able to perceive the other person's state or condition. They also must know something about how conditions of trouble or sorrow can be relieved, and they must be willing to give of themselves to others. As for adult modeling and nurturance, their effectiveness is evident in many areas of development.

SOCIAL RESPONSIBILITY VERSUS RECIPROCITY. Children are exposed quite early to the adult norms of social responsibility and reciprocity. *Social responsibility* requires a person to aid those who are dependent on him or her without expecting to be rewarded. *Reciprocity* refers to the belief that people should help those who help them and also that they should not injure those who help them. Studies have shown that emphasis on these norms varies by social class. Middle-class people are more likely to be influenced by the norm of reciprocity than are lower-class people. Lower-class people, on the other hand, tend to be more influenced by the norm of social responsibility.

With these differences in mind, Dreman and Greenbaum (1973) investigated sharing behavior in Israeli kindergarten children. The children were grouped by social class, ethnic group, and sex. An experiment was designed that would assess the willingness of children to share candy under two conditions. In one, the child who was giving the candy would be identified to the child who was receiving it. In the other, the giver of the candy would not be identified. Each child was given two bags. One of the bags contained seven pieces of candy; the other was empty. The child was told to do whatever he or she liked with the candy, but was also told that some of the other children would not be given candy. The child was then given the opportunity to take some of the candy out of one bag and put it into the other bag to be given to another child. The experimenter said he would not watch the child divide the candy, but after the child had done so, he or she was asked, "Who has more candies, you or the other child?" and "Is there any reason why you wanted the other child to have the candies?"

The majority of the children donated either three or four pieces of candy. It is likely that they wanted to donate half of the candy but could not. Hence, they debated between giving a little more or a little less than half. Middle-class boys were more generous in condition 1 (reciprocity) than in condition 2 (social responsibility). Middle-class girls and lower-class children of both sexes were not significantly affected by the difference between the conditions, nor were any significant ethnic differences found. These results, coupled with the findings of other investigators, indicate that middle-class boys, especially those whose parents' work is financial or commercial in nature, are more likely to be influenced by the reciprocity norm. Children from large families are more likely to stress social responsibility and those from small families, reciprocity. Thus children are sensitive to the value systems of their families and communities.

Analysis of children's verbal responses to questions such as those asked in the experiment reveals interesting differences. Children who give answers such as "The divider must always give more" seem to be following social responsibility norms without thinking about them. This reflects a less sophisticated level of cognitive development than that attained by children who give answers such as "I gave to him so he'll play with me"—answers that move beyond the present and indicate that the child has thought about prior debts and future rewards. Dreman and Greenbaum point out, however, that verbal responses and actual sharing behavior do not always coincide. In fact, the relationships between the two are quite complex, and neither should be regarded as *the* measure of the child's generosity.

MODELING AND NURTURANCE. Modeling and adult nurturance seem to be important factors in children's acquisition of altruistic behaviors. When a child watches someone else helping or giving, he or she is likely to engage in similar behavior. However, various studies have shown that what an adult model says ("It is good to give" or "Giving will make other children happy") is less influential than what the model actually does (Bryan, 1975). When adults demonstrate altruistic behavior—and especially when they accompany such actions with expressions of pleasure in what they are doing ("Gee, I'm glad I gave candy to those kids")—children are likely to follow suit. Moreover, children's evaluations of altruistic people are more favorable than their judgments of people who behave selfishly. Thus they are more likely to imitate helpful, charitable people.

When adults do one thing and say another, children do not seem to be bothered by the contradiction. They tend to do what the model does and say what the model says, apparently without recognizing the incongruity. However, the long-term effects of such inconsistent modeling are unclear. There is evidence that inconsistency reduces the model's later ability to influence the child (Bryan, 1975).

An interesting study of how children learn helping behavior was conducted by Yarrow, Scott, and Waxler (1973). They explored effects of adult modeling combined with nurturant behavior. These investigators created a naturalistic situation that continued for some time and used a variety of techniques to assess children's concern for others. Essentially, there were four conditions: (1) a nurturant adult responding to both symbolic and real-life distress, (2) a nurturant adult responding to symbolic distress but not to real-life distress, (3) a nonnurturant adult responding to both symbolic and real-life distress, and (4) a nonnurturant adult responding only to symbolic distress. Only in the first condition, in which the model treated the children in a nurturant way *and* responded to the full range of distress situations, was there a significant increase in the children's altruistic behavior. Such a finding suggests that a generalized form of altruism in the adult leads to generalized altruism in the child.

AGGRESSIVE BEHAVIOR

Just as prosocial behavior consists of a multitude of different behaviors involving different forms of friendliness, concern, and generosity, so, too, children's aggressive behavior appears in different forms with different purposes. Sometimes aggressive behavior is appropriate to the situation; sometimes it is not. In discussing aggressive behavior, it is important to keep in mind its purpose. One child may hit another because he or she wants a toy that the other child is unwilling to give up or because he or she dislikes that child. In the former case, the child's goal—getting the toy—is nonaggressive. In the latter case, the goal—inflicting injury or pain—is aggressive. In early childhood, it is often difficult to distinguish between these two goals. As a result, the "assertive" child may be considered "aggressive" even though that child does not intend to hurt others.

Researchers have found patterns of developmental changes in aggressive behavior. Green (1933) noted that the frequency of quarrels among young children reaches a peak at around age 3. Similarly, the number of undirected, diffuse temper tantrums increases gradually until age 3 and then drops abruptly. At the same time, children begin to retaliate more frequently; that is, they try to get revenge for an injury through either physical or verbal means. In the preschool years, verbal aggression increases, along with sulking and resentment following aggressive episodes (Goodenough, 1931). It may be that aggressive verbal responses enable the child to maintain aggressive attitudes when physical aggression is discouraged (Feshbach, 1970).

The ways in which parents respond to aggressive behavior in children also change with the age of the child. With younger children, parents use techniques such as physical force, diverting the child's attention, and ignoring the outburst. Techniques used with older children include scolding, threatening, and isolation (such as sending the child to his or her bedroom and sometimes straight to bed). Also, parents are more likely to yield to older children. They are more authoritarian with younger children and are more likely to use verbal controls as children grow older (Feshbach, 1970).

Every society trains children so that they can participate in the society without engaging in mutually destructive behavior. But cultures differ in the kind and amount of aggression they will tolerate. Headhunters like the Iatmul encourage the scalping of enemies; the Hutterites of North America, by contrast, stress pacifism as a way of life. This contrast is reflected in the child-rearing practices of these societies. The training of Iatmul youths involves a series of experiences in which pain or humiliation is inflicted on the younger members of the society while the older members receive social approval for those acts. The training of Hutterite children is equally severe, but aggressive behavior is never rewarded (Bandura and Walters, 1963).

Aggressive behavior is one area in which sex differences are quite noticeable. Cultures differ in the degree of aggressiveness they expect of boys and girls. In some cultures, in fact, aggressiveness is virtually equated with masculinity. In the United States, cultural expectations lead to the labeling of less aggressive boys as "sissies" and more aggressive girls as "tomboys." Expectations of this sort are a major source of sex differences in behavior. For instance, it may be harder to control aggression in males or to encourage it in females. There is evidence, mostly from experiments using animals, that this is the case. However, it is likely that whatever biologically based differences there are, they are reinforced (perhaps even exaggerated) by cultural factors and individual experience.

In our society, by the age of 2, boys are already more aggressive than girls. Studies of physical aggression conducted over the past 40 years have consistently reported this difference, which, incidentally, persists into adulthood (Feshbach, 1970). When other forms of aggression are measured, however, the findings are less consistent, but it appears that girls are likely to make use of verbal and other indirect forms of aggression (Feshbach, 1969). Girls, for example, are more likely to refuse to play with someone they do not like, to make critical remarks, to reject a newcomer's suggestions, and so forth.

Theories of aggression differ in the degree to which they emphasize biological processes or learning as the source of aggressive behavior. Ethologists see aggression as designed to help organisms survive in a given environment. They point out that animals prey on others in order to obtain food; they fight to protect themselves, their young, or their territory. Psychoanalytic theorists see aggression as a natural drive. They believe instinctual needs to hate as well as to love are present from birth. In contrast to ethologists, psychoanalytic theorists do not see aggression as an adaptive behavior. Instead, it is viewed as a personality force that needs to be diverted and restrained through socialization processes. Other investigators have argued that aggressive behaviors depend on experience. Behavior theorists believe that behaviors are acquired by a process of reinforcement. A child takes a toy away from another child and is reinforced by gaining possession of a desired object. Behavior theory proposes that a random act of aggression occurs, is reinforced, and therefore occurs more frequently. The initial random act of aggression can be explained as a manifestation of modeling or imitation. There is considerable evidence that children can acquire aggressive behavior simply by observing others — peers and adults — engaging in such behavior.

How Are Aggressive Behaviors Acquired?

The case for a biological origin of aggressive behavior is a good one. Anger seems to be a universal human emotion and can be observed even in very young infants. The agitated flailing of arms and legs that accompanies infant rage may be the source of later physical aggression. That is, with social experience these motor elements of anger may gradually be organized into direct assaults on others. However, as we have seen, social experience determines when and how a person's anger is expressed.

SELECTIVE REINFORCEMENT. Laboratory studies as well as observations of child-rearing practices have shown that aggression can be learned (or unlearned) through *selective reinforcement.* In an experiment by Lovaas (1961), for example, children were rewarded with a toy whenever they made aggressive verbal responses to a doll; another group was rewarded for nonaggressive responses. Then the children were given an opportunity to play with a nonaggressive or an aggressive toy. The children who had been reinforced for verbal aggression used the aggressive toy more often than those who had been reinforced for nonaggression. Similar studies have been conducted in nonlaboratory settings. In one such study (Brown and Elliot, 1965), nursery school teachers were told to ignore aggressive behaviors and to reinforce nonaggressive, cooperative behaviors. This was done for periods of two weeks, separated by three-week intervals. Both physical and verbal aggression declined markedly during the second week of each treatment period.

It is easy to see how selective reinforcement might operate in the home and other nonlaboratory settings. The parent who gives in to a child whenever he or she has a temper tantrum is reinforcing the tantrum. The teacher who scolds a repeatedly aggressive child may be rewarding the child for attention-seeking behavior. Children who yield to the desires of a bully are reinforcing the bully's aggressive behavior. The selective reinforcement of aggression among nursery school children was the subject of a study by Patterson et al., (1967). These investigators observed and recorded aggressive interactions among 3- and 4-year-olds over a period of 26 weeks, taking note of the aggressive action, the victim's reaction, and the teacher's behavior. They hypothesized that the victim's reaction would have a significant effect on the aggressor's later behavior: "If the victim complied with the aggressor's wish or otherwise reinforced the aggressive act, it was predicted that the aggressor would be more likely

Behavioral theorists believe that aggressive behaviors are acquired through processes of modeling and reinforcement. (Elizabeth Hamlin, Stock, Boston)

to aggress against that same child on a subsequent occasion. However, if the victim counterattacked or the teacher intervened, it was predicted that the aggressive response would be temporarily suppressed and redirected to another child" (p. 290). The observations confirmed this hypothesis. Thus selective reinforcement can be an important factor in the acquisition of aggressive behavior.

MODELING. A less direct but equally potent factor in the development of aggressive behavior is *modeling*. As we have seen, both adults and peers may serve as models. A series of pioneering studies of the role of imitation in the development of aggressive behavior was conducted by Bandura and his associates. In one study (Bandura, Ross, and Ross, 1961), children were exposed to models who either behaved aggressively toward a toy "Bobo" doll or ignored the doll. Later, the children were given an opportunity to play with a group of toys, including a Bobo doll. The children's behavior toward the doll reflected that of the model they had observed. Those children who had watched the aggressive model were both verbally and physically aggressive toward the Bobo doll. In addition, they showed more nonimitative aggression than did the other children. These results were most noticeable among boys.

Bandura and his associates also have studied the effects of modeling in combination with reinforcement. They showed nursery school children films in which an aggressor was either punished or rewarded for aggressive actions. The version in which the model was rewarded produced significantly more imitative aggression than the other version. Children who saw the punished model behaved similarly to children in a control group who were not shown a model. Interestingly, the children who imitated the aggressive model did so despite the fact that they had evaluated the model's behavior negatively. Thus reinforcement was more effective in producing imitative behavior than the children's values.

The conclusions of Bandura's studies of imitative aggression may be summed up as follows:

1. Children are more prone to imitate "real" models than cartoon characters.
2. When the model is reinforced, children show more imitative aggression, even though they may criticize the model's behavior.
3. Even though children are not likely to imitate a model who has been punished, they will perform the aggressive behavior if appropriately rewarded.

Parental Influences   Aggression in children reflects the way they are treated by their parents. Children who receive little affection or attention and who are often criticized and scolded tend to be hostile in their relations with others. But parental attitudes can encourage aggressiveness even in children who are loved and who receive positive attention from their parents. For example, some parents condone aggression in the name of self-defense, especially in boys: "Don't let him pick on you—hit him back!"

Parents' responses to aggressive behavior such as temper tantrums, destruction of household objects, or conflicts with siblings vary considerably. Parents may ignore or encourage the behavior in question; they may restrain or punish the child; they may try to distract the child or reason with him or her (Feshbach, 1970). Some parents punish aggression but fail to teach the child socially desirable alternative behaviors. The child knows what he or she should *not* do but has very little idea of what kind of behavior *will* win approval (Feshbach and Feshbach, 1972).

There is evidence that parental punishment of aggressive behavior does not result in reduced aggression. It appears that the parent who uses physical punishment becomes an aggressive model and is imitated by the child. Moreover, severe punishment has been associated with a high degree of aggressiveness in children's doll play and other forms of fantasy (Feshbach and Feshbach, 1972).

If physical punishment is not successful as a means of suppressing aggressive behavior for more than a brief period—and, indeed, can be seen as encouraging such behavior—how can aggression be inhibited? Before discarding punishment entirely, we should note that not all punishments have the same effect. The timing and type of punishment used and the consistency with which it is used will partly determine its effectiveness. Also, there is some evidence that "loving" psychological (as opposed to physical) punishment may inhibit aggression (Allinsmith, 1954; Sears, 1961; Feshbach and Feshbach, 1972). More research is needed in this area.

Inhibition and Expression of Aggression

An even more effective tool for inhibiting aggression is the internalization of moral standards. The development of conscience in children is related to factors such as parental affection and use of reasoning (Baumrind, 1967; Feshbach and Feshbach, 1972). A child with a strong conscience will refrain from behaving aggressively even when he or she is unlikely to be punished for doing so.

It has been hypothesized that children's aggressive behavior fulfills a tension-releasing function. This is known as the *catharsis hypothesis.* Do aggressive play, exposure to aggression on TV, and similar experiences serve as an outlet for aggressive tendencies in the child? If so, one would expect a decrease in aggressive behavior following such an experience. Studies of the effects of both aggressive play and aggression portrayed in films have not supported this hypothesis. In fact, usually the opposite effect—increased aggressiveness—has been observed (Bandura, Ross, and Ross, 1963; Feshbach, 1956).

CHILD REARING AND SOCIAL DEVELOPMENT

Most people would agree that parental behaviors have a major effect on children's social behavior, personality, and intellectual performance. But *how* this influence operates is an important question. If parents knew the answer, they might be able to modify their child-rearing practices in order to help their children acquire more desirable social skills and attitudes. Baumrind has devoted extensive study to the effects of parenting styles on children.

In a study of nursery school children, Baumrind (1967) found certain relationships between parental behaviors and social and personality characteristics of their children. The children who were most self-reliant, self-controlled, explorative, and content had parents who were controlling and demanding yet also warm and receptive to the child. Baumrind labeled the combination of high control and positive encouragement *authoritative* parental behavior. Children who were relatively distrustful, withdrawn, and discontent had parents who were controlling but detached and less warm than authoritative parents. This parenting style is called *authori-*

Patterns of Parental Authority

tarian. The least self-reliant, self-controlled, and explorative children had parents who were warm but noncontrolling and nondemanding. Baumrind called this pattern *permissive.* She described the three patterns of parental authority as follows:

The authoritative *parent . . . attempts to direct the child's activities but in a rational, issue-oriented manner. She encourages verbal give and take, and shares with the child the reasoning behind her policy. . . . She exerts firm control . . . , but does not hem the child in with restrictions. She recognizes her own special rights as an adult, but also the child's individual interests and special ways. The authoritative parent . . . uses reason as well as power to achieve her objectives. (1968, p. 261)*

The authoritarian *parent attempts to shape, control and evaluate the behavior and attitudes of the child in accordance with a set standard of conduct, usually an absolute standard . . . formulated by a higher authority. She values obedience as a virtue and favors punitive, forceful measures to curb self-will at points where the child's actions or beliefs conflict with what she thinks is right conduct. She believes in . . . respect for authority, respect for work, and respect for the preservation of order and traditional structure. She does not encourage verbal give and take, believing that the child should accept her word for what is right. (1968, 261)*

The permissive *parent attempts to behave in a nonpunitive, acceptant and affirmative manner towards the child's impulses, desires, and actions. She consults with him about policy decisions and gives explanations for family rules. She makes few demands for household responsibility and orderly behavior. She presents herself to the child as a resource for him to use as he wishes, not as an active agent responsible for shaping or altering his on-going or future behavior. She allows the child to regulate his own activities as much as possible, avoids the exercise of control, and does not encourage him to obey externally-defined standards. She attempts to use reason but not overt power to accomplish her ends. (1968, p. 256)*

Baumrind concludes that authoritative parents can teach their children responsible conformity to social standards without the loss of individual independence or self-assertiveness (1966).

The types of behaviors most parents want to see in their children may be grouped under Baumrind's (1972) label *instrumental competence.* These behaviors include friendliness, cooperation, achievement orientation, dominance (as opposed to submissiveness), and purposiveness. In short, the behaviors that characterize instrumental competence may be described as *socially responsible* and *independent.* These two dimensions of competence are of obvious value in an achievement-oriented society.

The dimension of socially responsible behavior has to do with the child's attitudes toward achievement and his or her willingness to cooperate with others in attaining a common goal. The socially responsible child is willing to continue a task in the face of frustration and tries to comply with the cognitive demands of teachers and other adults. Such behavior is highly correlated with willingness to cooperate with adults. Children who display these qualities also tend to be friendly toward their peers. Baumrind's observations suggest that adult modeling of socially responsible behavior leads to the development of such behavior in children. Both authoritative and authoritarian parents demand socially responsible behavior, but authoritarian parents are more likely to let their own needs take precedence over those of the child. Social responsibility is also stimulated by firmness on the part of the parent, provided that the parent makes clear what types of behavior are desirable. In other words, it is important for parents to make sure the child knows the rules as well as to make sure the rules are followed, using punishment if necessary. Permissive parents are reluctant to do this, and their children show less prosocial and achievement-oriented behavior than the children of authoritative parents. When punishment is accompanied by verbal explanations of why the behavior in question is undesirable, the child is more likely to learn desirable behaviors. Thus authoritarian parents, who engage in less verbal exchange with their children, are less successful than authoritative parents in producing socially responsible behavior.

With regard to the dimension of independence, Baumrind's studies have shown that an intellectually stimulating environment is conducive to greater independence in young children. Such an environment is usually provided by authoritative parents. Firm control also may be linked to independence. Firm control consists of enforcement of rules, resistance to unreasonable demands, and guidance of the child. Restrictive control entails the use of a multitude of rules in every area of the child's life, which hinder or prohibit vigorous interaction with other people and a resulting sense of individuality and self-expression.

Punishment

Is punishment useful? Is it harmful? These are controversial questions, and the answers are by no means clear. There are many variables that affect the value of punishment in controlling children's behavior. One such variable is the relationship between the parent and the child. Punishment is more effective when this relationship is close and affectionate. In such cases, physical punishment involves both the punishment itself and the temporary withdrawal of affection. Reasoning also plays an important role in determining the effectiveness of punishment for children over 4 or 5 years of age. Studies have shown that punishment is more effective when it is accompanied by an explanation of why the behavior is undesirable: "That toy will break if you treat it like that" (Parke, 1969). Parke and Murray (1971) found that a rationale by itself is more effective than punishment by itself; the combination of the two is most effective.

Another significant variable is the timing of the punishment. The longer the delay between the undesirable behavior and the punishment, the less effective the punishment is as a means of inhibiting that behavior. Moreover, the child is less likely to learn from punishment that is delayed. Walters, Parke, and Cane (1965) conducted an experiment in which 6- to 8-year-olds were rebuked ("No, that's for the other boy") when they touched an attractive toy. Children in one group were punished in this way before they actually touched the toy; those in another group were punished after having picked up the toy and held it for 2 seconds. The children were then seated before a display of toys similar to those used in the first part of the experiment and reminded not to touch them. The test consisted of leaving each child alone for 15 minutes with an unattractive German-English dictionary and the forbidden toy. An observer behind a one-way screen recorded the extent to which each child touched the toy. The data from these observations showed that the children who had been punished earlier touched the toy less than those who had been punished later, supporting the belief that immediate punishment is preferable to delayed punishment. Aronfreed (1965) found, however, that when a verbal explanation accompanied a punishment, early and late punishments were equally effective in correcting unwanted behaviors.

Of course, punishment can have undesirable consequences as well as desirable ones. As mentioned earlier, an adult who uses physical punishment may serve as an aggressive model. In addition, punishment may cause the child to avoid the adult who administers the punishment, thereby damaging the parent-child relationship. Thus, although punishment can be an effective means of controlling children's behavior, its effectiveness depends on several factors and it must be used with care. Moreover, punishment alone is unlikely to be very effective. It should be used with other socialization techniques such as reasoning and reinforcement so that the child is encouraged to behave in desirable ways as well as to avoid behaviors for which he or she will be punished.

SUMMARY

The social world of the infant is composed primarily of adults. By age 3, however, children begin to come into increasingly frequent contact with other children their own age or slightly older. Family groups, peer groups, and work groups all provide opportunities for face-to-face encounters with others who play crucial roles in the acquisition of new social knowledge and in the transmission of knowledge already gained. The role of the peer group varies from one culture to another, although it is generally recognized that the peer group fulfills a socializing function.

Certain behavioral characteristics — helping, cooperative, altruistic (or *prosocial*) behaviors on the one hand and aggressive (or *agonistic*) behaviors on the other—are factors governing the quality of group life. They may determine how well a group transmits knowledge to its members and how successful it is in its problem-solving efforts.

By the age of 2, children are already responsive to peers, although investigators disagree about the quality and quantity of the responsiveness observed. Interaction with peers stimulates children to make use of the unique properties of toys and to find creative and unusual ways to use them.

By the age of 3, children have acquired some specific techniques for initiating and maintaining social encounters. One such technique takes the form of ritualized patterns of turns and rounds between two children. Both children recognize that a play situation exists, that the rules of the interaction apply to both children, and that the theme around which the interaction is organized can be modified by either child.

As children grow older, turn patterns become longer and more varied. Other aspects of peer play change also: More sophisticated forms of play are observed; group play increases and solitary play decreases; the size of the play group increases. The number of quarrels peaks between the ages of 3 and 4 during the shift from solitary play to play with one other child.

With age, the overall pattern of group behavior changes. There is an increase in sociodramatic play. Children also become more verbal in their social exchanges, but most of the changes occur in the language used in dramatic play and not in the language used in ordinary social contacts. Both prosocial and hostile behaviors increase within the context of dramatic play but not in reality situations. Environments that promote dramatic play are those in which parents and children discuss topics of interest to children that can serve as bases for dramatic play.

Studies indicate that in human children, the *quality* of peer behavior acquired at an early age may be more important for social development than the number of opportunities for social interaction. It is also possible that peers can provide social nurturance and protection if these elements are otherwise lacking.

When children become members of a peer group, they often acquire new behaviors, both desirable and undesirable. Preschool children are more likely to choose as models those peers with whom they have already had positive social exchanges. Although children readily imitate the behavior of their peers, adults probably provide better models in areas such as language learning. Imitation of adult language increases with age, whereas imitation of peer language decreases.

Peers reinforce each other's behavior, but the conditions under which such reinforcement occurs are complex. Peers may also function as sources of new information. Older children are often effective teachers of younger children; young children profit from teaching behaviors of older siblings.

An early sign that children have acquired the concept of "friend" is the appearance of imaginary companions in the absence of (or in addition to) real ones. Children may also create an imaginary self and then come up with imaginary companions to go with the imaginary self. Still another imaginary companion is the toy that takes on a name and a personality.

Investigators measure the presence of friendship in young children by the *sociometric test* and by observation of group settings. Both methods have shown that by age 4 children prefer some companions to others and that these preferences are moderately stable. Sociometric analyses indicate that although some children are more popular than others, less popular children also form stable relationships.

Friendliness is not a cause of popularity. The relationship between friendliness and popularity is probably reciprocal: Sociable children are more easily accepted by the group, and being accepted encourages sociability. Several characteristics that are consistently associated or correlated with popularity include being outgoing, kind, sensitive to the social overtures of peers, cooperative, accepting of routines, and eager partners in group enterprises. Popular children are more likely to be imitated than less popular children. Dependence on adults interferes with acceptance by peers; dependence on peers may enhance a child's popularity. Socially mature behavior with adults and peers seems to facilitate peer acceptance. Aggressive children are usually rejected by peers, although nonaggressive children are not necessarily popular. Popularity appears to involve non-aggressiveness combined with an orientation toward other children and a willingness to accommodate to their wishes. Popular children tend to seek help and support from peers and are generally more outgoing than less accepted children. By the age of 4, children's group experiences may already be characterized as positive, negative, or middling.

As children grow older, their social behavior becomes more refined and differentiated. By the age of 4, generosity—one form of which is helping others—has become a stable dimension of children's behavior. Children who offer help to others are generally more *nurturant*—giving of positive attention—than less helpful children. They tend to be emotionally expressive and to seek help as well as give it. Generous children are also more aggressive, probably as a result of the greater number of social contacts in which they participate. They tend to be less competitive in situations in which competition is possible but not encouraged. However, in situations that encourage competition, even generous and helpful children strive for personal gain rather than social sharing.

Another measure of altruism is *empathy,* the ability to perceive and to understand the feelings or motives of others. Many observers believe that preschool children not only are aware that other people have feelings but that they also make an effort to understand those feelings, without necessarily sharing them. Young children are also sensitive to what others intend to do as opposed to what they do by accident. Attention to the perceptions and feelings of others increases as children grow older and become less "egocentric."

Children are exposed quite early to the adult norms of social responsibility and reciprocity. *Social responsibility* requires people to aid without expectation of reward those who are dependent on them. *Reciprocity* refers to the belief that people should help those who help them and also that they should not injure those who help them. Middle-class children are more likely to be influenced by reciprocity; lower-class children, by social responsibility. Children from large families are more likely to stress social responsibility and those from small families, reciprocity.

Modeling and adult nurturance seem to be important factors in children's acquisition of altruistic behaviors. What an adult model says is less influential than what the model actually does although when adults do one thing and say another, children do not seem to be bothered by the contradiction.

Children's aggressive behavior appears in different forms with different purposes. In young children, it is often difficult to distinguish between assertive behavior and aggressive behavior. Researchers have found patterns of developmental changes in aggressive behavior; for example, frequency of quarrels and diffuse temper tantrums seem to subside after the age of 3, when children also begin to retaliate more frequently. The ways in which parents respond to aggressive behavior in children also change with the age of the children. They are more authoritarian with younger children and are more likely to use verbal controls as children grow older. Cultures differ in the kind and amount of aggression they will tolerate as well as in the degree of aggressiveness they expect of boys and girls. Whatever biologically based differences there are, they are reinforced by cultural factors and individual experience.

Theories of aggression differ in their emphasis on biological processes or learning as the source of aggressive behavior. Ethologists see aggression as designed to help organisms survive in a given environment. Psychoanalytic theorists see aggression as a natural drive, as a personality force that needs to be diverted and restrained through socialization processes. Behavior theorists believe that aggressive behaviors depend on a process of reinforcement: A random act of aggression occurs, is reinforced, and therefore occurs more frequently. There is considerable evidence that children can acquire aggressive behavior simply by observing others engaging in such behavior.

A good case for a biological origin of aggressive behavior is that anger seems to be a universal human emotion and can be observed even in very young infants. However, social experience determines when and how anger is expressed. Laboratory studies and observations of child-rearing practices have shown that aggression can be learned (or unlearned) through *selective reinforcement.* A less direct but equally potent factor in the development of aggressive behavior is *modeling.*

There is evidence that parental punishment of aggressive behavior does not result in reduced aggression and that the parent who uses physical punishment becomes an aggressive model and is imitated. A more effective tool for inhibiting aggression is the internalization of moral standards. The *catharsis hypothesis* claims that children's aggressive behavior fulfills a tension-releasing function, but studies have not supported this hypothesis.

Baumrind has identified three patterns of parenting and their effects on children's social behavior, personality, and intellectual performance: (1) *Authoritative* parenting is a combination of high control and positive encouragement. Children of this type of parents tend to be self-reliant, self-controlled, explorative, and content. (2) *Authoritarian* parents are controlling but detached. Their children tend to be relatively distrustful, withdrawn, and discontent. (3) *Permissive* parenting is warm but noncontrolling and nondemanding. Children of this type of parents tend to be the least self-reliant, self-controlled, and explorative. The types of behaviors most parents want to see in their children may be grouped under Baumind's label *instrumental competence,* which includes friendliness, cooperation, achievement orientation, dominance, and purposiveness— all behaviors that may be described as *socially responsible* and *independent.*

There are many variables that affect the value of punishment in controlling children's behavior. Punishment is more effective when the relationship between parents and children is close and affectionate and when the punishment is accompanied by an explanation of why the behavior is undesirable. Punishment is less effective the longer the delay between the behavior and the punishment. Punishment may have some undesirable effects too: Adults who use physical punishment may serve as aggressive models and children may avoid adults who administer punishment, thereby damaging the parent-child relationship.

PART IV

Middle Childhood

(Visiting a friend in Boston; 9 years old)

April 10, 1965

Dear Mommy and Daddy,
We went to a zoo farm with all the woods animals—my favorite animal is all the animals. I'm having a very good time in Boston!

Love, Susan

P.S. I'm not homesick.

(From Girl Scout camp; 10 years old)

August 8, 1966

Dear Grandma and Grandpa,
I miss you very much. I am glad you had a good time at the art fair.
    On Saturday we are going to have a costume party. Melanie and I are going to be one person. Mel is on my back and she has a suit that we will put on.
    Oh well, good bye.

Love, Susan

(On a camping trip with his father; 11 years old)

August, 1970

Dear Mom,
We are haveing a good time. first we stoped for a night at a motel. I
wanted to camp but soon I was glad we didn't because at night a
terrible electric storm came.

   Later on we found this dock — it had a beach and at the end of
the beach was a rock cliff. And I looked down at a rock and at the
face of the rock there was a fossil!! I calculate that the fossil was about
500,000,000 years old. Then I said to dad and dad said to me there must
be more and thair was! Millions, and billions of other smaller fossils.
But they were all the same because they were the first animals that
you can call microscoppic. Rember when we went to the museum and
you were reading that thing about life on the earth? We broke off
pieces to bring home.

Jon.

CHAPTER 11

Cognitive and Social Development: The Changing Child

DEVELOPMENTAL SHIFTS IN MIDDLE CHILDHOOD

By the age of 6, children can think operationally, although only about fairly concrete objects and problems. Their mental skills are sufficient to master basic mathematical and physical principles, and their minds can begin to stretch to places they have never seen and to people they have never encountered. The child can conceive of a world populated by dinosaurs or cave people, although the span of time that separates such a world from our own may not be firmly fixed in the child's mind. It is not unusual for children at this age to draw pictures of cave men battling dinosaurs. The child becomes curious about the heavens—the stars, the clouds, the planets, and the solar system. The idea that some brightly shining lights in the sky are hotly burning suns whereas others are cold, light-reflecting planets is appealing. The child is fascinated by the discovery that things may not be what they seem—that a simple object is made up of unimaginable numbers of rapidly moving atoms and that even the apparent nothingness of air contains countless unseeable particles. Profound changes occur in the child between the ages of 6 and 11. Children in middle childhood become capable of more complex cognitive and social behaviors. This transformation has been studied in different contexts by clinicians, teachers, parents, and psychologists. In this chapter we describe changes in the way children think, process information, learn, understand others and the social system in which others live. According to psychoanalytic theorists, these changes are facilitated (perhaps made possible) by a period of relative emotional calm which begins when the child is about 6 years old.

According to Freud, sexual feelings develop first in relationship to one's parents. Young children attach erotic significance to their relationship with the opposite-sex parent and identify themselves with the same-sex parent. Eventually, as sexual wishes become more intense, they perceive the same-sex parent as the obstacle to gratification. Hostility, anger, and the desire to do away with the older rival are expressed in dreams, jokes, and fantasy play. A new psychological component, the *superego,* arises to control and dominate the erotic urges of the *id.* The superego is comprised of masculine and feminine elements drawn from both parents' personalities, but the traits of the same-sex parent usually predominate. By the age of 4, formation of the superego is complete and repression of sexual feelings begins. The waning importance of erotic energy signifies the onset of the *latency* period, which, according to Freud, lasts from age 6 to age 11. Thus, in the classic psychoanalytic model, middle childhood is the least erotic life stage.

Erikson's (1968) elaboration of Freudian theory assigns a special developmental role to the child's interactions with the social environment. It is the fourth stage in Erikson's model, *industry versus inferiority,* that parallels the Freudian concept of latency. In this period, children are temporarily free of erotic conflicts and begin to acquire new cognitive powers. They learn to reason deductively and to play by elaborate sets of rules. The range of games and activities available to them is dramatically expanded. Later in this chapter we describe in more detail changes in the games children play, the jokes they laugh at, and the stories they make up during this period.

During the latency period, then, children are preparing themselves to enter the adult world, emotionally and cognitively. They are busy acquiring new skills, winning recognition by making things and completing projects. The usual result of this development is a sense of industry, that is, pride and pleasure in creativity. The rewards of learning change, too. Children place increasing emphasis on the abstract, intellectual reinforcement of having the correct information, and less emphasis on the social rewards of praise and attention (White, 1966). Some children, however, continue to require a great deal of social support. Some emerge from this stage with a sense of inferiority, because they continue to experience the turmoil of unresolved conflicts. For example, they may be more interested

In middle childhood, children derive pride and pleasure from making things and from completing projects.
(The Merrill-Palmer Institute)

in being the pampered baby at home (and school) than in being the independent young boy or girl.

Both teachers and parents are instrumental in enhancing a child's sense of industry. Praise at home may be undermined by failure or criticism at school. On the other hand, a sensitive teacher can create self-confidence through reward and attention, even when parents are not filling this need (Elkind, 1970b). But boredom, dull routine, too few challenges might be even greater threats to children at this age. Children are eager to learn when parents and teachers provide opportunities for them to do so.

Changes in the use of language signify other kinds of cognitive growth. Whereas young children talk aloud to themselves as much as to others, older children internalize more of this dialogue, using it for planning and representation. Thus speech becomes the foundation for abstract and symbolic thought (Vygotsky, 1962). Free association patterns show an increasing awareness of grammar. Younger children make free associations among words that share a meaningful relationship but are grammatically different, for example, "water, wet, spill, cold." Older children not only respond with meaningfully related words, they also tend to give noun for noun and verb for verb (Erwin, 1961).

Changes in perception and orientation also occur. From age 3 to age 9, children pay increasing amounts of attention to sights and sounds and proportionately less attention to the sense of touch (White, 1966). At approximately 6 years, they learn to distinguish between left and right, from their own point of view. Sometime later, they learn to distinguish left and right of a person facing them. They also show increased ability to discriminate reversed letters, forms, and words (White, 1966). Another change that takes place during this period is increased ability to deal with distracting information while problem solving. Young children are easily distracted, but after age 6 or 7, their ability to learn is hampered less, and is sometimes even increased, by extraneous cues (Gollin, 1960, 1961).

We have mentioned many diverse changes that begin to occur when children reach 6 years of age. The period of emotional calm seems to set the stage for sweeping changes in the way children think, learn, and respond to others. Some of these changes will be described in more detail in this chapter. It is important to realize that although some changes may begin when children are 6, these changes continue to unfold over the next 5 years. And of course there is always some individual variation in the pattern of development.

COGNITIVE DEVELOPMENTS IN MIDDLE CHILDHOOD

In the period between the ages of 6 and 11, children learn to think in new and complex ways. The difference between the cognitive styles of early and middle childhood is best summarized as increased flexibility, independence, and relativism. Flavell (1977) cites four major cognitive developments that occur in middle childhood. These are: reliance on *inferred reality* rather than outward appearances, *decentration* (the ability to attend to more than one kind of information at the same time), *transformational thought,* and *reversible* mental operations. All of these changes have been explored by Piagetian researchers in connection with conservation tasks.

Development Within a Piagetian Framework

INFERRED REALITY VERSUS PERCEIVED APPEARANCES. Preschoolers are usually unable to conserve. When asked which beaker has more water, a short, wide container or a tall, thin one, they typically point to the tall, thin container. They place more importance on the appearance of things than do children in middle childhood. Preschoolers make their judgments largely on the basis of superficial perceptions.

Older children, on the other hand, rely less on perceived appearances and more on the results of internally performed mental operations. They do not accept as conclusive the fact that one container looks as if it holds more liquid. Older children are sensitive to the important difference between things as they seem and things as they really are. Where the preschooler quickly turns perceived appearances into judgments about quantity, the older child incorporates other, conflicting evidence into the final conclusion, (Flavell, 1977). Faced with the appearance of more versus the knowledge that beaker B contains exactly what was in beaker A, the child who conserves infers that the amount of liquid is the same.

Flavell (1977) is careful to point out that younger children sometimes make inferences about unperceived reality and that children who can conserve still occasionally base their conclusions on superficial appearances. The important cognitive difference between the two stages is the increased ease and frequency in middle childhood of making inferences about unperceived reality.

DECENTRATION VERSUS CENTRATION. *Decentration* refers to the way in which older children allocate attention and consideration to several phases or aspects of the conservation experiment. Preschoolers are more likely to focus their attention on the one or two features that seem the most important or interesting. In the case of the two beakers of liquid, their attention is drawn mainly to the difference in height. They neglect to fully consider the difference in width or the fact that the experimenter has neither added nor taken away any liquid. Piaget theorizes that the preschooler's centration often expresses itself in heavy reliance on ordinal relationships such as "ahead of," "first," and "in front of." Because this kind of comparison is so important in preoperational thought, the preschooler often applies it inappropriately. For example, when one 3-inch pencil is slid out in front of another, the preschooler usually says it is longer. Older children, by contrast, are more likely to consider all the relevant information. In water conservation experiments, they attend to height, width, and observation of the pouring process.

Studies of visual perception patterns support Piaget's hypothesis (O'Bryan and Boersma, 1971). With the aid of a special camera that recorded eye movements during conservation experiments, researchers observed that nonconservers concentrate on one prominent part of the visual field. Children in transition to the cognitive style of middle childhood pay attention to two or more important features, but they have difficulty shifting their attention. Children who can conserve look at many different aspects of the visual field; they move their eyes easily from one kind of stimulus to another and seem completely "decentered."

TRANSFORMATIONS VERSUS UNCHANGING STATES. The shift from centration to decentration involves a change in the visual area or the dimensions the child considers to be important. A similar shift occurs in the time span the child takes into consideration. Younger children tend to focus on the present rather than the past or future. Thus, in problem solving, not only do they fail to utilize historical information stored in memory that describes an earlier event or stimulus, they also fail to anticipate future or potential appearances. Just as their visual activity is limited to only the most salient features, the temporal range under consideration is limited largely to present sensory stimuli.

By contrast, conservers, when asked to explain their answers, readily refer to past, present, and future states and the processes of transformation that have occurred or might occur. For example, they might explain that the intervening process of pouring water from one beaker to another did not involve either adding or spilling. Or they might offer to support their conclusion by pouring the water back into the original container. This reference to a future or potential state reveals an awareness of nonpresent states and the transformations that produce them.

REVERSIBILITY VERSUS IRREVERSIBILITY. The thinking of preschoolers does not exhibit reversibility of thought. That is, once an object, person, or situation has somehow changed, the younger child is unable to recognize that the change can be undone by reversing the action that brought about the change. Older children are more adept at understanding that some transformations can be reversed. In conservation experiments, older children exhibit reversibility in two ways. First, older children understand the possibility of negation, an act that will reverse the effect of the initial pouring. They explain that pouring the water back into the original container will support their conclusion that the amount of water remains unchanged. But children do not simply learn that operations are reversible nor learn to undo certain transformations. They also learn something more subtle, that is, which transformations can be reversed by which operations. For example, pouring water from one container to another is reversible by one set of procedures; melting an ice cube requires another. The second aspect of reversible thought is recognition of compensatory or counterbalancing features. For example, the older child may point out that the increased height of the second container is offset by its narrower width. The changes in the dimensions counterbalance each other, and the result is the same.

Comprehension of counterbalancing factors seems to develop toward the end of middle childhood. In one study (Gelman and Weinberg, 1972), children were given two beakers, one of standard size and one that was either thinner and taller or shorter and wider, plus a pitcher of water. They were asked to pour water into the second beaker until it was the same as the amount in the first. Children did not begin to compensate even roughly (producing a higher water level in the tall, thin beaker or a lower level in the short, wide beaker) until the third grade. Even at age 11¾ only a minority of the children explicitly justified their response with compensatory explanations.

Up to now, we have been discussing cognitive development primarily in terms of changes in perception and reasoning. Other cognitive functions also undergo important transformations during middle childhood. For example, the power of memory takes on new characteristics that are closely related to other aspects of cognitive growth, according to Piaget's model.   *New Schemes*

In order to understand Piaget's notion of how memory develops during this stage, we must first define and clarify a number of theoretical terms. Piaget distinguished between the *operative* and the *figurative* components of cognitive skills. Remember that *operative* refers to those actions or operations that transform reality, changing an object from one state to another. *Figurative*, on the other hand, refers to the representation of a state, independent of the processes that produced it. Figurative processes include perception and imitation (Inhelder, 1969).

Somewhat similar to the difference between operative and figurative is the distinction between *scheme* and *schema*. A *scheme* is a conceptual framework of actions and operations. For example, the hierarchical and comparative concepts we use to arrange a group of objects from the smallest to the largest constitutes a scheme. A *schema*, on the other hand, is a simplified internal representation of the result of an operation. A schema is static; it represents an end-state, a steady-state. It does not involve past operations that produced this result, nor is it influenced by possible future operations that could transform this state into something new and different (Inhelder, 1969).

Piaget's hypothesis of how memory develops during middle childhood holds that performance is influenced not only by the figurative representation, or the external appearance perceived by the child, but also by the operative schemes the child uses to remember things. A study by Inhelder (1969) that presented children of different ages with the same memory task illustrates this hypothesis. A group of children, ages 3 to 8, was shown a collection of ten sticks, arranged in a row from the shortest to the longest. Experimenters told the children to look carefully at the sticks for as long as they wanted, in order to remember them later. One week later, the children were asked to describe, with gestures and drawings, the arrangement of sticks. Several months later, they were again asked to recall the stick arrangement (each time without seeing the sticks in the interim).

The results showed that each age group tended to use a characteristic type of organization in recalling the stick sequence. The youngest children, ages 3 and 4, drew a number of sticks, all about the same length, lined up in a row. Four- and 5-year-olds showed a greater ability to organize the recalled elements, but they used incorrect organizing principles. For example, some of them depicted pairs of long and short sticks. Others divided the sticks into two separate groups, big and small. Still others arranged three or four sticks in groups of small, big, and middle-sized. Starting at age 6 or 7, children showed the ability to recall the correct serial organization of the sticks. In other words, the ability to memorize and recall a serial arrangement seems to be dependent on an understanding of serial relationships. But other evidence suggests that this might not be the case.

The retest after 6 or 8 months revealed a very interesting development.

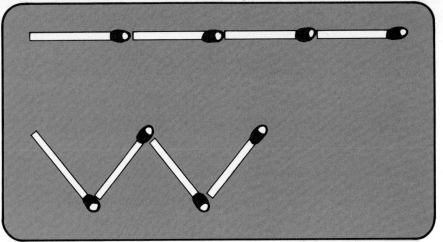

FIGURE 11–1
*Two different
arrangements of
match sticks used
to test children's
understanding of
schemes of length
and number*

An overwhelming majority of the children drew stick arrangements that were more complex and closer to the original arrangement than their first drawing. Within a few months, their ability to recall and duplicate the stick arrangement progressed to the next substage of complexity. Even though they had not seen the sticks for several months, their recall improved. Inhelder argues that the underlying development of operative schemes of seriation during the 6- or 8-month time lapse improved memory function, even in the absence of the figurative schema of the sticks. Subsequent research (Liben, 1976) seems to support the notion that memory is dependent on a basic understanding of the underlying scheme (in this case, seriation). There is less support, however, for the hypothesis that long-term memory of figurative schemas previously perceived is improved by later development of operative schemes.

Operative schemes do not develop at identical rates. One interesting study (Piaget, Inhelder, and Szeminska, 1960) illustrates actual conflict between the schemes of length and number. The problem is that an understanding of identity of number develops before the ability to conserve space or length. When asked to recall two different arrangements of match sticks (Figure 11–1), children of different ages drew pictures that demonstrated confusion over whether to duplicate the number of matches or the length of the line (Figure 11–2). Preoperational children understand the sameness of number. They do not, however, understand that a straight line converted into a zigzag has the same length it had before transformation (Inhelder, 1969).

One of the characteristics of cognitive development in middle childhood is a quantitative approach to problems. The grade-school pupil, unlike the preschooler, understands that many problems have precise solutions that can be derived with logical reasoning and measurement.

Seriation and *classification* are two important elements in the development of number concepts. *Seriation* is arrangement by increasing or

*Mathematical
Concepts*

decreasing size. *Classification* is organization of numbers into groups in accordance with some organizing principle, for example, whole numbers, multiples of 10, integers divisible by 3. Children's ability to seriate develops in stages. At first, they arrange the objects in small groups of two or three items. Within each group, there is seriation, but children are unable to arrange all the objects into a single series of gradated size. Next, children use trial and error until they have found the proper sequence. Finally, they develop a systematic approach, seeking out the smallest element first, then the smallest of the elements still remaining, and so on.

The first stage of the systematic method entails an understanding that object B is smaller than object A but bigger than object C. A refinement of this knowledge occurs when the child understands that if $A > B$ and $B > C$ then $A > C$. This cognitive development is termed *transitivity*, and it is usually assumed to occur around age 7 (Piaget and Inhelder, 1969). One set of experiments (Bryant and Trabasso, 1971), however, indicates that children as young as 4 can be trained to make transitive inferences. Thorough training and testing must be done to ensure that the children remember the elements they are supposed to combine. This line of research suggests that the ability to make transitive inferences is present at an earlier age than researchers previously thought, but that it usually lies dormant until the memory is sufficiently developed to expedite the operation.

Ability to classify also develops gradually. As we saw in Chapter 7, 3-year-olds can group objects according to similar or different characteristics, and curiously, they usually arrange their groupings in rows, squares, and circles. Five- and 6-year-old children group objects by char-

FIGURE 11–2
Types of memory reproductions of the match stick arrangement in Figure 11–1
(From Inhelder, 1969, Figure 9, p. 351)

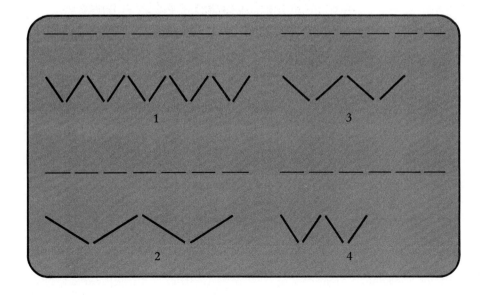

acteristics, but they do not form spatial figures (rows, squares, circles) with their groupings. Children of this age can even find groups within groups, or subsets. Suppose, for instance, you show a 6-year-old child a group B of 12 flowers within which there is a subset A of 6 roses. If you ask the child to identify the flowers (B) and then the roses (A), he or she can do so. He designates first the whole, and then the part. But if you ask if there are more flowers or roses, the child cannot answer correctly. If he thinks of the subset A, he fails to conserve the group B as a unit. In response to the question, he is likely to compare group A to the items that are left (the 6 flowers that are not roses) and answer that the number of flowers and roses are the same. Only at around age 8 do children conserve the relative size of a subset in relation to the whole set. This, according to Piaget, signifies full development of operative classification (Piaget and Inhelder, 1969).

The ability to measure also develops gradually and without explicit teaching (Piaget, 1953). Piaget tested measuring skill in an experiment involving an unstructured pile of blocks and a tower of blocks already erected on a small table. The child is asked to build (from the floor up) a tower of equal height. Young children pile up their blocks until the top levels are roughly similar; they disregard the different base levels. Older children, when they become aware of this discrepancy, try to move their tower onto the table on which the other tower rests. Since the rules of the game do not permit this, the children look for a measuring standard. Six-year-olds use their hands spaced apart, confident that the distance remains constant when the child moves from one tower to the other. Older children use two points on their bodies as references. Eventually, they realize the value of an independent measuring tool. Their first measure is a third tower, built to the height of the second tower and then moved onto the base of the first tower (the rules allow this) and compared. This is an act of transitivity. If Tower 3 is the same height as Tower 2, and Tower 3 is the same height as Tower 1, then Tower 1 must be the same height as Tower 2.

The second type of independent measure typically used is a rod, but in order to be useful to the child, it must be the same height as the towers. The beginning of true measurement comes when the child realizes that a shorter rod can be used by applying it several times to the tower. According to Piaget, this discovery involves two new operations of logic. First, the child uses *division,* an awareness that the whole is made up of many parts added together. The second logical operation is *displacement,* or *substitution,* the process of adding one part on to many others, thus creating a system of parts.

According to Piaget, changes in the child's thinking are reflected in the way children understand ordinary events in the world around them. Piaget has spent a great deal of time investigating children's explanations

Causal Explanation

of movement, because he believes they represent "the central point to which all the child's ideas about the world converge" (Piaget, 1951, p. 60). In particular, children have a great deal of difficulty distinguishing a body's own spontaneous movement from movement that is produced by an outside force. They view all bodies as having some ability to move of their own will, although they believe that bodies also are controlled by outside influences.

One topic about which Piaget has questioned many children is the movement of clouds. From the children's answers, he has noted five different stages in the development of causal explanations. The first stage is a magical belief that the clouds move "when we walk": "We make them move by walking." This view is characteristic of 5-year-olds, although Piaget has found traces of it in older children.

—*What makes them (the clouds) move?*
—*When we move along, they move along, too.*
—*And at night, when everyone is asleep . . . ?*
—*They always move. The cats, when they walk, and then the dogs, they make the clouds move along.*

The second stage, characteristic of age 6, adheres to the view that clouds move because God or people push them along. That is, the child senses the importance of some external factor. Nevertheless, clouds are still seen as somehow alive and conscious. After all, they have to have the ability to obey commands.

In the third stage, at about age 7, children believe that clouds move by themselves, but in response to other heavenly bodies like the sun and moon. The force exerted on the clouds is still seen as a personal act by the heavenly bodies, rather than a physical cause and effect.

—*What makes the clouds move along?*
—*It's the sun.*
—*How?*
—*With its rays. It pushes the clouds.*

The fourth stage, typical of 9-year-olds, is represented by the view that the wind pushes the clouds, but that the wind itself comes out of the clouds. There is still obvious difficulty in distinguishing between self-willed movement and actions caused by external forces. Finally, by age 10, children arrive at the mechanical explanation that the wind does push the clouds, but that the wind is not in any way produced by the clouds.

Piaget (1951) has found similar developmental patterns in children's causal explanations of a variety of things—in explanations of the movement of the sun, the moon, and water (rivers, lakes, seas); in explanations of the origin of wind and breath; and in explanations of how machines such as the bicycle and the steam engine work.

INFORMATION PROCESSING, LEARNING, AND MEMORY

In middle childhood, children eagerly organize and incorporate information about the outside world into their own thinking. The complex and interdependent development of information-processing skills is an important part of the cognitive growth that occurs in this period. As we mentioned in Chapter 1, the information-processing model is a useful framework for studying what mental processes account for improved performance in information-seeking strategies, attention, problem solving, learning, and memory in middle childhood.

Seeking and using information are major requirements for effective functioning in life. A study involving variations on the old game of Twenty Questions (Mosher and Hornsby, 1966) sheds light on how children develop information-seeking strategies.

Information Seeking and Symbolic Ability

Two versions of the guessing game were employed. In the first game, children were shown more than 40 pictures of familiar objects and were asked to guess which one the experimenter had in mind. A number of possible solutions was presented; the child's goal was to pinpoint the correct picture. In the second, more complex game, the children were given such problems as "John left school in the middle of the morning. Find out why." This variation required the children first to construct possible answers, and then to determine which one of these was correct. In both versions of the game, the children were limited to questions that could be answered with a simple "yes" or "no."

The children's attempts to solve the problems revealed two major strategies of questioning. At one extreme was *constraint seeking,* an attempt to narrow systematically the boundaries within which the correct answer lay. Constraint seeking proceeds on the assumption that all alternatives are equally likely. By dividing all possible solutions into two general categories, one question immediately eliminates half of the alternatives. For example, a typical question of this sort is, "Can you wear it?" Both a "yes" and a "no" answer are useful in this search. Successive questions narrow the number of possibilities until there is only one answer left.

The second major strategy used was *hypothesis scanning*. This technique involves testing a specific hypothesis that is not necessarily related to questions asked either earlier or later. A typical question here might be, "Did John get a stomachache all of a sudden?" Relationships between questions, if there are any at all, are likely to be associative. For example, a subsequent question could be, "Did he have to see the nurse?" Hypothesis scanning, unlike constraint seeking, depends completely on positive answers. A "no" to the stomachache question yields few clues about how to proceed, because the question was aimed at one specific possibility, which was completely eliminated by the answer.

The simple method of hypothesis scanning was the predominant form of questioning used by younger children (first graders). Older children, on the other hand, resorted to increasing numbers of constraint-seeking questions in their attempts to solve the problems.

In the first version of the guessing game, 6-year-olds relied almost completely on hypothesis scanning; 8-year-olds used some constraint seeking before jumping to hypotheses; and 11-year-olds deliberately narrowed the alternatives with at least one set of constraints before using hypotheses. The developmental pattern that Mosher and Hornsby found was one of increasingly connected strategies designed to focus in on relevant solutions by more economical but less direct questioning.

A different developmental picture emerged from the second game, in which children were forced to rely primarily on verbal skills rather than on pictures or objects. In this set of tests, the 8-year-olds behaved more like the 6-year-olds than like the 11-year-olds. The 8-year-olds used the younger children's strategy of hypothesis scanning more than the older children's approach of establishing constraints. When questioned later about which system they used to solve the problem, few of the 6-year-olds understood the question. Some of the 8-year-olds said they tried to figure what was most probable, but none mentioned the use of an initial general question to narrow the possibilities. On the other hand, almost all of the 11-year-olds had some description for the approach they used, and almost half mentioned the idea of using general questions.

The work of Mosher and Hornsby yields some general conclusions about the growth of information-seeking skills. First, increased reliance on symbolic representation, rather than representation by action or image, is essential to the complex function of constraint seeking. The more a child can use symbols and group them into manipulable categories, the more efficiently he or she can eliminate entire classes of possibilities. Second, the child needs a basic understanding that strategy and advance planning are required. In this case, the child needs to see that general questions will aid the search. Younger children, particularly in the second game, tend to get involved with the story action, visualizing the event in the hope that a cause will somehow enter the picture. Older children have acquired the ability to "stand outside" the information in their attempt to solve the problem. Mosher and Hornsby made the interesting observation that a sense of strategy appears at roughly the same age (8 years) as the use of self as a reference point. Both developments, they say, indicate "a new-found freedom from the perceptual and immediate properties of the environment" (1966, p. 101).

Selective Attention

In the course of processing information from the environment, children attend to some things and ignore others. A command from a teacher or a mother to "pay attention" may equal a demand that the child shift his or her attention from one area to another, or it may mean to increase concentration on something the child is already observing closely. In the second case, the child is being asked to intensify the selectiveness of his or her attention and to make an increased effort to ignore distracting and irrelevant information.

The more selectively children can attend, the more efficiently they can seek out and process information. Selectivity improves with age. One important factor is maturation and increased control over sensory receptors. For example, studies of eye movements indicate that children improve in their ability to scan those points of a picture that contain the most relevant and useful information and to disregard the rest. One experiment (Vurpillot, 1968) presented children with pairs of pictures of houses. Each house had several windows showing various objects. Some of the pairs of houses had identical window displays, others did not. The subjects were asked to say which pairs were the same. Before age 6, few children exhibited the appropriate behavior of comparing each set of windows in the two houses. After age 6, most children had discovered this approach.

Attentional patterns become crucial when children begin to read. In order to tell the difference between the letters P and R, for example, children must look in the lower right corner of the figure. Between the letters N and K, they must look in the upper right corner. When the eye movements of kindergartners are compared with those of third graders, it becomes evident that the younger children scan the letters in a diffuse, unplanned way. With age, visual fixation patterns become simpler and more concise. Also with age, there is a greater tendency to look at the parts of the figures that contain the information about whether the figures are the same or different. With age and experience, children acquire more efficient strategies for assembling relevant information (Nodine and Steuerle, 1973).

Similarly, children gradually become more selective in their hearing. When presented with a different message in each ear, the ability to report accurately one of the messages improved steadily between the ages of 5 and 14 (Maccoby, 1967).

Broadbent (1958) has suggested that there are "filtering mechanisms" at work in the process of selective attention. According to this theory, incoming information is initially stored in short-term memory. There, it is "filtered," and if found relevant, it is passed on to other areas of the brain for further analysis. Information that is filtered out fades rapidly from short-term memory. However, according to Broadbent, short-term memory itself improves with age, partly because of the improved ability to deal with certain cues and simply to ignore others. As children increasingly encounter tasks that provide more information than they can handle, they learn to ignore incidental information and concentrate on cues that are most relevant to their performance of the task at hand. This ability also improves with age. In an experiment by Hagen (1972), children who were deliberately distracted from the central task showed progressive improvements in their performance with increased age. A more natural-istic study involved a vivid and entertaining film shown to grade-school students (Hale, Miller, and Stevenson, 1968). After the film, the students were quizzed on different aspects of the narrative. Some of the questions asked were central to the plot and others were merely incidental. Interest-ingly, recall of incidental details increased steadily up to the seventh grade (about age 12), when it showed a marked drop. In early adolescence, then, the ability to focus attention on task-related information is nearly complete.

Problem Solving

Problem solving is one of the more important ways people use informa-tion. Gagné (1968) has proposed a cumulative learning theory, based on an assumed hierarchy of increasingly complex operations. This learning hierarchy may be broken down into a series of distinctive, but interre-lated states or abilities that in combination form successive layers of cognitive competence. Some researchers have recently used an analytical approach to construct models of human cognition and problem solving. Using a limited set of processes, borrowed from computer models of cog-nitive functioning, they have attempted to simulate the operations that comprise performance of advanced problem solving (Resnick and Glaser, 1976).

Models that describe how people perform tasks are called *production systems.* A production system is basically a symbolic representation of incoming information and action taken with respect to the information, which leads to a change in the state of the problem. New information stemming from the changed problem enters similarly, is acted upon, and modifies the next action.

A production-system approach was used with a group of fifth graders asked to determine the area of a parallelogram (Morris and Resnick, 1974; Resnick and Glaser, 1976). Earlier, the children had learned to determine the area of a rectangular parallelogram by placing 1-inch cubes over the figure and counting the number of cubes. In the experimental task, how-ever, this approach was useless, since the figure presented was not a rec-tangle (see Figure 11–3). The solution was to use scissors to cut off the nonrectangular portion and rearrange the pieces into a figure with four right angles (*transformation*). Transformation was not taught to the sub-jects. Table 11–1 illustrates the production system used in the study.

Of the 24 children tested, 5 spontaneously discovered the method of cutting off the nonrectangle. The others persisted with the established method of applying the cubes until the experimenter said, "You can't do that." The children then responded in two strikingly different ways. Some cleared the cubes from the figure and eventually discovered the cutting solution on their own. The others stuck with the cube technique, rearrang-ing them to make them "fit" better. They never discovered the transforma-tion secret. Resnick and Glaser explain the different responses in terms

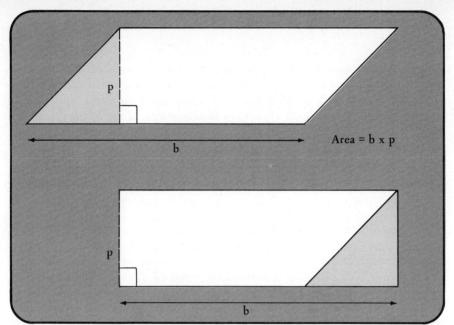

Area = b x p

FIGURE 11–3
Area-of-a-parallelogram problem and solution
(*Adapted from Resnick and Glaser, 1976, Figure 2, p. 213*)

of the children's conception of their goal. The children who defined their goal as "test for applicability of blocks" interpreted the teacher's intervention to mean that the blocks did not fit. Thus they cleared the figure and sought a new approach. Clearing the figure in itself gave the children a second opportunity to notice its features and thus formulate a new goal— transformation. These children who saw their goal as "using blocks" interpreted the intervention to mean that they were using the blocks improperly.

Later experiments using the parallelogram problem sought ways of stimulating inventiveness. Pillegrino and Schadler (1974) used the same general task but first asked the children, "What do you think I want you to do?" By encouraging the children to plan strategies and verbalize goals before beginning, they significantly increased the number of children who spontaneously discovered transformation.

In the last 15 years, learning theorists have begun to acknowledge that a major transition in learning occurs around age 5. Children younger than 5 respond to some learning tests in a way that conforms to simple stimulus-response associations. After age 5, children's responses change in a way that suggests more complicated processes (White, 1966).

In Chapter 8, we discussed the mediating role of verbal ability in tests of transposition. Children between the ages of 3 and 6 generally are able to transpose on a near test. Ability to verbalize the relevant dimension appears to enable children to transpose on a far test.

An experiment designed by the Kendlers and their associates (Kendler, 1963) yielded findings that seem to support those that emerged from

Learning

342

studies of transposition. Suppose that over several trials a child is shown the series of stimulus pairs illustrated in Figure 11–4. The child receives a reinforcement (candy or praise) every time he or she chooses the white square, regardless of its size, and never receives a reinforcement for choosing the yellow square. In order to pick a winner every time, the child must figure out that color is the relevant dimension—that white is the correct value—and that size is irrelevant. When the child solves the problem and chooses the white square on every trial, the experimenter changes the rules. Without warning the child about the rule change, the experimenter switches the choice for which the child will be reinforced. Now the child might be reinforced for choosing the yellow square rather than the white one. When the same dimension (here, color) continues to be relevant but the value of the correct stimulus is switched (for example, from white to yellow), the change is called a *reversal shift*. Or the experimenter might present the child with a nonreversal shift. In a *nonreversal shift*, the rules are changed so that another dimension (for example, size) becomes relevant. In our example, the child might be reinforced only when the larger square is chosen, regardless of its color. The child must shift responses and concentrate on a new dimension.

The question of interest to the experimenter is which type of shift (reversal or nonreversal) is easier for the child to learn. In our example, the child has been trained to choose the white square, regardless of size. Therefore, he has been reinforced every time he chose the large white square *and* every time he chose the small white square. He has never been reinforced for choosing a yellow square of either size. According to S→R

TABLE 11–1
Production System for Finding the Area in the Parallelogram Problem

---

GOAL: FIND AREA

Step 1: If you want to find how big a figure is, look at the figure.

Step 2: If you want to find how big a figure is, and you have a figure, then test to see if the blocks routine is applicable.

Step 3: If you want to find how big a figure is and it is a figure to which the blocks routine is applicable (a "yes-figure"), then use the blocks routine and the goal will be satisfied.

Step 4: If you want to find how big a figure is and it is a figure to which the blocks routine is not applicable (a "no-figure"), then try to transform the figure.

Source: Adapted from Resnick and Glaser, 1976, Figure 7, p. 223.

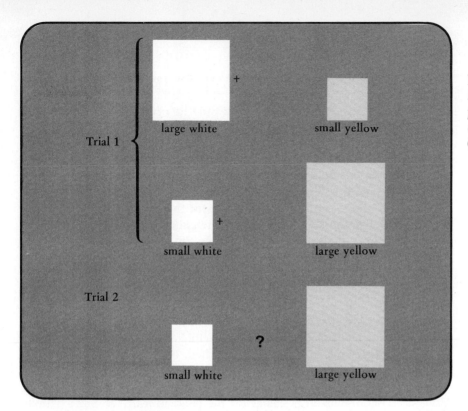

FIGURE 11–4
*Series of stimulus
pairs used in studies
of transposition
(Kendler, 1963)*

Trial 1

large white

small yellow

small white

large yellow

Trial 2

small white   ?   large yellow

learning theory, it is easier to strengthen a response that has been reinforced some of the time than it is to strengthen a response that has never
been reinforced. Therefore, learning theory proposes that a nonreversal
shift should be easier to learn. Mediational theory, on the other hand,
proposes that, *for children old enough to use mediators,* a reversal shift
should be easier to learn. The reason is that the child identified one dimension (color) as relevant in the initial learning session. Since the same
dimension (color) remains relevant in a reversal shift, the child simply has
to make *one* change—in this case, from white to yellow. Moreover, the
child can use mediators to coach himself to choose the right stimulus:
"Choose the yellow one."

Results of studies with humans and with rats support these theoretical
explanations. Kendler and Kendler (1962) found that rats accomplished
nonreversal shifts more easily, whereas adult humans found reversal shifts
easier to learn. Accordingly, young children who do not use mediators
should find the nonreversal shift problem easier than the reversal shift
problem. Results indicate that such is the case for children between the
ages of 3 to 5 years. Children over 7 are highly skilled at reversal shift
problems. Between 5 and 7 years of age, growth in use of mediators seems
to occur (Kendler, Kendler, and Learnard, 1962).

Thus there seems to be some support for the idea that mediational
processes influence the way people solve problems. It has been extremely

difficult, however, to identify how the hypothesized mediators operate. One way of looking at the problem is to assume that a particular cognitive process is called upon in learning situations. The mediational difficulties of younger children, then, would be determined by the way this process operates in learning situations. In accord with this notion, several investigators have focused on the study of children's memory.

Memory

Memory is an extremely important process, responsible in part for the retention of information and the accumulation of knowledge. The learning limitations of younger children have been attributed to their inability to identify or retain relevant information.

MEDIATION DEFICIENCY. Mediation refers to the use of verbal labels or symbols in problem-solving situations. As we have seen, young children rarely use mediation; older children use it frequently. This has led one researcher (Reese, 1962) to formulate the *mediation-deficiency hypothesis*, which holds that at one point in cognitive development, the child is able to make verbal or symbolic responses but does not use them to solve problems.

A study (Atkinson, Hansen, and Bernbach, 1964) testing short-term memory supports this hypothesis. In the experiment, 4- and 5-year-olds were presented with eight animal pictures. Each picture was displayed briefly, then laid face down on the table in a row. When all eight cards were lying face down, a cue card corresponding to one of the eight was presented, and the child was requested to point to the card in the face-down row that matched. In a series of such tasks, each child was eventually tested with the presentation card in each of the eight face-down positions. The results were analyzed in terms of the serial position of the presentation card. The important contrast is between the first card (i.e., the *primacy* position) and the last card (i.e., the *recency* position). Both groups of children had the highest recall for the recency positions (the last cards seen), and performed poorly with regard to primacy position. These results differ markedly from adult patterns. Adults, naturally, perform better overall. However, they show highest performance for the primacy position, lower performance for the recency position, and worst performance for the middle cards. The experimenters concluded that spontaneous use of verbal labels enabled the adults to recall earlier cards more easily than the younger subjects were able to.

A somewhat similar but more complicated experiment (Hagen and Kingsley, 1968) was designed to test the impact of verbal labeling on children at ages 6, 7, 8, and 10. Some children in each age group were required to label each card verbally as it was presented. The results demonstrated three principles. First, overall performance improved with age. Second, verbalizing improved the performance of those children who understood how to use labels but could not produce them spontaneously. (This included the 6-, 7-, and 8-year-olds.) Verbal labeling produced little improvement in the performance of the 10-year-olds, presumably because they were already using verbal mediation on their own. Finally, the serial performance of the older children bore increasing resemblance to adult patterns; that is, older children performed better on both the primacy card and the recency card.

PRODUCTION DEFICIENCY. One of the troubling questions in the study of children's memory is whether poor test performance results from failure to use a verbal symbol (mediation) or failure to articulate it or produce it for the tester. Flavell, Beach, and Chinsky (1966) suggested that the term *mediation deficiency* be applied only in instances where the child can produce a mediator, but still fails to recall. (An example is the experiment just mentioned in which children were prompted to verbalize labels.) Flavell proposed the term *production deficiency* to cover situations where children did not produce a mediator at all.

Flavell and his colleagues conducted a series of memorization tasks with two distinct groups—children who spontaneously rehearsed picture sequences that they were shown and asked to memorize and children who rarely rehearsed them (Keeny, Cannizzo, and Flavell, 1967). After the first testing session, both groups were given an opportunity to rehearse, whispering the names of the pictured objects over and over. The test was repeated, with instructions to rehearse. Finally, three more testing sessions were conducted in which the children had the opportunity to rehearse or not rehearse.

The spontaneous producers clearly outperformed the nonproducers. The nonproducers, however, were able to rehearse, under instruction, just as well as the producers. Their memory performance during the rehearsal was also comparable. These children, then, were production deficient but not mediation deficient. Encouragement to produce mediators resulted in markedly improved recall ability among the nonproducers. Thus verbal rehearsal itself can be a mediator that improves memory. The experiments seem to indicate that production deficiency is a more common obstacle to memory and learning than mediation deficiency. This conclusion has important practical ramifications for educators concerned with elementary and remedial education.

MEMORY STRATEGIES. Memory involves more than placing a certain piece of information into storage. It involves encoding and incorporating new knowledge into an internal conceptual representation. Because the process involves construction of a framework, as well as retention of items of information, this strategy is frequently referred to as *constructive memory* (Flavell, 1977). Another strategy, *retrieval,* is a similarly active operation of reconstruction and rearrangement. Memory, according to Flavell, is not an automatic recording device. Rather, memory involves relating new knowledge to old, encoding both the item and the relationship, and making spontaneous inferences and interpretations.

The "constructivists'" argument is supported by experiments that reveal how easily people confuse the material actually presented to the memory with the construction that they then elaborated. For example, after listening to sentences such as "the box is to the right of the tree" and "the chair is on top of the box," we may incorrectly recall one of the sentences as "the chair is to the right of the tree" (Paris and Mahoney, 1974). The incorrect sentence correctly describes what the actual sentences imply. People go beyond the information given and construct more elaborate, meaningful sets of relations.

Children frequently make this type of error. At the same time, they properly deny having heard sentences that are grammatically or semantically different from the ones actually presented. That is, children use constructive memory. Developmental studies show that as they grow older, children become increasingly sophisticated and adept at making inferences. This, in turn, creates fuller and more meaningful recall of earlier experiences (Paris, 1975).

Some recent studies have shown how children's memory processes and strategies change with age. Storage strategies (or *mnemonic* devices) are conscious efforts to store information in such a way that it is readily retrievable. We have already mentioned the strategy of *rehearsal* in connection with production deficiencies. Not only does rehearsal increase with age, but in middle childhood, *type* of rehearsal changes from item-only to cumulative. Ornstein, Naus, and Liberty (1975) found that in recall tasks third-graders tended to rehearse the item currently being presented either alone or in minimal combination with other words. Sixth-graders and older subjects rehearsed several different items together. Training children in more sophisticated rehearsal techniques improved their recall. Ornstein, Naus, and Stone (1977) found that the recall of second-grade subjects trained to rehearse several items together was similar to that of sixth graders who were not trained in rehearsal techniques. Another memory strategy is *organization*. Organization involves clustering information around a common feature. Bananas, apples, and pears might be grouped as kinds of fruit; plates, napkins, waiters, and menus might be grouped as items associated with dining out. The ability to organize appears at an early stage, well before kindergarten. However, awareness of the link between organization and improved recall does not occur until several years later. By the third grade (about age 8), many children demonstrate an organizational principle when asked to recall word lists, although some still rely somewhat on the less complex method of free association. By the sixth grade (age 11), most children adopt the organizational approach in many tasks to the exclusion of all other approaches (Tenney, 1975). Training children in the use of organizational techniques and sorting styles used by adults produces improvement in recall. Bjorklund,

Ornstein, and Haig (1977) found that improvements in children's sorting style accompany significant changes in recall. Thus, organization appears to be a mediating factor in memory performance and development. These changes in memory processes and strategies reflect the general cognitive trend toward increased use of deliberate strategies and planning in middle childhood, both of which enhance the child's ability to solve problems.

SOCIAL UNDERSTANDING AND SOCIAL RELATIONSHIPS

Social cognition is the term used to describe development of social skills and relationships. Social cognition involves knowledge and manipulation of people rather than physical objects or abstract ideas. In learning other people's intentions, abilities, emotions, memories, and thoughts, we must rely mainly on inferences, attributing overt, observable acts to inner, nonobservable mental states. Thus social cognition involves problems and skills that are different from other types of learning.

Social Cognition

Current research suggests that many important sociopersonal changes occur during middle childhood. Although the 4- to 6-year-old child understands the boundaries between himself and others, he does not realize that each person, including himself, acts on the basis of inner thoughts and feelings. Nor does he understand that these inner states vary markedly from one person to another. As Flavell (1977) puts it, "In his mind, there is only the reality; there are no personal constructions or interpretations of reality."

Between the ages of 6 and 8, children's egocentric perspective is transformed into a more complex and relative view of other people. They learn that people do have different cognitive perceptions, even regarding the same object or topic. They understand that people commonly obtain and interpret information from social events. They can distinguish between intended and unintended acts, and they understand that people often act on the basis of subjective, "personal" reasons (Flavell, 1977).

Social skills increase with age, but even third graders often fail to appreciate others' points of view. This was demonstrated in an experiment in which children of different ages were given the tasks of selling a tie to a stranger and of persuading their fathers to buy them a television set. Compare the attempts of the third graders with those of the seventh graders (from Flavell, 1968):

Grade three: "Here's a tie....Do you want to buy it?...Give it to him...."
Grade seven: "Ah...oh, ah...hello, sir. I'd like to introduce a new kind
of tie that we have brought out. I'm sure that you would like it.
It's a—it would be a wonderful Christmas present, or a birthday present, and of course you could wear it anywhere you

want. It doesn't cost very much. It's a very handsome tie, and you could match it with all your shirts, I'm sure." (p. 42)

Grade three: *"Oh Daddy, oh Daddy, please let me buy a television. I always wanted a television. Oh please, Daddy, please."*

Grade seven: *"Say, Dad, a lot of kids at school are getting televisions for Christmas. Can I have one? Gee, I know a lot of kids that want one, gee. I could really use it . . . for some of the educational programs, you know, that are on TV, and they're real good, and for homework at night some of our teachers want us to watch 'em, and—you know, Johnnie always wants to watch cowboys, and . . . and I—I'll never get a chance to watch it down there, so why can't I have it in my room? C'mon, Dad, please." (p. 144)*

Notice the shift to arguments based on advantages or benefits to others, a shift that is clearly based on greater ability to see things from another person's point of view.

By about 8 years of age, children also learn that people can make inferences about other people's cognitive perspectives. At first, this realization is limited to the notion that someone else is making an inference about a third person's perspective. Eventually, it matures into the understanding that they themselves may be the object of someone else's perceptions and inferences.

This development signifies the beginning of a new period, lasting roughly from age 8 to age 10. Now, children are better equipped to handle the complexities of social relationships. They realize that the way someone else views them and gauges their internal perspective can exert an important influence on their behavior. For example, if a child believes his mother suspects him of telling a fib in order to gain a prize or reward, the child may make elaborate displays of honesty and sincerity to alter her perceptions of his motives. According to Flavell (1977), the fundamental insight of this stage boils down to this:

I know I could conceivably tune in on your cognitive perspective because we are both subjects or persons rather than objects; I also know that you could do the same to me for the same reason; it follows that you may be doing so at the very moment I am, and that your tuning may therefore pick up my tuning (pp. 133–134).

Currently, theorists are attempting to integrate what is known about cognitive and social development into a broader, more cohesive framework. Flavell has been a leader in this field. He points out a number of parallel trends in social and nonsocial cognitive development. Children attempt to understand (impose structure) on the social environment in much the same way as they attempt to make sense of the physical environment. Both forms of development progress from reliance on superficial, overt indicators to probing examination of unperceived factors. Children are initially aware of only the most obvious types of social behavior, both in their own actions and feelings and in the actions and feelings of others. Gradually, they learn to detect concealed factors. Similarly, their social cognition is highly centrated; it focuses on the most salient aspects and neglects other important information. Centration of social cognition prevents children from piercing the social fronts that people, consciously or unconsciously, put up. They may perceive merely that a certain adult is acting gaily, whereas more mature observers might detect forced cheerfulness. Social cognition is also centrated in time. Children at first fail to make meaningful connections between past and present behavior; they are also unable to predict future behavior accurately (Flavell, 1977).

The most common impediment to social cognition is egocentrism, an inability to distinguish one's own view from those of other people. In Piagetian terms, *perceptual* egocentrism eventually recedes with the onset of operational thought. *Social* egocentrism is longer-lived; it continues in varying degrees to interfere with the perception of other people's feelings and point of view throughout life (Flavell, 1977).

In addition to learning to perceive other people's perspectives, children must learn about feelings for others and feelings of others. Shantz (1975) points out that it is important to distinguish between *social understanding* and *empathy*. Social understanding is cognition of another's feelings. Empathy, on the other hand, is sharing how another person feels. Researchers sometimes confuse the two in testing. For example, a child is presented with a story and a picture describing an event such as losing a pet. After asking "How does the child in the story feel?" some researchers judge the response to be one of social understanding; others score it for empathy. The question "How do *you* feel?" is scored for empathy.

Flavell (1977) cites three different kinds of reactions which are often taken as signs of empathy. The first is similar to contagion — expression of someone else's feelings triggers the same feelings in the child. This reaction has been noted in infancy. Six-month-old babies are more apt to cry in the presence of an angry adult than in the presence of a person with a neutral or positive attitude. The second kind of empathy involves not only related feelings, but also an inference about how the other person feels. Children of preschool age possess this ability. The third type of reaction is characterized primarily by an inference as to the other person's feelings. It is an inference because, in this case, the child does not share the same feelings. Preschoolers are capable of this kind of social cognition. Thus, a picture of a smiling child imparts the information that the child in the picture is happy, but it does not necessarily make the viewing child feel joyful. Nonempathetic inference grows from a general sense of "feel-

Boys and girls in middle childhood develop awareness of the motives, feelings, attitudes, and perceptions in themselves and others. (John Running, Stock, Boston)

ing good or bad" to finer distinctions of anger, fear, excitement, pride, and so forth. Eventually, older children also learn that the emotional expression of others may be calculated, controlled, or feigned.

How do children come to appreciate that others have thoughts quite different from their own? According to a developmental model drawn up by Selman and Byrne (1972, 1973, 1974) children pass through three major stages before adolescence. From ages 4 to 6, their outlook is primarily egocentric; the child is unaware that anyone's thoughts differ from his own. From 6 to 8, the child gradually comes to understand that he and other people are active, autonomous individuals with distinct views, even on the same subject. He also learns that people interpret and make judgments about events. From 8 to 10, the child comes to realize that one person's thinking can be the object of someone else's thought, with all the complications which that development entails. As they learn that others have thoughts different from their own, children also learn that individual characteristics—personalities—vary from person to person as well.

Personality is a difficult concept to grasp and, once understood, is often hard to articulate. It is not surprising, then, that young children have a great deal of difficulty assessing and describing personality. One study (Livescy and Bromley, 1973) asked hundreds of English children, ages 7 to 15, to describe the characters (but not the physical appearances) of themselves and people they knew. Despite the instructions, most 6- and 7-year-olds stuck to appearance, family, and possessions. Half of the 7-year-olds failed to mention even one psychological quality. Slightly older children seemed to have acquired more psychological acuity. They focused more on traits, attitudes, and abilities; they described character traits in increasingly precise terms. Still, the personality descriptions written in middle childhood showed little organization or sense of a coherent personality structure. Rather, they consisted of various behaviors, attitudes, and habits randomly strung together (Livesley and Bromley, 1973).

By the time children enter first grade, they have a fair amount of understanding about intentions and motives. They are familiar with the difference between wanting to do something and having to do it, and they can probably distinguish purposeful from accidental behavior. As with other aspects of social cognition, they become increasingly sensitive to the fact of hidden motives and more skilled at interpreting them (Flavell, 1977). One error young children commonly make, however, is placing undue emphasis on personal motives. For example, if father does not provide a desired toy, the young child attributes this to unwillingness rather than inability. Only gradually does the child learn that when people act under strong outside pressures (such as the family budget), behavior may not reflect true desire or motivation (Flavell, 1977).

Another aspect of social cognition is moral development. The most influential theories of moral development have come from Piaget and from Kohlberg. In order to probe children's sense of morality and justice, Piaget questioned them about the origins and alterability of rules in common games such as marbles. He also related stories about naughty children committing various misdeeds and asked his subjects for an evaluation of how guilty or blameworthy the child in the story was. From this research, Piaget evolved two general stages of moral growth. The earlier stage, sometimes called *moral realism,* is characterized by the child's belief that rules are sacred and inviolate. Behaviors are either right or they are wrong. The rightness of an act is determined by a number of factors. These include the seriousness of the consequences, the degree to which the act complies with or defies established rules, and whether or not it is followed by punishment. The young child fervently believes that transgressions are swiftly followed by harm or accidents that are deliberately caused by God or some other superior force (Hoffman, 1970).

The more advanced Piagetian stage of moral development, which begins to develop in the middle childhood years, is termed *autonomous*

Moral Development

morality or *morality of cooperation*. When they have reached this stage, children are no longer moral absolutists. They see rules as the result of social agreement and as a response to human needs, rather than as immutable laws. It follows logically that older children realize that rules and laws can be changed and that there are conflicting opinions about what constitutes right and wrong. Whereas formerly children stressed the consequences of an act, now they scrutinize the motive that prompted it.

Kohlberg (1958, 1963) has elaborated Piaget's model of moral development into a more complex and refined framework. Kohlberg based his theory on a series of 2-hour interviews conducted with boys aged 10 to 16. During the interview, he posed a variety of hypothetical moral dilemmas, all of which pitted obedience to authority against the well-being of some individual. For example:

Joe's father promised he could go to camp if he earned the $50 for it, and then changed his mind and asked Joe to give him the money he had earned. Joe lied and said he had only earned $10 and went to camp using the other $40 he had made. Before he went, he told his younger brother Alex about the money and about lying to their father. Should Alex tell their father? (Kohlberg, 1963, p. 13.)

Based on the results of these interviews, Kohlberg identified six separate stages of moral development, falling into three general categories. The first two stages fall under the general heading of *preconventional morality*. Conduct is controlled by forces external to the child—outer commands, externally imposed punishment, or rewards bestowed for compliance. Stage 1 is primarily oriented around obedience, punishment, and submission to higher authority. Stage 2 is hedonistic; the child defines as right those acts that are personally gratifying. At the same time, the child has some awareness that people's needs and perspectives vary.

The next two stages come under the category Kohlberg terms the *morality of conventional role-conformity*. Here, morality is defined as compliance with social conventions and expectations of others. This goes beyond mere observance of rules, however. It involves striving for the personal approval of other significant people whose opinions matter a great deal to the child. These "significant others" serve not only as sources of punishment and reward, but also as role models, enabling the child to evaluate the morality of his or her own conduct. Stage 3 of conventional role-conformity is characterized by a "good boy" or "good girl" mentality and the desire to please others. Stage 4 expands the concept of morality to the context of society at large, stressing duty and the importance of maintaining the social order for its own sake.

The last two stages in Kohlberg's model fall under the general heading of *morality of self-accepted principles*. Although this phase resembles the previous phases in the importance it places on shared social duties, it differs in one important regard. It acknowledges possible conflict between two socially accepted norms and seeks a resolution through internal, rather than external, processes. In Stage 5, duties and rights are cast in abstract, institutional terms, rather than in terms of performances personally owed to individuals. Although this view of morality recognizes that the law may sometimes be unjust and arbitrary, it demands that the law prevail over individuals for the long-range social benefits. Stage 6, the highest expression of morality in Kohlberg's scheme, is characterized by individual principles of conscience. The individual adheres both to established social norms and to internalized ideals of conscience. Moral dilemmas are usually resolved in favor of broad moral principles rather than the norms of the majority (Kohlberg, 1963). Not everyone reaches the highest level in Kohlberg's system; most adult Americans function at Stage 4.

Kohlberg and Piaget differ on major theoretical grounds. Kohlberg feels that Piaget imputes too much respect for authority to the young child and underestimates the conflict between parent and child. Respect for external authority appears later in Kohlberg's model than in Piaget's. On the other hand, Piaget views children aged 10 to 12 as almost fully matured, whereas Kohlberg sees such preadolescents as quite far from a mature, self-regulatory concept of morality.

Philosophical and political debates about the relationship between the individual and society, as well as the relationships among individual citizens, have been going on for centuries. Much of the discussion has been based on assumptions about basic human nature, that is, whether people are innately good or evil, aggressive or peace-loving, selfish or noble. Recent research in psychology indicates that none of these characteristics is preordained; rather, they are largely the product of social training. In particular, psychologists have been interested in cooperation versus competition and the way in which children are taught to value one mode of interaction over the other.

Cooperation and Competition

Cooperation may be defined as the sum total of individuals acting together with agreement to achieve a commonly desired goal. How do children learn that cooperation can produce a result that they are unable to obtain acting alone? Rewards based on group performance seem to be more effective reinforcers of cooperative behavior than rewards based on individual achievement. In experiments involving tasks that could be achieved only by a group of children, members of some groups were rewarded according to their collective performance. Members of other groups were rewarded on the basis of their personal effort, regardless of how the group did as a whole. In both cases, cooperation was enhanced. However, the increase in cooperative behavior was significantly greater in groups receiving a group reward—even when this resulted in fewer reinforcements for each group member (Bryan, 1975a). Furthermore, group dynamics were altered by the pattern of the reward. Rewards granted on the basis of group effort encouraged "taking turns," whereas individual rewards often led to dominant-submissive relationships among the children (Nelson and Madsen, 1968). In his studies of the Russian school system, Bronfenbrenner (1970) has noted that group rewards are frequently used intentionally to foster cooperation and responsibility among students for each other.

Group rewards have consistently been shown to encourage more cooperation than individual rewards. But the effectiveness of individual rewards in fostering cooperation depends in part on attitudes the child has already acquired at home and in society at large. For example, in a comparative study (Shapira and Madsen, 1969), individual and group rewards were administered to urban children and to children from a kibbutz. Both groups of children cooperated more when rewarded on a group basis, but their responses to individual reinforcement differed markedly. The kibbutz children continued to cooperate in the face of individual praise and reward, whereas the urban children displayed considerably less cooperative behavior.

In America, younger children are more likely to be cooperative than are older children (Bryan, 1975a). In addition, American children seem to be more competitive than children from some other cultures. One study (Kagan and Madsen, 1971) compared cooperative behavior among Anglo-American, Mexican-American, and Mexican children. In a game requiring cooperation in order to achieve maximum results, Mexican children showed more cooperation than Mexican-Americans, who in turn cooperated more than Anglo-Americans. Another set of studies (Richmond and Weiner, 1973; Sampson and Kardush, 1965) found that black children respond cooperatively to group rewards more than white children. White children competing with other white children for individual rewards were the most competitive of all.

Knowledge of the
Social Order

Up to now, we have discussed the psychological development of the child as a moralist. Now we turn to the child's growing knowledge of the social order. How do children move from a state of naiveté about social structure and status to an understanding of the attitudes, biases, and stereotypes of their culture?

Research suggests that children easily absorb abstract social concepts based on external, especially material, distinctions. One massive study (Simmons and Rosenberg, 1971), involving 2,000 black and white children from elementary and high schools in Baltimore, revealed that children have detailed and accurate ideas about the social hierarchy as early as the third grade (8 years of age). They understand that some occupations confer more prestige and money than others, and they have high hopes for reaching the top of the ladder themselves. As late as their senior year in high school, many of the children studied still had undiminished expectations of reaching their goals. In other words, they fervently believed in the concept and reality of upward mobility in American society (Simmons and Rosenberg, 1971).

Although the children studied had clear ideas about where they wanted to end up, their perception of their present social status was often surprisingly inaccurate. Many younger children had an inflated notion of their family's class status and occupational prestige. They also showed poor ability to discriminate the different class backgrounds of their peers. Interestingly, white children from relatively privileged families had a more highly developed awareness of social differences. On the other hand, black students who came from oppressed groups, and in whom we might expect hostility toward the existing order, had less class consciousness. In general, they lacked the ability to make fine distinctions of job prestige, had vague notions of the term "social class," and did not believe that they would be deprived of equal opportunity to develop and utilize their talents (Simmons and Rosenberg, 1971).

The major growth in social awareness seems to occur between grades 1 and 4. One study (Tudor, 1971) tested the development of awareness of social class by giving children pictures of individual men, women, and children from lower-, middle-, and upper-income groups. The children were asked to group the pictures into the appropriate families. Cues included clothing, hair styles, and facial expressions, as well as pictures of the family car and home. Tudor found that first graders are aware of a few class-related differences. By the sixth grade (age 11), however, most children were able to group the pictures with great accuracy. Girls performed better than boys on the test. The sex-related difference was most marked in the sixth grade. However, neither IQ scores nor social class, according to Tudor, is related to this kind of social perception.

Children recognize social inequality at an early age. By early adolescence, children in America come to accept inequality as an inevitable aspect of the social system (Esteven, 1952; Leahy, 1977). With age, children come to ascribe to a "just world" ideology in which people get what they deserve (Sampson, 1975). They first learn this notion at home. At school, it is reinforced by explanations of how one person eventually comes to occupy a more important position than another. Teachers, naturally, stress the role of academic success in gaining rewards and respect from society. By grade 2, children can accurately rank job categories according to adult value standards. By grade 4, they have developed rationalizations and justifications for the ranking; depending on their training, they may see the "filtering" process as the result of innate talent, family wealth, or the importance of the job to be done (Lauer, 1974). These findings raise interesting questions about the vitality of the "American dream," the common belief that ours is a classless society, and the willingness of our young citizens to work within the system for the promised rewards.

HUMOR, GAMES, AND FANTASY

Academic excellence, systematic problem solving, and social perceptions are not the only standards by which cognitive development can be measured. Imagination and humor are also important indicators of the young child's intellectual growth. Thus many recent studies that explore mental development have focused on the cognitive as well as the social aspects of children's jokes, fantasies, and games.

Humor

As we have already discussed in many different contexts, children between the ages of 6 and 11 begin to think in complex and abstract ways. One area in which this development is evident is the child's increasing ability to appreciate and generate humor. A child's "sense of humor" is a sign of the ability to sustain a sophisticated network of ideas or terms that are contradictory or incongruous. In order for the child to understand or tell a joke, he or she must first observe two contradictory or incongruous concepts and then discover how the ideas correspond. These two processes, which result in the resolution of incongruity, are central to the larger context of cognitive development.

Freud was one of the first psychologists to relate cognitive level to children's intellectual command of humor. He found that younger children responded favorably to both meaningful and nonsensical joke structures, whereas older children appreciated jokes based on incongruities that they could resolve (Ginsburg and Koslowski, 1976).

In an attempt to verify Freud's theory, Schultz and Horibe (1974) conducted a study in which they presented three versions of a joke to children aged 6 to 12. The original joke was "'Call me a cab.' 'You're a cab.'" The first variation was a *resolution-removed form,* which preserved an unexplained ambiguity: "'Call a cab for me.' 'You're a cab.'" The second variation ("'Call me a cab.' 'Yes, ma'am.'") presented an *incongruity-removed* form requiring no resolution whatsoever. Although 6-year-olds did not appreciate the incongruity-removed form, they responded to the original and resolution-removed forms with equal enthusiasm. Children aged 8 to 12 years old, on the other hand, preferred the original version of the joke. Schultz and Horibe concluded from their findings that children learn to appreciate pure incongruity (nonsense) before they can explain and manipulate the incongruous elements of a joke.

In a similar series of experiments, McGhee (1974) tested children's ability to perceive the humor in a joke or riddle and then to say something equally funny. Children in four age groups ranging from grades 1 to 6 listened to a total of 16 jokes, including 8 wordplays and 8 riddles. The humor in each of the wordplays was based on an ambiguous word or phrase. For example, "Why did the old man and his wife drive to the North Pole?" The humorous answer offered by the experimenter was

"They wanted to see the Christmas seals." The serious variation was: "They wanted to see what it was like to live in a really cold climate." The riddles, on the other hand, were funny because of some latent absurdity in the joke situation. For example, "Why did the elephant lie across the sidewalk?" The humorous response of the experimenter was "To trip the ants." The serious variant was "He wanted to rest."

Each child listened to the 16 jokes, receiving funny and serious responses on a random basis. They were then asked to rate each joke on a scale from 1 (not funny at all) to 5 (very funny). At the same time, the experimenters observed the children for smiles, laughter, or blank looks. Then, the experimenter reread the jokes, giving the version, either funny or serious, that the child had not heard before. Each child was then asked, for each joke, which version was funnier. Next, the experimenter pointed out to the child that while he had rated some of the wordplays and riddles as hilarious, others did not strike his funny bone at all. To test the ability to articulate a general statement about what constitutes humor, the experimenter asked, "What's different about the ones that are funny and the ones that aren't funny?"

Finally, the child was asked to create a similar joke or riddle. The result was evaluated in terms of the frequency of wordplays and absurd situations. McGhee found that children were generally better at mimicking concrete forms of humor than at stating a general principle of funniness. At age 7 or 8, many children were able to create joking relationships, but they were not able either to see the humor in jokes told by others or to formulate an abstract idea of humor. Ginsburg and Koslowski (1976) find a parallel between this aspect of cognitive growth and Flavell's (1977) findings on mediation and production deficiency. Remember Flavell's suggestion that children can use mediational devices (like rehearsal), if offered by instructors to improve memory, before the children have spontaneously developed mediational techniques by themselves.

Children's increasing capacity to appreciate jokes and riddles reflects changes in cognitive and linguistic skills. In experiments like those conducted by Schultz and Horibe (1974), the jokes were often based on an ambiguity of language. Schultz (1974) found that, in general, children appreciate jokes based on ambiguities of sound (for example, bare, bear) or word usage ("I'm bugged"), before they see the humor in jokes based on ambiguous sentence structure ("Call me a cab"). This development parallels the general pattern of linguistic growth. In nonhumorous situations, children first learn to detect ambiguities of sound, then word usage, then sentence structure.

The "make-believe" sociodramatic play of early childhood reaches its height between the ages of 4 and 6 and then declines drastically in middle childhood. Middle childhood ushers in a new era of leisure-time pursuits, namely, games with rules.

Games

Increasing cognitive, emotional, and social skills make games with rules more attractive in middle childhood. (Michal Heron, Monkmeyer)

The ability to interact with other children and stay within the boundaries of an agreed-upon game depends on physical, cognitive, emotional, and social skills. Not surprisingly, then, children's preferences for games change as they grow and become more capable. Infant games are primarily motoric and sensory. Gradually, symbolic elements and structures assume a larger role in play, until adulthood, when games are tests of strategy, physical strength, and luck (Herron and Sutton-Smith, 1971).

Games are important not only for the skills they test, but also for their outcome. The result of a game is a disparity between winners and losers. Herron and Sutton-Smith (1971) contrast this function with the overriding effort in other areas of life to achieve and maintain equilibrium. Similarly, games and play in middle childhood are valued for their ability to generate unexpected nonsense, whereas most mental activity is aimed at producing predictability.

Games governed by rules become particularly popular in middle childhood. Piaget (1932) used the game of marbles to chart the increasing importance of rules at different ages. He found that this common game is played in strikingly different ways at different ages. In describing the developmental course of rule assimilation, Piaget distinguished between the *application* of rules and the *consciousness* of rules.

He noted four stages of development in the *application* of rules. At first, children play marbles in an individual and motoric way; they handle the marbles the way they want. Between the ages of 2 and 5, children enter the second stage, that of egocentrism. In this phase, they can observe others playing by the rules, but they themselves do not observe rules, nor do they play to win. At age 7 or 8, the stage of cooperation begins. At this stage, children play to win and play with other marble shooters according to some general idea of what constitutes the rules of the game. But their notions of the rules are vague and often contradictory. Finally, at around 11 or 12, children achieve the final stage of the codification of rules. Not only are the children able to relate rules in detail, but there also is widespread agreement among the players as to what the rules really are (Piaget, 1932).

Piaget discovered a rather different sequence regarding *consciousness* of rules. Here, he found three different stages. During the first stage, rules have little coercive impact on behavior, either because they are purely physical ("Don't swallow the marble") or because the child sees them as interesting, but not mandatory. (One little girl, for instance, removed all the unlucky chance cards from the Monopoly game because she and her friends did not like to draw them.) In the second stage, egocentrism and budding cooperation blend. Rules are viewed as sacred, inviolate, and permanent. They originate, the children believe, from adult demands. In the third stage, rules are regarded as the product of mutual agreement that the child who wishes to be cooperative will observe. Children at this stage, however, are also aware that rules can be changed if one first seeks general support for the proposed change.

The work of a famous British couple, the Opies, deserves mention here as a treasury of children's games and rituals (Opie and Opie, 1959, 1969). The Opies have catalogued thousands of games, chants, and songs popular in British and other cultures. Most of the games involve either a set of rules or a sequence of tag and chase. They also, however, conjure up fantasies and major conflicts of the child's world.

For example, one common game in British Commonwealth countries is called "Old Man in the Well" or "Ghost in the Well." It involves a set dialogue in which mother sends child to the well for water, child finds old man at the bottom, and calls mother over to see.

Mother: *What are you doing here?*
Old Man: *Picking up sand.*
Mother: *What do you want sand for?*
Old Man: *To sharpen my needles.*
Mother: *What do you want needles for?*
Old Man: *To make a bag.*
Mother: *What do you want a bag for?*
Old Man: *To keep my knives in.*
Mother: *What do you want knives for?*
Old Man: *To cut off your heads.*
Mother: *Then catch us if you can.*
(Opie and Opie, 1969)

Games like this allow children to experience the thrill of danger and chase. The Opies also note that games frequently mirror actual contemporary conflicts. For example, children in Berlin were observed shooting at each other across miniature walls after that city was divided. After John Kennedy was killed, American children frequently played assassination games.

For children in every culture, play is an important way of developing physical and cognitive skills. Games played by children of various ages seem to reflect their dominant cognitive style or emotional state. Games also are a major means of socializing young children, of transmitting social values and concepts to them. Thus, interest in games may be *psychogenic* (stemming primarily from the needs and motives of the individual child) or *sociogenic* (resulting from social pressures and expectations). Games serve preparatory and training functions. For example, in hunting cultures, games of physical skill predominate. In primitive societies that rely on magic or ritual to solve major group problems and that punish individual achievement, games of chance are the major form of play (Roberts and Sutton-Smith, 1966). And in highly stratified societies, based on obedience, diplomacy, class interaction, and warfare, children learn many games of strategy (Roberts, Sutton-Smith, and Kendon, 1963).

Not surprisingly, the popularity of game forms changes with the historical era. In the late nineteenth century, singing games, team guessing, and acting games were played much more frequently than they are today. These games are played primarily by girls. Team games without distinct roles were played more frequently by boys a hundred years ago than they are today. Games that have apparently retained their popularity include tag and chase, imitative games, and games involving a central figure of low power (such as "Blindman's Bluff"). Some game forms are played more by American children today than formerly. These include leader games, organized sports, and games of physical skill played either indoors or outdoors (Sutton-Smith and Rosenberg, 1971). One of the most important changes involves the emerging similarity of boys' and girls' activities. Formerly, the provinces of the sexes were sharply defined. Now, it seems that children of both sexes are increasingly enjoying the games formerly reserved for children of the opposite sex.

There are, however, still important differences in the way the sexes play. Both boys and girls spend the great majority (about 75%) of their free time in play. But boys' games most frequently are played outdoors, whereas girls overwhelmingly prefer indoor games. Thus girls at play are more restricted in physical movement and vocal expression (Lever, 1976). Furthermore, although both sexes allocate a similar amount of play time to social play, boys tend to play in larger groups. Boys also are more likely to play in groups with children of a wide age range. Their games are competitive, involving rules and explicit goals (home runs, touchdowns). Girls' games, on the other hand, are more often cooperative interactions without winners or losers, goals, or end points. (This is true even if organized team sports are disregarded.) Finally, boys' games usually last longer than girls' games. Lever explains this last fact with the observation that boys are usually more physically skilled than girls and thus can keep an exciting game going longer. Furthermore, boys are more effective at resolving their disputes; they rarely end a game because of a quarrel. Lever suggests that the end product of this socialization through play is that girls get little training in the judicial process. They learn to take turns, rather than to outwit adversaries through strategy (Lever, 1976). These patterns may change as parents and other adults become increasingly aware of and make efforts to change subtle attitudes and behaviors that translate into differences between the sexes.

Although make-believe play declines during the middle childhood years, there is evidence that the fantasy elements of play "go underground," appearing both in the stories that children tell and in dreams.   *Fantasy*

FANTASY IN NARRATIVE STORIES. Fantasy narratives are a rich source of insight into the child's inner life. One way of viewing children's stories is through Piagetian analysis, which seeks out elements of conservation and reversibility. Sutton-Smith and his colleagues describe a sequence of five major stages, beginning at age 1 and culminating in maturity at age 9 (Sutton-Smith, Botvin, and Mahony, 1975).

Stage 1 consists of free association, observed in children under 2 years of age. Their stories are fragmented and lacking in unity of theme, time sequence, and coherent character. Full sentences are used but are not closely linked together. In Stage 2 (2 years), conservation of character can be observed. The same character remains in the story from beginning to end, but there is only one main actor. In Stage 3 (3 years), young storytellers employ characters that are not only conserved, but coordinated with others. These characters act or are acted upon by the main figure. The main figure is mentioned several times. Later in Stage 3, more complicated interaction among characters appears. Stage 4 (5 years) is characterized by conservation of plot. The different actions in the story are unified, usually following a pattern of initial state, transition, and return to initial state. Note the similarity of this pattern to the conceptual process involved in understanding that a ball of clay rolled into a sausage is still potentially a ball of clay. The first narrative scene or state is usually a place of equilibrium, such as home. Next, there is a transition to danger, or excitement, or some other marked change. Finally the narrative returns to the beginning situation. Children are now able to reverse narrative events in the same way that they can mentally reverse operations like pouring water into different beakers. For example:

I'll tell you a story. He's going to be a pumpkin man. Once upon a time there was a pumpkin man. And he lived in a little pumpkin house close by the city. So he went to the pumpkin mobile and he went faster than the speed of a bullet, more powerful than a locomotive. He could go down the highest hill in a single bound. And he went so fast that he passed the store that he wanted to go to. Then when he got back home he went to bed. And that's the end. (Sutton-Smith et al., 1975, p. 17)

Around the age of 8 or 9 (Stage 5), children add subplots to the main theme. They are able to conserve parallel stories occurring in different places ("Meanwhile, back at the ranch"). Furthermore, they can organize the whole story into discrete, coherent chapters. Such ability mirrors their increasingly organized and ordered understanding of the world around them. For instance, an 8-year-old told the following story:

Some boys were playing baseball. A man came and said they couldn't play there. "Why can't we play, we're in our own backyard." "Oh I never knew it was your backyard."

The mother came home and said it was time to come and play inside because it was going to rain. So they came in and played inside. Later they went out and played more baseball. (Sutton-Smith et al., 1975, pp. 17–18)

Thus, children make good use of the period of emotional calm ushered in by the latency period. In middle childhood, children are "tuned up" for learning and thinking. The intellectual changes that appear in this period reflect increased capacity and heightened eagerness to wrap their minds around knowledge, fascinating phenomena, and puzzles about the world at large.

SUMMARY

Between the ages of 6 and 11—the period known as middle childhood— profound changes occur in children; they become capable of more complex cognitive and social behaviors. According to psychoanalytic theorists, these changes are facilitated by a period of relative emotional calm that begins when children are about 6 years old. In this stage, children are busy acquiring new cognitive skills, which result in a sense of industry—pride and pleasure in creativity. Children also begin to place more emphasis on the abstract reinforcement of having the correct information and less emphasis on the social rewards of praise and attention.

Other kinds of cognitive growth are signified by changes in the use of language. Children begin to internalize more dialogue, using it for planning and representation. Their free association patterns show an increasing awareness of grammar. Changes in perception and orientation also occur. And children show an increased ability to deal with distracting information while problem solving.

In the period between the ages of 6 and 11, children learn to think in new and complex ways. Flavell cites four major cognitive developments that occur in middle childhood: (1) Reliance on *inferred reality* rather than outward appearances. (2) *Decentration.* (3) *Transformational thought.* (4) *Reversible* mental operations. In addition, the power of memory takes on new characteristics.

Another characteristic of cognitive development in middle childhood is a quantitative approach to problems. *Seriation* and *classification* are two important elements in the development of number concepts. The ability to classify also develops gradually as does the ability to measure, which comes about without explicit teaching.

Piaget has also found that children's causal explanations of such things as the movement of the sun, moon, clouds, and water; the origin of wind and breath; and the workings of machines such as the bicycle and the steam engine follow similar developmental patterns.

The complex and interdependent development of information-processing skills is an important part of the cognitive growth that occurs in middle childhood. Children's attempts to solve guessing game problems reveal two major strategies of questioning: *constraint seeking* and *hypothesis scanning.* Increased reliance on symbolic representation rather than representation by action or image is essential to the complex function of constraint seeking. In addition, children need a basic understanding that strategy and advance planning are required.

Learning theorists have begun to acknowledge that a major transition in learning occurs around age 5. Reversal and nonreversal shift problems indicate that mediational processes influence the way people solve problems, but it has been difficult to identify how the mediators operate. Investigators have focused on the study of memory in considering how mediation operates in learning situations.

Memory is an important process, responsible in part for the retention of information and the accumulation of knowledge. The learning limitations of younger children have been attributed to their inability to identify or retain relevant information. The *mediation deficiency hypothesis* holds that at one point in cognitive development, children are able to make verbal or symbolic responses but do not use them to solve problems. One of the troubling questions in the study of children's memory is whether poor test performance results from failure to use a verbal symbol (*mediation deficiency*) or failure to articulate it or produce it for the tester (*production deficiency*). Experiments seem to indicate that production deficiency is a more common obstacle to memory and learning than mediation deficiency.

Memory involves not only placing a certain piece of information into storage but also encoding and incorporating new knowledge into an internal conceptual representation. Because the process involves construction of a framework as well as retention of items of information, this strategy is frequently referred to as *constructive memory*. Another strategy, *retrieval*, is a similarly active operation of reconstruction and rearrangement. Memory is not an automatic recording device but, rather, involves relating new knowledge to old, encoding both the item and the relationship, and making spontaneous inferences and interpretations. Children use constructive memory and often go beyond the information given to construct more elaborate, meaningful sets of relations.

Rehearsal is one memory strategy that increases and changes with age. Another memory strategy is *organization,* which involves clustering information around a common feature, and which increases with age. Changes in memory processes and strategies reflect the general cognitive trend toward increased use in middle childhood of deliberate strategies and planning, both of which enhance the ability to solve problems.

Social cognition is the term used to describe development of social skills and relationships. It involves knowledge and manipulation of people and, therefore, involves problems and skills that are different from other types of learning. Between the ages of 6 and 8, children's egocentric perspectives are transformed into a more complex view of other people. At about ages 8 to 10 children learn that the way other people view them and gauge their internal perspective can exert an important influence on their behavior.

Flavell points out a number of parallel trends in social and nonsocial cognitive development. Both progress from reliance on superficial, overt indicators to examination of unperceived factors. Children are initially aware of only the most obvious types of social behavior, and they gradually learn to detect concealed factors. Similarly, their social cognition is highly centrated; it focuses on the most salient aspects and neglects other important information. The most common impediment to social cognition is *egocentrism,* the inability to distinguish one's own view from that of other people. In Piagetian terms, perceptual egocentrism eventually recedes with the onset of operational thought, but social egocentrism is longer-lived and continues to interfere with perception of other people's feelings and points of view throughout life.

In addition to learning to perceive other people's perspectives, children also learn about feelings for and of others. *Social understanding* is cognition of another's feelings. *Empathy* is sharing how another person feels. Preschoolers are capable of inferring another person's feelings without actually sharing them. And, eventually, older children learn that the emotional expressions of others may be calculated, controlled, or feigned.

Another aspect of social cognition is moral development. Piaget found two general stages of moral growth. The earlier stage, *moral realism,* is characterized by the belief that rules are sacred and inviolate and that behaviors are either right or wrong. The more advanced stage, which begins to develop in middle childhood, is termed *autonomous morality* or *morality of cooperation,* when children see rules as the result of social agreement and as a response to human needs rather than as immutable laws. Kohlberg elaborated Piaget's model by identifying six separate stages of moral development that fall into three general categories. In the *preconventional morality* category conduct is controlled by external forces. In the *morality of conventional role-conformity* category the child views morality as compliance with social conventions and expectations of others. The *morality of self-accepted principles* acknowledges possible conflict between two socially accepted norms and seeks a resolution through internal, rather than external, processes.

As children develop a sense of morality, they also gain a growing knowledge of the social order and their culture. Research suggests that children easily absorb abstract social concepts based on external, especially material, distinctions. Children recognize social inequality at an early age. By early adolescence, children in America come to accept inequality as an inevitable aspect of the social system. And with age, children come to ascribe to a "just world" ideology in which people get what they deserve.

Imagination and humor are important indicators of young children's intellectual growth. Children's "sense of humor" is a sign of the ability to sustain a sophisticated network of ideas or terms that are contradictory or incongruous. Children's increasing capacity to appreciate jokes and riddles reflects changes in cognitive and linguistic skills. In general, children appreciate jokes based on ambiguities of sound or word usage before they see the humor in jokes based on ambiguous sentence structure.

The ability to interact with other children and stay within the agreed-upon boundaries of a game depends on physical, cognitive, emotional, and social skills. Children's preferences for games change as they grow and become more capable. Infant games are primarily motoric and sensory. Gradually, symbolic elements and structures assume a larger role in play, until adulthood, when games are tests of strategy, physical strength, and luck. Games and play in middle childhood are valued for their ability to generate unexpected nonsense, whereas most mental activity is aimed at producing predictability.

Games governed by rules become particularly popular in middle childhood. In describing the developmental course of rule assimilation, Piaget distinguished between the *application* of rules and the *consciousness* of rules. By age 11 or 12, children are not only able to relate rules in detail but there is also widespread agreement among the players as to what the rules really are. Rules are regarded as a product of mutual agreement that children who wish to be cooperative will observe. Children are aware that rules can be changed if one first seeks general support for the proposed change.

Play is an important way of developing physical and cognitive skills. Games played by children of various ages seem to reflect their dominant cognitive style or emotional state. Games are also a major means of socializing young children, of transmitting social values and concepts to them. And games serve preparatory and training functions.

Although make-believe play declines during middle childhood, there is evidence that the fantasy elements of play "go underground," appearing both in the stories children tell and in dreams.

Thus, children make good use of the period of emotional calm ushered in by the latency period to bring increasing organization and order to their understanding of the world around them.

CHAPTER 12

Individual Differences in Middle Childhood

When Barker and Wright (1954) observed children who were playing in the playgrounds of housing projects, they found mostly children between the ages of 7 and 12. Younger children were at home or with adults, whereas adolescents roamed farther afield. During the middle years, children acquire the social skills needed to participate in large-group settings made up of children of their own age. They begin to seek out same-sex playmates as the desire to become similar to others of the same sex extends beyond members of the family. They are comfortable away from home and ready to transfer their affections and allegiances from parents to teachers. With the easing of the tensions produced by the Oedipal conflict, children become free to cultivate their intellectual and physical interests. Increased control of eyes and head makes it possible to learn to read and write; increased control of large motor muscles makes it possible to learn to ride a two-wheel bicycle, throw a ball, and do cartwheels. Children are emotionally, as well as mentally and physically, ready for the playground and the school.

Although differences among children are apparent from birth, these differences tend to become stabilized in middle childhood. Differences in the way children perform on intelligence and achievement tests, styles of problem solving, orientation to new information, and inventiveness begin to permeate their behavior at home, on the playground, and in school. Since school plays such an important role in the lives of American children, much of the research and the material covered in this chapter deal with differences in how children perform in academic situations.

INTELLIGENCE AND SCHOOL ACHIEVEMENT

Of all the ways in which children may differ from one another, the one that has been studied, discussed, and measured the most is intelligence. And yet, as we noted in Chapter 2, behavioral scientists and lay people alike may find it difficult to give a clear, precise definition of the term. In daily life, we judge other people as "intelligent" or "dull" by observing their behavior in concrete situations:

A person walks into a situation in which others are floundering, appraises it, and selects an effective course of action. If he does such a thing only once, we may say he is lucky. If he can do it only in particular kinds of situations, we may say he has a special knack or talent. But if he does it over and over again, in a wide variety of situations with which his prior familiarity is no greater than yours or mine, we say he is intelligent. (Loehlin, Lindzey, and Spuhler, 1975, p. 49)

Tests used to measure intelligence have recently come under serious criticism from psychologists as well as from the general public. In this section, we will discuss how intelligence tests are constructed, some of their characteristics, and some of the relationships children's scores have with other aspects of intellectual and social functioning. Before we present this material, it is important to understand how testing began and some of the social debates that have raged about how tests should be used.

Historical and Social Perspectives

The first intelligence test—and the model for all those that have followed it—was published in France in 1905 by Binet and Simon. Alfred Binet worked with retarded children and was concerned with the effects of the law, passed in France in 1881, that required compulsory education for all children. What would happen to children unable to keep up with the standard curriculum? The Ministry of Public Instruction in Paris commissioned Binet, along with Théodore Simon, to devise a test to identify students who would benefit from special education—or, as it was called, "mental orthopedics." Binet and Simon first had to determine average levels of development at different ages. Individual children could then be measured against the average, and the genuinely retarded could be distinguished from underachievers of normal intelligence (Sharp, 1972).

The Binet-Simon test was thus specifically designed to predict school performance. Binet and Simon observed children in school so as to understand better what teachers expected of them; the test items were deliberately designed to mimic school tasks. It should not surprise us, then, that IQ scores show a relationship to school learning. The correlation between IQ scores and school grades ranges between .40 and .60 at all levels from kindergarten to college. Children who score higher stay in school longer and like school better (Tyler, 1974). Findings such as these suggest that intelligence tests measure an aptitude for schooling.

INTELLIGENCE TESTING IN THE UNITED STATES. When the Binet-Simon test was brought to America, it was changed in several ways and used for purposes quite different from what its creators had intended. The first revision of the Binet test was published at Stanford University by Louis M. Terman in 1916. When the United States entered World War I in 1917, Terman designed the Army Alpha Examination, a group test given to all recruits in order to select those who would make good officers. Binet's test had been designed for individual administration, as part of a clinical examination. (Individual tests, as we will see, offer more reliable and valid scores than do group tests.) Group intelligence tests were soon used by school systems and colleges to sort students into ability groups and then into educational tracks. Two-and-a-half years after publication of the group IQ test, 4 million children had been tested (Cronbach, 1975). The mental-test movement gathered enormous momentum in the 1920s because it fit so well with the national mood—which stressed advancement according to merit rather than social class. No time or resource was to be wasted—each child must be schooled in the occupation to which he or she was best suited. As "streaming" children into ability groups at an early age became common, the results of IQ tests began to determine individual fates (Cronbach, 1975).

Despite the great momentum of the test movement, challenges to the validity of intelligence tests and the uses to which they were put did occur, even in the 1920s and 1930s. The early controversies—like the later ones of the 1960s—were over the nature-nurture issue and the ethnic slurs and chauvinism that followed. These controversies, though, were short-lived. Few people considered the implications of streaming children, and even fewer considered the narrow notions of education that justified the use of the tests. One exception was sociologist Allison Davis, who argued during the 1940s that a number of the verbal items on IQ tests were culture-laden and favored middle-class over working-class children. Davis's real challenge was to traditional education. But his challenge went largely unheard in an atmosphere where psychologists and the general public alike accepted the validity of traditional testing and traditional education.

All that is changing now. Both the validity of IQ tests and the wisdom of tracking children into different educational programs are being challenged. Some signs of the times: Several cities, including New York, Los Angeles, and Washington, D.C., have banned group intelligence testing in the public schools. In 1972, a federal court ruled that the state of Pennsylvania must provide an education for all mentally retarded children, even those classified as "uneducable and untrainable" by their performance on IQ tests. In 1971, the U.S. Supreme Court declared unlawful the Duke Power Company's use of an IQ test as part of the requirement for job promotion (Sharp, 1972).

What is causing the change in attitudes? Beliefs in the desirability of a pluralistic society, in affiliations within local communities, and in individual fulfillment rather than "perfection" are becoming more widespread. This change in vision is expressed in studies of the role parents play in intellectual development and in studies of the way education can be modified to maximize the skills of children. It is expressed in studies of the way test situations influence performance and in increased sensitivity to the negative consequences of labeling children (Mercer, 1972). More important, it is being expressed in a new stress on the development of tests that diagnose the state of childrens' skills so that they might be taught skills they have not developed (Feuerstein, 1972).

How Tests Are Constructed

At present, there are many different tests that claim to measure intelligence. Of these, the Stanford-Binet test is the best known and most widely used. This test requires children to be able to use a pencil; listen attentively; follow directions; repeat what is said to them; use labels to identify objects; concentrate on fine details; make reasonable inferences; and form analogies. A large number of tasks that measure these abilities were collected and then tried out on a great many children. Those tasks that almost all children at a given age could do and those tasks that very few children could do were discarded. Why? Because the purpose of the test was to identify *differences* among children, not similarities. The best items are those that some children pass and some children fail. Test constructors attempt to include items that 50% to 65% of the children will answer correctly. In this sense, the items used in IQ tests are based on current norms, or are *norm-referenced*.

IQ test items, then, vary in difficulty depending on the age of the child. A 3-year-old may be asked: "Point to the boy's nose; his eyes; his mouth." The same item, obviously, would not distinguish between bright and average 7-year-olds. Both a 3-year-old and a 7-year-old might be asked to describe the same picture, but the 3-year-old would be expected only to name the things in it ("woman," "doggie"), whereas the 7-year-old would be asked to describe what is happening ("The woman is walking the dog on a leash"). The Stanford-Binet test includes both performance and verbal tests of ability. Performance tests measure visual-spatial skills through items that include pictures and geometric shapes. For instance, children may be asked to complete the drawing of a man or to copy an abstract design from memory. Verbal tests include vocabulary items, general information questions, and problems involving language. Children may be asked to name words that rhyme with "head"; to say why two things like "wood" and "coal" are alike; to make analogies; to say why a certain statement ("In the year 1915 many more women than men got married in the United States") is silly; to repeat sentences; to use a given series of words to form a sentence.

Intelligence tests are deliberately constructed so as to force the scores to form a "bell-shaped" curve—that is, to have a *normal distribution*. If we assume that intelligence is distributed randomly, or normally, throughout the population—like height, for example—the vast majority of people would fall somewhere near the mean. About two-thirds of all individuals would fall within 15 or 16 IQ points of the mean, and fully 99.7% would be within 45 IQ points of the mean. Figure 12–1 shows an "idealized" distribution of IQ scores—the percentages of the population in each IQ range if IQ were distributed "normally." Figure 12–2 shows the *actual* distribution of IQ in the population. The major difference between the two curves is the "bump" between the IQs of 50 and 60. These low IQs are caused by conditions such as brain damage or chromosomal abnormalities, rather than by normal variation (Zigler, 1967). In fact, the actual distribution of IQ in the population is very like that of height, where genes that cause dwarfism account for a small bump in the group of extremely short people at the lower end of the scale.

An individual's IQ is not an absolute score, like a score of 90 out of a possible 100 right answers on an examination. Instead, an IQ score is a measure of a person's performance in relation to that of his or her peers. A 3-year-old's performance is measured against that of other 3-year-olds rather than against that of 8-year-olds. As we noted earlier, items in the Stanford-Binet test are age-graded. If a child passes all items through the 5-year-old level, his or her *mental age* (MA) is calculated at 5 years. If, in addition, he or she passes half the items at the 6-year-old level, his or her mental age is 5.5 years. In order to obtain the child's IQ, it is necessary to know his or her chronological age (CA). The old formula for calculating IQ was IQ = MA/CA × 100. Thus the 5-year-old child whose mental age

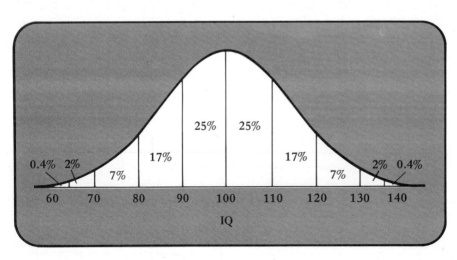

FIGURE 12–1
The normal theoretical distribution of IQs, showing percentages of the population expected to fall in each IQ range.*
(Jensen, 1969, Figure 1, p. 24)
*Due to rounding, the total is more than 100%.

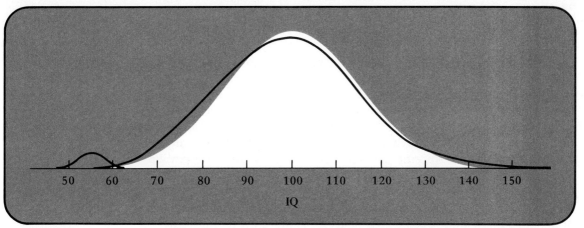

is 5.5 has an IQ of 110 (5.5/5 × 100 = 110). When this formula is used, the average child, by definition, will have an IQ of 100: His or her mental development is the same as that of most other children of the same age, so that the mental and chronological ages are the same.

Test constructors no longer calculate IQ by comparing mental and chronological ages, because the old formula posed certain statistical difficulties and did not work well for adults, whose intelligence does not change dramatically with age. IQ is now calculated from tables of norms in which the mean has been arbitrarily set at 100. Where do the norms come from? Test constructors calculate tables of norms "based on the actual test performances of a *standardization sample*, which is—or should be—a representative sampling of the population at the given ages" (Loehlin et al., 1975, pp. 52–53). Thus a child has an IQ of over 100 if his or her test performance is better than that of the average child of the same age in the standardization sample.

The standardization sample, therefore, affects how children will be rated on the test. A surprising number of intelligence tests widely used in the United States—among them the Peabody Picture Vocabulary Test, the Stanford-Binet IQ Test, and the Wechsler Intelligence Scale for Children—were standardized on white children only. Moreover, because standardization is expensive and time-consuming, the norms of many intelligence tests are based on the performance of a group of children years ago. For example, the Stanford-Binet was not restandardized when it was revised in 1960 but continues to use what the test constructors call "the irreplaceable original standardization sample" of 3,184 white, native-born people collected prior to 1937. Thus, the Stanford-Binet IQ scores of children tested in 1978 are actually a measure of how their performance compares to that of white children over 40 years ago (Sharp, 1972).

Intelligence tests are judged according to two criteria. They must be *reliable:* An individual's score must be essentially unchanged on repetition of the test after a short interval (Bayley, 1970). And a good test must be a *valid* measure of whatever it is supposed to measure. When a test is designed to predict something—for example, whether a 6-year-old is ready to learn to read, how well a high school student will perform in college—its validity is judged by the criterion of the individual's subsequent performance. If most of the children who pass reading-readiness tests do learn to read within a year, or if SAT scores prove to be highly correlated with college grades, then reading-readiness tests and College Boards are valid. Determining the validity of IQ tests is trickier, since the tests are not designed to predict a specific performance but to measure the psychological trait of intelligence.

"Intelligence" itself is an abstract concept. It is not one simple, observable behavior; rather it is a characteristic that shows itself in a wide range of behaviors. We judge people as intelligent or dull by their performance in many different kinds of situations, in the classroom, at work, in social conversations. Therefore, the validity of an intelligence test refers to two different things: (1) *content* validity—do the items of the test represent the range of abilities people mean when they talk about intelligence? and (2) *construct* validity—does people's behavior in other situations that require intelligence reflect how they score on this test? A given intelligence test is valid if the people who do well on it also do well on other intelligence tests; do well in school; are judged by teachers and other students as bright; achieve high occupational status; are successful in daily life.

However, the relationship between scores on different tests are influenced by several factors. An individual child's IQ may vary from test to test because of differences between the standardization samples. The test situation might also account for differences. For example, the difference between individual and group tests may account for variations in a child's IQ score. Individual tests are given to each child separately by an examiner, who can help to ensure that the child is paying attention and working to capacity. Individual tests are more reliable and valid than group tests (Bayley, 1970)—but they are also more expensive and time-consuming. In a large group of children taking a written IQ test, some may be working hard and with full attention, whereas others may not be working to capacity or with full attention.

Finally, differences in test content may cause a child's IQ score to vary. We have already seen that the Stanford-Binet yields scores for both performance and verbal IQ. Another test, the Wechsler scales, has been standardized for individuals from age 4 through age 74, for each of 10 or 11 different aspects of intelligence. The Wechsler test thus measures skills more precisely than the Stanford-Binet, offering, as Bayley (1970) notes, "the possibility of drawing for each person a 'profile' showing the more and less advanced aspects of his mental abilities" (p. 1168).

A feature of IQ tests that has created interest as well as confusion is the amount of correlation between test items. Such correlation is moderately high, and some items are more highly correlated than others. The person

What Is General Intelligence?

who does well on a vocabulary test is likely to do well on a test that consists of copying abstract designs. Spearman became interested in these positive correlations and hypothesized a single factor, "general intelligence," to account for them. This has come to be known as the "g factor." Spearman defines "general intelligence" as the "higher mental processes," and he argues that test items that are most highly correlated with other items are those that measure such higher processes (Jensen, 1969). Spearman's g is a *hypothetical* entity—like gravity in physics—an abstract concept intended to explain correlations between tests and individual differences in test scores.

The Nature of Intelligence

Spearman's description of general intelligence corresponds, interestingly, with a number of classic definitions of the nature of intelligence. Spearman characterizes the higher mental processes as the ability to generalize from particulars and to view the particular as an instance of the general.

Spearman's concept of general intelligence has been challenged by a number of psychologists, who argue that intelligence is better viewed as a series of special abilities rather than as a single capacity (Loehlin et al., 1975). Research in the 1930s showed that performance and verbal IQ, although somewhat correlated, are not interchangeable. This evidence suggests that intertest correlations may be explained by the interaction of *several* primary mental abilities rather than by one g factor (Tyler, 1976). How many of these primary mental abilities there are seems to be a function of the researcher: Different abilities appear as test items become increasingly specific. Memory, for example, can be divided into short-term and long-term and can be tested using numbers, letters, or words. Even short-term memory for digits can be changed by varying how fast the digits are presented; long-term memory for sentences can be changed by varying their meaning.

Resolving the question of whether intelligence represents one or many abilities is less important than recognizing that, in a general way, intelligence refers to how people *adapt* to the requirements of a given situation, environment, or culture. A society that values art or religious feeling will define intelligence differently from a society that values physical skill or mathematical reasoning. A situation in which a child is suspicious requires different skills from a situation in which the child is comfortable. There is a vivid contrast between the black child who answers in monosyllables—yes, no—in a test situation and the same child chatting animatedly in the playground. To be quiet in an unfamiliar and possibly unfriendly situation might be highly *adaptive,* even though it gets you a low score on a test.

Neisser (1976) has argued that the "intelligence" measured by our tests and rewarded in our schools actually represents a peculiar and narrow kind of adaptation. The skill involved in solving the "puzzles" of tests and schools, Neisser argues, is academic intelligence—which is different from the intelligence required "in the affairs of daily life." Intelligent behavior in daily settings outside of school typically involves a variety of motivations, as well as feelings and emotions, and the ability to respond to new facets of a situation as they are revealed. In such settings, the facts are not set out for you in the beginning, as they are in tests. In our discussion of cross-cultural issues in Chapter 2, we explored some of the problems of measuring intelligence in the isolated and artificial context of tests. Even performance in school may involve more complex kinds of adaptations than performance on intelligence tests. All intelligence tests are based on assumptions about the nature of intelligence. Thus the definition of intelligence may be related to the way the items are chosen, how the test is given, and how responses are evaluated as much as it is to the way people perform. There is a growing body of knowledge about the factors that influence performance on intelligence tests: what population groups tend to do well, how test performance is related to age or social change. In the next section, we will examine some of the findings.

THE CONSTANCY OF IQ. One of the questions most frequently asked about *The Data* intelligence has been: Is IQ constant? It is important to note first that IQ is not an absolute measurement like height or weight; it indicates a person's relative standing in a group. Therefore, the question should be rephrased: Do people maintain their relative standings throughout life?

As we noted in Chapter 5, the IQs of infants do not predict their adult positions in the group. Performance on tests of infant development is not highly correlated with performance on later intelligence tests—perhaps because intelligence is not a stable characteristic early in life, perhaps because there are no good ways of measuring intelligence before children are around 4 years old. IQ scores at age 5 correlate .70 with IQ at 17. This leaves plenty of room for scores to fluctuate. Longitudinal studies of children in California have shown that during the school years, scores of 9% of the children shifted up or down by as many as 30 IQ points, and 58% of the scores changed by as many as 15 points (Bayley, 1968).

TEMPORAL CHANGES IN IQ. Tests have been used to measure the intelligence of large groups of people for over half a century. Therefore, there is a growing body of data that helps us to answer the question: Has IQ changed markedly in the United States since the beginning of IQ testing? (Loehlin et al., 1975). The gene pool of a population cannot change dramatically over only a few generations. Any large-scale shifts in IQ level must be attributed to changes in the environment—as with the average increases in height during the past 50 years.

The studies that have compared IQs of population groups over long intervals of time have yielded contradictory findings. One group of studies shows essentially no change over time (Scottish Council for Research in Education, 1949; Cattell, 1950; Emmett, 1950; Terman and Merrill, 1937). Another group of studies suggests upward shifts of 5 to 15 IQ points over 10–20 years (Smith, 1942; Wheeler, 1942; Elley, 1969). How can the contradictions be explained? Loehlin et al. (1975) note that investigations that found small changes or none at all were those done in places where the educational system remained relatively stable between the two tests (such as elementary schools in the United States and Great Britain). Investigations that found larger IQ shifts were done on populations whose educational systems underwent major changes. Although environmental factors other than education may be involved, the upward shifts in the IQs of children in the Tennessee mountains, Hawaii, and New Zealand do seem to indicate that improving education can increase IQ scores.

SOCIAL CLASS AND RACE. Differences in IQ scores are also associated with differences in social class as well as race. On the Stanford-Binet test, children from the upper classes score an average of about 116; children from the lower classes average about 96 (Tyler, 1974). Various studies have shown average differences ranging from 10 to 20 points between the IQs of American blacks and whites. There are many ways of explaining the differences. For one thing, blacks tend to be poorer than whites, and poverty depresses intellectual achievement.

Children's experiences, of course, also influence performance on IQ tests. The white child from a New York suburb and the black child from a New York ghetto come from different environments—as, indeed, do the black child of a southern sharecropper and the black child of a factory worker in Gary, Indiana. We noted earlier in this chapter that a number of widely used intelligence tests—including the Stanford-Binet—were standardized on white, urban children. Rural children, as well as blacks, tend to obtain lower-than-average scores on such tests. In a study of test bias, Shimberg (1929) devised two tests, one using information likely to be available to urban children (sample question: "How can banks afford to pay interest on the money you deposit?") and one using information available to rural children ("Why does seasoned wood burn more easily than green wood?"). Not surprisingly, each group obtained inferior scores on the test designed for the other group. In tests where children are asked to draw a horse (the equivalent of the widely used Draw-a-Person Test), Pueblo Indian children score an average 26 points higher than urban white children (Norman, 1963). Recently, Williams (1972) has devised the BITCH (Black Intelligence Test of Cultural Homogeneity) Test, which is deliberately designed to draw on the words and phrases of the black culture. Not surprisingly, blacks obtain higher scores than whites on this test. Such a test may have value for identifying capable black children who, because of limited exposure to white culture, are underestimated by traditional tests (Loehlin et al., 1975).

The discrepancy between the scores of blacks and whites, as we might expect, is not equivalent throughout the nation. Scores for the two groups differ in areas where educational opportunities differ most (Tyler, 1974). A recent study showed that black-white discrepancies were widest among students who went to segregated schools in the South. Blacks in integrated schools, on the other hand, averaged only 3.3 points lower than whites (Bachman, 1970).

The purpose of achievement tests differs from that of intelligence tests. Intelligence tests are designed to measure the trait of intelligence, and they may be used to predict future performance. Achievement tests—whether a standardized reading test given to every ninth-grader in a public school system or the final exam for a college course—assess what students have already learned. Achievement tests differ from intelligence tests in three ways: (1) They are narrower in scope, since they do not measure "general intelligence" but the mastery of specific skills or information; (2) they are tied to a specific academic curriculum, and should be revised if the curriculum changes; (3) achievement tests primarily measure recent learning, and intelligence tests test older learning (Cleary, Humphreys, Kendrick, and Wesman, 1975). An achievement test is judged on the basis of its *content validity:* whether it covers adequately a given body of intellectual content (Nunnally, 1972).

Achievement and Its Measurement

The first standardized achievement tests were designed at the turn of the century, at the same time as the first intelligence tests. (In fact, Binet helped design some of the earliest achievement tests [Levine, 1976].) At the time when compulsory education was becoming universal, the practice of dividing school children into grades according to their age was becoming widespread. Achievement tests offered a way of identifying "slow learners," who could then be put into special classes, and a fairly objective way of determining which children should be promoted. They also offered a way of identifying schools that do a good job.

In fact, however, achievement tests do not adequately measure what children learn in school or how well schools teach. The first achievement tests—like the majority of those used today—were modeled on intelligence tests. The method of item selection, as in IQ tests, is geared to *stress* individual differences—even at the cost of content validity. One manual describes the principles of test construction.

No item which can be answered correctly by all pupils in a given group can be of any functional value in a general achievement test for that group....If instruction has been adequate, many...fundamental items have been so thoroughly taught as to have been mastered by all the pupils. Lists of fundamentals or of the minimal essentials in a course of study are therefore very often a poor source of material for general achievement test construction....Because of this necessity for a range of difficulty in the items, it may not

be possible to make the content of the test a representative or a random
sample of the content of the course of study. (Hawkes, Lindquist, and
Mann, 1936, pp. 29–32)

As Levine (1976) asks, "How then can the achievement test be measuring
what educators have been teaching?" College students might well object
to a professor who made up final exams on the principles described in
the quotation!

Achievement tests are constructed in three stages. First, teachers and
educational experts make up an outline of content. For a year of arithmetic,
such an outline might include understanding of currency, decimals, fractions, measurement, and number systems. Next, a pool of test items is
composed and classified according to skills. Finally, after the items have
been administered to a large number of students and the results statistically analyzed, those items that best discriminate between students are
chosen for the final test (Nunnally, 1972). It is at the third stage that dis-
tortions of content occur. If the original pool of items were used, children
would be tested on how well they have mastered the *skills* being taught
at each grade level. It would be possible for all the children to have
mastered some skills and for no children to have mastered others. The tests
would then reflect how well the school moves children from no knowledge
to complete mastery. However, when items are selected according to their
ability to discriminate *between* children, the emphasis shifts from what
children have learned to the things some children learn more easily than
others. Some skills may not be tested at all, whereas others may be over-
represented. If, for example, most children have mastered fractions and
few have memorized tables of weights and measures, the final test might
include few or no questions on fractions, and a large number of questions
based on the tables of weights and measures, such as "How many rods
are there in a mile?"

There are other and better ways of measuring achievement. Tests might
be given at the beginning and at the end of each school year; the difference
in scores would be a valid measure of what students had learned. Achievement tests might be designed in relation to an absolute standard. Present-
day achievement tests, whose purpose is to rank students in relation to
one another, are designed so that scores will be "normally distributed" to
form a bell-shaped curve. Norms are set so that fully half the children in
the country are performing below and half above their grade level. If
students were instead judged according to an absolute standard, their
scores would be based on the actual percentage of test items that they
answered correctly; 75 out of 100 might be passing score. Recently there
has been growing interest in *mastery testing*. The items in a mastery test
measure significant pieces of information or particular skills that should
be known as such to the people being tested (Cleary et al., 1975). In mastery tests, in principle, everyone can score 100%. Traditional achievement

tests are designed so that most children score 50%. Measures of individual differences are not appropriate for the assessment of how well schools teach.

Behavioral scientists have known for a long time that children growing up in impoverished environments earn low scores on intelligence and achievement tests. Whether a child's performance is above or below those of others of the same age depends on many factors. As we indicated earlier, some of these factors are associated with the way a test is constructed, the situation in which it is given, or the child's emotional state at the time. Other factors are associated with inadequate nutrition and poor health, and still others with the behavior or attitudes of parents or the life circumstances of the family.

Test Performance and Children's Experience

EFFECTS OF PARENTAL ATTITUDES AND BEHAVIORS. Much of the evidence relating the characteristics of parents and children's intellectual development is correlational. Parents who accept and approve of their children, encouraging them to interact freely with the environment tend to have children who perform well. On the other hand, parents who consistently reject their children, forbidding them to explore and punishing them harshly and coercively tend to have children who perform poorly on intellectual tasks. Children who learn early through aversive conditioning that exploring the world leads to unhappy experiences and punishment may simply stop thinking and so show less curiosity in exploring and manipulating the world (Hurley, 1965). In fact, the overwhelming majority of studies show that parental behaviors such as being accepting, encouraging independence, and valuing and rewarding achievement are positively correlated with their children's intellectual growth.

Researchers in the Berkeley Guidance Study (Honzik, 1967) found different achievement patterns for boys and girls. Between the ages of 6 and 18, boys' IQs were correlated with a close relationship between mother and son and with the father's occupational success and satisfaction. Girls, on the other hand, scored higher if their fathers were friendly to them and if their parents were happily married. Both sexes obtained higher scores if their parents were concerned about their achievement (Honzik, 1967).

Another study, the Berkeley Growth Study (Bayley and Schaefer, 1964), showed that the children's own behavior had an influence on their test scores. Girls who as babies were rated as happy, positive, and calm had high early scores, but this influence disappeared after they were 3 or 4. Boys who were happy and calm as babies tended to have low scores during the first 1 or 2 years but high scores after the age of 4 or 5. Boys who were rated as active before 15 months of age had high early scores but lower-than-average scores after 4 years. If they were active *after* 15

Test performance on both IQ and achievement tests is dependent on many factors — the test itself, the situation in which it is given, the child's physical and emotional state, parental attitudes. (Al Kaplan, DPI)

months, the pattern was reversed, and they tended to have high IQs at later ages (Bayley and Schaefer, 1964).

Once children reach school age, their academic *achievement* becomes an issue. Achievement and intelligence tend, of course, to be highly correlated, and we might expect that the same parental behaviors associated with high intelligence would also be associated with achievement. Studies have shown that the parents of high achievers tend to praise their children, to show interest in them and feel close to them, to make them feel as if they "belong" in their families. Children who are high achievers, in turn, identify with their parents. The parents of underachievers, on the other hand, tend to be domineering, restrictive, and punitive. They may either baby their children or push them too hard, and they may set exaggeratedly low or high demands for achievement (Morrow and Wilson, 1961).

Many studies measure children's achievement by only one criterion: performance in school. Success in school seems to be associated with parents' making explicit demands for achievement, and even with somewhat authoritarian parental behavior. But there are measures of "achievement" in addition to good grades in school. Some personality traits that are important for nonacademic achievement—such as curiosity, creativity, and internal motivation for achievement—may not be encouraged by authoritarian control or high demands for achievement. One study (Crandall and Battle, 1970) found that different kinds of parental behavior were correlated with two measures of adult achievement: academic effort (performance in courses in high school and college) and intellectual effort (intellectual pursuits outside of school). Academic effort was related to help-seeking behaviors and proximity-seeking dependency in the first 6 years of life. Adult *intellectual* effort, however, was associated with independence training at 3 to 6 years of age.

Maternal behavior that either encourages or discourages independence also seems to be associated with different kinds of cognitive capacity in children. We indicated earlier that the Stanford-Binet test measures two kinds of IQ—verbal and performance. Many children, of course, achieve approximately the same scores on both measures, but some show significant differences. In general, girls do better on verbal tests, boys on performance tests. One study of fifth-grade boys and girls with strikingly different scores showed that the high-verbal-group mothers were stricter and encouraged more dependence. High verbal abilities appeared to be associated with a demanding and somewhat intrusive mother; nonverbal abilities were associated with mothering that allows the child a considerable degree of freedom to experiment on his or her own (Bing, 1963).

Correlational evidence is often interpreted as meaning that parents influence the development of their children, although technically correlations only indicate the strength of a relationship, not the direction of the influence. Indeed, developmental psychologists are beginning to explore the idea that development is a bidirectional process, in which children influence parents just as parents influence children. According to this position, the influence is reciprocal rather than one-way from parent to child (cf. Sameroff and Chandler, 1975; Bell, 1968).

Not all psychologists, however, agree with this position. Hoffman (1975) has recently argued that bidirectional influence does not mean that the contributions of parent and child have equal weight in all things. Parents control material and social resources and make most of the day-to-day decisions regarding how these resources are to be used to satisfy their own needs as well as the needs of their child. Parents make decisions about books and playthings, about the management of household affairs,

In general, when parents value and model positive attitudes toward intellectual tasks, they instill these attitudes in their children.
(The Merrill-Palmer Insitute)

about the family's involvement with friends and relatives. Parents may deliberately or casually encourage children's interests in mechanical, scientific, civic, athletic, or literary things and attach to their encouragement different standards of achievement. They can respond positively, or they can ignore or belittle interests expressed by the child. In addition, there is a large body of research that demonstrates children's sensitivity to adults as models and as reinforcers (cf. Bandura and Walters, 1963; Risley and Baer, 1973) and another that demonstrates that children perceive their parents as powerful figures (Emmerich, 1959). Although children are far from passive members of the family, and although they may resist adult wishes or modify adult behavior, they are dependent during the early and middle years on adults and on environments created by adults. From this perspective, then, the evidence suggests that in general, when parents value achievement in themselves and their children —and themselves serve as models—they get it. When they value and model a positive attitude toward intellectual tasks, they instill this in their children.

EFFECTS OF FAMILY CONFIGURATION. Children's IQs are also related to family configuration—by family size, the presence or absence of the father, the number and ages of siblings, by being the oldest, youngest, or middle child. Parent-control models such as that advocated by Hoffman can be contrasted with models that stress sociological processes. These models see the family unit as a factor in determining the environment in which children are reared, the context in which psychological processes are expressed. We will examine those relationships in this section.

Father absence. Over 10% of children in the United States are reared in homes where there is no father. Countless others—the children of busy executives, traveling salesmen, night-shift workers—see their fathers only rarely. What effect does the fathers' absence have on the intellectual development of these children? The answer, of course, depends partially on other factors: whether the father's absence is caused by death, divorce, or occupation; how long the absence lasts; the child's age when the absence occurs; the child's relationship with his or her mother; the presence or absence of siblings; whether the child is a boy or a girl.

In general, father absence is associated with cognitive deficits (Hetherington and Deur, 1972; Zajonc, 1976). These deficits are apparent not only in school-aged children, but they also extend into young adulthood. Students—both boys and girls—whose fathers were absent when they were young do worse on college entrance examinations than those whose fathers were present (Sutton-Smith, Rosenberg, and Landy, 1968; Landy, Rosenberg, and Sutton-Smith, 1969; Carlsmith, 1964). Low father availability—under 6 hours a week—may be almost as severe in its consequences as father absence (Hetherington and Deur, 1972; Landy et al., 1969). The younger the child is when the absence occurs, the worse the consequences are for IQ (Zajonc, 1976).

In addition, father absence is associated with children's learning of their sex roles. Boys whose fathers are absent tend to be more feminine and less aggressive during early childhood, although they may exhibit "compensatory masculinity"—exaggeratedly masculine and assertive behavior—later on. Girls, on the other hand, seem to learn feminine behavior and roles whether their fathers are present or not. Father-absent girls, though, often have difficulties relating to the opposite sex—either excessive shyness or promiscuity—when they reach adolescence (Hetherington and Deur, 1972). The way children learn sex roles may explain these differences. Many psychologists believe that children learn sex-typed behavior through *identification* with the same-sex parent. Within the family, boys come to pattern their behaviors after the father and girls after the mother.

Sex-role identification may explain one effect of father absence on boys' cognitive development. As we have already seen, boys tend to have higher performance IQs than verbal IQs. This pattern continues through college age, when boys usually do better on the mathematical than the verbal sections of college entrance examinations. For father-absent boys, though, the masculine pattern is reversed: Father-absent boys showed relatively higher verbal than mathematical scores (Hetherington and Deur, 1972). Father-absent boys may, in the absence of a same-sex model, learn a cognitive style more characteristic of females. An alternative explanation for the reversal in scores is the *tension-interference hypothesis.* According to this theory, stress and tension interfere more with the development of mathematical than verbal ability. Some evidence supports this hypothesis: Reversed scores in college males are associated with the loss of *either* parent during childhood, and father absence lowers the mathematics scores of *girls* as well as boys (Hetherington and Deur, 1972). In one study, college girls whose fathers had worked night shifts when they were between 1 and 9 years old showed decreased quantitative scores — although whether the deficits were caused by tension in the household or by the simple lack of interaction with the father is not clear (Landy et al., 1969).

Father absence seems to affect children's cognitive development, academic achievement, development of conscience, sex-role orientation, and social relationships. All these effects are most severe if the father leaves home during the preschool years. Some of them can be modified, though: Boys will be more likely to learn masculine behavior if their mothers encourage and reward it and if they have an older brother; both sexes do better if the mother is loving and emotionally stable (Hetherington and Deur, 1972).

Birth order. At one time or another you may have heard people say: "First kids are smarter than others"; "Kids from large families don't do very well in school"; "Twins aren't as bright as other kids." Popular ideas about the importance of birth order reflect a truth: Intelligence is associated with family configuration.

In a study of over 800,000 students who took the National Merit Scholarship test in 1962 and in 1965, Breland (1974) found that after factors like parental education and socioeconomic status were controlled, students' scores were correlated to birth order and family size. Specifically,

1. Scores generally declined with increased family size — for *all* students from large families.
2. *Within families,* scores declined with birth order.
3. The rate of decline increased for closely-following siblings.
4. Only children scored lower than most other firstborns, even those from large families.
5. Twins in general had low scores (Breland, 1974).

Birth order had a particularly strong influence on verbal scores — not surprisingly, since early verbal stimulation and a close relationship with the mother are especially important for the development of verbal skills. Studies of family configuration and intelligence in the Netherlands, France, and Scotland reveal the same basic patterns. And a study of boys from two-child families who took the American College Entrance Exam-

Children's IQs are related to family size, the number and ages of siblings, and whether one is the oldest, youngest, or middle child. (Suzanne Szasz)

ination showed that firstborns had higher scores and that scores increased with larger age spacings (Zajonc, 1976; Zajonc and Markus, 1975; Rosenberg and Sutton-Smith, 1969).

How and why do family size and birth order influence intellectual development? According to the *confluence model,* the family's intellectual environment is a function of the average intellectual level of its members. (But, not, we should note, a function of their average IQs. A 4-year-old with an IQ of 140 still is not *absolutely* as knowledgeable as the average adult. The intellectual level is closer to being a measurement of mental age.) At the time of the birth of the first child, if we arbitrarily set the parents' intellectual level at 100 each and the newborn's at 0, then the average level is $(100 + 100 + 0)/3 = 67$. Suppose the couple waits to have their second child until the first has reached an intellectual level of 12. The second child would be born into an intellectual environment of $(100 + 100 + 12 + 0)/4 = 53$. The confluence model assumes that intellectual growth is shaped by family interaction and that the family as an intellectual environment is constantly changing. As children develop, they bring about changes in their environment by virtue of their own changes (Zajonc and

386

Markus, 1975). The environment changes most dramatically when there are additions to or departures from the family. According to the confluence theory, IQ differences are influenced entirely by the spacing between siblings. The wider the intervals between children, the more older children will be allowed to develop, thus creating a better intellectual environment for the newborn (Zajonc, 1976).

The confluence model is a neat explanation for the correlation between intelligence and family configuration. It explains why intelligence scores decline for closely spaced children and for successive children in large families. It also explains why, in *very* large families, the sixth or seventh or eighth child—as long as that child is not the last—is apt to be brighter than the next-oldest sibling: Families that include older siblings who have become young adults or adolescents may provide higher-than-average intellectual environments (Zajonc and Markus, 1975). The confluence model provides an alternative explanation for the intellectual deficits associated with father absence: The departure of any adult detracts significantly from the family as an intellectual atmosphere. And the theory explains why twins tend to have lower-than-average test scores. Twins have the shortest possible gap between successive siblings; therefore, their intellectual environment is lower than that for either of two singly born siblings.

Only one of the correlations we listed at the beginning of this section is puzzling in light of the confluence theory: Why do only children score below the expected level? Since they grow up in a family environment composed entirely of adults, we would expect them to do better than other firstborns, not worse. Breland (1974) offers one explanation: Firstborns, when there are other siblings, play a kind of "foreman" role, serving as a link between parents and younger siblings. That role would offer excellent opportunities for the development of verbal skills. Only children, of course, never play the foreman role, never have a chance to be teachers of younger siblings. In their families, they are the last-born children, and the intellectual ability of the last children—whether in families of two or ten—declines much more sharply than that of other siblings (Zajonc and Markus, 1975).

Family configuration may explain some of the IQ differences between population groups. Blacks tend to have larger families than whites, children are born closer together, and fathers are more often absent. The average IQs of American children from various ethnic groups are correlated with family size in those ethnic groups. And reading comprehension scores of children from 13 countries are correlated with the birth rates in those countries: the lower the birth rate, the higher are children's scores (Zajonc, 1976). Family configuration also may account for the steady decline in the average SAT scores since 1963. Educators have blamed this decline on everything from schools' failing to teach basic skills to too much TV watching, but demographic data offer another explanation. The average SAT scores may reflect birth-order fluctuations. Of births in 1947, 42% were first children; after that the percentage of firstborns declined steadily until 1962. Students taking SATs in the mid-sixties, then, included a high proportion of first and second children; since then, the average birth order of students has been declining. In 1963, for the first time since 1947, the percentage of newborns who were first children began to rise and has been increasing steadily since then. Children born in 1963 will take SATs in 1980, and if family configuration does explain the current decline in scores, we may expect that decline to begin to be reversed in the early 1980s (Zajonc, 1976).

COGNITIVE STYLES AND STRATEGIES

There is ample evidence that individuals differ in how well they perform on intelligence tests. However, these tests score only "right" and "wrong" answers; they do not provide any information on *how* the child arrived at the answer. Children differ both in how they do well and in how they do poorly. When they sit down to solve a problem, some children may spend time scanning and exploring its different parts. Some children scan systematically, whereas others scan in an erratic, haphazard way. Other children immediately focus in on a small part of the problem. Some children explore actively for solutions, and some children do so passively. Some children can see only one kind of solution, whereas other children are able to try different possibilities and to give up and start again when one solution fails to work. Some children are easily distracted by irrelevant noise or information, whereas others can control their concentration on the most important aspects of a problem. These kinds of differences among children are generally assumed to reflect cognitive styles and strategies of problem solving. In this section, we discuss two dimensions of individual difference in the way children approach intellectual tasks.

Reflectiveness-Impulsivity

One individual difference among children is the time they take to respond to cognitive problems. Kagan, Moss, and Sigel (1963) have studied this difference, which they term *conceptual tempo*. Styles of conceptual tempo are either *reflective* or *impulsive*. When confronted with a difficult problem —one with a high degree of response uncertainty—impulsive children respond quickly, giving the first answer that occurs to them, whereas reflective children take their time. Because they respond quickly, impulsive children make more errors than reflective children (Messer, 1976).

Kagan identifies children as impulsive or reflective by measuring their performance on two kinds of tests. In the Matching Familiar Figures test (MFF), children are shown one picture (the standard), and six very similar pictures, only one of which is identical to the first (see Figure 12–3). They are asked to choose the one that is identical. In the Haptic Visual Matching

FIGURE 12–3
Sample item from the Matching Familiar Figures (MFF) test

test (HVM), children are allowed to touch for as long as they like a wooden form that they cannot see. Then they are shown five visual stimuli, one of which corresponds to the form they have touched, and are asked to pick out that one. In both tests, children who respond quickly make more mistakes, and the children who respond quickly in one test tend to respond quickly in the other. Until age 10, children respond more slowly and make fewer mistakes as they grow older. Kagan claims that the change is caused not by "more mature cognitive structures" but by children's tendency to become more reflective as they grow older (Kagan, 1965). Recent evidence, however, suggests that response times decrease after 10 years of age and that fast response is then no longer associated with errors (Salkind, 1978). Although reflectiveness changes with age, Kagan argues that conceptual tempo is a relatively stable dimension of children's personalities.

According to Kagan, differences in conceptual tempo influence children's behavior in a wide range of situations. He has found that children already classified as impulsive or reflective on the basis of their MFF and HVM performances tend to display the same characteristics during interviews when they are asked questions which allow a number of different responses, such as "What games do you like best?" Impulsive children, when given a test where they are asked to repeat series of 12 words, tend to add extra words; reflective children censor incorrect responses. In another study, impulsive children made more simple reading errors — substitutions like "nose" for "noise," "ruck" for "trunk," "eight" for "eat," and the like. Kagan argues that reflective and impulsive children also behave differently in social situations such as nursery school and day camp. Impulsive children tend to join in games readily and show little fear of physical risk. Reflective children, on the other hand, tend to wait before joining groups, to withdraw from them more frequently, to avoid taking risks, and to work longer at difficult tasks.

Kagan argues that differences in conceptual tempo reflect fundamental differences in personality. Children are often confronted with two conflicting demands: to produce an answer quickly, but to do so without making a mistake. Kagan argues that "the impulsive child places a greater value on 'quick success' than he does on 'avoiding failure'" and that "the reflective child is a low-risk child who avoids situations that are potentially dangerous and productive of failure, humiliation, or harm. The impulsive child prefers a high-risk orientation" (Kagan, 1965, p. 155).

A recent study of black preschool children offers interesting support for Kagan's conclusions. The children were rated as impulsive-reflective on MFF tests and then given the Draw a Line Slowly and Walk Slowly Tests, which measure the ability to inhibit movement on request. The reflective children were significantly more able to inhibit movement than the impulsive children. This finding suggests that even a very young child may have an individual style that leads him or her to respond at a similar tempo to both cognitive and motor tasks (Harrison and Nadelman, 1972). Other research, however, suggests that the slower tempo of reflective children stems more from the use of sophisticated and time-consuming cognitive strategies than from a generalized disposition to respond hastily (McKinney, 1975).

It would seem that learning to slow down — at least in some situations — might be of real benefit to impulsive children. Impulsive children of average verbal ability tend to feel that they are "dumber" than reflective children whose ability is also average — perhaps because the impulsive children more often give wrong answers (Kagan, 1965). Can conceptual style and tempo be changed? Some evidence suggests that they can. Several studies modified these behaviors by reinforcement. For instance, fourth-grade boys classified as reflective, impulsive, and neutral were taught to increase or decrease the speed of their responses (Briggs, 1966).

Direct instruction can also cause children to modify their style and tempo. In one study, children who were asked to delay their responses not only did so, but also produced more analytic responses than did children who were instructed to speed up their responses (Kagan, Rosman, Day, Albert, and Phillips, 1964). However, training impulsive children to respond more slowly does not necessarily reduce error rates. Training children to change their problem-solving strategies, though, does slow down their responses and reduces errors (Meichenbaum and Goodman, 1969). Modeling can also cause children to change their conceptual tempo: second-grade boys who observed an adult performing a conceptual task changed their own tempo in the direction of the model (Denney, 1972). This experiment implies that parents and teachers influence children's conceptual tempo simply by their own example. One study showed that children who were placed in 20 different first-grade classes with teachers who were classified as impulsive or reflective had, by the end of the school year, changed their own tempo in the direction of the teacher's tempo (Yando and Kagan, 1968).

Field Dependence-Independence

Another dimension in which children differ is *field dependence* versus *independence*. This dimension is related to skill in analysis. Field-independent people are able to isolate a problem from its context, to focus on the clues that are relevant for solving it, and to ignore irrelevant information. People who are field dependent, by contrast, "lean" on external cues, seem not to make a clear separation between themselves and things external to themselves, and have difficulty focusing on relevant features of a problem and ignoring distractions.

There are three different tests that measure field dependence-independence. In the Body Adustment Test (BAT), the subject is seated in a tilted chair in a tilted room and asked to adust the chair to the true vertical while the room remains tilted. In the Rod-and-Frame Test (RFT), the subject, who is seated in a totally darkened room, is shown a luminous rod in a luminous frame and asked to adjust the rod to the true vertical, both when his or her own body is tilted and upright and when the rod and frame are tilted in the same or opposite directions. The Embedded Figures Test (EFT) is very much like a certain kind of puzzle in children's books and magazines, where there is a picture of something—say, a forest—and the instructions are to find the five faces hidden in it. In a children's form of the EFT (CHEF), complex figures (such as a car, man, and boat) are embedded in a whole that resembles a jigsaw puzzle, and the child is asked to remove the piece that corresponds to the correct figure (Goodenough and Eagle, 1963). Children's performance on the CHEF test between the ages of 5 and 8 predicts their later performance on field-dependence tests, and individuals' scores between the ages of 10 and 24 tend to be correlated (Kagan and Kogan, 1970). But even though field dependence-independence is a stable characteristic—individuals' relative ranks remain the same—field independence increases as children grow older, at least up to the age of 17.

Field dependence-independence is related to a number of other cognitive skills and personality characteristics. Field-independent children do better on conservation tasks. They tend to have higher IQs, especially on performance measures. Although field independence is not correlated with most verbal skills, field-independent children score high on tests of the ability to make their ideas intelligible to others. For example, field-independent children draw more detailed and complete human figures than do others (Kagan and Kogan, 1970). What kinds of personality characteristics are associated with field dependence? Studies show that field-dependent adults tend to be passive and dependent in interpersonal relationships. Children who score high in field independence tend to score high on such measures of achievement behavior—they persist in the face of a difficult task; they are eager to acquire complex motor skills and to do so without excessive reliance on others. Field-dependent children, by contrast, look to others for approval and are sensitive to changes in emotional climate. Disapproval is more likely to disrupt the performance of field-dependent children (Kagan and Kogan, 1970).

Mothers who encourage independence but also teach their children to control aggression seem to foster the development of field independence. Curiously, boys' field independence scores seem to resemble those of their mothers, whereas girls' scores are correlated with those of their fathers. Males, in general, do better on measures of field independence than females, although the difference is small and does not appear until after children are 8 years old. There are a number of possible explanations for the difference. Field independence is highly correlated with spatial ability, and girls generally do worse than boys on all kinds of spatial tasks, whether because of cultural sex-typing—boys play with blocks and erector sets, girls with dolls and tea sets—or because of biological factors. (Some investigators think that the ability to visualize spatial relationships may be influenced by a recessive gene on the X chromosome—a gene that would be more often unmasked in males than in females [Loehlin et al., 1975]).

Researchers have tended to assume that field independence is a desirable characteristic. But although field-independent children are highly task-oriented, to be this way is not always adaptive. Ruble and Nakamura (1972) compared field-dependent and -independent children in a task in which the adult sometimes offered information that would help the children solve the problem. Field-dependent children were more likely to make use of this information. Sometimes attention to incidental cues, whether in the physical environment or in the behavior of other people, can help in solving problems (Ruble and Nakamura, 1972). In problem solving, creativity may involve openness to seemingly irrelevant ideas and suggestions.

CREATIVITY

Creativity, like intelligence, is something most people agree is "good." Although we know intuitively that the two terms mean different things, they have sometimes been difficult to distinguish in practice. When teachers are asked to rate children for their creativity, the teachers give high ratings to children who score high on intelligence tests and do well in school. When children are asked to list the most creative children in their class, they tend to do the same thing. In this section, we discuss research that attempts to define what "creativity" really is by identifying the characteristics of creativity that are different from those of general intelligence.

Divergent and Convergent Thinking

According to Guilford (1957), "intelligence" and "creativity" represent two fundamentally different kinds of thinking: *convergent* and *divergent*. Convergent thinking, which is characteristic of intelligence, involves finding the one correct solution to a problem. IQ tests, achievement tests, and most activities students pursue in the classroom—whether solving math problems, memorizing spelling words, or using the card catalogue to find books in the library—are exercises in convergent thinking. Divergent thinking, which is characteristic of creativity, involves going out in a number of different directions, in situations where there is not one right answer, but many possible answers. Writing a story, painting a picture, and setting up a scientific experiment require divergent thinking (Nunnally, 1972).

Guilford and his colleagues designed a large number of tasks that attempt to identify particular aspects of divergent thinking. In Guilford's tests, children are asked to think of clever captions for pictures and to write clever endings for stories, to list words beginning with a specified letter or names of objects that roll on wheels, and to construct sentences using a given series of letters for the beginning of each word. Children are also asked to use a colored shape as the starting point for a picture or to draw specified objects using a given series of geometric shapes (see Figure 12–4). Another task measures children's ability to think of ingenious solutions to problems. For example,

A truck is rushing medical supplies to a flooded town. Ten miles from the city, the truck driver discovers that his truck is about 1 inch too tall to go under a railroad overpass. There are no roads nearby that will allow him to go around the overpass. Every minute is important. What should he do? (Nunnally, 1972, p. 427)

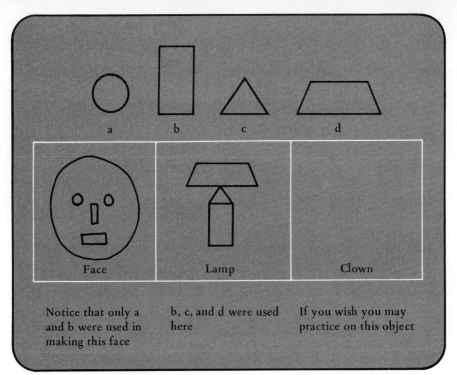

FIGURE 12–4
Sample item from Guilford's tests to measure divergent thinking. Here, children are asked to make the objects named in each box by using the figures provided.
(From the Southern California Tests of Divergent Production. Making Objects.)

In the Torrance tests of creative thinking, which are modeled on Guilford's, the "just suppose" item asks children to describe what would happen if clouds had strings attached that hung down to earth (Torrance, 1966).

Although the Guilford tests are designed to measure divergent thinking, the way in which they are administered may convey to children a mode appropriate to convergent (right answer) thinking. Children are given strict time limits for completing the Guilford tasks, and some of the items seem to limit the child to finding the "right" answer (Wallach, 1970). For example, in the story quoted above, there really seems to be only one correct answer: letting some air out of the truck's tires. Like the Guilford tasks, the Torrance tests are administered within relatively brief time limits. Moreover, they are given by the teacher, and the instructions imply that some answers are better than others. The time limits and the school testing situation are not conducive to creativity (Wallach and Kogan, 1965). Children given the Torrance tasks may well feel that they are just taking another test. Under these conditions, it would not be surprising to find a correlation between creativity and intelligence scores. Indeed, as a whole, the Guilford tests of creativity do correlate highly with tests of intelligence (Wallach, 1970). Many of the Guilford tasks, then—as with teachers being asked to say which students are "creative"—seem to measure general intelligence, not creativity. The one *type* of creative task that correlates with IQ less highly is the one designed to tap ideational fluency.

Ideational fluency refers to a person's ability to produce a large number of ideas appropriate to a given task (Wallach, 1970). When people are asked, for example, to name all the uses they can think of for bricks, the *first* ideas that come to mind are likely to be fairly conventional. Unusual or unique ideas are more likely to occur after conventional ideas have been generated. The more time given, the more relaxed and gamelike the atmosphere, and the more plentiful the individual's own flow of ideas, the more likely the person will be to hit upon original ideas. How is "originality" to be measured? As we use the word every day, it may have one of two meanings: "cleverness" or "unusualness." Some of the Guilford tasks — such as writing a caption for a picture or an ending for a story — measure cleverness, which is more a function of verbal intelligence than of ideational fluency. Ideational fluency, on the other hand, is independent of verbal skills, and cleverness is not a criterion for measuring it. In measures of ideational fluency, what counts is the number of responses the child can generate and how many of them are unusual — statistically unique. The two measures are related to each other, for children who can generate a lot of ideas also tend to come up with a good number of unusual or unique ones (Wallach, 1970). Ideational fluency is facilitated by testing contexts that convey a minimum of evaluation. The free and spontaneous flow of ideas can be blocked if children feel that each response is being judged as "right" or "wrong," "clever" or "dull."

The notion that creativity springs from ideational fluency — the free play of ideas that are not yet critically evaluated — is consistent with creative people's descriptions of how they discover new ideas. John Dryden wrote that his poetry involved the generating of "a confus'd Mass of Thoughts, tumbling over one another in the Dark" (quoted in Ghiselin, 1955, p. 80). Ingmar Bergman (1960) has written that each of his films began "with something very vague . . . split-second impressions that disappear as quickly as they come" (p. 15). Many creative artists have felt, like Mozart, that their ideas came to them from somewhere outside themselves: "*Whence* and *how* they come, I know not; nor can I force them" (quoted in Ghiselin, 1955, p. 44). If the "somewhere else" from which ideas come is the individual's own subconscious, then a context of freedom and play would facilitate their emerging to the surface.

The Remote Associates Test (RAT), developed by Mednick (1962), is a good example of a standardized test that focuses on ideational fluency. Children are given a series of items, each consisting of three words, and asked to find a word that is related by association to all three. Some sample items are: rat, blue, and cottage; go, poke, and molasses; sixteen, heart, and cookies; surprise, line, and birthday; railroad, girl, and class. (The answers are cheese; slow; sweet; party; and working.) At first glance, the RAT may look like a conventional test of convergent thinking, since it is standardized and there is only one correct answer for each item. The three words in each item, though, are connected *by association only*, not by logic. According to the theory behind the test, "the likelihood of solving this kind of associative problem should depend on how numerous—and therefore also how unusual—are the associates that the person produces in response to the three words that are offered. The greater this productivity, the easier it will be for the person to hit upon the word that provides an associative 'mediating link' to the other three" (Wallach, 1970, p. 1224).

In fact, several studies of RAT performance tend to confirm the theory. Individuals' scores on the RAT *are* highly correlated with productivity and uniqueness of content in tests of ideational fluency. They are *not* highly correlated with intelligence or academic achievement. Low RAT scorers do have a lower intelligence mean, but high and medium scorers have comparable levels of intelligence (Wallach, 1970). The intelligence-free variance in RAT scores also correlates with research creativity. What is the nature of the individual difference? Why do some people do well and some—equally intelligent—people do poorly?

People who score high on the RAT seem to employ their attention in a special way—from the center to the periphery of a set of ideas. A number of studies indicate that what the RAT measures is breadth of attention (Wallach, 1970). Once again, the descriptions of creative artists confirm the idea that breadth of attention—the tendency to let the mind wander to matters that seem peripheral, and perhaps to let it wander in several directions at once—is an important part of the creative process. John Dryden described poetic wit as "the faculty of imagination in the writer which, like a nimble spaniel, beats over and ranges through the field of memory till it springs the quarry it hunted after" (quoted in Miner, 1969, p. 112). People who do well on the RAT are able to diffuse their attention over a wide range of associations. They also pick up incidental cues from the external environment. When high RAT scorers take the test after seemingly irrelevant prompting from an experimenter, they use the cues, whereas low scorers do not (Mednick, Mednick, and Mednick, 1964).

Besides the RAT, the tests that best measure creativity in isolation from intelligence are those devised by Wallach and Kogan. Wallach and Kogan, who based their approach to creativity on the introspective accounts of creative people, concluded that the essentials of the creative process are "the production of associative content that is abundant and unique" and "the presence...of a playful, permissive task attitude" (Wallach and Kogan, 1965, p. 289). Because Wallach and Kogan recognized that stereotyped associations tend to come first and unique associations later, they set no time limit at all for the completion of their tasks. Be-

Behavioral Characteristics of Various Dimensions of Creativity and Intelligence

High creativity-high intelligence: These children can exercise within themselves both control and freedom, both adultlike and childlike kinds of behavior.

High creativity-low intelligence: These children are in angry conflict with themselves and with their school environment and are beset by feelings of unworthiness and inadequacy. In a stress-free context, however, they can blossom forth cognitively.

Low creativity-high intelligence: These children can be described as "addicted" to school achievement. Academic failure would be perceived by them as catastrophic, so that they must continually strive for academic excellence in order to avoid the possibility of pain.

Low creativity-low intelligence: Basically bewildered, these children engage in various defensive maneuvers ranging from useful adaptations such as intensive social activity to regressions such as passivity or psychosomatic symptoms.

Source: Wallach and Kogan, 1965, p. 303.

cause of the importance of a relaxed, playful atmosphere, the first Wallach-Kogan tasks were given to children not by their teachers, but by outside experimenters who were introduced as visitors interested in children's games. They presented the tasks to each child individually as "potential games" rather than as tests (Wallach, 1970).

The Wallach-Kogan tasks consist of items that measure five different kinds of associations. In the *instances* task, children are asked to name as many things as they can think of in a given category, such as "round things" or "things that move on wheels." The *alternative uses* requests children to give as many uses as possible for things like a shoe or a cork. In the *similarities* task, they are asked to think of all the ways in which a given pair of objects—cat-mouse, milk-meat—are alike. In the *pattern meanings* task, children are shown a number of abstract patterns and asked to think of all the possible meanings or interpretations for each design; the *line meanings* task requests them to do the same thing for line forms. The children's responses are scored according to two variables: the number of responses and their uniqueness.

The Wallach-Kogan tasks were first administered to 151 fifth graders under the experimental conditions described above. The same children were also given a series of conventional intelligence tests. When their scores were analyzed, the results showed that creativity measures of the different tasks were highly correlated with one another, as were scores on the different intelligence tests, but the cross-test correlations were low. These findings indicate that the Wallach-Kogan tasks, like the RAT, measure a general and pervasive dimension of individual differences that is independent of general intelligence (Wallach and Kogan, 1965).

Wallach and Kogan were interested not simply in measuring creativity, but in its psychological significance, in the ways creative children *behave* differently from others. They divided the fifth graders into four groups based on their scores on the two kinds of tests: high creativity-high intelligence; high creativity-low intelligence; low creativity-high intelligence; and low creativity-low intelligence. Before administering any tests, the experimenters had spent two weeks observing the children's behavior in school, both in the classroom and on the playground with their peers. The observers had then answered a series of questions for each child, such as "To what degree does this child seek attention in unsocialized ways like speaking out of turn or making noise?" "To what degree is this child's companionship sought after by his peers?" "How would you rate this child's attention span and concentration on academic work?" When the observers' findings were compared with the children's test scores, there emerged striking differences in the ways the four groups of children adapted to school.

The children who were both highly intelligent and highly creative had by far the best time in school. The girls in this group were the most self-confident and the least hesitant; they sought the companionship of their peers and were in turn sought after; they were highly attentive to and interested in their academic work. They also rated rather high in disruptive, attention-seeking behavior—which may have been the result of sheer high spirits. By contrast, the group that was worst off were the children who were highly creative but low in intelligence. They were the most cautious and least self-confident of all the groups; they both avoided and were avoided by their peers; they belittled their own academic work and had trouble concentrating; they engaged in disruptive behavior that seemed to be "an incoherent protest against their plight" (Wallach and Kogan, 1965). By comparison even the children who were low in *both* intelligence and creativity did rather well: They were more self-confident and less hesitant and much more outgoing in relationships with their peers (Wallach and Kogan, 1965).

Does creativity increase or decrease with age? Wallach and Kogan's findings suggest that, like intelligence, creativity is a relatively stable characteristic. When their original group of fifth graders was retested in the tenth grade, ideational productivity and uniqueness showed substantial stability over the intervening 5-year period (Kogan and Pankove, 1972). For girls, in grade 5 and later in grade 10, IQ was unrelated to creativity. For boys, however, creativity and intelligence scores began to converge in grade 10, as if for boys convergent and divergent thinking come to be mutually complementary.

SEX DIFFERENCES

"Boys are more aggressive than girls." "Girls are more compliant." "Girls are raised to have less self-esteem than boys." These statements, as well as many other generalizations, reflect a widespread popular belief that many of the most important differences between children are related to sex. Parents and teachers, who have many opportunities to observe children, may be convinced that boys and girls really do behave very differently—and they may see exactly what they expect to see. In one study, for example, teachers were asked to rate activity levels of each of their students. Teachers gave the boys higher average ratings—but when each child's activity was measured by machine (an "actometer"), no difference between the sexes was found (Maccoby and Jacklin, 1974). Stereotypes are powerful things that cause us to see behaviors that confirm our beliefs and to disregard behaviors that do not. The women's liberation movement has brought a new urgency to questions about sex differences: Which—if any—differences between boys and girls are genuine, and which are stereotypes? Maccoby and Jacklin's review (1974) of the literature on sex differences found that a number of widely accepted stereo-

By middle childhood, boys and girls have acquired sex-role behaviors and interests and play most often with others of the same sex. (Optic Nerve, Jeroboam; right, Peter Southwick, Stock, Boston)

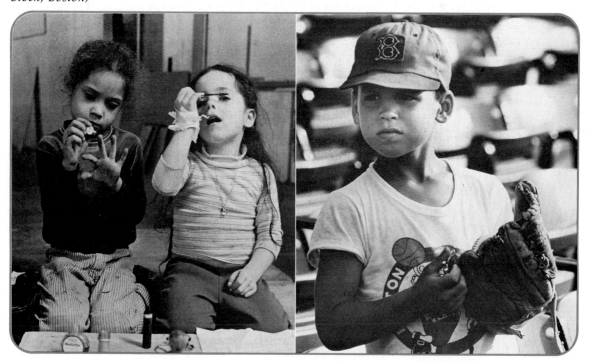

1. *Girls are more "social" than boys.* They are not. In early childhood, the sexes are equally dependent on their caregivers, equally responsive to social rewards, and spend equal amounts of time with other children. Boys are more peer-oriented and play in larger groups; girls get together in small groups and may be more adult-oriented.

2. *Girls are more "suggestible" than boys.* Both sexes are equally likely to imitate others spontaneously and to be influenced by "persuasive communications."

3. *Girls have lower self-esteem.* Boys and girls do not differ in overall self-esteem in childhood or adolescence, and what little information there is about adults does not show a sex difference. Girls tend to pride themselves on their social skills, boys on their strength and dominance.

4. *Girls are better at rote learning and simple repetitive tasks, boys at tasks that require higher-level cognitive processing and the inhibition of previously learned responses.* Boys and girls are equally proficient in rote learning and in higher-level cognitive tasks. Preschool boys may be somewhat more impulsive—lacking in inhibition—but this difference, if it exists, disappears by the time children reach school age, when the sexes are equal in their ability to wait for a reward and to inhibit first impulses on the Matching Familiar Figures Test.

5. *Boys are more "analytic."* Girls do as well as boys on tasks that involve field independence, *except when the tasks are visual-spatial.*

6. *Girls lack achievement motivation.* Observational studies and tests under "neutral" conditions show that girls are equal—and possibly even superior—to boys in achievement motivation. Boys' achievement motivation tends to be dormant until it is aroused by competition.

Source: Maccoby and Jacklin, 1974, pp. 349–351.

types are simply without foundation; others are still "open questions"; and there are a few genuine differences. (Of the three statements at the beginning of this paragraph, the first is true; the second is an open question; the third is false.)

Knowing that boys and girls behave differently is not enough to explain *why* they do so. Much debate about the origin of sex differences has centered on the old issue of heredity versus environment: Are sex differences primarily biological, or are they caused by differences in the ways boys and girls are raised? As we have argued in our discussions of hereditary and environmental influences on intelligence, it is not possible—nor theoretically justifiable—to treat heredity and environment as separate, mutually independent influences, nor to determine whether a given behavior is caused by one or the other. In the case of sex differences, genes and environment begin to interact as soon as the doctor says, "It's a boy" or "It's a girl," and parents begin calling the baby "he" or "she," dressing it in blue or pink. In the following discussion, we will examine three factors that influence the development of sex differences: biological differences, socialization, and the child's own spontaneous learning of sex-typed behavior. We should recognize at the outset, however, that "masculinity" and "femininity," like IQ, are shaped by a transactional relationship between genes and environment.

Maccoby and Jacklin (1974) argue that sex differences in aggression may, indeed, be biological in origin. The difference is cross-cultural; it also has been observed in primates; and there is reason to believe it is linked to hormones, the androgens that male fetuses receive prenatally. On the other hand, it does *not* seem to be true that parents or teachers "tolerate" or "encourage" aggression in boys more than in girls. In fact, teachers are more likely to interfere when one child picks on another if the child is a boy. Boys, then, may be more biologically predisposed toward aggression than girls. However, this difference by itself would not be enough to account for sex differences in dominance, competitiveness, and

Sex Differences That Are Fairly Well Established

1. *Girls have greater verbal ability than boys.* During the early school years, boys and girls are equal in verbal ability, but after age 11 female superiority increases. Girls score higher both in fluency and "higher-level" tasks like analogies, comprehension of difficult material, and creative writing.

2. *Boys excel in visual-spatial ability.* During childhood, boys and girls are equal in spatial skill, but male superiority increases during adolescence and through the high-school years.

3. *Boys excel in mathematical ability.* Boys begin to do better in math than girls after about age 12, but the difference is not as great, and is much more variable, than the difference in spatial skills—perhaps because solving math problems often involves both spatial and verbal skills.

4. *Males are more aggressive.* This sex difference has been observed in all cultures, and exists in children as young as 2 years, and continues through the college years. Boys are more aggressive verbally as well as physically.

Source: Maccoby and Jacklin, 1974, pp. 351–352.

activity level—much less for the many differences between boys and girls in sex-typed behavior.

The shaping of boy-like and girl-like behavior by parents, teachers, and relatives offers another way of explaining the differences between boys and girls. Many people believe that parents pay more attention to boys than to girls or that parents encourage boys to be more independent than girls. Maccoby and Jacklin, though, found that overall, the sexes are treated with equal affection and are equally encouraged to be independent. But there are some differences. Parents play more roughly with boys and more often punish them physically. And parents are much more anxious about boys' learning sex-typed behavior. Parents may tolerate—or even be proud of—their daughter's being a tomboy but may be extremely worried if their son is a "sissy" or plays with dolls. Socialization, though, does not explain all the differences between boys and girls. As Maccoby and Jacklin note, it does not account for differences in intellectual ability or even for all of children's sex-typed play. Girls, after all, are not specifically reinforced for doing poorly in math or for playing with jacks and jump-ropes.

If neither biology nor socialization explains sex differences, then what does? According to the psychoanalytic theory of identification, which we discussed earlier, the process of identification with the same-sex parent accounts for why children adopt the role appropriate for their sex. Social learning theory offers a somewhat different account. Maccoby and Jacklin (1974) explain that social learning theory "also emphasizes imitation, but argues that children are more often reinforced when they imitate a same-sex than an opposite-sex model, so that they acquire a generalized tendency to imitate not only the same-sex parent but other same-sex models as well" (p. 363). There are problems, though, with both theories. Studies of parent-child resemblances do not show that children resemble the same-sex more than the opposite-sex parent or that they are notably similar to either parent. When children under 5 years old are given a chance to imitate a same-sex or opposite-sex model, they are not more likely to choose the same-sex model—even though children's behavior at this age is clearly sex-typed. Moreover, much of children's sex-typed behavior does not resemble that of adult models: "Boys select an all-male play group, but they do not observe their fathers avoiding the company of females. Boys choose to play with trucks and cars, even though they may have seen their mothers driving the family car more frequently than their fathers" (Maccoby and Jacklin, 1974, p. 363). Imitation of parents and other adults, then, does not wholly account for sex-typed behavior.

Kohlberg (1966) has proposed a cognitive-developmental explanation for how children learn sex roles. He argues that children learn sex-typed behavior through a kind of "self-socialization." Children's notions about sexual identity are "cartoon-like" and based on observation of external features: Asked why the figure in a picture is a girl, the child is likely to

1. *Fear, timidity, and anxiety.* Experimenters who observe children have not found that girls behave more fearfully, but teachers report that girls are more timid, and girls themselves report more feelings of fear and anxiety. Girls may simply be more willing than boys to admit they are afraid.

2. *Activity level.* Boys and girls are equally active during infancy, but some studies show that boys are more active when children reach the age of social play. The presence of other boys appears to stimulate bursts of high activity.

3. *Competitiveness.* Some studies indicate that boys are more competitive, others that the sexes are similar.

4. *Dominance.* Dominance seems to be more of an issue in boys' groups; boys try more often to dominate each other and adults. It is difficult to tell whether males tend to dominate females, since boys and girls of school age usually play in separate groups. In mixed groups of adults, men usually take the lead initially, but women become more influential as authority comes to depend on individual skills.

5. *Compliance.* Girls are more compliant to adult demands than boys, but boys may be more vulnerable to pressure from their peers.

6. *Nurturance and "maternal" behavior.* Cross-cultural studies show that girls between age 6 and age 11 behave nurturantly more often than boys. The few studies of nurturant behavior in American children do not show a sex difference in this regard. Adult men and women are equal in altruism, or the willingness to help others in distress.

Source: Maccoby and Jacklin, 1974, pp. 352–354.

reply, "Because she wears a skirt." Children pick up information about boy-like and girl-like behavior from everywhere—parents, other children, television. And they may distort the information in the process, like the 4-year-old girl who insisted that girls could not be doctors, only nurses—even though her own mother was a doctor (Maccoby and Jacklin, 1974). Kohlberg's theory predicts that is is not until children have the requisite cognitive capacity (1) to know their own sex, (2) to see this sex as constant, and (3) to be able to identify the sex of others, that they can imitate a same-sex model. This cognitive capacity takes a long time to develop: 3-year-olds, for example, usually know their own sex but may not see it as constant. Differences in age are often more important to children than differences in sex, and "when I grow up" is a time when anything might happen. Thus some 3-year-old boys insist they will grow up to be "mommies." Four-year-olds may be able to identify other children as girls or boys but still lump all adults together as "grown-ups." Children cannot engage in selective imitation of same-sex models until they are sure about what other people's sexes are.

A number of studies seem to confirm Kohlberg's theory. Children before about 5 do not consistently choose to imitate same-sex models; afterward, they begin to show a preferences for models of their own sex. In two studies of children between ages 5 and 11, Wolf (1973, 1975) found that children played longer and more readily with a (so-called) sex-inappropriate toy (an oven for the boys, a truck for the girls) if they had first observed another child of the same sex playing with the toy. The children who had only observed an opposite-sex model playing with the toy were more reluctant to approach it. Another study demonstrates that by age 5½, children prefer to imitate the same-sex parent even in situations where the modeled behavior is not itself sex-typed (Duttamel and Biller, 1969). Although children may not be capable of selective imitation before age 5, sex-typed behavior begins much sooner. The children in Wolf's studies (1973, 1975), for example, seemed to have already acquired strong notions about what toys they ought to play with. In Kohlberg's view (1966), acquiring sexual identity is an active process on the part of the child. When the child knows his or her sex, he or she will begin to match behavior to the attributes believed appropriate for that sex.

SUMMARY

During the middle years, children acquire the social skills needed to participate in large-group settings made up of children of their own age. They are comfortable away from home and ready to transfer their affections and allegiances from parents to teachers. They are emotionally, as well as mentally and physically, ready for the playground and the school. Although differences among children are apparent from birth, they tend to become stabilized in middle childhood and to permeate behavior at home, on the playground, and in school.

Of all the ways in which children may differ from one another, the one that has been studied, discussed, and measured the most is intelligence. Yet behavioral scientists and lay people find it difficult to give a clear, precise definition of intelligence. And tests used to measure intelligence have recently come under serious criticism from psychologists as well as the general public. The first intelligence test—and the model for all those that have followed—was published in France in 1905 by Binet and Simon. It was specifically designed to predict school performance, and findings indicate that intelligence tests measure an aptitude for schooling. In recent years the validity of IQ tests, as they have come to be called, is being challenged. At present, there are many tests that claim to measure intelligence. The Stanford-Binet test attempted to include items that 50% to 65% of children will answer correctly, because the purpose of the test is to identify differences, not similarities, among children. It is norm-referenced, based on current norms. The items vary in difficulty for different age groups. The Stanford-Binet test includes both performance questions and verbal tests.

Intelligence tests are deliberately constructed so as to force the scores to form a bell-shaped or *normal distribution* curve. If it is assumed that intelligence is distributed randomly, or normally, throughout the population, then the vast majority of people would fall somewhere near the middle.

An individual's IQ is not an absolute score but a measure of performance in relation to peers. IQ used to be calculated by comparing mental and chronological ages, but because adult intelligence does not change with age, it is now calculated from tables of norms. The norms are based on the actual test performance of a *standardization sample* — a representative sampling of the population at given ages. But a number of intelligence tests were standardized on white children only and are based on the performance of a group of children years ago.

Intelligence tests are judged according to two criteria: They must be *reliable* and *valid*. Tests are reliable if an individual's score remains essentially unchanged on repetition after a short interval. Tests are valid in content if the items on the test represent the range of abilities people mean when they talk about intelligence. However, relationships between scores on different tests are influenced by several factors — differences in standardization samples, differences in test situations and differences in content. IQ is not an absolute measurement but, rather, indicates a person's relative standing in a group. The studies that have compared the IQs of population groups over long intervals have yielded contradictory findings.

Differences in IQ scores are also associated with differences in social class as well as race. Rural children, as well as blacks, tend to obtain lower than average scores on tests that were standardized on white, urban children. Poverty and life experiences both influence performance on IQ tests.

The purpose of achievement tests differs from that of intelligence tests. Intelligence tests are designed to measure the trait of intelligence, and achievement tests assess what students have already learned. Achievement tests are judged on the basis of *content validity*, whether they cover adequately a given body of intellectual content. In fact, however, achievement tests do not adequately measure what is learned in school.

Behavioral scientists have known for a long time that children growing up in impoverished environments earn low scores on intelligence and achievement tests. Children's performance on these tests depends on other factors as well. Studies show that parental behaviors such as being accepting, encouraging independence, and valuing and rewarding achievement are positively correlated with their children's intellectual growth. Researchers have also found different achievement patterns for boys and girls. And other studies show that children's own behavior influences their test scores.

Children's IQs are also related to family configuration — size, presence or absence of the father, number and ages of siblings, and by being the oldest, youngest, or middle child. Sociological models see the family unit as a factor in determining the environment in which children are reared, the context in which psychological processes are expressed. Father absence seems to affect children's cognitive development, academic achievement, development of conscience, sex-role orientation, and social relationships. Correlation of test scores to birth order and family size indicate: (1) scores decline with increased family size for all children from large families; (2) scores decline with birth order within families; (3) rate of decline increases for closely followed siblings; (4) only children score lower than most other firstborns, even those from large families; (5) twins have lower scores. These influences have been explained by the *confluence model,* which holds that IQ is determined by the average intellectual level of the members of a family.

Intelligence tests score only "right" and "wrong" answers without providing any information on how children arrive at their answers. Differences in the way children go about arriving at answers are assumed to reflect cognitive styles and strategies of problem solving. One individual difference among children is the time they take to respond to cognitive problems. Styles of conceptual tempo are either *reflective* or *impulsive.* Differences in conceptual tempo reflect fundamental differences in personality. Evidence suggests that conceptual style and tempo can be changed by reinforcement, direct instruction, and modeling.

Another dimension in which children differ is *field dependence* versus *independence.* Even though field dependence-independence is a stable characteristic — individuals' relative ranks remain the same — field independence increases as children grow older, at least to the age of 17. Field dependence-independence is related to a number of other cognitive skills and personality characteristics.

Creativity, like intelligence, is something most people agree is good. Creativity and intelligence represent two fundamentally different kinds of thinking: *convergent* and *divergent.* Convergent thinking, which is characteristic of intelligence, involves finding the one correct solution to a problem. Divergent thinking, which is characteristic of creativity, involves going out in a number of different directions, in situations where there are many possible answers.

Ideational fluency refers to a person's ability to produce a large number of ideas appropriate to a given task. In measures of ideational fluency, what counts is the number of responses and how many of them are unique. The two measures are related: Children who can generate a lot of ideas also tend to come up with a good number of unusual or unique ones. The Remote Associates Test (RAT) is a standardized test that focuses on ideational fluency and measures breadth of attention—the tendency to let the mind wander to matters that seem peripheral, and perhaps to let it wander in several directions at once—which is an important part of the creative process. Individuals' scores on the RAT are not highly correlated with intelligence or academic achievement.

There is a widespread, popular belief that the most important differences between children are related to sex. A number of widely accepted stereotypes are without foundation; others are still open questions; and a few genuine differences have been found. "Masculinity" and "femininity," like IQ, are shaped by a transactional relationship between genes and environment. There are three factors that influence the development of sex differences: biological differences, socialization, and spontaneous learning of sex-typed behavior.

CHAPTER 13

Beyond Home: The Child in School

Almost all children between the ages of 7 and 16 spend seven hours a day, thirty-five weeks a year, in the classroom. Going to school has become as central and time-consuming a part of childhood as going to the office and maintaining a home are for the child's parents. In a good school system, with talented teachers and motivated students, school can be a generally exciting, rewarding process of growth and maturity. All too often, though, schools fail to take full advantage of the child's eagerness and enthusiasm. Children might be pressured to meet unreasonably high standards or they might be hindered by low standards. Failure and boredom are the frequent outcomes of the social, educational, and economic conditions that prevent schools from contributing to the intellectual and emotional growth of children. Debates have swirled around traditional authoritarianism versus spontaneity; vocational training versus liberal arts; and standardization versus special programs for the gifted, the slow, and the disadvantaged. Individualizing education to suit the needs and characteristics of each and every child has been offered as a solution to the problem of matching schools to the immense diversity of intellectual and social styles, temperaments, interests, and abilities among children. And yet individualization places the total burden upon teachers, who must deal with countless interactions day by day and minute by minute.

In the study of child development, we are interested first and foremost in what happens to children when they begin to go to school. At what age are children ready to leave their homes and routines for school and a new and less intimate routine? How can children be prepared for the experience of going to school? What kinds of challenges will they meet in school? What systems and curricula are "best" for what types of children? What behavior problems beset the school-aged child? What are the characteristics of teacher-student relationships? What influence do family and peers have on children's success in school? These are some of the questions we will explore in this chapter. The assumption is that school—for better or for worse—influences the development of children. The influence may come about directly, through children's interactions with teachers, peers, and materials, or indirectly, through the way in which school and family work together in the child's interest.

GOING TO SCHOOL

The contrast between the infant and the school-age child is a dramatic one. Physically, the child is bigger and differently proportioned. In terms of body proportions, the 6-year-old's head is now relatively smaller and his or her arms and legs are relatively longer than the infant's. Small and large motor systems are coordinated. Physically, therefore, the school-age child is capable of learning to perform more complex activities. Progressing past the infant's preoccupation with mastering how to walk, the school-age child displays as much preoccupation with mastering how to ride a bike or jump rope. Cognitive changes occur as well. The problem of mastering the basic structure of language has become transformed into the problem of mastering the relation between oral and written language. The problem of how to use a lever has changed to that of how to measure distance and weight.

While children are meeting these new challenges, they are required to make significant social adjustments as well. One morning after breakfast, instead of settling into another day of activities at home with mother, brothers, sisters, and neighborhood playmates, the child is taken to school, where he or she encounters a strange but intriguing series of phenomena. The ratio of children to adults changes drastically. The child may at first feel lost in the crowd of children in the classroom or in a noisy playground. "Teacher" is not like a parent and not like a relative or neighbor either. Although such changes may make them apprehensive, most children are somewhat excited about the possibilities of their new environment. There, unlike home, many of the objects are scaled to the child's size and intended for the child's use. While sitting in their seats, children can reach the tops of their desks comfortably, with their feet on the floor (or close to it), not dangling in the air as when they sit in adult-sized chairs. Sinks are set at a lower, more reachable height than at home. Children learn that books, art supplies, playground equipment are going to be used—at appropriate times—and there is excitement in this promise. For some children, it is comforting to have one's *own* desk or one's *own* pencil. And "teacher" is an admired and respected adult figure. When school-age children are asked to rate adult occupations, they place teacher first, ahead of Supreme Court justice and doctor, although in most other respects their rankings are highly similar to the rankings of adults (Lauer,

Coordination of small and large muscle systems enables the school-age child to perform activities such as learning to print. (Marlis Müller)

1974; Lefebvre and Bohn, 1971). We might note that the tendency to rank teacher first is especially pronounced among black children.

How well the child adapts to the demands and challenges of the new school environment depends on many factors. One of these is the similarity between behavioral techniques used by the mother and those used by the teacher. In preparing their young children for school, different mothers emphasize different things. Some mothers impress their children with the importance of observing rules, obeying the teacher, and being neat. Other mothers try to make school seem appealing. They stress the teacher's role as friend and helpful guide, rather than as an authority figure, and they tell their children that they will make many new friends in class (Hess and Shipman, 1968). The degree to which the actual setting of the child's class matches the child's expectations will have something to do with the amount of success the child will achieve in school.

Types of Classrooms

TRADITIONAL CLASSROOMS. There was a time when almost all American children attended what is now called the "traditional" school. In the most rigid of these classrooms, desks were lined up in neat rows. Each child took an assigned seat and had to secure the teacher's permission to speak out or to get up from the seat. The activities of the school day followed the teacher's lesson plan. The day began with the pledge of allegiance and continued with recitation of multiplication tables, memorization of state capitals and U.S. presidents, and passages of verse. The idea behind traditional classrooms was that organization, structure, and discipline promoted the children's learning. They also, of course, helped teachers establish and maintain control in the classroom.

OPEN CLASSROOMS. In contrast to the traditional schoolroom is the *open classroom*. In open classrooms, the teacher and the students cooperate in planning the curriculum. By having the opportunity to express interest in particular areas of study, the children themselves become organizers of the learning process. Philosophically, the open classroom approach rests on a belief that children are naturally motivated to learn socially valued skills. Accordingly, the function of the open classroom is to tap the spontaneous will to learn by providing a number of appealing alternatives and allowing children to choose the ones they find most interesting.

Cognitively, this educational technique stresses process over results, means over ends. Direct involvement with concrete materials and everyday problems is considered important in developing learning skills, which may then be transferred to tasks such as learning to read and to perform mathematical computations. When it is possible, open classrooms try to teach several skills and subject matters at one time in an integrated lesson. For example, activity centered around an aquarium might include a science lesson on the presence of oxygen in water, an esthetic appreciation of the fishes' colors and movement, and a lesson on survival, that is, that big fish eat smaller ones and that cats like to eat fish. The children may also learn the practical skills of feeding the fish and cleaning out the tank.

Emotionally, the orientation is the "here and now." The children are taught to value expression of feelings, as well as of ideas. They are encouraged to express themselves creatively in drawing, acting, writing, dancing (Spodek, 1971). Feelings are accorded a legitimate status in the academic process. This is limited, of course, by the view that the teacher's primary goal is education, not child therapy.

All these aspects of the open classroom influence both the teachers' and the children's behavior. Resnick (1971) found that children's choices of activities were strongly influenced by the teacher. A good teacher in the open classroom was a leader and guide, effectively managing the child's experiences. The open classroom teacher must be sensitive to the individual personality and needs of each child. Obviously, this requires a great deal of one-to-one activity. Failure of the teacher to understand his or her managerial role diminishes the success of the open classroom as a vehicle for learning. An open classroom without a teacher who leads the children is simply a chaotic classroom.

Although the open classroom is often thought of as highly innovative and unconventional, it has a venerable history in the United States. John Dewey, the noted philosopher and educational reformer, sowed the seeds of this teaching approach in his writings and work at the turn of the twentieth century. Dewey emphasized the active participation of students, teachers, parents, and administrators in the life of the school.

Advocates for informal, open classrooms have surely had an impact on public education. Yet the enthusiasm for such methods seems to be waning. Many school systems are returning to more traditional forms of schooling. Effecting social change through education is a complex process involving numerous issues, such as stability and continuity of the community, economic and educational resources, and previous experiments with innovation. One maxim can be derived from the educational experiments that have been carried out recently: The more the new schooling technique diverges from the family backgrounds, community values, and previous experience of parents and students, the more resistance it will meet.

The distinction between traditional and open classrooms is but one way of describing different school environments. Classrooms—like homes—differ in pace and tempo, in warmth and sociability. Important differences emerge in the way children behave to one another and in the techniques teachers use to manage the social world of the classroom.

LEARNING TO BEHAVE

Perhaps the most important socialization function of the school is to teach children how to behave. There are many ideas about what constitutes "good" behavior. In the traditional classroom, good behavior may consist of being adjusted to the routine, being attentive during lessons, and looking to the teacher for help. In an open classroom, good behavior may be defined as self-initiated exploratory activity and interaction with peers in problem solving. Whatever the form of the classroom, however, the successful teacher learns to manage disruptive behavior that may occur.

Aggression in the classroom can describe a wide range of behavior—from wrestling at the wrong time in the wrong place, to punching the kid in the next seat, to verbally challenging the teacher. Redl (1969) suggests that teachers deal better with classroom aggression if they can identify its source. The child may be angry at something that has happened at home but may not dare express his or her anger anywhere but at school. Aggression may be excess energy from within that can be discharged in more socially acceptable ways. Or aggression may be the child's reaction to something in the immediate environment—boredom, confusion, or an emotional reaction to something the teacher or another student did or said. Redl suggests four techniques that can avert or tone down aggressive behavior. First, teachers can gracefully give children a chance to back off before a confrontation has become too heated. The child saves face, and the class is not overly distracted. Second, teachers can be alert for signals indicating that a child is heading for conflict and can signal him or her in a nonconfrontational way to stop. Third, teachers should avoid the "dare" situation, in which defiant students feel compelled to pit their defiance against the teacher's authority. Fourth, teachers should be aware of the aftereffects of classroom discipline. If a student responds to an early signal to abandon disruptive behavior, the teacher would be wise to have a brief chat with the student later, expressing appreciation for the student's cooperativeness.

There is no doubt that the peer group can exert a positive or negative influence on the incidence of aggressive behavior. This was illustrated in an experiment that has come to be called "Robber's Cave" (Sherif, Harvey, White, Hood, and Sherif, 1961). Two groups of well-adjusted 11-year-old boys were sent to an experimental camp run by researchers who wanted to see what variables encouraged and discouraged aggression. The first stage of the program involved competitive games between two rival factions. Although the contests started out in a spirit of sportsmanship, they soon became rough and hostile. Social events like movies and shared meals did not relieve the group hostility. The rival factions staged raids on each other's units; boys who had been best friends turned against each other. The second stage of the experiment aimed at reconciling the two groups. This was achieved in a few short weeks by contriving emergencies that required the cooperation of both groups. Feigned shortages of food and water that could not be overcome without the help of all gradually reconciled the most bitter of enemies. Sherif and his colleagues concluded that aggression and conflict are engendered by divergent, individual goals, whereas cooperation and harmony result when members of the group perceive one goal as more important than the personal desires of any one individual.

Behavior Modification

The school day is often plagued with a host of behaviors that interfere with the work to be done by student and teacher. Such behaviors include relatively small annoyances like talking out of turn, roaming around the room, and throwing things, as well as more serious problems such as tantrums or fighting. Techniques of behavior modification have proved successful in handling unwanted behaviors in the classroom.

The teacher's attention and approval are a major source of reinforcement for desired behaviors. A study done with a class of highly disruptive sixth graders exemplifies the method of reinforcement systems (Hall, Panyan, Rabon, and Broden, 1968). The first stage involved a *baseline* period, in which disruptive behaviors were simply noted and recorded at 30-minute intervals. After several days, the teacher was asked to increase the number of compliments and approving rewards to students who showed desired study behaviors. The incidence of desired study behaviors rose when reinforcement was given. When the teacher lowered the number of positive, approving reinforcements, desired study behaviors dropped off. They increased once again when the teacher resumed the frequent-approval approach. Thus, by making positive comments to students when they engage in desirable behavior and when they do *not* engage in undesirable behavior, teachers can increase the occurrence of desired behaviors and discourage less favored ones. In the study described above, Hall and his colleagues instructed the teacher to continue positive reinforcement for desired study behaviors, but to discontinue all comments on nonstudy behavior. (Up to this time, the teacher had given reprimands for nonstudy behavior.) When the reprimands were discontinued, there was no significant decline in desired study behaviors. The researchers concluded that the reliable correlation between teacher approval and increased study behavior, in the absence of other variables, indicated the effectiveness of the frequent approval. The insignificant effect that discontinuing reprimands had on study behavior indicated the relative uselessness of negative reinforcement (Hall et al., 1968).

Similar programs have been applied with success to increase concentration and desirable social behaviors and to decrease disruptions like tantrums and talking out of turn. Usually, desired behaviors have been praised and undesired behaviors ignored. Reprimands, when used at all, seem to be most effective when addressed quietly to the individual, rather than to the class at large. With some students, reprimands can backfire. If they receive frequent disapproval and insufficient approval, the result may be an increase in disruptive behavior. It seems that for these students, attention — whether positive or negative — has a reinforcement value in and of itself (Sherman and Bushnell, 1975).

Another behavior modification technique is the use of prizes or tokens to encourage desired behavior. Children are promised tokens or points for performance of specific desired behaviors. The tokens or points are redeemable for prizes such as dolls, comic books, or special privileges at the end of a specified interval ranging from a day to a week. The entire system of rewarding behaviors with prizes is referred to as a *token economy*.

Several different reinforcers may be provided, "priced" in varying numbers of tokens according to their desirability. In a token economy at home, washing the dishes might be worth 10 tokens, mowing the lawn might be worth 20, and finishing homework might be worth 30. Thus it becomes important to produce more instances of desired behavior in order to accumulate more tokens, in order to have a wider choice of reinforcers. Token economies have been used successfully at school to increase study behavior as well as to decrease aggressive behavior.

However, behavior modification techniques have been criticized on several points. First, behavior modification programs are not always effective. In particular, teacher approval by itself frequently fails to serve as a sufficiently powerful reinforcer. Students who are extremely disruptive are often immune to this influence. To alter their behavior, it may be necessary to go beyond the classroom and seek individual or family counseling. Second, some educators feel that the behaviors induced by these techniques are in and of themselves undesirable. Educators and psychologists stress the importance of getting students passionately involved not only with the materials used in learning, but also with the process of learning itself. This emphasis on exuberance and individualism seems at odds with the value placed by behavior modification advocates on conformity and manageability. Third, there is the question of the transferability of behaviors learned in the classroom. In the absence of tokens, the prize or the praise, will students revert to old ways? Will they have the motivation to pursue in real-life situations the rewards that often are elusive and uncertain? These questions remain sources of concern and controversy.

TEACHER EXPECTATIONS AND TEACHER BEHAVIOR

Most educators agree that a talented teacher is more effective in stimulating learning than the most sophisticated equipment. There is disagreement, however, on exactly how and why teachers influence their pupils. One of the most popular hypotheses, referred to variously as "teacher expectation," "teacher faith," or "self-fulfilling prophecy" suggests that teacher perceptions (sometimes inaccurate) of student ability are reflected in the way teachers teach and treat their pupils. The particular treatment in turn yields a particular performance by the students, and thus the teacher's prophecy for the student fulfills itself (Braun, 1976).

Attempts to verify this hypothesis have been influential but controversial. A study by Rosenthal and Jacobsen (1968) claimed to have documented the effects of teacher expectation. In this study, standard tests were administered to several classes, and then five children in each class were randomly designated as "intellectual spurters." It was casually mentioned to their teachers that these children would probably show significant growth during the school year. At the end of the year, the children were tested, and the randomly designated spurters showed marked gains. After one year of the experiment, first- and second-grade "spurters" showed the most improvement. Their teachers described them as being happier, more interesting, and more likely to succeed than the other (control) children. The Rosenthal and Jacobsen study aroused great interest among educators, but later experimenters had difficulty replicating their efforts.

One interesting experiment that supports, in part, the findings of Rosenthal and Jacobsen, is the work of Pippert (1969). On the pretext of validating an earlier test of creativity, children were randomly assigned to one of two groups, "inner controls" and "external controls." Teachers were given the names of several children in the "inner control" group who were supposedly exceptionally creative; they were urged to observe them closely but not to encourage them to any greater achievement. Subsequent testing revealed that explicitly named children made significantly more gains than did children in the "external control" group. Pippert concluded that the teacher's faith in the children who were singled out was related to higher expectations for the "inner control" group as a whole.

Changing teacher expectations is not an easy task, however, since such expectations are based on many different factors. In the experiments described above, pupils of teachers who had no suspicions regarding the supposed purpose of the experiment showed more gains than pupils of teachers who doubted the stated (and indeed false) purpose. Other researchers have shown that teacher expectations are more heavily influenced by "realistic" indicators such as cumulative records, teacher recommendations, and physical traits like attractiveness, motivation, sex, and status. Statements from a group of outside experimenters may not be accorded much credibility (Braun, 1976).

What are the characteristics that determine teachers' expectations for children's social and academic performance? Physical appearance is very important. Teachers judge attractive children as more intelligent, easier to teach, and more motivated than their less attractive classmates (Clifford and Walster, 1973). Unattractive children are more likely to be perceived as antisocial (Dion, 1972). The sex of the pupil may also influence the expectations of the teacher. One experiment indicates that if teachers believe that boys will learn to read as well as girls, this will happen. The opposite is also true (Palardy, 1969). In general, however, teachers express more approval toward girls than boys, probably in the expectation that boys will need more discipline.

Race and socioeconomic status are powerful sources of cues for teacher expectations. One study (Cooper, Baron, and Lowe, 1975) indicated that middle-class students are expected to perform better than lower-class students and that white middle-class students are more often held to be internally responsible for failure than any other students. Black middle-class students are perceived as potentially as successful as their white

classmates, but their failure is more often attributed to external causes.

The social setting of the school may also generate cues for expectations. For example, a novice teacher in a ghetto school may be warned to use a firm approach, which in turn may generate in the students defiance, aggression, and poor academic performance (Howe, 1972). The longer teachers stay in one school and become acquainted with several children from the same family, the more likely they are to base their expectations of a child on the performance of older siblings (Seaver, 1973).

And, of course, teachers deal with new information about children against a backdrop of ideas they already hold. Gaite (1974) believes that new information generates teacher expectations only when it conforms with opinions already held by the teacher. Dworkin (1975), on the other hand, argues that under certain conditions teachers may be led to form expectations on the basis of information that clashes with previously held beliefs. If teachers are at least indirectly involved in a program with a

417

success orientation and continual feedback, they may come to develop expectations of success, where they might otherwise have predicted failure.

How do teachers transmit their expectations to their students? One indication of their expectations is the amount of time a teacher spends interacting with a pupil. Teachers tend to devote more time to high achievers than to low achievers; they also tend to praise high achievers more often (Brophy and Good, 1970). Teachers encourage more responsiveness from children for whom they have high expectations, calling on them more often, posing harder questions, and prompting them to give the right answer (Rosenthal, 1973). Assignment to particular reading or study groups also conveys to the student information about teacher expectations. In a sociometric study of first graders, McGinley and McGinley (1970) found that members of lower-level reading groups chose fewer of their friends from their own reading group than might have been expected. Members of higher-level reading groups tended to choose more of their friends from their own reading group than might have been expected. Grouping can affect school achievement, as well. When children are placed in classes based on an overestimate of their abilities, they perform better on standardized tests than do children whose talents have been underestimated (Tuckman and Bierman, 1971).

And thus, the cycle is perpetuated. Learners who internalize the idea that they perform poorly in relation to their peers will act in accordance with that belief. Their teachers and their peers will then conclude that they were justified in their judgment, and the children are in danger of becoming "locked in" more or less permanently. Yet, whatever teacher expectations they encounter at school, the children's main base—the foundation upon which their academic progress and their reactions to school rest—is their family.

THE INFLUENCE OF THE FAMILY ON SCHOOL ACHIEVEMENT

Although children start their academic careers at about age 6, the family remains the dominant influence in their lives for quite some time. It appears that until the sixth or seventh grade, the child acts primarily on the basis of values and motivations transmitted by parents and other family members. Early in junior high school, a shift to peer orientation takes place. Until the shift to peer values occurs, however, family influence remains the most important determinant of behavior and achievement in school. In his comprehensive study of American education, Coleman (1966) attempted to assess the contribution to academic success of five major variables, ranging from family background to classmate characteristics. After surveying 600,000 children, Coleman concluded that the home environment (including parents' education and income) was the most profoundly influential variable. School characteristics were the second most important factor, but Coleman's data revealed that a strong, supportive home environment can effectively compensate for a deficient school system.

Many different components go into the totality of family life. We have already mentioned parental income and education. The individual personalities of parents also play a role in determining how their children will perform in school. Peterson, Becker, Hellmer, Shoemaker, and Quay (1959) compared two groups of approximately 30 families each to explore the relationship between parental personality and in-class behavior. One group was selected from families referred to a guidance center because of their children's disruptive behavior (the "clinic group"). The other group was composed of families with children rated as well adjusted by their teachers. All the children were 6 to 12 years old.

In general, mothers and fathers in the clinic group were evaluated as less democratic, less social, less well adjusted, and more likely to have problems with disciplining their children than parents in the second group. In particular, the attitudes of clinic fathers appeared to be very influential in generating maladjustment in their children. Personality traits observed frequently in clinic fathers included a lack of concern, autocratic treatment of their children, permissiveness, and low capacity for effective discipline. In addition, clinic fathers tended to be either rigidly organized and highly active or disorganized and poorly motivated in conducting their own affairs. The emphasis on paternal attitudes in Peterson et al.'s findings is interesting because of the doubt it casts on the widely held hypothesis that mothers are the dominant parental influence in middle childhood.

Indeed, there is a great deal of evidence pointing to the role mothers' attitudes play in shaping academic performance in this period. Studies comparing mothers of achievers with mothers of underachievers reveal important differences (Hilliard and Roth, 1969). Mothers of achievers are generally more accepting, whereas mothers of underachievers reject their children in small but important ways. Underachievers sense this rejection and frequently respond by creating crises, like failure in school, designed to elicit maternal attention and concern. When failure produces attention, and success does not, a child may become emotionally dependent on his or her identity as incompetent. In order to fill the primary need for maternal attention, the child may forego fulfillment of secondary needs like mastering new skills and developing a genuine sense of self-esteem (Hilliard and Roth, 1969).

The question of the influence of maternal versus paternal attitudes is further complicated by the sex of the child. It has been argued that parental attitudes influence girls more than boys (Crandall, Dewey, Katkovsky, and Preston, 1964). Forty children were rated for academic ability, using standard intelligence tests. Their parents were interviewed regarding general characteristics like nurturance, rejection, and affection,

How well children adapt to the demands of school depends on the values and motivations transmitted by the family as well as on the school environment. (Camilla Smith)

as well as their specific attitudes regarding academic performance. Although the results were complex, they tend to support the hypothesis that parents do exert more influence over daughters than over sons. Contrary to Peterson et al.'s findings, Crandall and his colleagues found that the mothers of academically competent girls tended to be less affectionate than other mothers. With respect to specific views on intellectual achievement, some attitudes and behaviors of the parents influenced performance; others did not. The *expressed* views of both parents appeared to play an insignificant role. (Crandall et al., 1964).

Finally, let us examine the relationship between socioeconomic status and academic achievement. There is the obvious fact that increased education, leisure time, and higher income enable parents to offer their children more toys, learning situations, and role models. There is an equally important, but more subtle factor at work here, too—the use of language in communicating parental instructions and desires. Parents of different social classes use different behavioral codes in controlling their children. People from the lower socioeconomic classes rely primarily on gestures, facial expressions, intonations, and "unwritten rules." Those from the middle class resort much more often to elaborate verbal communication, full of complex sentence structures, and to individual variations in modes of expression (Bernstein, 1965, 1966). These social class differences are reflected in parent-child interaction and informal teaching at home. In particular, Hess and Shipman (1966, 1968) found that middle-class mothers often use personal statements addressed to the individual child and his or her frame of mind. Their language is instructive and varied; they frequently take the initiative in encouraging new behavior. Lower-class mothers, on the other hand, tend to use commands addressed to their children as a group. Their sentences are shorter and more repetitious. Bernstein (1965) theorizes that these differences in language codes influence, for better or worse, later development in verbal skills. Other theorists have disputed Bernstein's conclusion, claiming that lower-class children do develop complex language codes, but that they frequently feel that the social situation does not call for elaborate self-expression (Fein and Clarke-Stewart, 1973).

LEARNING TO READ

Learning to read tops the list of objectives set for the school-age child by parents, teachers, administrators, and frequently by children themselves. School achievement usually hinges on how well a child can read. If children leave school illiterate, even though well adjusted and happy, the school has failed. Yet learning to read is a complex process. It entails understanding a set of marks as letters and, in combination, as meaningful words. Words must then be grouped into intelligible statements, and the statements grouped into informative or entertaining sequences. The psychology of reading has become over the past decade a major area in child development research.

Reading and Perceptual Theory

From the point of view of perceptual theory, learning to read involves a sequence of tasks of increasing complexity. One of the foremost analysts of the perceptual processes involved in learning to read is Eleanor Gibson (1965, 1968). According to Gibson, learning to read involves decoding written language into the spoken language that already is familiar to children. Gibson has broken down into three tasks the process of learning to read. The first task in the sequence is for children to learn the letters

Through practice of various word analysis skills, children learn to decode written symbols into the spoken language with which they are familiar. (Elizabeth Hamlin, Stock, Boston)

of the alphabet. Next they learn to decode the individual letters into familiar sounds. The final task in learning to read is learning to process larger units as wholes (reading by phrases or lines rather than word by word). The last stage distinguishes good readers from poor readers. If the process of learning to read has not been too painful, children may go on to learn another language with much greater efficiency, transferring their reading and spelling skills to a whole new body of symbols and meanings.

The task of learning to discriminate between letters involves the child's ability to focus on the distinctive features of letter-symbols. For example, to differentiate between similar letters like V and U, the child must attach significance to the characteristic of *curved* versus *angular*. To distinguish an F from a P, the child must attend to *closed* versus *opened*. Gibson, Gibson, Pick, and Osser (1962) found that the more features that two letter-like forms have in common, the more confusion there will be in distinguishing between them. Discrimination tests reveal that young children are most successful when they can apply perceptual rules drawn from their previous experience with three-dimensional objects to discrimination between letters. For example, differences in shape are important in distinguishing three-dimensional objects; the young child knows how to tell the difference between a ball and a stick. Rotation, on the other hand, is not very helpful in picking out objects. A stick put in a different position is still a stick. Thus the child has more difficulty discriminating between a P and a d than between an O and an l. To successfully distinguish letters, children must learn to attach significance to the subtle variations among them (Pick, 1972). The capacity to discriminate among forms that resemble letters improves between the ages of 4 and 8 (Gibson et al., 1962).

Gibson's second perceptual task in learning to read is association of sound and symbol. Unfortunately, the spoken word and the written word do not always match (*know, no; buy, by*). The alphabet is a system that helps us remember letters, but it carries the child only part of the way. (The letter *g*, for example, changes sounds in the word *garage*. And think of the peculiarities of *c, k,* and *s* in words such as *capacity, constant, task,* and *sack.*) The alphabet is efficient because a relatively small number of symbols serves to transcribe the huge number of sounds and words in spoken language. In theory, the child must learn a small number of sound-sight symbols in order to be able to read everything. But attached to the system are a number of rules that must also be learned if the child is to read. Research suggests that reading in English involves phonology (the study of the speech sounds of a language). In a recent review of the literature, Rozin and Gleitman (1977) suggest that beginning readers connect print to sounds and then assign meaning. With increasing reading skill, there seems to be a shift away from phonology to the direct conversion of print to meaning. The shift is not complete, however. Fluent English readers still make phonological errors, and if someone is asked to recall the letter E shown with other letters, he is more likely, if he errs, to give C or D (which are phonologically similar) than he is to give F (which is visually similar).

The evidence seems to indicate that children who have difficulty learning to read fail to understand the fundamental relationship between sound and writing. In one study, children were shown pairs of words such as *mow* and *motorcycle* and then told "one of these words is *mow* and the other is *motorcycle.*" They were then asked, "Which one is *mow?*" The pairs could always be discriminated by spoken and written length (Rozin, Bressman, and Taft, 1974). The study found that poor readers have difficulty distinguishing between the words, even though they can pronounce the words and understand what they mean. Poor readers also have difficulty telling whether the words *pat* and *bat* are the same or different, although they are able to repeat the words correctly when spoken by the tester and, in ordinary conversation, rarely confuse their meanings. Children hear phonological distinctions and must achieve phonological awareness so that what they know can be applied to the task of learning to read. Although perceptual processes may be important in learning to read, mediating mechanisms may also play a crucial role. In addition, experiments have also shown that children are quicker to associate single sounds with single letters than they are to associate complex sounds with an entire word (Bishop, 1964).

The final perceptual task in Gibson's analysis of learning to read takes place over a number of years. Gradually, the eye learns to span longer and more complex units of writing. Gibson (1965) suggests that beginning readers start by learning spelling patterns that have regular pronunciations according to the rules of English. The length and complexity of spelling patterns that children can perceive as *units* increases with development of reading skill (Gibson, Osser, and Pick, 1963). Eventually, readers become attentive to elements of meaning and syntax that help them deal with strings of words of increasing length.

There are four word analysis techniques that are essential for the beginning reader to master. These are *sight word analysis, phonic analysis, context analysis,* and *structural analysis* (Guszak, 1972). Reading programs that are prepared by individual teachers or that are commercially packaged are based on these techniques.

Word Analysis Techniques

Sight word analysis is also sometimes called *look-and-say teaching.* Typically, the teacher holds up a flash card to the class and pronounces the word printed on the card. The class looks at the flash card and repeats the word. This process is repeated over and over, in workbooks, readers, and chalkboard work until the children have mastered the 220 words that make up our basic reading vocabulary. The first words introduced are usually nouns and proper nouns, associated with a picture of the person, animal, or thing named. Next, action verbs such as *look, run, come* are taught so that the children can follow a simple story line. Gradually, new words are introduced into the basic text. The difficulty of primers may be graded by the percentage of sight words that each contains. For example, 52% of a sixth-grade reader is composed of basic sight words. This is similar to the difficulty level of the average American newspaper (Guszak, 1972). Sight analysis is usually a quick, efficient means of starting the reading process. Sight analysis is not very helpful, though, in developing analytical skills or rules that can be usefully transferred to reading new words. This function is better filled by phonic analysis.

Phonic analysis involves linking sounds to letter symbols or combinations of letters. It is both useful and confusing to young readers. Although rules on how to pronounce certain vowels and consonants yield many correct pronunciations, they also yield many mistakes. Because the English language is derived from many diverse linguistic traditions, no one rule always holds true. Phonic teaching usually begins with initial consonants like the *t* in *t*op, *t*able, *t*urn, since such sounds have a high degree of

Two Innovative Reading Programs

The Pittsburgh reading program is designed so that each child can progress at his or her own pace after receiving initial individual instruction from a teacher. The initial teaching first uses phonic analysis to teach a few sounds and then blends these into a small basic vocabulary. When the child has learned basic sound-symbol correspondences and how to blend them, self-paced materials take him or her on to phrases and then whole sentences. Next, the children start to work their way individually through cassettes, workbooks, and games. Reading for meaning is learned in reading groups. The children read to each other and the teacher leads discussions. The teacher also does diagnostic testing to determine when the child is ready for the next reading level, but the program is basically pupil-oriented. The Pittsburgh program is still in a developmental stage. Most important, a complete set of sequential curriculum materials has not yet been fully developed and refined. Thus, the effectiveness of this method is hard to evaluate, but its eclectic approach holds great promise.

The Stanford Computer Assisted Instructional (CAI) Reading Program is an example of a more controversial approach relying in part on sophisticated technology. Theoretically, the computer is a valuable teaching tool, since it possesses superior memory, flexibility, and ability to respond to the learner. In practice, it has proved difficult to develop the programs that must be fed into the computer.

The Stanford program is based on association of sound with written displays. The child sits in a booth equipped with a typewriter, an audio system, and a printout screen. The computer gives a visual printout such as IG, IT, IN. Then, over the audio system, the computer says, "Type out *IT*." If the child makes the correct response, the computer praises him or her and presents slightly more difficult material. If the child makes a mistake, the computer presents more questions of the same sort, and after a certain number of errors, gives the correct answer. Each child progresses at his own pace through different subject areas such as letter identification, vocabulary, spelling, phonics, and comprehension of sentences. Although each child uses the computer for only 12 minutes a day, many teachers object to the process as depersonalizing and uncreative. Nevertheless, children with CAI training give superior performances on a number of standard reading scales. The degree to which computer systems are adopted is probably as much a matter of economics as of teacher opposition, since computers are still vastly more expensive than traditional materials and methods (Gibson and Levin, 1975).

conformity with a simple rule. Gradually, the reader learns symbols of increasing sophistication and irregularity (Guszak, 1972).

Context analysis uses surrounding words, meanings, and pictures to discover the meaning of a word. This is not a guessing game, but a systematic process of narrowing the scope of possible meanings that will fit with those words in the sentence that are recognized. The more similarity

there is between the written text and the child's own language usage, the easier the context recognition will be. When teachers record children's own stories for the children to read, reading skills improve (Ruddell, 1965). This was demonstrated dramatically in the case of a 17-year-old whose ability to read was less than that needed to function in society. He related his experience as follows:

[The teacher and I] were talking about dating and girls and what's happening. And she'd go home and write it up. She'd say those are your words so why don't you read them. So we'd go over it. And that same day I'd know the words on that paper. I don't know how you learn to read, but sure, this is a big step. How many 17-year-old boys who can't read, learn about 50 words in one day. See, it amazes me, when she brings in something you said the next day; when you go over it, you can read some words. If you study those words, when you see them again, you will know them. ("From a Student," 1971, p. 190)

Goodman (1965) further demonstrated the utility of context analysis. He found that first-, second-, and third-grade children were able to recognize many words in context that they did not recognize when presented alone. Most children develop the reading strategy of context

426

analysis intuitively. Those who do not and who show poor ability to supply appropriate words may be bored by the text or may suffer from more serious learning problems. Poor context analysis should prompt teachers to give remedial work (Guszak, 1972).

Structural analysis often aids word recognition more quickly than does phonic analysis. In structural analysis, the reader learns to pick out parts of words, like plural endings, prefixes, suffixes, and root words. In this way, the student may discover common meaning in addition to common sounds. For example, after learning the word *place,* the child learns *some place, no place, any place.*

Through the use of all word analysis skills, the child gradually recognizes words in a shorter and shorter time. As a result, reading fluency increases. Table 13–1 shows minimal reading norms developed by McCracken (1967). There are two interesting aspects of the developmental pattern of reading. First, oral and silent reading rates start at the same levels of fluency. By the third grade, however, silent reading becomes comparatively much faster. This continues until the seventh grade, when silent reading is almost twice as fast as oral reading. Second, note the rapid jump between second- and fourth-grade reading levels. This is the fastest period of reading skill development.

Motivation

Modeling at home is one important aspect of the child's motivation to read. Parents who themselves take pleasure in reading and who frequently read to their children in a warm, affectionate atmosphere appear to instill a strong desire to read in the children. Children who are exposed to vividly illustrated books also acquire incentive to read (Guszak, 1972). Unfortunately, many parents neglect reading activities and permit their children to sit passively in front of the TV set for hours. This kind of nontraining fails to take advantage of the fact that young children love to imitate their parents and older brothers and sisters and could easily be led into a love for books. One father we know gave his 3-year-old daughter an early intro-

TABLE 13–1

Suggested Oral and Silent Minimum Reading Speeds, Grades 1–7 and Above

GRADE	ORAL WORDS PER MINUTE	SILENT WORDS PER MINUTE
1	60	60
2	70	70
3	90	120
4	120	150
5	120	170
6	150	245
7 and above	150	300

Source: McCracken, 1967, p. 85.

duction to books. He read her favorite story into a tape recorder that was simple enough for her to operate and indicated when it was time to turn the page by using a funny noise. When the little girl wanted to, she would get out the tape recorder and the book and follow the story and its pictures page-by-page as her father's voice read the story. She appeared to get great satisfaction from being able to entertain herself—and be entertained—in this way, particularly when her father was at work and her mother was busy with their new baby.

Parents can stimulate interest in the process of reading and writing by making readily available books, magazines, paper, pencils, crayons. Durkin (1966) studied early readers in public school systems in two different cities. Some important differences regarding home environment became apparent in interviews with the children's parents. As Tables 13–2 and 13–3 illustrate, parents of early readers provided opportunities to use reading and writing materials and were responsive to the children's requests for help in those activities. Durkin reports that the most common age at which children expressed interest in reading was 4 years. Children also take special interest and pride in books that are exclusively theirs. The Reading is FUNdamental (RIF) program, financially supported by foundations, business organizations, and the federal government, gives poor children paperback books of special interest to children. Surveys taken since the beginning of the program in 1966 indicate that 90% of the parents of children who have received books say that the program helped improve their children's reading skills. And 60% say that their children have encouraged them to buy them books (Gibson, 1976). In addition, word games like "I packed my grandmother's trunk," pig-latin, and rhyming games develop interest in language skills and convey the idea that learning about words is fun. Finally, frequent verbal interaction with the child and with others in the child's presence gives the child a chance to express himself or herself and to observe others do the same (Gibson and Levin, 1975).

	PERCENTAGE ANSWERING "YES"	
	Early readers	*Nonearly readers*
Availability of paper and pencil in home	83%	18%
Availability of reading materials in home	73%	14%
Availability of blackboard in home	57%	23%
Interest in the meaning of words	47%	9%

Source: Durkin, 1966.

TABLE 13–2
Factors Relating to Early Interest in Reading

TABLE 13–3
Help Requested on Reading Skills by Early and Nonearly Readers

	PERCENTAGE GIVING HELP	
	Early readers	*Nonearly readers*
With printing	93%	73%
With identification of written words	91%	27%
With the meaning of words	77%	27%
With spelling	73%	27%
With sounds of letters	67%	27%

Source: Durkin, 1966.

Problem Readers

Some children, however, have real difficulty learning to read. Failure to master reading at a level normal for one's age, when the failure is not the result of a disorder such as mental retardation, is termed *dyslexia* (Gibson and Levin, 1975). Dyslexia may occur because a child inverts letters and numbers, such as *p, d, b, g,* and *6.* Some children have orientation problems such as failing to sweep the eyes from left to right (Guszak, 1972). As we discussed earlier, many children have difficulty converting speech sounds to written language. The term dyslexia is used to indicate difficulties in learning to read. It is important for teachers, parents, and children to understand that difficulties in learning to read do *not* imply mental deficiency. Knowing that reading problems can be remedied is important to the child's self-concept and motivation in learning to read.

SPECIAL PROBLEMS OF DISADVANTAGED CHILDREN. One fact about reading problems is indisputable: So-called disadvantaged children in large-city school systems have the highest rate of failure in acquisition of reading skills. In addition to problems stemming from lack of reading and writing materials at home and from school systems with limited resources and overworked teachers, disadvantaged children may also be handicapped by differences in dialect. The English they hear at home and in the street is very different from that found in traditional grade-school readers.

The majority of research done on reading difficulties of disadvantaged children has focused on problems of black children. Unquestionably, it is difficult for a child of any background—Hispanic, Slavic, Oriental—to learn to read and write a language different from the one in which he or she communicates at home. Yet, for speakers of Black English, the problem is more subtle. It is obvious that English is a foreign language for speakers of Spanish, Polish, and Japanese. It requires a sensitive teacher to understand that standard English may be equally foreign to speakers of Black English, especially when many children do, in fact, master both forms.

Some early researchers believed that Black English was illogical and generally inferior to standard English. This belief is called the *cultural deficit hypothesis.* Its main thrust is that the very structure of Black English (dropping possessive endings, for example, and simplifying past and future tenses to the present) made it difficult for black children to think logically, formulate and manipulate concepts, and express themselves in full sentences. According to this view, deficient language impeded general cognitive growth as well as reading skills. The early researchers thought that the solution, therefore, was to teach black children standard English, rich in analytic and logical structures.

Later researchers have repudiated the cultural deficit hypothesis as the product of scholarly insensitivity. Black English, they argue, is not deficient in analytic and logical structures; rather, most (white) teachers have difficulty recognizing its structure. The problem is that Black English is different, not inferior.

The difference in dialects can create miscommunication between pupil and teacher and give rise to reading problems. This view is known as the *linguistic interference hypothesis.* For example, homonyms (words that sound alike) that are not recognized in standard English may occur in Black English. Pairs like *toll-toe, fault-fought, sore-so* may have identical sound values to the black student, but not to the white teacher (Labov, 1967). In Black English, it is common to omit the verb *to be,* as in "We late again." Such differences cause difficulties in "translating" one dialect to another.

What is the best means of helping black children deal with language differences in the course of the already formidable task of learning to read? No one formula or technique has proved completely effective to date, but there are a variety of promising approaches. These include books that incorporate more Black English, or at least do not penalize the young reader for being unfamiliar with standard English. Teachers who are sensitive to black linguistic styles and can switch between them and standard English, while motivating their students to achieve academically, are probably the most valuable asset. Unfortunately, there is, as yet, no systematized training program to help teachers develop these skills. Coleman's research (1966) indicates, however, that school programs addressed to the needs of disadvantaged children and conducted by well-trained teachers *can* set the disadvantaged child on the track of academic success.

SUMMARY

Almost all children between the ages of 7 and 16 spend seven hours a day, 200 days a year, in the classroom. The contrast between infants and school-going children is drastic. Six-year-olds are capable of learning to perform more complex physical and mental activities. How well children adapt to the demands and challenges of the new school environment depends on many factors. One is the similarity between behavioral techniques used by the mother and those used by the teacher.

There was a time when almost all American children attended what is now called the *traditional* school. The idea behind traditional classrooms was that organization, structure, and discipline facilitated both children's learning and teachers' control. In contrast to the traditional schoolroom is the *open classroom*. Philosophically, the open classroom approach rests on a belief that children are naturally motivated to learn socially desirable values and skills. The function of the open classroom is to tap the spontaneous will to learn by providing a number of appealing alternatives and by allowing children to choose the ones they find most interesting. Cognitively, this technique stresses process over results, means over ends. Emotionally, the orientation values expression of feelings as well as of ideas. Advocates of informal, open classrooms have had an impact on public education, yet enthusiasm for such methods seems to be waning. The more that schooling techniques diverge from family backgrounds, community values, and previous experiences of parents and students, the more resistance they meet.

Perhaps the most important socialization function of the school is to teach children how to behave. Aggression in the classroom can describe a wide range of behavior; and it helps teachers if they can identify its source. The peer group can also exert a positive or negative influence on the incidence of aggressive behavior. Techniques of behavior modification have proved successful in handling small unwanted behaviors that interfere in the classroom. The teacher's attention and approval is a major source of reinforcement for desired behaviors. Another behavior modification technique, known as a *token economy,* is the use of prizes or tokens to encourage desired behavior. Behavior modification techniques have been criticized on the grounds that they are not always effective, that they induce behaviors that are in and of themselves undesirable, and that the resulting behaviors are not transferrable. These questions remain sources of concern and controversy.

Most educators agree that a talented teacher is more effective in stimulating learning than the most sophisticated equipment. There is more disagreement on exactly how and why teachers influence their pupils. One of the most popular hypotheses, referred to as "teacher expectation," "teacher faith," or "self-fulfilling prophecy," suggests that teacher perceptions of student ability are reflected in the ways teachers teach and treat their pupils. This different treatment in turn yields different performance by the students, and thus the teacher's prophecy for the student fulfills itself. Attempts to verify this hypothesis have been controversial. The physical appearance, sex, race, and socioeconomic status of the student; the social setting of the school; and the ideas already held by the teacher determine teachers' expectations for children's social and academic performance. Teachers transmit their expectations to students by the way they interact with and treat each student.

Until the shift to peer-orientation takes place in early junior high school, family influence is the single most important determinant of behavior and achievement in school. Parental income, education, and personalities play a role in determining how children will perform in school.

Learning to read tops the list of objectives set for school-age children by parents, administrators, and frequently by children themselves. Reading is a complex process that involves understanding a set of marks as letters which in combination form meaningful words. Words are then grouped into intelligible statements and informative or entertaining sequences. From the point of view of perceptual theory, learning to read involves a sequence of tasks of increasing complexity: (1) learning the letters of the alphabet; (2) relating the individual letters to familiar sounds; (3) processing larger units as wholes (reading by phrases or lines rather than word by word). There are four word-analysis techniques that are essential for the beginning reader to master: sight word analysis, phonic analysis, context analysis, and structural analysis. In *sight word analysis* (also called look-and-say teaching) the teacher presents a flash card to the class, pronounces the word on the card, and asks the class to repeat the word. This process is repeated until students have mastered a basic reading vocabulary of about 220 words. *Phonic analysis* involves linking sounds to letter symbols or combinations of letters. It begins with initial consonants and progresses to letter combinations of increasing sophistication or irregularity. *Context analysis* uses surrounding words, meanings, and pictures to discover the meaning of a word; it is a systematic process of narrowing the number of possible meanings, not a guessing game. In *structural analysis,* readers learn to pick out words or parts of words, such as endings, prefixes, and root words, that will help them discover common meanings and sounds. Through the use of all word-analysis skills, children gradually recognize words in a shorter and shorter time, and their reading abilities increase.

Modeling at home is one important aspect of children's motivation to read. Parents who themselves take pleasure in reading and who frequently read to their children in a warm, affectionate atmosphere appear to instill a strong desire to read in their children. Children who are exposed to vividly illustrated books also acquire incentive to read. Parents can stimulate interest in the process of reading and writing by making books, magazines, papers, pencils, and crayons readily available. In addition, word games and rhyming games develop interest in language skills and convey the idea that learning about words is fun. Finally, frequent verbal interaction with children and others in the presence of children gives them a chance to express themselves and to observe others doing the same.

Failure to master reading at a level normal for a particular age, when the failure is not the result of a disorder such as mental retardation, is termed *dyslexia*. Disadvantaged children in large-city school systems have the highest rate of failure in acquisition of reading skills. In addition to other problems, they may often be handicapped by differences in dialect. For speakers of Black English, standard English may sound like a foreign language. Early researchers proposed the *cultural deficit hypothesis,* which claimed that Black English is illogical and that the logical deficiency impedes cognitive growth as well as reading skills. Later researchers argue that Black English is not inferior, but that it is different. The *linguistic intereference hypothesis* claims that the difference in dialects can create miscommunication between pupil and teacher and give rise to reading problems.

PART V

Adolescence

Dear Diary,
I am the shepherdess in a play. It is a French play but not in French.

Dear Diary,
I went ice skating with Bobby, Jane, Carol, and Kent. Kent kissed me. I was very astonished.

Dear Diary,
I went ice skating today, too. The ice was great. Got home at 6:30. Made a date to go to the movies Saturday. Kent may take me.

April 13, 1977

Dear Folks,
Things here are slow, but steady. School is starting to go well, as hard work finally shows signs of paying off. Professor M. seems pleased but not overwhelmed. I'm not socializing enough to give any decent run-down on my friends, except one, a next-door neighbor who I drove to the doctor Tues. to have a broken jaw wired shut. Poor thing can't open her mouth for a month.

   It's been hot here, and nice, weather-wise. I'm looking forward to summer-time. Dreading the factory (I've written to Mr. C., but not yet had confirmation), but looking forward to spending weekends on the beach.

Thanks for finding the car registration, Mom. The car is OK. Mended the horn which was blowing when it wasn't wanted.

I want you all to lift pens & pencils and frantically (well, furiously... no, *fervently*) write to me. I like to get mail, you know.

Love,
Jon

P.S. Just heard from Mr. C. today (4/14). It's *10-1/2* hours a day in the factory at $3/hr.! Four days a week, sometimes overtime Fri. & Sat. (goodbye, beach). What do you think? Is it worth it? Will I have the energy for night school?

CHAPTER 14

Physical, Intellectual, and Social Development

Up to this point, we have traced the development of the child from infancy through the middle years of childhood. We have seen how the infant, though dependent on adults for survival, is nevertheless an active force in bringing about interactions with people and things. We have noted the dramatic change that occurs between infancy and middle childhood. This process of change continues as the child enters adolescence. But now it takes on added significance (at least in Western societies) because adolescence marks the transition to adulthood. As Muuss (1974) points out, "sociologically, adolescence is the transition period from dependent childhood to self-sufficient adulthood. Psychologically, it is a 'marginal situation' in which new adjustments have to be made, namely those that distinguish child behavior from adult behavior in a given society" (p. 4). We might add that, biologically, adolescence covers the period from the onset of *puberty* (when sexual maturation begins) to the completion of bone growth. Although the biological transition occurs in all children wherever they might be, the sociological and psychological transition depends upon the culture in which a child lives. In the United States, the age of legal adulthood is an uncertain thing. The ages at which a person can vote, buy liquor, face charges for criminal behavior, join the army, drive, or work differ, have changed over the past decade, and may not be the same from one state to another.

Many important changes take place in adolescents. Physically, they are growing rapidly and maturing sexually. Intellectually, they are becoming able to use more abstract means of thought and expression. Socially, they are breaking ties with parents and forming more intense relationships with peers. These physical, intellectual, and social changes are the subject of this chapter.

Before we describe these changes in detail, it is important to note that adolescence is a critical period of human development not only because of the physical, sociological, and psychological transformations that take place during these years, but also because it is a vulnerable time for the child. For one thing, it is a new and sometimes frightening experience. As Neimark (1975) puts it, "The world of the adolescent is qualitatively different from the world of the child; it is far bigger, richer, and more complex. It is, in many respects, like the world of the adult except that much of it is new, and the adolescent does not yet have relevant experience to bring to bear upon it" (p. 541). In addition, the rapid pace at which the physical, and especially sexual, changes of adolescence occur may lead to confusion and embarrassment. Adolescents are anxious to become adults but have very little time to prepare themselves for adult roles and responsibilities.

No one has expressed the poignancy of adolescence better than Anne Frank (1952) in *The Diary of a Young Girl*. Anne's confused emotions, as well as her growing detachment from her mother, may be seen in the following excerpt:

. . . Margot and Mummy told me that they were going into the town to look at something or buy something. . . I wanted to go, too, but was not allowed to, as I had my bicycle with me. Tears of rage sprang into my eyes, and Mummy and Margot began laughing at me. Then I became so furious that I stuck my tongue out at them in the street just as an old woman happened to pass by, who looked very shocked! I rode home on my bicycle, and I know I cried for a long time.

It is queer that the wound that Mummy made then still burns, when I think of how angry I was that afternoon. (p. 116)

In the following passage from Anne Frank, we see the intensity of the adolescent's first sexual feelings:

I woke . . . this morning and knew at once, quite positively, what I had dreamed. I sat on a chair and opposite me sat Peter. . . . We were looking together at a book of drawings. . . . Suddenly Peter's eyes met mine and I looked into those fine, velvet brown eyes for a long time. Then Peter said very softly, "If I had only known, I would have come to you long before!" I turned around brusquely because the emotion was too much for me. And after that I felt a soft, and oh, such a cool kind cheek against mine and it felt so good. . . . (p. 119)

Another point that should be kept in mind throughout this chapter is that the physical, intellectual, and social changes of adolescence are highly interdependent. Physical and social changes, in particular, interact to produce what to many parents seems to be a completely unfamiliar and unpredictable creature: the teenager.

Finally, cultural differences have a significant effect on adolescence as a social phenomenon. If, for instance, a society is characterized by a high level of technological development, the period of adolescence will be prolonged by the length of time the adolescent must spend preparing for a specialized occupation — time during which self-sufficiency, marriage, and other aspects of adulthood are usually postponed. Another way in which cultures differ in their treatment of adolescents is in the presence or absence of puberty rites. The completion of these ceremonies entitles a person to recognition as a young adult. In societies such as our own, where the requirements for admission to adulthood are less clearly defined, the adolescent often goes through a long, confused struggle to gain adult status.

BIOLOGICAL ADOLESCENCE

Adolescence is the period from puberty to maturity. *Puberty* refers to the physical changes that occur during this period, particularly in the reproductive organs. These physical changes, as well as the "growth spurt" typical of the adolescent, are the subject of this section.

The Adolescent Growth Spurt

Because of the immense change in the *velocity* or *rate* of growth that occurs during this period, adolescents are said to experience a "growth spurt." A 13-year-old boy, for example, may find himself growing as quickly as he grew when he was 2 years old. Figure 14–1 illustrates this change.

There are differences between boys and girls not only in the amount of growth that takes place at puberty but also in the timing of the growth spurt. The average girl begins her growth spurt at about age 10½ and reaches a peak at 12; the average boy lags 2 years behind. Girls are generally shorter than boys, but because of the delay in the boys' growth spurt, an 11-year-old girl may be taller than most boys her age. During the period of most rapid growth, a girl will grow 2.4–4.4 inches, a boy 2.8–4.8 inches. However, the age at which this peak occurs varies according to environmental conditions such as socioeconomic class, nutrition, disease, and psychological disturbances, as well as genetic differences.

The amount of height added during the growth spurt is largely under hormonal control and thus is independent of the height attained before the spurt. However, at age 9, it is possible to predict with 90% accuracy a

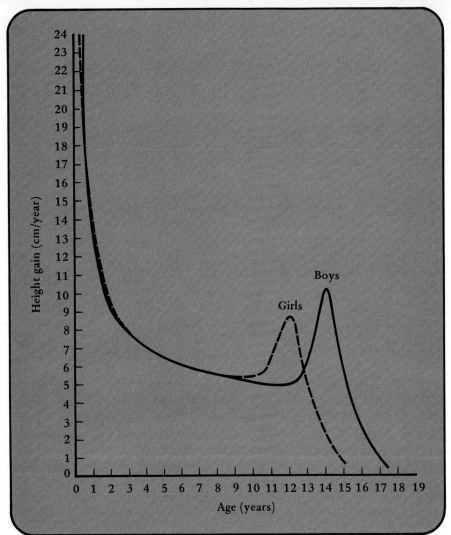

FIGURE 14–1
Typical velocity curves of growth for boys and girls from birth through adolescence
(Tanner, Whitehouse, and Takaishi, 1966)

person's adult height within 1½ inches on the basis of interrelated factors such as chronological age, bone age, and present height. Most of the increase in height occurs first in the legs and later in the trunk or torso (Faust, 1977). The hands, head, and feet reach adult proportions first, the shoulders last. This accounts for the proverbial awkwardness of the adolescent—the boy who grows out of his pants a year before he grows out of his jackets; the girl who complains that her feet are like boats.

The changes in other body measurements that occur in puberty follow the growth curve for height, so that for a while girls have larger muscles than boys. Boys may find this fact acutely embarrassing if their athletic performance fails to reach their expectations. In an effort to save face, they may call girls names like "Kong" or "Bigfoot." In boys, muscle growth is accompanied by actual loss of fat, whereas in girls fat accumulation merely slows down. At the same time, boys' hearts become larger and their pulse rates slow. Increases in muscle size in both girls and boys result in increased strength. Here the differences between the sexes are especially noticeable: Boys continue to show a marked increase in strength throughout the adolescent period, whereas girls reach their maximum strength at the age of *menarche* (onset of menstruation).

The changes just described have metabolic and nutritional implications that are familiar to any parent of an adolescent child. The food intake of both boys and girls increases. But the differences in muscle size and fat accumulation result in a higher daily caloric expenditure by boys than by girls and, hence, a tendency for boys to eat vast quantities of food, especially protein. Iron requirements increase also, but in this case girls need more than boys, since they lose more iron during menstruation.

Sexual Development

Sexual development occurs in an orderly sequence, though the age at which this sequence starts varies considerably. In boys, the first sign of puberty is accelerated growth of the testes and scrotum and appearance of pubic and underarm hair. This usually occurs around age 12, but normal limits for the change encompass ages 10 to 13½. Once the sequence begins, the order of events shows little variation. About a year after the testes have begun their accelerated growth, the penis begins to develop to adult size. This process may be completed as early as age 13½ or as late as age 16½. Thus boys who are in the early-maturing group may complete this process before late-maturing boys have even begun the sequence. About 2 years after puberty begins, facial hair appears—again in a definite sequence (corners of upper lip, whole upper lip, upper part of cheeks). This is followed by the "breaking" or lowering of the voice. These changes are accompanied by the first ejaculation of seminal fluid, which usually occurs about a year after the beginning of accelerated penis growth.

In girls, puberty begins with the appearance of unpigmented, downy hair in the pubic area followed by appearance of the "breast bud." At the same time, the uterus and vagina begin their development to mature dimensions. Menarche occurs relatively late in puberty—*after* the peak of the growth spurt—but here again there is considerable individual variation. Menarche may occur anywhere between 10 and 16½ years of age. There is also much variation in the time between breast development and menarche. A 16-year-old girl may have passed her growth peak and have fully developed breasts and pubic hair, yet not have experienced her first menstrual period, whereas some of her friends and classmates may have gone through all the stages of puberty between the ages of 12 and 14.

Sexual Dimorphism

The term *sexual dimorphism* refers to the differential growth of various parts of the body during adolescence that increases the difference in body composition between boys and girls. It means, in short, that boys and girls end up looking very different from each other. Among the more obvious sexual dimorphisms is the width of shoulders and hips. Hip width increases markedly in adolescent girls; similarly, boys show a marked increase in shoulder width. This dimorphism is often used as a measure of bodily *androgyny* (that is, the quality of having the characteristics of both sexes.)

Sexual dimorphism obviously does not develop only during adolescence. The basic genital differences are present in the fetus, and at birth girls have a wider pelvic outlet, which will be necessary for childbearing. It is hypothesized that the more noticeable changes (the secondary sexual characteristics) that occur during adolescence are intended to attract the opposite sex. Some of these characteristics, such as penis and breast changes, play a direct role in stimulating sexual activity. Other secondary sexual characteristics, such as the widening of the hips, the growth of pubic and facial hair, and the lowering of the voice, on the other hand, may be indirect releasers of mating behavior (Tanner, 1970).

Early and Late Maturation

As should be evident from the preceding discussion, there are enormous individual differences in rate of growth, especially during adolescence. Faust (1977) found that the range for onset of puberty extends from age 7½ to nearly age 16. Early developers tend to have pubertal periods of longer duration, and early developers gain more in height than do late developers. At the onset of puberty, early-maturing girls tend to be smaller on skeletal measures such as leg length, shoulder and hip width, and total height. But since they make greater gains than do late-maturing girls, the size difference tends to diminish during the growth period, so that there is no relationship between age at the onset of puberty and size at age 18. Early-developing girls simply pass through the successive stages of pubic hair growth and breast development at younger ages than do late-developing girls (Faust, 1977). In highly favorable social environments — that is, environments that are free from stress and provide adequate nutrition — differences in rate of growth and time of onset of puberty are largely under genetic control. However, unfavorable environmental factors — especially malnutrition and illness — may have a strong effect.

Secular, or long-term, data on age of menarche and height and weight at puberty reveal that puberty is occurring earlier today than it did 30 or 40 years ago. That is, today's 11-year-old is the size of the average 12-year-old in 1940, and girls begin menstruating now about a year earlier than they did then (Tanner, 1967). Nutrition is an important factor in such trends. For example, girls of Japanese descent born and raised in California (where nutrition is better than it is in Japan) mature earlier than those born in California but raised in Japan (Ito, 1942; Donovan and van der Werff ten Bosch, 1965). Similarly, black girls living in the West Indies, where nutrition is poor, experience later menarche than those living in the United States (Hafez, 1973). The physical and social environ-

The timing of the growth spurt as well as genetic differences can account for differences in growth among adolescents such as these seventh-grade girls. (Alice Kandell, Rapho/Photo Researchers)

ments have an effect too. Although climate has little effect on the age of menarche, high altitudes delay it (Hafez, 1973). Girls who live in urban areas tend to mature earlier than those who live in rural areas, possibly because of better nutrition and hygiene (Zacharias and Wurtman, 1969).

Children who are physically mature score higher, on the average, on tests of mental ability than do children who are physically immature. In addition, it has been demonstrated repeatedly that adolescent girls score higher than boys of the same age on tests of verbal ability, whereas the boys score higher on tests of spatial ability. Waber (1976) hypothesized that these differences may be due to differences in cortical organization which are related to maturation rate. She predicted that children who matured early (regardless of sex) would have relatively higher verbal than spatial scores, and those who matured late would show the reverse pattern. The results of her study of 80 adolescent boys and girls supported this prediction. Since, as we have seen, girls usually mature earlier than boys, their higher test scores may be explained by Waber's hypothesis.

How biological factors such as maturation rate operate is not entirely clear, but there is no doubt that early or late maturation is related to social and emotional as well as intellectual aspects of development. Studies conducted at the University of California (Mussen and Jones, 1957, 1958) found that late-maturing boys engage in more attention-seeking behavior and tend to be more restless, talkative, and bossy than their early-maturing peers. They are also less popular. Early-maturing boys have higher social status and are more likely to become leaders. For girls, the relationship between maturational level and social status is less clear. Studies of adolescent girls (e.g., Faust, 1960) have found that although physical maturity does contribute to a girl's social status, several other factors—such as emotional and personality changes—are also involved. Moreover, girls who are ahead of their classmates in physical maturity in the early years of puberty (around the fifth and sixth grades) may find themselves at a social *dis*advantage.

COGNITIVE CHANGES DURING ADOLESCENCE

In earlier chapters, we described the cognitive changes that occur between infancy and middle childhood. Though there are other possible explanations for these changes, we stressed the contributions of Piaget and his colleagues, because their theories make the nature of these changes explicit. The lack of useful alternative theories is even more evident when it comes to the changes in the organization of thought that take place during adolescence.

Philosophers, teachers, and parents have long commented on the adolescent's fascination with religious systems and scientific abstractions;

with serious questions (such as "Is there a God?" or "Will the human race destroy itself?"); with intense personal questions (such as "What am I like?" or "What career shall I choose?"); with the uniqueness of his or her own feelings. Piaget's theories provide a basis for understanding how certain features of the adolescent's thought make possible—if not inevitable—the mental and emotional symptoms of adolescence.

Fondness for intellectual puzzles, grand thoughts, emotional turmoil, and conflicts with parents do not characterize adolescents in *all* societies, nor even all adolescents in American society. However, the capacity for engaging in certain kinds of mental operations *does* appear during adolescence, and this makes possible for the adolescent a variety of experiences that are not possible for the younger child.

Formal Operations   Consider the following situations:

1. A child dips sticks into dishes that contain water, oil, molasses, sugar, and powder. The child is asked to explain wetting and sticking.
2. The child is shown water being distilled in a distillation apparatus in which two flasks are connected by a transparent glass tube. The passage of steam in the tube is invisible. The child is asked why the liquid decreases in one flask and increases in the other.
3. The child plays with a yoyo. Why does the spool rise?
4. Air is allowed to escape from a filled balloon. Why does the balloon move?
5. Light from a flashlight is shined onto a screen from different distances. Why is the size of the circle larger at greater distances?

It is not until early adolescence that children become capable of understanding the physical explanations of the above situations. They then begin to attribute the properties of substances to molecular structures— they begin to see steam as a step in the transfer of water from one flask to another, they understand wave motion and the principle of reciprocity expressed in Newton's law of action and reaction (Piaget, 1974). It is not until children are about 13 years old that they admit the existence of light between the flashlight and the spot, and it is not until a year or so later that children understand a cone of light with rays that widen with distance in such a way that the quantity of light decreases as the circle of light gets larger.

Formal operations—the stage of cognitive development in Piagetian theory that follows concrete operations—are characterized by the following aspects of thought: (1) a clear distinction between the actual and the possible, (2) the ability to use symbols to represent other symbols, and (3) the ability to coordinate variables (that is, to take several factors into account at the same time).

Formal operations enable adolescents to study successfully such subjects as algebra, chemistry, philosophy, and literature. (Peeter Vilms, Jeroboam)

THE ACTUAL VERSUS THE POSSIBLE. Suppose you ask a child to write down all the different addresses that could be made up from the numbers 1, 2, and 3. The child who is able to reason at the level of formal operations will first list all the one-number addresses (1, 2, 3), then all the two-number combinations (11, 12, 13, 21, 22, 23, 31, 32, 33), and then all the three-number combinations. This is an example of *combinatorial logic,* that is, the ability to consider all factors in a problem-solving situation.

A person who has reached the level of formal operations is able to take all the possible solutions to a problem into account before trying to determine which alternative actually applies. He or she is able to use the *hypothetical-deductive* method of thought, in which one inspects the data, hypothesizes that a particular theory may explain those data, deduces from it that certain phenomena ought or ought not to occur in reality, and tests the theory accordingly. This is in contrast to the reasoning of younger children in that it begins with the possible rather than with the actual. According to Piaget, this ability to let the possible take precedence over the actual is the basis of experimentation and scientific thinking.

The adolescent's capacity to deal with combinatorial logic and to consider all possible factors in a problem-solving situation has social as well as intellectual implications. For example, suddenly a large number of alternatives seem available. Thus decision making becomes a problem. Adolescents want to know *why* they are being asked (or told) to do certain things and are eager to debate parental decisions. And although adoles-

446

cents may have trouble deciding among possible alternatives, they do not want anyone else—notably parents—to make those decisions for them. This obviously can result in conflict between parents and children (Elkind, 1970a). The person who is capable of formal operations can also think about contrary-to-fact situations without confusing the possible with the actual. This ability, too, has social implications. The adolescent can conceive of ideal families and societies, and when he or she compares these ideals with reality, the real ones may be found wanting. This, in turn, often leads to rebellion against adult society (Elkind, 1970a).

USING SYMBOLS FOR SYMBOLS. The child who has reached the level of formal operations has acquired the ability to use a second symbolic system, that is, the ability to let symbols stand for other symbols. This makes thought more flexible. Words can take on more than one meaning, so the adolescent begins to understand figures of speech such as the metaphor and double entendre. Similarly, adolescents can begin to learn algebra because they can use symbols (such as x and y) to represent other symbols (such as 1 and 2).

A person who has acquired the capacity to use symbols in this way can consider the *logical* relationships between statements as well the *factual* relationship between a statement and an empirical (that is, real) event. Piaget calls this *interpropositional logic.* Consider the following example (from Flavell, 1977):

An experimenter and a subject face one another across a table strewn with poker chips of various solid colors. . . . The experimenter explains he is going to say things about the chips and that the subject is to indicate whether what the experimenter says *(i.e., his* statement*) is true, false, or uncertain ("can't tell"). He then conceals a chip in his hand and says, "Either the chip in my hand is green or it is not green," or alternatively, "The chip in my hand is green and it is not green." On other trials, he holds up either a green chip or a red chip so that the subject can see it, and then makes exactly the same statement. (p. 101)*

Children who have not yet reached the level of formal operations try to solve the problem on the basis of visual evidence alone. When the chip is hidden, they say they "can't tell" what color it is. Adolescents, on the other hand, are likely to base their answers on the verbal assertions, or propositions, themselves. Thus, without having seen the chip, they can tell the experimenter that the statement "The chip in my hand is green and it is not green" is false.

One effect of the adolescent's capacity to "think about thinking" is the tendency toward introspection. The adolescent can think about his or her own mental and personality traits, and this leads to increased self-consciousness and, sometimes, self-criticism. In practical terms, this tendency sometimes results in religiously followed diets and exercise programs as well as in intellectual regimes such as daily meditation.

COORDINATING VARIABLES. Formal operations involve the ability to consider several variables simultaneously. This ability is illustrated in the "balance problem," which uses a balance with unit weights and with arms marked in unit intervals. The experimenter tips the balance and asks the child to rebalance it and explain his solution for doing so. A child aged 3 to 5 uses his hand to raise or to lower one side of the balance, expecting that the correction will remain effective after he removes his hand. Between the ages of 5 and 7, the child has come to know something about the principle of weights; thus he adds or subtracts weights to achieve balance. A child between ages 7 and 9 recognizes both weight and length and achieves balance by use of one *or* the other. If he does attempt to use both modes, he will be able to balance the arms only through a process of trial and error. By the time a child is completely capable of concrete operations (at ages 9 to 11), he uses both variables— weight and length—*together*. He can use combinations of heavy weight with short length of the balance arms and light weight with long length of the arm. The child makes systematic use of two variables treated as one operation. Finally, the adolescent capable of formal operations combines the two variables and, in addition, expresses their quantitative relationship in terms of proportions (Neimark, 1975).

A method of testing the firmness of children's concepts of conservation has been devised by Miller, Schwartz, and Stewart (1973). These investigators rigged the balance with electromagnets, so that it would give false information. Thus a ball of clay could be made to seem lighter after it had been flattened. The results of the experiment showed that elementary school children tend to abandon their belief in conservation in the face of such evidence, whereas most college students will try to explain the discrepancy somehow (such as "You took some clay away" or "The scale isn't working right"). Miller and his colleagues conclude that the certainty with which a concept such as conservation of weight is held may be influenced by developmental changes.

Does Everyone Reach the Level of Formal Operations?

In the experiment just described, a few of the adolescent subjects were convinced by the visual evidence that the principle of conservation does not always hold true. Although the capacity for formal operations does not appear until adolescence, not all adolescents (nor adults, for that matter) demonstrate this capacity. Nor do those who have the ability to use formal operations use the ability effectively every time a task calls for it. Why is this so? In the first place, cultural differences have an effect. Some groups have more training and practice in formal operations than others. Yet there is no doubt that groups such as the Kpelle rice farmers and Puluwat Islanders mentioned in Chapter 2 are capable of using very complex cognitive skills in culture-appropriate tasks.

The matter of cognitive *capacity* is emphasized by Flavell (1977). He points out that performance is seldom a reliable indicator of capacity. A person faced with a cognitive problem "may misunderstand or fail to accept the task demands, may feel a different approach is more appropriate to the situation, or may just be having an off day intellectually.... In addition, an adult is likely to... find some types of reasoning operations more unnatural and difficult than others, and may therefore not perform them ...efficiently, accurately, or at all" (p. 116). Even well-educated adults often make errors on reasoning problems. Indeed, Piaget (1972) suggests that adults may be capable of formal operations only in areas where their interest and experience are greatest. Even though adolescents may make logical mistakes (for instance, conclude that if A implies B, B implies A), they are aware of the type of reasoning involved. As Flavell (1977) puts it, "Skill in actually playing the logic game and other abstract games may vary considerably...., but even the poorer players may know something about the general *sort* of game it is" (p. 118).

COGNITION AND SOCIAL PERSPECTIVES

In view of the preceding discussion, one should not be surprised to discover that changes in the way children think about logical problems are related to the way they think about personal problems. In previous chapters, we have described how the egocentrism of early childhood diminishes as the child grows older. There is evidence that this process continues during middle childhood. Scarlett, Press, and Crockett (1971), for instance, demonstrated that between the ages of 5 and 12, children shift from egocentric to nonegocentric judgments of others (for example, from "He hit me" to "He plays baseball"). In adolescence, however, a new form of egocentrism emerges.

Adolescent Egocentrism

As we have seen, formal operations permit the adolescent to consider all the possible solutions to a problem and to imagine contrary-to-fact situations. In addition, the young person is able to reason about his or her own mental activities. This new skill is also applied to the thoughts of others. Elkind (1970a) maintains that in applying this new skill to the thoughts of others, the adolescent fails to recognize that the concerns of others may be different from his or her own. As a result, adolescents believe others are preoccupied with the same things with which they themselves are preoccupied. This belief is the basis of adolescent egocentrism.

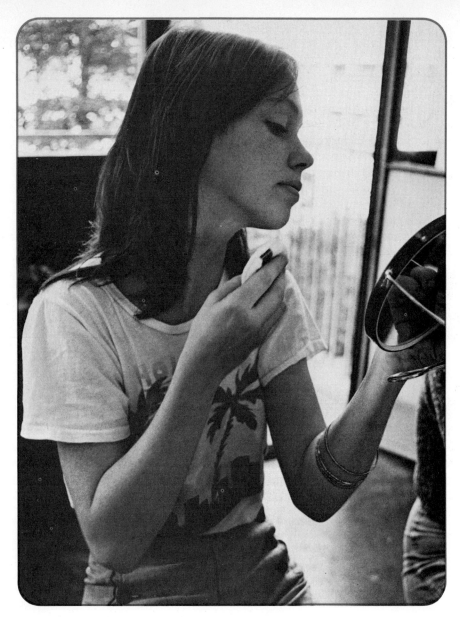

Adolescents are unusually sensitive to anticipated reactions of an imaginary audience to their appearance and behavior.
(Russell Abraham, Jeroboam)

THE IMAGINARY AUDIENCE. The adolescent is continually anticipating the reactions of other people to his or her appearance and behavior. The adolescent can and does, therefore, create an *imaginary audience*, in contrast to the younger child who creates an imaginary companion. "It is an audience," writes Elkind (1970a), "because the adolescent believes that he will be the focus of attention, and it is imaginary because, in actual social situations, this is not usually the case" (p. 67).

The presence of an imaginary audience may explain the extreme self-consciousness of the adolescent. Suppose a 15-year-old girl is feeling

450

critical of herself. Her imaginary audience must be critical too. And since that audience has been created by the girl herself, it knows just what to criticize: her shoulders, which may be a bit broader than those of her friends, her hair, which didn't curl right, her nervousness in talking to boys.

At the same time, the adolescent may be unrealistically self-admiring—and the imaginary audience will follow suit. This may explain why a young person often cannot understand why peers and adults fail to appreciate his or her dress and behavior. It can also be applied to adolescent behavior toward the opposite sex. The boy who spent a long time before a date combing his hair may be more concerned with his date's reaction to his hair than he is with his appreciation of something equally significant to her (Elkind, 1970a).

THE PERSONAL FABLE. The adolescent's belief that he or she is important to many people (the imaginary audience) leads to the notion that his or her feelings are special and unique. One has only to turn to any page of J. D. Salinger's *The Catcher in the Rye* to get an idea of the emotional torments of this period. Adolescents' convictions that their emotional experiences are unique may be viewed as a *personal fable*—a story told by the young person to himself or herself. Evidence of the personal fable may sometimes be seen in adolescent diaries, like that of Anne Frank.

Elkind (1970a) believes that the concepts of the imaginary audience and the personal fable can be used to explain a variety of adolescent behaviors, including middle-class delinquency and teenage pregnancies. In the former case, the young person is performing a daring act for the imaginary audience; in the latter, the young girl's personal fable leads her to believe that pregnancy—like death—is something that happens only to other people. This kind of egocentrism usually diminishes by the age of 15 or 16 (the age at which formal operations are firmly established). The young person becomes able to view himself or herself somewhat more realistically and can engage in real—as opposed to self-centered—interpersonal relations.

Adolescent Perceptions of Others

According to several investigators (Shantz, 1975; Flavell, 1977), cognitive development determines adolescents' perceptions of themselves and of others. The type of research being done in this area is illustrated in a study by Livesley and Bromley (1973). These investigators instructed children between the ages of 7 and 15 to write descriptions of themselves and of other people they knew well. The children were told not to describe a person's physical appearance but to indicate what sort of person he or she was. The 7-year-olds in the study tended to describe the other person's appearance, possessions, family, and so forth, despite the instructions. Older children showed greater ability to focus on personality attributes (for example, "considerate," "helpful," "nasty"), but their descriptions did not attempt to *explain* these attributes or to *integrate* those that were contradictory. (For example, one 10-year-old answered, "Her behavior is quite good most of the time but sometimes she is quite naughty and silly most of the time.") By contrast, the adolescents constructed organized, integrated portraits of other people, trying to explain their characteristics rather than to merely describe them. In some cases, these descriptions were quite impressive: "She is curious about people but naive, and this leads her to ask too many questions so that people become irritated with her and withhold information, although she is not sensitive enough to notice it."

In earlier chapters, we presented evidence that even children as young as 3 years of age are sensitive to the feelings of others. This sensitivity increases and deepens during middle childhood, when children begin to infer the feelings and motives of others. Rothenberg (1970) found that preadolescence is a period of life when extensive growth occurs in the ability to attribute feelings, thoughts, and motives to other people. She suggests that the increases in social sensitivity that occur between third and fifth grade may be directly related to growth in intellectual or cognitive development alone (Rothenberg, 1970).

If this is the case, cognitive growth affects adolescents' social perceptions as well. Concepts of other people may be expected to become increasingly complex and sophisticated with age. A study by Peevers and Secord (1973) strongly confirms this prediction. In this study, 80 subjects ranging from kindergarten to college age were asked to describe three people they liked ("friends") and one person they disliked. Their descriptions were analyzed from the standpoint of four qualities: descriptiveness, personal involvement, evaluative consistency, and depth. In the case of descriptiveness, the younger children often failed to differentiate a person from his or her environment (for example, "John lives in a big house") or used superficial characteristics (such as, "John is nice"). However, the results for liked and disliked peers differed in a number of ways for *all* age groups. Fewer items were used in describing disliked peers than in describing liked peers and descriptions of disliked peers contained more behavioral traits (for example, "John is talkative").

The measure of personal involvement referred to the degree to which the person doing the describing involved himself or herself in a particular item. Here again there was a significant difference between descriptions of liked and disliked peers. The hypothesis that younger children would use more egocentric items than older children was confirmed, but when it came to descriptions of disliked peers, college students were found to be as egocentric as kindergartners.

The results in the area of evaluative consistency (that is, assigning desirable qualities to liked peers and undesirable ones to disliked peers) varied from one age level to another. Third and seventh graders were more consistent than kindergartners and eleventh graders, and college students were about as consistent as seventh graders. On the other hand, depth (or the degree to which personal characteristics are seen as depending on situational factors) shows a definite increase with age.

To sum up, as the child grows older, he or she becomes more aware of people as unique individuals with specific personality traits, abilities, and interests. Liked people are increasingly perceived according to "other oriented" characteristics, whereas disliked people are seen in terms of the personal harm they do. The adolescent is able to recognize that the feelings or actions of others can cause changes in their emotional states. He or she can appreciate the feelings or condition of some distant group as well as the distress of a familiar person and eventually becomes aware of the possibilities of pretended or disguised feelings.

THE ACQUISITION OF IDENTITY

During adolescence, as we have seen, children become increasingly conscious of their own and others' psychological processes. As a result, they become both more introspective and more self-conscious. A related change may be termed *identity formation* and is described by Flavell (1977) as follows:

Children gradually come to think of themselves and others as stable human beings who conserve, over time and circumstances, their personhoods, personalities, social and sexual roles and identities, and many other attributes. Day to day changes in one's own or another's mood and behavior come to be construed as variations on an enduring theme, rather than as a succession of unrelated melodies. (p. 123)

Identity Versus Role Diffusion

In Chapter 1 we discussed Erikson's view of the stages of development as a series of crises whose outcomes may range along a continuum between extremes such as identity and identity confusion (or role diffusion). The adolescent identity crisis is perhaps the best known of these encounters between the individual and the environment. Erikson (1968) points out that in a technological society, the period of adolescence is prolonged by the need to prepare for specialized occupations and thus can be seen as a stage of life separate in many ways from childhood and adulthood. And yet the crisis of adolescence includes many elements of what has occurred before. The infant's need for someone to trust is reflected in the adolescent's search for people and ideas to have faith in. The young child's efforts to determine the limits of his or her autonomy may be seen in the adolescent's indecisiveness and rebellion against authority. The school-age child's desire to produce things is mirrored in the adolescent's worry over the choice of an occupation. According to Erikson, young people are troubled most by the inability to discover an occupational identity. Erikson uses the terms *identity confusion* and *role diffusion* to describe the experience of adolescents during this difficult period.

Elder's study (1974) of children during the Great Depression carries Erikson's notion of occupational identity somewhat further. Children from families who suffered severe income deprivation assumed more work responsibilities both in and outside the home at an earlier age than did children from families who suffered less. These children formulated occupational goals at an earlier age and seemed to acquire a clearer sense of identity with less conflict than did children from more advantaged homes.

Erikson's approach to adolescent egocentrism may be contrasted with Elkind's. Elkind would argue that the conflict described by Erikson (in psychoanalytic terms) is a consequence of cognitive egocentrism. Role diffusion represents the multiple and changing nature of the imaginary audience, whereas identity is the construction of a constant and permanent self. Erikson's approach emphasizes that identity formation does not begin at adolescence; childhood identities are continually forming and changing. At adolescence, however, several factors coincide to make the need for self-definition more critical.

Recent research suggests that the development of self-concept shows a sequence of development that parallels the sequence found for the development of concepts of others. In one study (Montemayor and Eisen, 1977), children between the ages of 9 and 18 were asked to write 20 answers to the question "Who am I?" With age, there were significant increases in the percentage of children who used occupational role (such as hoping to become a paper deliverer or a doctor) and personality characterizations related to occupational success (for example, ambitious, hard-working) to describe themselves. Just as adolescents tend to refer to others with terms that are abstract, interpersonal, and psychological, so they also increasingly tend to refer to themselves with such terms. For example, adolescents are more likely than younger children to refer to their interpersonal style (how they typically act, such as friendly, fair, shy) or their psychic style (how they typically feel, such as happy, calm). At the same time, the use of terms describing the physical self (height, weight) declines. There were significant decreases in the use of other self-characterizations. With age, children were less likely to use territorial terms ("an American living on Oak Street") or to see possessions (owning a dog or a bike) as a symbol of self. In general terms, then, the younger children described themselves in terms of concrete objective categories (address, physical appearance, possessions), whereas adolescents used more abstract and subjective descriptions (such as personal beliefs, motivations, and interpersonal style).

Here is how a 9-year-old saw himself:

The Development of Identity

The school-age child's desire to produce things is mirrored in the adolescent's worry over abilities, interests, and the choice of an occupation.
(Kenneth Karp)

My name is Bruce C. I have brown eyes. I have brown hair. I have brown eyebrows. I'm nine years old. I LOVE! Sports. I have seven people in my family. I have great! eye site. I have lots! of friends. I live on 1923 Pinecrest Dr. I'm going on 10 in September. I'm a boy. I have an uncle that is almost 7 feet tall. My school is Pinecrest. My teacher is Mrs. V. I play Hockey! I'am almost the smartest boy in the class. I LOVE! food. I love fresh air. I LOVE School. (Montemayor and Eisen, 1977, p. 317)

And here is how a 17-year-old described herself:

I am a human being. I am a girl. I am an individual. I don't know who I am. I am a Pisces. I am a moody person. I am an indecisive person. I am an ambitious person. I am a very curious person. I am not an individual. I am a loner. I am an American (God help me). I am a Democrat. I am a liberal person. I am a radical. I am a conservative. I am a pseudoliberal. I am an atheist. I am not a classifiable person (i.e., I don't want to be). (Montemayor and Eisen, 1977, p. 318)

455

The idea that the self remains invariant in the face of physical and other changes develops slowly throughout childhood. This concept is termed *self-and-other constancy*. The concept of physical identity develops before the concept of psychological identity. By the age of 6, the child learns that boys remain boys and girls remain girls, that blue-eyed people remain blue-eyed, that dogs remain dogs, and so on. But what about learning the intentions of self and other others—their motives, their tendencies to be affectionate or hostile? Here sex plays a very important part.

Identity formation occurs at varying rates. Some children establish an identity very early, perhaps in order to avoid anxiety or conflict. Such identities may be rather narrowly defined, as in the case of the athletic star or the "young genius." Or they may be based on the norms of their families and friends, as in the case of youngsters who almost without question go from preparatory school to college to brokerage houses or banks, in the same pattern as their parents and peers (Douvan and Adelson, 1966b, p. 17). At the other extreme are the cases of delayed identity formation in which adolescents cannot "find themselves" and make a point of keeping themselves uncommitted to any particular identity. Some adolescents feel driven to choose a *negative* or deviant identity, characterized by socially prohibited or feared qualities. As we will see, sex makes a considerable difference in identity formation. Boys tend to build their identities around occupational choices. Girls do not tend to make occupational choices as early as do boys, and thus their identities usually remain diffuse for a longer period.

There are two reasons to believe that sex roles are a key factor in the adolescent identity crisis. First, sex roles are learned very early, and even young children define themselves in terms of sex ("Who are you?" "I'm a little boy named Larry"). Moreover, this aspect of identity, assigned at birth, remains unchanged throughout life; hence, sex roles tend to be very stable. The second reason for considering sex roles to be a crucial factor in the identity crisis is the fact that the sex roles assigned by American society parallel the two worlds of home and "outside." The home is connected with child rearing and with "feminine" roles; the world outside the home is supposedly tougher and more "masculine." During adolescence, the individual must make a final transition from the home to the adult world outside the home. The sex-role connotations of these two worlds may be a source of added confusion to the person who is trying to establish an identity.

Sex-Role Identity

The impact of the early assignment of sexual identity was revealed in a study of *hermaphrodites*—children who at birth were not clearly male or female (Money, Hampson, and Hampson, 1957). Some of these children were assigned a sex on the basis of the appearance of their genitals. Later it was discovered that the internal sexual organs of these children were closer to those of the opposite sex. A family that had been raising a child as a boy thus might have to switch to treating the child as a girl. It was found that if the change was made before the age of 4, the child's later sexual adjustment would be normal; if the change was made after age 4, serious maladjustment could result.

In psychoanalytic theory, sex-role differences are considered to be characteristics of the individual. Biological differences between the sexes are important in that they may predispose a child to particular encounters. But there is considerable overlap between the sexes in most of these characteristics (such as activity level or aggressiveness) so that cultural preferences have ample opportunity to shape and modify biological dispositions. To anthropologists sex-role differences are largely a function of culture. This view was expressed by Linton (1936) as follows:

All societies prescribe different attitudes and activities to men and to women. Most of them try to rationalize these prescriptions in terms of the physiological difference between the sexes or their different roles in reproduction. While such factors may have served as a starting point for the development of a division, the actual ascriptions are almost entirely determined by culture. (p. 18)

There are two major cultural influences on sex-role development. First, the family setting varies. In our culture, the nuclear family prevails. In other cultures, extended families may include married sons and daughters and their spouses; mother and children may live without the father; or children may be raised communally, apart from their parents. All these arrangements can have dramatic effects on sex-role development. Second, more diverse types of sex roles are possible in some other cultures than the two that are generally recognized in American society. Consider the following list:

married females who bear children; married males who beget and provide for children; adult males who do not marry and beget children but who exercise some prescribed social function involving celibacy, sexual abstinence, and renunciation of procreation; adult males who assume female roles; adult females who assume male roles, including transvestism; adult females (or, less frequently, males) who maintain themselves economically by the exploitation of sex relationships with extramarital partners; adults whose special, nonprocreative ceremonial role is important; adults of whom various forms of transvestitism and adoption of the behavior of the opposite sex are expected. (Mead, 1961, p. 1456)

Many—perhaps all—of these roles can be found in the same society. These different sex roles may be thought of as *stereotypes,* and cultural differences in the sex-role training of boys and girls are in the direction of these stereotypes. The role of the stereotype was studied by Barry, Bacon, and

Child (1957). These investigators found that the most extreme sex differences are associated with societies whose way of life depends on the
superior strength of the male and with societies in which social customs
result in large family groups that have a high degree of cooperative interaction. By comparison, in American society the emphasis on sex differences is moderate.

AMERICAN SEXUAL STEREOTYPES. In recent years, the women's movement
has focused attention on the sex-role stereotyping that occurs in American
society. Broverman, Vogel, Broverman, Clarkston, and Rosenkrantz (1972)
devised a questionnaire to assess people's perceptions of "typical"
masculine and feminine behavior. On the basis of responses from men
and women, they identified the male and female stereotypes as consisting
of the following "clusters" of attributes:

The male-valued items seem . . . to reflect a "competency" cluster. Included
in this cluster are attributes such as being independent, objective, active,
competitive, logical, skilled in business, worldly, adventurous, able to make
decisions easily, self-confident, always acting as a leader, ambitious. A
relative absence of these traits characterizes the stereotype perception
of women; that is, relative to men, women are perceived to be dependent,
subjective, passive, noncompetitive, illogical. . . .

The female-valued stereotypic items, on the other hand, consist of
attributes such as gentle, sensitive to the feelings of others, tactful, religious,
neat, quiet, interested in art and literature, able to express tender feelings. . . .
Men are stereotypically perceived as lacking in these characteristics,
relative to women. (pp. 66–67)

Broverman and her associates also reviewed a number of studies of sex-
role stereotyping and arrived at several significant conclusions:

1. Sex-role stereotypes are pervasive and persistent in the United States.
   Not only are they widely approved of; they are often idealized, so that
   people who do not measure up to these stereotypes are considered
   "unmasculine" or "unfeminine."
2. Masculine characteristics are valued more highly than feminine characteristics in American society. There are many more girls who wish
   they were boys than boys who wish they were girls; parents are happier
   about boy babies than girl babies; and "masculine" characteristics are
   considered more socially desirable than "feminine" ones. There is
   also a double standard for mental health: Mental health experts tend
   to describe a "healthy man" in the same terms as a "healthy adult,"
   whereas a "healthy woman" is described in less positive terms.
3. Sex-role stereotypes have some effect on a person's self-concept and,
   hence, on his or her behavior. For example, women who perceive them-

selves as more competent than the average woman often plan to have fewer children and to combine employment with child rearing.

4. Maternal employment is a central factor in sex-role stereotyping. Not only does it affect the roles of the parents; it also influences the sex-role stereotypes developed by the child. Children whose parents do the things men and women have traditionally done (that is, whose mother is a full-time homemaker while the father is employed outside the home) see the roles of men and women as very different, whereas those whose parents both work outside the home—and share the housework—see sex roles as similar. In addition, daughters of mothers who work are more likely to seek a career outside the home.

BIOLOGY AND SOCIAL LEARNING. In Chapter 12, we reviewed the myths, realities, and uncertainties of sex differences in children. Although sexual stereotypes are clear and well articulated in American society, girls do not necessarily differ in all the ways suggested by the stereotypes. The question thus arises, to what extent are sex-role differences due to social learning? To put it another way, are sex roles determined by biological forces, with superficial differences assigned by the culture? Let us approach this question from each point of view.

As indicated earlier, boys are stronger and generally more active than girls. Structural and hormonal differences of this sort led to Freud's famous dictum that "anatomy is destiny." However, modern technology makes biological differences, although present, largely irrelevant factors in the development of sex roles (Matteson, 1975). Women can program computers; men can operate dishwashers. Why does the myth that men are necessary in certain roles (mining, truck driving, armed combat) still prevail in American society?

The answer to this question lies in social learning. There is a great deal of evidence that sex-role behavior is "taught" by adult modeling and reinforcement. For example, Bandura and his associates (1962) found that boys performed more imitative aggression than girls. However, when both boys and girls were offered rewards if they imitated the behavior of the model, their performances were almost identical. This finding indicates that sex differences in aggressive behavior can be heightened or muted by social learning.

Imitative learning often occurs through the medium of the toys parents give their children, and this occurs in a variety of cultures. In some societies, playthings linked to the roles of either sex are equally available to children of both sexes, and the activities of both parents are equally visible to their children. In Western industrial societies, however, mothers are usually more visible to their children than fathers. How, then, do boys learn the social norms of masculine behavior?

This is where direct reinforcement comes in. Fathers are particularly likely to reinforce "masculine" behavior in their sons. Mussen (1961) found that boys with strong "masculine" interests tend to describe their fathers as positive in their attitudes toward them. An earlier study (Payne and Mussen, 1956) found that boys who are very similar to their fathers perceive them as highly rewarding and affectionate.

It seems likely that a combination of modeling and direct reinforcement is responsible for the social learning of sex roles. Such a combination was illustrated in a study (Bandura, Ross, and Ross, 1963a) that used three-person groups to represent the nuclear family. In one condition of the experiment, an adult (male or female) played the part of the dispenser of resources. Another adult (male or female) was the recipient of the resources. The third person, a child, was an observer. A second condition of the experiment switched the roles of the child and the second adult, so that the child became the recipient and the adult was the powerless observer. In half of the groups in each condition, the male was the dispenser of resources; in the other half, the female controlled the resources. These conditions were designed to simulate husband-dominant families and wife-dominant families, respectively. In both conditions, the model who had the power to provide reinforcement was imitated; thus the children clearly identified with the source of reward. When the traditional sources of reward were reversed (that is, when the wife was dominant and the child was male), cross-sex imitation occurred. However, the tendency to imitate a model of the opposite sex was stronger in girls, probably reflecting the greater reinforcement for "masculine" behavior provided by our society.

If sex-role learning begins so early in life, why do adolescents experience a sex-role identity crisis? Some investigators suspect that the crisis does not have to do with whether an individual is male or female, or with what, if anything, other people might be thinking about him or her. Rather, given the special characteristics of adolescent thought, the crisis has to do with the nature of the stereotype itself, with whether the individual is or wants to be like that stereotype. Adolescents are well aware of what others *might* be thinking, but they are uncertain of what others—especially peers—are *actually* thinking at any given time. Thus the crisis may be less a matter of knowledge of sex roles (a developmental or maturational issue) and more a matter of evaluating one's particular role. Matteson (1975) expresses this view as follows: "The task of adolescence is not simply the discovery of the male or female role but the creation and affirmation of the individual's particular *style* of being a man or woman" (p. 145; emphasis added). *Why the Crisis?*

When the adolescent identity crisis is viewed in this light, it is clear that a wide variety of factors plays a part in determining how an individual's special identity—sexual and otherwise—will develop. In the first place, as we have seen, males and females are taught different roles and different attitudes toward sexuality. But parents are not the only, nor even the most important, influences in this respect. It is true that mothers and daughters exchange more information about sex than do mothers and sons or fathers and sons or daughters. However, most of what children learn about sex they learn from their peers.

PEER GROUP INFLUENCES. The influence of the peer group on boys and girls differs. Since the visible physical changes that occur in girls have to do with the "figure" rather than the reproductive organs themselves, girls' peer groups become preoccupied with clothes and other aspects of attractiveness and with romantic ideals. Not until the occurrence of menarche do they become interested in sexual matters. In boys, on the other hand, early sexual awareness is genital. Genital maturity in males often occurs before the rest of the body finishes its adolescent growth. The first ejaculation is not discussed with parents, but boys are frank with each other about wet dreams, masturbation, and the like. Unfortunately, most adolescent boys (and girls) seem to think there is something wrong with masturbation and feel guilty about it.

The peer group may be a factor in the development of homosexuality in some individuals. Since young adolescents spend most of their time with same-sexed peers and learn about sexual matters from those peers, it is not surprising to find that some of their erotic feelings are directed toward intimate friends of the same sex. This seems to occur more frequently among boys than girls, perhaps because of the earlier genital development of boys. However, the peer group also provides incentive to go on to heterosexual experience.

"WHEN GIRL MEETS BOY." With regard to heterosexual experience, there have been some significant changes in the past few decades. Preadolescent boys do not shun girls the way they used to. When preadolescents and adolescents were asked to indicate a choice of companion for certain activities, the number of heterosexual choices at each age level studied (sixth, ninth, and twelfth grades) increased compared to the number found in a 1942 study. However, as Matteson (1975) points out, it is unclear whether these results indicate that more heterosexual interaction is actually occurring or simply that more is desired.

Peer pressure plays a role in the age at which dating begins. Apparently, girls, who are at least a year ahead in physical maturation, manage to interest boys in the "dating game," thereby reinforcing the sex roles modeled by their parents. The interactions that do occur appear to be changing too. Dating appears to be more casual and less planned than it was in the past. Yet, whatever form, the process by which boys and girls get together is a difficult one at best. They have been taught different roles and find that they have different attitudes, desires, and goals, particularly in sexual matters. Each, therefore, has much to learn from the other.

SUMMARY

Many important changes take place during adolescence, the last stage of childhood to be completed before a person can gain adult status or be recognized as having adult abilities. Adolescents mature physically, sexually, intellectually, and socially, and these changes are highly interdependent. The term *adolescence* is used to designate the period from puberty to maturity. *Puberty* refers to the state of physical development when sexual reproduction first becomes possible.

Because of the immense changes in the velocity or rate of growth that occurs during this period, adolescents are said to experience a "growth spurt." The average girl begins her growth spurt at about age 10½ and reaches a peak at 12; the average boy lags 2 years behind. Most of the increase in height occurs first in the legs and later in the trunk or torso. Sexual development occurs in an orderly sequence, though the age at which this sequence starts varies considerably. *Sexual dimorphism* refers to the differential growth of various parts of the body that increases the difference in body composition between boys and girls.

There are enormous differences in rates of growth, especially at adolescence, and these differences are largely under genetic control, although environmental factors may have a telling effect. *Secular,* or long-term, trends indicate that puberty is occurring earlier than it did 30 or 40 years ago and that girls now begin menstruating about a year earlier than they did then. Nutrition and physical and social environments are important factors in such trends. Early or late maturation is related to social and emotional as well as to intellectual aspects of development.

Piaget's theories provide a basis for understanding how certain features of the adolescent's thought make possible—if not inevitable—the mental and emotional symptoms of adolescence. Formal operations are characterized by the following aspects of thought: (1) a clear distinction between the actual and the possible; (2) the ability to use symbols to represent other symbols; and (3) the ability to coordinate variables. The ability to let the possible take precedence over the actual is the basis of experimentation and scientific thinking. The ability to let symbols stand for other symbols makes thought more flexible and enables adolescents to consider *logical* relationships between statements as well as the *factual* relationship between a statement and an empirical event. Piaget calls this ability *interpropositional logic.* Although the capacity for formal operations does not appear until adolescence, not all adolescents (or adults) display this capacity. Performance is seldom a reliable indicator of capacity. Even though they may make logical mistakes, adolescents are aware of the type of reasoning involved. Piaget suggests that people may be capable of formal operations only in areas where their interest and experience are greatest.

Changes in the way children think about logical problems are related to the way they think about personal problems. In adolescence, a new form of egocentrism, different from that of early childhood, emerges. Adolescents are able to reason about the thoughts of others. But they fail to recognize that the concerns of others may be quite different from their own.

Adolescents continually anticipate the reactions of other people to their own appearance and behavior. They, therefore, create an *imaginary audience* (as opposed to the imaginary companions of younger children). Adolescents' beliefs that they are important to many people leads to the notion that their feelings are special and unique, which may be viewed as a *personal fable* — a story told by the young person to himself or herself.

The adolescent identity crisis is perhaps the best-known encounter between the individual and the environment. According to Erikson, the inability to discover an occupational identity is what most troubles young people, hence the terms *identity confusion* and *role diffusion.*

According to several investigators, cognitive development determines not only adolescents' perceptions of themselves but also their perceptions of the characteristics of others. As children reach adolescence, they become more aware of people as unique individuals with specific personality traits, abilities, and interests. Adolescents are able to recognize that the feelings or actions of others can cause changes in emotional states. They can appreciate the feelings or condition of some distant group as well as the distress of a familiar person and can eventually become aware of the possibilities of pretended or disguised feelings.

At adolescence, the need for self-definition or *identity formation* becomes critical. Personal qualities must be related to social opportunities and social ideals. Identity formation occurs at varying rates.

The concept of self-and-other constancy develops slowly throughout childhood. The concept of physical identity develops before the concept of psychological identity. Sex roles are a key factor in the adolescent identity crisis. During adolescence, the individual must make a final transition from the home to the outside adult world, and the sex-role connotation of these two worlds may be a source of added confusion to the person who is trying to establish an identity.

There are two major cultural influences on sex-role development: the society of the family and the number of types of sex roles possible. In recent years, the women's movement has focused attention on the sex-role stereotyping that occurs in American society. Although sexual stereotypes are clear and well articulated in American society, boys and girls do not necessarily differ in all ways suggested by the stereotypes. There is a great deal of evidence that sex-role behavior is taught by adult modeling and reinforcement. Some investigators suspect that the adolescent sex-role identity crisis does not have to do with whether an individual is male or female but rather with the nature of the stereotype itself — whether the individual is or wants to be like that stereotype.

CHAPTER 15

Adolescence, Family, and Society

STORM AND STRESS

In 1844, Henry Ward Beecher addressed a youthful audience:

A young man knows little of life; less of himself. He feels in his bosom various impulses, wild desires, restless cravings he can hardly tell for what, a sombre melancholy when all is gay, a violent exhilaration when others are sober. (Beecher, 1844, p. 21)

An audience deliberately composed of young people and addressed by an eminent speaker on a topic pertaining to the psychological characteristics of youth reflected a striking change in the status of young people during the early decades of the nineteenth century. According to Demos and Demos, historians of the American family, the change in America from an agricultural to an urban and industrial society brought with it a separation of children from adults, a grouping of children by age, and the discovery of adolescence as a troublesome period of childhood (Demos and Demos, 1977). Although books and pamphlets about or directed to young people were becoming popular at that time, the widespread notion that adolescence is a period of storm and stress *(Sturm und Drang)* achieved scientific respectability in the work of G. Stanley Hall (1904). Believing that it is typical for adolescents to shift from one psychological extreme to another, Hall emphasized the contrasting moods that may be seen in rapid succession in almost any adolescent: gaiety and optimism one day, hopelessness and depression the next; generosity one moment, selfishness the next. This tendency to shift from one mood to another within a short time became known as *adolescent turmoil.*

Some writers have gone so far as to consider adolescent behaviors in their extreme forms as similar to schizophrenic episodes, and indeed, it is during adolescence that true schizophrenic breakdowns may first occur. In fact, many normal adolescent characteristics (for example, feelings of dislocation, extreme docility, emotional volatility, and talk of suicide) in their extreme forms resemble schizophrenic behavior (Rogers, 1969). Eissler (1958) suggested that the child's psychic structure "dissolves" during adolescence. The result, naturally, is psychological chaos. Unable to control his or her impulses, the adolescent becomes a slave to them, and a variety of symptoms appear—antisocial behavior, looseness of thinking, intensity and volatility of feelings, a search for immediate gratifications.

In addition to the sociohistorical account given by Demos and Demos, there is support in psychological theory for the view of adolescent turmoil as a major phenomenon in psychological development. For one thing, it is compatible with traditional psychoanalytic theories, in which the child passes through a series of stages—oral, anal, phallic, latent, adolescent—before reaching adulthood. For another, clinical studies of disturbed adolescents seem to support the psychoanalytic viewpoint. On the other hand, there are arguments against such a view. Offer (1969) points out, for example, that "adolescent turmoil" as a universal concept is too vague and unclear to be useful as a psychiatric diagnosis. There is also evidence from normative studies (e.g., Douvan and Adelson, 1966a) of relatively little turmoil during adolescence. In one study, over 11,000 adolescents were given a personality test (the Minnesota Multiphasic Personality Inventory) initially designed to diagnose psychiatric problems. The percentage of adolescents (10–20%) whose scores fell in a range suggesting psychopathology did not differ from the percentage found in adult samples (Hathaway and Monachesi, 1963).

Similar results were obtained by Offer (1969), who conducted a 6-year longitudinal study of 73 normal boys. The period of study ended with the boys' graduation from high school. Interviews with the boys and their parents, teacher ratings, and psychological testing failed to produce evidence of widespread adolescent turmoil. "The concept of adolescent turmoil," writes Offer, "should be seen as only one route for passing through adolescence, one that the majority of our subjects did not utilize" (p. 179). Additional analyses of the data led to the division of the boys into three groups. Boys in the *continuous* growth group (23%) sailed through adolescence with ease. They were "happy human beings" with a realistic self-image and a sense of humor. They could cope with pressures and accepted societal norms. Members of the *surgent* group (35%) did well most of the time; under stress, however, they tended to lose control. It was the *tumultuous* group (22%) which most resembled the description of adolescence offered by G. Stanley Hall. Boys in this group experienced

Trust	I feel that life is just great.	
vs.		
Mistrust	I worry about the future.	
Autonomy	I can make up my mind without making	
vs.	mistakes.	
Shame and Doubt	I need more self-confidence.	
Initiative	I think of exciting and worthwhile things to	
vs.	do and do them.	
Guilt	I am afraid to really let myself go.	
Industry	I am known as a good worker.	
vs.		
Inferiority	I feel that other people do things much better than I do.	
Identity	I know my place in life and feel that it is	
vs.	right for me.	
Role Diffusion	I wonder what the real me is like.	
Intimacy	I have very close relations with other people.	
vs.		
Isolation	I am lonely.	

Source: McClain, 1975, p. 530.

TABLE 15–1
Sample Items From a "Self-Description" Blank Based on Erikson's Stages of Psychosocial Development

sharp mood swings; they experienced more anxiety and depression and were more likely to respond to small frustrations as major tragic events (Offer and Offer, 1974). For this reason, Offer suggests the term *normative crisis* to describe the experience most children undergo during adolescence.

This is not to deny that there is some degree of "turmoil" in adolescence, even under the best of conditions. Between the ages of 12 and 14, the *modal* adolescent (the most typical adolescent) shows a tendency to rebel against his or her parents in various ways. However, this conflict—or "bickering"—is usually over trivial issues: whether to have the stereo on while studying, whether to wear jeans or a skirt to Grandma's house for dinner. As a rebellion, this sort of behavior is not very severe; the adolescent and his or her parents become irritants to each other, but the adolescent continues to respect the parents' opinions.

Adolescent turmoil appears to ease during the high school years. In fact Erikson (1968) refers to these years as a "psycho-social moratorium"— "a period that is characterized by a selective permissiveness on the part of society and provocative playfulness on the part of youth" (p. 157). It is as if the student has been given an opportunity to test his or her environment in ways that will not result in intensified inner turmoil. However, whereas behavioral disruptions are at their worst during junior high school (that is, early adolescence), psychic distress increases in later adolescence. This pattern was illustrated in a recent study of adolescents in six communities in the United States and Europe (McClain, 1975). Self-descriptive statements were prepared (sample items from which are shown in Table 15–1, based on Erikson's stages of psychosocial development. Subjects from 12 to 18 years old were asked to indicate how much of the time (ranging from "never" to "always") each item was true for them. The responses showed a common pattern for each category: 12- and 13-year-olds showed "a naive certainty" about identity, presumably because they did not yet fully appreciate the problems they would have to deal with; 14- to 16-year-olds, in the midst of questioning their identities, showed "shaken confidence and disequilibrium"; and 17- and 18-year-olds showed "restoration of some confidence and balance."

Clearly, with respect to emotional development—that is, what is going on *inside* the child—it is the middle years of adolescence, from 14 to 16, that are the hardest. Everyone knows that adolescence is far from sublime but, as we have seen, neither is it inevitably marked by turmoil and conflict. What, then, is the nature of the social and emotional changes that appear during this period of development? In this chapter, we will discuss the adolescent's relationships with family, peers, and society, and some implications of these relationships in terms of adolescent behavior.

GENERATIONAL CONFLICT

Is generational conflict myth or reality? The question of generational conflict is a complex one consisting of at least three parts. First, there is the matter of conflict within the family: Do adolescents reject family values, and are the teen years filled with strife and contention between parent and child? The second part of the question deals with the presence of a "youth subculture" that emphasizes conformity to the values of the peer group—values that conflict with those of adults. Does the peer group channel and reinforce adolescent rebellion? Finally, there is the adolescent's relationship to secondary institutions—the school or, more generally, the community. What causes delinquent behavior in school or in the community? What makes some students alienated, others radical?

The Family Battleground

THE CASE FOR CONFLICT. Several influential viewpoints—both psychological and sociological—assume that conflict between adolescents and their parents is a fact of life. However, they explain the conflict in different ways.

According to psychoanalytic theory, there is an upsurge of sexual excitement during adolescence. During childhood, the sexual instinct is primarily autoerotic, taking the form of thumb-sucking or masturbation. As we have seen, however, the body undergoes some fundamental changes during puberty. The state of sexual "readiness" that results brings with it a renewal of the Oedipal conflict. But now the child cannot repress his or her sexual desires. Moreover, the adolescent has acquired a nagging superego, or conscience, which monitors his or her behavior and enforces the taboo against incest. Since the adolescent can reject neither sexuality nor superego, what remains is to reject his or her parents.

Other psychoanalytic theorists believe it is the parents of adolescents who are responsible for generational conflict. According to Freidenberg (1959), for instance, parents are frightened by the spontaneity, irreverence, and questioning of youth. The biological signs of adulthood they see developing in their children remind them of their own advancing age. The conflict that arises from such feelings is made worse by the dreams of success and achievement parents have for their children. In order to realize such dreams, which usually require long and thorough preparation in college and sometimes graduate school, the adolescent must remain in a position of enforced dependency—and as long as parents pay the bills, they expect "good" behavior in return.

Theorists who view the conflict in *intrapsychic* terms (that is, in terms of the child rejecting the parents or the parents rejecting the child) see it not only as inherent in the development of personality but as a necessary part of the struggle for independence and self-definition. Through active opposition or rebellion, young people gain a better understanding of the world around them and come to grips with who they are and where they stand. In challenging parental values, they come to understand those values better. In exposing adult hypocrisy, they acquire some understanding of the basis of moral judgment and the difficulty of translating possibility into reality. In turning away from the love objects of childhood, they find new love objects with whom sexual energies can be released in a socially acceptable manner.

Still other theorists see generational conflict as a social phenomenon. Davis (1940), for instance, believes a "generation gap" is inevitable in a fast-changing society. Parents raise their children according to their own experience, and that experience quickly becomes outdated. In other words, parents prepare children to live in a society that no longer exists. The generation gap, therefore, is not simply a problem of communication; rather, it is a result of the fact that young people can sense the inadequacy of the wisdom of past generations for life in the present and the future world.

Sociologists such as Davis also noted that the generation gap is a result of occupational and educational mobility and cultural differences. Differences are inevitable between children who go to college and their parents who did not, between children who were born in this country and their parents who were born in "the old country." These differences are aggravated by conflicting status roles—parents encourage economic reliance by stressing the need for education, yet berate their children (who would rather be independent) for being "irresponsible" and "dependent." Adding fuel to this fire is the fact that authority figures often disagree with one another. For example, parents may encourage their children to hit back when attacked, whereas the school may try to teach them to settle their conflicts by "talking it out." Or mothers and fathers may disagree. Mothers, for example, tend to be less lenient than fathers toward their daughters' sexual experimentation, with the situation reversed for sons. Fathers may be "soft" on daughters, while mothers are demanding and tough on them. Mothers may dote on sons, despite Dad's resentment.

Adolescents are sensitive to such contradictions and critical of them. Some investigators believe that this criticism serves a cultural function (Matteson, 1974; Braungart, 1974). In this view, the adolescent is a link in the transmission and revision of human culture. By looking at traditional values with a critical eye, he or she makes fresh contact with established customs and opens the way for new interpretations and social innovations. Generational conflict thus represents an effort to change whatever is inappropriate in the value system handed down by adults. Note that this is a two-way relationship. Just as the young are socialized by adults, so adults may be resocialized by the young. If adults become too remote from their children, this process becomes more difficult and conflict is more intense.

Another sociological view attributes generational conflict to the isolation of young people from the workings of modern technological society. Adolescents are segregated into high schools, cut off from employment opportunities, and unable to participate in adult decision making. Isolation leads to alienation, skepticism, and detachment—which, in turn, lead to rebellion.

THE EVIDENCE. Upon becoming an adolescent, the child faces a paradox: He or she must remain in the role of son or daughter while at the same time gradually moving away from the position of a dependent child to that of an independent adult. For most adolescents, this transition is accomplished without extreme conflict. Their autonomy shows striking increases, yet they do not abandon their emotional ties to their parents. (This is especially true of girls.) Adolescents apparently settle for "ritual signs of independence" such as holding part-time jobs, having some money of their own, having a social life independent from that of their families (Gold and Douvan, 1969). Moreover, the results of a study by Bandura (1964) contradict the stereotype of the rebellious teenager in conflict with parents. Although parents are thought to become more restrictive during their children's teenage years, Bandura found that parents

tend to relax their control over their children as the children become increasingly able to take responsibility for their own behavior. Although parents and adolescents are supposed to be in continual conflict, Bandura found that such conflicts are greatly reduced during the teenage years. And although parents are supposed to disapprove of their adolescent children's friends and companions, Bandura found that the peer group actually reinforces parental standards of behavior and thus serves as a substitute for parental control.

In general, there is an increase in moral autonomy (control of impulses, correct behavior, knowledge of right and wrong) during adolescence, as well as some growth in emotional autonomy. But the degree of change is surprisingly small compared to what might be expected on the basis of accounts of adolescent turmoil, rebellion, and so forth. Accordingly, some researchers believe such accounts are exaggerated. Offer (1969), for instance, believes that many investigators have overgeneralized from studies of disturbed adolescents to the population as a whole.

Offer's longitudinal study (1969), which was mentioned earlier, concentrated on normal, "modal" adolescent boys from two suburban middle-class communities. The boys and their parents were interviewed regularly throughout the boys' high school years. The results of the study provide a sharp contrast to the view of adolescents in conflict with parents and society. The teenage boys functioned well within their own families. For example, they could discuss most of their concerns—with the exception of sexual feelings—with their parents. More important, they appeared to share their parents' basic values in areas such as religion, ethics, and politics, as well as their attitudes toward education, work, and social relations. Some of Offer's specific findings are of interest. As noted earlier, whatever conflict occurred seemed to be confined largely to the years between the twelfth and fourteenth birthdays and was usually over seemingly insignificant issues. During the high school years, on the other hand, the values and judgments of the boys were in remarkable agreement with those of their parents. Moreover, though mothers and fathers were interviewed separately, they tended to agree with each other in assessments of their sons.

The boys were often critical of their parents and sometimes complained that their parents were not consistent in matters of discipline. Basically, though, the boys reflected their parents' middle-class values. For example, almost 90% of them planned to go to college. If any real "rebellion" may be said to have occurred among these teenagers, it took place at school, rather than at home.

PARENTAL ATTITUDES. The question naturally arises: What parental attitudes make the transition from childhood to adulthood easy, and what attitudes make it difficult? The Offers (1974) note that parents of boys in the continuous growth group supported independence in their children and seemed confident and in agreement about social values. By contrast, parents of boys in the tumultuous group were distressed by the strivings of their sons for independence and were uncertain and inconsistent in the values they expressed to their children. Other studies have shown that a democratic style of parental control results in greater autonomy in the adolescent than either an autocratic or a very lenient style. Autocratic or very lenient parents tend to have children who are either dependent or rebellious (Douvan and Adelson, 1966a; Elder, 1962). The children themselves provide clues to the most desirable parental behavior. The more autonomous children report that their parents give them a voice in making the rules they must follow and that their parents expect them to show autonomy in their behavior. Dependent and rebellious children, by contrast, report that their parents expect obedience above all else (Gold and Douvan, 1969).

Parental attitudes and behaviors may have a profound influence on an adolescent's confidence in being in control of his or her life. Wichern and Nowicki (1976) have studied the children of parents who provide early independence training—parents who begin during the preschool years to prepare their children for later independence by teaching skills that will make the child self-reliant and allowing opportunities for cause-and-effect learning to take place. They found that children who receive early independence training develop an "internal locus of control." That is, they tend to attribute the events of their lives to their own efforts rather than to external forces (such as fate). An internal locus of control, in turn, is associated with better intellectual functioning (Handel, 1975).

Kandel and Lesser (1972) compared parent-adolescent relationships and adolescent independence in Denmark and the United States. They found no evidence that adolescents in either country are generally estranged from their parents. However, Danish and American families show vastly different child-rearing styles, with resultant differences in how the children feel they are treated. American adolescents are more likely to describe parental discipline as "authoritarian" and less likely to report that their parents explain their decisions. American adolescents tend to have more rules to follow. Danish adolescents, on the other hand, report greater participation in decisions and a greater feeling that they are treated as adults and that their sense of independence is increasing.

There is evidence, then, that when parents use more democratic child-rearing methods, more explanation, and logical reasoning, children become more responsible, more alert to ethical and moral principles, and more self-directed. It may well be that children brought up in this way require fewer explicit rules, since they are more likely to have internalized parental values.

PARENTS AND PEERS. During childhood, parents are valued more highly than peers, but between the ages of 12 and 18, parents gradually become less important. It is generally assumed that friends and companions become more attractive to the child during adolescence, but Curtis (1975) has found that adolescents' valuations of their peers do not change appreciably during their teens. Moreover, teenagers' judgments of their parents are likely to become more positive during later adolescence. It should be noted, however, that the data in Curtis's study come from the later 1950s and early 1960s. One wonders whether the 1970s have brought any changes in this pattern.

Adolescents today may not feel estranged from their parents and may even turn to them for advice. There is evidence, however, that some ethical judgments may be influenced more by peers than by parents. Lasseigne (1975) has studied the question of whether peer group influence has increased since 1964. Her results support the hypothesis that the moral beliefs of adolescents are influenced significantly more today than a decade ago by the opinions of a majority of the members of their peer group. However, Lasseigne's findings do not support the hypothesis that adults have less influence on adolescents today. Instead, the influence of adults appears to have increased. Lasseigne (1975) summarizes the results of her study as follows:

Overall, the results of this study supported the widely held belief that the adolescent was extremely vulnerable where the peer group was concerned. In matters related to moral courage, responsibility, loyalty, honesty and friendliness, adolescents were influenced by the opinions of their peers to a significantly greater degree than they were by their parents. This was particularly true of the very young adolescent. While parents had gained in terms of the influence they wielded upon adolescents, it was still the higher court of peers who exercised the final authority. (p. 229)

In short, today's adolescent appears to be seeking guidance from *both* parents and peers. There is some evidence that democratically reared children are especially likely to benefit from both parents and peers; these children are more interested in acquiring information than in rebelling (Purnell, 1970).

In some areas, however, adolescents tend not to seek their parents' advice. The studies just described show that the modal adolescent is neither rebellious nor alienated from his or her family. Yet there are definite tensions at this stage of development, centering primarily on sexual standards. Parents are more conservative than their children in their sexual attitudes, not so much because of the age difference as because their roles in life have changed. The clash between mothers and daughters with respect to premarital sex is especially likely to be tense. There is evidence that the mother-daughter conflict over sex is so deep that by the time the daughter is 20, they disagree about whether the subject can even be discussed. Bell (1966) found that 83% of the mothers interviewed felt that daughters should answer mothers' questions about their sexual behavior, whereas only 37% of the daughters felt that they should do so.

Conflict with Authority

What about conflict with authority figures other than parents? While adolescents think less highly of their parents during their teens than they did at younger ages, their opinions of other adults is even lower. Offer (1969), for instance, noted that the adolescents in his study were more critical of teachers than of parents. In an effort to discover how attitudes toward authority change as a person grows older, Matteson (1974) examined the responses of students to questions about nonparental authority figures both before and after entering college. He predicted that when adolescents left home, the conflict with their parents would decrease and their negative attitudes toward authority would decrease correspondingly. The results of Matteson's study are of considerable interest. On the first test (that is, before starting college), the students who planned to move away from home and live on campus were found to be more negative toward authority and more self-assertive than those who planned to live at home. On the second test, however, the two groups of students showed similar attitudes toward authority; the "home" group's attitudes had become more negative. How can these findings be explained? Matteson (1974) suggests that "perhaps it is the more independent student who is ready to leave home.... And perhaps the increase in negative attitudes among the subjects staying at home is an indication that they are beginning to mature" (p. 343). The increase in negative attitudes toward authority in adolescents, Matteson concludes, "may...have more to do with a healthy increase in critical thought than with family conflict and rebellion" (p. 347). This conclusion must be considered tentative, however, since few studies of this age group adequately sample diverse regional, ethnic, and socioeconomic groups.

THE PEER GROUP

The shift to peer associations is a distinguishing mark of adolescence. Peer relationships differ from family relationships in two important ways: (1) Family relationships are "given" and permanent, whereas peer relationships must be formed and are more easily changed. (2) Friendship is "enlarging." That is, it exposes one to new behaviors and allows one to try on new roles and self-images that relationships in the family do not generally allow (Gold and Douvan, 1969).

The adolescent's concepts of friendship change continuously between the ages of 11 and 18. In middle childhood, the child sees friendship as a partnership based on a common activity, with relatively little emotional exchange and little conflict. During adolescence, the friendship itself becomes important and sometimes involves intense emotional interaction and considerable conflict. However, the adolescent's choice of friends may not be entirely "free." Friends tend to come from the same social background and the same neighborhood and to be similar in personal characteristics such as mental age, moral standards, sociability, and willingness to criticize self or others.

Much study has been devoted to the effects of the adolescent's association with peers in view of the age segregation that prevails in American society. Adolescents are separated from their parents and other people of different ages by the high school. According to some investigators, the result is that the peer group, not the family, dominates their lives. Moreover, it is claimed that some parents abdicate their child-rearing responsibility to the peer group. Bronfenbrenner (1970) stresses the fact that adolescents and their parents are spending less and less time together. He, too, believes parents are failing to fulfill their responsibilities and views the increased participation of children in the peer group as harmful.

Readiness to comply with peer-sponsored misbehavior increases between the ages of 7 and 13 and then declines. (Joel Gordon, DPI)

Without adult participation in child rearing and adult direction of peer relations, says Bronfenbrenner, the adolescent's involvement in the peer group may lead to undesirable behavior.

Other research has provided a somewhat different picture of peer group influence (Elder, 1968; Hirschi, 1969). These studies have found that adolescents' reliance on peers for companionship or guidance varies according to the degree and type of attention they receive from parents. Those whose parents are absent or fail to show affection and concern for them are likely to rely heavily on peers for their emotional needs. In a recent study, Condry and Siman (1974) compared adolescents who were peer-oriented with those who were adult-oriented. Peer-oriented adolescents tended to have a negative view of themselves; they judged themselves to be less dependable, "meaner," and less obedient than adult-oriented adolescents did. They were pessimistic about the future, and in accord with the pessimism, they did not do as well in school. These adolescents spent most of their free time in diffuse, "filler" activities—hanging around, "rapping," and partying. They were also more likely to become involved in delinquent behavior. The parents of peer-oriented adolescents failed either to support or control their children; their mode of response can be best characterized as passive neglect.

How readily do children yield to peer pressure—specifically, peer-sponsored misbehavior? Generally, readiness to comply with such pressure increases between the ages of 7 and 13 and then declines. Moreover, during the years from 7 to 13, conformity to peers increases relative to conformity to parents. It is assumed that the readiness to comply with peers even when it comes to breaking rules is related to the child's increased respect for peers. But Bixenstine, DeCorte, and Bixenstine (1976) have shown that children become more critical of their peers between the third and eighth grades. However, the same investigators have found that there is a correlation between readiness to conform to peer-sponsored misbehavior and lack of respect for parents and other adults. In fact, the relationship is stronger in the case of other adults: The child who has a low regard for other adults is more likely to yield to peer pressure than the child who has a high regard for other adults. Thus

it is not an advancing regard for and loyalty to peers . . . that accounts for the child's growing readiness to affirm peer-sponsored antisocial behavior, but an intense disillusionment with adult veracity, strength, wisdom, importance, good will, and fairmindedness. The child is not won away from parents to children, rather he is, at least for a time, lost to adults. (Bixenstine et al., 1976, p. 235)

What, exactly, is the peer group, then, and what is its true role? In a landmark study, Coleman (1961) found that high school students develop value systems centering on athletic abilities and social leadership and that students who are not skilled in these areas generally are excluded from the group. He concluded that the adolescent peer group constitutes a separate society distinct from that of adults.

Coleman's idea of an adolescent "subculture" caught on quickly. One had only to look at any group of adolescents to see clothing and hair styles, musical fads, language, and dance forms that seemed shared by teenagers and very different from those of adults. Sometimes they were so different as to seem bizarre. Coleman's view that adolescents have a separate culture was supported by the fact that the peer group obviously has a strong claim on its members' loyalty. Even though adolescents seek their parents' advice in making important decisions, in less important matters the values of the peer group make themselves felt to a large and highly visible extent. However, Coleman's methods were challenged by Epperson (1964). Coleman had asked adolescents whether they would be more disturbed by their parents' disapproval or by breaking with their closest friend. This made "disapproval" emotionally equivalent to "breaking." But disapproval undoubtedly occurs much more often than "breaking," so that the adolescent is likely to see breaking with a friend as the more significant of the two events. To overcome this difficulty, Epperson constructed the following question: "Which one of these things would make you the most unhappy? (a) If my parents did not like what I did; (b) If my (favorite) teacher did not like what I did; (c) If my best friend did not like what I did." His results were very different from those of Coleman

TABLE 15–2
Relative Concern over Negative Evaluation by Others

	EPPERSON		COLEMAN	
	Boys	*Girls*	*Boys*	*Girls*
Parent	80.4%	80.5%	53.8%	52.9%
Teacher	3.6%	1.2%	3.5%	2.7%
Best friend	15.8%	18.1%	42.7%	43.4%

Source: Epperson, 1964, Table 1, p. 94.

(see Table 15-2): 80% of the adolescents tested said they would be most unhappy if their parents disliked what they did. Epperson also compared the responses of elementary shcool and high school students to the same question. He found no evidence that high school students are less concerned about their parents' disapproval than elementary school students. If anything, the data show greater parental attachment in the high school years. Thus it is clear that the results of a study may depend on the questions asked.

If there is *not* a true adolescent subculture, how does the peer group influence its members? Although peer contact does increase during adolescence, peers seem to influence some attitudes, values, and behaviors but not others. At least during the high school years, the deeper beliefs—social, political, and religious—tend to reflect the views of the family, whereas more superficial behaviors tend to follow those of the peer group (especially when peers are present). Kandel (1974) writes, ''The extent of adolescent separateness from adults varies with the issue involved, and is always relative. No behavior comes under the exclusive dominance of a particular generation, either peers or parents. When the issues involve immediate gratifications,...adolescents tend to be particularly responsive to pressures from members of their own generation'' (p. 128). Drug use is a prime example of these ''immediate gratifications.'' Thus Kandel points out that the adolescent's use of drugs does not necessarily mean rejection of parents and family.

To sum up, at one time the peer group was seen in global terms as a ''peer culture.'' This concept, however, is a vague, undifferentiated one that obscures the very different ways in which adolescents may associate with one another. It may be that different forms of peer association have different implications for the adolescent's relations with parents and for his or her susceptibility to peer influence. Accordingly, we will turn our attention to the structures of peer association (dating, crowds and cliques, gangs) that emerge during adolescence.

Dating

During adolescence, children have their first experience with heterosexual social life. This usually begins with a period of heterosexual group activity and progresses to dating. According to Douvan and Adelson

477

Adolescent dating is a way of introducing young people to heterosexual social life through a system of prescribed roles. (Lyn Gardiner, Stock, Boston)

(1966), an important change occurs for girls around the age of 14. Before the fourteenth birthday, girls tend to share active team sports with boys and do not distinguish sharply between activities that are appropriate for all-girl groups and those that are appropriate for mixed groups. Around age 14, however, girls tend to engage in individual sports such as tennis and swimming, as well as social activities with boys, but they do not share team sports with boys. The distinction between all-girl and mixed activities becomes clearer.

Dating usually begins around age 14 for girls and age 15 for boys. It is generally agreed that adolescent dating is not "courting behavior" but, rather, a way of introducing children to heterosexual social life through a system of prescribed roles. As Gold and Douvan (1969) describe it, "Dating behavior is as ritualized as medieval courtly love, but has, at least in its early stages, much less to do with sex. The obligations of a good date include cheerfulness, the capacity to control moods and impulses, and good manners" (p. 177).

Almost all girls have dated by the age of 17, and 30% have formed a steady relationship with one boy. Such relationships are more common

478

today than they were before World War II, but they seem not to lead to early marriage. Indeed, dating and "going steady" may serve very different purposes. The results of a study by Larson, Spreitzer, and Snyder (1976) suggest that going steady may reflect lower educational or occupational aspiration and may be a way of compensating for personal insecurity.

What determines the attractiveness of members of the opposite sex? Sociometric testing has shown that popularity in general is associated with athletic ability and interest, sociability, and social adjustment (Horowitz, 1967). Boys prefer girls who are interested in sports, are friendly, have leadership ability, do well academically, and are relatively well off economically. Girls' preferences are similar, though they value sports less.

A recent study (Place, 1975) illuminates some of the problems girls encounter when they begin dating: parental resistance to dating, the relative immaturity of boys of the same age, and parental disapproval of the boys they date. The most difficult obstacle to overcome is parental resistance to the first date. As mentioned earlier, parents usually want their daughters to wait until they are 16, but most girls want to begin dating at an earlier age. They develop a variety of strategies to obtain this privilege. One girl in the study said, "You can't ask them [parents], just go— just tell them." For others, however, it is not so easy. They may nag their parents until they give in, or give examples of other girls who are "going out." Even when permission to date has been granted, however, there is continued conflict over matters such as how often, how late, and where. In such cases, the girl may play one parent against the other, for example: "Dad, can I go to the show? (Dad: I don't know, ask your mother.) Mom, Dad said it's OK to go to the show if you say yes. Then, my Mom says yes and then I say to my Dad, Mom said yes" (cited in Place, 1975, p. 159). Other techniques are peer group pressure—"As long as I name off a whole group of girls that are going, my Mom lets me go"—and examples of older brothers and sisters who have obtained similar privileges (Place, 1975). When it comes to getting their parents to approve of a particular boy, girls are less manipulative and more likely to keep their parents' values in mind. But parents are at a disadvantage in that their impressions often depend largely on the boy's appearance and manners, and these characteristics may not truly represent the boy. Parents are thus as likely to make bad judgments as they are to make good ones.

In addition to dealing with their parents, girls have had to cope with the stereotype in which the boy is expected to play the aggressive role. Since most adolescent boys do not date as early as girls, they usually date girls somewhat younger than themselves and tend to go around with a particular girl rather than dating at random. Thus girls who feel they must wait to be asked for a date may spend a lot of time at home waiting for the phone to ring.

Adolescents tend to form "crowds" and "cliques." A crowd is a group of young people who "hang out" together. It is the center of organized social activities such as parties and dances, provides the framework for heterosexual contacts, and serves as a sort of reservoir of friends who can be called upon for various social activities. Not surprisingly, adolescents view members of their crowd as more attractive physically than outsiders consider them to be (Cavior and Dokecki, 1973).

Crowds and Cliques

A clique is a subset of a crowd. It is smaller (about 6 members as opposed to 20), and therefore more intimate than a crowd. Cliques are more cohesive and more clearly defined; indeed, "exclusion of those who do not belong is the express purpose of the clique" (Hollingshead, 1949, p. 448). Clique leaders manage most of the communication between the clique and the crowd and thus give some structure to the clique's activities. The leaders tend to date more and, in general, are more mature in their heterosexual relations, often acting as advisors to other clique members. Furthermore, membership in a clique seems to be a prerequisite of membership in a crowd. Dunphy (1963) found no case in which an individual was a member of a crowd without at the same time being a member of a clique. However, a person could be a clique member without being a crowd member.

Cliques and crowds play an important role in the development of heterosexual groups. This development takes place in five stages: (1) the formation of the preadolescent unisexual clique, (2) interaction between unisexual cliques of opposite sexes in a group setting (such as a church youth group), (3) the formation of heterosexual cliques and the beginning of dating (members of these cliques still belong to their original unisexual clique), (4) reorganization of the group's structure so that the basic clique is heterosexual, and (5) the formation of couples who are going steady or are engaged (Dunphy, 1963).

Crowd activities occur outside the school, but clique activities occur in school as much as outside of it. In fact, the high school is where most group activity occurs. Cusick (1973) points out, "The school places practically no barriers to student group interaction. There are two reasons for this: (1) Students are always in the company of others who . . . are identical, and (2) there is a tremendous amount of school time taken up with procedural and maintenance details during which students, within broad limits, are free to do what they wish" (p. 118).

Clique activities have also been studied by Siman (1977), who compared peer and parent values in clique members. Siman concluded that the clique acts as a "filter" of parent norms. It reinterprets parental values for the group and homogenizes the values of its members around the *modal* parental standard. For example, in a clique of 6 members, if four sets of parents fix midnight as a curfew and two sets cite 11 P.M., the parents who wanted their kids in at 11 will probably agree to the later curfew.

There is evidence, then, that because membership in a group is initial-

Cliques and crowds provide group settings for social interaction (Mitchell Payne, Jeroboam)

ly determined by shared values on the part of the youngsters, group membership reflects family values. The peer group thus extends the socialization process beyond the family, but in such a way that basic agreement with family values is maintained. Viewed in this light, the homogenization process that occurs as a result of peer group membership may be seen as modernizing rather than revolutionizing social standards.

Gang Activity

Gangs present a different form of social grouping from crowds and cliques —a form with very different implications for the individual and for society. Gangs have a high degree of structure. Leadership roles and responsibilities in the gang are carefully defined, and the gang has a name and a specific territory. Since gangs usually are associated with illegal and delinquent activities, they have aroused considerable social concern. Researchers have suggested several characteristics that distinguish young people who join gangs from those who do not. These include "poverty, broken home, lack of adequate educational and vocational models, parents with criminal histories, lower intelligence test scores, lack of adequate preparation for educational experience, lack of impulse control, reliance on physical and verbal aggression as coping mechanisms within the gang, and a potential for dangerous behavior" (Friedman, Mann, and Friedman, 1975, p. 564).

Gangs of black and Puerto Rican youths have emerged primarily in the slum areas of large cities—New York, Philadelphia, Detroit—where protection is a necessity. The gang organization is usually inherited from previous residents of the neighborhood.

An intensive study of gangs in Philadelphia (Friedman et al., 1975) found that the characteristic most street gang members have in common

481

is a tendency for violent behavior. Gang members' second most signifi-cant characteristic is defiance of parents—arguing with, cursing at, and hitting parents, actions which are, of course, closely associated with a tendency toward violence. Gang membership is also marked by more arrests for illegal activities, more frequent truancy, more alcohol abuse, and more permissive attitudes toward drug use.

Gangs are more likely to be noticed in poor, urban neighborhoods—black as well as white. Yet it would be a mistake to assume that large num-bers of young people join gangs, even though it may be to their advantage (in terms of protection) to do so. One study of black youth (Himes, 1961) suggests that gang organization may be a relatively unusual form of ado-lescent organization. As an alternative to forming gangs, "low-prestige youths tend to participate habitually in loose, fluid, shifting bands. Such bands appear to lack regular leaders, well-defined membership, and clear-cut organization" (Himes, 1961, p. 534).

Nor do all young people who live in urban slums engage in delinquent activities. Scarpitti (1965) compared a group of low-income, 14- to 15-year-old boys who engaged in delinquent activities with a group who did not and with a middle-class control group. Scarpitti considered the following three hypotheses regarding the origins of delinquency:

1. Delinquency in working-class boys results from a feeling of frustration at the lack of opportunity to move upward socially. For example, they cannot afford to go to college; they cannot find well-paying jobs.
2. Delinquency grows out of a rejection of middle-class values, which are replaced by a new value system emphasizing cleverness, toughness, and excitement.
3. Delinquency is caused by an unhealthy self-concept due to unfavorable social experiences.

The results of the study appeared to support the first two hypotheses. Delinquents tend to reject middle-class values and feel that their op-portunities to achieve the rewards available to middle-class children are very limited. Nondelinquent lower-class boys feel the same way, but not as strongly. However, the nondelinquent lower-class and middle-class boys are similar in their feelings of self-worth. Although the nonde-linquent lower-class boys share many attitudes with delinquents, their self-concepts are closer to those of middle-class boys. In short, measures of self-concept reveal the greatest gap between delinquent and non-delinquent groups (and between gang members and nongang members).

There is much debate over whether the family or the gang plays a more important role in determining delinquent behavior. Stanfield (1966) be-lieves that these two influences interact. Pleasant family experiences reinforce family values. Unpleasant or unsatisfying family experiences weaken beliefs in family value systems and increase susceptibility to outside influences such as the gang. The socioeconomic status of the group is important in the production of delinquent behavior. The relationship between social class and family and peer behavior is complex. Middle- and lower-class gangs may engage in equally delinquent (though different) behavior. Differences between the groups may reside more in their resources than in the destructiveness of their activities. Middle-class gangs may have easy access to cars and to money, which allow them to escape their own neighborhoods for pool halls and cafés where they are not known by the community and the police. Thus they may avoid being labeled as delinquents. Lower-class gangs, on the other hand, tend to hang around their own neighborhoods where they are perceived by the community and by the police as delinquent. The activities of the two groups may be equally delinquent. But middle-class gang members generally leave adolescence to follow paths consistent with the expectations of the middle class. Although some lower-class gang members do leave adolescent delinquency behind, Chambliss notes "it is more likely that their noticeable deviance will have been so reinforced by police and community that their lives will be effectively channelled into careers consistent with their adolescent background" (p. 150).

ALIENATION AND PARTICIPATION

Alienation

Alienation is a popular term without precise meaning, frequently used to describe American youth, especially college students. The sense of alienation expressed by many young people seems to involve a number of complaints—despair over the corruption of politicians, bureaucrats, and business people; anger at the hypocrisy of U.S. foreign policy; frustration at the impossibility of finding a rewarding job; impatience with the materialism of modern society; and so on. Keniston (1968) has noted that alienation suggests the loss of a previous or desirable relationship. But it is necessary to specify what a person is alienated from, what replaces the old relationship, and how the alienation is expressed. In a clinical study of students at Harvard College during the period from 1957 to 1962, Keniston compared a highly alienated group, a highly nonalienated group, and a third, middle-of-the-road group. The alienated group was characterized by distrust of human nature, fear of intimacy or attachment to a group, and a negative view of American culture. Indeed, these students viewed any kind of commitment negatively.

The alienated students viewed life in terms of darkness, isolation, and lack of meaning. Morality was egocentric and arbitrary, and politics was considered a children's game. The outward signs of such a view, as might be expected, were scorn, bitterness, and anger. Keniston points out, however, that alienated students, although highly negative in their explicit views, implicitly emphasized "the positive value of passion and feeling, the search for awareness, contact, intensity, . . . and the need somehow to express their experience of life" (p. 330).

Keniston found that the life style of alienated students was not very different from that of nonalienated students—at least on the surface. But there were important differences in *how* they did things. Alienated students were characterized by "intellectual passion"; they became intensely involved in their intellectual interests. In group situations, they avoided positions of responsibility and acted as detached observers. When it came to personal relationships they were ambivalent; every friendship was examined from every possible viewpoint. In Keniston's words, they combined "an agonizing desire for closeness with a great fear of it" (p. 332).

What kind of background produced these alienated individuals? According to Keniston, intense feelings of alienation result from the interaction between a particular type of family environment and certain aspects of American society. The alienated students in Keniston's study portrayed both their parents as frustrated and dissatisfied. The mothers were "talented, artistic, intense, and intelligent girls who gave up promise and fulfillment for marriage"; the fathers were "failures in their own eyes, . . . disappointed, frustrated, and disillusioned men." The mothers were dominant and possessive and had succeeded in controlling the fathers (but not the sons). It was believed that the fathers had once had youthful, idealistic dreams, but that these had been crushed by the realities of adult life. The result of such perceptions was "the unconscious assumption that apparently admirable men were really weak and impotent; and that apparently nurturing and loving women were really controlling, possessive, and even emasculating" (Keniston, 1968, p. 338). Particularly evident among alienated students was an unwillingness to conform to traditional sex roles. The young men in Keniston's study had found the arrival of adult sexuality very disturbing and had feelings of anxiety or discomfort in connection with sex.

Keniston points out that the kind of families that produce alienated students are becoming increasingly common in American society. Moreover, the cultural factors that contribute to alienation will not go away soon. As a result, there will probably always be a group of talented, sensitive young people who are sufficiently repelled by the technological, specialized, highly organized nature of modern society to feel a deep sense of alienation from that society.

Participation

In contrast to the alienated student, the radical is committed to changing "the system" through political and social participation. The radical feels more competent and confident than the alienated student and is more concerned with social injustice than with inner experience and personal development. Both groups may be highly critical of society, but they express their disenchantment in dramatically different ways.

Both alienated and radical students seem to have experienced turmoil during their adolescent years, but with different results. The alienated turned their attention inward, the radical outward. Recent studies suggest, however, that the differences between the two groups may be more complex. Studies of student protest during the late 1960s (Block, Haan, and Smith, 1969; Haan, Smith, and Block, 1968) found that social protesters made moral judgments at a higher level than did uninvolved students. (Recall our discussion of moral stages in Chapter 11, in which we described how the basis of moral judgments ranges from punishment and obedience orientation to individual principles of conscience.) Protesters also tended to be intellectually gifted and academically superior. Their parents had succeeded in their careers, were liberal in their political philosophies, and were well off economically.

The students who participated in the protests of the 1960s may be divided into two groups: the activists and the dissenters. The differences between these groups are correlated with differences in their parents' child-rearing practices. The parents of dissenters were more "permissive" than those of activists. They made fewer demands on the child for independent mature behavior, were more tolerant of assertiveness, and put little emphasis on self-control. The parents of activists, by contrast, made more demands on their children for independence and mature behavior. They did not use physical punishment, but they made it clear that they expected responsible behavior. Activists and dissenters can also be distinguished on the basis of their parents' political philosophy. Activists' parents and their children generally have the same political outlook; hence, activists are rebelling against the social order rather than against their parents. Dissenters, on the other hand, are rebelling against their parents' conservative outlook as well as against "the system" (Block et al., 1969).

The "syndromes" of alienation and radicalism just described do not appear in high school students. Accordingly, some investigators believe these syndromes are due to extended or prolonged adolescence. The concept of adolescence as a distinct stage of life developed after the Industrial Revolution. Preparation for adulthood takes longer in an industrial society than in an agricultural one. More education is required for the tasks to be done, and this results in the segregation of young people into colleges and graduate schools.

Other factors, too, operate to prolong adolescence. In the past decade, the growth of junior and community colleges and specialized training schools (for computer programmers, secretaries, paramedical workers, and so forth) has made education after high school more readily available to young people from different social and economic groups. Increasingly, teenagers are graduating from high school (80%) and going on to some form of higher education (60%). Thus an extended adolescence, with all its implications (such as continued dependence on parents and postponement of marriage and career), will soon characterize most of the youth in America. It is not yet clear how this trend will influence young people—whether it will lead to alienation, participation, or "business as usual."

EARNING A LIVING

A 20-year-old college junior, intending to be funny, recently said to his mother, "I can't decide what to be when I grow up." His dilemma is a very real one, though. Few adolescents—college students included—are ready to make serious and fulfilling career decisions. At one time, what to "be" when one grew up was not an important question. A boy would be what his father was (or wanted him to be), and a girl would marry and become a mother. Parents arranged matters such as apprenticeships and marriages. Today, however, the choices facing young people are more complex and numerous. This aspect of the identity crisis is made even more complicated by the complete separation between "school" and "work" in American society, and by the lack of job opportunities for young people—even those who would rather work than go to school. Thus "What will I be?" is linked to "What *can* I be?" as well as "What will someone *let* me be?"

Another important factor in the choice of an occupation is the changing role of women. Changes in the American family (later marriage, fewer children), desire for greater affluence, and the women's movement have combined to produce a major shift in the aspirations of women toward equal and continuing participation in the work force. Yet as recently as 1968, there remained important differences between boys and girls with regard to their career aspirations (Thompson, 1968). Boys stressed being a leader or boss, well-paid, and famous, whereas girls were more likely to value jobs that allowed them to demonstrate their abilities and help other people. Girls tended to set lower goals for themselves; they tended to aim toward jobs as nurses rather than doctors, secretaries rather than lawyers, teachers rather than professors. Girls who set their goals higher, aiming toward traditionally male occupations such as medicine, mathematics, and science, had interests similar to those of boys and markedly different from those of girls who planned to prepare for traditionally female occupations such as nursing or teaching.

Between the eighth and twelfth grades, both boys and girls begin making clearer statements of their interests. In doing so, they shift from

Part-time jobs give adolescents their first taste of the working world and help them assess what they like to do and what they do well.
(Emilio A. Mercado, Jeroboam)

idealistic aspirations such as "adventure" or "service to humanity" to more realistic concerns — marriage, career preparation, jobs with high employment opportunity and a "future" (Putnam and Hansen, 1972; Gribbons and Lohnes, 1965). But whether they were idealistic or realistic, boys and girls still differed, with girls more people- and service-oriented and boys more task- and career-oriented. Boys and girls also differ in their achievement orientation. By the time they reach adolescence, boys from middle-class homes are under pressure to prepare for careers, and this pressure causes them to set higher standards of performance as well as to become more competitive.

As children become more realistic in their vocational planning, they also become better informed about the nature of occupations (DeFleur and DeFleur, 1967). Elementary school children have vague and often inaccurate notions about the work done by people such as janitors, carpenters, engineers, and secretaries. Children's knowledge of occupations increases during the elementary school years, especially for those occupations with which children have direct contact (teacher, mail carrier) and those which are portrayed on television (lawyer, reporter, waiter). By ninth grade, children's descriptions of representative occupations become highly accurate (Nelson, 1963). Elementary school children may be vague about the work lives of adults, but they tend to respond positively and uncritically to most jobs when asked if they would like to do that kind of work. As children become more accurate in their descriptions, they become more negative in their reactions. By ninth grade, adolescents respond negatively to most of the occupations tested — such as janitor, teacher, bookkeeper, manager (Nelson, 1963). A few occupations — doctor and engineer — continue to evoke positive reaction, whereas some less prestigious jobs — truck driver and mechanic — evoke a stable but less positive reaction. Findings such as these have led to the suggestion that vocational aspirations develop through the acquisition of dislikes rather than likes (Hess, 1970; Tyler, 1955). Children narrow their possible occupational choices by a process of *elimination* rather than selection.

In early adolescence, the elimination process is governed by the external characteristics of occupations. By mid-adolescence, personal self-estimates become involved (Gribbons and Lohnes, 1965; Tierney and Herman, 1973). Young people begin to apply what they know about themselves — their interests, capacities, and values — to the task of choosing an occupation. By this age, adolescents' self-concepts incorporate an accurate assessment of what they like to do and what they do well. The person who at an earlier age fantasized about being a research scientist begins to realize that she becomes impatient with detailed work; or the person who once dreamed of becoming a pilot begins to take account of his interests in painting and drawing. Adolescents acquire a deeper, more psychological understanding of themselves, and as they do so they apply their understanding to practical vocational goals.

In a classic 12-year longitudinal study, Tyler (1964) studied children's vocational interests as the children moved from the first through the twelfth grades. By the twelfth grade, the children could be clearly differentiated in terms of vocational interests. The question was: What characteristics differentiated these children in the earlier grades? One of Tyler's most interesting findings concerned girls who made career rather than family choices in the twelfth grade. By the eighth grade, these girls were more responsible and more achievement-oriented than those who planned to become homemakers, and they showed higher levels of self-control. Tyler notes that children's earlier choices of activities involve how they will use their time—reading, playing ball, building a playhouse, visiting a friend, watching TV, and so forth. Later, their vocational interests develop out of the skills they have acquired in the course of these activities. Occupational choices—and sex differences in the making of these choices—may not be *directly* reinforced or modeled by parents and other adults to the same extent as earlier choices of childhood activities, but childhood activities have a significant effect on later choices.

It should be noted that occupational choices are also influenced by the broader economic context. During the Depression, for example, the hardships suffered by many families led to an emphasis on "instrumental" rather than "companionship" values; earning money became more important than self-expression (Elder, 1974). Children in deprived households were needed; they helped out in any way they could. One result was that they decided on their occupational goals earlier than children from families that were better off economically. Children today are not subject to the same pressures; indeed, they may be viewed as "members of a surplus category" (Elder, 1974). Moreover, even if they want to enter the job market early and rise to the top, this is much less feasible in today's crowded society. Hence, students' occupational values tend less toward economic gain and more toward jobs that offer opportunities for personal growth and the chance to perform well.

SOCIAL CHANGE

There is little doubt that today's adolescents are different from adolescents 20 or even 10 years ago. But the extent of the differences is not clear. One of the more dramatic changes that took place during the 1960s (and that was supported by changes in the structure of the nation's economy) was the shift in attitudes toward traditional sex roles. A major factor in this change was the increase in service occupations—jobs that require intelligence and skill rather than strength. At the same time, as we have pointed out, more and more women entered the labor force, and men became more willing to share household duties. One result was that while more mothers acquired occupational identities other than "housewife," fathers participated more in the raising of their children. Children thus began to see their parents in less differentiated sex roles.

All this has produced adolescents who are less concerned with sex roles than their parents were at the same age. Girls are less likely to avoid intellectual achievement because it is "unfeminine," and "the imperative of male superiority is giving way to the ideal of companionship between equals" (Komarovsky, 1972, p. 876). Men's responses to psychological tests are becoming more like those of women, and vice versa (Brown, 1971). The cross-sex hostility that used to be characteristic of younger adolescents is declining, and there is some evidence that among teenagers the illogical "double standard" for males and females is fading.

Will these attitudes persist? Starr (1974) believes they will, pointing out that the "peace and love generation" has had a marked effect on American society and is still making itself felt. On the other hand, students in the 1970s appear to have become less interested in social issues and more concerned with academic achievement and professional goals. For example, when asked what made them proud of themselves, 93% of the students interviewed in 1975 gave responses that were achievement-oriented, compared to 76% in 1969 (McKinney, Hotch, and Truhon, 1977).

In the study of adolescence, individual differences become sharpened so that it is difficult to talk about the "typical" adolescent. Studies of social change also suggest that the opinions and attitudes of adolescents change from year to year, so that the personal characteristics of even the "model" adolescent will not necessarily be the same in all eras. More startling is recent evidence that personality attributes, once considered stable, individual characteristics, may also change in response to changes in the general social climate. A recent study by Nesselroade and Bates (1974) of almost 2,000 adolescents between the ages of 12 and 16 years, demonstrated that over the years 1970 to 1972, adolescents as a group tended to become more extroverted and more independent, less serious, conscientious, inhibited, and anxious. Sex differences did not change appreciably during this period: males continued to be more extroverted, tough-minded, autonomous, individualistic, aloof, aggressive and achievement-oriented and less apprehensive than females. There was also a tendency for males to become more autonomous and less anxious, whereas females became less autonomous over the 3-year period. In view of the changes in confessed social values, this pattern of results is somewhat disconcerting. Clearly, some personal characteristics of adolescents tend to bend with the times, but more deeply rooted differences (such as sex differences) may not change so easily.

It will be interesting to read what is written during the 1980s about the students of the 1970s. Will attitudes continue to be at odds with personality orientation? Or if the discrepancies become resolved, which will win out?

SUMMARY

The change in nineteenth-century America from an agricultural to an urban, industrial society brought with it the discovery of adolescence as a troublesome period of childhood. The tendency of adolescents to shift from one mood to another within a short time is known as *adolescent turmoil*. There is evidence to support the view of adolescent turmoil as a major stage in psychological development. For one thing, it is compatible with traditional psychoanalytic theories according to which children pass through a series of stages before reaching adulthood. On the other hand, there are arguments against this view from researchers who claim that not all adolescents experience adolescent turmoil and who propose that the term *normative crisis* is more appropriate to describe the experience most children undergo during adolescence. This is not to deny that there is some degree of turmoil in adolescence even under the best of conditions. Between the ages of 12 and 14, the modal adolescent shows a tendency to rebel against parents in various ways, but this conflict or bickering is usually over trivial issues. And adolescent turmoil appears to ease during the high-school years. Whereas behavioral disruptions are at their worst during junior high school (early adolescence), psychic distress increases in later adolescence. With respect to psychosocial development—what is going on *inside* the child—it is the middle years of adolescence, from 14 to 16, that are the hardest.

The question of generational conflict is complex. First, there is possible conflict within the family. Second, there is the presence of a "youth subculture" that emphasizes conformity to the values of the peer group—values that often conflict with those of adults. Third, there is the adolescent's relationship to secondary institutions—the schools or, more generally, the community.

Several influential viewpoints, both psychological and sociological, assume that conflict between adolescents and their parents is a fact of life. According to psychoanalytic theory, there is an upsurge of sexual excitement during adolescence that brings with it a renewal of the Oedipal conflict. Since adolescents can reject neither sexuality nor superego, all that remains is to reject their parents. Other psychoanalytic theorists believe it is the parents who are responsible for generational conflict. Theorists who view the conflict in *intrapsychic* terms—child rejecting parents or parents rejecting child—see it not only as inherent in the development of personality but as a necessary part of the struggle for independence and self-definition.

Still other theorists see generational conflict as a social phenomenon. Parents prepare children to live in a society that no longer exists. The "generation gap" is not simply a problem of communication but is a result of the fact that young people sense the inadequacy of the wisdom of past generations for life in the present and future world. Generational conflict represents an effort to change whatever is inappropriate in the value system handed down by adults. Another sociological view attributes generational conflict to the isolation of young people from the workings of modern technological society.

Upon becoming adolescents, children face a paradox: They must remain in the role of sons or daughters and at the same time gradually move away from the position of dependent children to that of independent adults. For most adolescents, this transition is accomplished without extreme conflict.

During childhood, parents are valued more highly than peers, but between the ages of 12 and 18, parents gradually become less important. Even though adolescents may not feel estranged from their parents, there is evidence that some ethical judgments may be influenced more by peers than by parents. Parents are more conservative than their children in sexual attitudes, for instance. Although adolescents think less highly of their parents during their teens than they did at younger ages, their opinion of other adults is even lower.

The shift to peer associations is a distinguishing mark of adolescence. During adolescence, friendship itself becomes important and sometimes involves intense emotional interaction and considerable conflict. Friends tend to come from the same social background and the same neighborhood and to be similar in personal characteristics.

Readiness to comply with peer pressure increases between the ages of 7 and 13 and then declines. During these years, conformity to peers increases relative to conformity to parents. Readiness to comply with peers, even when it comes to breaking rules, is related to children's increased respect for peers. However, there is also a correlation between readiness to conform to peer-sponsored misbehavior and lack of respect for parents and adults. Different forms of peer association may have different implications for adolescents' relations with parents and their susceptibility to peer influence.

Around adolescence, children have their first experience with heterosexual social life, which usually begins with a period of group activity and progresses to dating. Sociometric testing has shown that popularity in general is associated with athletic interest and ability, sociability, and social adjustment.

Adolescents tend to form crowds and cliques. A *crowd* is a group of young people who hang out together. A *clique* is smaller than a crowd, more cohesive, and more clearly defined. Crowd activities occur outside the school, but clique activities occur in school as much as outside of it. In fact, the high school is where most group activity occurs.

Gangs present a different form of social grouping from crowds and cliques. They have a high degree of structure and are usually associated with illegal and delinquent activities. Gangs are more likely to be recognized in poor, urban neighborhoods. Yet it would be a mistake to assume that large numbers of young people join gangs or that all young people who live in urban slums engage in delinquent activities.

The sense of alienation expressed by many young people seems to involve a number of complaints and can be defined as an explicit rejection of what are seen as the dominant values of American culture. In contrast to the alienated student, the radical is committed to changing the system through political and social action. The syndromes of alienation and radicalism do not usually appear in high school students. Some investigators believe these syndromes are due to extended or prolonged adolescence.

Choosing an occupation is an aspect of the identity crisis made more complicated by the complete separation between school and work in American society and by the shortage of job opportunities for young people. Another important factor in the choice of an occupation is the changing role of women. Despite these changes, boys and girls still differ, with girls more people- and service-oriented and boys more task- and career-oriented. Students' occupational values tend less toward economic gain and more toward jobs that offer opportunities for personal growth and the chance to perform well.

As children become more realistic in their vocational planning, they also become better informed about the nature of occupations. As their descriptions of jobs become more accurate, children become more negative in their reactions to various occupations. Children may narrow their occupational choices by a process of elimination rather than selection.

Students in the 1970s appear to have become less interested in social issues and more concerned with academic involvement and professional goals. There has also been a shift in attitude toward traditional sex roles — more women enter the labor force and men are more involved in household duties. The personal characteristics of adolescents tend to bend with the times, but recent research indicates that more deeply rooted differences (such as sex differences) may not be likely to change so easily.

PART VI

Some Problems

February 3, 1978

Dear Mom and Dad,

Friday, at last. The end of my first week as a student teacher in the Community Preschool for Emotionally Disturbed Children. It's un-gluing. One boy (5 years old) sits in a corner just rocking back and forth. Another seems to be in good shape until something gets him going and then—look out! On Tuesday he wanted to play with clay, and I went with him to a play table where he started making things for "dinner"— plates, cups, "hamburgers," and then some little "cookies." He was really into it, and it was great to see his pleasure as his dinner took shape. We had been talking while he played with the clay, and I felt I was right with him all the way. He announced it was time for dinner, then all of a sudden he got angry and destroyed his entire project. He pounded it all up, then threw himself on the floor and started screaming. I don't know what went wrong. Was it him, or me, or both of us? The experience left me upset and worried—what could I have done to help him? My head teacher was helpful and encouraging—basically, she said I need more time and experience but that I was on the right track.

The parents bring the kids by 9 in the morning and pick them up at 2:30 in the afternoon. Most of them seem really interested in their children and their progress at school, but a few seem annoyed or dis-appointed by them. One mother in particular leaves her daughter in the morning and picks her up later with no more than a goodbye and hello. Not even a smile. The little girl is extremely shy and withdrawn. She stands outside play groups observing but not joining in. She was very afraid of me the first few days I was here. I said hello one morning and she ran away. Now she just avoids me. The teacher says that the child hardly ever says anything and that she knows only isolated words. At 4 years old, she apparently doesn't know words even for parts of her body, pieces of clothing, or names of colors, so she can't understand a lot of what happens in class. She does seem to trust the teacher and has started to follow her around everywhere she goes. That's a start, I guess.

The other day, we took photos of each of the children and of the teacher and me, and put them up on the wall for the children to look at. One boy recognized the picture of everyone in the class — except himself. We talked about what people look like and that all people look different from other people, and can act different too. That stimulated some questions and comments from some of the children, especially about brothers and sisters and parents.

A couple of the kids are active (overactive?) most of the time. They'll start an activity but soon lose interest in it or be easily distracted by what someone else is doing. Others constantly need pushing. If no one makes an effort to arouse them or include them, they just sit still, apparently doing nothing.

Already I can feel that this occupation will have its sad and frustrating sides — but it's also challenging and worthwhile. Fortunately, I am working with a beautiful woman who has devoted her life to helping kids like these. Her calm, patience, affection, and determination is inspiring. I'll soon find out if *I* have enough of those qualities to stay in this field. I hope so!

Love,
Susan

CHAPTER 16

Disturbances in Development

We are deeply moved when we see handicapped children. Perhaps we think of how hard and frustrating their life must be, how awkward and embarrassed they may feel when they compare themselves with their "normal" peers. Somehow we want to reach out and help them—or we may turn away, overwhelmed or offended by their appearance or disturbing behavior.

Handicapped children have existed in all human societies, but people have not always looked upon them with sympathy or understanding. Earlier societies abandoned or destroyed their handicapped offspring. Others tolerated them, but treated them with neglect and cruelty. We might like to believe that the treatment of the handicapped has improved as our civilization matured, yet in our own time some of these children are still "stored" in custodial institutions under distressing conditions of neglect, if not abuse. We can take encouragement, however, from the growing efforts to help the handicapped to develop their abilities and live productive, satisfying lives.

The magnitude of the problem of childhood misfortunes may have something to do with the increasing attention it has attracted. Federal agencies estimate that there are about 1 million preschool-age children with handicaps and another 6 million of school age (Swets, 1974). These numbers include 1,200,000 mentally retarded; 1,000,000 emotionally disturbed; 2,000,000 with organic or functional speech disorders; and 500,000 with learning disabilities. Physical handicaps account for another 300,000 with hearing impairments; 60,000 with visual defects; 300,000 with crippling or other health impairments; and 40,000 with multiple handicaps.

Whether we are moved by sympathy or by pragmatic considerations of social and economic costs, we are compelled to explore ways of helping children with problems to attain some degree of self-sufficiency. In previous chapters, we dealt with development "as usual." Here we deal with the not-so-usual—the diagnosis, source, and treatment of developmental troubles.

DIAGNOSIS AND LABELING

People come in virtually infinite variety, whether they are described by appearance, abilities, behaviors, or any other attribute. If those with problems are to be helped, we must define the various kinds of problems in some organized, methodical fashion. This leads to diagnostic labeling.

To be useful, diagnostic labels should refer to conditions that can be observed or measured objectively. However, in dealing with variability among individuals and with such a complex organ as the human brain, the most experienced professionals are hard put to find simple indicators for particular problems. In the absence of some clear-cut functional cause or behavior pattern, there is a tendency to confuse value judgments with diagnostic labels (Bandura and Walters, 1963). Deviant behavior may be characterized by some as "abnormal," "disturbed," "mentally ill," "maladaptive." Attaching such global labels to behavior is prejudicial and counterproductive. It stigmatizes the child and impedes progress toward useful discovery of causes and effective treatment. In an earlier day, a label that signified a negative value judgment was enough to condemn a child to exclusion from school and, possibly, to confinement in an institution.

Our present expectations and objectives demand meaningful analysis of problems, and this, in turn, calls for a valid system of labels. Responding to that pressure, educators and psychologists concerned with developing the potential of handicapped children often find the diagnostic methods and labels used by doctors quite attractive. Unfortunately, the medical model presents serious disadvantages when we try to apply it to the behavioral problems of handicapped children. The concept of diagnosis in the medical model presumes a disease within the patient, a pathological condition that has a particular cause or origin, a definite set of observable symptoms, and a predictable outcome (prognosis). Ideally, the disease will respond to some specific treatment.

When we yield to the temptation to use medical labels for behavioral problems, we find that the method may fail to meet the basic criteria for diagnosis. The cause is seldom determinable, and often it is multidetermined; the course is not common to most cases of a particular disorder; the syndromes (combinations of symptoms) are not consistent; and the predictions are grossly unreliable.

The lack of regularity in syndrome patterns is responsible for wide inconsistency in the diagnosis of the same patients by different practitioners, even in the case of a gross psychosis like schizophrenia. Clarizio and McCoy (1976) cite the case of a 4-year-old child who was variously diagnosed as brain-damaged, retarded, schizophrenic, and autistic by different practitioners.

The medical model fares no better in predicting the outcome of diagnosed behavioral disorders. In the Berkeley Guidance Study, nearly 50%

of the children grew up to be "more stable and effective adults" than the pessimistic predictions of the psychologists, and 20% of the subjects turned out worse than the predictions—hardly a confirmation of diagnostic reliability (Clarizio and McCoy, 1976). Practitioners, of course, face serious problems in evaluating children's behavior. The children they are likely to meet have limited ability (in language skill or life experience) to describe their feelings, and they also tend to be shy, distractible, and uncooperative. The practitioner rarely has the opportunity to observe the child or in a variety of situations. Failing to get a clear reading of the child's world and how the child perceives that world, the diagnostician is inclined to overestimate the significance of symptoms and underestimate the flexibility and adaptability of the child as he or she passes through the striking changes of normal development.

Surely we need a sound labeling scheme and diagnostic methodology in order to prevent or correct the problems of the handicapped or troubled child. In view of developing evidence of the reciprocal impact of organism and environment, new interest is being focused on the notion of the *transactional system*. In this view, the vulnerable organism interacts with the provocative environment in an escalating process that intensifies the vulnerability of the organism and the hostility of the environment (Smith and Neisworth, 1975). The transactional system may be more useful than labels derived from the medical model, which tended to locate the problem *in* the child.

THE INTERACTIVE POSITION

The medical model served a useful purpose, during the last century and early part of this century, in that it changed the public's view of the handicapped as disgraceful and hopeless objects to be ridiculed and abused to an enlightened attitude that opened the way to humane treatment. A view of behavioral disorders as a treatable disease carried more hope than a view that stressed supernatural forces. As we have seen, the model is now being challenged. How is our view of childhood handicaps changing, and what are the implications for evolving approaches to treatment?

First, we are taking a closer look at the occurrence of the various handicaps in relation to environmental conditions—in particular, the reciprocal effects of the child's handicap on his or her environment (especially, the family) and of the environment (family, teachers, and peers) on the child's behavior. The interactive view of behavioral problems sees both personal and environmental factors as contributors to malfunctioning. We are as interested in the problems in the child's environment as in his or her physical dysfunction.

Among the chief environmental sources of childhood well-being are the parents. As Baldwin and Baldwin (1974) point out, "we now know that a handicapped child, from whatever cause, creates a situation to which the family must adapt." Thomas, Chess, and Birch (1968) found that the critical factor in determining whether "difficult" babies develop behavior disorders was parental reaction to the troublesome child. Difficult babies with warm, nurturing parents developed normally, whereas easy babies with disturbed parents were more likely to develop disorders. Thus we see how faulty parental reaction can produce the effects of an organic disorder. (Note, however, that brain-damaged children become disturbed in spite of good parenting.)

Studies have been done to determine whether families with disturbed children interact differently from families with normal children. Mishler and Waxler (1968) recorded family conversations, comparing those involving schizophrenic children with those involving nonschizophrenic children. Among their findings: Normal families were more responsive to each other's remarks, were more expressive, and were more affectionate.

Handicapped children are especially susceptible to the development of low self-esteem, which can aggravate their behavioral problems in social situations (including the classroom). They are prone to generalize their handicap to a belief that they cannot do anything right. Because of their painful self-consciousness, they are extremely sensitive to the opinions of others and need much social approval. Unfortunately, this may be denied them by their peers. Richardson, Goodman, Hastorf, and Dornbusch (1961) reported that their subjects ranked normal children highest in terms of how well they liked the children, whereas children in wheelchairs, those on crutches, those with facial disfigurements, and the obese were ranked lower, in that order. Peer rejection is one of the most destructive environmental factors to the handicapped child.

The problems posed by environmental interaction raise questions about the value of *mainstreaming*. Should handicapped children be educated with their nonhandicapped peers, to gain the benefits of experience in normal give-and-take situations? Or should they be protected from peer rejection and given the benefit of special programs geared to their needs and limitations? We will consider these alternatives in our discussion of therapeutic and educational interventions.

CHILDHOOD DISABILITIES

The new emphasis on transactional systems suggests a new definition of "disability." Deviations that make no difference in a particular environmental context cannot properly be called disabilities. Underaverage height is a disabling handicap on the basketball court, but very tall people are handicapped on the raceway. Skin color can be an advantage or a handicap, according to the culture. The visually impaired child often has no

A blind girl is read to by a sighted classmate. (Mitchell Payne, Jeroboam)

problem until faced with the requirement of reading what is written on the chalkboard. In a blackout, the blind are unhampered. Thus "disability is the product of the interaction of an individual difference with an environment" (Smith and Neisworth, 1975, p. 169). In the following discussion, we use the term disability in the interactional sense.

Sensorimotor Disabilities

DEAFNESS. Some degree of deafness affects about 5% of school-age children. Most of these children have some hearing. Only about one-tenth of 1% are profoundly deaf (hearing loss of 80 decibels or more). The use of hearing aids can increase hearing levels from 30 to 60 decibels, giving most deaf children some degree of hearing. Age of onset and introduction of amplification are critical factors.

The causes of deafness may be hereditary or external. However, it is more useful to know the time of onset than to know the cause of hearing loss. Because the loss of language (rather than loss of sound) is the most devastating effect of deafness, deafness that occurs before acquisition of speech is distinguished from deafness that occurs after speech acquisition. Thus congenital deafness and deafness acquired from prenatal, perinatal (during labor and delivery), or postnatal infections or injuries all cause deprivation of speech if proper measures are not taken in time.

501

> *1 year:* If the child fails to localize sounds that should have become famil-
> iar, or gives the response typical of hearing a sound for the first time, or
> still responds by a startle reflex, deafness must be suspected. Failure in
> speech development is also a danger sign.
>
> *2 years:* A child at this age who fails to understand speech or to talk must
> be suspected of deafness.
>
> *3 to 5 years:* A simple speech test should be used to detect deafness in
> this group.
>
> *Over 5 years:* All children should have a hearing test (screening test and,
> if failed, an audiogram). (Whetnall and Fry, 1964)

Hearing is not an all-or-none, now-or-never function. Although the
ear structures and auditory nerve channels are organically sound, their
function must be developed through use. Initially intact nerves deprived
of stimulating sound during the critical development period will deteriorate and forever lose their ability to transmit sound signals. Early screening is imperative since loss of function becomes more difficult to correct
after 8 months of age. The HEAR Foundation studied the effect of hearing
aids on 42 children with varying degrees of deafness and found that 74%
became "normally responsive" (no longer needed a hearing aid); the rest
continued to use the hearing aids successfully. All of the normally responsive children were under 8 months and 1 week old when treatment began
(Griffiths, 1967).

Since most deaf children have a hearing loss of less than 60 decibels,
they can receive (with amplification) and respond to oral language. This
capability has given rise to a sharp debate over the advantages and disadvantages of teaching deaf children either oral language only (forbidding
sign gestures) or both oral and sign languages simultaneously (bimodal-
ism) in a "total communication" environment. The basis for the oral-only
argument is the doctrine of "least effort"—that is, if allowed to use sign
language, the deaf child will neglect the more difficult oral mode, thereby
losing his or her residual hearing and oral speech abilities. However,
there seems to be no clear evidence for the least-effort doctrine.

Moreover, a number of studies show that bimodally trained children
are superior to oral-only children in speed of acquisition of vocabulary
and language competence. In fact, in one study (Schlesinger and Meadow,
1972) the subject—a girl whose parents were also deaf—had a vocabulary
of 156 signs and manual letters at age 19½ months, comparatively ahead
of hearing children who at that age are expected to know fewer than 50
words (Lenneberg, 1967). The richness of language interaction with the
parents, rather than hearing ability alone, seems to determine the pace
of speech development.

Schlesinger (1974) has shown that deaf children who use Ameslan (the American Sign Language consisting of pantomimic gestures) follow the same maturational sequence in language development that Lenneberg plotted for normal children (see Chapter 6). They even proceed through the same order of emergence of grammatical forms as hearing children do. However, their sentences tend to be shorter and contain more gross grammatical errors than those of hearing children. Deaf children exposed only to oral language are quite retarded in their rate of acquisition compared with both hearing and deaf bimodal children.

Curiously, deaf parents seem to provide their deaf children with an advantage in learning written and reading language. Such children score consistently higher on written and reading language tests than deaf children of hearing parents. Comparisons by Schlesinger and Meadow (1972) of two deaf children showed that the one whose parents consistently used both oral and sign modes eventually developed a strong preference for oral speech, showing no lapse in the use of residual hearing in a bimodal environment. Since deaf children experience special problems

A student at the Clarke School for the Deaf practices sound formation with his teacher. (Michael Philip Manheim, Photo Researchers)

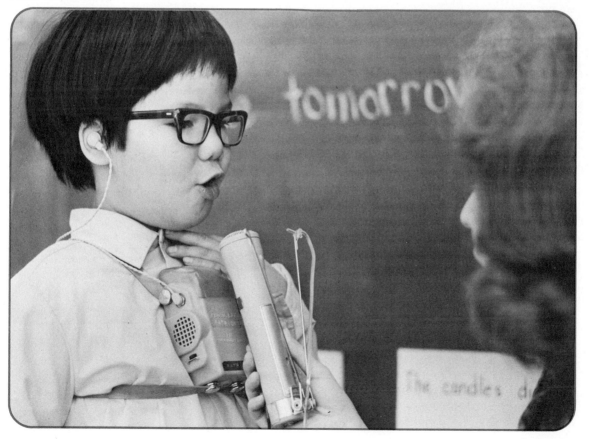

with the confusion of language sounds against background noise, and since they are also poorly reinforced by the inappropriate responses of others who misunderstand the deaf child's faulty verbalizations, the use of sign language and lip reading in the total environment helps to develop the natural language learning ability. The development of verbal concepts in one mode (Ameslan) probably transfers to the other modes (oral, reading, writing).

We saw in Chapter 6 that cognitive development in formal operations (reasoning) after initial language acquisition depends on verbal proficiency. As we might expect, therefore, in cognitive tasks reported by Best (1970) and Silverman (1967), hearing children surpassed deaf children in performance, and bimodally trained deaf children outperformed their oral-only peers. Deaf children score within normal ranges on intelligence tests with nonverbal instructions, but with lower mean scores than hearing children. In general, deaf children rank much lower in academic achievement (reading and arithmetic) than their cognitive performance would predict. It is noted that although deaf children do more poorly in digit arithmetic, they have a better memory for geometric forms than hearing children have, possibly because of their special training in sign language forms and lip contours (Meadow, 1975).

Slower social development of deaf children may be a consequence of limited verbal interaction with peers due to slower language acquisition and of confinement in residential schools for the death. Deaf children, of course, have special problems in adjusting to life with their formidable handicap, and the protective settings in which they grow up may deprive them of opportunities to work those problems out in normal give-and-take encounters.

BLINDNESS. Blindness in children is a handicap that slows, but does not disrupt, the development of cognitive and perceptual skills. One question relating to childhood blindness is the extent to which visual impairment interferes with the child's use of other sensory systems. Research indicates that with age blind children may acquire special sensitivity to touch or to sensations of movement. In general, although congenitally blind children seem to catch up with their sighted peers in most perceptual and cognitive tasks, they experience more difficulty in mastering them and reach similar levels of proficiency at somewhat later ages.

In considering the comparative proficiency of blind children in cognitive tasks, remember that verbal ability underlies cognitive performance. We saw in Chapter 6 that blind children's language acquisition, after a brief, initial lag, matches the pace of that of sighted children. In fact, they generally reach the same level of speech competence as sighted babies by the age of 2. Although blind children make more grammatical errors on the average, their thinking does not seem impeded by verbal differences.

A number of researchers have used conservations tasks to evaluate cognitive skills of blind children. Tobin's (1972) experiment considered how the blind child's lack of sight affects his understanding of conservation. He presented blind and blindfolded subjects with two soft plasticene balls of equal size and weight. One ball was rolled into a sausage shape, and the child was asked if it contained as much material as the round ball. He was then asked to explain why he thought it did or did not. The sighted children gave comparable levels of conservations responses about a year earlier than the blind children did. However, the blind children did reach 100% performance, and, indeed, the best of them attained conservation at ages 6 and 7, equal to the best of the sighted children. However, among the blind children, there was a greater spread in age of acquisition of conserving (extending beyond age 10).

Cromer (1973) found no difference in conservation performance between blind and sighted children on a task that required the subjects to place equal numbers of pingpong balls into cylinders of different shapes (tall and narrow versus short and wide), and then, upon feeling the height of the balls in the wire-mesh cylinders, to decide which held more balls. Although performance was about equal, the blind children handled the balls and cylinders in ways that differed from those employed by the sighted children, indicating different learning patterns.

No significant conclusions about the effect of blindness on cognitive ability can be drawn from the available findings, however. Differences in performance can be accounted for by differences in the educational backgrounds of blind and sighted children and by difficulties in making tests comparable. And, the experimental evidence, of course, is limited to special tasks. But, still, it seems clear that the blind child's visual disadvantage is neither constant nor decisive in handicapping his progress. Using the manifold resources of the human mind and body, he usually is able to make up for his loss.

MOTOR DISORDERS. Motor disorders afflict many fewer children than emotional disorders, retardation, and minimal brain dysfunction, but they seem more prevalent because of their visibility. The largest category of crippling disorders is cerebral palsy (CP), which affects about 1 to 3 out of every 1,000 school-age children (Smith and Neisworth, 1975). CP is a consequence of inherited conditions, lack of oxygen or other prenatal or perinatal accidents, or Rh blood incompatibility. Difficult deliveries, postnatal head injuries, and infections are also causative factors. Brain damage inflicted through child abuse is found to be a major cause of cerebral palsy ("Child Abuse Contributes to Palsy," 1977).

The disorder manifests itself in a variety of motor disabilities, such as spasms, tremors, and rigidity, and is sometimes accompanied by mental retardation. Special methods of training, physical therapy, drugs, and orthopedic surgery have been developed to improve the child's motor control and increase his or her independence.

Epilepsy, largely a childhood disorder, affects about 1 per 1,000 school-age children (Smith and Neisworth, 1975). It involves a functional disturbance in the discharge of neural energy, which causes motor spasms. Although the child is apparently normal between seizures, their sudden and (possibly) frequent occurrence constitutes a serious handicap, since teachers and others usually find it difficult to cope with the frightening, convulsive behavior. Some cases of epilepsy can be controlled through drug therapy. In severe cases where normal living is impossible, brain surgery is, at present, the only effective recourse.

Since motor disorders, as well as many auditory and visual disabilities, have their origins in the central nervous system, it is not surprising that a number of children suffer more than one handicap as a result of CNS defects. Mental retardation is often accompanied by visual deficits and motor disorders. In a study of about 9,000 blind children, Graham (1968), found that 80% were mentally retarded, nearly 40% with speech difficulties, 35% with brain damage, and an assortment of cerebral palsy, epilepsy, hearing loss, emotional and other medical problems. Multiple handicapped children are subject to the tragic likelihood that only their most prominent disorder will be diagnosed and treated, leaving their other defect(s) to impede their progress and frustrate them and their therapists, teachers, and parents.

DIFFUSE EMOTIONAL DISTRESS. Most children show behavior that is disturbing to others at one time or another. A spirited, outgoing child becomes subdued and tearful; a zesty eater becomes picky and choosy; a sound sleeper goes through a period of wakefulness at night and irritability during the day. Many more children show less extreme patterns or less abrupt changes. The common issue that brings these children to the attention of clinicians is often that parents and teachers become alarmed and uncertain about what to do. A large proportion of problems in childhood are characterized by behaviors that are perturbing to others but not in themselves terribly serious—such as nailbiting, stuttering, nightmares, tantrums, shyness, or a more general state of apprehensiveness. Sometimes these behaviors are short-lived; the precipitating "cause"—a new baby, a new neighbor, tension in the school—works its way out as the child discovers how to cope with the situation. Often the child needs help from sensitive parents and teachers—time alone with mother, a visit to the neighbor, or help with a school assignment. Sometimes help is not available and social responses to the behavior set up the cycle we described in an earlier section. In one survey of special classes for socially disturbed pupils (Clarizio and McCoy, 1976), 60% of the children were judged to be suffering from such problems. What causes these disturbances?

Emotional Problems

Psychoanalytic theory traces troubles such as these (often called neuroses) to unresolved childhood conflicts brought on by sudden traumas or chronic threats. The child's inability to handle his or her over-whelming impulses to resist the threat provokes defensive reactions by the ego, which generate persistent anxiety. The nature of the anxiety depends on the dominant motivations (oral, anal, phallic) that prevail during the period when the conflict occurs. The anxiety impels the child to develop some response (such as obsession, aggression, overachieve-ment, phobia) that relieves the tension.

Behavior, or learning, theory holds that the anxiety is evoked by some highly unpleasant experience (parental neglect or abuse, a dark bedroom, a frightening dog) and finds release through some escape or avoidance behavior, possibly discovered by chance. The behavior reduces the anxiety level and thus is reinforced. As the child grows and no longer faces the earlier, threatening situation, repetition of the once-effective behavior becomes maladaptive.

Symptoms of neurosis vary widely. The anxiety itself is often a prom-inent symptom in the so-called "nervous" child. In some cases, the anxiety resolves itself into a definite fear, expressed as a specific phobia associated with the dark, death, school, animals, or other objects. It is important not to overdiagnose childhood phobias, which may be normal events in the course of the child's development. The anxiety-ridden child may seek relief in food fads and fetishes or in deviant sexual practices. Psychosomatic disorders provide an outlet for the troubled child. Asthma and other allergic reactions are common effects of psychic disturbance in children. In some cases, sensitivity to certain allergens is heightened by emotional distress. Frightful wheezing and gasping may become a powerful means of controlling the parents or punishing them for insensi-tive treatment or failure to satisfy needs for affection or indulgence.

The principal characteristic of the child's neurotic disorder is that it represents an inefficient response to a present situation. It tends to persist either because the child cannot muster more appropriate behaviors to meet the negative reactions provoked by his or her disturbed style, or because the disturbed behavior gains some control over the significant people in the child's life.

CHILDHOOD PSYCHOSIS. *Childhood schizophrenia* and other early-life psy-choses are uncommon disorders, but because their effects are so disastrous and may be precursors of adult psychosis, they are the focus of much study. The signs of schizophrenia in children are physiological, emotional, and intellectual deviations. They include loss of personal identity, grossly disturbed relationships, general intellectual deficiencies, abnormal per-ceptions, distorted and stereotyped movements with occasional out-bursts of violent hyperactivity, and acute anxiety that may escalate to inexplicable terror (Davison and Neale, 1974). Speech may be retarded or marked by peculiar utterances.

Although earlier theorists—notably the psychoanalytic school—centered their attack on the role of disordered family or parent relations in the cause of childhood schizophrenia, recent studies point to genetic predisposition as a likely contributing factor. The strongest evidence is presented by a number of concordance studies, which differ on rates but agree on the high coincidence of schizophrenia among monozygotic twins. Kallman and Roth (1956) reported an MZ concordance rate of more than 88% and a DZ rate of almost 23%; Gottesmann and Shields (1966) found an MZ rate of nearly 42% and a DZ rate of more than 9%. We must, of course, raise the question about possibly similar effects of growing up in the same pathogenic (disease-producing) environment. Unfortunately, there is a lack of data on MZ twins reared in separate households.

Since even the high schizophrenic concordance rates for twins show that a significant number of schizophrenic children are paired with non-schizophrenic birthmates, genetic factors cannot be charged with the entire responsibility for causing schizophrenia. Other influences must trigger the psychotic reaction in the genetically predisposed child. To determine how such influences might work, Mednick and Schulsinger (1968) studied a group of schizophrenic "high-risk" children, children whose risk of becoming schizophrenic in adulthood was greater than average. Using a variety of tests and behavior reports from midwives, teachers, and others, the investigators discovered that the high-risk children who subsequently developed psychiatric disturbances shared some characteristics. They reacted more intensely to stressful stimuli; their word associations were deviant; they generally had experienced difficult births; when they were upset, they maintained high levels of excitement for excessively long periods. In other words, their responses to environmental stresses were exaggerated. The abnormally high rate of pregnancy and birth complications (70%) suffered by mothers of disturbed, high-risk children seems to be more than a casual coincidence.

Does birth trauma trigger the schizophrenic psychosis in the genetically predisposed child? Or do birth trauma and genetic predisposition create an organism that is primed to respond psychotically to a series of environmental insults? Studies of family relations and interactions have revealed some possible familial provocations to the high-risk child. Mednick (1958) suggests that high-risk children are extremely sensitive to aversive stimuli, and so protect themselves by means of avoidance behavior that may involve distortion of reality or total withdrawal. One type of family provocation that might precipitate such pathological responses is called the "double bind," a hypothesis proposed by Bateson, Jackson, Haley, and Weakland (1956). In this interaction, the child receives two related but contradictory messages from someone with whom he or she has an intense relationship, usually the mother. Acceptance of one message implies a threatened loss or punishment resulting from rejection of the other mes-

Childhood psychoses may result from the interaction of organic predisposition and environmental stress.
(Costa Manos, Magnum Photos)

sage. Moreover, the child cannot escape the impossible decision. There is no rational response that the child can make. Thus, for example, the mother urges the child to be more sociable, and then proceeds to criticize the friends he or she makes. While the double bind might be ignored by a normal child, the hypersensitive, high-risk child has no tolerance for the confusion of intentions.

Investigators have found that the patterns of communication in families with schizophrenic children show distinct differences from those of other families. Mishler and Waxler (1968) analyzed the conversations of a number of families and found that the style of communication of families when schizophrenic children were present was stilted and less spontaneous. The parents set up a defensive screen that discouraged expression of anxious or uncomfortable feelings.

The evidence builds strong support for a theory that describes childhood schizophrenia as the outcome of environmental stress applied to a child sensitized by a predisposition to the psychosis. The chances of recovery from childhood schizophrenia are poor; most children with this psychosis are eventually diagnosed as adult schizophrenics.

Infantile autism is a psychosis of very early onset (during the child's first year). Some consider it a prelude to schizophrenia, but its symptoms are quite distinctive: virtually total lack of communication (in some cases, mutism), avoidance of eye contact, absence of crying, unresponsiveness to adult efforts at engaging in play, obsessive requirement of unchanging routines and object arrangements, bizarre stereotyped movements (Page, 1975; Rimland, 1964). Autistic children often show preference for objects that move in repetitive ways or that can be opened and closed, screwed and unscrewed. They will engage in operating such objects endlessly, to the exclusion of all other activity. One of the most serious autistic behaviors is self-destruction. These children may bang their heads against the wall until they suffer a concussion, or chew on their fingers until they are raw.

Autistic behavior is often accompanied by intellectual deficits, although the child's lack of communication and refusal to cooperate prevent thorough testing. About half of all autistic children never learn to speak (Rutter, 1966). If the child has remained mute until age 5, there is little likelihood that he or she will ever acquire speech or become well adjusted. Since language mastery is a key factor in intellectual competence, the mute autistic child may be permanently retarded, requiring lifetime institutionalization (Rimland, 1964).

Although many autistic children do not use expressive communication, they demonstrate awareness of environmental situations and demands. Some practice a form of defiance in which they perform exactly the opposite of what is requested. Others engage in echolalia, the repeating of what others say. A change in the fixed arrangement of objects or in a constant ritual may provoke a hysterical tantrum that continues until the "standard" order is restored.

In all of their responses, autistic children appear to be indifferent to the reactions of others to their frustrating behavior. Such studied indifference suggests that they have "turned off" the world of offensive stimuli. Such a dramatic withdrawal might indicate an organic defect in the autistic child's sensory mechanism that makes him or her hypersensitive to stimuli. The extremely high autistic concordance rate for MZ twins seems to confirm the role of inherent defect (Page, 1975). Again, we are inclined toward the interactive effects of environmental insult and organic predisposition. There is little evidence that neurological defects alone can account for all of the autistic child's behaviors, such as his or her preoccupation with mechanical objects to the exclusion of appropriate response to people.

A clue to the home environment of autistic children was provided by Kanner, who, in 1943, first identified autism. He observed that the parents of autistic children were generally people of intellectual pretensions, who were preoccupied with many interests outside of the family circle. They tended to be cold in manner, unable or unwilling to focus on their child's needs. Accordingly, he named them "icebox parents," although he later denied indicting them as the original cause of the autism.

A classic example of the "icebox parent" effect has been described by Bettelheim (1959) in the case of Joey, the 9-year-old "mechanical boy." Joey lived like a machine. He attached wires and various devices to his body and "plugged" them in to provide the energy and pump the fluids for "running" his body. Nurses carefully avoided his network of wires and tubes when they attended him, so they would not interrupt the energy and fluid flow to the mechanism that Joey claimed "lived" him. The notable fact about Joey's case is that he seemed healthy at birth, but had been treated indifferently by his withdrawn mother, who virtually ignored the boy, treating him as little more than a machine. Joey apparently responded by assuming his assigned, mechanical role. Of course, as we noted earlier, Joey's mother might have been responding to a nonresponsive baby.

What does cause infantile autism? The autistic behavior observed in some infants at birth indicates a prenatal or perinatal accident or a genetic factor aggravated by ineffective early care. The very early appearance of symptoms poses problems for the psychoanalytic view of autism as a psychic disturbance brought on by the child's confusion of object relations — in particular, the child's inability to distinguish self from other objects in the world. But this difficulty should not have such a drastic effect so early in life, certainly not at birth.

Not only does the psychoanalytic interpretation raise questions, but psychoanalytic methods have not been very successful in treating severe cases of infantile autism. Bettelheim (1950), a psychoanalytic practitioner, has proposed a completely supportive treatment, with instant gratification of all demands. However, behaviorists argue that this procedure merely reinforces all of the undesirable autistic behaviors. The most effective results in treatment of autism have been obtained by such practitioners as Lovaas, using operant behavior modification (Lovaas and Bucher, 1974). The operant method of successive approximation has taught autistic children to speak, and aversive training (including mild electric shock) has stopped self-destructive behavior. However, in spite of some therapeutic successes, most autistic children at present are doomed to a lifetime psychosis.

Adolescent troubles are largely the product of the stressful impact of new social demands on a young person in the throes of gross physiological changes, complicated by the youth's lack of experience and, in some cases, by family conflicts.

In Chapters 14 and 15, we discussed normal development during adolescence. We observed that many of the behavioral variations during this period are appropriate developmental forms of adaptation to physiological changes and new environmental demands. The great changes in the bodies and perceptions of adolescents make them vulnerable to frustration, anxiety, depression, and general confusion in establishing a mature identity and a meaningful purpose. Increased independence, mobility, capacity for planning, and access to peers can channel anger and distress into socially dangerous or self-destructive pathways. Delinquency, drug addiction, suicide, and violent crime increase dramatically in adolescence, and these forms of behavior have increased over the past decade.

We have selected the problem of runaways from the array of adolescent troubles to illustrate the operation of environmental and personal factors on the vulnerable young person. The runaway problem is widespread, crosses social classes, and takes in other, more serious problems. Estimates of incidence range up to 500,000 a year, but no reliable figures are available, since most cases are not reported (D'Angelo, 1974). One study showed that only one out of six runaways was reported missing. Moreover, one-third of those surveyed who never ran away had seriously considered doing so (Shellow, Schamp, Liebow, and Unger, 1967).

All runaways are not alike in background, personality, or motivation. The majority consist mainly of one-time runaways and some repeaters. This group is not significantly different from nonrunaways in relative stability and social adaptability. A smaller segment of runaways are frequent repeaters and constitute the category of deeply troubled adolescents. The frequent repeaters shared problems of disrupted family situations, school failures, and delinquency.

The one-timers appear to be fairly sound in their personal development, but find conflict with rigid parents or deadening school systems to be intolerable. They "take a breather" by running away, at the same time issuing a warning to parents that they have had enough and want a change. Thus running away becomes, for these one-timers, both a demonstration of dissatisfaction and a means of coping with pressures.

Quite a different picture is presented by the frequent repeaters. D'Angelo (1974) investigated the personal, family, and social problems of teenage runaways whose records were bad enough to warrant residence in an institution. The comparison with nonrunaways revealed that frequent runaways came predominantly from broken homes (although apparently "intact" homes also produced runaways). They had negative impressions of their parents, who were prone to administer physical abuse and were less receptive to discussions of their children's problems than parents of nonrunaways. The runaways generally had a history of failure in school. In their peer relationships, they had few, if any, friends, and argued more with their parents over friends than did nonrunaways. Their self-image and self-acceptance were much lower than those of nonrunaways. A strong indication of the locus of the problem came from members of the clergy and social agencies, who reported that the most common problems brought to them by teenagers were family conflict and personal adjustment.

The major burden of responsibility for the serious runaway problem seems to fall on the family. Difficulties within families center around two factors: parent modeling and styles of discipline. Where maternal warmth and paternal acceptance prevail, there is a tendency for children to copy their parents' internalization of moral strictures against wrongdoing. On the other hand, power-assertive modes of parental discipline are associated with children's efforts to escape punishment, encouraging the belief that getting caught is the only crime. Since middle childhood is the period when the superego is internalized, adolescence is the critical time for appropriate internalization of moral values and a willingness to conform to social prohibitions. A faulty parental model can disrupt the normal process of acquiring a healthy conscience. McCord, McCord, and Zola (1959) found that one loving parent (especially a mother) can considerably counteract the effect of one rejecting parent. McCord et al. found the following percentages of boys convicted of crimes, as a function of loving and rejecting parents: loving mother and loving father, 32%; loving mother and rejecting father, 36%; rejecting mother and loving father, 46%; rejecting mother and rejecting father, 70%. Given the vulnerability induced by the maturational and physical developments that mark adolescence, it is easy to see how disastrous the impact of stressful demands can be. The transactional model offers an especially productive approach to adolescent problems.

Learning Problems   The profusion of learning problems challenges the vast resources of professionals in special education. Some problems seem to be specific to one skill (children who do well in all subjects but arithmetic or reading, for example). Other problems may lie outside the cognitive area, in the sphere of emotional disturbance (children who may be hyperactive and have trouble attending to school-type tasks). Still other problems may involve general intellectual deficits. We consider here requirements for definition, diagnosis, and intervention in each type of learning problem.

MENTAL RETARDATION. Diagnosis and treatment of mental retardation have improved since the time when such a label condemned a person to little more than custodial care in an institution. However, mental retardation is still a catchall category in which organic impairments are combined with cultural-familial deficiencies.

Zigler (1966, 1967) has proposed a way of differentiating two main subdivisions of mental subnormality. *Mental deficiency* is described as an organic dysfunction resulting from a physiological or anatomical defect. IQ levels tend to be lower (below 50) and the incidence of physical disabilities (including sensory and motor defects) higher. *Mental retardation* is a consequence of familial or cultural deprivation or inheritance. This group includes IQ scores of 50 to 75. The health and physical responses of the mentally retarded are generally good. In fact, Zigler sees mental retardation as a part of the continuous normal distribution of intelligence, with retardates differing only in degree from those at higher IQ levels.

The American Association for Mental Deficiency emphasizes another distinction in their definition of mental retardation as "a subaverage general intellectual functioning which originates during the developmental period and is associated with impairment in adaptive behavior" (Heber, 1961). Here we are asked to take into account the individual's social development as well as his or her IQ score. Some low IQ individuals are quite capable of functioning adequately in social situations, enabling them to engage in partially or fully self-supporting employment. By basing the application of the retardate label entirely on IQ score, we risk including many minority group children who are otherwise competent in social performance. Mercer (1972) conducted an extensive study of the correlation between the number of Anglo cultural characteristics possessed by blacks and Chicanos (Mexican-Americans) and their IQ scores. Those whose family characteristics matched those of Anglos (for instance, skilled fathers, small families) tended to have higher IQ scores than those with fewer Anglo cultural characteristics. Use of any of the standard cut-off scores for mental retardation traps many socially competent children under the retardate label with its tragic consequences.

Intervention measures in mental retardation are both preventive and corrective. Preventive measures include improved maternal care (especially for low socioeconomic status mothers), genetic counseling, diagnostic services for newborns (to detect correctable conditions), control of infectious diseases, and elimination of toxic agents in the environment (such as lead-based paints and gasoline) (Smith and Neisworth, 1975).

Programs to enhance the potential of the mentally retarded have their roots in the pioneering work of Itard and Seguin early in the nineteenth century. Their principles of sensory stimulation were developed into modern methods by educators like Montessori, who succeeded in teaching retarded children to read and write. Today, mildly retarded children are considered educable, and all but the most profoundly retarded are trainable at some level, at least in self-care and communication. Many attain a high degree of independence and employability. Special education programs are widespread, and increasing numbers of children whose IQ scores would classify them as retarded are being trained to lead productive lives.

HYPERACTIVITY AND DISTRACTIBILITY. The presence of children diagnosed as *hyperactive* in virtually every school in the country indicates a problem of epidemic proportions. The fact that the "symptoms" respond to stimulant drug treatment suggests that we have here a genuine medical disorder of a specific nature. However, closer examination of the problem and the currently popular method of treatment raises some disturbing questions.

Hyperactivity is commonly associated with an organic condition called *minimal brain dysfunction* (MBD), which is marked by excessive motor activity, short attention span, and lack of self-inhibition (disruptive behavior). The reason for calling the dysfunction "minimal" is that there are usually no definite signs of neurological damage.

Reacting to the disturbing frequency of the diagnosis and the fact that in the absence of hard symptoms, the diagnosis is often based on the acceptance by the physician of the symptom (that is, behavior and performance) reports of the referring teacher or parent, a number of medical practitioners and psychologists have challenged the basis for such a diagnostic entity. Schmitt (1975) questions the validity of MBD as a syndrome, pointing out that observed brain dysfunctions (such as epilepsy) are seldom accompanied by hyperactivity and that there is an extremely low correlation among hyperactivity, cognitive functioning, and soft neurological signs. McIntosh and Dunn (1973) report that only 20% of children with an MBD diagnosis display hyperactivity, which hardly qualifies it as a primary symptom of brain dysfunction. Sroufe (1975) defines MBD as an impairment of the central nervous system that causes impairment of perception, leading to learning disabilities. However, Sroufe, too, finds that the diagnostic requirement of uniform symptoms is not satisfied. Furthermore, he finds that, paradoxically, MBD is often defined in terms of a positive response to the drug.

Many educators argue, in defense of drug therapy for hyperactive children, that the children cannot be taught unless their inability to remain calm and attentive is controlled. Sroufe (1975) maintains that the use of amphetamines in such cases encourages dependence on drugs for behavior control, a typical approach to problems in our drug-oriented culture. Recourse to drugs also reduces efforts to explore alternative educational methods. Finally, the ready use of drugs as a simple solution to educational and behavior problems reduces disruptive children to a compliant state but fails to prepare them for the challenges that will confront them in adult life.

LEARNING DISABILITIES. The concept of *learning disabilities* (LD) suffers from the same shortcomings and dangers that we found in such diagnostic categories as MBD and mental retardation. In an effort to deal with a constellation of problems, educators, aided and abetted by psychologists and neurologists, attempt to classify them under one diagnostic label. The result, as we saw, is the arbitrary grouping of children with dissimilar "symptoms" and the basing of intervention on fuzzy theories.

In broad terms, LD applies to children of normal intelligence who experience extreme difficulty in learning academic subjects. Reading deficiency is generally considered the principal learning disability, because of its common occurrence and its implications for academic achievement. Some children read well but have difficulty with the mechanics of writing, telling time, or manipulating numbers.

A specialty area in the field of education has been developed to focus on LD. It is revealing of the "state of the art" in special education that there is no consensus in defining LD. Bateman's technical definition (1965) is widely accepted: "Children who have learning disorders are those who manifest an educationally significant discrepancy between their estimated intellectual potential and actual level of performance related to basic disorders in the learning processes, which may or may not be accompanied by demonstrable central nervous system dysfunction, and which are not secondary to generalized mental retardation, educational or cultural deprivation, severe emotional disturbance, or sensory loss" (p. 220). In other words, LD children may or may not have organic CNS defects, but they do not tend to be retarded, poor, or disturbed. The effect of this definition has been to exclude poor children from LD corrective programs, consigning them by default to the mentally retarded category. Such a label has a negative effect on the child's self-image and self-expectation.

The term "learning disabilities" was not originally designed to represent a diagnostic category. It was a convenient label for a collection of disparate problems, including MBD and perceptual disorders. As is usually the case, the term developed, through common use, into a formal diagnostic entity with a spectrum of symptoms: perceptual motor defects, hyperactivity, general orientation and laterality defects, disorders of attention, impulsivity, disorders of memory and conceptual thinking, specific learning defects (McCarthy and McCarthy, 1969).

Clearly, that conglomeration of symptoms does not constitute a coherent syndrome. It is neither necessary nor likely that all, or even most, of them would be present in a particular case. In fact, it is not even possible to rank them in order of primary or secondary importance. Note, also, that neurological impairment is neither assumed nor excluded.

Explanations of LD run the gamut from word blindness, lack of cerebral dominance, and glandular disturbances to such non-neurological notions as inadequate teaching and lack of motivation, which transfer the responsibility from the child to the educator. Each theory carries a prescription for remedial programs that center around the proposed cause.

There is an increasingly favored view that LD is not a disorder with a specific cause. This view removes the focus on global defects and promotes analysis of each child's problem in terms of response to task requirements in the particular area of academic deficiency. Attention is directed to the child's emotional background, environmental circumstances, and learning experience, as well as to diseases and accidents that he or she has suffered. By this procedure, physiological defects are detected or ruled out, and a program that concentrates on specific emotional as well as intellectual factors can be designed.

The disastrous effects of environmental disturbances are critical, yet were minimized or overlooked in the earlier diagnostic approach to LD. The case of Larry is a classic example (Clarizio and McCoy, 1976). His parents were anxious and overprotective as Larry grew up, communicating their fears to him and giving him a sense of inadequacy. He withdrew from active exploration and became reluctant to try new experiences. Lack of such activity retarded the development of his auditory and visual memory and his ability to organize stimuli. In first grade, he recognized the alphabet but not words. His continued failures in the early grades made him more anxious and less confident and led his parents to expect his successive failures. Larry, sensing their hopelessness, fulfilled their expectations, thereby qualifying for a diagnosis of LD. Current views would identify Larry with children with visual, motor, and auditory disabilities, specific language disabilities, and general cognitive deficits. Recognition of the transactional nature of the factors that were responsible for his learning problems helps suggest the proper focus for remedial action. In Larry's case, the parents must be central figures in a remedial program.

ETIOLOGY

In many of our life experiences, we see the consequences of nature's work and of our own actions. From such observations, we develop a cause-and-effect view of our universe. Everything that happens has a cause; often it may be the end result of a causal sequence or chain, consisting of many links. Some developmental problems begin with physical conditions; others cannot be traced to organic origins. In many cases, the initial cause interacts with factors in the child's environment to aggravate, correct, or compensate for the problem. The factors—physiological or environmental —that cause the development of a disease or disorder are its *etiology*.

When a physically defective child is born, we search for the genetic or physical accidents that caused the defect. At least, we recognize the defect and take measures to deal with it. More harmful is the hidden organic defect whose manifestations elicit the wrong responses from the mother and others in the child's environment, thereby initiating a vicious circle of reciprocal insults, leading to some behavioral pathology far removed from the original defect.

In this section, we discuss the kinds of biological and environmental influences that contribute to the complex nature of childhood problems.

Genetic Factors

CHROMOSOMAL ERRORS. Chromosomal errors are responsible for birth defects that result in severe mental disorders. Remember from Chapter 2 that there are 23 X chromosomes in the normal ovum and 23 Y chromosomes in the sperm. When there is an extra X or Y chromosome, one of the fetal chromosomes will be triple—either an XXY or XYY pattern. An extra X chromosome causes Down's syndrome, commonly called mongolism. It is marked by a variety of physiological defects, including defective heart structure, and also by mental retardation at severe to profound levels. Another condition caused by an extra X chromosome is referred to as Klinefelter's syndrome, whose symptoms include underdeveloped testes, infertility, enlarged hips, and, occasionally, mental retardation. An extra Y chromosome has been associated with highly aggressive, sociopathic behaviors.

Since the body tends to abort malformed fetuses, biologists have wondered why fetuses with such chromosome defects are carried through pregnancy and delivered. Stott (1971) did a comparative study of Down's syndrome cases and other retarded children. The mothers of mongoloids had suffered prolonged stress early in their pregnancies that appeared to upset the body's chemical balance and block spontaneous abortion of the fetuses. Other studies have linked similar failure of the natural abortion function to prenatal stress. Stott further maintains that emotional stress during pregnancy is, in fact, a contributing cause of birth malformations, as well as a critical factor in preventing abortion.

METABOLIC ERRORS. Metabolic errors occur in the genes, which compose the chromosomal material. This material consists essentially of the DNA

Toddlers with Down's syndrome playing. (Hank Lebo, Jeroboam)

TABLE 16–1
*Common Inherited
Metabolic Errors*

DISEASE	COMPOUND INVOLVED	CONSEQUENCE
Phenylketonuria (PKU)	Phenylalanine (too much)	Mental retardation, seizures, eczema.
Sickle cell anemia	Hemoglobin (wrong one made)	Poor delivery of oxygen to tissues. Abnormal red blood cells are easily destroyed by body and clog blood vessels.
Tay-Sachs disease	Ganglioside (fatty substance in brain)	Excess stored in brain. Deterioration of all brain function leading to death in first or second year.
Diabetes	Insulin (protein) not made	High blood sugar. Possible early development of degenerative changes in nearly all body tissues.
Galactosemia	Galactose (sugar) increased in blood	Mental retardation, cataracts, liver disease.

Source: Smith and Neisworth, 1975, Table 3–4, p. 57.

molecules that determine the operation of the body's functional systems. The molecules are subject to *mutation*—changes in certain characteristics. Such inherited errors result in malfunction of the various chemical mechanisms in the body, such as the metabolism of sugar into energy. Table 16–1 lists just a few of the nearly 2,000 metabolic errors that the fetus is subject to. A closer look at one of these errors—sickle cell anemia—shows how such errors develop and how they are perpetuated through many generations.

Sickle cell anemia is a disease that is largely confined to blacks, with an incidence of between 10% and 20% in that ethnic group. It consists of distorted hemoglobin cells with a bowed, hooked, or angled shape instead of the normal disc shape. The hook shape (like a farmer's sickle) causes the cells to get tangled, clogging arteries and hair-thin capillaries. The resulting jam blocks the vessels, cutting off the oxygen supply to body tissues, causing deterioration of the brain and the various organs. Sickle cell attacks generally occur when the body is chilled or under stress, conditions that impede circulation and thus promote the clumping of the sickle cells. Infection, which places extra demands on circulation, also precipitates anemic attacks.

How did the incidence of sickle cells concentrate almost exclusively

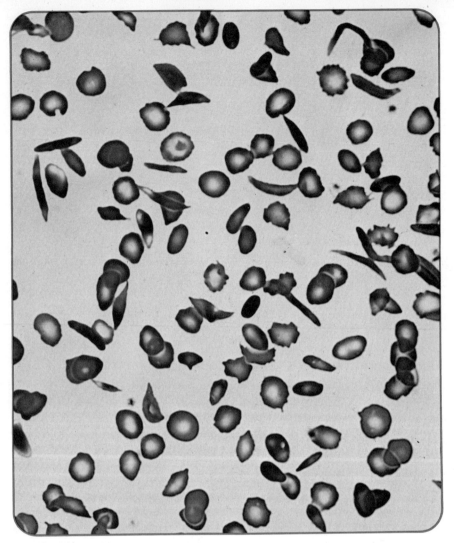

The crescent-shaped blood cells of sickle cell anemia can be seen here among the normal blood cells. (C.D. Conley, M.D., The Johns Hopkins Hospital)

among blacks? Researchers have discovered that children with sickle cell blood were especially resistant to malaria and respiratory diseases. At some point in the evolutionary process, the hemoglobin gene in black Africans had mutated, producing a malaria-resistant, sickle cell formation. The survival of children with sickle cells in a malarial environment assured the concentration and persistence of sickle cell blood among black Africans. Since there is virtually no malaria in the United States, 2½ million American blacks with sickle cell anemia are paying a heavy price for protection against a nonexistent threat.

Similarly, other ethnically confined diseases—Tay-Sachs among Jews, PKU among whites—tend to persist because of inbreeding or environmental conditions that select a particular genetic mutation because of its survival properties.

Environmental
Factors

PRENATAL DANGERS. Prenatal dangers have been discussed previously in connection with various psychological disturbances and dysfunctions. In Chapter 2, we showed how such maternal problems as toxemia and the Rh factor may damage the fetus. Infections like rubella (German measles) produce retarded infants. Diseases that precipitate or necessitate premature birth expose the newborn to the risk of hyaline membrane disease, a lung impediment that deprives the brain of vital oxygen, resulting in irreversible brain damage. Babies born of diabetic mothers often have blood-sugar problems that can be corrected with prompt treatment. Poor nutrition during pregnancy, during the spurt in brain growth (beginning about the fourth or fifth month), may cause reduced body size and brain development. An undersized brain is restricted in its capacity for cognitive development.

PERINATAL AND POSTNATAL DANGERS. Perinatal and postnatal dangers appear to have a highly interactive relationship. Studies indicate that whereas perinatal stress (difficult labor and delivery) is often associated with problems (neurological responses and illnesses) during the first year or two of life, virtually all correlation between perinatal complications and subsequent dysfunction disappears within 3 or 4 years (Drage, Berendes, and Fisher, 1969). However, when perinatal difficulty and socioeconomic status (SES) are combined, the effects are clear-cut and persistent.

In an elaborate study of a multiracial Hawaiian population, Werner, Bierman, and French (1971) found a definite interaction between perinatal complications and environmental factors. Among high-SES families or where the mother had a high IQ, IQ differences were minimal between with-complication and without-complication children. IQ differences between the two children's groups were substantial among low-SES and low-maternal-IQ families.

Studies made in many countries show a strong correlation between low birth weight and low SES. The linkage is not a simple one, however. It seems that low birth weight alone does not account for poor performance, but in poor environments (low SES and limited education of parents), inadequate prenatal and postnatal nutrition combine with impoverished stimulation to yield physiological and intellectual deficits. When the family's social background conditions are improved, early malnutrition does not have the expected depressing effect on intellectual functioning (Richardson, 1976). Further evidence of the close relationship between nutrition and low social background conditions comes from studies of the effect of supplemental nutrition on test performance in Latin America. Positive results of supplementation were observed almost exclusively in the lowest SES families (Ricciuti, 1976).

It would seem that factors like perinatal complications and early malnutrition can have depressing effects on later developmental progress when they are not counteracted by improved nutrition and stimulating environments. Poverty goes hand in hand with malnutrition, poor health, and inadequate medical care. These deficiencies may well result in impaired physiological and neurological functioning, which would, of course, be reflected in depressed performance scores.

PARENT BEHAVIORS AND FAMILY PATTERNS. Parent behaviors and family patterns are the dominant elements in the child's environment. A good deal of the influence on child development that we have attributed to the environment relates directly to family dynamics. The powerful effect of family interaction on the child's deviant behavior is most dramatically illustrated in the etiology of schizophrenic psychoses. When we look at schizophrenia in the light of behavioral theory, we see clearly the role that parental responses play. Ullman and Krasner (1975) traced schizophrenic behavior to faulty parental reinforcements of the child's responses to social stimuli. If children are criticized for sharing some candy with a friend, they may find this confusingly inconsistent with their parents' suggestion that they make friends. Eventually, exposed to such inconsistent reinforcement, they learn to look for particular attributes of stimuli that would not be noticed by normal children. This idiosyncratic behavior results from failure to receive positive reinforcement for normal responses to social stimuli. According to this theory, the schizophrenic's behavior is controlled by the "wrong" stimuli. Conflicting and incompatible demands generate stress in the defenseless child, as we have seen in our discussion of the "double bind" hypothesis. Children learn to protect themselves from the painful effects of such irrational treatment either by adopting equally irrational responses or by withdrawing completely into a shell of indifference. They accomplish their defensive maneuver at the cost of a normal view of reality.

Families in which the children manifest disturbed behavior exhibit characteristic patterns of disordered interaction. They engage in frequent conflict, adopt inappropriate roles (that is, the "taking" mother, the withdrawn father), and have rejecting attitudes toward unacceptable behavior. Ackerman (1968) describes the parents' use of the child as a pawn in ongoing conflicts. Of course, we must acknowledge that such families are studied after their offspring have been identified as deviant. We may be looking at the aftermath of a mother's disturbed reaction to a difficult or unresponsive child, leading to mutually maladaptive behaviors that have caught the rest of the family in a whirlpool of conflict. The vulnerable child and the disordered environment provide the basic elements in the transactional formula.

According to the Children's Bureau of the Department of Health, Education, and Welfare (1968a), 27 million children—40% of those below age 18—are members of families with an annual income under $6,000. The Bureau of the Census (1970) reported that more than 10.7 million persons under

Poverty and Its Cost

Programs such as Head Start aim at helping children break out of the cycle of poverty. (Herb Levart, Photo Researchers)

18 were below the poverty level in this country. Of these, 6.4 million were whites and 4.4 million were nonwhites. In other words, 10% of the white and 33.5% of the nonwhite population were below the poverty level. We can only speculate on the substantially greater proportion of the population of less advantaged countries that live at similarly depressed levels.

A considerable amount of evidence demonstrates that poverty is associated with poor performance in academic areas. There are three prevailing views of how poverty produces a cycle of school failure and low paying jobs that becomes self-perpetuating.

1. *The malnutrition view* focuses on a pattern of multiple deprivation: economic deprivation, lack of intellectual stimulation, inadequate reinforcements in the family which lead to cognitive deficits due to lack of stimulation of maturing biological structures.
2. *The cultural disparity view* emphasizes the failure of the child's home environment to provide him or her with learned behaviors that are useful in middle-class society, and the failure of social institutions to understand and respond sympathetically to the child of poverty.
3. *The social structural view* posits inherent biases in the social class system, which put the low-SES child into competition for scarce jobs and services, at the same time limiting his or her access to the skills, influence, and contacts required to compete effectively.

The three views are, of course, complementary, and together characterize the child of poverty as a social victim.

One of the critical deprivations specified in the malnutrition model— lack of stimulation of biological mechanisms during maturation—works its damage in what are called the bioneural results of poverty. Birch and Gussow (1970) demonstrated the prevalence of illness and generally poor health resulting from inadequate diets among families at poverty levels. This manifests itself in anemia and fatigue, handicapping the child in school, the parents in caring for their children and working to support the family. Deteriorated homes present more hazards: peeling, lead-based paint (a source of lead poisoning, which causes neural damage) and structural defects that promote accidents. As a consequence, poor children are subject to neurologically based disabilities.

It is clear that there is no single cause or starting point that initiates the poverty cycle. We cannot yet identify the primary factors. In all likelihood, poverty and its effects are part of the larger system that takes in our entire social system and, therefore, must be dealt with in the broader context of social structures.

Child Abuse

The magnitude of the child abuse problem is only beginning to be recognized in this country. There are no reliable figures, and estimates range from 60,000 to 500,000 incidents of child abuse (Light, 1973). Reported cases represent the tip of the iceberg: 11,000 in 1968, and double that number in 1972. But the data come from hospitals and social agencies, where low-SES cases are discovered; middle- and upper-class cases of child abuse are treated by private physicians, who are not inclined to report such cases. In New York City, physicians reported only 8 of 3,000 recorded cases (Light, 1973).

The visible effects of child abuse are bone and brain injuries and death. Approximately 1,500 cases of cerebral palsy presented in 1975 resulted from brain injury associated with child abuse ("Child Abuse Contributes to Palsy," 1977). Other consequences, such as mental retardation and sociopathic behavior, are not as readily apparent yet are nonetheless destructive.

The causal relationship in child abuse is not as clear and direct as we might believe. In approaching the problem, we consider three general models — psychiatric, sociological, and sociosituational — as presented by Parke and Collmer (1975).

The psychiatric model offers the tempting invitation to blame the "sick" parent. However, except for the observation that abusive parents have aggressive impulses, attempts to develop a discriminative personality profile for abusive parents have proved disappointing. In several studies, few of the abusing parents showed severe psychotic tendencies (Parke and Collmer, 1975).

One common environmental factor did emerge from these studies: Many of the abusive parents had a history of being abused by their parents (who often were victims of similar abuse when they were children). Family patterns of abuse extended across the generations in a significant number of cases. Oliver and Taylor (1971) found that in 27 out of 40 cases of abuse, the parent had been subjected to battering, cruelty, and abandonment in childhood. The operative effect of such treatment on these parents when they were children was a "lack of mothering." Instead of experiencing a model of caring and nurturing, these abusing parents got their parental training from models of physical abuse and neglect (Steele and Pollack, 1968).

The sociological model indicts cultural factors: public attitudes toward violence, the structure of the family, environmental stress as related to socioeconomic status. Our American culture cherishes a historic belief in the efficacy of violence — in particular, the use of physical force in settling conflicts and crises. Our tradition of "gun justice" and "the hanging cure" matched our puritanical principles of order and discipline. Spanking and whipping have been strongly entrenched child-rearing practices in the United States. Corporal punishment is accepted in some school systems and has been sanctioned by the Supreme Court. This has had an inhibiting influence on the reporting of child abuse and on efforts to give social agencies investigatory resources to deal directly with the problem.

There is some uncertainty about the association between child abuse and class level. The fact that low-SES families are exposed to more environmental stress invites the expectation that they will, therefore, be more prone to child abuse. Indeed, a pair of studies by Gil (1970) showed that 48% of child abusers had incomes under $5,000; only 25% of U.S. families are at that economic level. Gil found also that abusing parents were poorly educated: 41% had not completed high school, and 24% had less than 9 years of schooling. However, we must qualify these findings by recalling the bias in the reporting of cases of child abuse.

Social isolation is a not-so-obvious characteristic of abusive families. Among subjects in a study by Young (1964), 95% of the severe-abuse families and 83% of the moderate-abuse families had "no continuing relationship with others outside the family" and participated in no organized group. Of course, there are families that are socially isolated that do not abuse their children, but lack of contact with supportive persons outside the family leaves parents alone with pressing problems.

Another sociological variable of uncertain relationship to child abuse is family size. Larger families are associated with greater incidence of abuse. The effective factor may not be crowding as much as an inability to take care of a larger number of children (Parke and Collmer, 1975).

The sociosituational model relates the punitive parent's own background with the conditions under which punishment is administered to his or her children. As we have noted, exposure to aggressive models of discipline teaches aggression as well as discipline. If punishment is inconsistent or of low intensity, the child's undesirable behavior may persist, leading to escalation of intensity of punishment. In effect, the child's differential responses to varying degrees of punishment "trains" the parent up to high-intensity levels, which may prove effective as discipline but which may cause serious injury to the child.

The role of the child as provocateur of abuse is receiving more attention in recent studies. Observers have noted that abuse is selective; usually only one of the children in a family is the target. When the injured child is removed from the abusive family, he or she often gets less favorable attention from nurses in the hospital and may continue to be singled out for abuse in different foster homes.

Why do some children have such a negative effect on their caregivers? In some cases, the child's unattractive appearance or slow development may disappoint the high expectations of the parents. Rejection of the child may start a chain of reciprocal, negative behaviors between parent and child. Or the child's manner of expressing his or her demands—excessive, persistent crying or ambiguous cues—may be difficult or irritating to the worn-out caregiver. Developmental deviance may be a contributing provocation: high levels of activity may exhaust caregivers or lethargy and dullness may frustrate them.

On the other hand, the infant may be the victim of birth problems. Abnormally low birth weight is associated with later child abuse in a high percentage of cases (Simons, Downs, Hurster, and Archer, 1966;

Fontana, 1968). Low birth weight is often the precursor to medical difficulties, developmental problems, and feeding disturbances, all of which may provoke impatient reactions in vexed parents who are disappointed by their child's retarded motor and cognitive development. Many low-birth-weight infants are premature, requiring separation from the mother during the first days or weeks of life. Such immediate and prolonged separation seems to interfere with development of normal maternal affection (Klaus and Kennell, 1970).

Broussard and Hartner's inquiry (1971) into maternal attitudes reveals the transactional nature of the child abuse problem in terms of the progressive interaction between parent and child. Responses to questionnaires given to new mothers both a few days and a month after delivery showed a high correlation with the mothers' estimate after 1 month and the need for clinical intervention at age 4. Within 1 month, the mothers had developed a pattern of responses to their newborns' possibly disturbing behaviors that set the stage for developmental disaster. What we see when we look closely at the problem of child abuse is a constellation of negative factors that leads to abuse—including socioeconomic status, birth problems and deficiencies, level of education, stability of the family, and the child's vulnerability to aversive treatment.

THERAPY AND PREVENTION

Psychotherapy and Behavior Therapy

Although children manifest most of the neuroses, psychoses, and other psychophysiological disorders that adults suffer, their maturational development produces drastic changes that often result in outcomes quite different from adult disorders. Children show a remarkable capability for spontaneous improvement, often emerging from early disorders relatively intact and unscathed. In fact, their capacity for "outgrowing" their problems rivals the efficacy of psychotherapy. Levitt (1957) reported overall improvement of 67% after therapy and 78% at a 5-year follow-up. The corresponding improvement rates for nontreated children were approximately the same! Therapy included behavior modification, environmental manipulation, counseling, and drugs. Similar results were obtained in a comparative study (treatment versus nontreatment) of prevention of juvenile delinquency among high-risk children (Levitt, 1963). Many childhood problems are probably transient responses to environmental stress.

Behaviorists focus on the "symptoms"—the deviant behaviors, which they attempt to modify directly. Behavior modification operates on the basis of learning theory principles: Deviant and undesirable "symptoms" are maladaptive responses learned through inappropriate reinforcements. Psychodynamic therapy seeks to discover the hidden intrapsychic conflict, relieving the pressure of anxiety that motivates maladaptive behavior. Psychodynamic therapists believe that if the internal cause is not extinguished, removing the overt symptom will compel its replacement by a substitute symptom. However, behavior therapists deny this, pointing out that there is no evidence of symptom substitution after conditioning therapy. In the event of substitution, the behavior therapist would continue symptom extinction until appropriate behavior ensued.

Follow-up studies indicate that behavioral effects are durable up to periods of several years when treatment is undertaken before behaviors have become chronic and when the new environmental contingencies are maintained in the home. Unfortunately, generalization of specific behavioral improvement does not carry over to other situations. Attention is being directed to the problem of transfer of benefits to other areas of the child's experience.

An important advantage of behavior therapy over psychodynamic treatment for children is that it does not demand the verbal skill and intellectual sophistication required of psychoanalytic clients. Another advantage is that nonprofessionals—especially parents—can be trained in behavioral techniques and can maintain the contingency procedures at home. Psychodynamic therapy, on the other hand, can be administered only by professionally trained analysts in an office setting.

Behavior therapy recognizes the role of the family in inciting and maintaining deviant behaviors. Techniques have been developed for involving the family (especially the parents) in the therapeutic process. A notable example is the "behavioral contract" in which the parent and child agree to a formal statement of the target behaviors and applicable rewards and punishments for suitable or unacceptable behaviors.

Hawkins, Peterson, Schweid, and Bijou (1966) describe an elaborate program for in-home behavior modification performed by the mother after training by one of the experimenters. The mother learned appropriate prohibiting, punishing, and rewarding responses to her son's objectionable target behaviors. Baseline readings were taken during periods of ordinary response to the behaviors. Improvement was noted after only 6 training sessions. Within 24 sessions, the rate of objectionable behavior was reduced to one-sixth of the baseline rate.

A great deal of research has been directed toward the education and training of mentally retarded children, using behavioral methods. The "token economy" is an outstanding example of the effective use of learning theory techniques and is ideally suited to institutional settings where the mentally retarded reside. Successful programs have turned out to be ones in which tokens exchangeable for consumable reinforcers were given for accomplishment of useful behaviors, principally self-care. Tokens were also used as compensation for vocational learning. Such token economy programs work even with the profoundly retarded.

Reality Therapy

The reality therapy approach to childhood problems emphasizes behavior that fits the real world and seeks to correct the child's distorted view of his or her own feelings and needs (Clarizio and McCoy, 1975). The central theme is the individual's *responsibility* for the choices he or she makes and the actions he or she takes. Children are questioned about their objectives whenever they perform a disruptive act. They must make a value judgment about their own behavior. Their teachers or therapists help them to formulate sensible plans to achieve their goals. They learn what they must do for others and how others' cooperation (or resistance) affects the success of their plans. Once they agree to a specific plan, they must commit themselves to follow it. Reality therapy is essentially a behavioral approach that lends itself to school and home situations.

Drug Therapy

We have discussed the pros and cons of drug use as a means of controlling hyperactive and other disturbed behaviors. Stimulant drugs are widely prescribed for suspected minimal brain dysfunction as a means of reducing hyperactive symptoms. Other drugs, such as tranquilizers, antidepressants, and narcotics, are also used for managing problems of excessive arousal, excitability, and apathy.

The principal arguments offered in support of drug therapy center around the need to reduce the interference with the child's attention and concentration and to enhance his ability to exercise patience and respond effectively. Among the chief objections to drug treatment is danger of overmedication, without due regard for toxic side effects and without full consideration of alternative behavioral treatments. The common occurrence of insomnia, loss of appetite, dizziness, headache, and other side effects warrants extreme restraint in the use of drugs as "fast cures" for problem conditions in children.

Prevention

The ideal treatment for childhood disorders is to prevent them. Some serious disabilities can now be prevented by what is called the "new science of birth"—the timely treatment of defects and deficiencies almost immediately on delivery, thanks to advance detection of dangerous prenatal conditions by means of amniocentesis and fetal monitoring during childbirth (Seligmann, Gosnell, and Shapiro, 1976). Other problems, whose solution has long been at hand, seem more resistant to prevention. These are the consequences of economic privation: malnutrition, impoverished environment, pervasive illness, lack of medical attention. In spite of our affluence, we seem not to have made significant gains in this area since Franklin D. Roosevelt found one-third of Americans "ill-clothed, ill-housed, and ill-fed." Better education in proper nutrition and child rearing offers great promise of improvement in parenting, which seems to be a decisive factor in breaking the endless chain of child abuse and mental handicaps passed from generation to generation. What we need is a new "science of living" to plan a broad reconstruction of our social environment. When we can prevent predisposing neurological dysfunctions and reduce stresses in the environment, we will have changed the two critical factors in the transactional formula, and may thereby improve the quality of life for everyone.

SUMMARY

Handicapped children have existed in all human societies. To help them, it is important to define their various kinds of problems in some organized, methodical fashion. In the absence of some clear-cut functional cause or behavior pattern, there is a tendency to confuse value judgments with diagnostic labels. Attaching global labels to behavior can be prejudicial and counterproductive. Using medical labels for behavioral problems has many disadvantages, since behavioral problems do not necessarily conform to a medical model. The lack of regular clusters in syndrome patterns is responsible for wide inconsistency in the diagnosis of the same patients by different practitioners. The practitioner faces difficulties in evaluating children's behavior, because children have only limited ability to describe their feelings.

In view of developing evidence of the reciprocal impact of organism and environment, new interest is being focused on the notion of the transactional system. The interactive view of behavioral problems sees both personal and environmental factors as contributors to malfunctioning. The emphasis on transactional systems suggests a new definition of "disability." Deviations that make no difference in a particular environmental context cannot properly be called disabilities. Disability is a product of the interaction of an individual difference with an environment.

The loss of language is the most devastating effect of deafness. Hearing is not an all-or-none, now-or-never function. Although the ear structures and auditory nerve channels may be organically sound, their function must be developed through use. Initially intact nerves deprived of stimulating sound during a critical period of development will deteriorate and forever lose their ability to transmit sound signals. Early screening is necessary, since loss of function becomes more difficult to correct after 8 months of age.

Cognitive development depends somewhat on verbal proficiency and, therefore, hearing children score higher than deaf children on intelligence tests. In general, deaf children rank much lower in academic achievement than their cognitive performance would predict. Slower social development of deaf children may be a consequence of limited verbal interaction with peers.

In comparison with deaf children, relatively little research concerns children who are blind. Research indicates that, with age, blind children may acquire special sensitivity to touch or to sensations of movement. In terms of cognitive skills, blind children as a group are somewhat delayed in comparison to sighted children. No significant conclusions about the effect of blindness on cognitive ability can be drawn from these findings, however; differences can be accounted for by differences in the educational backgrounds of blind and sighted children and by difficulties in making tests comparable.

Motor disorders afflict many fewer children than emotional disorders, retardation, and minimal brain dysfunction, but they seem more prevalent because of their visibility. The largest category of crippling disorders is cerebral palsy, which manifests itself in a variety of motor disabilities and is sometimes accompanied by mental retardation. Since motor disorders have their origins in the central nervous system (CNS), a number of children suffer more than one handicap as a result of CNS defects. Children with multiple handicaps are subject to the likelihood that only the most prominent disorder will be diagnosed and treated.

Most children at one time or another show behavior that is disturbing to others. Often these problems are short-lived, receding as the child learns to deal with the precipitating cause. Psychoanalytic theory traces emotional troubles (often called *neuroses*) to unresolved childhood conflicts brought on by sudden traumas or chronic threats. Behavioristic, or learning, theory holds that the anxiety, which is evoked by some highly unpleasant experience, finds release through some escape or avoidance behavior, probably discovered by chance. The behavior reduces the anxiety level and thus is reinforced. Symptoms of neurosis vary widely, ranging from anxiety to definite fear. The principal characteristic of a neurotic disorder is that it represents an inefficient response to a present situation.

Childhood schizophrenia and other early-life psychoses are uncommon disorders, but because their effects are so disastrous and may be precursors of adult psychosis, they are the focus of much study. Recent studies point to genetic predisposition as a likely contributing factor but not the entire cause of schizophrenia. Evidence strongly indicates that childhood schizophrenia is an outcome of environmental stress applied to a child sensitized by a predisposition to the psychosis.

Infantile autism is a psychosis of early onset. In all of their responses, autistic children appear to be indifferent to the reactions of others to their frustrating behavior. Such studied indifference suggests that they have turned off the world of offensive stimuli. Since neurological defects alone cannot account for all of the autistic child's behaviors, this psychosis also appears to arise from the interactive effects of environment and organic predisposition. The most effective results in treatment of autism have been obtained using operant behavior modification.

Adolescent troubles are largely the product of the stressful impact of new social demands on young people in the throes of physiological changes complicated by lack of experience and, in some cases, by family conflicts. The problem of runaways illustrates the operation of environmental and personal factors on vulnerable young people. Two factors emerge as determinants of adolescent problems: parent modeling and styles of discipline. The transactional model offers an especially productive approach to adolescent problems.

The profusion of learning problems challenges the resources of professionals in special education. *Mental deficiency* is described as an organic dysfunction resulting from a physiological or anatomical defect. *Mental retardation* is a consequence of familial or cultural deprivation or inheritance and takes into account social development as well as IQ score. Intervention measures in mental retardation are both preventive and corrective. Today, mildly retarded children are considered educable, and all but the most profoundly retarded are trainable at some level, at least in self-care and communication.

Hyperactivity is commonly associated with an organic condition called minimal brain dysfunction (MBD). Many psychologists question the validity of MBD as a syndrome and define it as an impairment of the central nervous system that causes impairment of perception leading to learning disabilities. Drug therapy is most often used to control hyperactivity, although many psychologists and parents object to its use.

The concept of learning disabilities (LD) covers a wide range of problems but generally applies to children of normal intelligence who experience extreme difficulty in learning academic subjects, particularly reading. Explanations of LD are many and varied, and each carries a prescription for remedial programs. There is an increasingly favored view that LD is not a disorder with a specific cause. This position promotes analysis of each child's problem in terms of response to the particular area of academic deficiency.

The physiological or environmental factors that cause the development of a disease or disorder are its *etiology*. Chromosomal errors are responsible for birth defects that result in severe mental disorders. An extra X chromosome causes Down's syndrome (also called mongolism); an extra Y chromosome causes Klinefelter's syndrome. Metabolic errors occur in the genes, which compose the chromosomal material. Changes in certain characteristics of the DNA molecules result in malfunction of the various chemical mechanisms in the body. Sickle cell anemia, a disease largely confined to blacks, is one of these metabolic errors.

Prenatal dangers are connected with various physiological disturbances and dysfunctions. Perinatal and postnatal dangers appear to have a highly interactive relationship. Poverty goes hand in hand with malnutrition, poor health, and inadequate medical care that may well result in impaired physiological and neurological functioning.

Parent behaviors and family patterns are the dominant elements in the child's environment. Conflicting and incompatible demands may generate stress in defenseless children, and they may learn to protect themselves from the painful effects of such irrational treatment by adopting equally irrational responses or by withdrawing completely into a shell of indifference.

Evidence demonstrates that poverty is associated with poor academic performance. There are three prevailing views that explain how poverty produces a cycle of school failure and low-paying jobs. The *malnutrition model* focuses on a pattern of multiple deprivation as the root of poverty. The *cultural disparity model* emphasizes the failure of the home environment and social institutions to provide the behaviors and the understanding necessary in society. The *social structural model* posits inherent disadvantages in the hierarchical social system. The three models complement each other and together characterize the child of poverty as a social victim.

There are three major views that attempt to explain the causes of child abuse. The *psychiatric view* blames the "sick" parent. The *sociological view* indicts cultural factors. The *socio-situational view* relates punitive parents' background with the conditions under which punishment is administered to the children. Recently, the role of the child as provocateur of abuse has been receiving more attention. A whole constellation of negative factors leads to abuse, including socio-economic status, birth problems and deficiencies, level of education, stability of the family, and the child's vulnerability to aversive treatment.

Although children manifest most of the neuroses, psychoses, and other psychophysiological disorders that adults suffer, children show remarkable capability for spontaneous improvement, often emerging from early disorders relatively intact and unscathed. In fact, their capacity for outgrowing their problems rivals the efficacy of psychotherapy in childhood. Behaviorists focus on the "symptoms"—the deviant behaviors—that they attempt to modify directly. An important advantage of behavioral therapy over psychotherapy for children is that nonprofessionals, especially parents, can be trained in behavioral techniques and can maintain the contingency procedures at home. The reality therapy approach to childhood problems emphasizes behavior that fits the real world and seeks to correct the child's distorted view of his or her feelings and needs. Reality therapy is essentially a behavioral approach which lends itself to school and home situations. The use of drug therapy raises many objections, but the principal arguments offered in support of it center around the need to reduce the interference with the child's attention and concentration and to enhance his or her ability to exercise patience and respond effectively.

The ideal treatment for childhood disorders is to prevent them. The "new science of birth" permits the timely treatment of defects and deficiencies almost immediately on delivery. Problems that are the consequences of deprivation seem more resistant to prevention.

Glossary

accommodation to Piaget, the tendency to change in response to the environment

achievement tests tests designed to assess what students have learned

adaptation to Piaget, the ability to modify the environment, as well as the ongoing change that occurs in response to the environment

adolescence period that begins with puberty and spans the teenage years, during which the individual passes from dependent childhood to self-sufficient adulthood

adolescent turmoil tendency of adolescents to shift moods within a short period of time

affectional system reciprocal relationship between 2 persons, marked by strong feelings and mutual caring

agonistic aggressive

amniocentesis procedure used to detect genetic abnormality and sex of a fetus by analysis of amniotic fluid extracted from the mother's uterus

androgyny resemblance to the opposite sex

Apgar score scoring system administered a few minutes after birth to assess the newborn's physical condition

aphasia loss of speech function

assimilation to Piaget, incorporation of new events or elements of the external world into one's own activities

association areas areas of the human brain that link the primary sensory centers of vision, audition, and touch

assortative mating tendency for people to marry people who are like themselves

attachment affectional bond between a child and an individual with whom the child has a stable, long-term relationship

attractive elements hypothesis hypothesis that newborns refer to attractive parts of a figure rather than to the figure as a whole

autism *see* infantile autism

autonomous morality second of Piaget's 2 stages of moral development; the child believes that rules result from social agreement, that rules can be changed, and that there is conflict about what constitutes right and wrong; also called morality of cooperation

autosomes the 22 pairs of chromosomes that do not affect sex

Babinski reflex reflex response to stroking the sole of an infant's foot, in which the toes spread apart

Bayley Infant Scale (BIS) infant motor and mental scale that measures sensory perception, fine motor skills, adaptability to social situations, and some language ability from birth to age 3½

behavior modification technique that uses conditioning procedures to change or shape behavior

behavior therapy modification of deviant behaviors through learning theory principles to remove undesirable behaviors and reinforce desirable ones

Binet-Simon intelligence test first standardized intelligence test; published in France in 1905, it was the model for subsequent intelligence tests

biphasic attention ability to watch outward objects and to have sufficient control to shift or withdraw attention as well

blastula hollow sphere of embryonic cells whose center is filled with fluid

Brazelton Neonatal Behavior Scale neurological examination for infants to discover early neural dysfunction

canalization Waddington's concept that at sensitive periods environmental pressures may deflect a genetic trait from its normal course

case grammar Fillmore's grammar that explains children's semantic relations by identifying case roles of verbs and nouns

catch-up growth accelerated growth, following a period of environmental deprivation

catharsis hypothesis hypothesis suggesting that aggressive behavior fulfills a tension-releasing function

chromosome threadlike structure on which genes are strung

circular reactions to Piaget, repetition of actions that produced interesting results in order to obtain the same result again

classical conditioning learning process in which an associative connection is made through paired presentation of stimuli

classification grouping in accordance with some organizing principle

cleavage cell division; *see* mitosis

clique small, intimate group of about 6 people

cognition process of knowing and understanding

cognitive hypothesis Piaget's explanation of the relationship between thought and language: thought precedes and prepares the way for language

cognitive style way in which an individual approaches cognitive tasks, organizes information and uses it to solve problems

conceptual tempo time that individuals take to respond to cognitive problems

concordant in agreement; twins are concordant when both have a particular trait or disorder

concrete operations to Piaget, third period of intellectual development, from 7 to 11, when actions that the child performs mentally are applied only to objects that are present

conditioned response (CR) in classical conditioning, a response produced by the subject upon presentation of the conditioned stimulus, in the absence of the unconditioned stimulus

conditioned stimulus (CS) in classical conditioning, a neutral stimulus that elicits no response until after repeated pairing with an unconditioned stimulus

confluence model model that explains the family's intellectual environment as a function of the average intellectual level of its members

congenital defects environmentally caused structural deformities that do not affect the organism's chromosome structure and therefore are not passed on to succeeding generations

conjugate reinforcement learning model in which the amount of reinforcement depends upon the amount of effort expended by the subject

conservation maintenance of an object as invariant during such physical changes as amount, number, weight, volume

constraint seeking strategy of questioning that attempts to narrow systematically the boundaries within which an answer lies

construct validity quality of an intelligence test to reflect people's intelligence in situations other than the test

constructive memory memory strategy involving construction of a framework in which to "store" knowledge

content validity quality of an intelligence test to represent the range of abilities referred to as intelligence

context analysis word analysis technique that uses surrounding words, meanings, and pictures to discover the meaning of a word

convergent thinking cognitive style, characteristic of intelligence, which involves finding the one correct solution

correlation degree of relative relationship between factors

covariance process in which 2 factors mutually influence each other

critical age hypothesis Lenneberg's hypothesis that sets approximate age boundaries for language acquisition

crossover process occurring during meiosis that ensures a random assortment of genes in offspring

cross-sectional study research method in which different groups of subjects at various ages are observed

crowd group of about 20 people who "hang out" together; center of organized social activities providing the framework for heterosexual contacts

cultural deficit hypothesis suggestion, now repudiated, that the structure of Black English made it difficult for black children to think logically, formulate and manipulate concepts, or express themselves in full sentences

decentration ability to attend to more than one kind of information at once

deep structure in linguistic theory, an internal representation of the speaker's intended meaning

deferred imitation ability to form a mental image of an action and reproduce it later

deficit hypothesis assumption that poor families are culturally and intellectually deprived

development changes in living things as they move forward in time

discordant not in agreement; twins are discordant when only one has a particular trait or disorder

discrimination ability to distinguish between 2

very similar but slightly different stimuli

divergent thinking cognitive style, characteristic of creativity, which involves mentally exploring many directions in situations where several solutions exist

diversive exploratory behavior behavior directed toward change for its own sake

dizygotic (DZ) twins twins formed when the mother releases 2 ova during one menstrual cycle, each of which is fertilized by a different sperm; fraternal twins

DNA deoxyribonucleic acid; chemical code carrier for all the cells in the body

dominant gene gene that dominates a recessive gene and expresses its characteristic in the organism

Down's syndrome chromosomal abnormality caused by an extra X chromosome, marked by defects including a round head and face, mongoloid eyes, and mental retardation at severe to profound levels; also called mongolism

drive reduction theories theories that explain human activities as efforts to satisfy basic physiological needs such as hunger or thirst

drug therapy use of drugs to manage such disturbed behaviors as hyperactivity, excessive arousal, apathy, depression

dyslexia failure to master reading at a level normal for one's age that is not the result of a disorder such as mental retardation

echolia automatic repetition of what others say

effectance power to cause the environment to respond in ways over which one has control

ego in psychoanalytic theory, the personality structure that monitors the relation between drives (instincts) and reality

egocentric speech Piaget's term for the speech of young children, unable to distinguish between their own points of view and those of others

embryo developing human organism, from weeks 2 through 7 following conception

embryonic period weeks 2 through 7 after conception

empathy ability to perceive and understand the feelings or motives of others

endogenous originating internally

epigenetic crises sensitive periods of development

equilibration to Piaget, the process of balancing elements of the environment and internal structures of thought and action

erythroblastosis disease of the developing fetus or neonate, caused by incompatibility of RH factors in the blood of the mother and infant

estimators cognitive processes by which one determines some quantity

ethology observation and study of animal behavior in natural settings

etiology physiological or environmental factors that cause the development of a disease or disorder

exogenous originating externally

exploratory behavior behavior directed toward seeking information

extinction in operant conditioning, the return of an operant behavior to its previous state when reinforcement or punishment is discontinued

family configuration family structure, in terms of size, presence or absence of parents, number and ages of siblings, and whether one is the oldest, youngest, or middle child

far test experimental situation in which the stimulus pair presented in a test of transposition differs considerably from the stimulus pair presented during training

fertilization joining of a sperm with an egg cell to form a new organism

fetus developing human organism from 8 weeks after conception to birth

field dependence cognitive style in which a person depends on external clues, seems not to make a clear separation between the self and external things, and has difficulty focusing on relevant features of a problem and ignoring distractions

field independence cognitive style in which a person is able to isolate a problem from its context, to focus on clues relevant to the solution, and to ignore irrelevant information

figurative intelligence to Piaget, the aspect of intelligence that produces mental images

fine (manual) motor system motor system that governs movement of eyes, hands, and fingers

fixation in psychoanalytic theory, persistent attachment to an object or person that provides either too much frustration or too much gratification in some stage of development

fixed action patterns reflexes caused by genetic messages that are therefore constant in each animal species

formal operations to Piaget, most advanced stage of cognitive development beginning at about age 11 and characterized by distinction between the actual and the possible, the ability to use symbols to represent other symbols, and the ability to coordinate variables

fraternal twins *see* dizygotic twins

function words designations in the child's early

vocabulary for direction, request, and inquiry

functional core model Nelson's explanation of how children acquire meanings for words, based on functional features of objects and a core meaning of the named object

gag reflex reflex response that causes an infant to spit up liquids blocking breathing passages

gametes *see* germ cells

gang highly structured group, often associated with illegal or delinquent activities

gene unit of heredity

generalization extension of a learned response to situations similar to that in which the response was learned.

generative grammar system of rules that enables speakers to produce an unlimited variety of grammatically acceptable sentences

genotype biological inheritance of an organism

germ cells reproductive cells of the body; sperm and ova

Gesell Developmental Schedules lists showing normal development in motor, adaptive, language, and personal-social behaviors in the first year

grammar rule system that guides speakers in learning the relations and structures of language

gross chromosomal abnormality absence of a chromosome or a part of one, or the presence of an extra one, that causes a genetic defect in an individual

gross (large) motor system motor system that governs movement of the head, torso, legs, and arms

habituation phenomenon that occurs after repeated presentation of the same stimulus: the subject becomes used to the stimulus and no longer responds to it

heritability population statistic that measures the proportion of individual variation caused by genetic inheritance and environmental differences

holophrase single word used by an infant to communicate a thought, request, or feeling; single-word sentence

horizontal décalage to Piaget, irregularity in the appearance of similar mental operations

hyperactivity excessive motor activity

hyperplasia increase in the number of cells by cell division

hypertrophy enlargement of the components of a cell

hypothesis scanning strategy of questioning that attempts to find an answer by testing specific hypotheses not necessarily related to other questions asked

id in psychoanalytic theory, the first basic personality structure, which represents the infant's unregulated pleasure-seeking instincts

ideational fluency ability to produce many ideas appropriate to a given task

identical twins *see* monozygotic twins

identification *see* modeling

identity confusion to Erikson, failure to establish a firm sense of occupational identity; also called role diffusion

identity formation change during adolescence when children begin to think of themselves as individuals who maintain their personalities and social roles over time and in various circumstances

imaginary audience group believed to be watching and judging one's appearance and behavior

infantile autism psychosis of early onset whose symptoms are total lack of communication, absence of crying, unresponsiveness to adult attention, obsessive requirement of unchanging routines, and bizarre stereotyped movements

inferred reality to Piaget, perception of reality based on internally performed mental operations (inferences) rather than on perceived appearances

information-processing model mechanistic model of development that examines such processes as perception, memory, attention, and problem solving that occur between the S and the R of the S→R equation to convert specific inputs into specific outputs

instrumental competence Baumrind's label for the types of behavior most parents want in their children, such as friendliness, cooperation, achievement orientation, and purposiveness

intelligence (IQ) tests tests designed to measure intelligence

interpropositional logic ability to consider the logical relationships between statements as well as the factual relationship between a statement and an actual event

invariances stable and permanent concepts

kernel sentence in transformational grammar, a simple declarative sentence from which more complex sentences may be made by application of transformational rules

Klinefelter's syndrome chromosomal abnormality caused by an extra X chromosome, marked by such defects as underdeveloped testes, infertility, enlarged hips, and, occasionally, mental retardation

language acquisition device (LAD) in transformational grammar, a hypothetical system that has the inherent capability to learn any language

latency period to Freud, the life stage from about ages 6 to 11, in which erotic energy is at its lowest

lateralization focus in one hemisphere of the brain (usually the left) of the association areas responsible for speech functions

learning process in which behavior is changed by positive or negative reinforcement

learning disabilities (LD) term applied to multiple problems that cause children of normal intelligence to experience extreme academic difficulty

linguistic interference hypothesis view that differences in dialects can create miscommunication and give rise to reading problems

linguistic universals such basic syntactic forms as noun and verb phrases that Chomsky claims are common to all languages

longitudinal study research method in which the same group is observed over a period of time

look-and-say teaching *see* sight word analysis

low-birth-weight infant infant weighing less than 5½ pounds (2,500 grams) at birth

mainstreaming putting students with special needs in classes with nonhandicapped, "normal" students

mastery tests tests designed to measure the extent to which people have learned significant information or particular skills

mechanistic model model of development that likens behavior to the workings of a machine: a stimulus (input) applied to the organism results in a change in the organism's behavior (output of the machine)

mediation use of labels or symbols in problem-solving situations

mediation deficiency failure to use a mediator, although the child has produced it

mediation deficiency hypothesis view that the child is able to make verbal or symbolic responses (mediators) but does not use them to solve problems

meiosis halving process by which germ cells reproduce

menarche onset of menstruation

mental deficiency organic dysfunction, resulting from a physiological defect, associated with IQ levels below 50 and the incidence of sensory and motor defects

mental retardation intellectual dysfunction, resulting from familial inheritance or cultural deprivation, associated with IQ levels between 50 and 75 and good health and physical responses

minimal brain dysfunction (MBD) organic condition marked by excessive motor activity, short attention span, and disruptive behavior but seldom associated with neurological damage

mitosis process by which somatic cells divide and reproduce

modeling process in which behaviors are learned by observation; also called identification

mongolism *see* Down's syndrome

monozygotic (MZ) twins twins formed when one ovum fertilized by one sperm divides completely into 2 separate individuals; identical twins

moral realism first of Piaget's 2 stages of moral development; the child believes that rules are sacred and inviolate, that behaviors are either right or wrong, and that punishment follows transgression

morality of conventional role-conformity Kohlberg's second category of moral development; morality is defined as compliance with social conventions and expectations of others

morality of cooperation *see* autonomous morality

morality of self-accepted principles Kohlberg's third category of moral development; the person recognizes possible conflict between 2 socially accepted norms and seeks resolution of the conflict through internal processes

Moro reflex reflex response to a sudden change in stimulation, in which an infant arches his back, tosses back his head, spreads his arms and legs outward from his body, and then hugs them close to the middle of his body

morphemes semantic elements that compose words

morula sphere-shaped solid mass of embryonic cells

mundane cognition observation of cognitive capacities applied in everyday life

mutation variation in an inheritable characteristic

myelinization development of a myelin sheath around cranial nerves which marks the capacity for full neural functioning

near test experimental situation in which the stimulus pair presented in a test of transposition differs slightly from the stimulus pair presented during training

neurosis mental disorder characterized by one or more of the following: anxiety, phobia, depression, obsession

nonreversal shift in transposition studies, a change in the correct response from one dimension to another (e.g., color to size)

normal distribution random distribution throughout a population so that a graph of the distribution forms a bell-shaped curve

norm-referenced based on current norms

normative crisis Offer's term for the experience of relatively little turmoil that he believes characterizes most adolescence

numerosity how many items there are in a set

nurturant giving positive attention to others

object permanence understanding that objects continue to exist when absent

one-to-one correspondence operation that establishes that 2 sets of objects are equivalent in number

open classroom classroom in which the students organize the learning process; based on the belief that children are naturally motivated to learn socially valued skills

operant in learning theory, a voluntary, spontaneous behavior, whose frequency is changed by application of a stimulus

operant conditioning learning process in which an associative connection is made through application of a stimulus that gradually causes a change in the frequency of a voluntary behavior (the operant)

operations to Piaget, systems of cognitive actions; organized networks of related acts

operative intelligence to Piaget, the aspect of intelligence that produces physical or mental actions by which one deals with the environment

operators to Piaget, the cognitive processes by which one determines the consequences of transforming a quantity

optical blink reflex reflex response that causes an infant's eyes to close in order to protect them from bright light

organismic/structural model model of development that sees the organism as a self-regulating system whose structure and functional abilities change over time

organization to Piaget, the tendency to combine physical and psychological processes into coherent systems or structures

organized congenital patterns of behavior behavior patterns such as sucking and crying that are present at birth, to some extent the result of the child's act, and of longer duration than a reflex response

orienting response form of attention in which a subject turns toward a new stimulus, ceases other activities, and observes the new stimulus with interest

ova female reproductive cells

overgeneralization maladaptive extension of a learned response to situations similar to that in which the response was learned

palmar response reflex response that causes a baby's fingers to close around an object placed in his palm

perception process of organizing sensory information into meaningful patterns and hierarchies

period of the ovum first 2 weeks after conception

personal fable story told to oneself to convince oneself that one's feelings are special and unique

phenotype group of characteristics that emerges from the interaction of genetic potential and the working of the environment on the organism

phonemes set of sounds that are the "atoms" that form words

phonic analysis word analysis technique that involves linking sounds to letter symbols or combinations of letters

phonology study of a language's speech sounds

pivot-open grammar Braine's grammar that attempts to explain syntactic patterns of telegraphic speech by dividing words into pivot and open classes

placenta structure through which the embryo receives food and oxygen from the mother and excretes waste; it also acts as a barrier between the embryo and maternal infections

play nonserious and self-contained activity engaged in for its own satisfaction

polygenic inheritance inheritance that results from the cumulative effect of multiple genes whose messages are small and similar

preconventional morality Kohlberg's first category of moral development; conduct is controlled by external forces — commands, punishment, rewards

preoperational period to Piaget, second period of intellectual development, from 2 to 7, when the child acquires the understanding of conservation and the ability to symbolize one thing by another

private speech speech of young children which is

not addressed or adapted to a listener

production deficiency failure to produce a mediator

production system symbolic representation of incoming information and action taken with respect to the information, leading to a change in the state of the problem

prosocial helpful; cooperative; altruistic

psychogenic stemming from one's needs and motives; of psychic origin

psychosis major mental disorder in which contact with reality is seriously affected

psychotherapy treatment of mental disorder by means of communication between a trained professional and the patient, involving counseling and analysis to resolve the conflicts that produce anxiety and maladaptive behavior

puberty state of physical development during which the reproductive organs mature so that sexual reproduction becomes possible

punishment in operant conditioning, a stimulus that suppresses the frequency of a behavior

reaction range range of phenotypes that can develop from the same genotype under varying environmental conditions

reality therapy therapeutic approach that emphasizes behavior that fits the real world, seeks to correct the patient's view of his feelings and needs, and stresses the individual's responsibility for choices and actions

recessive gene gene that expresses its characteristic in the organism only when paired with another recessive gene

reciprocity belief that people should help and not injure those who help them

recognitory assimilation to Piaget, the child's recognition of external events

reflexes automatic, involuntary responses

reinforcer in operant conditioning, a stimulus that increases the frequency of a behavior

response reaction of an organism to a stimulus

reversal shift in transposition studies, a change in the correct response from one value to another (e.g., white to yellow), but within the same dimension (color)

rich interpretation approach to early speech analysis which credits the child with knowing more than he can express and using extralinguistic cues to complete his meaning

RNA ribonucleic acid; the molecule that transmits genetic instructions from DNA in a cell nucleus to the rest of the cell

role diffusion *see* identity confusion

role taking ability to understand another's point of view

rooting reflex reflex response that causes an infant to turn his head in search of a nipple toward an object that strokes his cheek

Sapir-Whorf hypothesis view that perception and thought are determined by language, that language affects how people observe and evaluate environment and experience

schema to Piaget, a simplified internal representation of the result of a mental operation

scheme to Piaget, an organized pattern of behavior, either behavioral or intellectual

schizophrenia psychosis whose symptoms include loss of personal identity, disturbed relationships, general intellectual deficiencies, abnormal perceptions, distorted and stereotyped movements

selective reinforcement process of changing the frequency of a behavior by responding with a reinforcer to a particular behavior and ignoring others

self-and-other constancy idea that the self remains invariant in the face of physical, emotional, and social changes

semantic feature hypothesis Clark's explanation of how children acquire meanings for words; accretions of features narrow the definition until the child's word corresponds in meaning to adult usage

sensorimotor period to Piaget, first period of intellectual development, from birth to age 2, in which thinking and learning center on bodily sensations and movements

separation anxiety distress of varying intensity caused by a young child's separation from the caregiver

seriation arrangement in a series of increasing or decreasing order

sex-role identity understanding of behaviors available and appropriate to one's sex

sexual dimorphism difference in body composition between males and females

shifting staring alternately at 2 stimuli

short-gestation-period infant infant born before 37 weeks of pregnancy

sickle cell anemia disease caused by a metabolic error in which blood cells take a hooked shape instead of the normal disc shape; it occurs mostly among blacks and may have been a mutation that once served as protection against malaria

sight word analysis word analysis technique in

which the teacher presents a flash card, pronounces the word on the card, and asks the class to repeat it; also called look-and-say teaching

sign arbitrary symbol whose meaning is agreed on by social convention

signal stimulus pattern associated with a particular object, such as a smell, tone, track, or gesture

social cognition development of social skills and relationships

social learning theory theory that explains learning processes as based on the observation of a model

social responsibility belief that people should aid without expectation of reward those who are dependent on them

social understanding cognition of another's feelings

sociogenic stemming from social pressures and expectations

sociogram graphic representation of the results of a sociometric test

sociometric test study that identifies patterns of relationships among a group

somatic cells cells in the body that govern the formation of bones, muscles, and organs

speech human language; the expression and reception of ideas and feelings by means of verbal symbols

sperm male reproductive cell

standardization sample representative sampling of the population, upon which tables of norms for IQ tests are based

state pattern of recurring self-generated behaviors

stimulus any action or agent that causes or changes the subject's activity

structural analysis word analysis technique that teaches readers to pick out parts of words, such as prefixes or suffixes, to help them discover common meanings and sounds

substantive words object names, action verbs, and event labels in the child's early vocabulary

sucking reflex reflex response that causes an infant to suck a nipple when one is presented

superego in psychoanalytic theory, the personality structure that makes a person feel uncomfortable when violating a moral prohibition; conscience

surface structure in linguistic theory, an external utterance

symbol something that stands for or represents another object, yet is separable from it

symbolic function to Piaget, the ability to represent one thing with another

teacher expectation view that teachers' perceptions of student ability are reflected in the ways they teach and treat pupils, which in turn yield performances by the students based on the teachers' original expectations

telegraphic speech children's 2-word combinations which resemble telegrams because items such as words and word endings are dropped

tension-interference hypothesis view that attempts to explain that father-absent boys may learn a cognitive style characteristic of females; supposedly, the stress and tension associated with a single-parent family interfere more with the development of mathematical than verbal ability

teratogens environmental stresses that cause fetal malformations

time tally hypothetical growth tempo for each individual

token economy in behavior modification, a system of rewarding behaviors with prizes or tokens that can later be "spent" on special privileges or items

tonic neck response reflex response in which, when a baby's head is turned sharply to one side and held there, the arm and leg on that side extend and the other arm bends at the elbow

traditional classroom classroom organized around the belief that structure, organization, and discipline facilitate both the children's learning and the teacher's control

transformational grammar Chomsky's grammatical system, which explains that all sentences are kernel sentences or transformations of kernel sentences

transitivity understanding that if $A > B$ and $B > C$, then $A > C$

unconditioned response (UCR) in classical conditioning, a reflex action that occurs regularly in response to a natural external stimulus

unconditioned stimulus (UCS) in classical conditioning, a natural external stimulus that normally elicits a particular reflex response

universal primitives hypothesis Bierwisch's explanation that traces the child's learning of meanings to a biological mechanism of perception and cognition

verbal mediation use of language to assist in problem solving

voluntary control capacity of "planfulness," including the ability to anticipate an outcome; to choose and employ means for achieving a goal; and to coordinate behavior to reach the goal

withdrawal reflex reflex response that causes an infant to pull away from a source of pain and to cry in outrage

X chromosome chromosome that determines sex; an organism with 2 X chromosomes is female; an organism with one X and one Y chromosome is male

Y chromosome chromosome that determines sex; the presence of a Y chromosome, contributed only by the father, makes a male organism

zygote fertilized ovum before cleavage

Bibliography

Abrahamson, P., Brackbill, Y., Carpenter, Y., & Fitzgerald, H. E. Interaction of stimulus and response in infant conditioning. *Psychosomatic Medicine,* 1970, *32,* 319–325.

Ackerman, N. The role of the family in the emergence of child disorders. In E. Miller (ED.), *Foundations of child psychiatry.* New York: Pergamon, 1968.

Ainsworth, M. D. S., Bell, S. M., & Stayton, D. J. Individual differences in the strange-situation behavior of one-year-olds. In H. R. Schaffer (Ed.), *The origins of human social relations.* London: Academic Press, 1971.

Aldrich, C. A., & Hewitt, E. S. A self-regulating feeding program for infants. *Journal of the American Medical Association,* 1947, *135,* 340–342.

Allinsmith, B. B. Parental discipline and children's aggression in two social classes (Doctoral dissertation, University of Michigan, 1954). *Dissertation Abstracts,* 1954, *14,* 708. (University Microfilms No. A54-1084).

Altman, L. K. Oxygen monitor may reduce birth defects. *New York Times,* June 13, 1976, pp. 1; 50.

Amsterdam, B. Mirror self-image reactions before age two. *Developmental Psychobiology,* 1972, *5,* 297–305.

Anderson, J. E. Dynamics of development: Systems in process. In D. B. Harris (Ed.), *The concept of development.* Minneapolis: University of Minnesota Press, 1957.

Anderson, J. W. Attachment behavior out of doors. In N. Blurton-Jones (Ed.), *Ethological studies of child behaviour.* London: Cambridge University Press, 1972.

André-Thomas, & Autgaerden, S. *Locomotion from pre- to post-natal life: How the newborn begins to acquire psycho-sensory functions* (Clinics in Developmental Medicine, No. 24). London: Heinemann Medical Publications, 1966.

Appleton, T., Clifton, R., & Goldberg, S. The development of behavioral competence in infancy. In F. D. Horowitz (Ed.), *Review of child development research* (Vol. 4). Chicago: University of Chicago Press, 1975.

Aronfreed, J. *Punishment learning and internalization: Some parameters of reinforcement and cognition.* Paper presented at the biennial meeting of the Society for Research in Child Development, Minneapolis, 1965.

Atkinson, R. C., Hansen, D. N., & Bernbach, H. A. Short-term memory with young children. *Psychonomic Science,* 1964, *1,* 255–256.

Atlee, H. B. Fall of the queen of heaven. *Obstetrics and Gynecology,* 1963, *21,* 514–519.

Avedon, E. M., & Sutton-Smith, B. *The study of games.* New York: Wiley, 1971.

Avers, C. J. *Biology of sex.* New York: Wiley, 1974.

Baird, R. R., & Bee, H. L. Modification of conceptual style preference by differential reinforcement. *Child Development,* 1969, *40,* 903–910.

Baldwin, C. P., & Baldwin, A. L. Children's judgments of kindness. *Child Development,* 1970, *41,* 29–47.

Baldwin, C. P., & Baldwin, A. L. Personality and social development of handicapped children. In C. E. Sherrick & others, *Psychology and the handicapped child* (DHEW Publication No. OE 73-05000). Washington, D. C.: U. S. Government Printing Office, 1974.

Bandura, A. *The influence of rewarding and punishing consequences to the model on the acquisition and performance of imitative responses.* Unpublished manuscript, Stanford University, 1962.

Bandura, A. The stormy decade: Fact or fiction? *Psychology in the Schools,* 1964, *1,* 224–231.

Bandura, A., Grusec, J. E., & Menlove, F. L. Vicarious extinction of avoidance behavior. *Journal of Personality and Social Psychology,* 1967, *5,* 16–23.

Bandura, A., Ross, D., & Ross, S. A. Transmission of aggression through imitation of aggressive models. *Journal of Abnormal and Social Psychology,* 1961, *63,* 575–582.

Bandura, A., Ross, D., & Ross, S. A. A comparative test of the status envy, social power, and secondary reinforcement theories of identificatory learning. *Journal of Abnormal and Social Psychology,* 1963, *67,* 527–534. (a)

Bandura, A., Ross, D., & Ross, S. A. Imitation of film-mediated aggressive models. *Journal of Abnormal and Social Psychology,* 1963, *66,* 3–11. (b)

Bandura, A., & Walters, R. H. *Social learning and personality development.* New York: Holt, Rinehart and Winston, 1963.

Bane, M. J., & Jencks, C. Five myths about your IQ. *Harper's Magazine,* February 1973, pp. 28 ff.

Barker, R. G., & Wright, H. F. *Midwest and its children: The psychological ecology of an American town.* Evanston, Ill.: Row, Peterson, 1954.

Barnes, K. E. Preschool play norms: A replication. *Developmental Psychology,* 1971, *5,* 99–103.

Barry, H., III, Bacon, M. K., & Child, I. L. A cross-cultural survey of some sex differences in socialization. *Journal of Abnormal and Social Psychology,* 1957, *55,* 327–332.

Bateman, B. An educator's view of a diagnostic approach

to learning disorders. In J. Hellmuth (Ed.), *Learning disorders* (Vol. 1). Seattle: Special Child Publications, 1965.

Bates, P. B., & Nesselroade, J. R. Cultural change and adolescent personality development: An application of longitudinal sequences. *Developmental Psychology,* 1972, *7,* 244–256.

Bateson, G. The message "This is play." In J. B. Schaffner (Ed.), *Group processes* (transactions of the 2nd conference). New York: Josiah Macy Foundation, 1956.

Bateson, G., Jackson, D. D., Haley, J., & Weakland, J. Toward a theory of schizophrenia. *Behavioral Science,* 1956, *1,* 251–264.

Baumrind, D. Effects of authoritative parental control on child behavior. *Child Development,* 1966, *37,* 887–907.

Baumrind, D. Child care practices anteceding three patterns of preschool behavior. *Genetic Psychology Monographs,* 1967, *75,* 43–88.

Baumrind, D. Authoritarian vs. authoritative parental control. *Adolescence,* 1968, *3,* 255–272.

Baumrind, D. Current patterns of parental authority. *Developmental Psychology Monograph,* 1971, *4* (1, Pt. 2).

Baumrind, D. Socialization and instrumental competence in young children. In W. W. Hartup (Ed.), *The young child: Reviews of research* (Vol. 2). Washington, D. C.: National Association for the Education of Young Children, 1972.

Bayley, N. On the growth of intelligence. *American Psychologist,* 1955, *10,* 805–818.

Bayley, N. Behavioral correlates of mental growth: Birth to thirty-six years. *American Psychologist,* 1968, *23,* 1–17.

Bayley, N. Development of mental abilities. In P.H. Mussen (Ed.), *Carmichael's manual of child psychology* (3rd ed.) (Vol. 1). New York: Wiley, 1970.

Bayley, N., & Schaefer, E. S. Correlations of maternal and child behaviors with the development of mental abilities: Data from the Berkeley Growth Study. *Monographs of the Society for Research in Child Development,* 1964, *29* (6, Serial No. 97).

Beckmann, H. Die entwicklung der zahlleistung bei 2-6 jährigen kindern. *Zeitschrift für Angewandte Psychologie,* 1923, *22,* 1–72.

Bee, H. L., Nyman, B. A., Sarason, I. G., & Van Egeren, L. F. *A study of cognitive and motivational variables in lower and middle class preschool children: An approach to the evaluation of the Head Start* (Vol. 1) (University of Washington Social Change Evaluation Project, Contract 1375). Washington, D. C.: Office of Economic Opportunity, 1968.

Bee, H. L., Van Egeren, L. F., Streissguth, A. P., Nyman, B. A., & Leckie, M. S. Social class differences in maternal teaching strategies and speech patterns. *Developmental Psychology,* 1969, *1,* 726–734.

Beecher, H. W. *Lectures to young men on various important subjects.* Boston: J. P. Jewett, 1844.

Beintema, D. *A neurological study of newborn infants* (Clinics in Developmental Medicine, No. 28). London: Heinemann Medical Publications, 1968.

Bell, R. Q. A reinterpretation of the direction of effects in studies of socialization. *Psychological Review,* 1968, *75,* 81–95.

Bell, R. Q. Contributions of human infants to caregiving and social interaction. In M. Lewis & L. A. Rosenblum (Eds.), *The effect of the infant on its caregiver.* New York: Wiley, 1974.

Bell, R. R. Parent-child conflict in sexual values. *Journal of Social Issues,* 1966, *22*(2), 34–44.

Bell, S. M., & Ainsworth, M. D. S. Infant crying and maternal responsiveness. *Child Development,* 1972, *43,* 1171–1190.

Benedict, R. Continuities and discontinuities in cultural conditioning. *Psychiatry,* 1938, *1,* 161–167.

Bergman, I. Introduction: Bergman discusses film-making. In *Four screenplays of Ingmar Bergman* (L. Malmstrom & D. Kushner, trans.). New York: Simon and Schuster, 1960.

Bergman, T., Haith, M., & Mann, L. *Development of eye contact and facial scanning in infants.* Paper presented at the meeting of the Society for Research in Child Development, Minneapolis, 1971.

Berko, J. The child's learning of English morphology. *Word,* 1958, *14,* 150–177.

Berlyne, D. E. Curiosity and exploration. *Science,* July 1, 1966, pp. 25–33.

Bernstein, B. Social class and linguistic development: A theory of social learning. In A. H. Halsey, J. Floud & C. A. Anderson (Eds.), *Education, economy, and society.* New York: Free Press, 1961.

Bernstein, B. Aspects of language and learning in the genesis of the social process. In D. Hymes (Ed.), *Language in culture and society.* New York: Harper and Row, 1965.

Bernstein, B. Elaborated and restricted codes: Their social origins and some consequences. In A. G. Smith (Ed.), *Communication and culture.* New York: Holt, Rinehart and Winston, 1966.

Best, B. *Development of classification skills in deaf children with and without early manual communication.* Unpublished doctoral dissertation, University of California, Berkeley, 1970.

Bettelheim, B. *Love is not enough.* New York: Free Press, 1950.

Bettelheim, B. Joey: A "mechanical boy." *Scientific American,* March 1959, pp. 116–127.

Biblow, E. Imaginative play and the control of aggressive behavior. In J. L. Singer (Ed.), *The child's world of make-believe: Experimental studies of imaginative play.* New York: Academic Press, 1973.

Bierwisch, M. Some semantic universals of German adjectives. *Foundations of Language,* 1967, *3,* 1–36.

Bing, E. Effect of childrearing practices on development of differential cognitive abilities. *Child Development,* 1963, *34,* 631–648.

Birch, H. G., & Gussow, J. D. *Disadvantaged children: Health, nutrition, and school failure.* New York: Harcourt, Brace and World, 1970.

Birkbeck, A., & Moore, M. *Controlled childbirth* (rev. ed.).

North Pomfret, Vt.: David & Charles, 1975.

Birns, B., & Golden, M. Prediction of intellectual performance at 3 years from infant tests and personality measures. *Merrill-Palmer Quarterly*, 1972, *18*, 53–58.

Bishop, C. H. Transfer effects of word and letter training in reading. *Journal of Verbal Learning and Verbal Behavior*, 1964, *3*, 215–221.

Bishop, D. W., & Chace, C. A. Parental conceptual systems, home play environment, and potential creativity in children. *Journal of Experimental Child Psychology*, 1971, *12*, 318–338.

Bixenstine, V. E., DeCorte, M. S., & Bixenstine, B. A. Conformity to peer-sponsored misconduct at four grade levels. *Developmental Psychology*, 1976, *12*, 226–236.

Bjorklund, D. F., Ornstein, P. A., & Haig, J. R. Developmental differences in organization and recall: Training in the use of organizational techniques. *Developmental Psychology*, 1977, *13*, 175–183.

Blank, M. *Teaching learning in the preschool: A dialogue approach.* Columbus, Ohio: Merrill, 1973.

Blank, M. Cognitive functions of language in the preschool years. *Developmental Psychology*, 1974, *10*, 229–245.

Blauvelt, H., & McKenna, J. Capacity of the human newborn for mother-infant interaction. II. The temporal dimensions of a neonate response. *Psychiatric Research Reports*, 1960, *13*, 128–154.

Bleier, I. J. *Maternity nursing: A textbook for practical nurses* (3rd ed.). Philadelphia: Saunders, 1971.

Block, J. H., Haan, N., & Smith, M. B. Socialization correlates of student activism. *Journal of Social Issues*, 1969, *25*(4), 143–177.

Block, N. J., & Dworkin, G. (Eds.). *The IQ controversy: Critical readings.* New York: Pantheon, 1976.

Bloom, L. *Language development: Form and function in emerging grammars.* Cambridge: MIT Press, 1970.

Bloom, L. *One word at a time: The use of single word utterances before syntax.* The Hague: Mouton, 1973.

Borke, H. Interpersonal perception of young children: Egocentrism or empathy? *Developmental Psychology*, 1971, *5*, 263–269.

Bornstein, M. H. Hue is an absolute code for young children. *Nature*, 1975, *256*, 309–310. (a)

Bornstein, M. H. Qualities of color vision in infancy. *Journal of Experimental Child Psychology*, 1975, *19*, 401–419. (b)

Bornstein, M. H. Infants' recognition memory for hue. *Developmental Psychology*, 1976, *12*, 185–191.

Bornstein, M. H., Kessen, W., & Weiskopf, S. The categories of hue in infancy. *Science*, January 16, 1976, pp. 201–202. (a)

Bornstein, M. H., Kessen, W., & Weiskopf, S. Color vision and hue categorization in young human infants. *Journal of Experimental Psychology*, 1976, *105*, 115–129. (b)

Bower, T. G. R. The visual world of infants. *Scientific American*, December 1966, pp. 80–92.

Bower, T. G. R. The object in the world of the infant. *Scientific American*, October 1971, pp. 30–38.

Bower, T. G. R. Object perception in infants. *Perception*,

1972, *1*, 15–30.

Bowerman, M. *Early syntactic development: A cross-linguistic study with special reference to Finnish.* London: Cambridge University Press, 1973.

Bowes, W. A., Jr. Obstetrical medication and infant outcome: A review of the literature. *Monographs of the Society for Research in Child Development*, 1970, *35*(4, Serial No. 137), 3–23.

Bowlby, J. A symposium on the contribution of current theories to an understanding of child development. **I.** An ethological approach to research in child development. *British Journal of Medical Psychology*, 1957, *30*, 230–240.

Bowlby, J. The nature of the child's tie to his mother. *International Journal of Psychoanalysis*, 1958, *39*, 350–373.

Bowlby, J. Beginnings of attachment behavior. In J. Bowlby, *Attachment and loss* (Vol. 1: *Attachment*). New York: Basic Books, 1969.

Bradley, R. H., & Caldwell, B. M. Early home environment and changes in mental test performance in children from 6 to 36 months. *Developmental Psychology*, 1976, *12*, 93–97.

Braine, M. D. S. The ontogeny of English phrase structure: The first phrase. *Language*, 1963, *39*, 1–13.

Braun, C. Teacher expectation: Sociopsychological dynamics. *Review of Educational Research*, 1976, *46*, 185–213.

Braungart, R. G. The sociology of generations and student politics: A comparison of the functionalist and generational unit models. *Journal of Social Issues*, 1974, *30*(2), 31–54.

Brazelton, T. B. *Neonatal behavioral assessment scale* (Clinics in Developmental Medicine, No. 50). London: Heinemann Medical Publications, 1973.

Brazelton, T. B., & Young, G. C. An example of imitative behavior in a nine-week-old infant. *Journal of the American Academy of Child Psychiatry*, 1964, *3*, 53–67.

Breland, H. M. Birth order, family configuration, and verbal achievement. *Child Development*, 1974, *45*, 1011–1019.

Briggs, C. H. An experimental study of reflection-impulsivity in children. (Doctoral dissertation, University of Minnesota, 1966). *Dissertation Abstracts*, 1968, *28*, 3891B–3892B. (University Microfilms No. 68–1610).

Broadbent, D. E. *Perception and communication.* New York: Pergamon, 1958.

Bronfenbrenner, U. *Two worlds of childhood: U. S. and U. S. S. R.* New York: Basic Books, 1970.

Bronson, G. W. Infants' reactions to unfamiliar persons and novel objects. *Monographs of the Society for Research in Child Development*, 1972, *37*(3, Serial No. 148).

Brophy, J. E., & Good, T. L. Teachers' communication of differential expectations for children's classroom performance: Some behavioral data. *Journal of Educational Psychology*, 1970, *61*, 365–374.

Broussard, E. R., & Hartner, M. S. S. Further consideration regarding maternal perception of the first born. In J. Hellmuth (Ed.), *The exceptional infant: Studies in abnormalities* (Vol. 2). New York: Brunner/Mazel, 1971.

Broverman, I. K., Vogel, S. R., Broverman, D. M., Clarkson, F. E., & Rosenkrantz, P. S. Sex-role stereotypes: A current appraisal. *Journal of Social Issues,* 1972, *28*(2), 59–78.

Brown, P., & Elliot, R. Control of aggression in a nursery school class. *Journal of Experimental Child Psychology,* 1965, *2,* 103–107.

Brown, R. (Ed.). *Psycholinguistics* (Part 1). New York: Free Press, 1970.

Brown, R., & Fraser, C. The acquisition of syntax. In C. N. Cofer & B. S. Musgrave (Eds.), *Verbal behavior and learning: Problems and processes.* New York: McGraw-Hill, 1963.

Bruner, J. S. The course of cognitive growth. *American Psychologist,* 1964, *19,* 1–15.

Bruner, J. S. On cognitive growth. In J. S. Bruner, R. R. Olver, & P. M. Greenfield (Eds.), *Studies in cognitive growth.* New York: Wiley, 1966.

Bruner, J. S. Eye, hand, and mind. In D. Elkind & J. H. Flavell (Eds.), *Studies in cognitive development: Essays in honor of Jean Piaget.* New York: Oxford University Press, 1969. (a)

Bruner, J. S. Processes of growth in infancy. In A. Ambrose (Ed.), *Stimulation in early infancy.* New York: Academic Press, 1969. (b)

Bruner, J. S. Nature and uses of immaturity. *American Psychologist,* 1972, *27,* 687–708.

Bruner, J. S. Organization of early skilled action. *Child Development,* 1973, *44,* 1–11. (a)

Bruner, J. S. Pacifier-produced visual buffering in human infants. *Developmental Psychobiology,* 1973, *6,* 45–51. (b)

Bryan, J. H. Children's cooperation and helping behaviors. In E. M. Hetherington (Ed.), *Review of child development research* (Vol. 5). Chicago: University of Chicago Press, 1975. (a)

Bryan, J. H. "You will be well advised to watch what we do instead of what we say." In D. J. DePalma & J. M. Foley (Eds.), *Moral development: Current theory and research.* New York: Wiley, 1975. (b)

Bryant, P. E., & Trabasso, T. Transitive inferences and memory in young children. *Nature,* 1971, *232,* 456–458.

Buder, L. High school graduation standards to be stiffened by New York City. *New York Times,* April 25, 1977, pp. 1; 57.

Burt, C. Intelligence and social mobility. *British Journal of Statistical Psychology,* 1961, *14,* 3–24.

Caldwell, B. M., & Richmond, J. B. The impact of theories of child development. *Children,* 1962, *9,* 73–78.

Cann, M. A. *An investigation of a component of parental behavior in humans.* Unpublished Master's thesis, University of Chicago, 1953.

Caplan, F. (Ed.). *The first twelve months of life: Your baby's growth month by month.* New York: Grosset and Dunlap, 1973.

Carlsmith, L. Effect of early father absence on scholastic aptitude. *Harvard Educational Review,* 1964, *34,* 3–21.

Carroll, J. B. (Ed.). *Language, thought, and reality: Selected writings of Benjamin Lee Whorf.* New York: Wiley, 1956.

Cattell, R. B. The fate of national intelligence: Test of a thirteen-year prediction. *Eugenics Review,* 1950, *42,* 136–148.

Cavior, N., & Dokecki, P. R. Physical attractiveness, perceived attitude similarity, and academic achievement as contributors to interpersonal attraction among adolescents. *Developmental Psychology,* 1973, *9,* 44–54.

Chambliss, W. J. The saints and the roughnecks. In T. J. Cottle (Ed.), *Readings in adolescent psychology: Contemporary perspectives.* New York: Harper and Row, 1977.

Charlesworth, W. R. *Development of the object concept: A methodological study.* Paper presented at the meeting of the American Psychological Association, New York, September, 1966.

Charlesworth, W. R. The role of surprise in cognitive development. In D. Elkind & J. H. Flavell (Eds.), *Studies in cognitive development: Essays in honor of Jean Piaget.* New York: Oxford University Press, 1969.

Chavez, A., Martinez, C., & Yaschine, T. The importance of nutrition and stimuli on child mental and social development. In J. Cravioto, L. Hambraeus & B. Vahlquist (Eds.), *Early malnutrition and mental development.* Uppsala, Sweden: Almquist and Wiksell, 1974.

Cherry, L. & Lewis, M. Mothers and two-year-olds: A study of sex-differentiated aspects of verbal interaction. *Developmental Psychology,* 1976, *12,* 278–282.

Child abuse contributes to palsy. *Detroit Free Press,* March 28, 1977.

Chomsky, N. *Syntactic structures.* The Hague: Mouton, 1957.

Chomsky, N. Review of *Verbal Behavior* by B. F. Skinner. *Language,* 1959, *35,* 26–58.

Chomsky, N. *Aspects of the theory of syntax.* Cambridge: MIT Press, 1965.

Chukovsky, K. I. [*From two to five*] (M. Morton, Ed. & trans.). Berkeley: University of California Press, 1963.

Cicirelli, V. G. Relationship of sibling structure and interaction to younger sib's conceptual style. *Journal of Genetic Psychology,* 1974, *125,* 37–49.

Clarizio, H. F., & McCoy, G. F. *Behavior disorders in children* (2nd ed.). New York: Crowell, 1976.

Clark, E. V. What's in a word? On the child's acquisition of semantics in his first language. In T. E. Moore (Ed.), *Cognitive development and the acquisition of language.* New York: Academic Press, 1973.

Clark, H., & Clark, E. *Psychology and language: An introduction to psycholinguistics.* New York: Harcourt Brace Jovanovich, 1977.

Clarke-Stewart, K. A. Interactions between mothers and their young children: Characteristics and consequences. *Monographs of the Society for Research in Child Development,* 1973, *38* (6–7, Serial No. 153).

Cleary, T. A., Humphreys, L. G., Kendrick, S. A., & Wesman, A. Educational uses of tests with disadvantaged students. *American Psychologist,* 1975, *30,* 15–41.

Clifford, M. M., & Walster, E. The effect of physical attractiveness on teacher expectation. *Sociology of Education,* 1973, *46,* 248–258.

Cohen, L. B. Attention-getting and attention-holding processes of infant visual preferences. *Child Development, 1972, 43,* 869–879.

Cohen, L. B., & Gelber, E. R. Infant visual memory. In L. B. Cohen & P. Salapatek (Eds.), *Infant perception: From sensation to cognition* (Vol. 1: *Basic visual processes*). New York: Academic Press, 1975.

Cohen, L. J. The operational definition of human attachment. *Psychological Bulletin, 1974, 81,* 207–217.

Cole, M., & Bruner, J. S. Cultural differences and inferences about psychological processes. *American Psychologist, 1971, 26,* 867–876.

Coleman, J. S. *The adolescent society.* New York: Free Press, 1961.

Coleman, J. S., & others. *Equality of educational opportunity.* Washington, D. C.: U.S. Dept. of Health, Education and Welfare, Office of Education, 1966.

Collard, R. R., & Rydberg, J. E. Generalization of habituation to properties of objects in human infants. *American Psychological Association, Proceedings, 1972, 7,* 81–82.

Condon, W. S., & Sander, L. W. Neonate movement is synchronized with adult speech: Interactional participation and language acquisition. *Science,* January 11, 1974, 99–101.

Condry, J., & Siman, M. L. Characteristics of peer- and adult-oriented children. *Journal of Marriage and the Family, 1974, 36,* 543–554.

Conel, J. L. Histologic development of the cerebral cortex. In *The biology of mental health and disease.* New York: Hoeber, 1952.

Conway, E. & Brackbill, Y. Delivery medication and infant outcome: An empirical study. *Monographs of the Society for Research in Child Development, 1970, 35* (4, Serial No. 137), 24–34.

Cooke, R. E. The behavioral response of infants to heat stress. *Yale Journal of Biology and Medicine, 1952, 24,* 334–340.

Cooper, H. M., Baron, R. M., & Lowe, C. A. The importance of race and social class information in the formation of expectancies about academic performance. *Journal of Educational Psychology, 1975, 67,* 312–319.

Craik, F. I. M., & Lockhart, R. S. Levels of processing: A framework for memory research. *Journal of Verbal Learning and Verbal Behavior, 1972, 11,* 671–684.

Crandall, V. & Battle, E. S. The antecedents and adult correlates of academic and intellectual achievement effort. In J. P. Hill (Ed.), *Minnesota Symposia on Child Psychology* (Vol. 4). Minneapolis: University of Minnesota Press, 1970.

Crandall, V., Dewey, R., Katkovsky, W., & Preston, A. Parents' attitudes and behaviors and grade-school children's academic achievements. *Journal of Genetic Psychology, 1964, 104,* 53–66.

Critchley, M. Language. In E. H. Lenneberg & E. Lenneberg (Eds.), *Foundations of language development: A multidisciplinary approach* (Vol. 1). New York: Academic Press, 1975.

Cromer, R. The development of language and cognition: The cognitive hypothesis. In B. Foss (Ed.), *New perspectives in child development.* Harmondsworth, England: Penguin, 1974.

Cronbach, L. J. Five decades of public controversy over mental testing. *American Psychologist, 1975, 30,* 1–14.

Curtis, R. L., Jr. Adolescent orientations toward parents and peers: Variations by sex, age, and socioeconomic status. *Adolescence, 1975, 10,* 483–494.

Cusick, P. A. Adolescent groups and the school organization. *School Review, 1973, 82,* 116–119.

D'Angelo, R. *Families of sand: A report concerning the flight of adolescents from their families.* Columbus: Ohio State University School of Social Work, 1974.

Danziger, K. *Interpersonal communication.* New York: Pergamon, 1976.

Dargassies, S. S. The first smile. *Developmental Medicine and Child Neurology, 1962, 4,* 531–553.

Davis, K. The sociology of parent-youth conflict. *American Sociological Review, 1940, 5,* 523–535.

Davison, G. C., & Neale, J. M. *Abnormal psychology: An experimental-clinical approach.* New York: Wiley, 1974.

Dayton, D. H. Early malnutrition and human development. *Children, 1969, 16,* 211–217.

Dearden, R. F. The concept of play. In R. S. Peters (Ed.), *The concept of education.* London: Routledge and Kegan Paul, 1967.

DeFleur, M. L., & DeFleur, L. B. The relative contribution of television as a learning source for children's occupational knowledge. *American Sociological Review, 1967, 32,* 777–789.

de Laguna, G. A. *Speech: Its function and development.* Bloomington: Indiana University Press, 1927.

DeLoache, J. *Individual differences in infant visual memory.* (Doctoral dissertation, University of Illinois, 1973). *Dissertation Abstracts International, 1974; 34,* 6234B–6235B. (University Microfilms No. 74–12,001)

Demos, J., & Demos, V. Adolescence in historical perspective. In T. J. Cottle (Ed.), *Readings in adolescent psychology: Contemporary perspectives.* New York: Harper and Row, 1977.

Denney, D. R. Modeling effects upon conceptual style and cognitive tempo. *Child Development, 1972, 43,* 105–119.

Descoeudres, A. *La développement de l'enfant de deux à sept ans.* Paris: Delachaux et Niestlé, 1921.

Desor, J. A., Maller, O., & Andrews, K. Ingestive responses of human newborns to salty, sour, and bitter stimuli. *Journal of Comparative and Physiological Psychology, 1975, 89,* 966–970.

Dion, K. K. Physical attractiveness and evaluation of children's transgressions. *Journal of Personality and Social Psychology, 1972, 24,* 207–213.

Dodwell, P. C., Muir, D., & DiFranco, D. Responses of infants to visually presented objects. *Science,* October 8, 1976, 209–211.

Donovan, B. T., & van der Werff ten Bosch, J. J. *Physiology of puberty.* London: Edward Arnold, 1965.

Douvan, E., & Adelson, J. (Eds.). *The adolescent experience.* New York: Wiley, 1966. (a)

Douvan, E., & Adelson, J. The self and identity. In E. Douvan & J. Adelson (Eds.), *The adolescent experience.* New York: Wiley, 1966. (b)

Drage, J. S., Berendes, H. W., & Fisher, P. D. The Apgar score and four-year psychological examination performance. In *Perinatal factors affecting human development* (Scientific Publication, No. 185). Pan American Health Organization, World Health Organization, 1969.

Dreman, S. B., & Greenbaum, C. W. Altruism or reciprocity: Sharing behavior in Israeli kindergarten children. *Child Development,* 1973, *44,* 61–68.

Dreyfus-Brisac, C. The bioelectric development of the central nervous system during early life. In F. Falkner (Ed.), *Human development.* Philadelphia: Saunders, 1966.

Dubos, R. Biological individuality. *Columbia Forum,* 1969, *12*(1), 5–9.

Dunphy, D. C. The social structure of urban adolescent peer groups. *Sociometry,* 1963, *26,* 230–246.

Durkin, D. *Children who read early.* New York: Teachers College Press, 1966.

Dworkin, N. E. Changing teachers' negative expectation towards educationally vulnerable children through the use of a brief interactive process. (Doctoral dissertation, Hofstra University, 1974). *Dissertation Abstracts International,* 1975, *35,* 5921A. (University Microfilms No. 76–6995)

Dwyer, J. M. *Human reproduction: The female system and the neonate.* Philadelphia: F. A. Davis, 1976.

Eckerman, C. O., Whatley, J. L., & Kutz, S. L. Growth of social play with peers during the second year of life. *Developmental Psychology,* 1975, *11,* 42–49.

Eckland, B. K. Genetics and sociology: A reconsideration. *American Sociological Review,* 1967, *32,* 173–194.

Eibl-Eibesfeldt, I. Concepts of ethology and their significance in the study of human behavior. In H. W. Stevenson, E. H. Hess & H. L. Rheingold (Eds.), *Early behavior: Comparative and developmental approaches.* New York: Wiley, 1967.

Eibl-Eibesfeldt, I. [*Ethology: The biology of behavior*] (E. Klinghammer, trans.). New York: Holt, Rinehart and Winston, 1970.

Eimas, P. D., Siqueland, E. R., Jusczyk, P., & Vigorito, J. Speech perception in infants. *Science,* January 22, 1971, pp. 303–306.

Eisenberg, R. B. *Auditory competence in early life: The roots of communicative behavior.* Baltimore: University Park Press, 1975.

Eissler, K. R. Notes on problems of technique in the psychoanalytic treatment of adolescents: With some remarks on perversions. *Psychoanalytic Study of the Child,* 1958, *13,* 223–254.

Elardo, R., Bradley, R., & Caldwell, B. M. The relation of infants' home environments to mental test performance from six to thirty-six months: A longitudinal analysis. *Child Development,* 1975, *46,* 71–76.

Elder, G. H., Jr. Structural variations in the child rearing relationship. *Sociometry,* 1962, *25,* 241–262.

Elder, G. H., Jr. Adolescence in the life cycle: An intro-

duction. In S. E. Dragastin & G. H. Elder, Jr. (Eds.), *Adolescence in the life cycle: Psychological change and social context.* New York: Wiley, 1968. (a)

Elder, G. H., Jr. *Adolescent socialization and personality development.* Chicago: Rand-McNally, 1968. (b)

Elder, G. H., Jr. *Children of the Great Depression: Social change in life experience.* Chicago: University of Chicago Press, 1974.

Elkind, D. Giant in the nursery—Jean Piaget. *New York Times Magazine,* May 26, 1968, pp. 25–27 ff.

Elkind, D. *Children and adolescents: Interpretive essays on Jean Piaget.* New York: Oxford University Press, 1970. (a)

Elkind, D. Erik Erikson's eight ages of man. *New York Times Magazine,* April 5, 1970, pp. 25–27 ff. (b)

Elley, W. B. Changes in mental ability in New Zealand school children, 1936-1968. *New Zealand Journal of Educational Studies,* 1969, *4,* 140–155.

Emmerich, W. Young children's discriminations of parent and child roles. *Child Development,* 1959, *30,* 403–419.

Emmett, W. G. The trend of intelligence in certain districts of England. *Population Studies,* 1950, *3,* 324–337.

Englund, S. Birth without violence. *New York Times Magazine,* December 8, 1974, pp. 113 ff.

Epperson, D. C. A re-assessment of indices of parental influence in *The Adolescent Society. American Sociological Review,* 1964, *29,* 93–96.

Erikson, E. *Childhood and society* (rev. ed.). New York: Norton, 1964.

Erikson, E. *Identity, youth and crisis.* New York: Norton, 1968.

Ervin, S. M. Changes with age in the verbal determinants of word-association. *American Journal of Psychology,* 1961, *74,* 361–372.

Estvan, F. J. The relationship of social status, intelligence, and sex of ten- and eleven-year-old children to an awareness of poverty. *Genetic Psychology Monographs,* 1952, *46,* 3–60.

Fagan, J. F., III. Infants' delayed recognition memory and forgetting. *Journal of Experimental Child Psychology,* 1973, *16,* 424–450.

Fallender, C. A., & Heber, R. Mother-child interaction and participation in a longitudinal intervention program. *Developmental Psychology,* 1975, *11,* 830–836.

Fantz, R. L. The origin of form perception. *Scientific American,* May 1961, pp. 66–71.

Faust, M. S. Development maturity as a determinant in prestige of adolescent girls. *Child Development,* 1960, *31,* 173–184.

Faust, M. S. Somatic development of adolescent girls. *Monographs of the Society for Research in Child Development,* 1977, *42*(1, Serial No. 169).

Feffer, M. H., & Gourevitch, V. Cognitive aspects of role-taking in children. *Journal of Personality,* 1960, *28,* 383–396.

Fein, G. G. The effect of within-pair variation and instructions on the transposition behavior of kindergarten and third grade children. *Journal of Experimental Child Psychology,* 1972, *14,* 379–397.

Fein, G. G. A transformational analysis of pretending.

Developmental Psychology, 1975, *11,* 291–296.

Fein, G. G. Play: The elaboration of possibilities. In K. F. Riegel & J. A. Meacham, *The developing individual in a changing world* (Vol. 2). Chicago: Aldine, 1976.

Fein, G. G., & Clarke-Stewart, A. *Day care in context.* New York: Wiley, 1973.

Fein, G. G., & Robertson, A. *Cognitive and social dimensions of pretending in two-year-olds* (Children's Bureau Report No. OCD-CB-98). Washington, D. C.: U.S. Government Printing Office, 1976. (ERIC Document Reproduction Service No. ED 119 806)

Fein, G. G., Robertson, A., & Diamond, E. *Materials and persons: Influences on pretend play.* Paper presented at the meeting of the Society for Research in Child Development, 1973.

Feshbach, N. D. Sex differences in children's modes of aggressive responses toward outsiders. *Merrill-Palmer Quarterly,* 1969, *15,* 249–258.

Feshbach, N. D., & Feshbach, S. Children's aggression. In W. W. Hartup (Ed.), *The young child: Reviews of research* (Vol. 2). Washington, D. C.: National Association for the Education of Young Children, 1972.

Feshbach, N. D., & Roe, K. Empathy in six- and seven-year-olds. *Child Development,* 1968, *39,* 133–145.

Feshbach, S. The catharsis hypothesis and some consequences of interaction with aggressive and neutral play objects. *Journal of Personality,* 1956, *24,* 449–462.

Feshbach, S. Aggression. In P. H. Mussen (Ed.), *Carmichael's manual of child psychology* (3rd ed.) (Vol. 2). New York: Wiley, 1970.

Feuerstein, R. Cognitive assessment of the socio-culturally deprived child and adolescent. In L. J. Cronbach & P. J. Drenth (Eds.), *Mental tests and cultural adaptation.* Atlantic Highlands, N. J.: Humanities Press, 1972.

Fillmore, C. The case for case. In E. Bach & R. T. Harms (Eds.), *Universals in linguistic theory.* New York: Holt, Rinehart and Winston, 1968.

Final natality statistics, 1975. *Monthly Vital Statistics Report,* December 30, 1976, *25*(10).

Fishbein, H. D. *Evolution, development, and children's learning.* Pacific Palisades, Calif.: Goodyear, 1976.

Flaste, R. Scientists wonder what's on a baby's mind. *New York Times,* August 27, 1976, p. B4.

Flavell, J. H. *The developmental psychology of Jean Piaget.* Princeton, N. J.: Van Nostrand, 1963.

Flavell, J. H. *The development of role-taking and communication skills in children.* New York: Wiley, 1968.

Flavell, J. H. Concept development. In P. H. Mussen (Ed.), *Carmichael's manual of child psychology* (3rd ed.) (Vol. 1). New York: Wiley, 1970.

Flavell, J. H. *Cognitive development.* Englewood Cliffs, N. J.: Prentice-Hall, 1977.

Flavell, J. H., Beach, D. R., & Chinsky, J. M. Spontaneous verbal rehearsal in a memory task as a function of age. *Child Development,* 1966, *37,* 283–299.

Forfar, J. O., & Nelson, M. M. Epidemiology of drugs taken by pregnant women: Drugs that may affect the fetus adversely. *Clinical Pharmacology and Therapeutics,* 1973, *14*(4), 632–642.

Fraiberg, S. Blind infants and their mothers: An examination of the sign system. In M. Lewis & L. A. Rosenblum (Eds.), *The effect of the infant on its caregiver.* New York: Wiley, 1974.

Francis-Williams, J., & Davies, P. A. Very low birthweight and later intelligence. *Developmental Medicine and Child Neurology,* 1974, *16,* 709–728.

Frank, A. [*The diary of a young girl*] (B. M. Mooyart-Doubleday, trans.). New York: Pocket Books, 1953.

Freud, A., & Dann, S. An experiment in group upbringing. *Psychoanalytic Study of the Child,* 1951, *6,* 127–168.

Freud, S. [*An outline of psycho-analysis*] (J. Strachey, trans.). London: Hogarth, 1949. (Originally published, 1940.)

Freyberg, J. T. Increasing the imaginative play of urban disadvantaged kindergarten children through systematic training. In J. L. Singer (Ed.), *The child's world of make-believe: Experimental studies of imaginative play.* New York: Academic Press, 1973.

Friedenberg, E. Z. *The vanishing adolescent.* Boston: Beacon Press, 1959.

Friedlander, B. Z. Receptive language development in infancy: Issues and problems. *Merrill-Palmer Quarterly,* 1970, *16,* 7–51.

Friedman, C. J., Mann, F., & Friedman, A. S. A profile of juvenile street gang members. *Adolescence,* 1975, *10,* 563–607.

From a student—William (Mannix) Smith. In J. Bremer & M. von Moschzisker, *The school without walls: Philadelphia's Parkway Program.* New York: Holt, Rinehart and Winston, 1971.

Fulker, D. (Review of *The science and politics of IQ* by L. J. Kamin). *American Journal of Psychology,* 1975, *88,* 505–522.

Gagné, R. M. *The conditions of learning.* New York: Holt, Rinehart and Winston, 1965.

Gagné, R. M. Learning hierarchies. *Educational Psychologist,* 1968, *6,* 1–9.

Gaite, A. J. H. Teachers' expectations: An influence on pupil performance? *Instructor,* October 1974, p. 38.

Garvey, C. Some properties of social play. *Merrill-Palmer Quarterly,* 1974, *20,* 163–180.

Garvey, C., & Hogan, R. Social speech and social interaction: Egocentrism revisited. *Child Development,* 1973, *44,* 562–568.

Gelman, R. Conservation acquisition: A problem of learning to attend to relevant attributes. *Journal of Experimental Child Psychology,* 1969, *7,* 167–187.

Gelman, R. The nature and development of early number concepts. In H. W. Reese (Ed.), *Advances in child development and behavior* (Vol. 7). New York: Academic Press, 1972.

Gelman, R., & Weinberg, D. H. The relationship between liquid conservation and compensation. *Child Development,* 1972, *43,* 371–383.

Gentry, E. F., & Aldrich, C. A. Rooting reflex in the newborn infant: Incidence and effect of it on sleep. *American Journal of Diseases of Children,* 1948, *75,* 528–539.

Gewirtz, J. L. A distinction between attachment and dependency in terms of stimulus control. In J. L. Gewirtz (Ed.), *Attachment and dependency.* New York: Halsted Press, 1972.

Ghiselin, B. (Ed.) *The creative process*. New York: Mentor, 1955.

Gibson, E. J. Learning to read: Experimental psychologists examine the process by which a fundamental intellectual skill is acquired. *Science*, May 21, 1965, pp. 1066–1072.

Gibson, E. J. Perceptual learning in educational situations. In R. Gagné & W. Gephart (Eds.), *Learning research and school subjects*. Itasca, Ill.: Peacock, 1968.

Gibson, E. J., Gibson, J. J., Pick, A. D., & Osser, H. A developmental study of the discrimination of letter-like forms. *Journal of Comparative and Physiological Psychology*, 1962, *55*, 897–906.

Gibson, E. J., & Levin, H. *The psychology of reading*. Cambridge: MIT Press, 1975.

Gibson, E. J., Osser, H., & Pick, A. D. A study of the development of grapheme-phoneme correspondences. *Journal of Verbal Learning and Verbal Behavior*, 1963, *2*, 142–146.

Gibson, J. T. *Psychology for the classroom*. Englewood Cliffs, N. J.: Prentice-Hall, 1976.

Gil, D. G. *Violence against children: Physical child abuse in the United States*. Cambridge: Harvard University Press, 1970.

Ginsburg, H., & Koslowski, B. Cognitive development. In M. R. Rosenzweig & L. W. Porter (Eds.), *Annual review of psychology* (Vol. 27). Palo Alto, Calif.: Annual Reviews, 1976.

Ginsburg, H., & Opper, S. (Eds.). *Piaget's theory of intellectual development: An introduction*. Englewood Cliffs, N. J.: Prentice-Hall, 1969.

Gladwin, T. *East is a big bird: Navigation and logic on Puluwat atoll*. Cambridge: Harvard University Press, 1970.

Glick, J. Cognitive development in cross-cultural perspective. In F. D. Horowitz (Ed.), *Review of child development research* (Vol. 4). Chicago: University of Chicago Press, 1975.

Gold, M., & Douvan, E. (Eds.). *Adolescent development: Readings in research and theory*. Boston: Allyn and Bacon, 1969.

Goldberg, S. Infant care and growth in urban Zambia. *Human Development*, 1972, *15*, 77–89.

Gollin, E. S. Tactual form discrimination: A developmental comparison under conditions of spatial interference. *Journal of Experimental Psychology*, 1960, *60*, 126–129.

Gollin, E. S. Tactual form discrimination: Developmental differences in the effects of training under conditions of spatial interference. *Journal of Psychology*, 1961, *51*, 131–140.

Golomb, C. *Young children's sculpture and drawing: A study in representational development*. Cambridge: Harvard University Press, 1974.

Goodenough, D. R., & Eagle, C. J. A modification of the embedded-figures test for use with young children. *Journal of Genetic Psychology*, 1963, *103*, 67–74.

Goodman, K. S. A linguistic study of cues and miscues in reading. *Elementary English*, 1965, *42*, 639–643.

Gornick, V. Here's news: Fathers matter as much as mothers. *Village Voice*, October 13, 1975, pp. 10–11.

Gottesman, I. I. Genetic aspects of intelligent behavior. In N. Ellis (Ed.), *Handbook of mental deficiency: Psychological theory and research*. New York: McGraw-Hill, 1963. (a)

Gottesman, I. I., & Shields, J. Schizophrenia in twins: 16 years' consecutive admissions to a psychiatric clinic. *Diseases of the Nervous System, Supplement*, 1966, *27*, 11–19.

Graham, M. D. *Multiply-impaired blind children: A national problem*. New York: American Foundation for the Blind, 1968.

Gratch, G. A study of the relative dominance of vision and touch in six-month-old infants. *Child Development*, 1972, *43*, 615–623.

Gratch, G., & Landers, W. F. Stage IV of Piaget's theory of infant's object concepts: A longitudinal study. *Child Development*, 1971, *42*, 359–372.

Green, E. H. Group play and quarreling among preschool children. *Child Development*, 1933, *4*, 302–307.

Greenberg, D. J., Hillman, D., & Grice, D. Infant and stranger variables related to stranger anxiety in the first year of life. *Developmental Psychology*, 1973, *9*, 207–212.

Gribbons, W. D., & Lohnes, P. R. Shifts in adolescents' vocational values. *Personnel and Guidance Journal*, 1965, *44*, 248–252.

Griffiths, C. *Conquering childhood deafness*. New York: Exposition Press, 1967.

Grimm, E. R. Psychological and social factors in pregnancy, delivery, and outcome. In S. A. Richardson & A. F. Guttmacher (Eds.), *Childbearing: Its social and psychological aspects*. Baltimore: Williams and Wilkins, 1967.

Guilford, J. P. Creative abilities in the arts. *Psychological Review*, 1957, *64*, 110–118.

Guszak, F. J. *Diagnostic reading instruction in the elementary school*. New York: Harper and Row, 1972.

Guttmacher, A. F. *Pregnancy, birth, and family planning: A guide for expectant parents in the 1970's*. New York: Viking Press, 1973.

Haan, N., Smith, M. B., & Block, J. Moral reasoning of young adults: Political-social behavior, family background, and personality correlates. *Journal of Personality and Social Psychology*, 1968, *10*, 183–201.

Hafez, E. S. E. Reproductive life cycle. In E. S. E. Hafez & T. N. Evans (Eds.), *Human reproduction: Conception and contraception*. New York: Harper and Row, 1973.

Hagen, J. W. Attention and mediation in children's memory. In W. W. Hartup (Ed.), *The young child: Reviews of research* (Vol. 2). Washington, D. C.: National Association for the Education of Young Children, 1972.

Hagen, J. W., Jongeward, R. H., Jr., & Kail, R. V., Jr. Cognitive perspectives on the development of memory. In H. W. Reese (Ed.), *Advances in child development and behavior* (Vol. 10). New York: Academic Press, 1975.

Hagen, J. W., & Kingsley, P. R. Labeling effects in short-term memory. *Child Development*, 1968, *39*, 113–121.

Haith, M. M. *Organization of visual behavior at birth.* Paper presented at the 22nd International Congress of Psychology, Symposium on Perception in Infancy, Paris, July 1976.

Haith, M. M., & Campos, J. J. Human infancy. In M. R. Rosenzweig & L. W. Porter (Eds.), *Annual review of psychology* (Vol. 28). Palo Alto, Calif.: Annual Reviews, 1977.

Hale, G. A., Miller, L. K., & Stevenson, H. W. Incidental learning of film content: A developmental study. *Child Development*, 1968, *39*, 69–77.

Hall, G. S. *Adolescence: Its psychology and its relations to physiology, anthropology, sociology, sex, crime, religion and education (1904)*. New York: Appleton, 1916.

Hall, R. V., Panyan, M., Rabon, D., & Broden, M. Instructing beginning teachers in reinforcement procedures which improve classroom control. *Journal of Applied Behavior Analysis*, 1968, *1*, 1–12.

Halverson, H. M. Mechanisms of early infant feeding. *Journal of Genetic Psychology*, 1944, *64*, 185–223.

Hamilton, M. L., & Stewart, D. M. Peer models and language acquisition. *Merrill-Palmer Quarterly*, 1977, *23*, 45–55.

Handel, A. Attitudinal orientations and cognitive functioning among adolescents. *Developmental Psychology*, 1975, *11*, 667–675.

Harlow, H. F., & Harlow, M. The affectional systems. In A. M. Schrier, H. F. Harlow & F. Stollnitz (Eds.), *Behavior of nonhuman primates* (Vol. 2). New York: Academic Press, 1965.

Harlow, H. F., & Harlow, M. Learning to love. *American Scientist*, 1966, *54*, 244–272.

Harrison, A., & Nadelman, L. Conceptual tempo and inhibition of movement in Black preschool children. *Child Development*, 1972, *43*, 657–668.

Hartley, R. E., Frank, L. K. & Goldenson, R. M. *Understanding children's play*. New York: Columbia University Press, 1952.

Hartup, W. W. Peer interaction and social development. In P. H. Mussen (Ed.), *Carmichael's manual of child psychology* (3rd ed.) (Vol. 2). New York: Wiley, 1970.

Hartup, W. W. The origins of friendships. In M. Lewis & L. A. Rosenblum (Eds), *Friendship and peer relations*. New York: Wiley, 1975.

Hartup, W. W., & Coates, B. Imitation of a peer as a function of reinforcement from the peer group and rewardingness of the model. *Child Development*, 1967, *38*, 1003–1016.

Hartup, W. W., & Keller, E. D. Nurturance in preschool children and its relation to dependency. *Child Development*, 1960, *31*, 681–690.

Hathaway, S. R., & Monachesi, E. D. *Adolescent personality and behavior: MMPI patterns of normal, delinquent, dropout and other outcomes*. Minneapolis: University of Minnesota Press, 1963.

Hawkes, H. E., Lindquist, E. F., & Mann, C. R. (Eds.). *The construction and use of achievement examinations*. Boston: Houghton, Mifflin, 1936.

Hawkins, R. P., Peterson, R. F., Schweid, E., & Bijou, S. W. Behavior therapy in the home: Amelioration of problem parent-child relations with the parent in a therapeutic role. *Journal of Experimental Child Psychology*, 1966, *4*, 99–107.

Haynes, H., White, B. L., & Held, R. Visual accommodation in human infants. *Science*, April 23, 1965, pp. 528–530.

Heber, R. A manual on terminology and classification in mental retardation (2nd ed.). American Association of Mental Deficiency, 1961.

Heber, R. *Rehabilitation of families at risk for mental retardation*. Regional Rehabilitation Center, University of Wisconsin, 1969.

Herron, R. E., & Sutton-Smith, B. *Child's play*. New York: Wiley, 1971.

Hess, E. H. Ethology and developmental psychology. In P. H. Mussen (Ed.), *Carmichael's manual of child psychology* (3rd ed.) (Vol. 1). New York: Wiley, 1970.

Hess, R. D., & Shipman, V. C. Early experience and socialization of cognitive modes in children. *Child Development*, 1965, *36*, 869–886.

Hess, R. D., & Shipman, V. C. *Maternal attitude toward the school and the role of the pupil: Some social class comparisons.* Paper prepared for the Fifth Work Conference on Curriculum and Teaching in Depressed Urban Areas, Columbia University, Teachers College, New York, June 1966.

Hess, R. D., & Shipman, V. C. Maternal influences upon early learning: The cognitive environments of urban preschool children. In R. D. Hess & R. M. Bear (Eds.), *Early education: Current theory, research, and action*. Chicago: Aldine, 1968.

Hetherington, E. M., & Deur, J. L. The effects of father absence on child development. In W. W. Hartup (Ed.), *The young child: Reviews of research* (Vol. 2). Washington, D. C.: National Association for the Education of Young Children, 1972.

Hewes, G. W. The current status of the gestural theory of language origin. In S. R. Harnad, H. D. Steklis & J. Lancaster (Eds.), *Origins and evolution of language and speech. New York Academy of Sciences, Annals*, 1976, *280*, 489–504.

Hill, D. E. Placental insufficiency and brain growth of the fetus. In D. B. Cheek, *Fetal and postnatal cellular growth*. New York: Wiley, 1975.

Hilliard, T., & Roth, R. M. Maternal attitudes and the non-achievement syndrome. *Personnel and Guidance Journal*, 1969, *47*, 424–428.

Himes, J. S. Negro teen-age culture. In J. Bernard (Ed.), *Teen-age culture. American Academy of Political and Social Sciences, Annals*, 1961, *338*, 91–101.

Hinde, R. A. Analyzing the roles of the partners in a behavioral interaction: Mother-infant relations in rhesus macaques. In E. Tobach (Ed.), Experimental approaches to the study of emotional behavior. *New York Academy of Sciences, Annals*, 1969, *159*, 651–667.

Hinde, R. A., & Spencer-Booth, Y. Social influences on the mother-infant relations in rhesus monkeys. In

D. Morris (Ed.), *Primate ethology.* Chicago: Aldine, 1967.

Hirschi, T. *Causes of delinquency.* Berkeley: University of California Press, 1969.

Hirschman, R., & Katkin, E. S. Psychophysiological functioning, arousal, attention, and learning during the first year of life. In H. W. Reese (Ed.), *Advances in child development and behavior* (Vol. 9). New York: Academic Press, 1974.

Hockett, C. D. The origin of speech. *Scientific American,* September 1960, pp. 88–111.

Hoffman, M. L. Moral development. In P. H. Mussen (Ed.), *Carmichael's manual of child psychology* (3rd ed.) (Vol. 2). New York: Wiley, 1970.

Hoffman, M. L. Moral internalization, parental power, and the nature of parent-child interaction. *Developmental Psychology,* 1975, *11,* 228–239.

Hollingshead, A. B. *Elmtown's youth.* New York: Wiley, 1949.

Honzik, M. P. Environmental correlates of mental growth: Prediction from the family setting at 21 months. *Child Development,* 1967, *38,* 337–364.

Honzik, M. P. *Resemblance in Wechsler patterns in three generations.* Paper presented at the biennial meeting of the Society for Research in Child Development, Minneapolis, April 2, 1971.

Horowitz, H. Prediction of adolescent popularity and rejection from achievement and interest tests. *Journal of Educational Psychology,* 1967, *58,* 170–174.

How children grow (Clinical Research Advances in Human Growth and Development, DHEW Publication No. NIH 72–166). Washington, D. C.: U. S. Government Printing Office, 1972.

Howe, M. J. *Understanding school learning: A new look at educational psychology.* New York: Harper and Row, 1972.

Hubel, D. H., & Wiesel, T. N. Receptive fields of cells in striate cortex of very young, visually inexperienced kittens. *Journal of Neurophysiology,* 1963, *26,* 996–1002.

Humphrey, J. H. Comparison of the use of active games and language workbook exercises as learning media in the development of language understandings with third grade children. *Perceptual and Motor Skills,* 1965, *21,* 23–26.

Humphrey, J. H. An exploratory study of active games in learning of number concepts by first grade boys and girls. *Perceptual and Motor Skills,* 1966, *23,* 341–342.

Hunt, J. McV. Intrinsic motivation and its role in psychological development. In D. Levine (Ed.), *Nebraska Symposium on Motivation: 1965.* (Vol. 13). Lincoln: University of Nebraska Press, 1965.

Hunt, W. A., Clarke, F. M., & Hunt, E. B. From the Moro reflex to the mature startle pattern. In Y. Brackbill & G. G. Thompson (Eds.), *Behavior in infancy and early childhood.* New York: Free Press, 1967.

Hurley, J. R. Parental acceptance-rejection and children's intelligence. *Merrill-Palmer Quarterly,* 1965, *11,* 19–31.

Hutt, S. J. Lenard, H. G., & Prechtl, H. F. R. Psychophysiological studies in newborn infants. In L. P. Lipsitt & H. W. Reese (Eds.), *Advances in child development and behavior* (Vol. 4). New York: Academic Press, 1969.

Illingworth, R. S. *The normal child* (6th ed.). Edinburgh: Churchill Livingstone, 1975.

Inhelder, B. Memory and intelligence in the child. In D. Elkind & J. H. Flavell (Eds.), *Studies in cognitive development: Essays in honor of Jean Piaget.* New York: Oxford University Press, 1969.

Inhelder, B., Bovet, M., & Sinclair, H. [Development and learning.] *Schweizerische Zeitschrift für Psychologie und ihre Anwendungen,* 1967, *26*(1), 1–23. (*Psychological Abstracts,* 1967, *41,* No. 10248.)

Ito, P. K. Comparative biometrical study of physique of Japanese women born and reared under different environments. *Human Biology,* 1942, *14,* 279.

Jencks, C., Smith, M., Acland, H., Bane, M. J., Cohen, D., Gintis, H., Heyns, B., & Michelson, S. *Inequality: A reassessment of the effect of family and schooling in America.* New York: Basic Books, 1972.

Jensen, A. R. How much can we boost IQ and scholastic achievement? *Harvard Educational Review,* 1969, *39*(1), 1–123.

Jesperson, O. *Language: Its nature, development, and origin.* London: Allen and Unwin, 1922.

Kagan, J. Impulsive and reflective children: Significance of conceptual tempo. In J. D. Krumboltz (Ed.), *Learning and the educational process.* Chicago: Rand McNally, 1965.

Kagan, J. Continuity in cognitive development during the first year. *Merrill-Palmer Quarterly,* 1969, *15,* 101–119.

Kagan, J. *Change and continuity in infancy.* New York: Wiley, 1971.

Kagan, J. Do infants think? *Scientific American,* March 1972, pp. 74–82.

Kagan, J., Henker, B. A., Hen-Tov, A., Levine, J., & Lewis, M. Infants' differential reactions to familiar and distorted faces. *Child Development,* 1966, *37,* 519–532.

Kagan, J., Kearsley, R. B., & Zelazo, P. R. *The effects of infant day care on psychological development.* Paper presented at a symposium of the American Association for the Advancement of Science, Boston, February 1976.

Kagan, J., & Klein, R. E. Cross-cultural perspectives on early development. *American Psychologist,* 1973, *28,* 947–961.

Kagan, J., & Kogan, N. Individual variation in cognitive processes. In P. H. Mussen (Ed.), *Carmichael's manual of child psychology* (3rd ed.) (Vol. 1). New York: Wiley, 1970.

Kagan, J., Moss, H. A., & Sigel, I. E. Psychological significance of styles of conceptualization. In J. C. Wright & J. Kagan (Eds.), *Basic cognitive processes in children. Monographs of the Society for Research in Child Development,* 1963, *28*(2, Serial No. 86), 73–124.

Kagan, J., Rosman, B. L., Day, D., Albert, J., & Phillips, W. Information processing in the child: Significance of analytic and reflective attitudes. *Psychological Monographs,* 1964, *78* (1, Whole No. 578).

Kagan, S., & Madsen, M. C. Cooperation and competition of Mexican, Mexican-American, and Anglo-American children of two ages under four instructional sets. *Developmental Psychology,* 1971, *5,* 32–39.

Kallmann, F. J. *Heredity in health and mental disorder.* New York: Norton, 1953.

Kallmann, F. J., & Roth, B. Genetic aspects of preadolescent schizophrenia. *American Journal of Psychiatry,* 1956, *112,* 599–606.

Kalnins, I. V., & Bruner, J. S. The coordination of visual observation and instrumental behavior in early infancy. *Perception,* 1973, *2,* 307–314.

Kamin, L. J. *The science and politics of IQ.* Potomac, Md.: Erlbaum, 1974.

Kandel, D. Inter- and intragenerational influences on adolescent marijuana use. *Journal of Social Issues,* 1974, *30*(2), 107–135.

Kandel, D., & Lesser, G. S. *Youth in two worlds: United States and Denmark.* San Francisco: Jossey-Bass, 1972.

Karnes, M. B., Teska, J. A., Hodgins, A. S., & Badger, E. D. Educational intervention at home by mothers of disadvantaged infants. *Child Development,* 1970, *41,* 925–935.

Keeney, T. J., Cannizzo, S. R., & Flavell, J. H. Spontaneous and induced verbal rehearsal in a recall task. *Child Development,* 1967, *38,* 953–966.

Kendler, H. H., & Kendler, T. S. Vertical and horizontal processes in problem solving. *Psychological Review,* 1962, *69,* 1–16.

Kendler, T. S. Development of mediating responses in children. In J. C. Wright & J. Kagan (Eds.), Basic cognitive processes in children. *Monographs of the Society for Research in Child Development,* 1963, *28*(2, Serial No. 86).

Kendler, T. S., Kendler, H. H., & Learnard, B. Mediated responses to size and brightness as a function of age. *American Journal of Psychology,* 1962, *75,* 571–586.

Keniston, K. Alienation in American youth. In K. Keniston, *Young radicals.* New York: Harcourt, Brace and World, 1968.

Kennell, J. Evidence for a sensitive period in the human mother. In M. H. Klaus, T. Leger & M. A. Trause (Eds.), *Maternal attachment and mothering disorders: A round table.* Johnson and Johnson Baby Products Co., 1975.

Kessen, W. Research design in the study of developmental problems. In P. H. Mussen (Ed.), *Handbook of research methods in child development.* New York: Wiley, 1960.

Kessen, W. Sucking and looking: Two organized congenital patterns of behavior in the human newborn. In H. W. Stevenson, E. H. Hess & H. L. Rheingold (Eds.), *Early behavior: comparative and developmental approaches.* New York: Wiley, 1967.

Kessen, W., Haith, M. M., & Salapatek, P. H. Human infancy: A bibliography and guide. In P. H. Mussen (Ed.), *Carmichael's manual of child psychology* (3rd ed.) (Vol. 1). New York: Wiley, 1970.

Kessen, W., Leutzendorff, A., & Stoutsenberger, K. Age, food deprivation, nonnutritive sucking, and movement in the human newborn. *Journal of Comparative and Physiological Psychology,* 1967, *63,* 82–86.

Kessen, W., Salapatek, P., & Haith, M. The visual response of the human newborn to linear contour. *Journal of Experimental Child Psychology,* 1972, *13,* 9–20.

King, M. The development of some intention concepts in young children. *Child Development,* 1971, *42,* 1145–1152.

Klaus, M. H., & Kennell, J. H. Mothers separated from their newborn infants. *Pediatric Clinics of North America,* 1970, *17,* 1015–1037.

Koch, J. *Total baby development.* New York: Wyden Books, 1976.

Kogan, N., & Pankove, E. Creative ability over a five-year span. *Child Development,* 1972, *43,* 427–442.

Kohlberg, L. *The development of modes of moral thinking and choice in the years 10 to 16.* Unpublished doctoral dissertation, University of Chicago, 1958.

Kohlberg, L. The development of children's orientations toward a moral order. I. Sequence in the development of moral thought. *Vita Humana,* 1963, *6,* 11–33.

Kohlberg, L. A cognitive-developmental analysis of children's sex-role concepts and attitudes. In E. E. Maccoby (Ed.), *The development of sex differences.* Stanford: Stanford University Press, 1966.

Kohlberg, L. Stage and sequence: The cognitive-developmental approach to socialization. In D. A. Goslin (Ed.), *Handbook of socialization theory and research.* Chicago: Rand McNally, 1969.

Komarovsky, M. Cultural contradictions and sex roles: The masculine case. *American Journal of Sociology,* 1972, *78,* 873–884.

Konner, M. J. Aspects of the developmental ethology of a foraging people. In N. Blurton-Jones (Ed.), *Ethological studies of child behaviour.* London: Cambridge University Press, 1972.

Korner, A. F. The effect of the infant's state, level of arousal, sex, and ontogenetic stage on the caregiver. In M. Lewis & L. A. Rosenblum (Eds.), *The effect of the infant on its caregiver.* New York: Wiley, 1974.

Koslowski, B., & Bruner, J. S. Learning to use a lever. *Child Development,* 1972, *43,* 790–799.

Kotelchuck, M., Zelazo, P. R., Kagan, J., & Spelke, E. Infant reaction to parental separations when left with familiar and unfamiliar adults. *Journal of Genetic Psychology,* 1975, *126,* 255–262.

Krauss, R. M., & Glucksberg, S. The development of communication: Competence as a function of age. *Child Development,* 1969, *40,* 255–266.

Kuenne, M. R. Experimental investigation of the relation of language to transposition behavior in young children. *Journal of Experimental Psychology,* 1946, *36,* 471–490.

Kuhn, T. S. *The structure of scientific revolutions* (2nd ed.). Chicago: University of Chicago Press, 1970.

LaBarbera, J. D., Izard, C. E., Vietze, P., & Parisi, S. A. Four- and six-month-old infants' visual responses to joy, anger, and neutral expressions. *Child Development,* 1976, *47,* 535–538.

Labov, W. Some sources of reading problems for Negro speakers of nonstandard English. In A. Frazier (Ed.), *New directions in elementary English.* Champaign, Ill.:

National Council of Teachers of English, 1967.

Labov, W. The logical nonstandard English. In F. Williams (Ed.), *Language and poverty*. Chicago: Markham, 1970.

Labov, W., Cohen, P., Robins, C., & Lewis, J. *A study of the nonstandard English of Negro and Puerto Rican speakers in New York City* (Final Report, U. S. Office of Education Cooperative Research Project No. 3288). New York: Columbia University Press, 1968.

Lamb, M. E. Fathers: Forgotten contributors to child development. *Human Development*, 1975, *18*, 245–266.

Lamb, M. E. A re-examination of the infant social world. *Human Development*, 1977, *20*, 65–85.

Landers, W. F. Effects of differential experience on infant's performance in a Piagetian stage IV object-concept task. *Developmental Psychology*, 1971, *5*, 48–54.

Landy, F., Rosenberg, B. G., & Sutton-Smith, B. The effect of limited father absence on cognitive development. *Child Development*, 1969, *40*, 941–944.

Larson, D. L., Spreitzer, E. A., & Snyder, E. E. Social factors in the frequency of romantic involvement among adolescents. *Adolescence*, 1976, *11*, 7–12.

Lasseigne, M. W. A study of peer and adult influence on moral beliefs of adolescents. *Adolescence*, 1975, *10*, 227–230.

Lauer, R. H. Socialization into inequality: Children's perception of occupational status. *Sociology and Social Research*, 1974, *58*, 176–183.

Leahy, R. L. The development of the conception of social class. *Rockefeller University, Institute for Comparative Human Development, Quarterly Newsletter*, 1977, *1*, 3–5.

LeCompte, G. K., & Gratch, G. Violation of a rule as a method of diagnosing infants' level of object concept. *Child Development*, 1972, *43*, 385–396.

Lee, C. L. *Social encounters of infants: The beginnings of popularity*. Paper presented at the meeting of the International Society for the Study of Behavioral Development, Ann Arbor, Michigan, August 1973.

Lefebvre, A., & Bohn, M. J., Jr. Occupational prestige as seen by disadvantaged black children. *Developmental Psychology*, 1971, *4*, 173–177.

Lenneberg, E. H. The natural history of language. In F. Smith & G. A. Miller (Eds.), *The genesis of language*. Cambridge: MIT Press, 1966.

Lenneberg, E. H. *Biological foundations of language*. New York: Wiley, 1967.

Lenneberg, E. H. On explaining language. *Science*, May 9, 1969, pp. 635–643.

Lenrow, P. B. Studies in sympathy. In S. S. Tomkins & C. E. Izard (Eds.), *Affect, cognition, and personality: Empirical studies*. New York: Springer, 1965.

Leventhal, A. S., & Lipsitt, L. P. Adaptation, pitch discrimination, and sound localization in the neonate. *Child Development*, 1964, *35*, 759–767.

Lever, J. Sex differences in the games children play. *Social Problems*, 1976, *23*, 478–487.

Levine, M. The academic achievement test: Its historical context and social functions. *American Psychologist*, 1976, *31*, 228–238.

Levitt, E. E. The results of psychotherapy with children: An evaluation. *Journal of Consulting Psychology*, 1957, *21*, 189–196.

Levitt, E. E. Psychotherapy with children: A further evaluation. *Behavior Research and Therapy*, 1963, *1*, 45–51.

Levy, J. Evolution of language lateralization and cognitive function. In S. R. Harnad, H. D. Steklis & J. Lancaster (Eds.), Origins and evolution of language and speech. *New York Academy of Sciences, Annals*, 1976, *280*, 810–820.

Lewis, M. Infant intelligence tests; Their use and misuse. *Human Development*, 1973, *16*, 108–118.

Liben, L. S. Piagetian investigations of the development of memory. In R. V. Kail & J. W. Hagen (Eds.), *Memory in cognitive development*. Hillsdale, N. J.: Lawrence Erlbaum Associates, 1976.

Light, R. J. Abuse and neglected children in America: A study of alternative policies. *Harvard Educational Review*, 1973, *43*, 556–598.

Linton, R. *The study of man*. New York: Appleton-Century, 1936.

Lipsitt, L. P. Learning in the human infant. In H. W. Stevenson, E. H. Hess & H. L. Rheingold (Eds.), *Early behavior: Comparative and developmental approaches*. New York: Wiley, 1967.

Lipsitt, L. P., & Levy, N. Electrotactual threshold in the neonate. *Child Development*, 1959, *30*, 547–554.

Lipton, E. L., Steinschneider, A., & Richmond, J. B. Swaddling, a child care practice: Historical, cultural, and experimental observations. *Pediatrics*, 1965, *35*(3, Pt. 2), 521–567.

Livesley, W. J., & Bromley, D. B. *Person perception in childhood and adolescence*. London: Wiley, 1973.

Lockett, H. C., Midwives and childbirth among the Navajo, *Plateau*, 1939, *12*, 15–17.

Loehlin, J., Lindzey, G., & Spuhler, J. *Race differences in intelligence*. San Francisco: Freeman, 1975.

Lorenz, K. Z. Die angeborenen formen möglicher erfahrung. *Zeitschrift für Tierpsychologie*, 1943, *5*, 235–409.

Lövaas, O. I. Effect of exposure to symbolic aggression on aggressive behavior. *Child Development*, 1961, *32*, 37–44.

Lövaas, O. I., & Bucher, B. D. (Eds.). *Perspectives in behavior modification with deviant children*. Englewood Cliffs, N. J.: Prentice-Hall, 1974.

Luria, A. R. *The role of speech in the regulation of normal and abnormal behavior*. New York: Liveright, 1961.

Maccoby, E. E. Selective auditory attention in children. In L. P. Lipsitt & C. C. Spiker (Eds.), *Advances in child development and behavior* (Vol. 3). New York: Academic Press, 1967.

Maccoby, E. E., & Jacklin, C. N. *The psychology of sex differences*. Stanford: Stanford University Press, 1974.

Manosevitz, M., Prentice, N. M., & Wilson, F. Individual and family correlates of imaginary companions in preschool children. *Developmental Psychology*, 1973, *8*, 72–79.

Markey, F. V. *Imaginative behavior of preschool children*

(Child Development Monographs, Monograph No. 18). New York: Teachers College, Columbia University, 1935.

Marquis, D. P. Can conditioned responses be established in the newborn infant? *Journal of Genetic Psychology,* 1931, *39,* 479–492.

Marquis, D. P. Learning in the neonate: The modification of behavior under three feeding schedules. *Journal of Experimental Psychology,* 1941, *29,* 263–282.

Marshall, H. R. Relations between home experiences and children's use of language in play interactions with peers. *Psychological Monographs,* 1961, *75*(5, Whole No. 509).

Marshall, H. R., & McCandless, B. R. Relationships between dependence on adults and social acceptance by peers. *Child Development,* 1957, *28,* 413–419. (a)

Marshall, H. R., & McCandless, B. R. A study in predictions of social behavior of preschool children. *Child Development,* 1957, *28,* 149–159. (b)

Martin, B. Parent-child relations. In F. D. Horowitz (Ed.), *Review of child development research* (Vol. 4). Chicago: University of Chicago Press, 1975.

Matteson, D. R. Changes in attitudes toward authority figures with the move to college: Three experiments. *Developmental Psychology,* 1974, *10,* 340–347.

Matteson, D. R. (Ed.). *Adolescence today: Sex roles and the search for identity.* Homewood, Ill.: Dorsey, 1975.

Maudry, M., & Nekula, M. Social relations between children of the same age during the first two years of life. *Journal of Genetic Psychology,* 1939, *54,* 193–215.

Maurer, D., & Salapatek, P. Developmental changes in the scanning of faces by young infants. *Child Development,* 1976, *47,* 523–527.

McCall, R. B. Exploratory manipulation and play in the human infant. *Monographs of the Society for Research in Child Development,* 1974, *39*(2, Serial No. 155).

McCall, R. B., Hogarty, P., & Hurlburt, N. Transitions in infant sensorimotor development and the prediction of childhood IQ. *American Psychologist,* 1972, *27,* 728–748.

McCall, R. B., & Melson, W. H. Amount of short-term familiarization and the response to auditory discrepancies. *Child Development,* 1970, *41,* 861–869.

McCarthy, J. J., & McCarthy, J. F. *Learning disabilities.* Boston: Allyn and Bacon, 1969.

McClain, E. W. An Eriksonian cross-cultural study of adolescent development. *Adolescence,* 1975, *10,* 527–541.

McClearn, G. E. Genetic influences on behavior and development. In P. H. Mussen (Ed.), *Carmichael's manual of child psychology* (3rd ed.) (Vol. 1). New York: Wiley, 1970.

McCord, W., McCord, J., & Zola, I. K. *Origins of crime: A new evaluation of the Cambridge-Somerville youth study.* New York: Columbia University Press, 1959.

McCracken, R. The informal reading inventory as a means of improving instruction. In T. C. Barrett (Ed.), *The evaluation of children's reading achievement.* Newark,

Del.: International Reading Association, 1967.

McGhee, P. E. Development of children's ability to create the joking relationship. *Child Development,* 1974, *45,* 552–556.

McGhee, P. E. Children's appreciation of humor: A test of the cognitive congruency principle. *Child Development,* 1976, *47,* 420–426.

McGinley, P., & McGinley, H. Reading groups as psychological groups. *Journal of Experimental Education,* 1970, *39*(2), 35–42.

McGraw, M. B. Swimming behavior of the human infant. *Journal of Pediatrics,* 1939, *15,* 485–490.

McIntosh, D., & Dunn, L. Children with specific learning disabilities. In L. M. Dunn (Ed.), *Exceptional children in the schools.* New York: Holt, Rinehart and Winston, 1973.

McKeon, R. P. *Introduction to Aristotle.* Chicago: University of Chicago Press, 1973.

McKinney, J. D. Problem-solving strategies in reflective and impulsive children. *Journal of Educational Psychology,* 1975, *67,* 807–820.

McKinney, J. P., Hotch, D. F., & Truhon, S. A. The organization of behavioral values during late adolescence: Change and stability across two eras. *Developmental Psychology,* 1977, *13,* 83–84.

McLennan, C. E., & Sandberg, E. C. *Synopsis of obstetrics* (9th ed.). St. Louis: Mosby, 1974.

McNeill, D. *Explaining linguistic universals.* Paper presented at the 19th International Congress of Psychology, London, July 1969.

McNeill, D. *The acquisition of language: The study of developmental psycholinguistics.* New York: Harper and Row, 1970. (a)

McNeill, D. The development of language. In P. H. Mussen (Ed.), *Carmichael's manual of child psychology* (3rd ed.) (Vol. 1). New York: Wiley, 1970. (b)

Mead, M. Cultural determinants of sexual behavior. In W. C. Young (Ed.), *Sex and internal secretions.* (Vol. 2). Baltimore: Williams and Wilkins, 1961.

Mead, M., & Newton, N. Cultural patterning of perinatal behavior. In S. A. Richardson & A. F. Guttmacher (Eds.), *Childrearing: Its social and psychological aspects.* Baltimore: Williams and Wilkins, 1967.

Meadow, K. P. The development of deaf children. In E. M. Hetherington (Ed.), *Review of child development research* (Vol. 5). Chicago: University of Chicago Press, 1975.

Mednick, S. A. A learning theory approach to research in schizophrenia. *Psychological Bulletin,* 1958, *55,* 316–327.

Mednick, S. A. The associative basis of the creative process. *Psychological Review,* 1962, *69,* 220–232.

Mednick, S. A., & Schulsinger, F. Some premorbid characteristics related to breakdown in children with schizophrenic mothers. In D. Rosenthal & S. S. Kety (Eds.), *The transmission of schizophrenia.* New York: Pergamon Press, 1968.

Mednick, M. T., Mednick, S. A., & Mednick, E. V. Incubation of creative performance and specific associative priming. *Journal of Abnormal and Social Psychology,* 1964, *69*, 84–88.

Meichenbaum, D., & Goodman, J. Reflection-impulsivity and verbal control of motor behavior. *Child Development,* 1969, *40*, 785–797.

Mendel, G. Children's preferences for differing degrees of novelty. *Child Development,* 1965, *36*, 453–465.

Mendelson, M. J., & Haith, M. M. The relation between nonnutritive sucking and visual information processing in the human newborn. *Child Development,* 1975, *46*, 1025–1029.

Menyuk, P. *The development of speech.* New York: Bobbs-Merrill, 1972.

Mercer, J. R. IQ: The lethal label. *Psychology Today,* September 1972, pp. 44–47 ff.

Meredith, H. V. Growth in body size: A compendium of findings on contemporary children living in different parts of the world. In H. W. Reese (Ed.), *Advances in child development and behavior* (Vol. 6). New York: Academic Press, 1971.

Meredith, H. V. Relation between tobacco smoking of pregnant women and body size of their progeny: A compilation and synthesis of published studies. *Human Biology,* 1975, *47*, 451–472.

Messer, S. B. Reflection-impulsivity: A review. *Psychological Bulletin,* 1976, *83*, 1026–1052.

Millar, W. S. Conditioning and learning in early infancy. In B. Foss (Ed.), *New perspectives in child development.* Harmondsworth, England: Penguin, 1974.

Miller, S. Ends, means, and galumphing: Some leitmotifs of play. *American Anthropologist,* 1973, *75*, 87–98.

Miller, S., Schwartz, L. C., & Stewart, C. An attempt to extinguish conservation of weight in college students. *Developmental Psychology,* 1973, *8*, 316.

Miller, W., & Ervin, S. The development of grammar in child language. In U. Bellugi & R. Brown (Eds.), The acquisition of language. *Monographs of the Society for Research in Child Development,* 1964, 29(1, Serial No. 92), 9–34.

Miner, E. (Ed.). *Selected poetry and prose of John Dryden.* New York: Random House, 1969.

Mischel, W. *Introduction to personality.* New York: Holt, Rinehart and Winston, 1971.

Mischler, E. G., & Waxler, N. E. *Interaction in families.* New York: Wiley, 1968.

Moerk, E. L. Verbal interactions between children and their mothers during the preschool years. *Developmental Psychology,* 1975, *11*, 788–794.

Money, J., & Ehrhardt, A. A. *Man and woman, boy and girl.* New York: Mentor, 1974.

Money, J., Hampson, J. G., & Hampson, J. L. Imprinting and the establishment of gender role. *Archives of Neurology and Psychiatry,* 1957, *77*, 333–336.

Montemayor, R., & Eisen, M. The development of self-conceptions from childhood to adolescence. *Developmental Psychology,* 1977, *13*, 314–319.

Moore, K. L. *The developing human: Clinically oriented embryology* (2nd ed.). Philadelphia: Saunders, 1977.

Moore, O. K., & Anderson, A. R. Some principles for the design of clarifying educational environments. In D. A. Goslin (Ed.), *Handbook of socialization theory and research.* Chicago: Rand McNally, 1969.

Moore, S. G. Correlates of peer acceptance in nursery school children. In W. W. Hartup & N. L. Smothergill (Eds.), *The young child: Reviews of research* (Vol. 1). Washington, D. C.: National Association for the Education of Young Children, 1967.

Morehead, D., & Morehead, A. From signal to sign: A Piagetian view of thought and language during the first two years. In R. L. Schiefelbusch & L. L. Lloyd (Eds.), *Language perspectives: Acquisition, retardation, and intervention.* Baltimore: University Park Press, 1974.

Morgan, G. A., & Ricciuti, H. N. Infants' responses to strangers during the first year. In B. M. Foss (Ed.), *Determinants of infant behavior* (Vol. 4). New York: Wiley, 1969.

Morris, L., & Resnick, L. B. *Assembling component processes in problem solving.* Paper presented at the meeting of the Midwestern Psychological Association, Chicago, May 1974.

Morrone, W. W. Which way do you (and he) want to have your baby? *Glamour Magazine,* May 1976, pp. 164–165ff.

Morrow, W. R., & Wilson, R. C. Family relations of bright high-achieving and under-achieving high school boys. *Child Development,* 1961, *32*, 501–510.

Mosher, F. A., & Hornsby, J. R. On asking questions. In J. S. Bruner, R. R. Olver & P. M. Greenfield (Eds.), *Studies in cognitive growth.* New York: Wiley, 1966.

Moss, H. A. Sex, age, and state as determinants of mother-infant interaction. *Merrill-Palmer Quarterly,* 1967, *13*, 19–36.

Mueller, E. *Clustering and socially-directed behaviors in toddlers' playgroups.* Paper presented at the meeting of the Society for Research in Child Development, Philadelphia, 1972. (a)

Mueller, E. The maintenance of verbal exchanges between young children. *Child Development,* 1972, *43*, 930–938. (b)

Mueller, E., & DeStefano, C. Sources of toddlers' peer interaction in a play group setting. In *Early child development and care.* In press.

Mussen, P. H. Some antecedents and consequences of masculine sex-typing in adolescent boys. *Psychological Monographs,* 1961, *75*(2, Whole No. 506).

Mussen, P. H., & Jones, M. C. Self-conceptions, motivations, and interpersonal attitudes of late- and early-maturing boys. *Child Development,* 1957, *28*, 243–256.

Mussen, P. H., & Jones, M. C. The behavior-inferred motivations of late- and early-maturing boys. *Child Development,* 1958, *29*, 61–67.

Muuss, R. E. *Theories of adolescence* (3rd ed.). New York: Random House, 1974.

National Research Council, Food and Nutrition Board, Committee on Maternal Nutrition. *Maternal nutrition and the course of pregnancy.* Washington, D. C.: National Academy of Sciences, 1970.

Neimark, E. D. Intellectual development during adolescence. In F. D. Horowitz (Ed.), *Review of child development research* (Vol. 4). Chicago: University of Chicago Press, 1975.

Neisser, U. General, academic, and artificial intelligence. In L. B. Resnick (Ed.), *The nature of intelligence.* New York: Wiley, 1976.

Nelson, K. Some evidence for the cognitive primacy of categorization and its functional basis. *Merrill-Palmer Quarterly,* 1973, *19,* 21–39. (a)

Nelson, K. Structure and strategy in learning to talk. *Monographs of the Society for Research in Child Development,* 1973, *38*(2, Serial No. 149). (b)

Nelson, K. Concept, word, and sentence: Interrelations in acquisition and development. *Psychological Review,* 1974, *81,* 267–285.

Nelson, L., & Madsen, M. C. Cooperation and competition in four-year-olds as a function of reward contingency and subculture. *Developmental Psychology,* 1969, *1,* 340–344.

Nelson, R. C. Knowledge and interests concerning sixteen occupations among elementary and secondary school students. *Educational and Psychological Measurement,* 1963, *23,* 741–754.

Nesselroade, J. R., & Bates, P. B. Adolescent personality development and historical change: 1970-1972. *Monographs of the Society for Research in Child Development,* 1974, *39*(1, Serial No. 154).

Neubauer, P. B. (Ed.). *Children in collectives: Child-rearing aims and practices in the kibbutz.* Springfield, Ill.: Charles C. Thomas, 1965.

Nickerson, D., & Newhall, S. M. A psychological color solid. *Journal of the Optical Society of America,* 1943, *33,* 419–422.

Nodine, C. F., & Steuerle, N. L. Development of perceptual and cognitive strategies for differentiating graphemes. *Journal of Experimental Psychology,* 1973, *97,* 158–166.

Norman, R. D. Intelligence tests and the personal world. *New Mexico Quarterly,* 1963, *33,* 153–184.

Nunnally, J. C. *Educational measurement and evaluation* (2nd ed.). New York: McGraw-Hill, 1972.

Nunnally, J. C., & Lemond, L. C. Exploratory behavior and human development. In H. W. Reese (Ed.), *Advances in child development and behavior* (Vol. 8). New York: Academic Press, 1973.

O'Bryan, K. G., & Boersma, F. J. Eye movements, perceptual activity and conservation development. *Journal of Experimental Child Psychology,* 1971, *12,* 157–169.

Offer, D. *The psychological world of the teen-ager: A study of normal adolescent boys.* New York: Basic Books, 1969.

Offer, D., & Offer, J. Normal adolescent males: The high school and college years. *Journal of the American College Health Association,* 1974, *22,* 209–215.

Oliver, J. E., & Taylor, A. Five generations of ill-treated children in one family pedigree. *British Journal of Psychiatry,* 1971, *119,* 473–480.

Opie, I., & Opie, P. *The lore and language of school children.* Oxford: Oxford University Press, 1959.

Opie, I., & Opie, P. *Children's games in street and playground.* Oxford: Oxford University Press, 1969.

Ornstein, P. A., Naus, M. J., & Liberty, C. Rehearsal and organizational processes in children's memory. *Child Development,* 1975, *46,* 818–830.

Ornstein, P. A., Naus, M. J., & Stone, B. P. Rehearsal training and developmental differences in memory. *Developmental Psychology,* 1977, *13,* 15–24.

Page, J. D. *Psychopathology: The science of understanding deviance* (2nd ed.). Chicago: Aldine, 1975.

Palardy, J. M. What teachers believe—what children achieve. *Elementary School Journal,* 1969, *69,* 370–374.

Papoušek, H. Experimental studies of appetitional behavior in human newborns and infants. In H. W. Stevenson, E. H. Hess & H. L. Rheingold (Eds.), *Early behavior: Comparative and developmental approaches.* New York: Wiley, 1967.

Papoušek, H., & Papoušek, M. Mirror image and self-recognition in young human infants: I. A new method of experimental analysis. *Developmental Psychobiology,* 1974, *7,* 149–157.

Paris, S. G. *Developmental changes in constructive memory abilities.* Paper presented at the meeting of the Society for Research in Child Development, Denver, Colorado, April 1975.

Paris, S. G., & Mahoney, G. J. Cognitive integration in children's memory for sentences and pictures. *Child Development,* 1974, *45,* 633–642.

Parke, R. D. Effectiveness of punishment as an interaction of intensity, timing, agent nurturance, and cognitive structuring. *Child Development,* 1969, *40,* 213–235.

Parke, R. D. Some effects of punishment on children's behavior. In W. W. Hartup (Ed.), *The young child: Reviews of research* (Vol. 2). Washington, D. C.: National Association for the Education of Young Children, 1972.

Parke, R. D. Father-infant interaction. In M. H. Klaus, T. Leger & M. A. Trause (Eds.), *Maternal attachment and mothering disorders: A round table.* Johnson and Johnson Baby Products Co., 1975.

Parke, R. D., & Collmer, C. W. Child abuse: An interdisciplinary analysis. In E. M. Hetherington (Ed.), *Review of child development research* (Vol. 5). Chicago: University of Chicago Press, 1975.

Parke, R. D., & Murray, S. *Re-instatement: A technique for increasing stability of inhibition in children.* Unpublished manuscript, University of Wisconsin, 1971.

Parten, M. B. Social participation among pre-school children. *Journal of Abnormal and Social Psychology,* 1932, *27,* 243–269.

Patterson, G. R., Littman, R. A., & Bricker, W. Assertive behavior in children: A step toward a theory of aggression. *Monographs of the Society for Research in Child Development,* 1967, *32*(5, Serial No. 113).

Payne, D. E., & Mussen, P. H. Parent-child relations and father identification among adolescent boys. *Journal of Abnormal and Social Psychology,* 1956, *52,* 358–362.

Peevers, B. H., & Secord, P. F. Developmental changes in attribution of descriptive concepts to persons. *Journal of Personality and Social Psychology,* 1973, *27,* 120–128.

Pellegrino, J. W., & Schadler, M. *Maximizing performance in a problem solving task.* Unpublished manuscript, University of Pittsburgh, Learning Research and Development Center, 1974.

Peterson, D. R., Becker, W. C., Hellmer, L. A., Shoemaker, D. J., & Quay, H. C. Parental attitudes and child adjustment. *Child Development,* 1959, *30,* 119–130.

Piaget, J. [*Judgment and reasoning in the child*] (M. Warden, trans.). New York: Harcourt, Brace, 1926. (Originally published, 1924.)

Piaget, J. [*The child's conception of the world*] (J. Tomlinson & A. Tomlinson, trans.). Totawa, N. J.: Littlefield, Adams, 1975. (Originally published in 1929.)

Piaget, J. [*The moral judgment of the child*] (M. Gabain, trans.). New York: Free Press, 1932.

Piaget, J. [*The construction of reality in the child*] (M. Cook, trans.). New York: Basic Books, 1954. (Originally published, 1937.)

Piaget, J. [*The psychology of intelligence*] (M. Percy & D. E. Berlyne, trans.). Totawa, N. J.: Littlefield, Adams, 1973. (Originally published, 1947.)

Piaget, J. [*Play, dreams, and imitation in childhood*] (C. Gattegno & F. M. Hodgson, trans.). New York; Norton, 1951.

Piaget, J. [*The origins of intelligence in children*] (M. Cook, trans.). New York: International Universities Press, 1952.

Piaget, J. [*The child's conception of number*] (C. Gattegno & F. M. Hodgson, trans.). New York: Norton, 1965. (Originally published, 1952.)

Piaget, J. How children form mathematical concepts. *Scientific American,* November 1953, pp. 74–79.

Piaget, J. [*Six psychological studies*] (A. Tenzer & D. Elkind, trans.). New York: Random House, 1967. (Originally published, 1964.)

Piaget, J. Piaget's theory. In P. H. Mussen (Ed.), *Carmichael's manual of child psychology* (3rd ed.) (Vol. 1). New York: Wiley, 1970.

Piaget, J. [*Understanding causality*] (D. Miles & M. Miles, trans.). New York: Norton, 1974.

Piaget, J., & Inhelder, B. [*The child's conception of space*] (F. J. Langdon & J. L. Lunzer, trans.). London: Routledge and Kegan Paul, 1956.

Piaget, J., & Inhelder, B. [*The psychology of the child*] (H. Weaver, trans.). New York: Basic Books, 1969.

Piaget, J., Inhelder, B., & Szeminska, A. [*The child's conception of geometry*] (E. A. Lunzer, trans.). New York: Basic Books, 1960. (Originally Published, 1948.)

Pick, A. D. Some basic perceptual processes in reading. In W. W. Hartup (Ed.), *The young child: Reviews of research* (Vol. 2). Washington, D. C.: National Association for the Education of Young Children, 1972.

Pippert, R. A. *A study of creativity and faith.* Manitoba Department of Youth and Education Monograph No. 4, 1969.

Place, D. M. The dating experience for adolescent girls. *Adolescence,* 1975, *10,* 157–174.

Plumb, J. H. "Children, the victims of time." Chapter 5 of J. H. Plumb, *In the light of history.* Boston: Houghton, Mifflin, 1973.

Polanyi, M. *Science, faith, and society.* Chicago: University of Chicago Press, 1964.

Prader, A., Tanner, J. M., & von Harnack, G. A. Catch-up growth following illness or starvation. *Journal of Pediatrics,* 1963, *62,* 646–659.

Prechtl, H., & Beintema, D. *The neurological examination of the full-term newborn infant* (Clinics in Developmental Medicine, No. 12). London: Heinemann Medical Publications, 1964.

Premack, D. Language in chimpanzee? *Science,* May 21, 1971, pp. 808–822.

Pulaski, M. A. Play as a function of toy structure and fantasy predisposition. *Child Development,* 1970, *41,* 531–537.

Pulaski, M. A. *Understanding Piaget: An introduction to children's cognitive development.* New York: Harper and Row, 1971.

Pulaski, M. A. The rich rewards of make believe. *Psychology Today,* January 1974, pp. 68–74.

Purnell, R. F. Socioeconomic status and sex differences in adolescent reference-group orientation. *Journal of Genetic Psychology,* 1970, *116,* 233–239.

Putnam, B. A., & Hansen, J. C. Relationship of self-concept and feminine role concept to vocational maturity in young women. *Journal of Counseling Psychology,* 1972, *19,* 436–440.

Redl, F. Aggression in the classroom. *Today's Education,* September 1969, pp. 30–32.

Reed, E. W. Genetic anomalies in development. In F. D. Horowitz (Ed.), *Review of child development research* (Vol. 4). Chicago: University of Chicago Press, 1975.

Reese, H. W. Verbal mediation as a function of age level. *Psychological Bulletin,* 1962, *59,* 502–509.

Reese, H. W., & Overton, W. F. Models of development and theories of development. In L. R. Goulet & P. B. Baltes (Eds.), *Life-span developmental psychology: Research and theory.* New York: Academic Press, 1970.

Resnick, L. B. *Teacher behavior in an informal British infant school.* Pittsburgh: Learning Research and Development Center, University of Pittsburgh, 1971.

Resnick, L. B., & Glaser, R. Problem solving and intelligence. In L. B. Resnick (Ed.), *The nature of intelligence.* New York: Wiley, 1976.

Rheingold, H. L. A comparative psychology of development. In H. W. Stevenson, E. H. Hess & H. L. Rheingold (Eds.), *Early behavior: Comparative and developmental approaches.* New York: Wiley, 1967.

Ricciuti, H. N. Object grouping and selective ordering behavior in infants 12 to 24 months old. *Merrill-Palmer Quarterly,* 1965, *11,* 129–148.

Ricciuti, H. N. *Interaction of adverse social and biological influence on early development: Research and remediation.* Paper presented at a symposium of the American Association for the Advancement of Science, Boston, February 1976.

Richards, M. P. M., Bernal, J. F., & Brackbill, Y. Early behavioral differences: Gender or circumcision?

Developmental Psychobiology, 1976, *9,* 89–95.

Richardson, S. A. The relation of severe malnutrition in infancy to intelligence of school children with differing life histories. *Pediatric Research,* 1976, *10,* 57–61.

Richardson, S. A., Goodman, N., Hastorf, A. H., & Dornbusch, S. M. Cultural uniformity in reaction to physical disabilities. *American Sociological Review,* 1961, *26,* 241–247.

Richmond, B. O., & Weiner, G. P. Cooperation and competition among young children as a function of ethnic grouping, grade, sex, and reward condition. *Journal of Educational Psychology,* 1973, *64,* 329–334.

Rimland, B. *Infantile autism.* New York: Appleton-Century-Crofts, 1964.

Risley, T. R., & Baer, D. M. Operant behavior modification: The deliberate development of behavior. In B. M. Caldwell & H. N. Ricciuti (Eds.), *Review of child development research* (Vol. 3). Chicago: University of Chicago Press, 1973.

Roberts, J. M., & Sutton-Smith, B. Cross-cultural correlates of games of chance. *Behavior Science Notes,* 1966, *1,* 131–144.

Roberts, J. M., Sutton-Smith, B., & Kendon, A. Strategy in games and folk tales. *Journal of Social Psychology,* 1963, *61,* 185–199.

Robinson, W. P. The elaborated code in working class language. *Language and Speech,* 1965, *8,* 243–252.

Rogers, D. (Ed.). *Issues in adolescent psychology.* New York: Appleton-Century-Crofts, 1969.

Rosen, C. E. The effects of sociodramatic play on problem-solving behavior among culturally disadvantaged preschool children. *Child Development,* 1974, *45,* 920–927.

Rosenbaum, A. L., Churchill, J. A., Shakhashiri, Z. A., & Moody, R. L. Neuropsychologic outcome of children whose mothers had proteinuria during pregnancy. *Obstetrics and Gynecology,* 1969, *33,* 118–122.

Rosenberg, B. G., & Sutton-Smith, B. Sibling age spacing effects upon cognition. *Developmental Psychology,* 1969, *1,* 661–668.

Rosenthal, R. The Pygmalion effect lives. *Psychology Today,* September 1973, pp. 56–58 ff.

Rosenthal, R., & Jacobson, L. *Pygmalion in the classroom: Teacher expectation and pupil's intellectual development.* New York: Holt, Rinehart and Winston, 1968.

Ross, H. S. Forms of exploratory behavior in young children. In B. M. Foss (Ed.), *New perspectives in child development.* Harmondsworth, England: Penguin, 1974.

Rothenberg, B. B. Children's social sensitivity and the relationship to interpersonal competence, intrapersonal comfort, and intellectual level. *Developmental Psychology,* 1970, *2,* 335–350.

Rovee, C. K., & Rovee, D. T. Conjugate reinforcement of infant exploratory behavior. *Journal of Experimental Child Psychology,* 1969, *8,* 33–39.

Rozin, P., Bressman, B., & Taft, M. Do children understand the basic relationship between speech and writing? The mow-motorcycle test. *Journal of Reading Behavior,* 1974, *6,* 327–334.

Rozin, P., & Gleitman, L. R. The structure and acquisition of reading. II. The reading process and the acquisition of the alphabetic principle. In A. S. Reber & D. L. Scarborough (Eds.), *Toward a psychology of reading.* New York: Wiley, 1977.

Rubenstein, J., & Howes, C. The effects of peers on toddler interaction with mother and toys. *Child Development,* 1976, *47,* 597–605.

Rubenstein, J., & Sandberg, C. *The effects of peers in the toddler's interaction with his mother and with his toys.* Paper presented at the meeting of the Society for Research in Child Development, Denver, Colorado, April 1975.

Rubin, K. H. Egocentrism in childhood: A unitary construct? *Child Development,* 1973, *44,* 102–110.

Rubin, K. H., Hultsch, D. F., & Peters, D. L. Non-social speech in four-year-old children as a function of birth order and interpersonal situation. *Merrill-Palmer Quarterly,* 1971, *17,* 41–50.

Ruble, D. N., & Nakamura, C. Y. Task orientation versus social orientation in young children and their attention to relevant social cues. *Child Development,* 1972, *43,* 471–480.

Ruddell, R. B. The effect of oral and written patterns of language structure on reading comprehension. *Reading Teacher,* 1965, *18,* 270–275.

Ruff, H. A. The function of shifting fixations in the visual perception of infants. *Child Development,* 1975, *46,* 857–865.

Rugh, R., & Shettles, L. B. *From conception to birth: The drama of life's beginnings.* New York: Harper and Row, 1971.

Rutherford, E., & Mussen, P. Generosity in nursery school boys. *Child Development,* 1968, *39,* 755–765.

Rutter, M. Prognosis: Psychotic children in adolescence and early adult life. In J. K. Wing (Ed.), *Childhood autism: Clinical, educational, and social aspects.* New York: Pergamon Press, 1966.

Saayman, G, Ames, E. W., & Moffett, A. R. Response to novelty as an indicator of visual discrimination in the human infant. *Journal of Experimental Child Psychology,* 1964, *1,* 189–198.

Salapatek, P., & Kessen, W. Visual scanning of triangles by the human newborn. *Journal of Experimental Child Psychology,* 1966, *3,* 155–167.

Salk, L. The effects of the normal heart beat sound on the behavior of the newborn infant: Implications for mental health. *World Mental Health,* 1960, *12,* 168–175.

Salk, L. Mothers' heartbeat as an imprinting stimulus. *New York Academy of Sciences, Transactions,* 1962, *24,* 753–763.

Salkind, H. *Norming the MFF: Developmental trends in cognitive tempo.* Paper presented at the meeting of the American Education Research Association, Toronto, 1978.

Saltz, E., & Johnson, J. Training for thematic-fantasy play in culturally disadvantaged children: Preliminary results. *Journal of Educational Psychology,* 1974, *66,* 623–630.

Sameroff, A. J. The components of sucking in the human

newborn. *Journal of Experimental Child Psychology,* 1968, *6,* 607–623.

Sameroff, A. J., & Chandler, M. J. Reproductive risk and the continuum of caretaking casuality. In F. D. Horowitz (Ed.), *Review of child development research* (Vol. 4). Chicago: University of Chicago Press, 1975.

Sampson, E. E. On justice as equality. *Journal of Social Issues,* 1975, *31*(3), 45–64.

Sampson, E. E., & Kardush, M. Age, sex, class, and race differences in response to a two-person non-zero-sum game. *Journal of Conflict Resolution,* 1965, *9,* 212–220.

Sander, L. The longitudinal course of early mother-child interaction: Cross-case comparison in a sample of mother-child pairs. In B. M. Foss (Ed.), *Determinants of infant behavior* (Proceedings of the 4th Tavistock Seminar on Mother-Infant Interaction.) London: Methuen, 1969.

Sander, L. The regulation of exchange in the infant caretaker system and some aspects of the context-content relationship. In M. Lewis & L. A. Rosenblum (Eds.), *Origins of behavior communication and language.* New York: Wiley, 1976.

Saxen, L. & Rapola, J. *Congenital defects.* New York: Holt, Rinehart and Winston, 1969.

Scarlett, H. H., Press, A. N., & Crockett, W. H. Children's descriptions of peers: A Wernerian developmental analysis. *Child Development,* 1971, *42,* 439–453.

Scarpitti, F. R. Delinquent and non-delinquent perceptions of self, values and opportunity. *Mental Hygiene,* 1965, *49,* 399–404.

Scarr-Salapatek, S. Race, social class, and IQ. *Science,* December 24, 1971, pp. 1285–1295. (a)

Scarr-Salapatek, S. Unknowns in the IQ equation. *Science,* December 17, 1971, pp. 1223–1228. (b)

Scarr-Salapatek, S. Genetics and the development of intelligence. In F. D. Horowitz (Ed.), *Review of child development research* (Vol. 4). Chicago: University of Chicago Press, 1975.

Schaffer, H. R. *The growth of sociability.* England: Penguin, 1971.

Schaffer, H. R., & Emerson, P. E. The development of social attachments in infancy. *Monographs of the Society for Research in Child Development,* 1964, *29*(3, Serial No. 94). (a)

Schaffer, H. R., & Emerson, P. E. Patterns of response to physical contact in early human development. *Journal of Child Psychology and Psychiatry and Allied Disciplines,* 1964, *5,* 1–13. (b)

Scheinfeld, A. *Heredity in humans* (Rev. ed.). Philadelphia: Lippincott, 1972.

Schlesinger, H. S. *The acquisition of sign language.* Unpublished manuscript, University of California, Department of Psychiatry, San Francisco, 1974.

Schlesinger, H. S., & Meadow, K. P. *Sound and Sign: Childhood deafness and mental health.* Berkeley: University of California Press, 1972.

Schmitt, B. D. The minimal brain dysfunction myth. *American Journal of Diseases of Children,* 1975, *129,* 1313–1325.

Scholtz, G. J. L., & Ellis, M. J. Repeated exposure to objects and peers in a play setting. *Journal of Experimental Child Psychology,* 1975, *19,* 448–455.

Schultz, T. R. Development of the appreciation of riddles. *Child Development,* 1974, *45,* 100–105.

Schultz, T. R., & Horibe, F. Development of the appreciation of verbal jokes. *Developmental Psychology,* 1974, *10,* 13–20.

Schwarz, J. C., Krolick, G., & Strickland, B. S. Effects of early day care experience on adjustment to a new environment. *American Journal of Orthopsychiatry,* 1973, *43,* 340–346.

Schwarz, J. C., Strickland, R. G., & Krolick, G. Infant day care: Behavioral effects at preschool age. *Developmental Psychology,* 1974, *10,* 502–506.

Scottish Council for Research in Education. *The trend of Scottish intelligence: A comparison of the 1947 and 1932 surveys of the intelligence of eleven-year-old pupils.* London: University of London Press, 1949.

Scrimshaw, N. S. Early malnutrition and central nervous system function. *Merrill-Palmer Quarterly,* 1969, *15,* 375–388.

Sears, R. R. Relation of early socialization experiences to aggression in middle childhood. *Journal of Abnormal and Social Psychology,* 1961, *63,* 466–492.

Seaver, W. B. Effects of naturally induced teacher expectancies. *Journal of Personality and Social Psychology,* 1973, *28,* 333–342.

Seligman, M. E. P. On the generality of the laws of learning. *Psychological Review,* 1970, *77,* 406–418.

Seligmann, J., Gosnell, M., & Shapiro, D. New science of birth. *Newsweek,* November 15, 1976, pp. 55–60.

Selman, R. L., & Byrne, D. F. *Manual for scoring social roletaking stages in moral dilemmas.* Unpublished Report (No. RSIA) of the Moral Education and Research Foundation, Harvard University, December 1972.

Selman, R. L., & Byrne, D. F. *Manual for scoring social roletaking in social dilemmas.* Unpublished Report (No. RSIB) of the Moral Education and Research Foundation, Harvard University, March 1973.

Selman, R. L., & Byrne, D. F. A structural-developmental analysis of levels of roletaking in middle childhood. *Child Development,* 1974, *45,* 803–806.

Shantz, C. U. The development of social cognition. In E. M. Hetherington (Ed.), *Review of child development research* (Vol. 5). Chicago: University of Chicago Press, 1975.

Shapira, A., & Madsen, M. C. Cooperative and competitive behavior of kibbutz and urban children in Israel. *Child Development,* 1969, *40,* 609–617.

Sharp, E. *The IQ cult.* New York: Coward, McCann & Geoghegan, 1972.

Shatz, M., & Gelman, R. The development of communication skills: Modifications in the speech of young children as a function of listener. *Monographs of the Society for Research in Child Development,* 1967, *38* (5, Serial No. 152).

Shellow, R., Schamp, J. R., Liebow, E., & Unger, E. Suburban runaways of the 1960's. *Monographs of the*

Society for Research in Child Development, 1967, *32,* (3, Serial No. 111).

Sherif, M., Harvey, O. J., White, B. J., Hood, W. R., & Sherif, C. W. *Intergroup conflict and cooperation: The robbers cave experiment.* Norman, Oklahoma: Institute of Group Relations, University Book Exchange, 1961.

Sherman, J. A., & Bushnell, D., Jr. Behavior modification as an educational technique. In F. D. Horowitz (Ed.), *Review of child development research* (Vol. 4). Chicago: University of Chicago Press, 1975.

Sherrick, C. E. Sensory processes. In C. E. Sherrick & others, *Psychology and the handicapped child* (DHEW Publication No. OE/73-05000). Washington, D. C.: U. S. Government Printing Office, 1974.

Shimberg, M. E. An investigation into the validity of norms with special reference to urban and rural groups. *Archives of Psychology,* 1929, No. 104.

Siklóssy, L. Problem-solving approach to first-language acquisition. In S. R. Harnad, H. D. Steklis & J. Lancaster (Eds.), Origins and evolution of language and speech. *New York Academy of Sciences, Annals,* 1976, *280,* 257–261.

Silverman, T. R. Categorization behavior and achievement in deaf and hearing children. *Exceptional Children,* 1967, *34,* 241–250.

Siman, M. L. Application of a new model of peer group influence to naturally existing adolescent friendship groups. *Child Development,* 1977, *48,* 270–274.

Simmons, R. G., & Rosenberg, M. Functions of children's perceptions of the stratification system. *American Sociological Review,* 1971, *36,* 235–249.

Simons, B., Downs, E. F., Hurster, M. M., & Archer, M. Child abuse: Epidemiologic study of medically reported cases. *New York State Journal of Medicine,* 1966, *66,* 2783–2788.

Sinclair-de-Zwart, H. Developmental psycholinguistics. In D. Elkind & J. H. Flavell (Eds.), *Studies in cognitive development: Essays in honor of Jean Piaget.* New York: Oxford University Press, 1969.

Singer, J. L. Imagination and waiting ability in young children. *Journal of Personality,* 1961, *29,* 396–413.

Singer, J. L. (Ed.). *The child's world of make-believe: Experimental studies of imaginative play.* New York: Academic Press, 1973.

Singer, J. L., & Singer, D. G. *Fostering imaginative play in preschool children: Effects of television-viewing and direct adult modeling.* Paper presented at the meeting of the American Psychological Association, New Orleans, 1974.

Siqueland, E. R., & DeLucia, C. A. Visual reinforcement of nonnutritive sucking in human infants. *Science,* September 12, 1969, pp. 1144–1146.

Skeels, H. M. Adult status of children with contrasting early life experiences. *Monographs of the Society for Research in Child Development,* 1966, *31* (3, Serial No. 105).

Skinner, B. F. *Science and human behavior.* New York: Macmillan, 1953.

Skinner, B. F. *Verbal behavior.* New York: Appleton-Century-Crofts, 1957.

Skinner, B. F. *Beyond freedom and dignity.* New York: Bantam, 1971.

Skodak, M., & Skeels, H. M. A final follow-up of one hundred adopted children. *Journal of Genetic Psychology,* 1949, *75,* 85–125.

Slobin, D. I. The acquisition of Russian as a native language. In F. Smith & G. A. Miller (Eds.), *The genesis of language.* Cambridge: MIT Press, 1966.

Slobin, D. I. Cognitive prerequisites for the development of grammar. In C. A. Ferguson & D. I. Slobin (Eds.), *Studies of child language development.* New York: Holt, Rinehart and Winston, 1973.

Smedslund, J. The acquisition of conservation of substance and weight in children. II. External reinforcement of conservation of weight and of the operation of addition and subtraction. *Scandinavian Journal of Psychology,* 1961, *2,* 71–84.

Smilansky, S. *The effects of sociodramatic play on disadvantaged preschool children.* New York: Wiley, 1968.

Smith, R. M., & Neisworth, J. T. *The exceptional child: A functional approach.* New York: McGraw-Hill, 1975.

Smith, S. Language and non-verbal test performance of racial groups in Honolulu before and after a fourteen-year interval. *Journal of General Psychology,* 1942, *26,* 51–93.

Smith, T. L., & Hall, G. S. Curiosity and interest. In G. S. Hall, *Aspects of child life and education.* Boston: Ginn, 1907.

Sokolov, E. N. Neuronal models and the orienting reflex. In M. A. Brazier (Ed.), *The central nervous system and behavior.* New York: Josiah Macy Foundation, 1960.

Sokolov, E. N. [*Perception and the conditioned reflex*] (S. W. Waydenfeld, trans.). London: Pergamon, 1963.

Spitz, R. A., & Wolf, K. M. The smiling response: A contribution to the ontogenesis of social relations. *Genetic Psychology Monographs,* 1946, *34,* 57–125.

Spodek, B. Alternatives to traditional education. *Peabody Journal of Education,* 1971, *48,* 140–146.

Sroufe, L. A. Drug treatment of children with behavior problems. In F. D. Horowitz (Ed.), *Review of child development research* (Vol. 4). Chicago: University of Chicago Press, 1975.

Sroufe, L. A., & Waters, E. The ontogenesis of smiling and laughter: A perspective on the organization of development in infancy. *Psychological Review,* 1976, *83,* 173–189.

Sroufe, L. A., & Wunsch, J. P. The development of laughter in the first year of life. *Child Development,* 1972, *43,* 1326–1344.

Stanfield, R. E. The interaction of family variables and gang variables in the aetiology of delinquency. *Social Problems,* 1966, *13,* 411–417.

Starr, J. M. The peace and love generation: Changing attitudes toward sex and violence among college youth. *Journal of Social Issues,* 1974, *30*(2), 73–106.

Stayton, D. J., & Ainsworth, M. D. S. Individual differences in infant responses to brief, everyday separations as related to other infant and maternal behaviors.

Developmental Psychology, 1973, *9,* 226–235.

Stayton, D. J., Ainsworth, M. D. S., & Main, M. B. Development of separation behavior in the first year of life: Protesting, following, and greeting. *Developmental Psychology,* 1973, *9,* 213–235.

Steele, B. F., & Pollack, C. B. A psychiatric study of parents who abuse infants and small children. In R. E. Helfer & C. H. Kempe (Eds.), *The battered child.* Chicago: University of Chicago Press, 1968.

Stein, A. H., & Friedrich, L. K. Impact of television on children and youth. In E. M. Hetherington (Ed.), *Review of child development research* (Vol. 5). Chicago: University of Chicago Press, 1975.

Strauss, M. E., Lessen-Firestone, J. K., Starr, R. H., Jr., & Ostrea, E. M., Jr. Behavior of narcotics-addicted newborns. *Child Development,* 1975, *46,* 887–893.

Streissguth, A. P., & Bee, H. L. Mother-child interactions and cognitive development in children. In W. W. Hartup (Ed.), *The young child: Reviews of research* (Vol. 2). Washington, D. C.: National Association for the Education of Young Children, 1972.

Stott, D. H. The child's hazards in utero. In J. G. Howells (Ed.), *Modern perspectives in international child psychiatry.* New York: Brunner/Mazel, 1971.

Sutton-Smith, B. The role of play in cognitive development. In W. W. Hartup & N. L. Smothergill (Eds.), *The young child: Reviews of research* (Vol. 1). Washington, D. C.: National Association for the Education of Young Children, 1967.

Sutton-Smith, B. Play, games, and controls. In J. P. Scott (Ed.), *Social control.* Chicago: University of Chicago Press, 1970.

Sutton-Smith, B. Boundaries. In R. E. Herron & B. Sutton-Smith, *Child's play.* New York: Wiley, 1971.

Sutton-Smith, B., Botvin, G., & Mahony, D. *Developmental structures in fantasy: Narratives.* Paper presented at the meeting of the American Psychological Association, Chicago, September 1975.

Sutton-Smith, B., & Rosenberg, B. G. Sixty years of historical change in the game preferences of American children. In R. E. Herron & B. Sutton-Smith (Eds.), *Child's play.* New York: Wiley, 1971.

Sutton-Smith, B., Rosenberg, B. G., & Landy, F. Father-absence effects in families of different sibling compositions. *Child Development,* 1968, *39,* 1213–1221.

Sweet, A. Y. Classification of the low-birth-weight infant. In M. H. Klaus & A. A. Fanaroff (Eds.), *Care of the high-risk neonate.* Philadelphia: Saunders, 1973.

Swets, J. A. Introduction. In C. E. Sherrick & others, *Psychology and the handicapped child* (DHEW Publication No. OE 73-05000). Washington, D. C.: U. S. Government Printing Office, 1974.

Switzky, H. N., Haywood, H. C., & Isett, R. Exploration, curiosity, and play in young children: Effects of stimulus complexity. *Developmental Psychology,* 1974, *10,* 321–329.

Tanner, J. M. Puberty. In A. McClaren (Ed.), *Advances in reproductive physiology* (Vol. 2). London: Logos, 1967.

Tanner, J. M. Physical growth. In P. H. Mussen (Ed.),

Carmichael's manual of child psychology (3rd ed.) (Vol. 1). New York: Wiley, 1970.

Tanner, J. M. The regulation of human growth. In F. Rebelsky and L. Dorman (Eds.), *Child development and behavior.* New York: Knopf, 1973.

Tanner, J. M., Whitehouse, R. H., & Takaishi, M. Standards from birth to maturity for height, weight, height velocity and weight velocity: British children 1965. *Archives of Disease in Childhood,* 1966, *41,* 454–471; 613–635.

Templin, M. C. *Certain language skills in children: Their development and interrelationships.* Minneapolis: University of Minnesota Press, 1957.

Terman, L. M., & Merrill, M. A. *Measuring intelligence: A guide to the administration of the revised Stanford-Binet tests of intelligence.* Boston: Houghton, Mifflin, 1937.

Ter Vrugt, D., & Pederson, D. R. The effects of vertical rocking frequencies on the arousal level in two-month-old infants. *Child Development,* 1973, *44,* 205–209.

Thoman, E. B. Sleep and wake behaviors in neonates: Consistencies and consequences. *Merrill-Palmer Quarterly,* 1975, *21,* 295–314.

Thomas, A., Chess, S., & Birch, H. G. *Temperament and behavior disorders in children.* New York: New York University Press, 1968.

Thomas, A., Chess, S., & Birch, H. G. The origin of personality. *Scientific American,* August 1970, pp. 102–109.

Thomas, H. Psychological assessment instruments for use with human infants. *Merrill-Palmer Quarterly,* 1970, *16,* 179–223.

Thompson, O. E. Student values in transition. *California Journal of Educational Research,* 1968, *19,* 17–86.

Thompson, W. R., & Grusec, J. E. Studies of early experience. In P. H. Mussen (Ed.), *Carmichael's manual of child psychology* (3rd ed.) (Vol. 1). New York: Wiley, 1970.

Tierney, R. J., & Herman, A. Self-estimate ability in adolescence. *Journal of Counseling Psychology,* 1973, *20,* 298–302.

Tikhomirov, O. K. [On the formation of voluntary movement in children of pre-school age.] In A. R. Luria (Ed.), [*Problems of the higher neural activity of the child*] (Vol. 2). Moscow, 1958.

Torrance, E. P. *Torrance tests of creative thinking: Directions manual and scoring guide; verbal test, booklet A, research edition.* Princeton, N. J.: Personnel Press, 1966.

Toynbee, A. J. *Greek historical thought.* New York: Mentor, 1952.

Tuckman, B. W., & Bierman, M. L. *Beyond Pygmalion: Galatea in the schools.* Paper presented at the meeting of the American Educational Research Association, New York, April 1971.

Tudor, J. F. The development of class awareness in children. *Social Forces,* 1971, *49,* 470–476.

Tulkin, S. R., & Covitz, E. *Mother-infant interaction and intellectual functioning at age six.* Paper presented at the meeting of the Society for Research in Child Development, Denver, Colorado, April 1975.

Tyler, L. E. The development of "vocational interests":

I. The organization of likes and dislikes in ten-year-old children. *Journal of Genetic Psychology,* 1955, *86,* 33–44.

Tyler, L. E. The antecedents of two varieties of vocational interests. *Genetic Psychology Monographs,* 1964, *70,* 177–227.

Tyler, L. E. *Individual differences: Abilities and motivational directions.* New York: Appleton-Century-Crofts, 1974.

Tyler, L. E. The intelligence we test: An evolving concept. In L. B. Resnick (Ed.), *The nature of intelligence.* New York: Wiley, 1976.

Ulich, R. (Ed.). *Three thousand years of educational wisdom: Selections from great documents* (2nd ed.). Cambridge: Harvard University Press, 1954.

Ullmann, L. P., & Krasner, L. *A psychological approach to abnormal behavior* (2nd ed.). Englewood Cliffs, N. J.: Prentice-Hall, 1975.

U. S. Bureau of the Census. *1970 Census of population: Subject reports* (Final Reports; Series PC[2]; Vol. 2, 9A & 9B. Washington, D. C.: U. S. Government Printing Office, 1970.

U. S. Bureau of the Census. *Statistical abstract of the United States: 1975.* Washington, D. C.: U. S. Government Printing Office, 1975.

U. S. Department of Health, Education and Welfare. *Perspectives on human deprivation: Biological, psychological, and sociological.* Washington, D. C.: U. S. Government Printing Office, 1968. (a)

U. S. Department of Health, Education and Welfare, Children's Bureau. *The nation's youth* (Children's Bureau Publication No. 460–1968). Washington, D. C.: U. S. Government Printing Office, 1968. (b)

U. S. Department of Health, Education and Welfare, Children's Bureau. *Prenatal care* (DHEW Publication No. OCD 73–17, Children's Bureau Publication No. 4). Washington, D. C.: U. S. Government Printing Office, 1973.

Updike, J. *Couples.* New York: Knopf, 1968.

Uzgiris, I. C. Infant development from a Piagetian approach: Introduction to a symposium. *Merrill-Palmer Quarterly,* 1976, *22,* 3–10. (a)

Uzgiris, I. C. Organization of sensorimotor intelligence. In M. Lewis (Ed.), *The origins of intelligence.* New York: Plenum, 1976. (b)

Uzgiris, I. C., & Hunt, J. McV. *Assessment in infancy: Ordinal scales of psychological development.* Urbana: University of Illinois Press, 1975.

Veitch, J. *The rationalists: Rene Descartes.* New York: Doubleday, 1974.

Vine, I. The role of facial visual signalling in early social development. In M. von Cranach & I. Vine (Eds.), *Social communication and movement: Studies of interaction and expression in man and chimpanzee.* London: Academic Press, 1973.

Von Bertalanffy, L. *Robots, men, and minds.* New York: Braziller, 1967.

Vurpillot, E. The development of scanning strategies and their relation to visual differentiation. *Journal of Experimental Child Psychology,* 1968, *6,* 632–650.

Vygotsky, L. S. [*Thought and language*] (E. Hanfmann & G. Vakar, trans.). Cambridge. MIT Press, 1962. (Originally published, 1934.)

Vygotsky, L. S. [*Selected psychological studies.*] Moscow: 1956.

Waber, D. P. Sex differences in cognition: A function of maturation rate? *Science,* May 7, 1976, pp. 572–574.

Waddington, C. H. *The strategy of genes.* London: Allen and Unwin, 1957.

Wahler, R. G. Child-child interactions in free field settings: Some experimental analyses. *Journal of Experimental Child Psychology,* 1967, *5,* 278–293.

Waldrop, M. F., & Halverson, C. F., Jr. Intensive and extensive peer behavior: Longitudinal and cross-sectional analyses. *Child Development,* 1975, *46,* 19–26.

Wallach, M. A. Creativity. In P. H. Mussen (Ed.), *Carmichael's manual of child psychology* (3rd ed.) (Vol. 1). New York: Wiley, 1970.

Wallach, M. A., & Kogan, N. *Modes of thinking in young children.* New York: Holt, Rinehart and Winston, 1965.

Walters, R. H., Parke, R. D., & Cane, V. A. Timing of punishment and the observation of consequences to others as determinants of response inhibition. *Journal of Experimental Child Psychology,* 1965, *2,* 10–30.

Wasz-Hockert, O., Lind, J., Vuorenkoski, V., Partanen, T., & Valanne, E. *The infant cry* (Clinics in Developmental Medicine, No. 29). London: Heinemann Medical Publications, 1968.

Watson, J. B. *Psychological care of infant and child.* New York: Norton, 1928.

Watson, J. B. *Behaviorism* (Rev. ed.). Chicago: University of Chicago Press, 1958.

Watson, J. B., & Rayner, R. Conditioned emotional reactions. *Journal of Experimental Psychology,* 1920, *3,* 1–14.

Watson, J. S. Perception of object orientation in infants. *Merrill-Palmer Quarterly,* 1966, *12,* 73–94.

Watson, J. S. Memory and "contingency analysis" in infant learning. *Merrill-Palmer Quarterly,* 1967, *13,* 55–76.

Watson, J. S. Smiling, cooing, and "the game." *Merrill-Palmer Quarterly,* 1972, *18,* 323–339.

Weir, R. H. *Language in the crib.* The Hague: Mouton, 1970.

Weisler, A., & McCall, R. B. Exploration and play: Résumé and redirection. *American Psychologist,* 1976, *31,* 492–508.

Werner, E. E., Bierman, J. M., & French, F. E. *The children of Kauai: A longitudinal study from the prenatal period to age ten.* Honolulu: University of Hawaii Press, 1971.

Werner, H. [*Comparative psychology of mental development*] (E. B. Garside, trans.). New York: Science Editions, 1948. (Originally published, 1926.)

Wheeler, L. R. A comparative study of the intelligence of East Tennessee mountain children. *Journal of Educational Psychology,* 1942, *33,* 321–334.

Whetnall, E., & Fry, D. B. *The deaf child* (2nd ed.). Springfield, Ill.: Charles C Thomas, 1971.

White, B. L. *Human infants: Experience and psychological development.* Englewood Cliffs, N. J.: Prentice-Hall, 1971.

White, B. L. Discussions and conclusions. In B. L. White

& J. C. Watts (Eds.), *Experience and environment: Major influences on the development of the young child.* Englewood Cliffs, N. J.: Prentice-Hall, 1973.

White, R. W. Motivation reconsidered: The concept of competence. *Psychological Review,* 1959, *66,* 297–333.

White, S. H. Evidence for a hierarchical arrangement of learning processes. In L. P. Lipsitt & C. C. Spiker (Eds.), *Advances in child development and behavior* (Vol. 2). New York: Academic Press, 1966.

Whiting, B. B., & Whiting, J. W. M. *Children of six cultures: A psychocultural analysis.* Cambridge: Harvard University Press, 1975.

Wichern, F., & Nowicki, S., Jr. Independence training practices and locus of control orientation in children and adolescents. *Developmental Psychology,* 1976, *12,* 77.

Williams, R. L. *A Black intelligence test of cultural homogeneity.* Paper presented at the 80th Annual Convention of the American Psychological Association, Honolulu, September 1972.

Wind, J. Phylogeny of the human vocal tract. In S. R. Harnad, H. D. Steklis & J. Lancaster (Eds.), *Origins and evolution of language and speech. New York Academy of Sciences, Annals,* 1976, *280,* 612–630.

Wingerd, J., Christianson, R., Lovitt, W. V., & Schoen, E. J. Placental ratio in white and black women: Relation to smoking and anemia. *American Journal of Obstetrics and Gynecology,* 1976, *124,* 671–675.

Winick, M., & Noble, A. Quantitative changes in DNA, RNA, and protein during prenatal and postnatal growth, in the rat. *Developmental Biology,* 1965, *12,* 451–466.

Winick, M., & Noble, A. Cellular response in rats during malnutrition at various ages. *Journal of Nutrition,* 1966, *89,* 300–306.

Witryol, S. L., & Thompson, G. G. A critical review of the stability of social acceptability scores obtained with the partial-rank-order and the paired-comparison scales. *Genetic Psychology Monographs,* 1953, *48,* 221–260.

Wolf, T. M. Effects of live modeled sex-inappropriate play behavior in a naturalistic setting. *Developmental Psychology,* 1973, *9,* 120–123.

Wolf, T. M. Response consequences to televised modeled sex-inappropriate play behavior. *Journal of Genetic Psychology,* 1975, *127,* 35–44.

Wolff, P. H. Observations on the early development of smiling. In B. M. Foss (Ed.), *Determinants of infant behaviour* (Vol. 2.). New York: Wiley, 1963.

Wolff, P. H. The natural history of crying and other vocalizations in early infancy. In B. M. Foss (Ed.), *Determinants of infant behaviour* (Proceedings of the 4th Tavistock Seminar on Mother-Infant Interaction). London: Methuen, 1969.

World Health Organization. The prevention of perinatal morbidity and mortality. *Public Health Papers,* 1972, no. 42.

Wyden, B. Growth: 45 crucial months. *Life,* December 17, 1971, pp. 93–95.

Yando, R. M., & Kagan, J. The effect of teacher tempo on the child. *Child Development,* 1968, *39,* 27–34.

Yang, R. K., & Halverson, C. F., Jr. A study of the "inversion of intensity" between newborn and preschoolage behavior. *Child Development,* 1976, *47,* 350–359.

Yarrow, L. J., Pederson, F. A. Attachment: Its origins and course. *Young Children,* 1972, *27,* 302–312.

Yarrow, L. J., Rubenstein, J. L., & Pedersen, F. A. *Infant and environment: Early cognitive and motivational development.* New York: Wiley, 1975.

Yarrow, M. R., Scott, P. M., & Waxler, C. Z. Learning concern for others. *Developmental Psychology,* 1973, *8,* 240–260.

Young, L. R. *Wednesday's children: A study of child neglect and abuse.* New York: McGraw-Hill, 1964.

Young, V. H. Family and childhood in a Southern Negro community. *American Anthropologist,* 1970, *27,* 269–288.

Zacharias, L., & Wurtman, R. J. Age at menarche: Genetic and environmental influences. *New England Journal of Medicine,* 1969, *280,* 868–875.

Zajonc, R. B. Family configuration and intelligence. *Science,* April 16, 1976, pp. 227–236.

Zajonc, R. B., & Markus, G. B. Birth order and intellectual development. *Psychological Review,* 1975, *82,* 74–88.

Zelazo, P. R. *Social reinforcement of vocalizations and smiling of three month old infants.* Unpublished doctoral dissertation, University of Waterloo, 1967.

Zelazo, P. R. *Differential three month old vocalizations to sex-of-strangers.* Paper presented at the 19th International Congress of Psychology, London, July 1969.

Zelazo, P. R., & Komer, M. J. Infant smiling to nonsocial stimuli and the recognition hypothesis. *Child Development,* 1971, *42,* 1327–1339.

Zelazo, P. R., Zelazo, N. A., & Kolb, S. "Walking" in the newborn. *Science,* April 21, 1972, 314–315.

Zigler, E. Mental retardation: Current issues and approaches. In L. W. Hoffman & M. L. Hoffman (Eds.), *Review of child development research* (Vol. 2). New York: Russell Sage Foundation, 1966.

Zigler, E. Familial mental retardation: A continuing dilemma. *Science,* January 20, 1967, pp. 292–298.

Zigler, E., Abelson, W. D., & Seitz, V. Motivational factors in the performance of economically disadvantaged children on the Peabody Picture Vocabulary Test. *Child Development,* 1973, *44,* 294–303.

Zigler, E., & Butterfield, E. C. Motivational aspects of changes in IQ test performance of culturally deprived nursery school children. *Child Development,* 1968, *39,* 1–14.

Acknowledgments

Acknowledgments continued from page iv

Figure 2–5: From *Heredity in humans* by Amram Schein-feld. Copyright © 1956, 1961, 1971 by Amram Schein-feld. Reproduced by permission of J. B. Lippincott Company and of Harold Ober Associates Incorporated.

Figure 2–7: Adapted from *Handbook of mental deficiency: Psychological theory and research.* Copyright © 1963 by McGraw-Hill, Inc. Used with permission of McGraw-Hill Book Company.

Figures 2–8 and 2–9: From H. M. Skeels, Adult status of children with contrasting early life experiences. *Monographs of the Society for Research in Child Development,* 1966, *31,* Serial No. 105. © 1966 The Society for Research in Child Development, Inc.

quotation, p. 64: From John Updike, *Couples.* Copyright © 1968 by Alfred A. Knopf, Inc. Used by permission of Alfred A. Knopf, Inc.

Table 3–1: Adapted from M. Winick and A. Noble, Quan-titative changes in DNA, RNA, and protein during prenatal and postnatal growth in the rat. *Developmental Biology,* 1965, *3,* 451–466; and from Cellular responses in rats during malnutrition at various ages. *Journal of Nutrition,* 1966, *89,* 300–306. By permission of *Developmental Biology* and of the *Journal of Nutrition.*

Table 3–3: From *Pregnancy, birth, and family planning: A guide for expectant parents in the 1970's* by Alan F. Guttmacher. Copyright 1937, 1947, 1950, © 1956, 1962, 1965, 1973 by Alan F. Guttmacher. Adapted by per-mission of The Viking Press.

Figure 3–1: From *The strategy of genes,* by C. H. Wadding-ton. Copyright © 1957 by Allen & Unwin. Used by permission of Allen & Unwin.

Figures 3–2 and 3–3: From Keith L. Moore, *The developing human: Clinically oriented embryology,* 2nd ed. © 1977 by the W. B. Saunders Company, Philadelphia, Pa.

Figure 3–4: From A. Prader, J. M. Tanner, and G. A. von Harnack, Catch-up growth following illness or starva-tion. *J. Pediatr. 62,* 1963, 646–659.

Figure 3–5: From J. M. Tanner, The regulation of human growth. *Child Development,* 1963, *34,* 817–848. © 1963 The Society for Research in Child Development, Inc.

Box, p. 135: Reprinted from *The origins of intelligence in children* by Jean Piaget. By permission of International Universities Press, Inc., and of Delachaux & Niestlé, Switzerland.

Figure 5–2: From "The origin of form perception," Robert

L. Fantz. Copyright © 1961 by Scientific American, Inc. All rights reserved.

Table 6–1: From E. H. Lenneberg, *Biological foundations of language.* By permission of John Wiley & Sons.

Table 7–2 and Figure 7–3: From L. A. Sroufe and J. P. Wunsch, The development of laughter in the first year of life. *Child Development,* 1972, *43,* 1326–1344. © 1972 The Society for Research in Child Development, Inc.

Figure 7–2: From J. S. Watson, Smiling, cooing, and "The Game." *The Merrill-Palmer Quarterly,* 1972, *18,* 323–339. By permission.

Figure 7–4: From K. A. Clarke-Stewart, Interactions between mothers and their young: Characteristics and consequences. *Monographs of the Society for Research in Child Development,* 1973, *38,* Serial No. 153. © 1973 The Society for Research in Child Develop-ment, Inc.

quotation, p. 226: From Ruth Weir, *Language in the crib.* The Hague: Mouton, 1962. By permission.

quotation, pp. 226–227: In *From two to five* by K. Chukov-sky. Copyright © 1963 by The Regents of the Univer-sity of California; reprinted by permission of the University of California Press.

quotation, p. 230: From J. H. Flavell, *The developmental psychology of Jean Piaget.* New York: D. Van Nostrand Company, 1963. By permission.

quotations, pp. 231 and 233: Selections reprinted from *Play, dreams and imitation in childhood* by Jean Piaget. Translated by C. Gattegno and F. M. Hodgson, with the permission of W. W. Norton & Company, Inc. Copyright 1962 by W. W. Norton & Company, Inc.

quotation, pp. 234–235: From Jean Piaget, *The psychology of intelligence.* London & Boston, Mass.: Routledge & Kegan Paul, 1964.

quotation, p. 238: From Jean Piaget, *Judgment and reason-ing in the child,* 1926. By permission of Humanities Press, Inc.

quotation, pp. 240–241: From Jean Piaget, *The child's conception of the world,* 1929. Reprinted by permission of Littlefield, Adams, & Co.

quotation, p. 243: Selection reprinted from *The child's conception of number* by Jean Piaget. Copyright 1965 by W. W. Norton & Company, Inc.

quotation, p. 257: From C. Garvey and R. Hogan, Social speech and social interaction: Egocentrism revisited.

Child Development, 1973, *44*, 562–568. © 1973 The Society for Research in Child Development, Inc.

quotation, pp. 260–261: From Marion Blank, *Teaching learning in the preschool: A dialogue approach.* Copyright © 1973 by Charles E. Merrill.

quotation, p. 262: From R. D. Hess and V. Shipman, Early experience and socialization of cognitive modes in children. *Child Development*, 1965, *36*, 869–886. © 1965 The Society for Research in Child Development, Inc.

Table 8–1: From P. E. McGhee, Children's appreciation of humor: A test of the cognitive congruency principle. *Child Development*, 1976, *47*, 420–426. © 1976 The Society for Research in Child Development, Inc.

Table 8–2: From R. Gelman, The nature and development of early number concepts. In H. W. Reese (Ed.), *Advances in child development and behavior* (Vol. 7). Copyright 1972 by Academic Press.

Figure 8–1: From J. Berko, The child's learning of English morphology. *Word*, 1958, *14*, 150–177.

Figures 8–2, 8–3, and 8–4: From C. Golomb, *Young children's sculpture and drawing: A study in representational development.* Cambridge: Harvard University Press, 1974. Copyright © 1974 by the President and Fellows of Harvard College.

Figure 8–12: From Krauss and Glucksberg, 1969.

quotation, pp. 275–276: From R. E. Hartley et al., *Understanding children's play.* New York: Columbia University Press, 1952, by permission of the publisher.

quotation, p. 317: From D. Baumrind, Authoritarian vs. authoritative parental control. *Adolescence*, 1968, *3*, 255–272. By permission.

Table 10–1: From C. Garvey, Some properties of social play. *The Merrill-Palmer Quarterly*, 1974, *20*, 163–180. By permission.

Figure 10–1: From E. H. Green, Group play and quarreling among preschool children. *Child Development*, 1933, *4*, 302–307. © 1933 The Society for Research in Child Development, Inc.

quotation, p. 349: From J. H. Flavell, *Cognitive development.* Englewood Cliffs, N.J.: Prentice-Hall, 1977. By permission.

quotation, p. 353: From L. Kohlberg, The development of children's orientations toward a moral order. 1. Sequence in the development of moral thought. *Vita Humana*, 1963, *6*, 11–33. By permission of *Vita Humana* and of S. Karger AG, Basel.

Table 11–1 and Figure 11–3: Reprinted with the permission of the authors and publishers from L. B. Resnick and R. Glaser, Problem solving and intelligence. In L. B. Resnick (Ed.), *The nature of intelligence.* Hillsdale, N.J.: Lawrence Erlbaum Associates, Publishers, 1976.

Figure 11–2: From *Studies in cognitive development: Essays in honor of Jean Piaget*, eds. David Elkind and John H. Flavell. Copyright © 1969 by Oxford University Press, Inc. Reprinted by permission.

quotation, p. 369: From *Race differences in intelligence*, by J. C. Loehlin, G. Lindzey, and J. N. Spuhler, Copyright © 1975 by W. H. Freeman and Company. Used by permission.

quotation, pp. 378–379: From Hawkes, Lindquist, and Mann, 1936. © American Council on Education.

Box, p. 397: From M. A. Wallach and N. Kogan, *Modes of thinking in young children.* By permission of John Wiley & Sons.

Boxes, pp. 400, 401, and 403: Adapted from *The psychology of sex differences* by Eleanor Emmons Maccoby and Carol Nagy Jacklin, with the permission of the publishers, Stanford University Press. © 1974 by the Board of Trustees of the Leland Stanford Junior University.

Figures 12–1 and 12–2: From A. R. Jensen, How much can we boost IQ and scholastic achievement? *Harvard Educational Review*, 1969, *39*, 1–123. Copyright © 1969 by the President and Fellows of Harvard College.

Table 13–1: Reprinted with permission of R. A. McCracken and the International Reading Association.

Tables 13–2 and 13–3: From Dolores Durkin, *Children who read early* New York: Teachers College Press, 1966. Used by permission of the publisher.

quotation, p. 455: From R. Montemayor and M. Eisen, The development of self-conceptions from childhood to adolescence. *Developmental Psychology*, 1977, *13*, 314–19. By permission.

Figure 14–1: From Tanner, Whitehouse, and Takaishi, 1966. Used by permission of the publisher.

quotation, p. 415: From M. W. Lasseigne, A study of peer and adult influence on moral beliefs of adolescents. *Adolescence*, 1975, *10*, 227–230. By permission.

Table 15–1: From E. W. McClain, An Eriksonian cross-cultural study of adolescent development. *Adolescence*, 1975, 10, 527–541. By permission.

Table 15–2: From David C. Epperson, "A re-assessment of indices of parental influence in *The Adolescent Society*," *American Sociological Review*, Vol. 29, 1964, Table 1, p. 94. By permission of the American Sociological Association.

Box, p. 504: From E. Whetnall and D. B. Fry, *The deaf child.* Copyright © 1964 by Charles C Thomas. Used by permission.

Table 16–1: From R. M. Smith and J. T. Neisworth, *The exceptional child: A functional approach.* Copyright © 1975 by McGraw-Hill, Inc. Used with permission of McGraw-Hill Book Company.

Author Index

Subject Index

To organismic theorists, abilities of thought are structural properties that define what the child can and cannot do in his or her interactions with the outside world at various stages of development.
(Stock, Boston)

Rousseau was interested in persuading his contemporaries to abandon authoritarianism in favor of freedom and independence. Accordingly, he urged educators to "give children full liberty to use their natural abilities." (cited in Ulich, 1954, p. 392)

Those who take the organismic approach to the study of development generally stress *structure-function* relations rather than stimulus-response relations. They take it as their task to describe the structures present in the behavior of the organism at any given time, the order in which they appear, and the rules determining the transition from one stage to another.

The study of structure—both biological and psychological—is justified by the argument that one cannot understand how the child functions or develops until one understands exactly *what* is functioning or developing. Structural analyses are illustrated by Jean Piaget's study of the structure of children's thought, and by the psychoanalytic analysis of feeling and emotion.

Jean Piaget may be the most eminent developmental psychologist of our time. He has linked research about early development to a comprehensive theory of how children move from one stage to another, with successively more stable and sophisticated modes of thought appearing at each stage. Piaget began his professional career as a biologist; thus it is not surprising that he would base his theory on an organismic model. Later, while working in Alfred Binet's laboratory in Paris, constructing an intelligence test for children, Piaget became interested in the *wrong* answers that children gave while being tested. He considered the possibility that those wrong answers came not as a result of children being less smart than adults, but from a totally different way of thinking and viewing the world. The problem that attracted Piaget was the origin of knowledge: What do children know and how do they acquire this knowledge? It was from the writings of the rationalist philosopher Immanuel Kant (1724–1804) that Piaget drew inspiration. Kant asserted that the mind at birth could not be "blank," for if it were, human beings could never acquire the ability to reason.

Piaget

According to Kant, the capacity to make causal judgments, to comprehend time, space, and number are inherent properties of mind that make it possible to make sense out of experience. Piaget set out to study how the categories of reason develop in young children. Does the infant at birth comprehend causality, time, space, and number? Or are there simpler, earlier structures that become transformed with experience into adult categories of reason? Beginning with the concept of structure as consisting of three key ideas—wholeness, transformation, and self-regulation— Piaget roughly defines a structure as "a system of transformations" and states that the structure as a whole (the system) is defined by laws governing the relations among its parts or elements.

What Piaget means is easier to illustrate than to explain. An example is his classic study of the "conservation problem," which Piaget used in order to study the origins of the child's concept of quantity. A child is shown two identical beakers (A and B) filled with equal amounts of liquid, as illustrated in Figure 1–2. He is asked whether the two contain the same amount, and most children agree that they do. The liquid from one beaker (say B) then is poured into a third beaker (C), which is shorter and wider. The child is again asked whether the two beakers (A and C) contain the same amount. In the same manner, the liquid is poured back into the original beaker (B), and then into another beaker (D), which is taller and thinner. If the child always says that the amount of liquid is the same, he is said to have conserved continuous quantity. The child who conserves quantity recognizes that pouring the liquid into beakers of different

FIGURE 1–2
*Conservation of
continuous quantity*

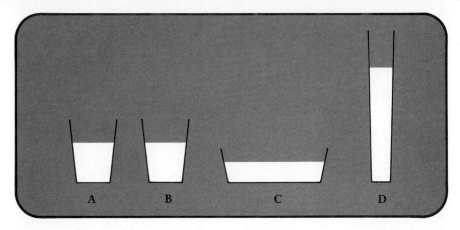

shapes does not change the amount. If the child does not assert that the quantity of liquid remains the same, then he has failed to conserve.

When the child performs the conservation problem ("same? more? less?") by reference to the surface appearance of things (that is, height or width), and again when he or she shifts from height to width without sensing a contradiction, the child is demonstrating *structural* characteristics of thinking. In the first case, the child's cognitive structure is organized on the basis of surface appearances such as height or width. In the second case, the child has replaced these properties with the "law of conservation of quantity" as an organizing principle. To Piaget, these modes of thought are structural properties. Their existence in the child defines what the child can and cannot do in his or her interactions with the outside world (Flavell, 1963).

In an elaboration of this study (Inhelder, Bovet, and Sinclair, 1967), the child was shown transparent jars filled with equal amounts of liquid. Instead of being poured out, the liquid emptied through taps into different-shaped jars and finally into jars identical to the original ones (see Figure 1–3). By experimenting with this arrangement, the child can perform both dimensional and quantitative comparisons and eventually arrive at an understanding of conservation of quantity. The results of the experiment showed, according to Piaget (1970), that the ease with which a child acquires a logical structure such as conservation depends on the child's level of development. For example, most very young children were unable to learn the logic underlying the principle of conservation. At higher levels of development, the ability to learn the principle of conservation—that is, to demonstrate a structural characteristic of thinking—increased progressively. If the child understood quantitative relations before taking part in the experiment, he or she could learn the principle of conservation from the comparisons made during the experiment. But the farther the child was from that ability, the less likely he or she was to use the experimental sequence to arrive at an understanding of conservation. It is at this point that Piaget's notion of the stages of development comes into play.

15

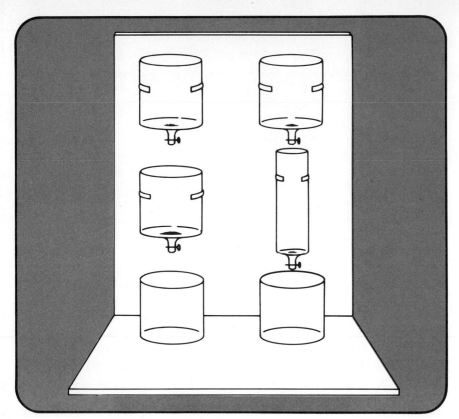

FIGURE 1–3
Experimental apparatus for learning the concept of conservation of quantity (Adapted from Inhelder, Bovet, and Sinclair, 1967)

THE CONCEPT OF STAGES. Thus far, we have used the term *stage* or *level* of development in a very general way, simply to indicate how far the child has progressed along the road from conception to maturity. But to Piaget, these terms have a more precise meaning. As the child progresses toward maturity, he or she goes through a series of stages. These stages occur in a fixed order because each one is a *prerequisite* for the one that follows. At each stage, certain organized patterns of behavior, or *schemes,* appear; these may be either behavioral (e.g., thumb-sucking) or intellectual (e.g., classification of objects). The term *scheme* includes both the child's activities and the structures underlying those activities.*

Piaget's stages are classified into four major periods: (1) the sensorimotor ("sensory-motor") period; (2) the preoperational period; (3) the period of concrete operations; and (4) the period of formal operations. These periods and their subdivisions will be described at length in later chapters; here we will present a brief summary by way of introduction.

The *sensorimotor* period extends from birth to about age 2. During this period, the first organized patterns of behavior appear. At first, the infant is completely egocentric—it does not distinguish between its own body

---

*Many authors refer to the same concept by the term *schema* (plural: *schemata*). *Schema* is a mistranslation of the French word for "scheme."

16